The Best Test Preparation for the

MSAT

Multiple Subjects Assessment for Teachers

Archibald Sia, Ph.D.
Associate Professor of Elementary Education
California State University at Northridge
Northridge, California

Linda Bannister, Ph.D.
Director of University Writing Programs
Associate Professor of English at Loyola Marymount
Los Angeles, California

Scott Cameron, M.S.
Chair of Science Department
San Marino High School
San Marino, California

Garrett T. Caples
Instructor of English
University of California at Berkeley
Berkeley, California

Eric Boime
Instructor of History
University of California at San Diego
San Diego, California

Research & Education Association
61 Ethel Road West
Piscataway, New Jersey 08854

The Best Test Preparation for the
MULTIPLE SUBJECTS ASSESSMENT
FOR TEACHERS (MSAT)

Printed in the United States of America

Library of Congress Catalog Card Number 97-69994

International Standard Book Number 0-87891-749-7

Research & Education Association
61 Ethel Road West
Piscataway, New Jersey 08854

REA supports the effort to conserve and
protect environmental resources by
printing on recycled papers.

CONTENTS

Chapter 5
SCIENCE REVIEW

Chapter 6
VISUAL AND PERFORMING ARTS REVIEW

Chapter 7
HUMAN DEVELOPMENT REVIEW

About Research & Education Association

Research & Education Association (REA) is an organization of educators, scientists, and engineers specializing in various academic fields. Founded in 1959 with the purpose of disseminating the most recently developed scientific information to groups in industry, government, high schools, and universities, REA has since become a successful and highly respected publisher of study aids, test preps, handbooks, and reference works.

REA's Test Preparation series includes study guides for all academic levels in almost all disciplines. Research & Education Association publishes test preps for students who have not yet completed high school, as well as high school students preparing to enter college. Students from countries around the world seeking to attend college in the United States will find the assistance they need in REA's publications. For college students seeking advanced degrees, REA publishes test preps for many major graduate school admission examinations in a wide variety of disciplines, including engineering, law, and medicine. Students at every level, in every field, with every ambition can find what they are looking for among REA's publications.

Unlike most test preparation books that present only a few practice tests which bear little resemblance to the actual exams, REA's series presents tests which accurately depict the official exams in both degree of difficulty and types of questions. REA's practice tests are always based upon the most recently administered exams, and include every type of question that can be expected on the actual exams.

REA's publications and educational materials are highly regarded and continually receive an unprecedented amount of praise from professionals, instructors, librarians, parents, and students. Our authors are as diverse as the subjects and fields represented in the books we publish. They are well known in their respective fields and serve on the faculties of prestigious universities throughout the United States.

Acknowledgments

We would like to thank Dr. Max Fogiel, President, for his overall guidance which has brought this publication to its completion; Larry B. Kling, Quality Control Manager of Books in Print, for his editorial direction; Bernadette Brick, Editorial Assistant, for coordinating the revision of the book; and Alyson DeMonte for her editorial contributions.

MSAT

Multiple Subjects Assessment for Teachers

CHAPTER 1

Passing the MSAT

Chapter 1

Passing the MSAT

ABOUT THIS BOOK

This text provides a complete and accurate representation of the Multiple Subjects Assessment for Teachers (MSAT), one of the most broad-based teacher certification exams in use today. Comprehensive review material for each of the seven test sections is included, along with two complete practice tests, based on the format of the most recently administered MSAT. These practice tests contain every type of question you can expect to encounter on the actual exam, and as with the MSAT itself you are allowed five hours to complete each of ours. Detailed explanations of each answer are included for the Content Knowledge test, and sample essays are provided for the Content Area Exercises to help you understand the test material more completely.

ABOUT THE TEST

Who Takes the Test and What is It Used For?

The MSAT is taken by individuals seeking multiple subject certification in California and Oregon. Candidates may be starting their teaching careers, or may be seeking additional certification.

Who Administers the Test?

The MSAT is administered by Educational Testing Service (ETS). A comprehensive test development process was designed and implemented specifically to ensure that the content and difficulty level of the exam are appropriate.

When and Where is the Test Given?

The MSAT is usually administered four times a year at several locations throughout the states of California and Oregon, generally on a Saturday. ETS also administers the test less frequently at testing centers outside of California and Oregon. Contact ETS for more information on upcoming test dates and locations. ETS can be reached at:

The Praxis Series
Educational Testing Service
P.O. Box 6051
Princeton, NJ 08541-6051
Phone: (800) 772-9476
Website: *www.ets.org/praxis*

Registration information, as well as test dates and locations, are provided in the registration bulletin. Information regarding testing accommodations for candidates with special needs is also included in this bulletin.

Is there a Registration Fee?

You must pay a registration fee in order to take the MSAT. A complete outline of registration fees is provided in your registration bulletin.

HOW TO USE THIS BOOK

When Should I Start Studying?

An eight-week study schedule is provided in this text to assist you in preparing for the exam. This study schedule allows for a great deal of flexibility. Thus, if your test date is only four weeks away, you can halve the time allotted for each section—but keep in mind that this is not the most effective way to study. If you have several months before your test date, you may want to extend the time allotted to each section. Remember, the more time you spend studying, the better your chances of achieving a passing score.

FORMAT OF THE MSAT

The Multiple Subjects Assessment for Teachers is really a group of three tests: Content Knowledge, Content Area Exercises 1, and Content Area Exercises 2. This group of tests is designed to assess your knowledge of the seven major subject areas, in order of their importance to a beginning educator.

The Content Knowledge Test is composed of 120 multiple-choice questions divided into seven subject areas. You have two hours to complete the exam. The breakdown is as follows:

Literature and Language Studies	24 questions
Mathematics	24 questions
History / Social Sciences	22 questions
Science	22 questions
Visual and Performing Arts	12 questions
Human Development	8 questions
Physical Education	8 questions

When preparing to take the actual MSAT, you should be aware that the test sections often fall in random order. The test questions are grouped by subject area, and an index on the back page of your test booklet lists the subject order and page locations, but they may not be placed in the same order as our practice tests. To facilitate your test preparation, our practice tests place the subjects in order if importance, determined by the percentage of the overall exam that the individual sections represent. Each question in the Content Knowledge test has four options, lettered A through D. In each case, only one answer is correct.

Content Area Exercises 1 and 2 are designed to measure higher-order thinking skills as well as your knowledge of subject matter. Candidates are required to produce short responses to questions in each of the content areas. You have two hours to complete Content Area Exercises 1. The breakdown is as follows:

Literature and Language Studies	3 questions
Mathematics	3 questions
Visual and Performing Arts	2 questions
Human Development	2 questions
Physical Education	2 questions

You have one hour to complete Content Area Exercises 2. The breakdown of this test is as follows:

History / Social Sciences	3 questions
Science	3 questions

About the Review Sections

The review material in this text has been compiled in accordance with explicit guidelines provided by Educational Testing Service and the California Commission on Teacher Credentialing. Oregon now accepts the same standards. By using the review material in conjunction with the practice tests, you should be well prepared for the actual MSAT. At some point in your educational experience, you have probably studied all the material that constitutes the test. For most candidates, however, this was most likely some time ago. The reviews will serve to refresh your memory of these topics, and the practice tests will help you gauge which areas you need to work on.

SCORING THE MSAT

How Do I Score My Practice Test?

ETS administers several versions of the MSAT, and these versions vary in level of difficulty. For this reason, there is no single formula that you may use to convert your raw score into a scaled score. It is a safe assumption, however, that if you have answered two thirds (89 items) of the questions on the Content Knowledge test correctly, you have achieved a passing score.

The Content Area Exercises are a bit more difficult to score. A scoring guide is included in the Content Area Exercises practice exam, as are sample essays against which you can judge your work. You may want to have a professor or another test candidate judge your work against our sample essays. If you are honest with yourself about the quality of your work, however, there is no reason why you cannot score your responses yourself. Each response is graded on a four-point scale, 0-3; therefore, the highest possible score you can receive on Content Area Exercises 1 is a 42. If you achieve a score of 28, it is safe to assume that you have passed this area of the test. The highest possible score you can achieve in Content Area Exercises 2 is a 24. If you score at least a 16, it is safe to assume that you have passed this area as well. A quick reference guide to minimum passing scores is presented below:

Test	Number of Questions	Minimum Score
Content Knowledge	134	89
Content Area Exercises 1	14	28
Content Area Exercises 2	8	16

If you do not achieve a passing score on your first practice test, don't worry. Review those sections with which you have had the most difficulty, and try the second practice test. With each practice test, you are sharpening the skills you need to pass the actual exam.

When Will I Receive My Score Report?

Your score report should arrive about six weeks after you take the test. No scoring information will be given over the telephone. Remember, the data on your score report will reflect your *scaled* score, *not* the number of questions you have answered correctly. Minimum scaled scores are as follows:

Test	Passing	Minimum
Content Knowledge	156	148
Content Area Exercises 1 and 2	155	147
Overall Passing Score		311

Even if you do not pass every section of the MSAT, if your individual scores are above the minimum, and your overall score is above 311, then you have passed the exam. If you have scored at or above the minimum on some sections of the exam, but have not achieved an overall passing score, you may combine passing or minimum scores from several administrations. However, you must achieve the overall passing score of the last test that you take.

STUDYING FOR THE MSAT

There is no one correct way to study for the MSAT. You must find the method that works best for you. Some candidates prefer to set aside a few hours every morning to study, while others prefer to study at night before going to sleep. Only you can determine when and where your study time will be most effective, but it is helpful to be consistent. You may retain more information if you study every day at roughly the same time. A study schedule appears at the end of this chapter to help you budget your time.

When taking the practice tests you should try to duplicate the actual testing conditions as closely as possible. A quiet, well lit room, free from such distractions as the television or radio is preferable. As you complete each practice test, score your test and thoroughly review the explanations. Information that is wrong for one item may be correct for another, so it will be helpful to you to absorb as much data as possible. Keep track of your scores so you may gauge your progress accurately, and develop a clear sense of where you need improvement.

MSAT TEST-TAKING TIPS

Although you may have taken standardized tests like the MSAT before, it is crucial that you become familiar with the format and content of each section of this exam. This will help to alleviate any anxiety concerning your performance. Listed below are several ways to help you become accustomed to the test.

> ➤ *Become comfortable with the format of the test.* The MSAT covers a great deal of information, and the more comfortable you are with the format, the more confidence you will have when you take the actual exam. Familiarize

yourself with the requirements of each section individually, and the overall test will be much less intimidating.

➤ *Read all of the possible answers.* Even if you believe you have found the correct answer, read all four options. Often answers that look right at first prove to be "magnet responses" meant to distract you from the correct choice.

➤ *Eliminate obviously incorrect answers immediately.* In this way, even if you do not know the correct answer, you can make an educated guess. Do not leave anything blank; it is always better to guess than to not answer at all. Even if you have absolutely no clue what the correct answer might be, you have a 25% chance of being correct. If you do not mark any answer, you have a 100% chance of being wrong.

➤ *Work quickly and steadily.* You have less than a minute to answer each item on the Content Knowledge test, so don't spend too much time on any one item. You have seven to eight minutes per item on the Content Area Exercises, so try to pace yourself. Timing yourself while you take the practice tests will help you learn to use your time wisely.

➤ *Be sure that the circle you are marking corresponds to the number of the question in the test booklet.* Multiple-choice tests like the MSAT are graded by a computer, which has no sympathy for clerical errors. One incorrectly placed response can upset your entire score.

THE DAY OF THE TEST

Try to get a good night's rest, and rise early on the day of the test. You should have a good breakfast so you will not be distracted by hunger. Dress in layers that can be removed or added as the conditions of the testing center require. There is no guarantee that the temperature in the testing center will be comfortable for *you*. Plan to arrive early. This will enable you to familiarize yourself with the testing center—and minimize the possibility of distraction during the test.

Before you leave for the testing center, make sure you have any admissions material you may need, as well as photo identification. You will also need to bring several sharpened no. 2 pencils, as none will be provided at the test site. In addition, you may bring a non-programmable calculator to the exam. None of the mathematics problems covered on the test requires scientific functions, so a scientific calculator is neither necessary nor permitted. No eating, drinking, or smoking will be permitted during the test, so be sure to get those things out of the way before the test.

During the test, follow the proctor's instructions carefully. Fill out any paperwork very carefully, because this information will be used to process your score reports.

When you have finished the test, turn in your test booklet, and proceed toward the exit in an orderly fashion.

MSAT STUDY SCHEDULE

The following study course schedule allows for thorough preparation to pass the Multiple Subjects Assessment for Teachers. Since this is a suggested eight-week course of study, you may want to use more time to study the MSAT review and other supplementary materials. Be sure to keep a structured schedule by setting aside ample time each day to study. Depending on your schedule, you may find it easier to study throughout the weekend. No matter which schedule works best for you, the more time you devote to studying for the MSAT, the more prepared and confident you will be on the day of the actual test.

Week	Activity
1	Take the first exam as a diagnostic exam. Your score will be an indication of your strengths and weaknesses. Review the explanations for the questions you answered incorrectly.
2	Study REA's MSAT review material. Highlight key terms and information. Take notes on the important theories and key concepts since writing will aid in the retention of information.
3 and 4	Review your references and sources. Use any other supplementary material which your counselor and the California Commission on Teacher Credentialing or the Oregon Teacher Standards and Practices Commission recommend.
5	Condense your notes and findings. You should have a structured outline detailing specific facts. You may want to use index cards to aid you in memorizing important facts and concepts.
6	Test yourself using the index cards. You may want to have a friend or colleague quiz you on key facts and items. Take the second full-length exam. Review the explanations for the questions you answered incorrectly.
7	Study any areas you consider to be your weaknesses by using your study materials, references, and notes.
8	Retake the tests using the extra answer sheets provided in the back of the book.

MSAT

Multiple Subjects Assessment for Teachers

CHAPTER 2

Literature and Language Studies Review

Chapter 2

Literature and Language Studies Review

The Literature and Language Studies section of the MSAT accounts for 20 percent of the overall exam. This 20 percent comprises 24 of the 120 multiple-choice questions (Content Knowledge), and three of the 18 free-response items (Content Area Exercises). This portion is divided into three sections, each represented in this chapter.

Literature (35 percent)
- Literary terms and concepts
- Literary genres
- Social and historical context
- Methods of interpretation

Language Studies (35 percent)
- Stages of language development
- Cultural influences on American English
- Principles of linguistics

Oral and Written Communication (30 percent)
- Applied communication skills
- Rhetorical methods and conventions
- Information retrieval and analysis

The review material that follows covers each of these topics in detail, providing you with all the information you'll need to achieve a passing score on this section. Be sure to complete the Practice Problems at the end of the review. This should isolate areas that you may need to re-read.

PROSE

General Rules and Ideas

Why do people write prose? Certainly such a question has a built-in counter: As opposed to writing what, poetry? One possible answer is that the person is a poor poet. The requirements and restrictions of the various genres make different demands upon a writer; most writers find their niche and stay there, secure in their private "comfort zone." Shakespeare did not write essays; Hemingway did not write poetry. If either did venture outside of his literary domain, the world took little note.

Students are sometimes confused as to what exactly is prose. Basically, prose is **not** poetry. Prose is what we write and speak most of the time in our everyday intercourse: unmetered, unrhymed language. Which is not to say that prose does not have its own rhythms—language, whether written or spoken, has cadence and balance. And certainly prose can have instances of rhyme or assonance, alliteration or onomatopoeia. Language is, after all, **phonic.**

Furthermore, **prose** may be either **fiction** or **non-fiction**. A novel (like a short story) is fiction; an autobiography is non-fiction. While a novel (or short story) may have autobiographical elements, an autobiography is presumed to be entirely factual. Essays are usually described in other terms: expository, argumentative, persuasive, critical, narrative. Essays may have elements of either fiction or non-fiction, but are generally classed as a separate subgenre.

Satire, properly speaking, is not a genre at all, but rather a **mode**, elements of which can be found in any category of literature—from poetry and drama to novels and essays. Satire is a manifestation of authorial attitude (tone) and purpose. Our discussion of satire will be limited to its use in prose.

But we have not addressed the initial question: "Why do people write prose?" The answer depends, in part, on the writer's intent. If he wishes to tell a rather long story, filled with many characters and subplots, interlaced with motifs, symbols, and themes, with time and space to develop interrelationships and to present descriptive passages, the writer generally chooses the novel as his medium. If he believes he can present his story more compactly and less complexly, he may choose the novella or the short story.

These subgenres require from the reader a different kind of involvement than does the essay. The essay, rather than presenting a story from which the reader may discern meaning through the skillful analysis of character, plot, symbol, and language, presents a relatively straightforward account of the writer's opinion(s) on an endless array of topics. Depending upon the type of essay, the reader may become informed (expository), provoked (argumentative), persuaded, enlightened (critical), or, in the case of the narrative essay, better acquainted with the writer who wishes to illustrate a point with his story, whether it is autobiographical or fictitious.

Encountering satire in prose selections demands that the reader be sensitive to the nuances of language and form, that he detect the double-edged sword of irony, and that he correctly assess both the writer's tone and his purpose.

Readers of prose, like readers of poetry, seek aesthetic pleasure, entertainment, and knowledge, not necessarily in that order. Fiction offers worlds—real and imagined—in which characters and ideas, events and language, interact in ways familiar and unfamiliar. As readers, we take delight in the wisdom we fancy we have acquired from a novel or short story. Non-fiction offers viewpoints which we may find comforting or horrifying, amusing or sobering, presented by the author rather than by his once-removed persona. Thus, we are tempted to believe that somehow the truths presented in non-fiction are more "real" than the truths revealed by fiction. But we must resist! Truth is not "genre-specific."

Reading Novels

Most literary handbooks will define a novel as an extended fictional prose narrative, derived from the Italian *novella*, meaning "tale, piece of news." The term "novelle," meaning short tales, was applied to works such as Boccaccio's *The Decameron*, a collection of stories which had an impact on later works such as Chaucer's *Canterbury Tales*. In most European countries, the word for **novel** is **roman**, short for **romance**, which was applied to longer verse narratives (Malory's *Morte d'Arthur*), which were later written in prose. Early romances were associated with "legendary, imaginative, and poetic material"—tales "of the long ago or the far away or the imaginatively improbable"; novels, on the other hand, were felt to be "bound by the facts of the actual world and the laws of probability" (*A Handbook to Literature*, C. Hugh Holman, p. 354).

The novel has, over some 600 years, developed into many special forms which are classified by subject matter: detective novel, psychological novel, historical novel, regional novel, picaresque novel, Gothic novel, stream-of-consciousness novel, epistolary novel, and so on. These terms, of course, are not exhaustive nor mutually exclusive. Furthermore, depending on the conventions of the author's time period, his style, and his outlook on life, his *mode* may be termed **realism, romanticism, impressionism, expressionism, naturalism,** or **neo-classicism** (Holman, p. 359).

Our earlier description of a novel ("...a rather long story, filled with many characters and subplots, interlaced with motifs, symbols, and themes, with time and space to develop interrelationships and to present descriptive passages") is satisfactory for our purposes here. The works generally included on the MSAT are those which have stood the test of time in significance, literary merit, and reader popularity. New works are incorporated into the canon which is a reflection of what works are being taught in literature classes. And teachers begin to teach those works which are included frequently among the questions. So the process is circular, but the standards remain high for inclusion.

Analyzing novels is a bit like asking the journalist's five questions: what? who? why? where? and how? The what? is the story, the narrative, the plot and subplots. Most students are familiar with Freytag's Pyramid, originally designed to describe the structure of a five-act drama but now widely used to analyze fiction as well. The stages generally specified are **introduction** or **exposition, complication, rising action, climax, falling action,** and **denouement** or **conclusion.** As the novel's events are charted, the "change which structures the story" should emerge. There are many events in a long narrative; but generally only one set of events comprises the "real" or "significant" story.

However, subplots often parallel or serve as counterpoints to the main plot line, serving to enhance the central story. Minor characters sometimes have essentially the same conflicts and goals as the major characters, but the consequences of the outcome seem less important. Sometimes the parallels involve reversals of characters and situations, creating similar yet distinct differences in the outcomes. Nevertheless, seeing the parallels makes understanding the major plot line less difficult.

Sometimes an author divides the novel into chapters—named or unnamed, perhaps just numbered. Or he might divide the novel into "books" or "parts," with chapters as subsections. Readers should take their cue from these divisions; the author must have had some reason for them. Take note of what happens in each larger section, as well as within the smaller chapters. Whose progress is being followed? What event or occurrence is being foreshadowed or prepared for? What causal or other relationships are there between sections and events? Some writers, such as Steinbeck in *The Grapes of Wrath*, use intercalary chapters, alternating between the "real" story (the Joads) and peripheral or parallel stories (the Okies and migrants in general). Look for the pattern of such organization; try to see the interrelationships of these alternating chapters.

Of course, plots cannot happen in isolation from characters, the **who?** element of a story. Not only are there major and minor characters to consider; we need to note whether the various characters are **static** or **dynamic**. Static characters do not change in significant ways—that is, in ways which relate to the story which is structuring the novel. A character may die, i.e., change from alive to dead, and still be static, unless his death is central to the narrative. For instance, in Golding's *Lord of the Flies*, the boy with the mulberry birthmark apparently dies in a fire early in the novel. Momentous as any person's death is, this boy's death is not what the novel is about. However, when Simon is killed, and later Piggy, the narrative is directly impacted because the reason for their deaths is central to the novel's theme regarding man's innate evil. A dynamic character may change only slightly in his attitudes, but those changes may be the very ones upon which the narrative rests. For instance, Siddhartha begins as a very pure and devout Hindu but is unfulfilled spiritually. He eventually does achieve spiritual contentment, but his change is more a matter of degree than of substance. He is not an evil man who attains salvation, nor a pious man who becomes corrupt. It is the process of his search, the stages in his pilgrimage, which structure the novel *Siddhartha*.

We describe major characters or "actors" in novels as **protagonists** or **antagonists**. Built into those two terms is the Greek word *agon,* meaning "struggle." The *pro*tagonist struggles **toward** or for someone or something; the *ant(i)*agonist struggles **against** someone or something. The possible conflicts are usually cited as man against himself, man against man, man against society, man against nature. Sometimes more than one of these conflicts appears in a story, but usually one is dominant and is the structuring device.

A character can be referred to as **stock**, meaning that he exists because the plot demands it. For instance, a Western with a gunman who robs the bank will require a number of stock characters: the banker's lovely daughter, the tough but kindhearted barmaid, the cowardly white-shirted citizen who sells out the hero to save his own skin, and the young freckle-faced lad who shoots the bad guy from a second-story hotel window.

Or a character can be a **stereotype**, without individuating characteristics. For instance, a sheriff in a small Southern town; a football player who is all brawn; a librarian clucking over her prized books; the cruel commandant of a POW camp.

Characters often serve as **foils** for other characters, enabling us to see one or more of them better. A classic example is Tom Sawyer, the Romantic foil for Huck Finn's Realism. Or, in Lee's *To Kill a Mockingbird*, Scout as the naive observer of events which her brother Jem, four years older, comes to understand from the perspective of the adult world.

Sometimes characters are **allegorical**, standing for qualities or concepts rather than for actual personages. For instance, Jim Casey (initials "J. C.") in *The Grapes of Wrath* is often regarded as a Christ figure, pure and self-sacrificing in his aims for the migrant workers. Or Kamala, Siddhartha's teacher in the art of love, whose name comes from the tree whose bark is used as a purgative; she purges him of his ascetic ways on his road to self-hood and spiritual fulfillment.

Other characters are fully three-dimensional, "rounded," "mimetic" of humans in all their virtue, vice, hope, despair, strength and weakness. This verisimilitude aids the author in creating characters who are credible and plausible, without being dully predictable and mundane.

The interplay of plot and characters determines in large part the **theme** of a work, the why? of the story. First of all, we must distinguish between a mere topic and a genuine theme or thesis; and then between a theme and contributing *motifs*. A **topic** is a phrase, such as "man's inhumanity to man"; or "the fickle nature of fate." A **theme**, however, turns a phrase into a statement: "Man's inhumanity to man is barely concealed by 'civilization.'" Or "Man is a helpless pawn, at the mercy of fickle fate." Many writers may deal with the same topic, such as the complex nature of true love; but their themes may vary widely, from "True love will always win out in the end," to "Not even true love can survive the cruel ironies of fate."

To illustrate the relationship between plot, character, and theme, let's examine two familiar fairy tales. In "The Ugly Duckling," the structuring story line is "Once upon a time there was an ugly duckling, who in turn became a beautiful swan." In this case, the duckling did nothing to merit either his ugliness nor his eventual transformation; but he did not curse fate. He only wept and waited, lonely and outcast. And when he became beautiful, he did not gloat; he eagerly joined the other members of his flock, who greatly admired him. The theme here essentially is: "Good things come to him who waits," or "Life is unfair—you don't get what you deserve, nor deserve what you get"? What happens to the theme if the ugly duckling remains an ugly duckling: "Some guys just never get a break"?

Especially rewarding to examine for the interdependence of plot and theme is "Cinderella": "Once upon a time, a lovely, sweet-natured young girl was forced to labor for and serve her ugly and ungrateful stepmother and two stepsisters. But thanks to her fairy godmother, Cinderella and the Prince marry, and live happily ever after."

We could change events (plot elements) at any point, but let's take the penultimate scene where the Prince's men come to the door with the single glass slipper. Cinderella has been shut away so that she is not present when the other women in the house try on the slipper. Suppose that the stepmother or either of the two stepsisters tries on the slipper—and it fits! Cinderella is in the back room doing the laundry, and her family waltzes out the door to the palace and she doesn't even get an invitation to the wedding. And imagine the Prince's dismay when the ugly, one-slippered lady lifts her wedding veil for the consummating kiss! Theme: "There is no justice in the world, for those of low or high station"; or "Virtue is not its own reward"?

Or let's say that during the slipper-test scene, the stepsisters, stepmother, and finally Cinderella all try on the shoe, but to no avail. And then in sashays the Fairy Godmother, who gives them all a knowing smirk, puts out her slipper-sized foot and cackles hysterically, like the mechanical witch in the penny arcade. Theme: "You can't trust anybody these days"; or, a favorite statement of theme, "Appearances can be deceiving." The link between plot and theme is very strong, indeed.

Skilled writers often employ **motifs** to help unify their works. A motif is a detail or element of the story which is repeated throughout, and which may even become symbolic. Television shows are ready examples of the use of motifs. A medical show, with many scenes alternately set in the hospital waiting room and operating room, uses elements such as the pacing, anxious parent or loved one, the gradually filling ashtray, the large wall clock whose hands melt from one hour to another. And in the operating room, the half-masked surgeon whose brow is frequently mopped by the nurse; the gloved hand open-palmed to receive scalpel, sponge, and so on; the various oscilloscopes giving readouts of the patient's very fragile condition; the expanding and collapsing bladder manifesting that the patient is indeed breathing; and, again, the wall clock, assuring us that this procedure is taking forever. These are all motifs, details which in concert help convince the reader that this story occurs in a hospital, and that the mood is pretty tense, that the medical team is doing all it can, and that Mom and Dad will be there when Junior or Sissy wakes up.

But motifs can become symbolic. The oscilloscope line quits blipping, levels out, and gives off the ominous hum. And the doctor's gloved hand sets down the scalpel and shuts off the oscilloscope. In the waiting room, Dad crushes the empty cigarette pack; Mom quits pacing and sinks into the sofa. The door to the waiting room swings shut silently behind the retreating doctor. All these elements signal "It's over, finished."

This example is very crude and mechanical, but motifs in the hands of a skillful writer are valuable devices. And in isolation, and often magnified, a single motif can become a controlling image with great significance. For instance, Emma Bovary's shoes signify her obsession with material things; and when her delicate slippers become soiled as she crosses the dewy grass to meet her lover, we sense the impurity of her act as well as its futility. Or when wise Piggy, in *Lord of the Flies,* is reduced to one lens in his specs, and finally to no specs at all, we see the loss of insight and wisdom on the island, and chaos follows.

Setting is the where? element of the story. But setting is also the **when** element: time of day, time of year, time period or year; it is the dramatic moment, the precise intersection of time and space when this story is being told. Setting is also the atmosphere: positive or negative ambiance, calm, chaotic, Gothic, Romantic. The question for the reader to answer is whether the setting is ultimately essential to the plot/theme, or whether it is incidental; i.e., could this story/theme have been told successfully in another time and/or place? For instance, could the theme in *Lord of the Flies* be made manifest if the boys were not on an island? Could they have been isolated in some other place? Does it matter whether the "war" which they are fleeing is WWII or WWIII or some other conflict, in terms of the theme?

Hopefully, the student will see that the four elements of plot, character, theme, and setting are intertwined and largely interdependent. A work must really be read as a whole, rather than dissected and analyzed in discrete segments.

The final question, how?, relates to an author's style. Style involves language (word choice), syntax (word order, sentence type and length), the balance between narration and dialogue, the choice of narrative voice (first person participant, third person with limited omniscience), use of descriptive passages, and other aspects of the actual words on the page which are basically irrelevant to the first four elements (plot, character, theme, and setting). Stylistic differences are fairly easy to spot among such diverse writers as Jane Austen, whose style is—to today's reader—very formal and mannered; Mark Twain, whose style is very casual and colloquial; William Faulkner, whose prose often spins on without punctuation or paragraphs far longer than the reader can hold either the thought or his breath; and Hemingway, whose dense but spare, pared-down style has earned the epithet, "Less is more."

Reading Short Stories

The modern short story differs from earlier short fiction such as the parable, fable, and tale, in its emphasis on character development through scenes rather than summary: through *showing* rather than *telling.* Gaining popularity in the 19th century, the short story generally was realistic, presenting detailed accounts of the lives of middle-class personages. This tendency toward realism dictates that the plot be grounded in *probabil-*

ity, with causality fully in operation. Furthermore, the characters are human with recognizable human motivations, both social and psychological. Setting—time and place—is realistic rather than fantastic. And, as Poe stipulated, the elements of plot, character, setting, style, point of view, and theme all work toward a single *unified* effect.

However, some modern writers have stretched these boundaries and have mixed in elements of nonrealism—such as the supernatural and the fantastic—sometimes switching back and forth between realism and nonrealism, confusing the reader who is expecting conventional fiction. Barth's "Lost in the Funhouse" and Allen's "The Kugelmass Episode" are two stories which are not, strictly speaking, *realistic*. However, if the reader will approach and accept this type of story on its own terms, he will be better able to understand and appreciate them fully.

Unlike the novel, which has time and space to develop characters and interrelationships, the short story must rely on flashes of insight and revelation to develop plot and characters. The "slice of life" in a short story is of necessity much narrower than that in a novel; the time span is much shorter, the focus much tighter. To attempt anything like the panoramic canvas available to the novelist would be to view fireworks through a soda straw: occasionally pretty, but ultimately not very satisfying or enlightening.

The elements of the short story are those of the novel, discussed earlier. However, because of the compression of time and concentration of effect, probably the short story writer's most important decision is **point of view**. A narrator may be *objective*, presenting information without bias or comment. Hemingway frequently uses the objective *third-person* narrator, presenting scenes almost dramatically, i.e., with a great deal of dialogue and very little narrative, none of which directly reveals the thoughts or feelings of the characters. The third-person narrator may, however, be less objective in his presentation, directly revealing the thoughts and feelings, of one or more of the characters, as Chopin does in "The Story of an Hour." We say that such a narrator is fully or partially *omniscient*, depending on how complete his knowledge is of the characters' psychological and emotional makeup. The least objective narrator is the *first-person* narrator, who presents information from the perspective of a single character who is a participant in the action. Such a narrative choice allows the author to present the discrepancies between the writer's/reader's perceptions and those of the narrator.

One reason the choice of narrator, the point of view from which to tell the story, is immensely important in a short story is that the narrator reveals character and event in ways which affect our understanding of theme. For instance, in Faulkner's "A Rose for Emily," the unnamed narrator who seems to be a townsperson recounts the story out of chronological order, juxtaposing events whose causality and significance are uncertain. The narrator withholds information which would explain events being presented, letting the reader puzzle over Emily Grierson's motivations, a device common in detective fiction. In fact, the narrator presents contradictory information, making the reader alternately pity and resent the spinster. When we examine the imagery and conclude that Miss Emily and her house represent the decay and decadence of the Old South which resisted the invasion of "progress" from the North, we see the importance of setting and symbol in relation to theme.

Similarly, in Mansfield's "Bliss," the abundant description of setting creates the controlling image of the lovely pear tree. But this symbol of fecundity becomes ironic when Bertha Young belatedly feels sincere and overwhelming desire for her husband. The third-person narrator's omniscience is limited to Bertha's thoughts and feelings; otherwise we would have seen her husband's infidelity with Miss Fulton.

In O'Connor's "Good Country People," the narrator is broadly omniscient, but the reader is still taken by surprise at the cruelty of the Bible salesman who seduces Joy-Hulga. That he steals her artificial leg is perhaps poetic justice, since she (with her numerous degrees) had fully intended to seduce him ("just good country people"). The story's title, the characters' names—Hopewell, Freeman, Joy; the salesman's professed Christianity, the Bibles hollowed out to hold whiskey and condoms, add to the irony of Mrs. Freeman's final comment on the young man: "Some can't be that simple... I know I never could."

The *initiation story* frequently employs the first-person narrator. To demonstrate the subtle differences which can occur in stories which ostensibly have the same point of view and general theme, let's look at three: "A Christmas Memory" (Capote), "Araby" (Joyce), and "A & P" (Updike).

Early in "A Christmas Memory," Capote's narrator identifies himself:

> The person to whom she is speaking is myself. I am seven; she is sixty-something. We are cousins, very distant ones, and we have lived together—well, as long as I can remember. Other people inhabit the house, relatives; and though they have power over us, and frequently make us cry, we are not, on the whole, too much aware of them. We are each other's best friend. She calls me Buddy, in memory of a boy who was formerly her best friend. The other Buddy died in the 1880's, when she was still a child. She is still a child.

Buddy and his cousin, who is called only "my friend," save their meager earnings throughout the year in order to make fruitcakes at Christmas to give mainly to "persons we've met maybe once, perhaps not at all... Like President Roosevelt.... Or Abner Packer, the driver of the six o'clock bus from Mobile, who exchanges waves with us everyday...." Their gifts to one another each year are always handmade, often duplicates of the year before, like the kites they present on what was to be their last Christmas together.

Away at boarding school, when Buddy receives word of his friend's death, it "merely confirms a piece of news some secret vein had already received, severing from me an irreplaceable part of myself, letting it loose like a kite on a broken string. That is why, walking across a school campus on this particular December morning, I keep searching the sky. As if I expected to see, rather like hearts, a lost pair of kites hurrying toward heaven."

Buddy's characterizations of his friend are also self-revelatory. He and she are peers, equals, despite their vast age difference. They are both totally unselfish, joying in the simple activities mandated by their economic circumstances. They are both "children."

The story is told in present tense, making the memories from the first paragraphs seem as "real" and immediate as those from many years later. And Buddy's responses from the early years ("Well, I'm disappointed. Who wouldn't be? With socks, a Sunday school shirt, some handkerchiefs, a hand-me-down sweater and a year's subscription to a religious magazine for children. *The Little Shepherd*. It makes me boil. It really does.") are as true to his seven-year-old's perspective, as are those when he, much older, has left home ("I have a new home too. But it doesn't count. Home is where my friend is, and there I never go.").

The youthful narrator in "A & P" also uses present tense, but not consistently, which gives his narrative a very colloquial, even unschooled flavor. Like Buddy, Sammy identifies himself in the opening paragraph: "In walks these three girls in nothing but bathing suits. I'm in the third checkout slot, with my back to the door, so I don't see them until they're over by the bread." And later, "Stokesie's married, with two babies chalked up on his fuselage already, but as far as I can tell that's the only difference. He's twenty-two, and I was nineteen this April." The girls incur the wrath of the store manager, who scolds them for their inappropriate dress. And Sammy, in his adolescent idealism, quits on the spot; although he realizes that he does not want to "do this" to his parents, he tells us "… it seems to me that once you begin a gesture it's fatal not to go through with it." But his *beau geste* is ill-spent: "I look around for my girls, but they're gone, of course…. I could see Lengel in my place in the slot, checking the sheep through. His face was dark gray and his back stiff, as if he'd just had an injection of iron, and my stomach kind of fell as I felt how hard the world was going to be to me hereafter."

Like Buddy, Sammy tells his story from a perch not too distant from the events he recounts. Both narrators still feel the immediacy of their rites of passage very strongly. Buddy, however, reveals himself to be a more admirable character, perhaps because his story occurs mainly when he is seven—children tend not to be reckless in the way that Sammy is. Sammy was performing for an audience, doing things he knew would cause pain to himself and his family, for the sake of those three girls who never gave him the slightest encouragement and whom he would probably never even see again.

In "Araby," the unnamed narrator tells of a boyhood crush he had on the older sister of one of his chums: "I thought little of the future. I did not know whether I would ever speak to her or not or, if I spoke to her, how I could tell her of my confused adoration. But my body was like a harp and her words and gestures were like fingers running upon the wires." She asks the boy if he is going to Araby, a "splendid bazaar," and reveals that she cannot. He promises to go himself and bring her something. But his uncle's late homecoming delays the boy's excursion until the bazaar is nearly closed for the night, and he is unable to find an appropriate gift. Forlornly, "I turned away slowly and walked down the middle of the bazaar…. Gazing up into the darkness I saw myself as a creature driven and derided by vanity; and my eyes burned with anguish and anger." This narrator is recounting his story from much further away than either Buddy or Sammy tells his own. The narrator of "Araby" has the perspective of an adult, looking back at a very important event in his boyhood. His "voice" reflects wisdom born of experience. The incident was very painful then; but its memory, while poignant, is no longer devastating. Like Sammy, this narrator sees the dichotomy between his adolescent idealism and the mundane reality of "romance." However, the difference is in the narrator's ability to turn the light on himself; Sammy is still so close to the incident that he very likely would whip off his checker's apron again if the girls returned to the A & P. The "Araby" narrator has "mellowed," and can see the futility—and the necessity—of adolescent love.

Reading Essays

Essays fall into four rough categories: **speculative**, **argumentative**, **narrative**, and **expository**. Depending on the writer's purpose, his essay will fit more or less into one or these groupings.

The **speculative** essay is so named because, as its Latin root suggests, it *looks* at ideas; explores them rather than explains them. While the speculative essay may be said to be *meditative*, it often makes one or more points. But the thesis may not be as obvious or clear-cut as that in an expository or argumentative essay. The writer deals with ideas in an associative manner, playing with ideas in a looser structure than he would in an expository or argumentative essay. This "flow" may even produce *intercalary* para-

narrative of sorts and thoughtful responses to the
s "The Ring of Time."

tative essay, on the other hand, are always clear: to
e, which may be factual or anecdotal, and to support
formal, as in a debate, with counterpositions and
ganizational pattern, the writer's intent in an argumen-
er of the validity of some claim, as Bacon does in "Of

ays have elements of both the speculative and argu-
ay may recount an incident or a series of incidents and
in order to make a point, as in Orwell's "Shooting an
torytelling makes the narrative essay less insistent than
directed than the speculative essay.

familiar with the expository essay, the primary purpose
of which is to explain and clarify ideas. While the expository essay may have narrative
elements, that aspect is minor and subservient to that of explanation. Furthermore, while
nearly all essays have some element of persuasion, argumentation is incidental in the
expository essay. In any event, the four categories—speculative, argumentative, narrative, and expository—are neither exhaustive nor mutually exclusive.

As non-fiction, essays have a different set of elements from novels and short
stories: **voice**, **style**, **structure**, and **thought**.

Voice in non-fiction is similar to the narrator's tone in fiction; but the major
difference is in who is "speaking." In fiction, the author is not the speaker—the **narrator**
is the speaker. Students sometimes have difficulty with this distinction, but it is necessary
if we are to preserve the integrity of the fictive "story." In an essay, however, the author
speaks directly to the reader, even if he is presenting ideas which he may not actually
espouse personally—as in a satire. This directness creates the writer's **tone**, his attitude
toward his subject.

Style in non-fiction derives from the same elements as style in fiction: word choice,
syntax, balance between dialogue and narration, voice, use of description—those things
specifically related to words on the page. Generally speaking, an argumentative essay
will be written in a more formal style than will a narrative essay, and a meditative essay
will be less formal than an expository essay. But such generalizations are only descriptive, not prescriptive.

Structure and thought, the final elements of essays, are so intertwined as to be
inextricable. We must be aware that to change the structure of an essay will alter its
meaning. For instance, in White's "The Ring of Time," to abandon the *intercalary* paragraph organization, separating the paragraphs which narrate the scenes with the young
circus rider from those which reflect on the circularity and linearity of time, would alter
our understanding of the essay's thesis. Writers signal structural shifts with alterations in
focus, as well as with visual clues (spacing), verbal clues—(*but, therefore, however*), or
shifts in the kind of information being presented (personal, scientific, etc).

Thought is perhaps the single element which most distinguishes non-fiction from
fiction. The essayist chooses his form not to tell a story but to present an idea. Whether
he chooses the speculative, narrative, argumentative, or expository format, the essayist
has something on his mind that he wants to convey to his readers. And it is this idea
which we are after when we analyze his essay.

Often anthologized is Orwell's "Shooting an Elephant," a narrative essay recounting the writer's (presumably) experience in Burma as an officer of the British law that

ruled the poverty-ridden people of a small town. Orwell begins with two paragraphs which explain that, as a white, European authority figure, he was subjected to taunts and abuse by the natives. Ironically, he sympathized with the Burmese and harbored fairly strong anti-British feelings, regarding the imperialists as the oppressors rather than the saviors. He tells us that he felt trapped between his position of authority, which he himself resented, and the hatred of those he was required to oversee.

The body of the essay—some eleven paragraphs—relates the incident with an otherwise tame elephant gone "must" which had brought chaos and destruction to the village. Only occasionally does Orwell interrupt the narrative to reveal his reactions directly, but his descriptions of the Burmese are sympathetically drawn. The language is heavily connotative, revealing the helplessness of the villagers against both the elephant and the miserable circumstances of their lives.

Orwell recounts how, having sent for an elephant gun, he found that he was compelled to shoot the animal, even though its destruction was by now unwarranted and even ill-advised, given the value of the elephant to the village. But the people expected it, demanded it; the white man realized that he did not have dominion over these people of color after all. They were in charge, not he.

To make matters worse, Orwell bungles the "murder" of the beast, which takes half an hour to die in great agony. And in the aftermath of discussions of the rightness or wrongness of his action, Orwell wonders if anyone realizes he killed the elephant only to save face. It is the final sentence of the final paragraph which directly reveals the author's feelings, although he has made numerous indirect references to them throughout the essay. Coupled with the opening paragraphs, this conclusion presents British imperialism of the period in a very negative light: "the unable doing the unnecessary to the ungrateful."

Having discovered Orwell's main idea, we must look at the other elements (voice, style, structure) to see *how* he communicates it to the reader. The voice of the first-person narrative is fairly formal, yet remarkably candid, using connotation to color our perception of the events. Orwell's narrative has many complex sentences, with vivid descriptive phrases in series, drawing our eye along the landscape and through the crowds as he ponders his next move. Structurally, the essay first presents a premise about British imperialism, then moves to a gripping account of the officer's reluctant shooting of the elephant, and ends with an admission of his own culpability as an agent of the institution he detests. Orwell frequently signals shifts between his role as officer and his responses as a humane personage with *but*, or with dashes to set off his responses to the events he is recounting.

Reading Satire

Satire is a *mode* which may be employed by writers of various genres: poetry, drama, fiction, non-fiction. It is more a perspective than a product.

Satire mainly exposes and ridicules, derides and denounces vice, folly, evil, stupidity, as these qualities manifest themselves in persons, groups of persons, ideas, institutions, customs, or beliefs. While the satirist has many techniques at his disposal, there are basically only two types of satire: gentle or harsh, depending on the author's intent, his audience, and his methods.

The terms **romanticism, realism,** and **naturalism** can help us understand the role of *satire*. Romanticism sees the world idealistically, as perfectible if not perfect. Realism sees the world as it is, with healthy doses of both good and bad. Naturalism sees the world as imperfect, with evil often triumphing over good. The satirist is closer to the naturalist than he is to the romantic or realist, for both the satirist and the naturalist focus on what is wrong with the world, intending to expose the foibles of man and his society. The difference between them lies in their techniques. The naturalist is very direct and does not necessarily employ humor; the satirist is more subtle, and does.

For instance, people plagued with overpopulation and starvation is not, on first glance, material for humor. Many works have treated such conditions with sensitivity, bringing attention to the plight of the world's unfortunate. Steinbeck's *Grapes of Wrath* is such a work. However, Swift's "A Modest Proposal" takes essentially the same circumstances and holds them up for our amused examination. How does the satirist make an un-funny topic humorous? And why would he do so?

The satirist's techniques—his weapons—include **irony, parody, reversal** or **inversion, hyperbole, understatement, sarcasm, wit, invective**. By exaggerating characteristics, by saying the opposite of what he means, by using his cleverness to make cutting or even cruel remarks at the expense of his subject, the writer of satire can call the reader's attention to those things he believes are repulsive, despicable, or destructive.

Whether he uses more harsh (Juvenalian) or more gentle (Horatian) satire depends upon the writer's attitude and intent. Is he merely flaunting his clever intellect, playing with words for our amusement or to inflate his own sense of superiority? Is he probing the psychological motivations for the foolish or destructive actions of some person(s)? Is he determined to waken an unenlightened or apathetic audience, moving its members to thought or action? Are the flaws which the satirist is pointing out truly destructive or evil, or are they the faults we would all recognize in ourselves if we glanced in the mirror, not admirable but not really harmful to ourselves or society? Is the author amused, sympathetic, objective, irritated, scornful, bitter, pessimistic, mocking? The reader needs to identify the satirist's purpose and tone. Its subtlety sometimes makes satire a difficult mode to detect and to understand.

Irony is perhaps the satirist's most powerful weapon. The basis of irony is inversion or reversal, doing or saying the opposite or the unexpected. Shakespeare's famous sonnet beginning "My mistress' eyes are nothing like the sun..." is an ironic tribute to the speaker's beloved, who, he finally declares is "as rare/As any she belied with false compare." At the same time, Shakespeare is poking fun at the sonnet form as it was used by his contemporaries—himself included—to extol the virtues of their ladies. By selecting a woman who, by his own description, is physically unattractive in every way imaginable, and using the conventions of the love sonnet to present her many flaws, he has inverted the sonnet tradition. And then by asserting that she compares favorably with any of the other ladies whose poet-lovers have lied about their virtues, he presents us with the unexpected twist. Thus, he satirizes both the love sonnet form and its subject by using irony.

Other notable poetic satires include Koch's "Variations on a Theme by William Carlos Williams," in which he parodies Williams "This is Just to Say." Koch focuses on the simplicity and directness of Williams' imagery and makes the form and ideas seem foolish and trivial. In "Boom!," Nemerov takes issue with a pastor's assertion that modern technology has resulted in a concomitant rise in religious activities and spiritual values. Nemerov catalogues the instant, disposable, and extravagant aspects of Americans' lifestyles, which result in "pray as you go... pilgrims" for whom religion is another convenience, commercial rather than spiritual.

Satire in drama is also common; Wilde's "The Importance of Being Earnest" is wonderfully funny in its constant word play (notably on the name *Ernest*) and its relentless ridiculing of the superficiality which Wilde saw as characteristic of British gentry.

Barrie's "The Admirable Crichton" has a similar theme, with the added assertion that it is the "lower" or servant class which is truly superior—again, the ironic reversal so common in satire. Both of these plays are mild in their ridicule; the authors do not expect or desire any change in society or in the viewer. The satire is gentle; the satirists are amused, or perhaps bemused at the society whose foibles they expose.

Classic novels which employ satire include Swift's *Gulliver's Travels* and Voltaire's *Candide*, both of which fairly vigorously attack aspects of the religions, governments, and prevailing intellectual beliefs of their respective societies. A modern novel which uses satire is Heller's *Catch-22*, which is basically an attack on war and the government's bureaucratic bungling of men and materiel, specifically in WWII. But by extension, Heller is also viewing with contempt the unmotivated, illogical, capricious behavior of all institutions which operate by that basic law: "catch-22." Like Swift and Voltaire, Heller is angry. And although his work, like the other two, has humor and wit, exaggeration and irony, his purpose is more than intellectual entertainment for his readers. Heller hopes for reform.

Heller's attack is frontal, his assault direct. Swift had to couch his tale in a fantastic setting with imaginary creatures in order to present his views with impunity. The audience, as well as the times, also affect the satirist's work. If the audience is hostile, the writer must veil his theme; if the audience is indifferent, he must jolt them with bitter and reviling language if he desires change. If he does not fear reprisals, the satirist may take any tone he pleases.

We can see satire in operation in two adaptations of the biblical story of King Solomon, who settled the dispute between two mothers regarding an infant: Cut the baby in two and divide it between you, he told them. The rightful mother protested, and was promptly awarded the child. The story is meant to attest to the King's wisdom and understanding of parental love, in this case.

However, Twain's Huck Finn has some difficulty persuading runaway slave Jim that Solomon was wise. Jim insists that Solomon, having fathered "'bout five million chillen," was "waseful.... *He* as soon chop a chile in two as a cat. Dey's plenty mo'. A chile er two, mo' er less, warn't no consekens to Solermun, dad fetch him!" Twain is ridiculing not only Jim's ingenuousness, as he does throughout the novel; he is also deflating time-honored beliefs about the Bible and its traditional heroes, as he earlier does with the account of Moses and the "bulrushers." While Twain's tone is fairly mild, his intent shows through as serious; Twain was disgusted with traditional Christianity and its hypocritical followers, as we see later in *Huck Finn* when young Buck Grangerford is murdered in the feud with the Shepherdsons: "I wished I hadn't ever come ashore that night to see such things."

A second satiric variation on the Solomon theme appears in Asprin's *Myth Adventures*, in the volume *Hit or Myth*. Skeebe, the narrator, realizes that he, as King pro-tem, must render a decision regarding the ownership of a cat. Hoping to inspire them to compromise, he decrees that they divide the cat between them: "Instead they thanked me for my wisdom, shook hands, and left smiling, presumably to carve up their cat." He concludes that many of the citizens of this realm "don't have both oars in the water," a conclusion very like Huck's: "I never see such a nigger. If he got a notion in his head once, there warn't no getting it out again." The citizens' unthinking acceptance of the infallibility of authority is as laughable as Jim's out-of-hand rejection of Solomon's wisdom because no wise man would "want to live in the mids' er sich a blim-blammin' all de time" as would prevail in the harem with the King's "million wives."

POETRY

Opening a book to study for an examination is perhaps the worst occasion on which to read poetry, or about poetry, because above all, poetry should be enjoyed; it is definitely "reading for pleasure." This last phrase seems to have developed recently to describe the reading we do other than for information or for study. Perhaps you personally would not choose poetry as pleasure reading because of the bad name poetry has received over the years. Some students regard the "old" poetry such as Donne's or Shelley's as effete (for "wimps" and "nerds" only, in current language), or modern poetry as too difficult or weird. It is hard to imagine that poetry was the "current language" for students growing up in the Elizabethan or Romantic eras. Whereas in our world information can be retrieved in a nanosecond, in those worlds time was plentiful to sit down, clear the mind and let poetry take over. Very often the meaning of a poem does not come across in a nanosecond and for the modern student this proves very frustrating. Sometimes it takes years for a poem to take on meaning—the reader simply knows that the poem sounds good and it provokes an emotional response that cannot be explained. With time, more emotional experience, more reading of similar experiences, more life, the reader comes to a meaning of that poem that satisfies for the time being. In a few more years that poem may take on a whole new meaning.

This is all very well for reading for pleasure but you are now called upon, in your present experience, to learn poetry for an important examination. Perhaps the first step in the learning process is to answer the question, "Why do people write poetry?" An easy answer is that they wish to convey an experience, an emotion, an insight, or an observation in a startling or satisfying way, one that remains in the memory for years. But why not use a straightforward sentence or paragraph? Why wrap up that valuable insight in fancy words, rhyme, paradox, meter, allusion, symbolism and all the other seeming mumbo-jumbo that explicators of poetry use? Why not just come right out and say it like "normal people" do? An easy answer to these questions is that poetry is not a vehicle for conveying meaning alone. Gerard Manley Hopkins, one of the great innovators of rhythm in poetry, claimed that poetry should be "heard for its own sake and interest even over and above its interest or meaning." Poetry provides intellectual stimulus of course, one of the best ways of studying a poem is to consider it a jigsaw puzzle presented to you whole, an integral work of art, which can be taken apart piece by piece (word by word), analyzed scientifically, labelled, and put back together again into a whole, and then the meaning is complete. But people write poetry to convey more than meaning.

T.S. Eliot maintained that the meaning of the poem existed purely to distract us "while the poem did its work." One interpretation of a poem's "work" is that it changes us in some way. We see the world in a new way because of the way the poet has seen it and told us about it. Maybe one of the reasons people write poetry is to encourage us to *see* things in the first place. Simple things like daffodils take on a whole new aspect when we read the way Wordsworth saw them. Why did Wordsworth write that poem? His sister had written an excellent account of the scene in her journal. Wordsworth not only evokes nature as we have never seen it before, alive, joyous, exuberant, he shows nature's healing powers, its restorative quality as the scene flashes "upon that inward eye/Which is the bliss of solitude." Bent over your books studying, how many times has a similar quality of nature's power in the memory come to you? Maybe for you a summer beach scene rather than daffodils by the lake is more meaningful, but the poet captures a moment that we have all experienced. The poet's magic is to make that moment new again.

If poets enhance our power of sight they also awaken the other senses as power-fully. We can hear Emily Dickinson's snake in the repeated "s" sound of the lines:

His notice sudden is—
The Grass divides as with a Comb—
A spotted shaft is seen—

and because of the very present sense of sound, we experience the indrawn gasp of breath of fear when the snake appears. We can touch the little chimneysweep's hair "that curled like a lamb's back" in William Blake's poetry and because of that tactile sense we are even more shocked to read that the child's hair is all shaved off so that the soot will not spoil its whiteness. We can smell the poison gas as Wilfred Owen's soldiers fumble with their gas masks; we can taste the blood gurgling in the poisoned lungs.

Poets write, then, to awaken the senses. They have crucial ideas but the words they use are often more important than the meaning. More important still than ideas and sense awakening is the poet's appeal to the emotions. And it is precisely this area that disturbs a number of students. Our modern society tends to block out emotions—we need reviews to tell us if we enjoyed a film, a critic's praise to see if a play or novel is worth our time. We hesitate to laugh at something in case it is not the "in" thing to do. We certainly do not cry—at least in front of others. Poets write to overcome that blocking (very often it is their own blocking of emotion they seek to alleviate), but that is not to say that poetry immediately sets us laughing, crying, loving, hating. The important fact about the emotional release in poetry is that poets help us explore our own emotions, sometimes by shocking us, sometimes by drawing attention to balance and pattern, sometimes by cautioning us to move carefully in this inner world.

Poets tell us nothing really new. They tell us old truths about human emotions that we begin to restructure anew, to reread our experiences in light of theirs, to reevaluate our world view. Whereas a car manual helps us understand the workings of a particular vehicle, a poem helps us understand the inner workings of human beings. Poets frequently write to help their emotional life—the writing then becomes cathartic, purging or cleansing the inner life, feeding that part of us that separates us from the animal. Many poets might paraphrase Byron, who claimed that he had to write or go mad. Writer and reader of poetry enter into a collusion, each helping the other to find significance in the human world, to find safety in a seemingly alien world.

This last point brings any reader of poetry to ask the next question: Why read poetry? One might contend that a good drama, novel or short story might provide the same emotional experience. But a poem is much more accessible. Apart from the fact that poems are shorter than other genres, there is a unique directness to them which hinges purely on language. Poets can say in one or two lines what may take novelists and playwrights entire works to express. For example, Keats' lines—

Beauty is truth, truth beauty,—that is all
Ye know on earth, and all ye need to know—

studied, pondered, open to each reader's interpretations, linger in the memory with more emphasis than George Eliot's *Middlemarch*, or Ibsen's *The Wild Duck*, which endeavor to make the same point.

In your reading of poems remember that poetry is perhaps the oldest art and yet surrounds us without our even realizing it. Listeners thrilled to Homer's poetry; tribes chanted invocations to their gods; today we listen to pop-song lyrics and find ourselves, sometimes despite ourselves, repeating certain rhythmic lines. Advertisements we chuckle over or say we hate have a way of repeating themselves as we use the catchy phrase or snappy repetition. Both lyricists and advertisers cleverly use language, playing on the reader's/listener's/watcher's ability to pick up on a repeated sound or engaging rhythm or inner rhyme. Think of a time as a child when you thoroughly enjoyed poetry: nursery rhymes, ball-game rhythms, jump-rope patterns. Probably you had no idea of the meaning of the words ("Little Miss Muffet sat on a tuffet..." a tuffet?!) but you responded to the sound, the pattern. As adults we read poetry for that sense of sound and pattern. With more experience at reading poetry there is an added sense of pleasure as techniques are recognized: alliteration, onomatopoeia; forms of poetry become obvious—the sonnet, the rondelle. Even greater enjoyment comes from watching a poet's development, tracing themes and ideas, analyzing maturity in growth of imagery, use of rhythm.

To the novice reader of poetry, a poem can speak to the reader at a particular time and become an experience in itself. A freshman's experience after her mother's death exemplifies this. Shortly after the death, the student found Elizabeth Jenning's poem "Happy Families." Using the familiar names of the cards, Mrs. Beef and Master Bun, the poet describes how strangers try to help the family carry on their lives normally although one of the "happy family" is "missing." The card game continues although no one wants it to. At the end the players go back to their individual rooms and give way to their individual grief. The student described the relief at knowing that someone else had obviously experienced her situation where everyone in the family was putting up a front, strangers were being very kind, and a general emptiness prevailed because of that one missing family member. The poem satisfied. The student saw death through another's eyes; the experience was almost the same, yet helped the reader to reevaluate, to view a universal human response to grief as well as encourage her to deal with her own.

On reading a poem the brain works on several different levels: it responds to the sounds; it responds to the words themselves and their connotations; it responds to the emotions; it responds to the insights or learning of the world being revealed. For such a process poetry is a very good training ground—a boot camp—for learning how to read literature in general. All the other genres have elements of poetry within them. Learn to read poetry well and you will be a more accomplished reader, even of car manuals! Perhaps the best response to reading poetry comes from a poet herself, Emily Dickinson, who claimed that reading a book of poetry made her feel "as if the top of [her] head were taken off!"

Before such a process happens to you, here are some tips for reading poetry before and during the examination.

Before the Exam

1. Make a list of poets and poems you remember; analyze poems you liked, disliked, loved, hated, and were indifferent to. Find the poems. Reread them and for each one analyze your *feelings*, first of all, about the poetry itself. Have your feelings changed? Now what do you like or hate? Then paraphrase the *meaning* of each poem. Notice how the "magic" goes from the poem, i.e., "To Daffodils:" the poet sees many daffodils by the side of a lake and then thinks how the sight of them later comforts him.

2. Choose a poem at random from an anthology or one mentioned in this introduction. Read it a couple of times, preferably aloud, because the speaking voice will automatically grasp the rhythm and that will help the meaning. Do not become bogged-down in individual word connotation or the meaning of the

poem—let the poetry do its "work" on you; absorb the poem as a whole jigsaw puzzle.

3. Now take the puzzle apart. Look carefully at the title. Sometimes a straightforward title helps you focus. Sometimes a playful title helps you get an angle on the meaning. "Happy Families," of course, is an ironic title because the family playing the card game of that name is not happy.

4. Look carefully at the punctuation. Does the sense of a line carry from one to another? Does a particular mark of punctuation strike you as odd? Ask why that mark was used.

5. Look carefully at the words. Try to find the meaning of words with which you are not familiar within the context. Familiar words may be used differently: ask why that particular use. Having tapped into your memory bank of vocabulary and you are still at a loss, go to a dictionary. Once you have the *denotation* of the word, start wondering about the *connotation*. Put yourself in the poet's position and think why that word was used.

6. Look carefully at all the techniques being used. You will gain these as you progress through this section and through the test preparation. As soon as you come across a new idea—"caesura" perhaps—learn the word, see how it applies to poetry, where it is used. Be on the lookout for it in other poetry. Ask yourself questions such as why the poet used alliteration here; why the rhythm changes there; why the poet uses a sonnet form and which sonnet form is in use. Forcing yourself to ask the WHY questions, and answering them, will train the brain to read more perceptively. Poetry is not accidental; poets are deliberate people; they do things for specific reasons. Your task under a learning situation is to discover WHY.

7. Look carefully at the speaker. Is the poet using another persona? Who is that persona? What is revealed about the speaker? Why use that particular voice?

8. Start putting all the pieces of the puzzle together. The rhythm helps the meaning. The word choice helps the imagery. The imagery adds to the meaning. Paraphrase the meaning. Ask yourself simple questions: What is the poet saying? How can I relate to what is being said? What does this poet mean to me? What does this poem contribute to human experience?

9. Find time to read about the great names in poetry. Locate people within time areas and analyze what those times entailed. For example, the Elizabethans saw a contest between secular love and love of God. The Romantics (Wordsworth, Coleridge, Keats, Shelley, Byron) loved nature and saw God within nature. The Victorians (Tennyson, Blake) saw nature as a threat to mankind and God, being replaced by the profit cash-nexus of the Industrial Age. The moderns (T.S. Eliot, Pound, Yeats) see God as dead and man as hollow, unwanted and unsafe in an alien world. The Post-Moderns see life as "an accident," a comic/cosmic joke, fragmented, purposeless—often their topics will be political: apartheid, abortion, unjust imprisonment.

10. Write a poem of your own. Choose a particular style; use the sonnet form; parody a famous poem; express yourself in free verse on a crucial, personal aspect of your life. Then analyze your own poetry with the above ideas.

During the Exam

You will have established a routine for reading poetry, but now you are under pressure, must work quickly, and will have no access to a dictionary. You cannot read aloud but you can:

1. Internalize the reading—hear the reading in your head. Read through the poem two or three times following the absorbing procedure.

2. If the title and poet are supplied, analyze the title as before and determine the era of the poetry. Often this pushes you toward the meaning.

3. Look carefully at the questions which should enable you to be able to "tap into" your learning process. Answer the ones that are immediately clear to you: form, technique, language perhaps.

4. Go back for another reading for those questions that challenge you—theme or meaning perhaps—analyze the speaker or the voice at work—paraphrase the meaning—ask the simple question "What is the poet saying?"

5. If a question asks you about a specific line, metaphor, opening or closing lines, highlight or underline them to force your awareness of each crucial word. Internalize another reading emphasizing the highlighted area—analyze again the options you have for your answers.

6. Do not waste time on an answer that eludes you. Move onto another section and let the poetry do its "work." Very often the brain will continue working on the problem on another level of consciousness. When you go back to the difficult question, it may well become clear.

7. If you still are not sure of the answer, choose the option that you *feel* is the closest to correct.

Go home, relax, forget about the examination—read your favorite poem!

Verse and Meter

As children reading or learning poetry in school, we referred to each section of a poem as a verse. We complained we had ten verses to learn for homework. In fact the word **verse** strictly refers to a line of poetry, perhaps from the original Latin word "versus": a row or a line, and the notion of turning, "vertere," to turn or move to a new idea. In modern use we refer to poetry often as "verse" with the connotation of rhyme, rhythm and meter but we still recognize verse because of the positioning of lines on the page, the breaking of lines that distinguish verse from prose.

The verses we learned for homework are in fact known as **stanzas:** a grouping of lines with a metrical order and often a repeated rhyme which we know as the **rhyme scheme.** Such a scheme is shown by letters to show the repeating sounds. Byron's "Stanzas" will help you recall the word, see the use of a definite rhyme and how to mark it:

"Stanzas"

(When a man hath no freedom to fight for at home)	
When a man hath no freedom to fight for at home,	*a*
Let him combat for that of his neighbors;	*b*
Let him think of the glories of Greece and of Rome,	*a*
And get knocked on the head for his labors.	*b*

To do good to mankind is the chivalrous plan,	c
And is always as nobly requited;	d
Then battle for freedom wherever you can,	c
And, if not shot or hanged, you'll get knighted.	d

The rhyme scheme is simple: *abab* and your first question should be "Why such a simple, almost sing-song rhyme?" The simplicity reinforces the **tone** of the poem: sarcastic, cryptic, cynical. There is almost a sneer behind the words "And get knocked on his head for his labors." It is as if the poet sets out to give a lecture or at least a homily along the lines of: "Neither a lender nor a borrower be," but then undercuts the seriousness. The **irony** of the poem rests in the fact that Byron joined a freedom fighting group in Greece and died, not gloriously, but of a fever. We shall return to this poem for further discussion.

Certain types of rhyme are worth learning. The most common is the **end rhyme**, which has the rhyming word at the end of the line, bringing the line to a definite stop but setting up for a rhyming word in another line later on, as in "Stanzas": home... Rome, a perfect rhyme. **Internal rhyme** includes at least one rhyming word within the line, often for the purpose of speeding the rhythm or making it linger. Look at the effect of Byron's internal rhymes mixed with half-rhymes: "combat... for that"; "Can/And... hanged" slowing the rhythm, making the reader dwell on the harsh long "a" sound, prolonging the sneer which almost becomes a snarl of anger. **Slant rhyme**, sometimes referred to as half, off, near or approximate rhyme, often jolts a reader who expects a perfect rhyme; poets thus use such a rhyme to express disappointment or a deliberate let-down. **Masculine rhyme** uses one-syllable words or stresses the final syllable of polysyllabic words, giving the feeling of strength and impact. **Feminine rhyme** uses a rhyme of two or more syllables, the stress not falling upon the last syllable, giving a feeling of softness and lightness, one can see that these terms for rhyme were written in a less enlightened age! The terms themselves for the rhymes are less important than realizing or at least appreciating the effects of the rhymes.

If the lines from "Stanzas" had been unrhymed and varying in metrical pattern, the verse would have been termed **free**, or to use the French term, *"Vers libre,"* not to be confused with **blank verse**, which is also unrhymed but has a strict rhythm. The Elizabethan poets Wyatt and Surrey introduced blank verse, which Shakespeare uses to such good effect in his plays, and later, Milton in the great English epic, *Paradise Lost*. Free verse has become associated with "modern" poetry, often adding to its so-called obscurity because without rhyme and rhythm, poets often resort to complicated syntactical patterns, repeated phrases, awkward cadences and parallelism. Robert Frost preferred not to use it because, as he put it, "Writing free verse is like playing tennis with the net down," suggesting that free verse is easier than rhymed and metrical. However, if you have ever tried writing such verse, you will know the problems. (Perhaps a good exercise after your learning about meter is to write some "free" verse.) T.S. Eliot, who uses the form most effectively in "The Journey of the Magi," claimed that no *"vers"* is *"libre"* for the poet who wanted to do a good job.

Such a claim for the artistry and hard work behind a poem introduces perhaps the most difficult of the skills for a poet to practice and a reader to learn: meter. This time the Greeks provide the meaning of the word from *"metron,"* meaning measure. **Meter** simply means the pattern or measure of stressed or accented words within a line of verse. When studying meter a student should note where stresses fall on syllables—that is why reading aloud is so important, because it catches the natural rhythm of the speaking voice—and if an absence of stressed syllables occurs there is always an explanation why. We "expect" stressed and unstressed syllables because that is what we use in everyday speech. We may stress one syllable over another for a certain effect, often using the definite article "THE well known author..." or the preposition "Get OUT of here!" Usually, however, we use a rising and falling rhythm, known as **iambic rhythm**. A line of poetry that alternates stressed and unstressed syllables is said to have **iambic meter**. A line of poetry with ten syllables of rising and falling stresses is known as **iambic pentameter**, best used by Shakespeare and Milton in their blank verse. The basic measuring unit in a line of poetry is called a **foot**. An **iambic foot** has one unstressed syllable followed by a stressed marked by ∪ /. Pentameter means "five-measure." Therefore **iambic pentameter** has five groups of two syllables, or ten beats, to the line. Read aloud the second and fourth, sixth and eighth lines of "Stanzas," tapping the beat on your desk or your palm, and the ten beat becomes obvious. Read again with the stresses unstressed and stressed (or soft and loud, short or long, depending on what terminology works for you) and the iambic foot becomes clear .

Tapping out the other alternate lines in this poem you will not find ten beats but twelve. The term for this line is **hexameter**, or six feet, rather than five. Other line-length names worth learning are:

monometer	one foot	**dimeter**	two feet
trimeter	three feet	**tetrameter**	four feet
heptameter	seven feet	**octameter**	eight feet

Other foot names worth learning are:

the **anapest** marked ∪ ∪ / the most famous anapestic line being:

"Twas the night before Christmas, when all through the house..."

the **trochee**, marked / ∪, the most memorable trochaic line being:

"Double double toil and trouble..."

the **dactyl** marked / ∪ ∪ / ∪ ∪, the most often quoted dactylic line being:

"Take her up tenderly..."

Old English poetry employs a meter known as **accentual meter**, with four stresses to the line without attention to the unstressed syllables. Contemporary poets tend not to use it, but one of the greatest innovators in rhythm and meter, Gerard Manley Hopkins, used it as the "base line" for his counterpointed "Sprung Rhythm." Living in the 19th century, Hopkins produced poetry that even today strikes the reader as "modern," in that the rhymes and rhythms often jar the ear, providing stressed syllables where we expect unstressed and vice versa. The rhythm was measured by feet of from one to four syllables, and any number of unstressed syllables. Underneath the rhythm we hear the "regular" rhythm we are used to in speech, and an intriguing counterpoint develops. One stanza from "The Caged Skylark" will show the method at work:

> As a dare-gale skylark scanted in a dull cage
> Man's mounting spirit in his bone-house, mean house, dwells—
> That bird beyond the remembering his free fells;
> This in drudgery, day-labouring-out life's age.

The stress on "That" and "This" works particularly well to draw attention to the two captives: the skylark and Man. The accentual meter in the second line reinforces the wretchedness of the human condition. No reader could possibly read that line quickly, nor fail to put the full length of the syllable on "dwells." The dash further stresses the length and the low pitch of the last word.

If at first the terms for meter are new and strange, remember that what is most important is not that you mindlessly memorize the terminology but are able to recognize the meter and analyze why the poet has used it in the particular context of the poem. For example, Shakespeare did not want the lyrical fall and rise of the iamb for his witches around the cauldron, so he employs the much more unusual trochee to suggest the gloom and mystery of the heath in "Macbeth." Many poets will "mix and match" their meter and your task as a student of poetry is to analyze why. Perhaps the poet sets up the regular greeting card meter, rising and falling rhythm, regular end-stopped rhyme. If the poet abruptly changes that pattern, there is a reason. If the poet subtly moves from a disruptive meter into a smooth one, then analyze what is going on in the meaning. If the poet is doing "a good job" as T.S. Eliot suggested, then the rhyme, rhythm and meter should all work together in harmony to make the poem an integral whole. Answer the test essay questions to practice the points in this section and the integrity of a poem as a single unit will become clearer.

Figurative Language and Poetic Devices

It will be becoming ever more obvious that a poem is not created from mere inspiration. No doubt the initial movement for a poem has something of divine intervention: the ancients talked of being visited by the Muse of Poetry; James Joyce coined the word "epiphany" for the clear moment of power of conception in literature, but then the poet sets to, working at the expression to make it the best it can be.

Perhaps what most distinguishes poetry from any other genre is the use of figurative language—figures of speech—used through the ages to convey the poet's own particular world-view in a unique way. Words have **connotation** and **denotation**, **figurative** and **literal** meanings. We can look in the dictionary for denotation and literal meaning, but figurative language works its own peculiar magic, tapping into shared experiences within the psyche. A simple example involves the word "home." If we free-associated for awhile among a group of twenty students we would find a number of connotations for the word, depending on the way home was for us in our experiences: comforting, scary, lonely, dark, creepy, safety, haven, hell…. However, the denotation is quite straightforward: a house or apartment or dwelling that provides shelter for an individual or family. Poets include in their skill various figures of speech to "plug into" the reader's experiences, to prompt the reader to say "I would have never thought of it in those terms but now I see!"

The most important of these skills is perhaps the **metaphor**, which compares two unlike things, feelings, objects, and the **simile**. Metaphors are more difficult to find than **similes**, which also compare two dissimilar things but always use the words "as if" (for a clause) or "like" (for a word or phrase). Metaphors suggest the comparison, the meaning is implicit. An easy way to distinguish between the two is the simple example of the camel. **Metaphor:** the camel is the ship of the desert. **Simile:** a camel is like a ship in the desert. Both conjure up the camel's almost sliding across the desert, storing up its water as a ship must do for survival for its passengers, and the notion of the vastness of the desert parallels the sea. The metaphor somehow crystallizes the image. Metaphors can be *extended* so that an entire poem consists of a metaphor or unfortunately they can be *mixed*. The latter rarely happens in poetry unless the poet is deliberately playing with his readers and provoking humor.

Start thinking of how many times you use similes in your own writing or speech. The secret is, as Isaac Babel once said, that similes must be "as precise as a slide rule and as natural as the smell of dill." The precision and naturalness coming together perfectly often set up an equation of comparison. A student once wrote "I felt torn apart by my loyalty to my mother and grandmother, like the turkey wishbone at Thanksgiving." We have all experienced divided loyalties. Using the graphic wishbone-tearing idea, something we have all done at Thanksgiving or have seen done lets us more easily relate to the student's experience. Another student wrote of his friends waiting for the gym class to begin "like so many captive gazelles." Again the visual point of comparison is important but also the sense of freedom in the idea of gazelle, the speed, the grace; juxtaposing that freedom with the word "captive" is a master stroke that makes a simile striking.

The same student went on to an *extended simile* to state precisely and naturally his feelings upon going into a fistfight: "I was like the kid whose parents were killed by the crooked sheriff, waiting for high noon and the showdown that would pit a scared kid with his father's rusty old pistol against the gleaming steel of a matched pair, nestled in the black folds of the sheriff's holsters. I knew there was no way out. Surrounded by friends, I marched out into the brilliant sun, heading for the back fields of the playground, desperately trying to polish the rusty old gun." Although this student was writing in prose, his use of figurative language is poetic. He plugs into readers' movie experience with the central idea of the showdown at high noon, an **allusion** that involves the reader on the same plane as the writer. The notion of the black holster extends the allusion of the old cowboy films where the "baddies" wore black hats and rode black horses. The use of the word "nestled" provokes some interesting connotations of something soft and sweet like a kitten nestling into something. But then the gun is an implement of destruction and death; maybe "nestles" takes on the connotation of how a snake might curl in the sun at the base of a tree. The metaphor then ends with the child going out into the sun. The "rusty gun" in context of the essay was in fact the outmoded ideas and morals his father and old books had inculcated in him. All in all a very clever use of figurative language in prose. If the same concept had been pursued in poetry, the metaphor would have moved more speedily, more subtly—a poet cannot waste words—and of course would have employed line breaks, rhythm and meter.

Personification is a much easier area than metaphor to detect in poetry. Usually the object that is being personified—referred to as a human with the personal pronoun sometimes, or possessing human attributes—is capitalized, as in this stanza from Thomas Gray's "Ode on a Distant Prospect of Eton College":

> Ambition this shall tempt to rise,
> Then whirl the wretch from high,
> To bitter Scorn a sacrifice,

And grinning Infamy.
The stings of Falsehood those shall try,
And hard Unkindness' altered eye,
That mocks the tear it forced to flow;
And keen Remorse with blood defiled,
And moody Madness laughing wild
Amid severest woe.

As the poet watches the young Eton boys, he envisions what the years have to offer them, and the qualities he sees he gives human status. Thus Ambition is not only capable of tempting, an amoral act, but also of "whirling," a physical act. Scorn is bitter, Infamy grinning, and so on. Coleridge employs a more visual personification in "The Ancient Mariner," for the sun whom he describes as:

...the Sun (was) flecked with bars
(Heaven's Mother send us grace!)
As if through a dungeon-grate he peered
With broad and burning face.

More so than with Gray's more formal personification, Coleridge's supplies an image that is precise—we can see the prisoner behind the bars, and what's more this particular prisoner has a broad and burning face... of course because he is the sun! The personification brings us that flash of recognition when we can say "Yes, I see that!"

The word **image** brings us to another important aspect of figurative language. Not a figure of speech in itself, the image plays a large role in poetry because the reader is expected to imagine what the poet is evoking, through the senses. The image can be **literal**, wherein the reader has little adjustment to make to see or touch or taste the image; a **figurative image** demands more from readers, almost as if they have to be inside the poet's imagination to understand the image. Very often this is where students of poetry, modern poetry particularly, find the greatest problems because the poetry of **imagism**, a term coined by Ezra Pound, is often intensely personal, delving into the mind of the poet for the comparison and connection with past memories that many readers cannot possibly share. Such an image is referred to as *free*, open to many interpretations. This concept suits the post-modern poet who feels that life is fragmented, open to multi-interpretations—there is no fixed order. Poets of the Elizabethan and Romantic eras saw the world as whole, steady, *fixed*, exactly the word used for their type of images. Readers of this poetry usually share the same response to the imagery. For example, the second stanza of Keats' "Ode to a Nightingale" sets up the taste imagery of a

draught of vintage that hath been
Cooled a long age in the deep-delvéd earth,
Tasting of Flora and the country green,
Dance, and Provençal song, and sunburnt mirth!
O for a beaker of the warm South,
Full of the true, the blushful Hippocrene,
With beaded bubbles winking at the brim,
And purple-stainéd mouth;

Even though Flora and Hippocrene are not names we are readily familiar with, the image of the cool wine, the taste, the look, the feeling evoked of the South and warmth, all come rushing into our minds as we enter the poet's imagination and find images in common.

Blake's imagery in "London" works in a similar way but as readers we have to probe a little harder, especially for the last line of the last stanza:

> But, most thro' midnight streets I hear
> How the youthful Harlot's curse
> Blasts the new-born Infant's tear,
> And blights with plagues the Marriage hearse.

Notice how the "Marriage hearse" immediately sets up a double image. Marriage we associate with happiness and joy; hearse we associate with death and sorrow. The image is troubling. We go back to the previous lines. The harlot curses her (?) new-born—the curse of venereal disease—that child marries and carries the disease to marriage? Or the young man consorting with the harlot passes on the disease to his marriage partner? Marriage then becomes death? The image is intriguing and open to interpretation.

Image in figurative language inevitably leads to symbol. When an object, an image, a feeling, takes on larger meaning outside of itself, then a poet is employing a symbol, something which stands for something greater. Because mankind has used symbols for so long many have become stock or conventional: the rose standing for love; the flag standing for patriotism, love of one's country (thus the controversy over flag-burning today); the color yellow standing for corruption (hence Gatsby's Daisy Buchanan—the white-dressed virginal lady with the center core of carelessness); the bird for freedom; the sea for eternity; the cross for suffering and sacrifice. If you are not versed in the Christian tradition it might be useful to read its symbols because the older poetry dwells on the church and the trials of loving God and loving Woman—the latter also has become a symbol deteriorating over the ages from Eve to the Madonna to Whore.

If the symbol is not conventional then it may carry with it many interpretations, depending on the reader's insight. Some students "get carried away" with symbolism, seeing more in the words than the poets do! If the poet is "doing a good job" the poetry will steer you in the "right" direction of symbolism. Sometimes we are unable to say what "stands for" what, but simply that the symbol evokes a mood; it suggests an idea to you that is difficult to explain. The best way to approach symbolism is to understand a literal meaning first and then shift the focus, as with a different camera lens, and see if the poet is saying something even more meaningful. Blake again supplies an interesting example. In his poem "The Chimney Sweeper" he describes the young child's dream of being locked up in "coffins of black." Literally of course coffins are brown wood, the color of mourning is black. Shift the focus then to the young child chimney sweeper, so young he can barely lisp the street cry "Sweep" so it comes out "'weep! 'weep! 'weep! 'weep!" (a symbolic line in itself). Your reading of the Industrial Age's cruelty to children who were exploited as cheap, plentiful, and an expendable labor force will perhaps have taught you that children were used as chimney brushes—literally thrust up the thin black chimneys of Victorian houses and factories, where very often they became trapped, suffocated, sometimes burned to death if fires were set by unknowing owners. Now the black coffins stand for the black-with-soot chimneys the little children had to sweep, chimneys which sometimes became their coffins. The realization of the symbol brings a certain horror to the poem. In the dream an Angel releases the children who then run down "a green plain leaping, laughing.../And wash in a river, and shine in the sun." The action is of course symbolic in that in real life the children's movements were restricted, living in monstrous cities where green plains would be enjoyed only by the rich, and totally limited by the size of the chimneys. They were always black with soot. They rarely saw the sun, never mind shone in it! Again the symbolism adds something to the poem. In many students there have been reactions of tears and anger when they *see* the symbolism behind such simple lines.

The idea of reading about the Industrial Age brings us to an important part of figurative language, briefly mentioned before: **allusion**. Poets tap into previous areas of experience to relate their insights, to draw their readers into shared experiences. Remember how the student writer alluded to old cowboy movies, the classic "High Noon." Poets will refer to history, myth, other older poems, plays, music, heroes, famous people. Allusion is becoming more and more difficult for the modern student because reading is becoming more and more a lost art. Core courses in schools have become hotbeds of controversy about what students should know. Fortunately modern poets are shifting their allusions so that contemporary readers can appreciate and join in with their background of knowledge. However, be aware that for the examination in poetry it will be useful to have a working knowledge of, at least a passing acquaintance with, "oldness." Think of areas of history that were landmarks: the burning of Catharge; Hannibal's elephants; Caesar's greatness; Alexander the Great; the first World War and its carnage of young men; the Second World War and the Holocaust. Think of the great Greek and Roman myths: the giving of fire to the world; the entrance of sin into the world; the labyrinth; the names associated with certain myths: Daedalus, Hercules, the Medusa. You may never have a question on the areas you read but your background for well-rounded college study will already be formulated.

If we now return to more specific figures of speech and other poetic devices, you may feel you can immediately get to grips with these rather than read for background! Alphabetical order may help in your studying:

Alliteration: the repetition of consonants at the beginning of words that are next door to each other or close by. The Hopkins' stanza quoted earlier provides some fine examples: "skylark scanted"; "Man's mounting… mean house"; "free fells"; "drudgery, day-labouring-out life's age." Always try to understand the reason for the alliteration. Does it speed or slow the rhythm? Is it there for emphasis? What does the poet want you to focus on?

Apostrophe: the direct address of someone or something that is not present. Many odes begin this way. Keats' "Ode to a Grecian Urn" for example: "Thou still unravished bride of quietness," and "Ode to Psyche": "O Goddess! hear these tuneless numbers."

Assonance: the repetition of vowel sounds usually internally rather than initially. "Her goodly eyes like sapphires shining bright." Here the poet, Spenser, wants the entire focus on the blue eyes, the crispness, and the light.

Bathos: deliberate anticlimax to make a definite point or draw attention to a falseness. The most famous example is from Pope's "Rape of the Lock": "Here thou, great Anna! whom three realms obey, /Dost sometimes counsel take—and sometimes tea."

The humor in the bathos is the fact that Anna is the Queen of England—she holds meetings in the room Pope describes but also indulges in the venerable English custom of afternoon tea. The fact that tea should rhyme with obey doubles the humor as the elongated vowel of the upper-class laconic English social group is also mocked.

Caesura: the pause, marked by punctuation (/) or not within the line. Sometimes the caesura (sometimes spelled cesura) comes at an unexpected point in the rhythm and gives the reader pause for thought.

Conceits: very elaborate comparisons between unlikely objects. The metaphysical poets such as John Donne were criticized for "yoking" together outrageous terms, describing lovers in terms of instruments, or death in terms of battle.

Consonance: similar to slant rhyme—the repetition of consonant sounds without the vowel sound repeated. Hopkins again frequently uses this as in "Pied Beauty": "All things counter, original, spare, strange;... adazzle, dim."

Diction: the word for word choice. Is the poet using formal or informal language? Does the poetry hinge on slang or a dialect? If so what is the purpose? Are the words "highfalutin" or low-brow? As always, the diction needs examining and questions like these answering.

Enjambment: the running-on of one line of poetry into another. Usually the end of lines are rhymed so there is an end-stop. In more modern poetry, without rhyme, often run-on lines occur to give a speedier flow, the sound of the speaking voice or a conversational tone.

Hyperbole: refers to large overstatement often used to draw attention to a mark of beauty or a virtue or an action that the poet disagrees with. Donne's instruction to the woman he is trying to seduce not to kill the flea, by contrasting her reluctance with "a marriage" of blood within a flea, reinforces the hyperbole used throughout the poem:

Oh stay, three lives in one flea spare,
Where we almost, yea, more than married are.

The example is also good for an unexpected caesura for emphasis at the second pause.

Irony: plays an important role in voice or tone, inferring a discrepancy between what is said and what is meant. A famous example is Shelley's "Ozymandias," which tells of the great ruler who thought that he and his name would last forever, but the traveller describes the huge statue in ruins with the inscription speaking truer than the ruler intended: "My name is Ozymandias, king of kings: /Look on my works, ye Mighty, and despair!"

Metonymy: the name for something closely related to it which then takes on a larger meaning. "You can't fight City Hall" has taken on the meaning of fighting against an entire bureaucracy. "You can't go home again" suggests that you can never emotionally return to your roots.

Onomatopoeia: a device in which the word captures the sound. In many poems the words are those in general use: the whiz of fireworks; the crashing of waves on the shore; the booming of water in a underground sea-cave. However, poets like Keats use the device to superb effect in, for example, " To Autumn,'' when he describes the gleaner sitting by the cider press watching the last "oozings hours by hours"... one can hear the last minute drops squeezed from the apples.

Oxymoron: a form of paradox in which contradictory words are used next to each other: "painful pleasure," "sweet sorrow."

Paradox: a situation or action or feeling that appears to be contradictory but on inspection turns out to be true or at least make sense. "The pen is mightier than the sword" at first glance is a contradiction of reality. One can hardly die by being stabbed by a pen... but in the larger world view the words of men, the signing of death warrants, the written issuing of commands to the gas chambers have killed. Or reason has prevailed by men writing out their grievances and as a result lives have been saved. Paradox always opens up the doors of thinking.

Pun: a play on words often for humorous or sarcastic effect. The Elizabethans were very fond of them; many of Shakespeare's comedies come from punning. Much of Donne's sexual taunting involves the use of the pun.

Sarcasm: when verbal irony is too harsh it moves into the sarcastic realm. It is the "lowest form of wit" of course but can be used to good effect in the tone of a poem. Browning's dramatic monologues make excellent use of the device.

Synecdoche: when a part of an object is used to represent the entire thing or vice versa. When we ask someone to give us a hand we would be horrified if they cut off the hand, what we want is the person's help, from all of the body!

Syntax: the ordering of words into a particular pattern. If a poet shifts words from the usual word order you know you are dealing with an older style of poetry (Shakespeare, Milton) or a poet who wants to shift emphasis onto a particular word.

Tone: the voice or attitude of the speaker. Remember that the voice need not be that of the poet's. He or she may be adopting a particular tone for a purpose. Your task is to analyze if the tone is angry, sad, conversational, abrupt, wheedling, cynical, affected, satiric, etc. Is the poet including you in a cozy way by using "you," or is he accusing "you" of what he is criticizing? Is the poet keeping you at a distance with coldness and third person pronouns. If so, why? The most intriguing of voices is Browning's in his **dramatic monologues**: poems that address another person who remains silent. Browning brought this type of poetry to an art. Think of all the variations of voices and attitudes and be prepared to meet them in poetry.

Types of Poetry

Having begun to grasp that poetry contains a great deal more than initially meets the eye, you should now start thinking about the various types of poetry. Of course, when reading for pleasure, it is not vital to recognize that the poem in hand is a sonnet or a villanelle, but for the exam you may well be asked to determine what sort of poem is under scrutiny. Certainly in discussing a poem it is also useful to know what "breed" you are dealing with because the form may dictate certain areas of rhyme or meter and may enhance the meaning.

The pattern or design of a poem is known as **form**, and even the strangest, most experimental poetry will have some type of form to it. Allen Ginsberg's "A Supermarket in California" caused a stir because it didn't read like poetry, but on the page there is a certain form to it. Some poets even try to match the shape of the poem to the subject. Find in anthologies John Hollander's "Swan and Shadow," and Dorthi Charles' "Concrete Cat." Such visual poems are not just fun to look at and read but the form adds to the subject and helps the reader appreciate the poet's world view. **Closed form** will be immediately recognizable because lines can be counted, shape determined. The poet must keep to the recognized form, in number of lines, rhyme scheme, and/or meter. **Open form** developed from "vers libre," which name some poets objected to as it suggested that there was little skill or craft behind the poem, simply creativity, as the name suggests, gives a freedom of pattern to the poet.

The most easily recognized closed form of poetry is the **sonnet**, sometimes referred to as a **fixed form**. The sonnet always has fourteen lines but there are two types of sonnets, the Petrarchan or Italian, and the Shakespearean or English. The word sonnet in fact comes from the Italian word "sonnetto" meaning a "little song," and Petrarch, the 14th century Italian poet, took the form to its peak with his sonnets to his loved one Laura. This woman died before he could even declare his love, and such poignant, unrequited love became the theme for many Elizabethan sonnets. As a young man might telephone a young woman for a date in today's society, the Elizabethan would send a sonnet. The Petrarchan sonnet is organized into two groups: eight lines and six: the **octave** and the **sestet**. Usually the rhyme scheme is abbaabba-cdecde, but the sestet can vary in its pattern. The octave may set up a problem or a proposition, and then the answer or resolution follows in the sestet after a turn or a shift. The Shakespearean sonnet organizes the lines into three groups of four lines: **quatrains** and a **couplet**: two rhyming lines. The rhyming scheme is always abab cdcd efef gg, and the turn or shift can happen at one of three places or leave the resolution or a "twist in the tail" at the end.

Couplet, mentioned earlier, leads us to a closed form of poetry that is very useful for the poet. It is a two-line stanza that usually rhymes with an end rhyme. If the couplet is firmly end-stopped and written in iambic pentameter it is known as an **heroic couplet**, after the use was made of it in the English translations of the great classical or heroic epics such as *The Iliad* and *The Odyssey*. Alexander Pope became a master of the heroic couplet, sometimes varying to the twelve-syllable line from the old French poetry on Alexander the Great. The line became known as the **Alexandrine**. Pope gained fame first as a translator of the epics and then went on to write **mock-heroic** poems like "The Rape of the Lock," written totally in heroic couplets which never become monotonous, as a succession of regularly stepped-out couplets can, because he varied the place of the caesura and masterfully employed enjambment.

Rarely in an exam will you be presented with an **epic** because part of the definition of the word is vastness of size and range. However, you may be confronted with an excerpt and will need to recognize the structure. The translation will usually be in couplets, the meter regular with equal line lengths, because originally these poems were sung aloud or chanted to the beat of drums. Because of their oral quality, repetition plays an important part, so that if the bard, or singer, forgot the line, the audience, who had heard the stories many times before, could help him out. The subject deals with great deeds of heroes: Odysseus (Ulysses), Hector, and Aeneus, their adventures and their trials; the theme will be of human grief or pride, divided loyalties—but all "writ large." The one great English epic, *Paradise Lost* is written by Milton and deals with the story of Adam and Eve and the Fall. Adam thus becomes the great hero. The huge battle scenes of *The Iliad* are emulated in the War of the Heavens when Satan and his crew were expelled into Hell; the divided loyalties occur when Adam must choose between obedience to God and love for his wife.

On much simpler lines are the **ballads**, sometimes the earliest poems we learn as children. Folk or popular ballads were first sung as early as the 15th century and then handed down through generations until finally written down. Usually the ballads are anonymous and simple in theme, having been composed by working folk who originally could not read or write. The stories—a ballad is a story in a song—revolve around love and hate and lust and murder, often rejected lovers, knights, and the supernatural. As with the epic, and for the same reason, repetition plays a strong part in the ballad and often a repeated refrain holds the entire poem together. The form gave rise to the **ballad stanza**, four lines rhyming abcb with lines 1 and 3 having 8 syllables and lines 2 and 4 having 6. Poets who later wrote what are known as **literary ballads** kept the same pattern. Read Coleridge's "The Rime of the Ancient Mariner" and all the elements of the ballad come together as he reconstructs the old folk story but writes it in a very closed form.

The earlier poetry dealt with narrative. The "father of English poetry," Geoffrey Chaucer, told stories within a story for the great *Canterbury Tales*. The Elizabethans turned to love and the humanistic battle between love of the world and love of God. Wordsworth and Coleridge marked a turning point by not only using "the language of men" in poetry but also by moving away from the narrative poem to the **lyric**. The word comes again from the Greek, meaning a story told with the poet playing upon a lyre. Wordsworth moves from story to emotion, often "emotion recollected in tranquillity" as we saw in "Daffodils." Although sometimes a listener is inferred, very often the poet seems to be musing aloud.

Part of the lyric "family" is the **elegy**, a lament for someone's death or the passing of a love or concept. The most famous is Thomas Gray's "Elegy Written in a Country Churchyard," which mourns not only the passing of individuals but of a past age and the wasted potential within every human being, no matter how humble. Often **ode** and elegy become synonymous, but an ode, also part of the lyric family, is usually longer, dealing with more profound areas of human life than simply death. Keats' odes are perhaps the most famous and most beloved in English poetry.

More specialized types of poetry need mentioning so that you may recognize and be able to explicate how the structure of the poem enhances the meaning or theme. For example the **villanelle**: a Courtly Love poem structure from medieval times, built on five three-line stanzas known as **tercets**, with the rhyme scheme aba, followed by a four-line stanza, a **quatrain** which ends the poem abaa. As if this were not pattern and order enough, the poem's first line appears again as the last line of the 2nd and 4th tercets; *and* the third line appears again in the last line of the 3rd and 5th tercets; *and* these two lines appear again as rhyming lines at the end of the poem! The most famous and arguably the best villanelle, as some of the older ones can be so stiff in their pattern that the meaning is inconsequential, is Dylan Thomas' "Do not go gentle into that good night." The poem stands on its own with a magisterial meaning of mankind raging against death, but when one appreciates the structure also, the rage is even more emphatic because it is so controlled. A poem well worth finding for "reading for pleasure." In James Joyce's *A Portrait of the Artist as a Young Man*, writing a villanelle on an empty cigarette packet turns the young boy, Stephen Daedalus, dreaming of being an artist, into a poet, a "real" artist.

Said to be the most difficult of all closed forms is the **sestina**, also French, sung by medieval troubadours, a "song of sixes." The poet presents six six-line stanzas, with six end-words in a certain order, then repeats those six repeated words in any order in a closing tercet. Find Elizabeth Bishop's "Sestina" or W.H. Auden's "Hearing of Harvests Rotting in the Valleys" and the idea of six images running through the poet's head and being skillfully repeated comes across very clearly. You might even try working out a sestina for yourself.

Perhaps at this stage an **epigram** might be more to your liking and time scale because it is short, even abrupt, a little cynical and always to the point. The cynical Alexander Pope mastered the epigram, as did Oscar Wilde centuries later. Perhaps at some stage we have all written **doggerel**, rhyming poetry that becomes horribly distorted to fit the rhymes, not through skill but the opposite. In contrast **limericks** are very skilled: five lines using the anapest meter with the rhyme scheme: aabba. Unfortunately they can deteriorate into types such as "There was a young lady from....," but in artful hands such as Shakespeare's (see Ophelia's mad song in *Hamlet*: "And will he not come again?"), and Edward Lear's, limericks display fine poetry. Finally, if you are trying to learn all the different types of closed-form poetry, you might try an **aubade**—originally a song or piece of music sung or played at dawn—a poem written to the dawn or about lovers at dawn—the very time when poetic creation is extremely high!

Although the name might suggest open-form, **blank verse** is in fact closed-form poetry. As we saw earlier, lines written in blank verse are unrhymed and in iambic pentameter. Open-form poets can arrange words on the page in any order, not confined by any rhyme pattern or meter. Often it seems as if words have spilled onto the page at random with a direct address to the readers, as if the poets are cornering them in their room, or simply chatting over the kitchen table. The lines break at any point—the dash darts in and out—the poets are talking to the audience with all the "natural" breaks that the speaking voice will demonstrate. Open-form poets can employ rhyme, but sometimes it seems as if the rhyme has slipped into the poem quite easily—there is no wrenching of the word "to make it rhyme." Very often there is more internal rhyme as poets play with words, often giving the sensation they are thinking aloud. Open-form poetry is usually thought of as "modern," at least post-World War I, but the use of space on the page, the direct address of the voice and the use of the dash clearly marks Emily Dickinson as an open-form poet, but she lived from 1830-1886.

LANGUAGE AND LINGUISTICS

"The meaning of a word," wrote Ludwig Wittgenstein in his *Philosophical Investigations*, "is its use in the language"; and by so writing, he revolutionized the study of language and linguistics. This association of the meaning of a word with the way people use it—as simple and common-sense a notion as that might seem—was a virtually unprecedented move in language philosophy, posing significant challenges to the prominent linguistic theories of the time. Its advantages as a construal of how human beings operate with language are several. To begin with, this approach dispenses with the notion that there is a single, underlying logic to human linguistic practice. Instead of conceiving of language as a monolithic, unified structure functioning according to strict rules, this principle of linguistic analysis allows for the multiple and even inconsistent ways in which people use language. Utterances are no longer seen to boil down to some "deep structure," whereby linguists would simplify or rearrange the grammar of a sentence to show what it "really means." The meaning is, rather, "on the surface," consisting in the various actions which result from the particular words read or spoken.

Meaning Is Use

This transfer of "meaning" from some hidden depth to the surface of an utterance parallels another shift in its location: from the "mind" to the "situation" of an utterance. Previously, it was assumed that meaning must be some sort of mental event or process, taking place in the mind, and the problem of how words meant things to people—how two people in conversation could be sure that they meant the same thing by the same words—remained an inscrutable mystery. The association of meaning with use, however, assures linguists that meaning is a public event, one which can be observed and measured by outward, shareable criteria. Our gaze is now trained on what happens when a person speaks or reads, what actions or consequences follow from a use of words and how the situation in which they are used changes. This allows us to avoid—in active situations—complicated and perhaps insoluble questions of the speaker's or writer's intention. Intention itself is removed from the mind and is instead seen to be manifested in the situation itself.

A third important consequence of the "meaning is use" assertion is that it avoids the problematic idea of correspondence, which also had frustrated much prior linguistic theory. It formerly was thought that a word had an inherent, one-to-one correspondence with the object it signified, and that the meaning of the word somehow lay in this relationship—as if, for example, the word "chair" had a natural connection to the object we call by that name and that is what "chair" means. The untenability of this notion, as indicated by the fact that different words in different languages are used to refer to the same thing and that the meanings of words sometimes change over the course of time, had already been recognized as early as 1915 by Ferdinand de Saussure in his *Course in General Linguistics*.

Word-Referent Connection

Saussure was one of the first linguists to insist on the idea that the connection between a word and its referent is arbitrary, the result of human conventional practices. He instead proposed that every "sign" consisted of a "signifier" (the word itself) and a "signified" (the idea or object to which the word refers), encouraging the notion in linguistic study that signifiers are detachable from their signifieds but remain in place through sheer force of convention. The trouble with Saussure's model, however, was that it continued to rely on reference as the criterion of meaning. A word, by this way of thinking, means what it refers to. Yet this presumes that all language operates the way nouns do, that all words are merely names for things. While this might be true in some cases, it is inadequate as a total description of linguistic behavior. To what, one might ask, does the word "of" refer? Even if this question had an answer, it is nonetheless obvious that the relationship between the word "of" and what it signifies would be quite a different matter from the relationship between "pug" and what it signifies. Clearly it would be a mistake to adopt this noun-oriented view in order to consider language more generally. The idea of meaning-as-use advocated thus far represents a significant advance beyond Saussure's more limited model.

Situational Meaning

Exactly what is at stake in this approach to linguistic analysis may be illustrated by the following crude but useful example: Suppose John walks into a room in which his roommate Steve is studying and says, "Gee, it's hot in here. Could you open the window, Steve?", whereupon Steve turns away from the book he is reading, says "Sure," opens the window, and resumes his studies. If the question then arose, "What did John mean when he said to Steve, 'Could you open the window?'?" it could be answered in the following manner. In this context, "Could you open the window?" is a request that Steve perform the action of opening the window. We could, to be sure, imagine other meanings for the sentence; but these other meanings would necessarily depend on other specific situations in which the sentence could be uttered. Suppose, for example, John was questioning Steve's strength or fine motor skills. "Could you open the window?" might then be a question demanding whether or not Steve was actually capable of performing such a task. Alternatively, they might be living in one of those dormitory rooms whose windows do not open sufficiently; John's question in this case might be an appeal to Steve, asking if he knew any possible way to circumvent the dormitory's restriction on air circulation.

The point to these linguistic contortions is that, while other possible meanings for the question "Could you open the window?" can be imagined, each of them depends upon an actual situation in which the words were uttered. It is important to note that, in our original example, when John asked Steve "Could you open the window?", Steve didn't have to translate the sentence into anything else in order to proceed with his action. That is, he didn't take the sentence "Could you open the window?", consider all of its possible meanings, and find the one that matched the situation he was in (as if saying to himself, "Oh, John actually is asking me if I *would* open the window"). Steve didn't have to move from the words of the question itself to any other set of words. Indeed, what would guarantee that the next set of words Steve settled on would be sufficiently clear and that he wouldn't have to move still further to another set of words in order to carry out John's request? This is why it is important to insist that the meaning of the words is "on the surface" and not hidden anywhere in "the mind" or in "deep structures." Steve only needed the question "Could you open the window?" as it stood in order to know what John wanted and to carry it out.

Meaning and Intention

How, it might be asked, can one be certain what John wanted by the question "Could you open the window?"? That is, how do we know what John's intention was and how do we know that Steve understood this intention? Surely, one might insist, such processes take place in the mind. One might be led to believe by such a line of reasoning that only John himself could know his intention, that it was private to him and that Steve could only guess what John intended by his question. But this is not at all the case. This is why we must insist that the intention of John's utterance is manifested in the situation. Various factors of the situation work to restrict the possibilities of what "Could you open the window?" means. It was hot in the room; John remarked on his discomfort. So far in their relationship, one might suppose, Steve's strength or fine motor skills have not been called into question. No doubt Steve has opened the window many times before, and they live at a college whose windowopening policies are fairly liberal. All of these factors—and no doubt innumerable others—combine to limit the possibilities of meanings for the sentence in this case. The shared knowledge and assumptions of John and Steve are a reasonable guarantee that John's intentions in uttering these words are clear and evident. This is not to say that there aren't cases in which confusion as to what somebody intends by an utterance cannot arise. No doubt, in certain situations, two or three or even more possible meanings for a given utterance might be available. But it is to say that such confusions can be rectified. John can always elaborate as much as necessary until his intentions are clear. If he couldn't, one might suppose, there would be no guarantee that John himself could know what he intended by the utterance. For how would he be able to explain it, even to himself? The only sensible conclusion one could draw from such an example is that intention, like meaning, is a public event, discernible within a given situation.

How, one might ask, can we be sure Steve understood John's intention? Simple. He opened the window. This was the action which followed from John's utterance, the consequence resulting from the meaning of his question. Like John's intention, Steve's understanding in this situation is a public event, able to measured by outward criteria.

Stages of Linguistic Development

The "meaning is use" conception of language has extended into many realms of linguistic study, including the basic stages of language development as considered by the philosopher/psychologist Maurice Merleau-Ponty in his study of *Consciousness and the Acquisition of Language.* As Merleau-Ponty suggests, one can—in a broad and general-ized way—divide the development of language in children into a number of stages. From two and one-half months onward, the child begins "babbling," pronouncing all manner of phonetic sounds without any particular reference to the surrounding environment. At approximately four months, the child begins to acquire the speech rhythms of the particu-lar language surrounding him or her, learning the stresses and tones of this language but still without any specific or meaningful content in his or her utterances. Around eight months the child might be able to repeat words said to him or her, and at one year, generate his or her own first word independently. From eighteen months to three years, the child sets about acquiring language in earnest, still predominantly through imitation, and gradually develops the capacity for abstract thoughts and the ability to refer to objects in their absence.

As Merleau-Ponty warns, however, "one must be wary of all artificial divisions into 'successive stages.' It appears that, from the beginning, all the possibilities are inscribed in the expressive manifestations of the child. There is never anything absolutely new, but there are anticipations, regressions, and retentions of older elements in new forms. There is, in other words, no strict or inherent logic by which children acquire language. Children may perform the stages outlined above in an overlapping and/ or non-sequential manner, and may move in and out of various stages at different times. They may, moreover, be exposed to and acquire the capacity for different uses of language long before they ever demonstrate such operations.

Language Acquisition

According to Merleau-Ponty's analysis, one sees that even in the acquisition of language, "use" plays the crucial role as it does in considerations of "meaning." Children seldom learn language through simple ostensive teaching, that is, by adults pointing at objects and saying, for example, "This is a chair." Rather, they absorb the language around them and gradually begin to imitate it. And, as Merleau-Ponty further suggests, "imitation is not preceded by a coming to consciousness of other people and an identification with them; it is on the contrary the act by which identification is produced" (50). Such assertions, once again, place the emphasis on the public, shareable aspects of language. The child is not seen as someone with his or her own inner meanings which he or she struggles to express to other people. Instead, the child acquires meanings through his or her absorption of the surrounding language. It is also suggested, in considering the relationship of intention to meaning, that "the self [of the child learning language] must become bound up with certain situations" and that "the ego ought to be defined as identical with the act in which it projects itself" (49). Thus again, intentions are seen as manifest in particular situations rather than in "the mind"; they are public phenomena which one can discern and assess.

Merleau-Ponty concludes this particular set of considerations by insisting that meaning "is not a question of a phenomenon on the level of pure thought or understanding. It is the *value of use* that defines language. Instrumental language precedes signification per se" (52). In other words, children learn how to use language in order to accomplish actions long before any questions arise as to what a given word signifies in the abstract. Merleau-Ponty goes on to insist that this is not merely the way that children acquire language, but, more often the not, the way adults do as well. He denies that there is a radical discontinuity between childhood and adult language-learning techniques. Adults, rather, pick up new words and new ways of saying previously-acquired words by exposure to their use in different situations. This is perhaps most dramatically apparent in the learning of technical terminologies, ranging anywhere from automobile repair to philosophy. Often, the sole criterion for assessing the meaning of the new term introduced is by examining how the writer or speaker uses it in the particular situation.

Standardization of Grammar

While "meaning-as-use" has led to new and valuable insights in the study of language and linguistics, it has also forced the re-conceptualization of teaching practices in challenging ways. For now the grammar which traditionally was taught in schools as the standard and correct way to speak and write, is seen to be an arbitrary construction—a set of rules not deduced from any logic inherent in language but rather an artificial code of conduct imposed upon it. This discovery has raised complex moral and ethical questions in the linguistic training of people who may not have learned "standard American English" as children before entering the educational system. In addition, it has called into question the efficacy of teaching a standard English, which may have little relationship to the way people in the world actually speak, to speakers of foreign languages. There is, arguably, no one particular standard by which Americans use the English language.

The idea of a standard American English has retained its viability in education and culture only through a major revision of its status. No longer considered the correct or proper way to speak and write, standard English is now conceived of as only one type of language among many, valuable for certain pedagogical uses. In the teaching of English to speakers of foreign languages, standard English can be used as a general, systematic convention by which to begin the process of learning the language. It is a convenience rather than a normative principle—a starting point rather than a goal—providing students with sets of rules with which to grasp the large, bewildering, and inconsistent whole of the language. Equipped with such guidelines, students may then be in a position to cope with the language in all of the various ways in which it is spoken. As is the case with native speakers of English, both children and adults, the only way for students to truly learn any language is to be immersed in it and observe how people are using it in various situations. Standard English provides a general understanding and competence in the language, enabling students to then learn English in all its spoken and written particularity.

Cultural Implications

Somewhat different issues are at stake in the teaching of standard American English to native speakers of the language. Given the cultural, ethnic, and geographic composition of the United States, various forms of English have proliferated among different groups and regions. The imposition of any particular form of English at the expense of others can therefore be seen as an oppressive exercise of power by one group of speakers over the majority. Rather than portray standard English as the proper way to speak and write—implying therefore that other varieties of English are improper or flawed—progressive teachers now recognize its conventional aspect and may teach it as a particular type of discourse for specific purposes. Standard English thus becomes a convenience, a common point of reference among the various types of English. It functions not as a castigating device or exclusionary practice but rather as a means by which members of disparate groups can communicate with one another via certain agreed-upon uses of words.

No one, to be sure, actually or naturally speaks with the fastidiousness and regularity of standard American English. Its function is largely to facilitate certain procedures, such as business or academic writing, by following a set of rules everyone can share. It is, of course, by no means an uncontroversial arrangement; there will no doubt always be disagreement as to which ways of speaking English should be codified as "standard" and which should be excluded from this status. Questions of power relations—for example, whose language does standard English most closely resemble and by whose authority have such decisions been made—will inevitably still arise. But with this reconceptualization of the nature of standard American English has come the belated but growing recognition that the life of the language is not in rigid and stagnant conformity but rather in the diverse and changing employments of words found among particular groups of speakers. The language continues to evolve only through the proliferation of different ways of speaking it, and the exposure of one variety of English to another is potentially a source of great richness. The more possibilities of ways to use words which people possess, the greater the variety and precision with which they can communicate and express themselves will be.

Language Across Disciplines

If the meaning of a word is its use in the language, it follows that the wider a person's exposure to various usages is, the more he or she will be able to comprehend the various linguistic situations with which he or she is confronted. And this is important because, of course, virtually every situation with which we are confronted involves the use of language. From reading a novel to reproducing a physics experiment, from watching television to cooking dinner to learning how to dance, every procedure we perform is dependent upon language. Humans are, with few exceptions, never without language and the importance of linguistic study can thus never be overestimated. Mathematics and perhaps even music can be considered varieties of language.

In a more obvious and practical sense, every profession requires of its members adequate reading and writing skills in order to succeed. The two practices are, moreover, intimately related. Often the difficulty in teaching people good compositional skills stems from the fact that many people do not read extensively. Reading texts is an essential component of writing texts, because the more one reads, the more one witnesses the various uses of language for various purposes. The avid reader is exposed many more varieties of English usage than the occasional or nonreader, and as we have seen, exposure is crucial to one's capacity to use language. Just as children acquire language from proximity to people using it, just as adults learn new uses of words from listening to other people, so too do actively reading people increase their linguistic skills relative to the breadth of texts which they encounter. The importance of this point cannot be stressed enough: the best writers are generally the best readers.

Even in intellectual pursuits outside of the humanities, people must rely on strong linguistic capabilities in order to achieve the most effective results possible. Scientific research, for example, is useless unless its results can be expressed cogently and convincingly. No experiment can be successful and accepted into the body of shared knowledge unless its procedures and results are expressed so that they may be followed and verified by other members of the field. Each professional discipline, skilled trade, or academic field depends upon its members' abilities to operate according to shared linguistic principles in order to ensure consistent communication. Just as the various strains of American English can enrich one another through extended contact, one's exposure to the broadest range of linguistic purposes available enables him or her to explore as many subjects and cultivate as many skills as desired.

Early in his career as a philosopher of language, Wittgenstein wrote: *"The limits of my language* mean the limits of my world." We might feel that this statement has a greater resonance than even that learned man intended at the moment he wrote it. For as we have seen, it is not merely the case that one's linguistic skills expand one's horizons and increase one's possibilities for experiencing the world, though both of these are true. It is above all language that enables both self and world to exist. The greater and broader our exposure to various uses of language are, the larger and more exciting that world will be.

References

Merleau-Ponty, Maurice. *Consciousness and the Acquisition of Language.* Trans. Hugh J. Silverman. Evanston, IL: Northwestern University Press, 1973.

Wittgenstein, Ludwig. *Tractatus Logico-Philosophicus* (1921). Trans. D. F. Pears and B. F. McGuinness. London: Routledge, 1974. §5.6

Wittgenstein, Ludwig. *Philosophical Investigations*. 3rd ed. Eds. G. E. M. Anscombe and Rush Rhees. Trans. G. E. M. Anscombe. New York: Macmillan, 1958. §43.

LEARNING ABOUT THE "OTHER" LITERATURE

In his recent book, *The Rhetoric of the "Other" Literature*, noted scholar W. Ross Winterowd argues that literature has been much too narrowly defined. Traditional genres (fiction, poetry, and drama) do not accommodate the huge volume of nonfictional texts that have been written over the past several centuries. According to Winterowd, any text of enduring value, regardless of its genre, is worthy of the name "literature."

Indeed, students may be exposed to a variety of these "other" literatures. Students may read the works of autobiographers, diarists, biographers, historians, critics, essayists, journalists, political commentators, scientific writers, and nature writers, among others. Whatever the discipline, excellent prose pieces share certain characteristics of style and arrangement. Similarly, there are strategies for critical reading that are useful for any prose passage.

A Brief Look at the Significance of the Essay

The "other" literature most often takes the form of an essay. Students will study essays written by writers from a variety of disciplines and periods. Over the last 400 years, many compelling essays have captured the audiences of their day with their powerful ideas and styles. The development of the essay as an art form is particularly interesting precisely because great essay writers have sprung from fields as diverse as politics and biology, education and art history. This fact speaks to the importance of conveying ideas in writing. The literary tradition of the essay has been shaped by thinkers who, regardless of their training, felt strongly about issues and ideas, and who had an impact on their audiences.

Despite its power to change people's thinking, the essay has not enjoyed the prestige of fiction, poetry, and drama. Montaigne, a sixteenth-century lawyer and writer, generally agreed upon by scholars as the father of the essay, helps us understand why. Montaigne articulated the problematic nature of the form when he defined the essay very loosely, saying anything could be included in it and that it could start and stop wherever it pleased. An essay could consequently include history and personal experience, fact and fiction, scientific discovery and philosophical musing. The "proper" length of an essay is nowhere specified, though it is generally read in one sitting. Essays are often written in the first person, and thus are easily seen as an expression of the author's persona or voice as well as the author's thoughts. An essay's style, therefore, is as significant as the information and opinion it contains. Essays are often superb examples of the marriage of form and content, the hallmark of great literature. It is indeed appropriate to consider essays the "other" literature.

Strategies for Critical Reading of Prose Passages

Critical reading is a demanding process. Linguists and language philosophers speak passionately of the importance of true literacy in human affairs. It is not enough to merely comprehend: true literacy lies in the ability to make critical judgments, to analyze, and to evaluate. It is with this end in mind—true literacy—that any reader should approach a text.

What Critical Readers Do

If you can summarize the main points of an essay, that's a start. If you can recall the plot twists in a short story, or articulate the line of reasoning in an argument, that's a start. But if you are able to offer an informed opinion about the purpose and merits of a text, then you are on the road to true literacy.

The MSAT seeks to identify critical readers, readers who not only can describe *what* happened in a text they've read, but *why* it happened and *how* it happened.

More specifically, as a critical reader, you will:

- summarize and outline complex material,

- critically examine a text's reasoning,

- analyze the way a text achieves its effects, especially through stylistic choice,

- evaluate a text, deciding whether it is accurate, authoritative, and convincing,

- determine a text's significance,

- compare and contrast different texts,

- synthesize information from one or more related texts, and

- apply concepts in one text to other texts.

As a critical reader, you'll be an active participant, not a passive recipient. It may help to envision yourself in a dialogue with the author and other critical readers. As rhetorician and critic Mikhail Bahktin argues, language operates in a dialogic mode, where receivers are just as essential to effective transmission of messages as senders.

There are six strategies a critical reader can employ to participate fully in the "re-creative act" that is reading.

1. Get the facts straight.

2. Analyze the argument.

3. Identify basic features of style.

4. Explore your personal response.

5. Evaluate the text overall and determine its significance.

6. Compare and contrast related texts.

1. Get the Facts Straight

Listen and read actively, pencil in hand, underlining important phrases or noting key points in the margin. Briefly record your reactions, questions, and conclusions. Though you may not have time to thoroughly annotate a prose passage during a test, if you rigorously practice annotating beforehand, you'll begin to do it less laboriously and with less written back-up.

Your first task as a critical reader is to learn everything you can about the text. You can begin by scrutinizing the implications of the title, trying to identify the author and general time period in which the text was written, and identifying the thesis. In short, a good reader looks for the main ideas, but also looks for other information (author, era, form) that may help him or her determine the slant of those ideas.

Once you've identified the essence of a passage, try to jot it down in your own words in a single sentence. This will help you focus on a text's meaning and purpose, a skill extremely useful when the detailed multiple-choice questions present you with "blind alleys" or slightly off-base interpretations of a text.

There are really four activities you perform in order to "get the facts straight":

a. **Previewing** – looking over a text to learn all you can *before* you start reading (This is, of course, much more difficult with excerpts.)

b. **Annotating** – marking up the text to record reactions, questions, and conclusions (Hint: It's especially useful to underline what you think the thesis is.)

c. **Outlining** – identifying the sequence of main ideas, often by *numbering* key phrases

d. **Summarizing** – stating the purpose and main idea, the "essence" of a text

Once you've got the facts straight, you're ready to tackle the analytic and evaluative aspects of critical reading. Before addressing those, let's test your ability to get the facts.

Here's an essay titled "Education of Women" by William Hazlitt, an essayist and scholar who wrote during the early nineteenth century. Try your hand at previewing, annotating, outlining, and summarizing it. Then look at the following pages, where a proficient critical reader has done those operations for you. Compare your responses and see where you can improve. Remember, you don't have to take copious notes to get to the essence of a text.

"Education of Women"

We do not think a classical education proper for women. It may pervert their minds, but it cannot elevate them. It has been asked, Why a woman should not learn the dead languages as well as the modern ones? For this plain reason, that the one are still spoken, and may have immediate associations connected with them, and the other not. A woman may have a lover who is a Frenchman, or an Italian, or a Spaniard; and it is well to be provided against every contingency in that way. But what possible interest can she feel in those old-fashioned persons, the Greeks and Romans, or in what was done two thousand years ago? A modern widow would doubtless prefer Signor Tramezzani to Aeneas, and Mr. Conway would be a formidable rival to Paris.[1] No young lady in our days, in conceiving an idea of Apollo, can go a step beyond the image of her favorite poet: nor do we wonder that our old friend, the Prince Regent,[2] passes for a perfect Adonis in the circles of beauty and fashion. Women in general have no ideas, except personal ones. They are mere egoists. They have no passion for truth, nor any love of what is purely ideal. They hate to think, and they hate every one who seems to think of anything but themselves. Everything is to them a perfect nonentity which does not touch their senses, their vanity, or their interest. Their poetry, their criticism, their politics, their morality, and their divinity, are downright affectation. That line in Milton is very striking—

'He for God only, she for God in him.'

Such is the order of nature and providence; and we should be sorry to see any fantastic improvements on it. Women are what they were meant to be; and we wish for no alteration in their bodies or their minds. They are the creatures of the circumstances in which they are placed, of sense, of sympathy and habit. They are exquisitely susceptible of the passive impressions of things: but to form an idea of pure understanding or imagination, to feel an interest in the true and the good beyond themselves, requires an effort of which they are incapable. They want principle, except that which consists in an adherence to established custom; and this is the reason of the severe laws which have been set up as a barrier against every infringement of decorum and propriety in women. It has been observed by an ingenious writer of the present day, that women want imagination. This requires explanation. They have less of that imagination which depends on intensity of passion, on the accumulation of ideas and feelings round one object, on bringing all nature and all art to bear on a particular purpose, on continuity and comprehension of mind; but for the same reason, they have more fancy, that is greater flexibility of mind, and can more readily vary and separate their ideas at pleasure. The reason of the greater presence of mind which has been re-marked in women is, that they are less in the habit of speculating on what is best to be done, and the first suggestion is decisive. The writer of this article confesses that he never met with any woman who could reason, and with but one reasonable woman. There is no instance of a woman having been a great mathematician or metaphysician or poet or painter: but they can dance and sing and act and write novels and fall in love, which last quality alone makes more than angels of them. Women are no judges of the characters of men, except as men. They have no real respect for men, or they never respect them for those qualities, for which they are respected by men. They in fact regard all such qualities as interfering with their own pretensions, and creating a jurisdiction different from their own. Women naturally wish to have their favourites all to themselves, and flatter their weaknesses to make them more dependent on their own good opinion, which, they think, is all they want. We have, indeed, seen instances of men, equally respectable and amiable, equally admired by the women and esteemed by the men, but who have been ruined by an excess of virtues and accomplishments.

—William Hazlitt (1815)

[1] Hazlitt was a theatre critic and had accused a popular Italian tenor, Tramezzani, of overacting in his love scenes. He also criticized actor William Conway in the role of Romeo.

[2] The Prince Regent was George, Prince of Wales, recently declared insane.

A. Previewing "Education of Women"

A quick look over the text of "Education of Women" reveals a few items worth mentioning. This short essay is probably most closely related to an Op-Ed (Opinion-Editorial) piece written in a newspaper. Published in the *Examiner* in 1815, the essay begins with a proclamation, "We do not think a classical education proper for women." The term "we" suggests the assurance of numbers and power. It's safe to assume Hazlitt speaks for a significant group (perhaps educated men?). And lastly, the year 1815 is relevant to our reading because it suggests a time when women did not enjoy the rights and privileges that are commonplace in the late twentieth century, at least in most of the major industrialized cultures. If the year were not stated you could infer from the debate over educating women that the piece was written before the late twentieth century.

B. Annotating "Education of Women"

An annotation records reactions, questions, and conclusions. Underlining key phrases may help you find the theme. Here are excerpts from Hazlitt's essay with underlining and annotations alongside to facilitate easy reference.

"Education of Women"

We do not think a classical education proper for women. It may pervert their minds, but it cannot elevate them. It has been asked, Why a woman should not learn the dead languages as well as the modern ones? For this plain reason, that the one are still spoken, and may have immediate associations connected with them, and the other not. A woman may have a lover who is a Frenchman, or an Italian, or a Spaniard; and it is well to be provided against every contingency in that way. But what possible interest can she feel in those old-fashioned persons, the Greeks and Romans, or in what was done two thousand years ago? A modern widow would doubtless prefer Signor Tramezzani to Aeneas, and Mr. Conway would be a formidable rival to Paris.[1] No young lady in our days, in conceiving an idea of Apollo, can go a step beyond the image of her favorite poet: nor do we wonder that our old friend, the Prince Regent[2], passes for a perfect Adonis in the circles of beauty and fashion. Women in general have no ideas, except personal ones. They are mere egoists. They have no passion for truth, nor any love of what is purely ideal. They hate to think, and they hate every one who seems to think of anything but themselves. Everything is to them a perfect nonentity which does not touch their senses, their vanity, or their interest. Their poetry, their criticism, their politics, their morality, and their divinity, are downright affectation. That line in Milton is very striking—
'He for God only, she for God in him.'
Such is the order of nature and providence; and we should be sorry to see any fantastic improvements on it. Women are what they were meant to be; and we wish for no alteration in their bodies or their minds. They are the creatures of the circumstances in which they are placed, of sense, of sympathy and habit. They are exquisitely susceptible of the passive impres-

1. The Thesis! But, what was a "classical" education in 1815? Probably Latin and Greek, philosophy and the "classics" of literature.

2. Perversion, not elevation, is the result of education of women—learning "taints" women.

3. Women learn modern languages only to be able to speak to their lovers—women have a shallow purpose for education.

4. Allusion to "poor" actors of the day (see footnote) who are preferable to historical figures (Aeneas, Paris)—women have little interest in history or politics, only romantic self-gratification.

5. Women don't think, are selfish, frivolous.

sions of things: but to form an idea of pure understanding or imagination, to feel an interest in the true and the good beyond themselves, requires an effort of which they are incapable. They want principle, except that which consists in an adherence to established custom; and this is the reason of the severe laws which have been set up as a barrier against every infringement of decorum and propriety in women. It has been observed by an ingenious writer of the present day, that women want imagination. This requires explanation. They have less of that imagination which depends on intensity of passion, on the accumulation of ideas and feelings round one object, on bringing all nature and all art to bear on a particular purpose, on continuity and comprehension of mind; but for the same reason, they have more fancy, that is greater flexibility of mind, and can more readily vary and separate their ideas at pleasure. The reason of that greater presence of mind which has been remarked in women is, that they are less in the habit of speculating on what is best to be done, and the first suggestion is decisive. The writer of this article confesses that he never met with any woman who could reason, and with but one reasonable woman. There is no instance of a woman having been a great mathematician or metaphysician or poet or painter: but they can dance and sing and act and write novels and fall in love, which last quality alone makes more than angels of them. Women are no judges of the characters of men, except as men. They have no real respect for men, or they never respect them for those qualities, for which they are respected by men. They in fact regard all such qualities as interfering with their own pretensions, and creating a jurisdiction different from their own. Women naturally wish to have their favourites all to themselves, and flatter their weaknesses to make them more dependent on their own good opinion, which, they think, is all they want. We have, indeed, seen instances of men, equally respectable and amiable, equally

6. Women's destiny—creatures of circumstance, habit. Women can't change.

7. They have impressions, not ideas. So women only feel, can't think? They aren't interested in any truths beyond what is true for them.

8. They "want principle...They "want" imagination...Want means lack, not desire.

9. They don't synthesize ideas but rather "separate" them. Does this mean they can't compare issues, seeing things only in isolation?

10. Women go with the first idea, don't reason through alternatives. Where is his evidence?

11. Oh, here's the proof...he's met only one reasonable women.

12. Women have accomplished little. Falling in love is their greatest skill. The double-standard in action; women are restricted to "non-cognitive" activity. The most they can aspire to: performing arts, romance.

admired by the women and esteemed by the men, but who have been ruined by an excess of virtues and accomplishments.

As these annotations illustrate, a reader approaching Hazlitt's text would have several questions and perhaps express surprise at Hazlitt's opinionated judgments. Your notes should, as the sample annotations do, reflect your reactions as the text progresses. Make sure you include any conclusions you have drawn as well as the questions that occur to you. The lines you underline or highlight, places where the text makes statement of "fact," will help you identify the main ideas later.

13. Women ruin men.

C. Outlining "Education of Women"

Go back to the statements you have underlined. Paraphrase and list them in numerical order, with supporting statements subsumed under key statements. Hazlitt's essay could be said to have the following key points, extrapolated from the underlining and written in outline form.

1. Classical education not proper for women

    a. modern language study better suits their romances

    b. no interest in history

2. Education is wasted on them because

    a. women have no ideas

    b. women have no passion for truth

    c. women hate to think

3. Women are what they are meant to be: frivolous, superficial

    a. creatures of circumstance, sympathy, and habit

    b. can't form ideas of understanding or imagination

    c. they lack principle

    d. they have fancy, flexibility of mind

    e. they can't synthesize ideas, but see ideas separately

    f. they take the first suggestion rather than speculate on what's best

    g. women can't reason

4. There are no examples of great women thinkers

5. Women are frivolous creatures

    a. women are only able to dance, sing, act, write novels, fall in love

    b. women cannot judge character

    c. women don't respect men for qualities considered good in women themselves (they're hypocrites)

D. Summarizing "Education of Women"

Read in this outline form, Hazlitt's essay is clearly an opinionated discussion of why women are not suited to education. Women are "born to" certain frivolous qualities of mind and behavior, and lack the mental capacity to reason, particularly in any principled fashion. The outline of key points and supporting statements lead the reader rather pointedly to this conclusion. Though at first Hazlitt's essay seems a disjointed litany of complaints, a sequence of reasons becomes more apparent after annotating and outlining the essay. It also becomes clearer how much Hazlitt relies on "accepted" opinion and his own experience rather than demonstrable proof.

We have just undertaken previewing, annotating, outlining, and summarizing the elements of "Get the Facts Straight." Very often at the conclusion of this stage of critical reading, the reader begins to get a handle on the text. The remaining five strategies after "Get the Facts Straight" seem to flow readily and speedily. To recap, these remaining five strategies are:

2. Analyze the argument.

3. Identify basic features of style.

4. Explore your personal response.

5. Evaluate the text overall and determine its significance.

6. Compare and contrast related texts.

Let's apply these remaining five strategies to Hazlitt's "Education of Women."

2. Analyze the Argument

An analysis examines a whole as the sum of its parts. Another brief look at the outline of "Education of Women" reveals the parts of Hazlitt's argument. In short, women should not be educated because they lack the qualities education enhances. They lack the capacity to entertain ideas because they have no passion for truth and hate to think. Women are naturally predisposed to acting precipitously rather than thoughtfully, with the use of reasoning. Evidence for these statements may be found in the lack of female contributions to human knowledge. Women can "perform" (and write novels, a less-than-respectable literary endeavor in 1815), and fall in love, but do little else. In short, things that require judgment are not suitable activities for women.

Hazlitt's essay has a rather simple argumentative structure. He asserts women are not educable and then provides "reasons" why. Hazlitt's "reasons" are primarily opinions, offered without any backing except the assertion that women have achieved little. The essay concludes with a final comment on the ability of women to ruin men, chiefly through flattery.

Analysis reveals that Hazlitt's essay has little to offer in support of the opinion it presents. Further, its statements seem more an emotional outpouring than a reasonable explanation. (The careful reader will also make note of how difficult it is to view Hazlitt's remarks in an unprejudiced fashion—the twentieth-century reader will, in all probability, find his assertions a bit ridiculous.)

3. Identify Basic Features of Style

Stylistically, Hazlitt's essay may be described as a series of blunt statements followed by reflection on how the statement is manifested in his culture. Hazlitt draws on anecdotal support—his observations of the women of his day, a line from Milton, and his own knowledge of the absence of women's accomplishments. Hazlitt's essay seems a collection of accepted or common knowledge: he writes as though his "reasons" are generally agreed upon, undisputed statements of fact. This structure suggests that because something is widely believed, readers should accept it. In all probability readers in 1815 did. Thus, the tone is both authoritative and perhaps a bit annoyed—annoyed with the problems women present.

Hazlitt's diction is largely straightforward, more plain than flowery. A few of the words and phrases he chooses have powerful or dramatic connotations, such as "pervert," "mere egoists," "perfect nonentity," "downright affectation," "hate to think," and "no passion for truth." But he relies largely on ordinary language and sentence structure. Only occasionally does he indulge in a syntactic permutation. For example, in the sentence "The writer of this article confesses that he never met with any woman who could reason, and with but one reasonable woman," Hazlitt shifts the modal verb "could reason" to the adjective "reasonable" with memorable effect. By and large, however, his sentences are simple declaratives, not difficult to read or interpret and not especially memorable stylistically.

This is an appropriate time to mention that most of the literary and rhetorical terms used in this discussion and the others that follow are included in the glossary at the end of these chapters on critical reading and writing.

4. Explore Your Personal Response

While nineteenth-century readers would probably have nodded in agreement as Hazlitt offered reasons why women shouldn't be educated, contemporary readers are probably surprised, dismayed, perhaps even angry. Review your responses in the annotations to the text. They will help recreate your personal reactions and the causes for those reactions. Do not always expect to agree with, or even appreciate a writer's point of view. You will find yourself disagreeing with texts rather regularly. The important thing is to be certain you can account for the sources and causes of your disagreement. Much of reader disagreement with Hazlitt's essay rests in what we would consider a more enlightened perspective on the abilities of women. An awareness of historical context does help explain "Education of Women," but probably doesn't increase twentieth-century sympathy for Hazlitt's position.

5. Evaluate the Text Overall and Determine its Significance

Hazlitt's essay "Education of Women" was a product of early nineteenth-century sensibilities. Its chief significance today is as a representative of its time, an indicator of a social and intellectual climate much different than our own. As a citizen of the Romantic period preceding the Victorian age, Hazlitt expresses an understanding of women that today we would deem, at the very least, incomplete.

6. Compare and Contrast Related Texts

A complete analysis of Hazlitt's essay would include a comparison of other essays of his, if available, on the subject of women and education. It would also be useful to examine other early nineteenth-century essays on this subject, and lastly, to contrast Hazlitt's essay with contemporary (i.e., late twentieth-century) essays that argue for and against the education of women. Through such comparison, a more complete understanding of Hazlitt's essay is possible. Occasionally you might be asked on the exam to contrast opposing (or similar) views on a single subject, but only within very narrow parameters. For instance, you might be questioned about two distinct styles used to approach the same subject and the resulting effects.

Although you may experience certain points of departure from the above discussion, most skilled readers will agree, in general, with its broad conclusions. This is because the text has been kept in mind and referred to throughout the discussion. If you read attentively, that is, if you attend to the text carefully, you are much more likely to reflect judiciously upon it. Thus, the components of our good reading definition—to read attentively, reflectively, and judiciously—are all present in the six broad strategies described and employed above.

The very *active* reading strategies employed on Hazlitt's essay "Education of Women" can be used with any text to help you "re-create" it with optimal effectiveness. That is to say, you as a reader should be able to very closely approximate the original authorial intentions, as well as understand the general audience response and your more particular individual response. Remember to work with the six strategies in sequence. They are:

1. Get the facts straight.

   a. Preview

   b. Annotate

   c. Outline

   d. Summarize

2. Analyze the argument.

3. Identify basic features of style.

4. Explore your personal response.

5. Evaluate the text overall and determine its significance.

6. Compare and contrast related texts.

LITERATURE AND LANGUAGE STUDIES
PRACTICE QUESTIONS

Questions 1–6 are based on the following passage. Read the passage carefully before choosing your answers.

1   We laymen have always been intensely curious to know—like the cardinal who put a similar question to Ariosto—from what sources that strange being, the creative writer, draws his material, and how he manages to make such an impression on us with it and to arouse in us emotions of which, perhaps, we had not even thought ourselves capable. Our
5   interest is only heightened the more by the fact that, if we ask him, the writer himself gives us no explanation, or none that is satisfactory, and it is not at all weakened by our knowledge that not even the clearest insight into the determinants of his choice of material and into the nature of the art of creating imaginative form will ever help to make creative writers of us.
10   If we could at least discover in ourselves or in people like ourselves an activity which was in some way akin to creative writing! An examination of it would then give us a hope of obtaining the beginnings of an explanation of the creative work of writers. And, indeed, there is some prospect of this being possible. After all, creative writers themselves like to lessen the distance between their kind and the common run of humanity;
15   they so often assure us that every man is a poet at heart and that the last poet will not perish till the last man does.
     Should we not look for the first traces of imaginative activity as early as in childhood? The child's best-loved and most intense occupation is with his play or games. Might we not say that every child at play behaves like a creative writer, in that he creates
20   a world of his own, or, rather, rearranges the things of his world in a new way which pleases him? It would be wrong to think he does not take that world seriously; on the contrary, he takes play very seriously and he expends large amounts of emotion on it. The opposite of play is not what is serious but what is real. In spite of all the emotion with which he cathects his world of play, the child distinguishes it quite well from reality; and
25   he likes to link his imagined objects and situations to the tangible and visible things of the real world. This linking is all that differentiates the child's "play" from "fantasying."

1.   What is the effect of the speaker's use of "we"?

    (A)   It separates the speaker and his/her colleagues from the reader.

    (B)   It involves the reader in the search for, yet distinguishes him/her from, the creative writer.

    (C)   It creates a royal and authoritative persona for the speaker.

    (D)   It makes the speaker the stand-in for all men.

2.   What is the antecedent of "it" (line 6)?

    (A)   "explanation" (line 6)   (C)   "interest" (line 5)

    (B)   "fact" (line 5)   (D)   "impression" (line 3)

3. Which of the following statements would the speaker be most likely to DISAGREE with?

   (A) A lay person cannot become a creative writer by studying the writer's methods.

   (B) All men are writers at heart.

   (C) Creative writers are fundamentally different from nonwriters.

   (D) Children understand the distinction between imagination and reality.

4. "Cathects" (line 24) can best be defined as

   (A) constructs.   (C) fantasizes.

   (B) distances.   (D) discourages.

5. The structure of the passage can best be described as

   (A) an initial paragraph that introduces an idea and two paragraphs that digress from that idea.

   (B) a series of paragraphs that answer the questions with which they begin.

   (C) a series of questions ascending in their inability to be answered.

   (D) paragraphs whose length or brevity parallel their depth or narrowness of inquiry.

6. It can be inferred that the speaker believes that creative writing is

   (A) an opposite of childhood play.

   (B) unrelated to childhood play.

   (C) a continuation of childhood play.

   (D) similar to the fantasizing of childhood play.

Questions 7–10 are based on the following passage.

1   Under the strange nebulous envelopment, wherein our Professor has now shrouded himself, no doubt but his spiritual nature is nevertheless progressive, and growing: for how can the "Son of Time," in any case, stand still? We behold him, through those dim years, in a state of crisis, of transition: his mad Pilgrimings, and general solution into
5 aimless Discontinuity, what is all this but a mad Fermentation; wherefrom, the fiercer it is, the clearer product will one day evolve itself.
   Such transitions are ever full of pain: thus the Eagle when he moults is sickly; and, to attain his new beak, must harshly dash-off the old one upon rocks. What Stoicism soever our Wanderer, in his individual acts and motions, may affect, it is dear that there
10 is a hot fever of anarchy and misery raging within; coruscations of which flash out: as, indeed, how could there be other? Have we not seen him disappointed, bemocked of

Destiny, through long years? All that the young heart might desire and pray for has been denied; nay, as in the last worst instance, offered and then snatched away. Ever an "excellent Passivity"; but of useful, reasonable Activity, essential to the former as Food
15 to Hunger, nothing granted: till at length, in this wild Pilgrimage, he must forcibly seize for himself an Activity, though useless, unreasonable. Alas, his cup of bitterness, which had been filling drop by drop, ever since that first "ruddy morning" in the Hinterschlag Gymnasium, was at the very lip; and then with that poison drop, of the Towngood-and-Blumine business, it runs over, and even hisses over in a deluge of foam.
20   He himself says once, with more justice than originality: "Man is, properly speaking, based upon Hope, he has no other possession but Hope; this world of his is emphatically the Place of Hope." What, then, was our Professor's possession? We see him, for the present, quite shutout from Hope; looking not into the golden orient, but vaguely all round into a dim copper firmament, pregnant with earthquake and tornado.

7. All of the following name the main character of the passage EXCEPT

(A) our Wanderer.   (C) he/him.

(B) the Eagle.   (D) our Professor.

8. Which phrase best summarizes the speaker's intent in examining this stage of the main character's life?

(A) "Such transitions are ever full of pain" (line 7)

(B) "Have we not seen him disappointed, bemocked of Destiny, through long years" (lines 11-12)

(C) "there is a hot fever of anarchy and misery raging within" (line 9-10)

(D) "What is all this but a mad Fermentation; wherefrom, the fiercer it is, the clearer product will one day evolve itself" (lines 5–7)

9. The accumulative painfulness of this time for the main character is illustrated primarily by the use of

(A) metaphors.   (C) hyperbole.

(B) digressions.   (D) oxymoron.

10. What is the function of the clause introduced by "nay" in line 13?

(A) It negates the clause that precedes it.

(B) It contradicts the clause that precedes it.

(C) It intensifies the clause that precedes it.

(D) It restates the clause that precedes it.

LITERATURE AND LANGUAGE STUDIES

ANSWERS TO PRACTICE QUESTIONS

1.	**(B)**	6.	**(D)**
2.	**(C)**	7.	**(B)**
3.	**(C)**	8.	**(D)**
4.	**(A)**	9.	**(D)**
5.	**(B)**	10.	**(C)**

MSAT

Multiple Subjects Assessment for Teachers

CHAPTER 3

Mathematics Review

Chapter 3

Mathematics Review

The Mathematics section of the MSAT focuses on the understanding of mathematical concepts necessary to elementary school teachers, as well as the ability to relate these concepts to others. The emphasis is on the candidate's ability to use logic and reason when solving problems. A basic four-function calculator is both necessary and permitted. Programmable or scientific calculators are neither required nor allowed by the test administrators. The Mathematics section of the MSAT accounts for 20 percent of the overall exam. There are 24 multiple-choice questions on the Content Knowledge exam, and three questions in the Content Area Exercises section. The Mathematics portion of the MSAT is divided into seven sections:

Number Sense and Numeration (20 percent)
- Understanding of concepts as they relate to problem solving

Geometry (20 percent)
- Understanding of both two- and three-dimensional relationships
- Ability to draw inferences on the basis of geometric concepts

Measurement (5 percent)
- Knowledge and application of both English and metric systems

Algebraic Concepts (10 percent)
- Application of algebraic concepts
- Describe patterns through formulae

Number Theory (10 percent)
- Understanding of numeric concepts, such as prime and composite numbers, divisibility rules, least common multiple, etc.

Real Number System (20 percent)
- Ability to solve real-world situational problems
- Work with both standard and alternate algorithms

Probability and Statistics (15 percent)
- Ability to understand data presented in various forms

- Ability to recognize valid and invalid assumptions
- Ability to make predictions based on data

The following Mathematics Review contains all the information you will need to do well on the mathematics portion of the MSAT. There is probably nothing in this section that you have not studied before, so most of the topics should be familiar to you. The review will serve to refresh your memory on some of the more difficult topics, and the practice tests will show what areas need more work.

KEY STRATEGIES FOR ANSWERING THE MATHEMATICS QUESTIONS

1. **Make effective use of your time.** You will have approximately 22 minutes to answer 24 questions on the mathematics section of the MSAT. This will allow you less than one minute to answer each question. If you find yourself taking longer than one minute on a given question, mark the answer you think is most likely correct, circle the number of the item in the test booklet, and come back to it later if time allows.

2. **Answer all questions on this section of the test.** There is no penalty for guessing on the MSAT, so do not leave any question unanswered. If you are not sure of the correct answer, narrow the choices to the two or three most likely, and choose one. Eliminate answers that could not possibly be correct before you choose.

3. **Read each question carefully.** Be sure you understand what the question is actually asking, not what a casual reading of the question might suggest. Be sure you have separated all the relevant information from the irrelevant information in the question.

4. **Devise a plan for answering the question.** This plan will be especially useful on the word problems and geometry items.

5. **Work the problem backwards to check your answer.** If time allows, check your work by substituting the answer into the original problem. Be certain that the answer meets all the conditions in the original question.

6. **Draw a diagram, sketch, or table to organize your work or to explain the question.** Not all questions will have an illustration. If you need an illustration to help you to understand a question, make one for yourself. This strategy may be especially useful in the geometry section.

7. **Write in the test booklet.** Mark up diagrams as needed. Write in the margins and other blank spaces. Write information directly into the statement of the problem, especially if you are having trouble setting up a solution.

8. **Look for similar questions.** Similar items may have appeared elsewhere on the test. You also may recall similar questions from classes you have taken previously. Apply suitable strategies from related work to the problem at hand.

PART I: ARITHMETIC

INTEGERS

Natural or counting numbers are 1, 2, 3, ...
Whole numbers are 0, 1, 2, 3, ...
Integers are ...−2, −1, 0, 1, 2, ...
As shown below, a number line is often used to represent integers.

The following are properties of integers:

Commutative property: $a + b = b + a$.
Example: $2 + 3 = 3 + 2$.

Associative property: $(a + b) + c = a + (b + c)$.
Example: $(2 + 3) + 4 = 2 + (3 + 4)$.

Distributive property: $a(b + c) = ab + ac$.
Example:
$$2(3 + 4) = (2 \times 3) + (2 \times 4)$$
$$2 \times 7 = 6 + 8$$
$$14 = 14$$

Additive identity: $a + 0 = a$.
Example: $2 + 0 = 2$.

Multiplicative identity: $a \times 1 = a$.
Example: $2 \times 1 = 2$.

PRIME AND COMPOSITE NUMBERS

When two whole numbers are multiplied, they yield a product. These two whole numbers can be called *factors* or *divisors* of the product. (An exception to this is 0. Zero can be a factor, but not a divisor, since division by 0 is undefined.)

Example: $2 \times 3 = 6$. 2 and 3 are factors or divisors of the product 6.
Example: $0 \times 3 = 0$. 3 is a factor and divisor of the product 0, but 0 is only a factor of the product 0, since $0 \div 0$ is undefined.

A *prime number* is a whole number greater than 1 which has only two different whole number factors, 1 and the number itself.

Example: 5 is a prime number, because it has only two different factors, 1 and 5.

A *composite number* is a whole number that has three or more whole number factors.

Example: 6 is a composite number, because it has four different factors, 1, 2, 3, and 6.

EVEN AND ODD NUMBERS

Even numbers are whole numbers that have 2 as a factor.

Example: 6 is an even number, since $2 \times 3 = 6$.

Odd numbers are whole numbers that do not have 2 as a factor.

Example: 5 is an odd number, since 2 is not a factor of 5.

PLACE VALUE

Our numeration system uses the *Hindu-Arabic numerals* (0, 1, 2, 3, 4, 5, 6, 7, 8, 9) to represent numbers.

Our numeration system follows a *base 10 place-value scheme*. As we move to the left in any number, each place value is ten times the place value to the right. Similarly, as we move to the right, each place value is one-tenth the place value to the left.

Example: In the number 543.21, the place value of the 5 (100's) is ten times the place value of the 4 (10's). The place value of the 1 ($^1/_{100}$'s) is one-tenth the place value of the 2 ($^1/_{10}$'s).

The concept of place value will be discussed in the section "Arithmetic Operations and Decimal Fractions."

POWERS AND ROOTS OF WHOLE NUMBERS

Exponents and Bases

In the expression 5^3, 5 is called the *base* and 3 is called the *exponent*. The expression $5^3 = 5 \times 5 \times 5$. The base (5) gives the factor used in the expression and the exponent (3) gives the number of times the base is to be used as a factor.

Examples: $4^2 = 4 \times 4.$
$3^5 = 3 \times 3 \times 3 \times 3 \times 3.$

When the base has an exponent of 2, the base is said to be *squared*. When the base has an exponent of 3, the base is said to be *cubed*.
The Basic Laws of Exponents are

1) $b^m \times b^n = b^{m+n}.$
Example: $2^5 \times 2^3 = 2^{5+3} = 2^8.$

2) $b^m \div b^n = b^{m-n}.$
Example: $2^5 \div 2^3 = 2^{5-3} = 2^2.$

3) $(b^m)^n = b^{m \times n}$.

Example: $(2^5)^3 = 2^{5 \times 3} = 2^{15}$.

Roots

Consider again the expression 5^3. If we carry out the implied multiplication, we get $5^3 = 5 \times 5 \times 5 = 125$. 5 is called the cube root of 125, since $5^3 = 125$. In general, when a base is raised to a power to produce a given result, the base is called the *root* of the given result.

If the power for the base is 2, the base is called the *square root*. If the power for the base is 3, the base is called the *cube root*. In general, if $b^n = p$, then b is the *nth root of p*.

Examples: **Since $4^2 = 16$, 4 is the square root of 16.**
            Since $2^3 = 8$, 2 is the cube root of 8.
            Since $3^5 = 243$, 3 is the 5th root of 243.

ARITHMETIC OPERATIONS AND INTEGERS

Integers are *signed numbers* preceded by either a "+" or a "–" sign. If no sign is given for the integer, one should infer that the integer is positive (e.g., 3 means +3). As previously illustrated, integers to the *left of zero are negative* and integers to the *right of zero are positive*.

The *absolute value* of an integer is the measure of the distance of the integer from zero. Since the measure of distance is always positive, absolute value is always positive. The absolute value of the real number a is denoted by $|a|$ (e.g., $|-3| = 3, |3| = 3$).

Addition

When two integers are added, the two integers are called *addends*, and the result is called the sum, as illustrated in the following:

$$
\begin{array}{ccccc}
5 & + & 3 & = & 8 \\
\text{(addend)} & & \text{(addend)} & & \text{(sum)}
\end{array}
$$

$$
\begin{array}{ll}
\text{or} \quad 5 & \text{(addend)} \\
\underline{+\,3} & \text{(addend)} \\
8 & \text{(sum)}
\end{array}
$$

When adding two integers, one of the following two situations might occur:

Situation 1: Both integers have the same sign. In this case, add the absolute values of the two addends and give the sum the same sign as the addends.

Examples: **$2 + 3 = 5$, and**

            $-2 + (-3) = -5$.

Situation 2: The two integers have different signs. In this case, subtract the addend with the smaller absolute value from the addend with the larger absolute value. The sum gets the sign of the addend with the larger absolute value.

Examples: **$-2 + 5 = 3$, but**

            $2 + (-5) = -3$.

Subtraction

In a subtraction sentence, the top or first number in the subtraction is the *minuend,* the bottom or second number is the *subtrahend,* and the result is the *remainder or difference.* These quantities are demonstrated in the following figure:

$$5 \quad - \quad 3 \quad = \quad 2$$
$$\text{(minuend)} \quad \text{(subtrahend)} \quad \text{(remainder)}$$

$$\text{or} \quad 5 \qquad \text{(minuend)}$$
$$\underline{-\,3} \qquad \text{(subtrahend)}$$
$$2 \qquad \text{(remainder)}$$

When subtracting a negative integer, change the sign of the subtrahend and add the resulting two integers, following the procedures given above.

Examples: $5 - 3 = 2$, but
$$5 - (-3) = 5 + (+3) = 5 + 3 = 8.$$

Multiplication

When multiplying two integers, the two integers are called *factors,* and the result is called the *product,* as illustrated in the following:

$$5 \quad \times \quad 3 \quad = \quad 15$$
$$\text{(factor)} \quad \text{(factor)} \quad \text{(product)}$$

$$\text{or} \quad 5 \qquad \text{(factor)}$$
$$\underline{\times\,3} \qquad \text{(factor)}$$
$$15 \qquad \text{(product)}$$

When multiplying two integers, multiply the absolute values of the factors. If the factors have the *same sign,* the product is *positive*; if the factors have *different signs,* the product is *negative.* If either factor is zero, the product is zero.

Examples: $3 \times 5 = 15$ and $(-3) \times (-5) = 15$, but
$$(-3) \times 5 = -15 \text{ and } 3 \times (-5) = -15.$$

Division

When dividing two integers, the number being divided is the *dividend,* the number being divided into another integer is the *divisor,* and the result is the *quotient,* as illustrated in the following:

$$10 \quad \div \quad 2 \quad = \quad 5$$
$$\text{(dividend)} \quad \text{(divisor)} \quad \text{(quotient)}$$

When dividing two integers, divide the absolute values of the dividend and divisor. The sign of the quotient can be obtained by following the same procedures given above in the multiplication section.

Examples: $10 \div 2 = 5$ and $(-10) \div (-2) = 5$, but
$$(-10) \div 2 = (-5) \text{ and } 10 \div (-2) = (-5).$$

ARITHMETIC OPERATIONS AND COMMON FRACTIONS

A *common fraction* is a number that can be written in the form $\frac{a}{b}$, where a and b are whole numbers. In the expression $\frac{a}{b}$, the dividend a is called the *numerator* and the divisor b is called the *denominator*.

Example: In the expression $\frac{3}{4}$, 3 is the numerator and 4 is the denominator.

A common fraction may not have 0 as a denominator, since *division by 0 is undefined*.

A fraction is in *lowest terms* if the numerator and denominator have no common factors.

Examples: $\frac{1}{2}, \frac{3}{4}$ and $\frac{5}{6}$ are in lowest terms, since the numerator and denominator of each have no common factors.

$\frac{2}{4}, \frac{9}{21}$ and $\frac{20}{24}$ are *not* in lowest terms, since the numerator and denominator of each have common factors.

Fractions are *equivalent* if they represent the same number.

Example: $\frac{8}{16}, \frac{4}{8}, \frac{2}{4}$, and $\frac{5}{10}$ are equivalent fractions, since each represents $\frac{1}{2}$.

A *mixed numeral* is a number that consists of an integer and a common fraction.

Example: $5\frac{3}{4}$ is a mixed numeral since it consists of the integer 5 and the common fraction $\frac{3}{4}$.

An *improper fraction* is a common fraction whose numerator is larger than its denominator. A mixed numeral can be expressed as an improper fraction by multiplying the denominator of the common fraction part times the integer part and adding that product to the numerator of the common fraction part. The result is the numerator of the improper fraction. The denominator of the improper fraction is the same as the denominator in the mixed numeral.

Example: $5\frac{3}{4} = \frac{23}{4}$, since $(4 \times 5) + 3 = 23$, and 4 was the denominator of the common fraction part, $\frac{23}{4}$ is an improper fraction, since the numerator 23 is larger than the denominator 4.

Addition

In order to *add* two fractions, the denominators of the fractions must be the same; when they are, they are called *common denominators*. The equivalent fractions with the smallest common denominator are said to have the *lowest common denominator*.

Examples: $\dfrac{3}{8} + \dfrac{2}{8} = \dfrac{5}{8}$, but

$\dfrac{3}{8} + \dfrac{1}{4} = \dfrac{3}{8} + \dfrac{2}{8} = \dfrac{5}{8}$. **Note that while 16, 24, 32, and so forth, could have been used as common denominators to obtain equivalent fractions, the lowest common denominator, 8, was used to generate like denominators.**

The procedures regarding the addition of signed numbers given in the addition section also apply for the addition of common fractions.

Subtraction

The procedures given for the addition of common fractions together with the procedures for subtraction of signed numbers form the basis for the subtraction of common fractions.

Examples: $\dfrac{3}{8} - \dfrac{2}{8} = \dfrac{1}{8}$, but

$\dfrac{3}{8} - \dfrac{1}{4} = \dfrac{3}{8} - \dfrac{2}{8} = \dfrac{1}{8}$.

As also suggested:

$\dfrac{3}{8} - \left(\dfrac{2}{8}\right) = \dfrac{3}{8} + \dfrac{2}{8} = \dfrac{5}{8}$ and

$\dfrac{3}{8} - \left(-\dfrac{1}{4}\right) = \dfrac{3}{8} + \dfrac{1}{4} = \dfrac{3}{8} + \dfrac{2}{8} = \dfrac{5}{8}$.

Multiplication

To *multiply* two common fractions, simply find the product of the two numerators and divide it by the product of the two denominators. Reduce the resultant fraction to lowest terms.

Example: $\dfrac{2}{3} \times \dfrac{9}{11} = \dfrac{18}{33} = \dfrac{6}{11}$.

In addition, the procedures regarding the multiplication of integers given in the "multiplication of integers" section apply to the multiplication of common fractions.

Division

To find the *reciprocal* of a common fraction, exchange the numerator and the denominator.

Examples: The reciprocal of $\dfrac{2}{3}$ is $\dfrac{3}{2}$.

The reciprocal of $\dfrac{21}{4}$ is $\dfrac{4}{21}$.

To *divide* two common fractions, multiply the fraction which is the dividend by the reciprocal of the fraction which is the divisor. Reduce the result to lowest terms.

Examples: $\dfrac{4}{9} \div \dfrac{2}{3} = \dfrac{4}{9} \times \dfrac{3}{2} = \dfrac{12}{18} = \dfrac{2}{3}$.

$\dfrac{7}{8} \div \dfrac{21}{4} = \dfrac{7}{8} \times \dfrac{4}{21} = \dfrac{28}{168} = \dfrac{1}{6}$.

In addition, the procedures regarding the division of integers given above apply for the division of common fractions.

ARITHMETIC OPERATIONS AND DECIMAL FRACTIONS

As previously discussed, our numeration system follows a base 10 place value scheme. Another way to represent a fractional number is to write the number to include integer powers of ten. This allows us to represent *decimal fractions* as follows:

$$\frac{1}{10} = 10^{-1} = 0.1 \text{ (said "one-tenth")}$$

$$\frac{1}{100} = 10^{-2} = 0.01 \text{ (said "one-hundredth")}$$

$$\frac{1}{1,000} = 10^{-3} = 0.001 \text{ (said "one-thousandth"), and so forth.}$$

Examples: 3.14 is said "**three and fourteen hundredths.**"
528.5 is said "**five hundred twenty-eight and five-tenths.**"

Addition

To *add decimal fractions*, simply line up the decimal points for each decimal numeral to be added, and follow the procedures for the addition of integers. Place the decimal point in the sum directly underneath the decimal point in the addends.

Examples:

$$
\begin{array}{r}
89.8 \\
152.9 \\
+\ 7.21 \\
\hline
249.91
\end{array}
\qquad
\begin{array}{r}
32.456 \\
6561.22 \\
+\ 2.14 \\
\hline
6595.816
\end{array}
$$

Subtraction

To *subtract decimal fractions*, place zeros as needed so that both the minuend and the subtrahend have a digit in each column.

Examples:	152.9	→	152.90
	−7.21		−7.21
			145.69

	32.456	→	32.456
	−2.14		−2.140
			30.316

Multiplication

To *multiply decimal fractions*, follow the procedures for multiplying integers and then place the decimal point so that *the total number of decimal places in the product is equal to the sum of the decimal places in each factor.*

Examples: (3.14) (0.5) = 1.570, and
(89.8) (152.9) = 13730.42

Division

To *divide decimal fractions,*

1) move the decimal point in the divisor to the right, until there are no decimal places in the divisor,

2) move the decimal point in the dividend the same number of decimal places to the right, and

3) divide the transformed dividend and divisor as given above.

4) The number of decimal places in the quotient should be the same as the number of decimal places in the transformed dividend.

Examples: 15.5 ÷ 0.5 → 155 ÷ 5 = 31, and
32.436 ÷ 0.06 → 3243.6 ÷ 6 = 540.6

PERCENT

Percent is another way of expressing a fractional number. Percent always expresses a fractional number in terms of $\frac{1}{100}$'s or 0.01's. Percents use the "%" symbol.

Examples: $100\% = \frac{100}{100} = 1.00$, and

$25\% = \frac{25}{100} = 0.25.$

As shown in these examples, a percent is easily converted to a common fraction or a decimal fraction. To convert a decimal to a common fraction, place the percent in the numerator and use 100 as the denominator (reduce as necessary). To convert a percent to a decimal fraction, divide the percent by 100, or move the decimal point two places to the left.

Examples: $25\% = \dfrac{25}{100} = \dfrac{1}{4}$ and

$25\% = 0.25.$

Similarly, $125\% = \dfrac{125}{100} = 1\dfrac{25}{100} = 1\dfrac{1}{4}$ and

$125\% = 1.25.$

To convert a *common fraction to a percent,* carry a division of the numerator by the denominator of the fraction out to three decimal places. Round the result to two places. To convert a *decimal fraction to a percent,* move the decimal point two places to the right (adding 0's as place holders, if needed) and round as necessary.

Examples: $\dfrac{1}{4} = 1 \div 4 = 0.25 = 25\%$, and

$\dfrac{2}{7} = 2 \div 7 \cong 0.28 = 28\%.$

If one wishes to find the *percentage* of a known quantity, change the percent to a common fraction or a decimal fraction, and multiply the fraction times the quantity. The percentage is expressed in the same units as the known quantity.

Example: To find 25% of 360 books, change 25% to 0.25 and multiply times 360, as follows: $0.25 \times 360 = 90.$ The result is 90 books.

(Note: The known quantity is the *base,* the percent is the *rate,* and the result is the *percentage.*)

ELEMENTARY STATISTICS

Mean

The average, or *mean,* of a set of numbers can be found by adding the set of numbers and dividing by the total number of elements in the set.

Example: The mean of 15, 10, 25, 5, 40 is

$$\dfrac{15 + 10 + 25 + 5 + 40}{5} = \dfrac{95}{5} = 19.$$

Median

If a given set of numbers is ordered from smallest to largest, the *median* is the "middle" number; that is, half of the numbers in the set of numbers are below the median and half of the numbers in the set are above the median.

Example: To find the median of the set of whole numbers 15, 10, 25, 5, 40, first order the set of numbers to get 5, 10, 15, 25, 40. Since 15 is the middle number (half of the numbers are below 15, half are above 15), 15 is called the median of this set of whole numbers. If there is an even number of numbers

in the set, the median is the mean of the middle two numbers.

Mode

The *mode* of a set of numbers is the number that appears most frequently in the set. There may be no mode or more than one mode for a set of numbers.

Example: In the set 15, 10, 25, 10, 5, 40, 10, 15, the number 10 appears most frequently (three times); therefore, 10 is the mode of the given set of numbers.

Range

The *range* of a set of numbers is obtained by subtracting the smallest number in the set from the largest number in the set.

Example: To find the range of 15, 10, 25, 5, 40, find the difference between the largest and the smallest elements of the set. This gives $40 - 5 = 35$. The range of the given set is 35.

PART II: ALGEBRA

ALGEBRAIC EXPRESSIONS

An *algebraic expression* is an expression using letters, numbers, symbols, and arithmetic operations to represent a number or relationship among numbers.

A *variable,* or unknown, is a letter that stands for a number in an algebraic expression. *Coefficients* are the numbers that precede the variable to give the quantity of the variable in the expression.

Algebraic expressions are comprised of *terms,* or groupings of variables and numbers.

An algebraic expression with one term is called a *monomial;* with two terms, a *binomial;* with three terms, a *trinomial;* with more than one term, a *polynomial.*

Examples: $2ab - cd$ is a binomial algebraic expression with variables a, b, c, and d, and terms $2ab$ and $(-cd)$. 2 is the coefficient of ab and -1 is the coefficient of cd.

$x^2 + 3y - 1$ is a trinomial algebraic expression using the variables x and y, and terms x^2, $3y$, and (-1);

$z(x - 1) + uv - wy - 2$ is a polynomial with variables z, x, u, v, w, and y, and terms $z(x - 1)$, uv, $(-wy)$, and (-2).

As stated above, algebraic expressions can be used to represent the relationship among numbers. For example, if we know there are ten times as many students in a school as teachers, if S represents the number of students in the school and T represents the number of teachers, the total number of students and teachers in the school is $S + T$.

If we wished to form an algebraic sentence equating the number of students and teachers in the school, the sentence would be $S = 10T$. (Note that if either the number of students or the number of teachers were known, the other quantity could be found.)

SIMPLIFYING ALGEBRAIC EXPRESSIONS

Like terms are terms in an algebraic expression that are exactly the same; that is, they contain the same variables and the same powers.

Examples: **The following are pairs of like terms:**
x^2 and $(-3x^2)$, *abc* and *4abc*, $(x-1)$
and $(x-1)^2$.
The following are not pairs of like terms:
x and $(-3x^2)$, *abc* and $4a^2bc$, $(x-1)$ and (x^2-1).

To simplify an algebraic expression, combine like terms in the following order:

1) simplify all expressions within symbols of inclusion (e.g., ( ), [ ], { }) using steps 2-4 below;

2) carry out all exponentiation;

3) carry out all multiplication and division from left to right in the order in which they occur;

4) carry out all addition and subtraction from left to right in the order in which they occur.

FACTORING ALGEBRAIC EXPRESSIONS

When two numbers are multiplied together, the numbers are called factors and their result is called the product. Similarly, algebraic expressions may be the product of other algebraic expressions.

In factoring algebraic expressions, first remove any monomial factors, then remove any binomial, trinomial, or other polynomial factors. Often one may find other polynomial factors by inspecting for the sum and difference of two squares; that is, $x^2 - y^2 = (x+y)(x-y)$.

Examples: $2a + 2b = 2(a+b)$
$4x^2y - 2xy^2 + 16x^2y^2 = 2xy(2x - y + 8xy)$
$x^2 - 4 = (x+2)(x-2)$
$4a^2 - 16b^2 = 4(a^2 - 4b^2) = 4(a+2b)(a-2b)$

In factoring polynomials, one often uses what is called the *"FOIL" method (First, Outside, Inside, Last).*

Examples: $x^2 + 3x - 10 = (x-2)(x+5)$
$6y^2 - y - 2 = (2y+1)(3y-2)$
$ab^2 - 3ab - 10a = a(b^2 - 3b - 10) = a(b+2)(b-5)$

SOLVING LINEAR EQUATIONS

To solve a linear equation, use the following procedures:

1) isolate the variable; that is, group all the terms with the variable on one side of the equation (commonly the left side) and group all the constants on the other side of the equation (commonly the right side);

2) combine like terms on each side of the equation;

3) divide by the coefficient of the variable;

4) check the result in the original equation.

Problem: Solve $3x + 2 = 5$ for x.
Solution: $3x + 2 = 5$ (add -2 to both sides)

$3x = 3$ (multiply by $\frac{1}{3}$)

$x = 1$

Problem: Solve $a + 3a = 3a + 1$ for a.
Solution: $a + 3a = 3a + 1$ (add $-3a$ to both sides)
$a = 1$

Problem: Solve $3(y - 2) + 5 = 3 + 5y$ for y.
Solution: $3(y - 2) + 5 = 3 + 5y$ (simplify)
$3y - 6 + 5 = 3 + 5y$ (combine like terms)
$3y - 1 = 3 + 5y$ (add 1 to both sides)
$3y = 4 + 5y$ (add $-5y$ to both sides)

$-2y = 4$ (multiply by $-\frac{1}{2}$)

$y = -2$

SOLVING INEQUALITIES

The equivalence properties of integers given in the "integers" section and the procedures for solving linear equations given in "solving linear equations" are used *to solve inequalities.* In addition, the following properties of inequalities should be noted:

If $x < y$ and $z > 0$, then $zx < zy$.
If $x > y$ and $z > 0$, then $zx > zy$.
If $x < y$ and $z < 0$, then $zx > zy$.
If $x > y$ and $z < 0$, then $zx < zy$.

In other words, if both sides of an inequality are *multiplied by a positive number, the sense of the inequality remains the same.* If both sides of an inequality are *multiplied by a negative number, the sense of the inequality is reversed.*

Examples: Since $3 < 5$ and 2 is positive,
$(2)(3) < (2)(5)$ or $6 < 10$.
But since $3 < 5$ and -2 is negative,
$(-2)(3) > (-2)(5)$ OR $-6 > -10$.

The above properties are also demonstrated in the following problems:

Problem: Find the values of y for which $2y > y - 3$.
Solution: $2y > y - 3$ (add $-y$ to both sides)
$y > -3$

Problem: Find the values of x for which $x > 4x + 1$.

Solution: $x > 4x + 1$ (add $-4x$ to both sides)

$$-3x > 1 \text{ (multiply by } -\frac{1}{3})$$

$$x < -\frac{1}{3}$$

EVALUATING FORMULAS

Formulas are algebraic sentences that are frequently used in mathematics, science, or other fields. Examples of common formulas are $A = l \times w$, $d = r \times t$, and $C = \left(\frac{5}{9}\right)(F - 32°)$. *To evaluate a formula*, replace each variable with the given values of the variables and solve for the unknown variable.

Example: Since $A = l \times w$, if $l = 2$ ft. and
           $w = 3$ ft.,
           then $A = 2$ ft. $\times 3$ ft. $= 6$ sq. ft.

Example: Since $d = r \times t$, if $r = 32$ m/sec^2 and
           $t = 5$ sec.,
           then $d = (32$ m/sec$) \times 5$ sec. $= 160$ m.

Example: Since $C = \left(\frac{5}{9}\right)(F - 32)$, if $F = 212°$,

           then $C = \left(\frac{5}{9}\right)(212° - 32°) = 100°$.

ELEMENTARY PROBABILITY

The likelihood or chance that an event will take place is called the *probability* of the event. The probability of an event is determined by dividing the number of ways the event could occur by the number of possible events in the given sample. In other words, if a sample space S has n possible outcomes, and an event E has m ways of occurring, then the probability of the event, denoted by $P(E)$, is given by

$$P(E) = \frac{m}{n}.$$

It should be noted that $0 \leq P(E) \leq 1$.

Problem: What is the probability of getting "heads" on the toss of a coin?

Solution: Since the number of possible outcomes in the toss of a coin is 2 and the number of ways of getting "heads" on a coin toss is 1, $P(\text{head}) = \frac{1}{2}$.

Problem: What is the probability of drawing an ace from a standard deck of playing cards?

Solution: Since the number of aces in a standard deck is 4 and the number of cards in a standard deck is 52, $P(ace) = \dfrac{4}{52} = \dfrac{1}{13}$.

ALGEBRA WORD PROBLEMS

A general procedure for solving problems was suggested by Polya. His procedure can be summarized as follows:

1) Understand the problem.

2) Devise a plan for solving the problem.

3) Carry out the plan.

4) Look back on the solution to the problem.

When taking the mathematics section of the MSAT, you can use this procedure by translating the word problem into an algebraic sentence, then following the procedures for solving an algebraic sentence. Find a variable to represent the unknown in the problem. Look for key synonyms such as "is, are, were" for "=", "more, more than" for "+", "less, less than, fewer" for "–", and "of" for "×."

Problem: The sum of the ages of Bill and Paul is 32 years. Bill is 6 years older than Paul. Find the age of each.

Solution: If p = Paul's age, then Bill's age is $p + 6$. So that $p + (p + 6) = 32$. Applying the methods from above, we get $p = 13$. Therefore, Paul is 13 and Bill is 19.

Problem: Jose weighs twice as much as his brother Carlos. If together they weigh 225 pounds, how much does each weigh?

Solution: If c = Carlos' weight, then Jose's weight is $2c$. So $c + 2c = 225$ pounds. Applying the methods above, we get $c = 75$. Therefore, Carlos weighs 75 pounds and Jose weighs 150 pounds.

Problem: Julia drove from her home to her aunt's house in 3 hours and 30 minutes. If the distance between the houses is 175 miles, what was the car's average speed?

Solution: As noted previously, distance = rate×time. Since we know $d = 175$ mph and $t = 3\frac{1}{2}$ hr., then 175 mph = $r \times 3\frac{1}{2}$ hr. Solving for the rate (r), we get $r = 50$ mph.

PART III: MEASUREMENT AND GEOMETRY

PERIMETER AND AREA OF RECTANGLES, SQUARES, AND TRIANGLES

Perimeter refers to the measure of the distance around a figure. Perimeter is measured in linear units (e.g., inches, feet, meters). *Area* refers to the measure of the interior of a figure. Area is measured in square units (e.g., square inches, square feet, square meters).

The *perimeter of a rectangle* is found by adding twice the length of the rectangle to twice the width of the rectangle. This relationship is commonly given by the formula $P = 2l + 2w$, where l is the measure of the length and w is the measure of the width.

Example: If a rectangle has $l = 10$ m and $w = 5$ m,
then the perimeter of the rectangle is given by
$P = 2(10 \text{ m}) + 2(5 \text{ m}) = 30$ m.

The *perimeter of a square* is found by multiplying four times the measure of a side of the square. This relationship is commonly given by the formula, $P = 4s$, where s is the measure of a side of the square.

Example: If a square has $s = 5$ feet,
then the perimeter of the square is given by
$P = 4(5 \text{ feet}) = 20$ feet.

The *perimeter of a triangle* is found by adding the measures of the three sides of the triangle. This relationship can be represented by $P = s_1 + s_2 + s_3$, where s_1, s_2, and s_3 are the measures of the sides of the triangle.

Example: If a triangle has three sides measuring
3 inches, 4 inches, and 5 inches,
then the perimeter of the triangle is given by
$P = 3 \text{ inches} + 4 \text{ inches} + 5 \text{ inches} = 12$ inches.

AREA OF RECTANGLES, SQUARES, AND TRIANGLES

The *area of a rectangle* is found by multiplying the measure of the length of the rectangle by the measure of the width of the triangle. This relationship is commonly given by $A = l \times w$, where l is the measure of the length and w is the measure of the width.

Example: If a rectangle has $l = 10$ m and $w = 5$ m,
then the area of the rectangle is given by
$A = 10 \text{ m} \times 5 \text{ m} = 50 \text{ m}^2$.

The *area of a square* is found by squaring the measure of the side of the square. This relationship is commonly given by $A = s^2$, where s is the measure of a side.

Example: If a square has $s = 5$ ft.,
then the area of the square is given by
$A = (5 \text{ ft})^2 = 25 \text{ ft}^2$.

The *area of a right triangle* is found by multiplying $\frac{1}{2}$ times the product of the base and the height of the triangle. This relationship is commonly given by $A = \frac{1}{2}bh$, where b is the base and h is the height.

Example: If a triangle has a base of 3 in. and a height of 4 in., then the area of the triangle is given by

$$A = \frac{1}{2}\ (3\ \text{in.} \times 4\ \text{in.}) = \frac{1}{2}\ (12\ \text{in}^2) = 6\ \text{in}^2.$$

CIRCUMFERENCE AND AREA OF CIRCLES

The *radius of a circle* is the distance from the center of the circle to the circle itself. The *diameter of a circle* is a line segment that passes through the center of the circle, the end points of which lie on the circle. The *measure of the diameter of a circle* is twice the measure of the radius.

The number π (approximately 3.14) is often used in computations involving circles.

The *circumference of a circle* is found by multiplying π times the diameter (or twice the radius). This relationship is commonly given by $C = \pi \times d$, or $C = 2 \times \pi \times r$.

The *area of a circle* is found by multiplying π by the square of the radius of the circle. This relationship is commonly given by $A = \pi \times r^2$.

Example: If a circle has a radius of 5 cm, then
$C = \pi \times 10\ \text{cm} = 3.14 \times 10\ \text{cm} \approx 31.4\ \text{cm}$, and
$A = \pi \times (5\ \text{cm})^2 \approx 3.14 \times (5\ \text{cm})^2 = 78.50\ \text{cm}^2.$

VOLUME OF CUBES AND RECTANGULAR SOLIDS

Volume refers to the measure of the interior of a three-dimensional figure.

A *rectangular solid* is a rectilinear (right-angled) figure that has length, width, and height. The volume of a rectangular solid is found by computing the product of the length, width, and height of the figure. This relationship is commonly expressed by $V = l \times w \times h$.

Example: The volume of a rectangular solid with
$l = 5$ cm, $w = 4$ cm, and $h = 3$ cm is given by
$V = 5\ \text{cm} \times 4\ \text{cm} \times 3\ \text{cm} = 60\ \text{cm}^3.$

A *cube* is a rectangular solid, the length, width, and height of which have the same measure. This measure is called the *edge of the cube*. The volume of a cube is found by cubing the measure of the edge. This relationship is commonly expressed by $V = e^3$.

Example: The volume of a cube with $e = 5$ cm is given by $V = (5\ \text{cm})^3 = 125\ \text{cm}^3.$

ANGLE MEASURE

An *angle* consists of all the points in two noncollinear rays that have the same vertex. An angle is commonly thought of as two "arrows" joined at their bases.

Two angles are *adjacent* if they share a common vertex, share only one side, and one angle does not lie in the interior of the other.

Angles are usually measured in *degrees*. A circle has a measure of 360°, a half circle 180°, a quarter circle 90°, and so forth. If the measures of two angles are the same, then the angles are said to be *congruent*.

An angle with a measure of 90° is called a *right angle*. Angles with measures less than 90° are called *acute*. Angles with measures more than 90° are called *obtuse*.

If the sum of the measures of two angles is 90°, the two angles are said to be *complementary*. If the sum of the measures of the two angles is 180°, the two angles are said to be *supplementary*.

If two lines intersect, they form two pairs of *vertical angles*. The measures of vertical angles are equivalent; that is, vertical angles are congruent.

PROPERTIES OF TRIANGLES

Triangles are three-sided polygons.

If the measures of two sides of a triangle are equal, then the triangle is called an *isosceles triangle*. If the measures of all sides of the triangle are equal, then the triangle is called an *equilateral triangle*. If no measures of the sides of a triangle are equal, then the triangle is called a *scalene triangle*.

The sum of the measures of the angles of a triangle is 180°.

The sum of the measures of any two sides of a triangle is greater than the measure of the third side.

If the measure of one angle of a triangle is greater than the measure of another angle of a triangle, then the measure of the side opposite the larger angle is greater than the side opposite the smaller angle. (A similar relationship holds for the measures of angles opposite larger sides.)

Related to the previous discussion of angles, if all of the angles of a triangle are acute, then the triangle is called an *acute triangle*. If one of the angles of a triangle is obtuse, then the triangle is called an *obtuse triangle*. If one of the angles of a triangle is a right angle, then the triangle is called a *right triangle*.

Two triangles are *congruent* if the measures of all corresponding sides and angles are equal. Two triangles are *similar* if the measures of all corresponding angles are equal.

Problem: Find the measures of the angles of a right triangle, if one of the angles measures 30°.

Solution: Since the triangle is a right triangle, a second angle of the triangle measures 90°. We know the sum of the measures of a triangle is 180°, so that, $90° + 30° + x° = 180°$. Solving for $x°$, we get $x° = 60°$. The measures of the angles of the triangle are 90°, 60°, and 30°.

THE PYTHAGOREAN THEOREM

In a right triangle, the side opposite the 90° angle is called the *hypotenuse* and the other two sides are called the *legs*. If the hypotenuse has measure c and the legs have measures *a* and *b,* the relationship among the measures, known as the *Pythagorean Theorem,* is given by

$$c^2 = a^2 + b^2.$$

Problem: Find the length of the hypotenuse of a triangle if the measure of one leg is 3 cm and the other leg is 4 cm.

Solution: By the Pythagorean Theorem, $c^2 = (3 \text{ cm})^2 + (4 \text{ cm})^2$, so that $c^2 = 9 \text{ cm}^2 + 16 \text{ cm}^2$, $c^2 = 25 \text{ cm}^2$. Taking the square root of both sides, we get $c = 5$ cm.

PROPERTIES OF PARALLEL AND PERPENDICULAR LINES

If lines have a point or points in common, they are said to *intersect.*

Lines are *parallel* if they do not intersect.

Lines are *perpendicular* if they contain the sides of a right angle.

If a third line intersects two other lines, the intersecting line is called a *transversal.*

Two lines crossed by a transversal form eight angles. The four angles that lie between the two lines are called *interior angles.* The four angles that lie outside the two lines are called *exterior angles.*

The interior angles that lie on the same side of the transversal are called *consecutive interior angles.* The interior angles that lie on opposite sides of the transversal are called *alternate interior angles.* Similarly, exterior angles that lie on the same side of the transversal are called *consecutive exterior angles,* and those that lie on opposite sides of the transversal are called *alternate exterior angles.*

An interior angle and an exterior angle that have different vertices and have sides that are on the same side of the transversal are called *corresponding angles.*

Properties of Parallel Lines

The following are true for parallel lines:

Alternate interior angles are congruent. Conversely, if alternate interior angles are congruent, then the lines are parallel.

Interior angles on the same side of the transversal are supplementary. Conversely, if interior angles on the same side of the transversal are supplementary, then the lines are parallel.

Corresponding angles are congruent. Conversely, if corresponding angles are congruent, then the lines are parallel.

Properties of Perpendicular Lines

If two lines are perpendicular, the four angles they form are all right angles.

If two lines are perpendicular to a third line, the lines are parallel.

If one of two parallel lines is perpendicular to a third line, so is the other line.

COORDINATE GEOMETRY

The rectangular coordinate system is used as a basis for coordinate geometry. In this system, two perpendicular lines form a plane. The perpendicular lines are called the *x-axis* and the *y-axis*. The coordinate system assigns an *ordered pair of numbers* (x, y) to each point in the plane. The point of intersection of the two axes is called the origin, O, and has coordinates (0,0).

As shown in the figure below, the x-axis has positive integers to the right and negative integers to the left of the origin. Similarly, the y-axis has positive integers above and negative integers below the origin.

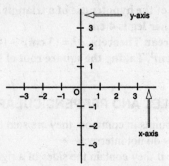

The distance between any two points in the coordinate plane can be found by using the *distance formula*. According to the distance formula, if P_1 and P_2 are two points with coordinates (x_1, y_1) and (x_2, y_2), respectively, then the distance between P_1 and P_2 is given by

$$P_1 P_2 = \sqrt{(x_2 - x_1)^2 + (y_2 - y_1)^2}$$

Problem: Compute the distance between the points A and B with coordinates (1,1) and (4, 5), respectively.

Solution: Using the distance formula,

$$AB = \sqrt{(4-1)^2 + (5-1)^2}$$

$$= \sqrt{3^2 + 4^2}$$

$$= \sqrt{9 + 16}$$

$$= \sqrt{25}$$

$$= 5$$

GRAPHS

To *plot a point* on a graph, first plot the x-coordinate, then plot the y-coordinate from the given ordered pair.

Problem: Plot the following points on the coordinate plane: A (1, 2), B (2, 1), C (-2, -1).

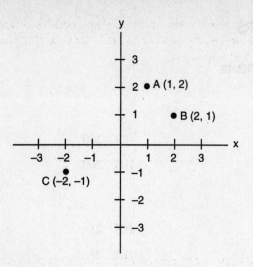

THE METRIC SYSTEM

The *metric system of measurement* is closely related to the base 10 place value scheme. The prefixes commonly used in the metric system are:

Prefix	Meaning
kilo-	thousand (1,000)
deci-	tenth (0.1)
centi-	hundredth (0.01)
milli-	thousandth (0.001)

The basic unit of linear measure in the metric system is the *meter*, represented by m. The relationship among the commonly used linear units of measurement in the metric system is as follows:

1 kilometer (km)	=	1,000 m
1 meter (m)	=	1.0 m
1 decimeter (dm)	=	0.1 m
1 centimeter (cm)	=	0.01 m
1 millimeter (mm)	=	0.001 m

The basic unit of measurement for mass (or weight) in the metric system is the *gram,* represented by g. The relationship among the commonly used units of measurement for mass in the metric system is as follows:

1 kilogram (kg)	=	1,000 g
1 gram (g)	=	1.0 g
1 milligram (mg)	=	0.001 g

The basic unit of measurement for capacity (or volume) in the metric system is the *liter,* represented by L or l. The most commonly used relationship between two metric units of capacity is

1 liter (l) = 1,000 milliliters (ml).

MATHEMATICS

PRACTICE QUESTIONS

1. $\sqrt{100} =$

    (A) 10   (C) 200

    (B) 50   (D) 500

2. $(2^2)^4 =$

    (A) $\sqrt{2}$ (C) 2^7

    (B) 2^6 (D) 2^8

3. $\dfrac{3}{4} \times \dfrac{8}{9} =$

    (A) $\dfrac{24}{9}$ (C) $\dfrac{2}{3}$

    (B) $\dfrac{32}{3}$ (D) $\dfrac{11}{13}$

4. Solve $2x + 5 = 9$ for x.

    (A) -5 (C) 2

    (B) -2 (D) 7

5. $5mn^2 \times 4mn^2 =$

    (A) $20m^2n^2$ (C) $9mn^2$

    (B) $20m^2n^4$ (D) mn^2

6. $x^4 - 1 =$

    (A) $(x^2 + 1)(x^2)$ (C) $(x^2 + 1)(x - 1)(x + 1)$

    (B) $(x^2 - 1)(x^2)$ (D) $(x - 1)(x^3 + 1)$

7. $3m + 2 < 7$

    (A) $m \geq \dfrac{5}{3}$ (C) $m \leq 2$

    (B) $m > 2$ (D) $m < \dfrac{5}{3}$

8. The circumference of a circle is 18π cm. Find the area of the circle.

    (A) 18π cm^2 (C) 36π cm^2

    (B) 81π cm^2 (D) 36π cm^2

9. Find the volume of a solid with $l = 4$ cm, $w = 3$ cm, and $h = 6$ cm.

    (A) 8 cm^3 (C) 36 cm^3

    (B) 9 cm^3 (D) 72 cm^3

10. $\angle a$ and $\angle b$ are supplementary angles and $\angle a = 3\angle b$. Find $\angle b$.

    (A) 22.5°   (C) 90°

    (B) 45°   (D) 135°

MATHEMATICS

ANSWERS TO PRACTICE QUESTIONS

1.	**(A)**	6.	**(C)**
2.	**(D)**	7.	**(D)**
3.	**(C)**	8.	**(B)**
4.	**(C)**	9.	**(D)**
5.	**(B)**	10.	**(B)**

MSAT

Multiple Subjects Assessment for Teachers

CHAPTER 4

History and Social Sciences Review

Chapter 4

History and Social Sciences Review

The History and Social Sciences portion of the MSAT accounts for about 18% of the overall exam, approximately 22 questions on the Content Knowledge Exam, and approximately four items in the Content Area Exercises. Subject matter in this area is divided into three sections:

World History (45 percent)
- Prehistory and early civilizations
- The classical world
- Development of world religions
- World cultural influences and developments
- Pre-Columbian America
- Rise and expansion of Europe
- Twentieth century ideologies and conflicts
- Political concepts and theories
- Global economics
- Geographical skills

United States History (50 percent)
- The American Revolution
- Civil War and Reconstruction
- Industrialization
- World War I and its aftermath
- World War II and its aftermath

Non-historical Perspective (5 percent)
- One social science question not posed in historical context

The review material that follow gives you all the substantive knowledge you'll need to achieve a passing score on this section of the MSAT. After you have completed the first practice test, you will have a better idea of which areas present the most difficulty for you. The more time you can spend working on these areas, the more confident you will be when you take the actual MSAT.

1. THE ANCIENT AND MEDIEVAL WORLDS

THE APPEARANCE OF CIVILIZATION

The earliest civilizations appeared in the Near East between 4000 and 3000 B.C.E. Between 6000 and 3000 B.C.E., humans invented the plow, utilized the wheel, harnessed the wind, discovered how to smelt copper ores, and began to develop accurate solar calendars. Small villages gradually grew into populous cities. The invention of writing in Mesopotamia around 3500 B.C.E., combined with heightened refinement in sculpture, architecture, and metal working from about 3000 B.C.E., marks the beginning of civilization and divides prehistoric from historic times.

Mesopotamia

Sumer (4000 to 2000 B.C.E.) included the city of Ur. The *Gilgamesh* is an epic Sumerian poem. The Sumerians constructed dikes and reservoirs and established a loose confederation of city-states. They probably invented writing, first in the form of pictograms, later in cuneiform (so called because of the wedge-shaped letters—from the Latin, *cuneus*, or wedge). The Akkadians (2300 to 2200 B.C.E.) conquered Sumer and eventually merged with that culture. The Amorites, or Old Babylonians (2000 to 1550 B.C.E.), established a new capital at Babylon, known for its famous Hanging Gardens. King Hammurabi (reigned 1792–1750 B.C.E.) promulgated a legal code which unified the entire lower Tigris-Euphrates Valley. It called for retributive punishment and provided that one's social class determined punishment for a crime.

The Assyrians (1100–612 B.C.E.) conquered Syria, Palestine, and much of Mesopotamia. They controlled a brutal, militaristic empire. The Chaldeans, or New Babylonians (612–538 B.C.E.), conquered the Assyrian territory, including Jerusalem. In 587 B.C.E., King Nebuchadnezzar (reigned ca. 605–562 B.C.E.) ordered the Temple of Solomon destroyed and the Jews brought to Babylon as slaves. In 538 B.C.E., Cyrus, king of the southern Persians, defeated the Chaldeans. The Persians created a huge empire and constructed a road network. Their religion, Zoroastrianism, promoted worship of a supreme being, Ahura Mazda, in the context of a cosmic battle with the forces of evil. After 538 B.C.E., the peoples of Mesopotamia came under the rule of a succession of dynasties and empires.

Egypt

Egypt's history is divided into seven periods. During the end of the Archaic Period (5000–2685 B.C.E.), Menes, or Narmer, probably unified Upper and Lower Egypt around 3200 B.C.E. During the Old Kingdom (2685–2180 B.C.E.), the pharaohs came to be considered living gods. The capital moved to Memphis during the Third Dynasty (ca. 2650 B.C.E.). The pyramids were built during the Fourth Dynasty (ca. 2613–2494 B.C.E.).

During the First Intermediate Period (2180–2040 B.C.E.), power reverted to regional authorities. The Middle Kingdom (2040–1785 B.C.E.) was one of brilliance. It was ended by the invasion of the Hyksos (Second Intermediate Period, 1785–1560 B.C.E.), who brought horses, chariots, and body armor to Egypt. The cult of Osiris was popular in this period. Osiris's resurrection promised the possibility of an afterlife, and funerary paintings show souls being judged on how much good or evil they had done.

The New Kingdom (1560–1085 B.C.E.) expanded into Nubia and invaded Palestine and Syria, enslaving the Jews. King Amenhotep IV or Akhenaton (reigned c. 1372–1362 B.C.E.) promulgated the idea of a single god, Aton, and closed other temples. He instructed his people to worship Aton through himself as a living god. His successor, Tutankhamen, returned to pantheism.

Following the Third Intermediate Period (1085–712 B.C.E.), Egypt came under the successive control of the Assyrians, the Persians, Alexander the Great, and finally, in 30 B.C.E., the Roman Empire. The Egyptians developed papyrus and made many medical advances. Other peoples would enlarge upon the Egyptian ideas of monotheism and the notion of an afterlife.

Palestine and the Hebrews

Phoenicians settled along the present-day Lebanon coast (Sidon, Tyre, Beirut, Byblos) and established colonies at Carthage and in Spain. They spread Mesopotamian culture through their trade networks. The Aramaeans lived in present-day Syria, with their capital at Damascus; in forming a number of Syrian states, they would become a major force for international economic and political stability.

Abraham, father of the Hebrews, left Ur sometime between 2000 and 1700 B.C.E. His grandson, Jacob, led the tribes into Palestine. The Hebrews probably moved to Egypt around 1700 B.C.E. and were enslaved about 1500 B.C.E. The Hebrews fled Egypt under Moses and around 1200 B.C.E. returned to Palestine. A loose confederation of 12 tribes, the Hebrews fought the Canaanites and Philistines for control of Palestine. Under King David (reigned ca. 1012–972 B.C.E.), the Philistines were defeated and a capital established at Jerusalem. Solomon (reigned ca. 972–932 B.C.E.) built huge public works projects. The tribes broke apart after his death, and Palestine divided into Israel (10 tribes) and Judah (two tribes). The 10 tribes of Israel (Lost Tribes) disappeared after Assyria conquered Israel in 722 B.C.E.

The poor and less attractive state of Judah continued until 586 B.C.E., when the Chaldeans transported the Jews to Israel as advisors and slaves (known as the Babylonian Captivity). There they preserved their faith and even converted King Nebuchadnezzar (Book of Daniel). When the Persians conquered Babylon in 539 B.C.E., the Jews were allowed to return to Palestine and they were tolerated by King Cyrus. Alexander the Great conquered Palestine in 325 B.C.E. During the Hellenistic period (323–63 B.C.E.) the Jews were allowed to govern themselves. Under Roman rule, Jewish autonomy was restricted, and as a result, the Jews revolted in 70 B.C.E. The Romans quashed the revolt and ordered the dispersion of the Jews. The Jews also revolted in 132-135 C.E. The result of the two revolts was the loss of their holy land. The Jews contributed the ideas of monotheism and humankind's covenant with God to lead ethical lives.

Greece

The Minoans (2600–1250 B.C.E.) lived on Crete. They established a vast overseas trading network and developed several written languages.

The Myceneans migrated to the Peloponnesian Peninsula before 2000 B.C.E. Their civilization peaked around 1400–1230 B.C.E. The Dorian invasion helped spark the Greek Dark Ages (1200–750 B.C.E.). Writing was reinvented in the eighth century.

Homer's *Iliad* and *Odyssey* were important in defining for ancient Greek civilization ideas like excellence (*arete*), courage, honor, heroism, and so on. Hesiod's *Works and Days* summarized everyday life. His *Theogony* recounted Greek myths. Greek religion was based on their writings.

In the archaic period (800–500 B.C.E.) Greek life was organized around the polis (city-state). Oligarchs controlled most of the poleis until the end of the sixth century, when individuals holding absolute power (tyrants) replaced them. By the end of the sixth century, democratic governments replaced many tyrants.

Sparta, however, developed into an armed camp. Sparta seized control of neighboring Messenia around 750 B.C.E. In 650 B.C.E., the Spartans crushed a revolt and enslaved the Messenians, who outnumbered them 10 to one. To prevent future rebellions, every Spartan entered lifetime military service (as hoplites) at age 7. Around 640 B.C.E., Lycurgus promulgated a constitution. Around 540 B.C.E., Sparta organized the Peloponnesian League.

Athens was the principal city of Attica. Between 1000 and 700 B.C.E., it was governed by monarchs (legendary kings such as Perseus and Theseus). In the eighth century, an oligarchy replaced the monarchy. Draco (ca. 621 B.C.E.) first codified Athenian law. His Draconian Code was known for its harshness. Solon (ca. 630–560 B.C.E.) reformed the laws in 594 B.C.E. He enfranchised the lower classes and gave the state responsibility for administering justice. The Athenian governing body was the Council of Areopagus, from which were selected archons (leaders). Growing indebtedness of small farmers and insufficient land strengthened the nobles. Peisistratus (ca. 605–527 B.C.E.) seized control and governed as a tyrant. In 527 B.C.E., Cleisthenes led a reform movement that established the basis of Athens's democratic government, including an annual assembly to identify and exile those considered dangerous to the state.

THE FIFTH CENTURY B.C.E. (CLASSICAL AGE)

The fifth century was the high point of Greek civilization. It opened with the Persian War. At Marathon (490 B.C.E.), the Athenians defeated Darius I's (reigned 522–486 B.C.E.) army. Ten years later, Darius's son Xerxes (reigned 486–465 B.C.E.) returned to Greece with 250,000 soldiers. The Persians burned Athens, but their fleet was defeated at the Battle of Salamis (480 B.C.E.) and they retreated.

After the Persian War, Athens organized the Delian League. Pericles (ca. 495–429 B.C.E.) used League money to rebuild Athens, including construction of the Parthenon and other Acropolis buildings. Athens's dominance spurred war with Sparta.

The Peloponnesian War between Athens and Sparta (431–404 B.C.E.) ended with Athens's defeat, but weakened Sparta as well. Sparta fell victim to Thebes, and the other city-states warred amongst themselves until Alexander the Great's conquest. That conquest unified the Greek city-states in the fourth century B.C.E., which marked the beginning of the Hellenistic Age.

A revolution in philosophy occurred in classical Athens. The Sophists emphasized the individual and his attainment of excellence through rhetoric, grammar, music, and mathematics. Socrates (ca. 470–399 B.C.E.) criticized the Sophists' emphasis on rhetoric and emphasized a process of questioning, or dialogues, with his students. Like Socrates, his pupil Plato (ca. 428–348 B.C.E.) emphasized ethics. His *Theory of Ideas* or *Forms* said that what we see is but a dim shadow of the eternal Forms or Ideas. Philosophy should seek to penetrate to the real nature of things. Plato's *Republic* described an ideal state ruled by a philosopher king.

Aristotle (ca. 384–322 B.C.E.) was Plato's pupil. He criticized Plato, arguing that ideas or forms did not exist outside of things. He contended that it was necessary to examine four factors in treating any object: its matter, its form, its cause of origin, and its end or purpose. Aristotle tutored Alexander the Great and later opened a school, the Lyceum, near Athens.

Greek art emphasized the individual. In architecture, the Greeks developed the Doric and Ionian forms. In poetry, Sappho (ca. 610–ca. 580 B.C.E.) and Pindar (ca. 522–438 B.C.E.) wrote lyric poems. In tragedy, Aeschylus (525–456 B.C.E.) examined the problem of hubris, most notably in his *Orestia* trilogy: *Agamemnon, The Libation Bear-*

ers, and *The Eumenides.* Sophocles (ca. 496–406 B.C.E.) used irony to explore the fate of Oedipus in *Oedipus Rex.*

Euripides (484–406 B.C.E.) is often considered the most modern tragedian because he was so psychologically minded. In comedy, Aristophanes (ca. 450–388 B.C.E.) was a pioneer who used political themes. The New Comedy, exemplified by Menander (ca. 342–292 B.C.E.), concentrated on domestic and individual themes.

The Greeks were the first to develop the study of history. They were skeptical critics, intent on banishing myth from their works. Herodotus (ca. 484–424 B.C.E.), called the "father of history," wrote *History of the Persian War.* Thucydides (ca. 460–400 B.C.E.) wrote *History of the Peloponnesian War.* The Greeks pioneered the study of metaphysics, ethics, politics, rhetoric, and cosmology.

THE HELLENISTIC AGE AND MACEDONIA

The Macedonians were a Greek people who were considered semibarbaric by their southern Greek relatives. They never developed a city-state system and had more territory and people than any of the poleis.

In 359 B.C.E. Philip II (382–336 B.C.E.) became king. To finance his state and secure a seaport, he conquered several city-states. In 338 B.C.E., Athens fell. In 336 B.C.E., Philip was assassinated.

Philip's son, Alexander the Great (356–323 B.C.E.) killed or exiled rival claimants to his father's throne. He established an empire that included Syria and Persia and extended to the Indus River Valley. His troops threatened to mutiny in 325 B.C.E. So he would not have to depend on the questionable loyalty of his Macedonian troops, Alexander married a Persian princess and ordered 80 of his generals to do likewise. At the time of his death, Alexander had established 70 cities and created a vast trading network.

With no succession plan, Alexander's realm was divided among three of his generals. Seleucus I established a dynasty in Persia, Mesopotamia, and Syria; Ptolemy I controlled Egypt, Palestine, and Phoenicia; and Lysimachus governed Asia Minor and Macedonia. Several Greek poleis rebelled against Macedonia and formed the Achaean and Aetolian leagues, the closest the Greeks ever came to national unity until modern times. By 30 B.C.E., all of the successor states had fallen to Rome.

ROME

The traditional founding date for Rome is 753 B.C.E. Between 800 and 500 B.C.E., Greek tribes colonized southern Italy, bringing their alphabet and religious practices to Roman tribes. In the sixth and seventh centuries, the Etruscans expanded southward and conquered Rome.

Late in the sixth century (the traditional date is 509 B.C.E.), the Romans expelled the Etruscans and established an aristocratically based republic in place of the monarchy (the rebellion was supposedly marked by the rape of Lucretia, a Roman matron, by an Etruscan).

In the early Republic, power was in the hands of the patricians (wealthy landowners). A Senate composed of patricians governed. The Senate elected two consuls to serve one-year terms. Roman executives had great power (the imperium). They were assisted by two quaestors, who managed economic affairs. The consuls' actions were supposed to be approved by the Senate and then by the Assembly, which represented all the people, but in practice, consuls in early times had near-despotic power.

Between 509 and 264 B.C.E., Rome conquered Italy through a mixture of diplomatic guile and brute force. It then turned its attention to Carthage, a powerful trading outpost.

In the three Punic Wars (264–146 B.C.E.), Rome defeated Carthage to gain control of the Mediterranean.

The First Punic War (264–241 B.C.E.) began when Carthage tried to dominate eastern Sicily. After its defeat, Carthage relinquished its interest and paid war reparations to Rome. The Second Punic War (218–202 B.C.E.) saw Carthage try to expand into Spain. Carthage's General Hannibal (247–183 B.C.E.) led 26,000 troops and 60 elephants across the Alps into Italy. He defeated the Romans at Cannae in 216 B.C.E. The Roman Pulibcus Scipio (died ca. 211 B.C.E.) defeated Carthage in a series of battles in Italy and Africa. The final Roman victory, in the Battle of Zama (202 B.C.E.) led to Carthage's surrender in 201 B.C.E. Carthage was reduced to a minor state.

Macedonia allied with Carthage in the Third Punic War (149–146 B.C.E.). The Macedonians' defeat brought Greek slaves, cultrue, and artifacts into Rome. In 146 B.C.E., the Romans burned Carthage and salted the earth to keep anything from growing again.

Rome's expansion and contact with Greek culture disrupted the traditional agrarian basis of life. Tiberius Gracchus (163–133 B.C.E.) and Gaius Gracchus (153–121 B.C.E.) led the People's party (or *Populares*). They called for land reform and lower grain prices to help small farmers. They were opposed by the *Optimates* (best men). Tiberius was assassinated. Gaius continued his work, assisted by the *Equestrians*. After several years of struggle, Gaius committed suicide.

Power passed into the hands of military leaders for the next 80 years. General Marius (157–86 B.C.E.) defeated Rome's Germanic invaders. A revolt (the Social War) broke out in 90 B.C.E. Sulla (138–78 B.C.E.), Marius's successor, restored order by granting citizenship to those who could not meet property qualifications. During the 70s and 60s, Pompey (106–48 B.C.E.) and Julius Caesar (100–44 B.C.E.) emerged as the most powerful men. In 73 B.C.E., Spartacus led a slave rebellion, which General Crassus suppressed.

In the 60s, Caesar helped suppress Cataline, who had led a conspiracy in the Senate. In 60 B.C.E., Caesar convinced Pompey and Crassus (ca. 115–53 B.C.E.) to form the First Triumvirate. When Crassus died, Caesar and Pompey fought for leadership. In 49 B.C.E., Caesar crossed the Rubicon, the stream separating his province from Italy, and a civil war followed. Caesar reformed the tax code and eased burdens on debtors. He instituted the Julian calendar, which remained in use until 1582. The Assembly under Caesar had little power.

In 47 B.C.E., the Senate proclaimed Caesar as dictator, and later named him consul for life. Brutus and Cassius believed that Caesar had destroyed the Republic. They formed a conspiracy, and on March 15, 44 B.C.E. (the Ides of March), Caesar was assassinated in the Roman Forum. His 18-year-old nephew and adopted son, Octavian, succeeded him.

In literature and philosophy, Plautus (254–184 B.C.E.) wrote Greek-style comedy. He also was an important advocate of the Roman Republic and an opponent of Caesar. Catullus (87–54 B.C.E.) was the most famous lyric poet. Lucretius's (ca. 94–54 B.C.E.) *Order of Things* described Epicurean atomic metaphysics, while arguing against the immortality of the soul. Cicero (106–43 B.C.E.), the great orator and stylist, defended the Stoic concept of natural law. His *Orations* described Roman life. Roman religion was family centered and more civic-minded than Greek religion.

THE ROMAN EMPIRE

Octavian (63 B.C.E.–14 C.E.), named as Caesar's heir, did not have enough power to control the state. He formed the Second Triumvirate in 43 B.C.E. with Mark Anthony (Caesar's lieutenant) and Lepidus, governor of the western provinces, to run the Republic and punish Caesar's assassins. Brutus's and Cassius's armies were defeated at Philippi in 42 B.C.E. The triumvirs divided the state, with Anthony getting Egypt and the east, Lepidus getting Africa, and Octavian getting Rome and the western provinces. Lepidus soon lost his position, and Octavian went to war with Anthony and Cleopatra, queen of Egypt. Octavian's army triumphed at Actium, in western Greece (31 B.C.E.), and Anthony and Cleopatra fled to Egypt, where they committed suicide (30 B.C.E.).

Octavian held absolute control while maintaining the appearance of a republic. When he offered to relinquish his power in 27 B.C.E., the Senate gave him a vote of confidence and a new title, "Augustus." Augustus ruled for 44 years (31 B.C.E.–14 C.E.) He introduced many reforms, including new coinage, new tax collection, fire and police protection, and land for settlers in the provinces.

Between 27 B.C.E. and 180 C.E., Rome's greatest cultural achievements occurred under the Pax Romana. The period between 27 B.C.E. and 14 C.E. is called the Augustan Age. Vergil (70–19 B.C.E.) wrote the *Aeneid,* an account of Rome's rise. Horace (65–8 B.C.E.) wrote the lyric *Odes.* Ovid (43 B.C.E.–18 C.E.) published the *Ars Amatoria,* a guide to seduction, and the *Metamorphoses,* about Greek mythology. Livy (57 B.C.E.–17 C.E.) wrote a narrative history of Rome based on earlier accounts.

The Silver Age lasted from 14 to 180 C.E. Writings in this period were less optimistic. Seneca (5 B.C.E. to 65 C.E.) espoused Stoicism in his tragedies and satires. Juvenal (50–127 C.E.) wrote satire, Plutarch's (46–120 C.E.) *Parallel Lives* portrayed Greek and Roman leaders, and Tacitus (55–120 C.E.) criticized the follies of his era in his histories.

Stoicism was the dominant philosophy of the era. Epictetus (ca. 60–120 C.E.), a slave, and Emperor Marcus Aurelius were its chief exponents. In law, Rome made a lasting contribution. It distinguished three orders of law: civil law *(jus civile),* which applied to Rome's citizens, law of the people *(jus gentium),* which merged Roman law with the laws of other peoples of the Empire, and natural law *(jus naturale),* governed by reason.

In science, Ptolemy, an Egyptian, and Galen worked in the provinces. Pliny the Elder's (23–79 C.E.) *Natural History* was widely known in the Middle Ages. In architecture, the Colosseum and Pantheon were constructed. The Romans developed the use of concrete as a building material.

After the Pax Romana, the third century was a period of great tumult for Rome. Marcus Aurelius's decision to name his son Commodus as his successor (reigned 180–192 C.E.), rather than the most talented governor, provoked vicious infighting. Commodus was ultimately strangled. Three emperors governed in the next 10 years. Civil war was nearly endemic in the third century. Between 235 and 284 C.E., 26 "barracks emperors" governed, taxing the population heavily to pay for the Empire's defense.

Rome's frontiers were attacked constantly. The Sassanians, a Persian dynasty, attacked Mesopotamia in 224 C.E. and took Emperor Valerian hostage in 259 C.E. By 250 C.E., the Germanic Goths had captured Rome's Balkan provinces. In the fourth century, the Huns under Attila (ca. 406–453) swept in from central Asia, driving out the Visigoths and other Germanic tribes before them. In 378 C.E., the Visigoths defeated Emperor Valens in the Battle of Adrianople. In 410 C.E., the Visigoths under Alaric (ca. 370–410) looted Rome.

Emperors Diocletian (reigned 285–305 C.E.) and Constantine (reigned 306–337 C.E.) tried to stem Rome's decline. Diocletian divided the Empire into four parts and moved the capital to Nicomedia in Asia Minor. Constantine moved the capital to Constantinople.

Some historians argue that the rise of Christianity was an important factor in

Rome's decline. Jesus was born around 4 B.C.E., and began preaching and ministering to the poor and sick at the age of 30. The Gospels provide the fullest account of his life and teachings. Saul of Tarsus, or Paul (10–67 C.E.), transformed Christianity from a small sect of Jews who believed Jesus was the Messiah into a world religion. Paul, a Hellenized Jew, had a conversion experience in 35 C.E. Early followers of Jesus believed that Christianity was a part of Judaism, and continued to follow Jewish law. Paul taught that Christians were justified by their faith in Jesus, and need no longer to follow Jewish law. Paul won followers through his missionary work. He also shifted the focus from the early followers' belief in Jesus's imminent return to concentrate on personal salvation. His *Epistles* (letters to Christian communities) laid the basis for the religion's organization and sacraments.

The Pax Romana allowed Christians to move freely through the Empire. In the Age of Anxiety, many Romans felt confused and alienated, and thus drawn to the new religion. And unlike other mystery religions, Christianity included women. By the first century, the new religion had spread throughout the Empire. Generally, the Romans tolerated other religions, including Christianity, but there were short, sporadic persecutions, reaching an apex under Diocletian.

Around 312 C.E., Emperor Constantine converted to Christianity and ordered toleration in the Edict of Milan (ca. 313 C.E.). In 391 C.E., Emperor Theodosius I (reigned 371–395 C.E.) proclaimed Christianity as the Empire's official religion.

By the second century, the church hierarchy had developed. Eventually, the Bishop of Rome came to have preeminence, based on the interpretation that Jesus had chosen Peter as his successor.

THE BYZANTINE EMPIRE

Emperor Theodosius II (reigned 408–450 C.E.) divided his empire between his sons, one ruling the East, the other the West. After the Vandals sacked Rome in 455 C.E., Constantinople was the undisputed leading city of the Empire. In 476 C.E., the Ostrogoth king, Odoacer, forced the last emperor in Rome, Romulus Augustulus (reigned 475–476 C.E.), to abdicate.

In 527 C.E., Justinian I (483–565 C.E.) became emperor in the East and reigned with his controversial wife, Theodora, until 565 C.E. The Nika revolt broke out in 532 C.E. and demolished the city. It was crushed by General Belisarius in 537 C.E., after 30,000 had died in the uprising. Justinian's campaigns to win back the western lands failed.

The Crusaders further weakened the state. In 1204 C.E., Venice contracted to transport the Crusaders to the Near East in return for the Crusaders capturing and looting Constantinople. The Byzantines were defeated in 1204 C.E. Though they drove out the Crusaders in 1261 C.E., the empire never regained its former power. In 1453 C.E., Constantinople fell to the Ottoman Turks.

ISLAMIC CIVILIZATION IN THE MIDDLE AGES

Mohammed was born about 570 C.E. and received a revelation from the Angel Gabriel around 610 C.E. In 630 C.E., Mohammed marched into Mecca. The Sharia (code of law and theology) outlines five pillars of faith for Muslims to observe. First is the belief that there is one God and that Mohammed is his prophet. In addition, the faithful must pray five times a day, perform charitable acts, fast from sunrise to sunset during the holy month of Ramadan, and make a hajj, or pilgrimage, to the holy city of Mecca. The Koran, which consists of 114 suras (verses), contains Mohammed's teachings. Mullahs (scholars or teachers) occupy positions of authority, but Islam did not develop a hierarchical system comparable to that of Christianity.

A leadership struggle developed after Mohammed's death. His father-in-law, Abu Bakr (573–634 C.E.), succeeded as caliph (successor to the prophet) and governed for two years, until his death in 634 C.E. Omar succeeded him. Between 634 and 642 C.E., Omar established the Islamic Empire. Khalid ibn-al-walid, called the Sword of Islam, defeated the Byzantines, gaining Jerusalem in 637 C.E. and the Persians in 643 C.E. He also claimed Egypt and much of North Africa.

The Omayyad caliphs, based in Damascus, governed from 661–750 C.E. They called themselves Shiites and believed they were Mohammed's true successors. (Most Muslims were Sunnites, from "sunna," oral traditions about the prophet.) They conquered Spain by 730 C.E. and advanced into France until they were stopped by Charles Martel (ca. 688–741 C.E.) in 732 C.E. at Poitiers and Tours. Muslim armies penetrated India and China. They transformed Damascus into a cultural center and were exposed to Hellenistic culture from the nearby Byzantine Empire.

The Abbasid caliphs ruled from 750–1258 C.E. They moved the capital to Baghdad and treated Arab and non-Arab Muslims as equals. Islam assumed a more Persian character under their reign. Caliph Harun-al-Rashid (reigned 786–809 C.E.) is known for the collection of stories called the *Thousand and One Arabian Nights*. Al-Maman (reigned 813–833 C.E.) was a great patron of the arts and sciences. In the late tenth century, the empire began to disintegrate. In 1055 C.E., the Seljuk Turks captured Baghdad, allowing the Abbasids to rule as figureheads. Genghis Khan (ca. 1162–1227 C.E.) and his army invaded the Abbasids. In 1258 C.E., they seized Baghdad and murdered the last caliph.

FEUDALISM IN JAPAN

Feudalism in Japan began with the arrival of mounted nomadic warriors from throughout Asia during the Kofun Era (300–710). Some members of these nomadic groups formed an elite class and became part of the court aristocracy in the capital city of Kyoto, in western Japan. During the Heian Era (794–1185), a hereditary military aristocracy arose in the Japanese provinces, and by the late Heian Era, many of these formerly nomadic warriors had established themselves as independent land owners, or as managers of landed estates *(shoen)* owned by Kyoto aristocrats. These aristocrats depended on these warriors to defend their *shoen,* and in response to this need, the warriors organized into small groups called *bushidan.* Members of these groups were often related by either blood or ties of personal loyalty, and were given rewards in the form of booty or land in return for service to the landowners.

As the years passed, these warrior clans grew larger, and alliances formed among them, led by imperial descendants who moved from the capital to the provinces. By the twelfth century, local warrior chieftains were serving as liaisons between the Kyoto and the provinces, and giving military support to the factions that were locked in a constant struggle for wealth and power. At this time, the dominant clans were the Taira (or Heike) and the Minamoto (or Genji), and in the bloody Taira-Minamoto War (1180–1185), the Taira were defeated.

After this victory, Minamoto no Yorimoto forced the emperor to award him the title of *shogun,* which is short for "barbarian subduing generalissimo." He used this power to found the Kamakura Shogunate which survived for 148 years. This was the first of the three feudal governments, or *bakfu,* which directly translated means "tent government," but is usually translated as shogunate. Under the Kamakura Shogunate, many vassals were appointed to the position of *jitro* or land steward, or the position of provincial governors *(shugo)* to act as liasons between the Kamakura government and local vassals.

By the fourteenth century, the *shugo* had augmented their power enough to become a threat to the Kamakura, and in 1333 lead a rebellion that overthrew the shogunate. After his crushing defeat of the Kamakura, Ashikaga Takauji founded the second *bakfu,* which would bear his name. Under the Ashikaga Shogunate, the office of *shogu* was made hereditary, and its powers were greatly extended. These new *shogu* turned their vassals into aggressive local warriors called *kokujin,* or *jizamurai.* Following this move, the Ashikaga shoguns lost a great deal of their power to political fragmentation, which eventually lead to the Onin War (1467–1477) and the Sengoku, or Warring States Era (1467–1568).

By the middle of the sixteenth century, the feudal system had evolved considerably. At the center of this highly evolved system was the *daimyo,* a local feudal lord who ruled over one of the many autonomous domains. Some *daimyo* were descendants of the *shogu* families, and others were simply opportunistic warriors who took advantage of political unrest to seize power by force. More than 100 *daimyo* once ruled the fragmented Japan, and saw their relationships to their vassals as nothing short of patriarchal.

Far reaching alliances of *daimyo* were forged under the national unifiers Oda Nobunaga, Toyotomi Hideyoshi, and Tokugawa Ieyasu, who together founded the Tokugawa Shogunate, the final and most unified of the three shogunates. Under the Tokugawa, the *daimyo* were considered direct vassals of the shoguns, and were kept under strict control. The warriors were gradually transformed into scholars and bureaucrats under the *bushido,* or code of chivalry, and the principles of Neo-Confucianism. A merchant class, or *chonin* gained wealth as the samurai class began to lose power, and the feudal system effectively ended when power was returned to the emperor under the Meji Restoration of 1868, when all special privileges of the samurai class were abolished.

CHINESE AND INDIAN EMPIRES

The Harappan or Indus civilization, which was confined to the Indus basin, was the early Indian civilization. That civilization was wealthy, being based on an intensive agriculture system and well-developed commerce, but it appears to have been unwarlike and easily overwhelmed by the Indo-Aryans coming down from the northwest. At around 1500 B.C.E., during the so-called Vedic age, India came to be ruled by the Indo-Aryans, a mainly pastoral people with a speech closely related to the major languages of Europe.

The religion of the Harappan peoples revolved around the god Siva, the belief in reincarnation, in a condition of "liberation" beyond the cycle of birth and death, and in the technique of mental concentration which later came to be called *yoga.* The religion of the Indo-Aryans was based on a pantheon of gods of a rather worldly type, and sacrifices were offered to them. These sacrifices were performed on behalf of kings and nobles by a hereditary class of priests called *Brahmas.* The traditional hymns that accompanied them were the Vedas, which form the basic scriptures for the religion of Hinduism. Indian society also came to be based on a *caste* system. The laws and usages of caste tended to become more and more strict as time went on and castes multiplied. Eventually, Hindu society became an aggregate of mutually exclusive groups which were nevertheless unified by a highly distinctive civilization and way of life.

In the third century B.C.E., the Indian kingdoms fell under the Mauryan Empire. The grandson of the founder of this empire, named Asoka, opened a new era in the cultural history of India by believing in the Buddhist religion. Buddha had disregarded the Vedic gods and the institutions of caste and had preached a relatively simple ethical religion which had two levels of aspiration—a monastic life of renunciation of the world and a high, but not too difficult morality for the layman. Buddhism had a wide appeal for a population in the midst of economic development and political upheaval, but it would hardly have attained the influence it did had it not been for the conversion of Asoka. The two religions of Hinduism and Buddhism flourished together for centuries in a tolerant rivalry, and in the end Buddhism virtually disappeared from India by the thirteenth century C.E.

Chinese civilization originated in the Yellow River Valley only gradually extending to the southern regions. The history of the first Chinese dynasty, the Xia or Hsia, is based more on legend than fact. The second dynasty, the Shang, originated in about 1500 B.C.E. This dynasty is famous for its oracle bones, which had inscriptions written on them and were used for divination. The Shang dynasty was agriculturally based with a dominant ruler and a class of feudal nobles and techniques of bronze casting. The Shang dynasty fell in 1122 B.C.E. to a conquering Zhou dynasty that lasted until 211 B.C.E.

After the Zhou dynasty, China welcomed the teachings of Confucius as warfare between states and philosophical speculation created circumstances ripe for such teachings. Confucius made the good order of society depend on an ethical ruler, who should be advised by scholar-moralists like Confucius himself. The disciples of Confucius formed a school that preached the duties of rulers and the need for honest and devoted officials.

In contrast to the Confucians, the Taoists professed a kind of anarchism; the best kind of government was none at all. The wise man did not concern himself with political affairs, but with mystical contemplation identified himself with the forces of nature. The founder of the first centralized empire, the Ch'in empire, persecuted the Confucians, and this empire lasted only 50 years. The next dynasty, the Han, which ruled China for the majority of four centuries, conciliated the Confucians, their teaching became a popular religion, and Buddhism was also introduced to China at this time.

SUB-SAHARAN KINGDOMS AND CULTURES

The Nok were a people that lived in the area now known as Nigeria. Artifacts indicate that they were peaceful farmers who built small communities consisting of houses of wattle and daub. They made jewelry of iron and tin, and beads have been found, indicating an interest in beauty and decoration. Perhaps the most revealing artifacts are the terra cotta figurines that they left behind. These are nearly life-sized figures of people and animals that show great skill on the part of the Nok.

The people referred to as the Ghana lived about 500 miles from what we now call Ghana. The Ghana peoples traded with Berber merchants. The Ghana offered these traders gold from deposits found in the south of their territory. Muslim influence in Ghana grew between 1054 and 1076, and for a century the country flourished under its new religion. Well-constructed stone houses replaced the older wooden ones and Muslim mosques appeared. In the 1200s the Mali kingdom conquered Ghana and the civilization mysteriously disappeared.

The people known as the Mali lived in a huge kingdom that mostly layed on the savanna bordering the Sahara Desert. The city of Timbuktu, built in the thirteenth century, was a thriving city of culture where traders visited stone houses, shops, libraries, and mosques. Although the religion of the kingdom was Islamic, the royal leaders and their subjects were reluctant to give up their belief in royal magic. In the fourteenth century, questions of succession to the throne weakened the kingdom, but the country did thrive for 400 years.

The Songhai lived near the Niger River and gained their independence from the

Mali in the early 1400s. The major growth of the empire came after 1464 C.E. under the leadership of Sunni Ali, who devoted his reign to warfare and expansion of the empire. Sunni Ali also professed to be Muslim but ruled as a magician king claiming the right to rule through his heritage. His successor was a devout Muslim who put Muslims in high government positions. In the 1500s people from Morocco came to find gold and salt deposits near Songhai territory and the people were forced to flee east of the Niger.

The Bantu peoples, numbering about 100 million lived across large sections of Africa. Bantu societies lived in tiny chiefdoms, starting in the third millennium B.C.E., and each group developed its own version of the original Bantu language. Instead of one Bantu people, they divided and redivided into a great number of distinct societies sharing some common forms of government and religious belief. Chiefs evolved into kings and some were buried with considerable worldly goods made of copper, iron, and ivory. The city of Great Zimbabwe, a walled city built of stone, was a major trading center providing gold and ivory to Swahili merchants. The Bantu fashioned bells, fine pottery, bark and raphia and, in some areas, cotton cloth.

CIVILIZATIONS OF THE AMERICAS

The great civilizations of early America were agricultural, and foremost of these was the Mayan, in Yucatan, Guatemala, and eastern Honduras. Here there developed a highly integrated society with elaborate religious observances, for which they built stone and mortar pyramid temples faced with carved stone. The Maya developed an elaborate calendar, a system of writing, and developed the concept of zero. Astronomy, engineering, and art were highly advanced. Maya priests used the calendar to commemorate the erection of stone monuments and kept elaborate historical scrolls.

Mayan history is divided into three parts, the Old Empire, Middle Period, and the New Empire. During the period known as the New Empire, the Mayans built the city of Chichen Itza, with its famous well in which human victims were sacrificed. By the time the Spanish conquerors arrived, most of the Mayan religious centers had been abandoned and their civilization had deteriorated seriously, perhaps due to the wide gulf between the majority of the people, who were peasants, and the priests and nobles.

Farther north in Mexico there arose a series of advanced cultures that derived much of their substance from the Maya. Such peoples as the Zapotecs, Totonacs, Almecs, and Toltecs evolved a high level of civilization. By 500 B.C.E. agricultural peoples had begun to use a ceremonial calendar and had built stone pyramids on which they performed religious observances. Their script was partly alphabetic and their codices dealt with history, religion, and secular affairs. Building in stone was characteristic of Mexican culture. The greatest site of the formative period of Mexican history is at San Juan Teotihuacan, which consists of more than a hundred pyramids arranged around a long plaza and was never finished.

The Aztecs then took over Mexican culture, and a major feature of their culture was human sacrifice in repeated propitiation of their chief god. Aztec government was centralized, with an elective king and a large army. Like their predecessors, they were skilled builders and engineers, accomplished astronomers and mathematicians. They built the famous city of Tenochtitlan, with 300 or more pyramids, palaces, plazas, and canals, and its population perhaps numbered five million.

Andean civilization was characterized by the evolution of beautifully made pottery, intricate fabrics, and flat-topped mounds called *huacas*. On the Andean plateaus, various highland cultures learned to cut stone and build palace structures, and in some cases stone pyramids. Andean cultural achievement reached a climax in the Chimu period, in which the various Andean cultures were welded into the Chimu Empire early in the common era.

The Incas, a tribe from the interior of South America who termed themselves "Children of the Sun," controlled an area stretching from Ecuador to central Chile. Sunworshippers, they believed themselves to be the viceregent on earth of the sun god; the Inca were all powerful; every person's place in society was fixed and immutable; the state and the army were supreme. Although not so advanced in scholarship as the Maya and Aztecs, the Incas had a well-developed system of roads and were very advanced politically. They were at the apex of their power just before the Spanish conquest.

In North America two major groups of mound builders are known as the Woodland and Mississippian peoples. The Woodland peoples lived in the Great Lakes and northern Mississippi area, and built burial mounds of several varieties dated from 500 B.C.E. to 1000 C.E. The Mississippian peoples lived in the middle and southern Mississippi areas. They built flat-topped mounds as sub-structures for wooden temples dated from 500 C.E. until historic times.

In the southwestern U.S. and northern Mexico, two varieties of ancient culture can be identified, the Anasazi and the Hohokam. The Anasazi developed adobe architecture, they worked the land extensively, had a highly developed system of irrigation, and made cloth and baskets. The Hohokam built separate stone and timber houses around a central plaza. Neither peoples developed a written language.

EUROPE IN ANTIQUITY

Between 486 and 1050 C.E., Europe saw the growth of many different ethnic groups. In antiquity, much of Europe was occupied by Germanic tribes. The northern tribes became the Vikings and Norsemen. The eastern tribes (Vandals, Burgundians, and Goths) settled east of the Elbe River. The Saxons and Lombards dominated the western tribes. In Eastern Europe and Russia, the Slavs were the dominant group.

Nomadic tribes from the central Asian steppes invaded Europe and pushed Germanic tribes into conflict with the Roman Empire. The Huns invaded in the fourth century, and led by Attila (ca. 406–453 C.E.), again in the fifth. In 410 C.E., the Visigoths sacked Rome, followed by the Vandals in 455 C.E. In 476 C.E., the Ostrogoth king forced the boy emperor Romulus Augustulus to abdicate, ending the empire in the West.

The Frankish Kingdom was the most important medieval Germanic state. Under Clovis I (reigned 481–511 C.E.), the Franks finished conquering France and the Gauls in 486 C.E. Clovis converted to Christianity and founded the Merovingian dynasty.

Pepin's son Charles, known as Charles the Great or Charlemagne (reigned 768–814 C.E.), founded the Carolingian dynasty. He defeated the Lombards in northern Italy, declaring himself their king, and pushed the Muslims out of northern Spain. He converted the Saxons to Christianity, and helped put down a revolt of Roman nobles in 799 C.E. In 800 C.E., Pope Leo III named Charlemagne Emperor of the Holy Roman Empire. In the Treaty of Aix-la-Chapelle (812 C.E.), the Byzantine emperor recognized Charles's authority in the West.

The Holy Roman Empire was intended to reestablish the Roman Empire in the West. Charles vested authority in 200 counts, who were each in charge of a county. Charles's son, Louis the Pious (reigned 814–840 C.E.), succeeded him. On Louis's death, his three sons vied for control of the Empire. After Louis II the German (ca. 804–876 C.E.), and Charles the Bald (823–877 C.E.) had sided against Lothair I (795–855 C.E.), the three eventually signed the Treaty of Verdun in 843 C.E. This gave Charles the Western

Kingdom (France), Louis the Eastern Kingdom (Germany), and Lothair the Middle Kingdom, a narrow strip of land running from the North Sea to the Mediterranean.

In the ninth and tenth centuries, Europe was threatened by attacks from the Vikings in the north, the Muslims in the south, and the Magyars in the east. The Vikings occupied England, leaving only Wessex under control of the English king Alfred (reigned 871–899 C.E.). King Alfred fought back and drove the invaders into an area called the Danelaw for which he earned the name "the Great." Viking invasions left France divided into small principalities. Danish Vikings seized control of Normandy and Brittany at the end of the ninth century. Under the leadership of William the Conqueror (reigned 1066–1087 C.E.), the Normans conquered England in 1066 C.E. (Battle of Hastings).

The Saxon king Otto I stopped the Magyar advance in the east and made the Saxons the most powerful group in Europe. In 962 C.E., Otto was crowned Holy Roman Emperor.

Rome's collapse ushered in the decline of cities, a reversion to a barter economy from a money economy, and a fall in agricultural productivity with a shift to subsistence agriculture.

Manorialism and feudalism developed in this period. Manorialism refers to the economic system in which large estates, granted by the king to nobles, strove for self-sufficiency. Large manors might incorporate several villages. The lands surrounding the villages were usually divided into long strips, with common land in-between. Ownership was divided among the lord and his serfs (also called *villeins*). The lord's property was called the demesne.

Feudalism describes the decentralized political system of personal ties and obligations that bound vassals to their lords. Serfs were peasants who were bound to the land. They worked on the demesne three or four days a week in return for the right to work their own land. In difficult times, the nobles were supposed to provide for the serfs.

The church was the only institution to survive the Germanic invasions intact. The power of the popes grew in this period. Gregory I (reigned 590–604 C.E.) was the first member of a monastic order to rise to the papacy. He is considered one of the four church Fathers (along with Jerome, Ambrose, and Augustine). He advanced the ideas of penance and purgatory. He centralized church administration and was the first pope to rule as the secular head of Rome.

Literacy nearly disappeared in Western Christendom during the early Middle Ages. Monasteries preserved the few remnants of antiquity that survived the decline. Outside the monasteries, the two most important literary works of the period were *Beowulf* (ca. 700 C.E.) and the Venerable Bede's (ca. 672–735 C.E.) *Ecclesiastical History of the English People.*

THE HIGH MIDDLE AGES (1050–1300)

1050 C.E. marked the beginning of the High Middle Ages. Europe was poised to emerge from five centuries of decline. Inferior to the Muslim and Byzantine empires in 1050 C.E., by 1300 C.E., the Europeans had surpassed them. Between 1000 and 1350 C.E., the population grew from 38 million to 75 million. Agricultural productivity grew, aided by new technologies, such as heavy plows, and a slight temperature rise which produced a longer growing season. Horses were introduced into agriculture in this period, and the three-field system replaced the two-field system.

As new lands came into cultivation, nobles needed an incentive to get serfs to move. Enfranchisement, or freeing of serfs, grew in this period, and many other serfs simply fled their manors for the new lands. Enfranchisement progressed most rapidly in England, and most slowly in Russia and Eastern Europe.

The Holy Roman Empire

Charlemagne's grandson, Louis the German, became Holy Roman Emperor under the Treaty of Verdun. Under the weak leadership of his descendants, the dukes in Saxony, Franconia, Swabia, Bavaria, and the Lorraine eroded Carolingian power. The last Carolingian died in 911 C.E. The German dukes elected the leader of Franconia to lead the German lands. He was replaced in 919 C.E. by the Saxon dynasty, which ruled until 1024 C.E. Otto became Holy Roman Emperor in 962 C.E. His descendants governed the Empire until 1024 C.E., when the Franconian dynasty assumed power, reigning until 1125 C.E.

A dispute over lay investiture (in which monarchs chose the high church officials in their realm) between Pope Gregory VII (pope 1073–1085 C.E.) and Emperor Henry IV (reigned 1084–1105 C.E.) came to a head in 1077 C.E., when the pope forced Henry to beg forgiveness for appointing church leaders. In revenge, Henry captured Rome in 1083 C.E. and sent the pope into exile. However, in the Concordat of Worms (1122 C.E.), the emperor received the right to grant secular, but not religious, authority to German bishops.

When the Franconian line died out in 1125 C.E., the Hohenstaufen family (Conrad III, reigned 1138–1152 C.E.) won power over a contending family. The Hapsburg line gained control of the Empire in 1273 C.E.

The Romans abandoned their last outpost in England in the fourth century. Around 450 C.E., the Jutes, Angles, and Saxons occupied different parts of the country. Danes began invading in the eighth century. Alfred the Great (ca. 849–899 C.E.) defeated the Danes in 878 C.E. In 959 C.E., Edgar the Peacable (reigned 959–975 C.E.) became the first king of all England.

William (reigned 1066–1087 C.E.) stripped the Anglo-Saxon nobility of its privileges and instituted feudalism. He ordered a survey of all property of the realm, which was recorded in the Domesday Book (1086 C.E.). His descendants, William II (reigned 1087–1100 C.E.) and Henry I (reigned 1100–1135 C.E.), continued to centralize the kingdom. Henry created the Office of the Exchequer to monitor receipt of taxes.

Nineteen years of civil war followed Henry's death. In 1154 C.E., his grandson, Henry II, was crowned king, founding the Plantagenet dynasty. Henry inherited Brittany from his mother. His reign was controversial, marked by a power struggle with the pope (during which Henry had Thomas Becket murdered) and his sons' revolt. In 1189 C.E., Richard the Lionhearted (reigned 1189–1199 C.E.) succeeded his father. He spent most of his reign fighting in the Crusades.

John I (reigned 1199–1216 C.E.) became king upon his brother's death. In 1215 C.E., the English barons forced him to sign the Magna Carta Libertatum, acknowledging their "ancient" privileges. The Magna Carta established the principle of a limited English monarchy. Henry III reigned from 1216–1272 C.E. In 1272 C.E., Edward I became king. His need for revenue led him to convene a parliament of English nobles, which would act as a check upon royal power.

France and the Capetian Dynasty

Creation of a strong national monarchy was slower in France than in England. Hugh Capet founded the dynasty in 987 C.E., but it had little power until 1108 C.E., when Louis the Fat subdued the most powerful vassals. Louis's grandson, Philip Augustus (reigned 1180–1223 c.e.), defeated King John of England (Battle of Bouvines, 1214) to win large territories in western France. Philip's son, Louis VIII, conquered most of southern France during his prosperous three-year reign. His grandson, Philip IV (1285–1314 c.e.), involved France in several wars. Philip also summoned a parliament, the Estates General, but it did not develop into a counterweight to royal power. In 1328 c.e., the Capetian dynasty ended with the death of Charles IV (reigned 1322–1328 c.e.). Since Edward III, king of England, had a claim to the French throne, the succession sparked the Hundred Years' War between England and France.

Spain Under the Muslims

In 710 c.e., the Muslims conquered Spain from the Visigoths. Under the Muslims, Spain enjoyed a stable, prosperous government. The caliphate of Córdoba became a center of scientific and intellectual activity. Internal dissent caused the collapse of Córdoba and the division of Spain into more than 20 Muslim states in 1031 c.e.

The Reconquista (1085–1340 c.e.), wrested control from the Muslims. Rodrigo Díaz de Bivar, known as El Cid (ca. 1043–1099 c.e.) was the most famous of its knights. The small Christian states of Navarre, Aragon, Castile, and Portugal organized the Reconquista. Each had a *cortes*, an assembly of nobles, clergy, and townspeople. The fall of Córdoba in 1234 c.e. completed the Reconquista, except for the small state of Granada.

Most of Eastern Europe and Russia was never under Rome's control, and it was cut off from Western influence by the Germanic invasions. Poland converted to Christianity in the tenth century, and after 1025 c.e. was dependent on the Holy Roman Empire. In the twelfth and thirteenth centuries, powerful nobles divided control of the country.

The Mongol Invasion of Russia

In Russia, Vladimir I converted to Orthodox Christianity in 988 c.e. He established the basis of Kievian Russia. After 1054 c.e., Russia broke into competing principalities. The Mongols (Tatars) invaded in 1221 c.e., completing their conquest in 1245 c.e., and cutting Russia's contact with the West for almost a century.

THE CRUSADES

The Crusades attempted to liberate the Holy Land from infidels. There were seven major crusades between 1096 and 1300 c.e. Urban II called Christians to the First Crusade (1096–1099 c.e.) with the promise of a plenary indulgence (exemption from punishment in purgatory). Younger sons who would not inherit their fathers' lands were also attracted.

Several months later, the organized Crusaders reached the Holy Land, capturing Jerusalem in 1099 c.e. They established four feudal states: Edessa, Antioch, Tripoli, and Jerusalem. The success of the First Crusade sparked a movement of pilgrims to the Levant and the organization of several religious and military orders to aid the pilgrims, including the Knights of St. John (Hospitalers), the Templars, and the Teutonic Knights. The Second Crusade (1147–1149 c.e.) attempted to recapture Edessa, and failed.

In 1187 c.e., the Muslim leader Saladin captured Jerusalem, sparking the Third Crusade, which failed to dislodge the Muslims, though Richard the Lionhearted negotiated the right of Christian pilgrims to visit shrines in Jerusalem.

In the Fourth Crusade (1202–1204 c.e.), the Crusaders never reached the Holy Land. They had hired the Venetians to transport them to Jerusalem, in payment for which they agreed to loot Constantinople, which fell in 1204 c.e. The Crusaders then established the Latin kingdom of Constantinople, but it was recaptured by the Byzantine emperor's troops 57 years later.

In the Fifth Crusade (1228–1229 C.E.), Frederick II negotiated what the Crusaders could not win by force: control of Jerusalem and Nazareth. In the Sixth Crusade (1248–1254 C.E.), Louis IX tried unsuccessfully to capture Egypt. In 1270 C.E., Louis IX died outside of Tunis in the Seventh Crusade. In 1291 C.E., Acre, the last Christian enclave in the Holy Land, fell.

The Crusades helped to renew interest in the ancient world. But thousands of Jews and Muslims were massacred as a result of the Crusades, and relations between Europe and the Byzantine Empire collapsed.

Charlemagne mandated that bishops open schools at each cathedral, and founded a school in his palace for his court. The expansion of trade and the need for clerks and officials who could read and write spurred an 1179 C.E. requirement that each cathedral set aside enough money to support one teacher. The first universities opened in Italy at Bologna (law) and Salerno, which became a center for medical studies.

Scholasticism was an effort to reconcile reason and faith and to instruct Christians on how to make sense of the pagan tradition.

Peter Abelard (ca. 1079–1144 C.E.) was a controversial proponent of Scholasticism, both for his love affair with Heloise, niece of the canon of Notre Dame, and for his views. In *Sic et Non* (Yes and No), Abelard collected statements in the Bible and by church leaders that contradicted each other. Abelard believed that reason could resolve the apparent contradictions between the two authorities, but the church judged his views as heretical.

Thomas Aquinas (ca. 1225–1274 C.E.), whose doctrines remained influential on church teachings for some time, believed that there were two orders of truth. The lower, reason, could demonstrate propositions such as the existence of God, but on a higher level, some of God's mysteries such as the nature of the Trinity must be accepted on faith. Aquinas viewed the universe as a great chain of being, with humans midway on the chain, between the material and the spiritual.

Latin was the language used in universities. Groups of satirical poets called Golliards also wrote in Latin. But the most vibrant works were in the vernacular. The *chansons de geste* were long epic poems composed between 1050 and 1150 C.E. Among the most famous are the *Song of Roland,* the *Song of the Nibelungs,* the Icelandic *Eddas,* and *El Cid.*

The fabliaux were short stories, many of which ridiculed the clergy. Boccaccio (1313–1375 C.E.) and Chaucer (ca. 1342–1400 C.E.) belonged to this tradition. The work of Dante (1265–1321 C.E.), the greatest medieval poet, synthesized the pagan and Christian traditions.

In this period, polyphonic (more than one melody at a time) music was introduced. In architecture, Romanesque architecture (rounded arches, thick stone walls, tiny windows) flourished between 1000 and 1150 C.E. After 1150 C.E., Gothic architecture, which emphasized the use of light, came into vogue because new building techniques, such as the peaked arch and the flying buttress, permitted thinner walls and larger windows.

2. THE RENAISSANCE, REFORMATION, AND THE WARS OF RELIGION (1300–1648)

THE LATE MIDDLE AGES

The Middle Ages were chronologically between the classical world of Greece and

Rome and the modern world. The papacy and monarchs, after exercising much power and influence in the high Middle Ages, were in eclipse after 1300. During the late Middle Ages (1300–1500), all of Europe suffered from the Black Death. While England and France engaged in destructive warfare in northern Europe, in Italy the Renaissance had begun.

The governments of medieval Europe did not have the control over their lands that we associate with modern governments. Toward the end of the period, monarchs began to assert their power and control. The major struggle, between England and France, was the Hundred Years' War (1337–1453).

The English king was the vassal of the French king for the duchy of Aquitaine, and the French king wanted control of the duchy; this was the event that started the fighting. The English king, Edward III, had a claim to the French throne through his mother, a princess of France. Thus, France faced a succession crisis.

Additionally, French nobles sought opportunities to gain power at the expense of the French king. England also exported its wool to Flanders, which was coming under control of the king of France. Finally, kings and nobles shared the values of chivalry which portrayed war as a glorious and uplifting adventure.

The war was fought in France, though the Scots (with French encouragement) invaded northern England. A few major battles occurred—Crécy (1346), Poitiers (1356), Agincourt (1415)—which the English won due to the chivalrous excesses of the French. The fighting consisted largely of sieges and raids. Eventually, the war became one of attrition; the French slowly wore down the English. Technological changes during the war included the use of English longbows and the increasingly expensive plate armor of knights.

Joan of Arc (1412–1431), an illiterate peasant girl who said she heard voices of saints, rallied the French army for several victories. Joan's victories led to Charles VII being crowned king at Rheims, the traditional location for enthronement. Joan was later captured by the Burgundians, allies of England, and sold to the English, who tried her for heresy (witchcraft). She was burned at the stake at Rouen.

England lost all of its Continental possessions, except Calais. French farmland was devastated, with England and France both expending great sums of money. Population, especially in France, declined.

Both countries suffered internal disruption as soldiers plundered and local officials left to fight the war. Trade everywhere was disrupted and England's wool trade with the Low Countries slumped badly. To cover these financial burdens, heavy taxation was inflicted on the peasants.

A series of factional struggles led to the deposition of Richard II in 1399. The Hundred Years' War ended with England finally stretched beyond its resources; it was evicted from Guyenne in 1453 and thus had its French territories pared down to Calais. The nobility continued fighting each other in the War of the Roses (1450–1485), choosing sides as Lancastrians or Yorkists.

In both countries, the war, fed by propaganda, led to the growth of nationalism.

Literature also came to express nationalism, as it was written in the language of the people instead of in Latin. Geoffrey Chaucer, the first of the great English poets, was inspired by Italian authors, particularly Boccaccio; his best known work is the unfinished *Canterbury Tales*. François Villon (1431–1463), in his *Grand Testament*, emphasized the ordinary life of the French with humor and emotion.

The New Monarchs

Nobles claimed various levels of independence under feudal rules or traditions.

Forming an assembly provided some sort of a meeting forum for nobles. Furthermore, the core of royal armies consisted of nobles. Many of the higher clergy of the church were noble-born.

Additionally, some towns had obtained independence during times of trouble. Church and clergy saw the pope as their leader.

The defeat of the English in the Hundred Years' War and of the duchy of Burgundy in 1477 removed major military threats. Trade was expanded, fostered by the merchant Jacques Coeur (1395–1456). Louis XI (1461–1483) demonstrated ruthlessness in dealing with his nobility as individuals and collectively in the Estates General.

The marriage of Isabella of Castile (reigned 1474–1504) and Ferdinand of Aragon (reigned 1474–1516) created a united Spain. The Muslims were defeated at Granada in 1492. Navarre was conquered in 1512.

A government organization called the Mesta encouraged sheep farming. An alliance with a group of cities and towns, the Hermandad, was formed to oppose the nobility. Finally, reform and control of the church was enacted through the Inquisition.

The "Black Death" and Social Problems

The bubonic plague ("Black Death") is a disease affecting the lymph glands. It causes death quickly. Conditions in Europe encouraged the quick spread of disease. There was no urban sanitation, and streets were filled with refuse, excrement, and dead animals. Living conditions were overcrowded, with families often sleeping in one room or one bed. Poor nutrition was rampant. There was also little personal hygiene.

Carried by fleas on rats, the plague was brought from Asia by merchants, and arrived in Europe in 1347. The plague affected all of Europe by 1350 and killed perhaps 25 million people—about a third of the population.

THE RENAISSANCE (1300–1600)

The Renaissance emphasized new learning, including the rediscovery of much classical material, and new art styles.

Italian city-states, such as Venice, Milan, Padua, Pisa, and especially Florence, were the home to many Renaissance developments, which were limited to the rich elite.

Jacob Burckhardt's *The Civilization of the Renaissance in Italy* (1860) popularized the study of the period and argued that it was a strong contrast to the Middle Ages. Subsequent historians have often found more continuity with the Middle Ages.

Literature, Art, and Scholarship

Humanists, as both orators and poets, were inspired by and imitated works of the classical past. The literature was more secular and wide-ranging than that of the Middle Ages.

Dante (1265–1321) was a Florentine writer who spent much of his life in exile after being on the losing side in political struggles in Florence. His *Divine Comedy*, describing a journey through hell, purgatory, and heaven, shows that reason can only take people so far and that God's grace and revelation must be used. Dealing with many other issues and with much symbolism, this work is the pinnacle of medieval poetry.

Petrarch (1304–1374), who wrote in both Latin and Italian, encouraged the study of ancient Rome, collected and preserved work of ancient writers, and produced much work in the classical literary style. He is best known for his sonnets, including many expressing his love for a married woman named Laura, and is considered the father of humanism.

Boccaccio (1313–1375) wrote *The Decameron*, a collection of short stories in Italian, which were meant to amuse, not edify, the reader.

Artists also broke with the medieval past, in both technique and content. Renaissance art sometimes used religious topics, but often dealt with secular themes or portraits of individuals. Oil paints, chiaroscuro, and linear perspectives produced works of energy in three dimensions.

Several artists became associated with the new style or art. Leonardo de Vinci (1452–1519) produced numerous works, including *The Last Supper* and *Mona Lisa*, as well as many mechanical designs, though few were ever constructed. Raphael (1483–1520), a master of Renaissance grace and style, theory and technique, represented these skills in *The School of Athens*. Michelangelo (1475–1564), a universal man, produced masterpieces in architecture, sculpture (*David*), and painting (the Sistine Chapel ceiling). His work was a bridge to a new, non-Renaissance style called Mannerism.

Renaissance scholars were more practical and secular than medieval ones. Manuscript collections enabled scholars to study the primary sources and to reject all traditions which had been built up since classical times. Also, scholars participated in the lives of their cities as active politicians.

Leonardo Bruni (1370–1444), a civic humanist, served as chancellor of Florence, where he used his rhetorical skills to rouse the citizens against external enemies. He also wrote a history of his city and was the first to use the term humanism.

Machiavelli (1469–1527) wrote *The Prince*, which analyzed politics from the standpoint of expediency, rather than faith or tradition. His work advocated the acquisition and maintenance of power by any means.

THE REFORMATION

The Reformation destroyed Western Europe's religious unity and introduced new ideas about the relationships between God, the individual, and society. Its course was greatly influenced by politics and led, in most areas, to the subjection of the church to the political rulers.

Earlier threats to the unity of the church had been made by the works of John Wycliffe and John Hus. The abuses of church practices and positions upset many people. Likewise, Christian humanists had been criticizing abuses.

Personal piety and mysticism, which were alternative approaches to Christianity and did not require the apparatus of the institutional church and the clergy, appeared in the late Middle Ages.

Martin Luther (1483–1546)

Martin Luther was a miner's son from Saxony in central Germany. At the urgings of his father, he studied for a career in law. While traveling, he underwent a religious experience that led him to become an Augustinian friar. Later he became a professor at the university in Wittenberg, Saxony.

Luther, to his personal distress, could not reconcile the problem of the sinfulness of the individual with the justice of God. How could a sinful person attain the righteousness necessary to obtain salvation? he wondered. During his studies of the Bible, especially of Romans 1:17, Luther came to believe that personal efforts—good works such as a Christian life and attention to the sacraments of the church—could not "earn" the sinner salvation, but that belief and faith were the only way to obtain grace. By 1515 Luther believed that justification is faith alone and that the scriptures are the sole source of faith.

Indulgences, which had originated in connection with the Crusades, involved the cancellation of the penalty given by the church to a confessed sinner. Indulgences had long been a means of raising money for church activities. In 1517 the pope was building the new cathedral of St. Peter in Rome. Also, Albrecht, archbishop of Mainz, had purchased three church positions (simony and pluralism) by borrowing money from the banking family, the Fuggers. A Dominican friar, John Tetzel, was authorized to preach and sell indulgences, with the proceeds going to build the cathedral and repay the loan. The popular belief was that "As soon as a coin in the coffer rings, the soul from purgatory springs," and Tetzel had much business. On October 31, 1517, Luther, with his belief that no such control or influence could be had over salvation, nailed 95 theses, or statements, about indulgences to the door of the Wittenberg church and challenged the practice of selling indulgences. At this time he was seeking to reform the church, not divide it.

In 1519 Luther presented various criticisms of the church and was driven to say that only the Bible, not religious traditions or papal statements, could determine correct religious practices and beliefs. In 1521 Pope Leo X excommunicated Luther for his beliefs.

In 1521 Luther appeared in the city of Worms before a meeting (diet) of the important figures of the Holy Roman Empire, including the Emperor, Charles V. He was again condemned. At the Diet of Worms Luther made his famous statement about his writings and the basis for them: "Here I stand. I can do no other." After this, Luther could not go back; the break with the pope was permanent.

Frederick III of Saxony, the ruler of the territory in which Luther resided, protected Luther in Wartburg Castle for a year. Frederick never accepted Luther's beliefs but protected him because Luther was his subject. The weak political control of the Holy Roman Emperor contributed to Luther's success in avoiding the pope's and the Emperor's penalties.

Other Reformers

Anabaptist (derived from a Greek word meaning to baptize again) is a name applied to people who rejected the validity of child baptism and believed that such children had to be rebaptized when they became adults.

Anabaptists sought to return to the practices of the early Christian church, which was a voluntary association of believers with no connection to the state.

Anabaptists adopted pacifism and avoided involvement with the state whenever possible. Today, the Mennonites, founded by Menno Simons (1496–1561), and the Amish are the descendants of the Anabaptists.

In 1536 John Calvin (1509–1564), a Frenchman, arrived in Geneva, a Swiss city-state which had adopted an anti-Catholic position. He left after his first efforts at reform failed. Upon his return in 1540, Geneva became the center of the Reformation. Calvin's *Institutes of the Christian Religion* (1536), a strictly logical analysis of Christianity, had a universal appeal.

Calvin brought knowledge of organizing a city from his stay in Strasbourg, which was being led by the reformer Martin Bucer (1491–1551). Calvin emphasized the doctrine of predestination (God knew who would obtain salvation before those people were born) and believed that church and state should be united.

Calvinism triumphed as the majority religion in Scotland, under the leadership of

John Knox (ca. 1514–1572), and in the United Provinces of the Netherlands. Puritans in England and New England also accepted Calvinism.

REFORM IN ENGLAND

England underwent reforms in a pattern different from the rest of Europe. Personal and political decisions by the rulers determined much of the course of the Reformation there.

Henry VIII (1509–1547) married Catherine of Aragon, the widow of his older brother. By 1526 Henry became convinced that he was unable to produce a legitimate son to inherit his throne because he had violated God's commandments (Leviticus 18:16, 20:21) by marrying his brother's widow.

Soon, Henry fell in love with Anne Boleyn and decided to annul his marriage to Catherine in order to marry Anne. Pope Clement VII, who had the authority necessary to issue such an annulment, was, after 1527, under the political control of Charles V, Catherine's nephew. Efforts by Cardinal Wolsey (ca. 1473–1530) to secure the annulment ended in failure and Wolsey's disgrace. Thomas Cranmer (1489–1556), named archbishop in 1533, dissolved Henry's marriage. Henry married Anne Boleyn in January 1533.

In 1536 Thomas More was executed for rejecting Henry's leadership of the English church.

Protestant beliefs and practices made little headway during Henry's reign, as he accepted transubstantiation, enforced celibacy among the clergy, and otherwise made the English church conform to most Catholic practices.

Under Henry VIII's son, Edward VI (1547–1553), who succeeded to the throne at age 10, the English church adopted Calvinism. Clergy were allowed to marry, communion by the laity expanded, and images were removed from churches. Doctrine included justification by faith, the denial of transubstantiation, and only two sacraments.

From 1553 to 1558, England was ruled by Queen Mary I, daughter of Henry VIII. An ardent Catholic, Mary sought to restore the Roman church in England. In 1554, Mary wed Philip II, heir to the Spanish throne, creating fear and suspicion among many who were anti-Catholic and anti-Spanish. Mary pursued a policy of carefully dismantling a number of the religious reforms undertaken by her brother and father, although she was met with fierce resistance along the way. Mary came to be known by the vivid moniker "Bloody Mary" in the wake of mass executions of Protestants who refused to acquiesce to her attempts to reintroduce Catholicism in England. Mary's own mental and physical condition was fragile, and her husband, upon ascending to the Spanish throne, was largely absent from England. She lapsed into depression and became delusional. Her death, in 1558, cleared the way for her sister, who had no intention of continuing Mary's Catholic program.

Under Elizabeth I (1558–1603), who was Henry VIII's daughter and half-sister to Edward and Mary, the church in England adopted Protestant beliefs again. The Elizabethan Settlement required outward conformity to the official church, but rarely inquired about inward beliefs.

Some practices of the church, including ritual, resembled the Catholic practices. Catholicism remained, especially among the gentry, but could not be practiced openly.

Some reformers wanted to purify (hence "Puritans") the church of its remaining Catholic aspects. The   resulting church, Protestant in doctrine and practice but retaining most of the physical possessions, such as buildings, and many of the powers, such as church courts, of the medieval church, was called Anglican.

THE COUNTER REFORMATION

The Counter Reformation brought changes to the portion of the Western church which retained its allegiance to the pope. Some historians see this as a reform of the Catholic church, similar to what Protestants were doing, while others see it as a result of the criticisms of Protestants.

Ignatius of Loyola (1491–1556), a former soldier, founded the Society of Jesus in 1540 to lead the attack on Protestantism. Jesuits, as the order's followers are known, became the leaders of the Counter Reformation. By the 1540s Jesuits, including Francis Xavier (1506–1552), traveled to Japan as missionaries.

Popes resisted reforming efforts, fearing what a council of church leaders might do to papal powers. The Sack of Rome in 1527, when soldiers of the Holy Roman Emperor captured and looted Rome, was seen by many as a judgment of God against the lives of the Renaissance popes. In 1534 Paul III became pope and attacked abuses while reasserting papal leadership.

THE WARS OF RELIGION (1560–1648)

The period from approximately 1560 to 1648 witnessed continuing warfare, primarily between Protestants and Catholics. Though religion was not the only reason for the wars—occasionally Catholics and Protestants were allies—it was the dominant cause. In the latter half of the sixteenth century, the fighting was along the Atlantic seaboard between Calvinists and Catholics; after 1600 the warfare spread to Germany, where Calvinists, Lutherans, and Catholics fought.

The Catholic Crusade

The territories of Charles V, the Holy Roman Emperor, were divided in 1556 between Ferdinand, Charles's brother, and Philip II (1556–1598), Charles's son. Ferdinand received Austria, Hungary, Bohemia, and the title of Holy Roman Emperor. Philip received Spain, Milan, Naples, the Netherlands, and the New World. Both parts of the Hapsburg family cooperated in international matters.

Philip was a man of severe personal habits, deeply religious, and a hard worker. Solemn (it is said he only laughed once in his life, when the report of the St. Bartholomew's Day Massacre reached him) and reclusive (he built the Escorial outside Madrid as a palace, monastery, and eventual tomb), he devoted his life and the wealth of Spain to making Europe Catholic. It was Philip, not the pope, who led the Catholic attack on Protestants.

The gold and silver of the New World flowed into Spain, especially following the opening of the silver mines at Potesi in Peru.

Spain dominated the Mediterranean following a series of wars led by Philip's half-brother, Don John, against Muslim (largely Turkish) forces. Don John secured the Mediterranean for Christian merchants with a naval victory over the Turks at Lepanto off the coast of Greece in 1571.

Portugal was annexed by Spain in 1580 following the death of the king without a clear successor. This gave Philip the only other large navy of the day as well as Portuguese territories around the globe.

Calvinism was spreading in England, France, the Netherlands, and Germany. Calvinists supported each other, often disregarding their countries' borders.

England and Spain

England was ruled by two queens, Mary I (reigned 1553–1558), who married Philip II, and then Elizabeth I (reigned 1558–1603), while three successive kings of France from 1559 to 1589 were influenced by their mother, Catherine de' Medici (1519–1589). Women rulers were a novelty in European politics.

Monarchs attempted to strengthen their control and the unity of their countries, a process which nobles often resisted.

Mary I was the daughter of Henry VIII and Catherine of Aragon, Mary sought to make England Catholic. She executed many Protestants, earning the nickname "Bloody Mary" from opponents.

To escape persecution, many English went into exile on the Continent in Frankfurt, Geneva, and elsewhere, where they learned more radical Protestant ideas.

Mary married Philip II, king of Spain, and organized her foreign policy around Spanish interests. They had no children.

Elizabeth I, a Protestant, achieved a religious settlement between 1559 and 1563 which left England with a church governed by bishops and practicing Catholic rituals, but maintaining a Calvinist doctrine. Though suppressed by Elizabeth's government, Puritans were not condemned to death.

Catholics participated in several rebellions and plots. Mary, Queen of Scots, had fled to England from Scotland in 1568, after alienating the nobles there. In Catholic eyes, she was the legitimate queen of England. Several plots and rebellions to put Mary on the throne led to her execution in 1587. Elizabeth was formally excommunicated by the pope in 1570.

In 1588, as part of his crusade and to stop England from supporting the rebels in the Netherlands, Philip II sent the Armada, a fleet of more than 125 ships, to convey troops from the Netherlands to England as part of a plan to make England Catholic. The Armada was defeated by a combination of superior English naval tactics and a wind which made it impossible for the Spanish to accomplish their goal.

A peace treaty between Spain and England was signed in 1604, but England remained an opponent of Spain.

The Thirty Years' War

Calvinism was spreading throughout Germany. The Peace of Augsburg (1555), which settled the disputes between Lutherans and Catholics, had no provision for Calvinists. Lutherans gained more territories through conversions and often took control of previous church-states—a violation of the Peace of Augsburg. A Protestant alliance under the leadership of the Calvinist ruler of the Palatinate opposed a Catholic League led by the ruler of Bavaria. Religious wars were common.

Not all issues pitted Protestants versus Catholics. The Lutheran ruler of Saxony joined the Catholics in the attack on Frederick at White Mountain, and the leading general for the Holy Roman Emperor, Ferdinand, was Albrecht of Wallenstein, a Protestant.

The war brought great destruction to Germany, leading to a decline in population of perhaps one-third, or more, in some areas. Germany remained divided and without a strong government until the nineteenth century.

After 1648, warfare, though often containing religious elements, would not be executed primarily for religious goals.

The Catholic crusade to reunite Europe failed, largely due to the efforts of the Calvinists. The religious distribution of Europe has not changed significantly since 1648.

Nobles, resisting the increasing power of the state, usually dominated the struggle. France, then Germany, fell apart due to the wars. France was reunited in the seventeenth century.

Spain began a decline which ended its role as a great power of Europe.

THE GROWTH OF THE STATE AND THE AGE OF EXPLORATION

In the seventeenth century the political systems of the countries of Europe began dividing into two types, absolutist and constitutionalist. England, the United Provinces, and Sweden moved towards constitutionalism, while France was adopting absolutist ideas.

Overseas exploration, begun in the fifteenth century, expanded. Governments supported such activity in order to gain wealth and to preempt other countries.

England

The English church was a compromise of Catholic practices and Protestant beliefs and was criticized by both groups. The monarchs, after 1620, gave leadership of the church to men with Arminian beliefs, a modified Calvinist creed that deemphasized predestination. Arminius (1560–1609), a Dutch theologian, had changed Calvinist beliefs to shift—if only slightly—the emphasis away from absolute predestination. English Arminians also stressed the role of ritual in church services and sought to enjoy the "beauty of holiness," which their opponents viewed as too Catholic. William Laud (1573–1645), Archbishop of Canterbury, accelerated the growth of Arminianism.

Opponents to this shift in belief were called Puritans, a term that covered a wide range of beliefs and people. To escape the church in England, many Puritans began moving to the New World, especially Massachusetts. Both James I and Charles I made decisions which, to Puritans, favored Catholics too much.

In financial matters, inflation and Elizabeth's wars left the government short of money. Contemporaries blamed the shortage on the extravagance of the courts of James I and Charles I. James I sold titles of nobility in an effort to raise money, annoying nobles with older titles. The monarchs lacked any substantial source of income and had to obtain the consent of a Parliament to levy a tax.

Parliament met only when the monarch summoned it. Though Parliaments had existed since the Middle Ages, there were long periods of time between parliamentary meetings. Parliaments consisted of nobles and gentry, and a few merchants and lawyers. The men in a Parliament usually wanted the government to remedy grievances as part of the agreement to a tax. In 1621, for the first time since the Middle Ages, the power to impeach governmental servants was used by a Parliament to eliminate men who had offended its members.

James I ended the war with Spain and avoided any other entanglements. The Earl of Somerset and then the Duke of Buckingham served as favorites for the king, doing much of the work of government.

Charles I inherited both the English and Scottish thrones at the death of his father, James I. Like his father, he claimed a "divine right" theory of absolute authority for himself as king and sought to rule without Parliament. That rule also meant control of the Church of England. Henrietta Maria, a sister of the king of France and a Catholic, became his queen.

Charles stumbled into wars with both Spain and France during the late 1620s. A series of efforts to raise money for the wars led to confrontations with his opponents in Parliament. A "forced loan" was collected from taxpayers with the promise it would be repaid when a tax was voted by a Parliament. Soldiers were billeted in subjects' houses during the wars. People were imprisoned for resisting these royal actions. In 1626 the Duke of Buckingham was nearly impeached. In 1628 Parliament passed the Petition of Right, which declared royal actions involving loans and billeting illegal.

Charles ruled without calling a Parliament during the 1630s. A policy of "thorough"—strict efficiency and much central government activity—was followed, which included reinstating many old forms of taxation.

In August 1642 Charles abandoned all hope of negotiating with his opponents and instead declared war against them. Charles's supporters were called Royalists or Cavaliers. His opponents were called Parliamentarians or Roundheads, due to many who wore their hair cut short. This struggle is called the Puritan Revolution, the English Civil War, or the Great Rebellion.

Charles was defeated. His opponents had allied with the Scots, who still had an army in England. Additionally, the New Model Army, with its general, Oliver Cromwell (1599–1658), was made up of common people, mostly volunteers, who could attain rank through merit rather than by aristocratic birth. The New Model Army became a cauldron of radical political ideas.

France

The regions of France had long had a large measure of independence, and local parliaments could refuse to enforce royal laws. The centralization of all government proceeded by replacing local authorities with intendants, civil servants who reported to the king.

As a result of the Edict of Nantes, the Huguenots had separate rights and powers. All efforts to unify France under one religion faced both internal resistance from the Huguenots and the difficulty of dealing with Protestant powers abroad.

By 1650 France had been ruled by only one competent adult monarch since 1559. Louis XIII came to the throne at age nine and Louis XIV at the age of five. The mothers of both kings, Maria de' Medici and Anne of Austria, governed until the boys were of age. Both queens relied on chief ministers to help govern: Cardinal Richelieu and Cardinal Mazarin (1602–1661).

Henry IV relied on the duke of Sully (1560–1641), the first of a series of strong ministers in the seventeenth century. Sully and Henry increased the involvement of the state in the economy, acting on a theory known as mercantilism. Monopolies on the production of gunpowder and salt were developed.

Louis XIII reigned from 1610 to 1643, but Cardinal Richelieu became the real power in France. Foreign policy was difficult because of the problems of religion. The unique status of the Huguenots was reduced through warfare and the Peace of Alais (1629), when their separate armed cities were eliminated. The nobility was reduced in power through constant attention to the laws and the imprisonment of offenders.

Cardinal Mazarin governed while Louis XIV (reigned 1643–1715) was a minor. During the Fronde, from 1649 to 1652, the nobility controlled Paris, drove Louis XIV and Mazarin from the city, and attempted to run the government. Noble ineffectiveness, the memories of the chaos of the wars of religion, and the overall anarchy convinced most people that a strong king was preferable to a warring nobility. The Fronde had little impact.

Louis XIV saw the need to increase royal power and his own glory and dedicated his life to these goals. He steadily pursued a policy of "one king, one law, one faith."

EXPLORATIONS AND CONQUESTS

Portugal: Prince Henry the Navigator (1394–1460) supported exploration of the African coastline, largely in order to seek gold. Bartholomew Dias (1450–1500) rounded the southern tip of Africa in 1487. Vasco da Gama (1460–1524) reached India in 1498 and, after some fighting, soon established trading ports at Goa and Calicut. Albuquerque (1453–1515) helped establish an empire in the Spice Islands after 1510.

Spain: Christopher Columbus (1451–1506), seeking a new route to the (East) Indies, "discovered" the Americas in 1492. Ferdinand Magellan (1480–1521) circumnavigated the globe in 1521–1522. Conquests of the Aztecs by Hernando Cortes (1485–1547), and the Incas by Francisco Pizarro (ca. 1476–1541), enabled the Spanish to send much gold and silver back to Spain.

Other Countries: In the 1490s the Cabots, John (1450–1498) and Sebastian (ca. 1483–1557), explored North America, and after 1570, various Englishmen, including Francis Drake (ca. 1540–1596), fought the Spanish around the world. Jacques Cartier (1491–1557) explored parts of North America for France in 1534.

Samuel de Champlain (1567–1635) and the French explored the St. Lawrence River, seeking furs to trade. The Dutch established settlements at New Amsterdam and in the Hudson River Valley. The Dutch founded trading centers in the East Indies, the West Indies, and southern Africa. Swedes settled on the Delaware River in 1638.

3. BOURBON, BAROQUE, AND THE ENLIGHTENMENT

Through the Treaty of Paris (1763), France lost all possessions in North America to Britain. (In 1762 France had ceded to Spain all French claims west of the Mississippi River and New Orleans.) France retained fishing rights off the coast of Newfoundland and Martinique and Guadeloupe, sugar islands in the West Indies. Spain ceded the Floridas to Britain in exchange for the return of Cuba.

France entered the French-American Alliance of 1778 in an effort to regain lost prestige in Europe and to weaken her British adversary. In 1779 Spain joined France in the war, hoping to recover Gibraltar and the Floridas. Rochambeau's (1725–1807) and Lafayette's (1757–1834) French troops aided Washington at Yorktown.

With the Treaty of Paris (1783), Britain recognized the independence of the United States of America and retroceded the Floridas to Spain. Britain left France no territorial gains by signing a separate and territorially generous treaty with the United States.

ECONOMIC DEVELOPMENTS

There were several basic assumptions of mercantilism: 1) Wealth is measured in terms of commodities, especially gold and silver, rather than in terms of productivity and income-producing investments; 2) Economic activities should increase the power of the national government in the direction of state controls; 3) Since a favorable balance of trade was important, a nation should purchase as little as possible from nations regarded as enemies. The concept of the mutual advantage of trade was not widely accepted; 4) Colonies existed for the benefit of the mother country, not for any mutual benefit that would be gained by economic development.

Absentee landlords and commercial farms replaced feudal manors, especially in

England. Urbanization, increased population, and improvements in trade stimulated the demand for agricultural products.

The design of farm implements improved. Drainage and reclamation of swamp land was expanded. Experiments with crops, seeds, machines, breeds of animals, and fertilizers were systematically attempted.

The construction of canals and roads was of fundamental importance. The major rivers of France were linked by canals during the seventeenth century.

Thomas Newcomen in 1706 invented an inefficient steam engine as a pump. James Watt, between 1765 and 1769, improved the design so that the expansive power of hot steam could drive a piston. Later Watt translated the motion of the piston into rotary motion.

The steam engine became one of the most significant inventions in human history. It was no longer necessary to locate factories on mountain streams where water wheels were used to supply power. Its portability meant that both steamboats and railroad engines could be built to transport goods across continents. Ocean-going vessels were no longer dependent on winds to power them.

At the same time, textile machines revolutionized that industry. John Kay introduced the flying shuttle in 1733. James Hargreaves patented the spinning jenny in 1770. Richard Arkwright perfected the spinning frame in 1769. Samuel Crompton introduced the spinning mule in 1779. Edward Cartwright invented the power loom in 1785.

Bourbon France

Louis XIV (reigned 1643–1715) was vain, arrogant, and charming. The king had hours of council meetings and endless ceremonies and entertainments. He aspired to be an absolute ruler.

The king believed in royal absolutism, where the most effective government was one in which the king had unquestioned authority. Louis XIV deliberately chose his chief ministers from the middle class in order to keep the aristocracy out of government. No members of the royal family or the high aristocracy were admitted to the daily council sessions at Versailles, where the king presided personally over the deliberations of his ministers.

Council orders were transmitted to the provinces by intendants, who supervised all phases of local administration (especially courts, police, and the collection of taxes). Additionally, Louis XIV nullified the power of French institutions which might challenge his centralized bureaucracy.

Louis XIV never called the Estates General. His intendants arrested the members of the three provincial estates who criticized royal policy, and the parlements were too intimidated by the lack of success of the *Frondes* to offer further resistance.

Control of the peasants, who comprised 95 percent of the French population, was accomplished by numerous means. Some peasants kept as little as 20 percent of their cash crops after paying the landlord, the government, and the Church. Peasants also were subject to the *corvée*, a month's forced labor on the roads. People not at work on the farm were conscripted into the French army or put into workhouses. Finally, rebels were hanged or forced to work as galley slaves.

Under Louis XV (reigned 1715–1774) French people of all classes desired greater popular participation in government and resented the special privileges of the aristocracy. All nobles were exempt from certain taxes. Many were subsidized with regular pensions from the government. The highest offices of government were reserved for aristocrats.

Promotions were based on political connections rather than merit. Life at Versailles was wasteful, extravagant, and frivolous.

There was no uniform code of laws and little justice. The king had arbitrary powers of imprisonment. Government bureaucrats were often petty tyrants, many of them merely serving their own interests. The bureaucracy became virtually a closed class. Vestiges of the feudal and manorial systems taxed peasants excessively compared to other segments of society. A group of intellectuals called the *philosophes* gave expression to these grievances as discontent grew.

When Louis XV died, he left many of the same problems he had inherited from his great-grandfather, Louis XIV. Corruption and inequity in government were even more pronounced. Ominously, crowds lined the road to St. Denis, the burial place of French kings, and cursed the king's casket just as they had his predecessor.

Louis XVI (reigned 1774–1792) was the grandson of Louis XV. He married Marie Antoinette (1770), daughter of the Austrian Empress Maria Theresa. Louis XVI was honest, conscientious, and sought genuine reforms, but he was indecisive and lacking in determination. He antagonized the aristocracy when he sought fiscal reforms. One of his first acts was to restore judicial powers to the French parlements. When he sought to impose new taxes on the undertaxed aristocracy, the parlements refused to register the royal decrees. In 1787 he granted toleration and civil rights to French Huguenots (Protestants).

In 1787 the king summoned the Assembly of the Notables, a group of 144 representatives of the nobility and higher clergy. Louis XVI asked them to tax all lands, without regard to privilege of family; to establish provincial assemblies; to allow free trade in grain; and to abolish forced labor on the roads. The Notables refused to accept these reforms and demanded the replacement of certain of the king's ministers.

The climax of the crisis came in 1788 when the king was no longer able to achieve either fiscal reform or new loans. He could not even pay the salaries of government officials. By this time one-half of government revenues went to pay interest on the national debt (at eight percent).

For the first time in 175 years, the king called for a meeting of the Estates General (1789). The Estates General formed itself into the National Assembly, and the French Revolution was under way.

England, Scotland, and Ireland

One of the underlying issues in the English Civil War (1642-1649) was the constitutional issue of the relationship between the king and Parliament. Could the king govern without the consent of Parliament, or go against the wishes of Parliament? In short, the question was whether England was to have a limited constitutional monarchy, or an absolute monarchy as in France and Prussia.

The theological issue focused on the form of church government England was to have—whether it would follow the established Church of England's hierarchical, episcopal form of church government, or acquire a presbyterian form. The episcopal form meant that the king, the Archbishop of Canterbury, and the bishops of the church would determine policy, theology, and the form of worship and service. The presbyterian form of polity allowed for more freedom of conscience and dissent among church members. Each congregation would have a voice in the life of the church, and a regional group of ministers, or "presbytery," would attempt to ensure "doctrinal purity."

The political implications for representative democracy were present in both issues. That is why most Presbyterians, Puritans, and Congregationalists sided with Parliament and most Anglicans and Catholics sided with the king.

The Parliament in effect bribed the king by granting him a tax grant in exchange for his agreement to the Petition of Right in 1628. It stipulated that no one should pay any tax, gift, loan, or contribution except as provided by an act of Parliament; no one should be imprisoned or detained without due process of law; all were to have the right to the writ of *habeas corpus;* there should be no forced billeting of soldiers in the homes of private citizens; and martial law was not to be declared in England.

In the midst of a stormy debate over theology, taxes, and civil liberties, the king sought to force the adjournment of Parliament. But when he sent a message to the Speaker ordering him to adjourn, some of the more athletic members held him in his chair while the door of the House of Commons was locked to prevent the entry of other messengers from the king. That famous date was March 2, 1629. A number of resolutions passed. Concessions towards Catholicism or Arminianism were to be regarded as treason. Whoever advised any collection of taxes without consent of Parliament would be guilty of treason. Whoever should pay a tax levied without the consent of Parliament would be considered a betrayer of liberty and guilty of treason.

A royal messenger was allowed to enter the Commons and declare the Commons adjourned, and a week later Charles I dissolved Parliament—for 11 years. Puritan leaders and leaders of the opposition in the House of Commons were imprisoned by the king, some for several years.

The established Church of England was the only legal church under Charles I, a Catholic. Archbishop of Canterbury William Laud (1573–1645) sought to enforce the king's policies vigorously. Arminian clergymen were to be tolerated, but Puritan clergymen silenced. Criticism was brutally suppressed. Several dissenters were executed.

The Scots invaded northern England. Charles called a Great Council of Lords, who arranged a treaty with the Scots to leave things as they were.

The king was cornered—he had no money, no army, and no popular support. He summoned the Parliament to meet in November 1640. The Commons immediately moved to impeach one of the king's principal ministers, Thomas Wentworth, Earl of Strafford (1593–1641). With mobs in the street and rumors of an army en route to London to dissolve Parliament, a bare majority of an underattended House of Commons passed a bill of attainder to execute the earl. Fearing mob violence as well as Parliament itself, the king signed the bill and Strafford was executed in 1641. Archbishop William Laud was also arrested and eventually tried and executed in 1645.

The House of Commons passed a series of laws to strengthen its position and protect civil and religious rights. The Triennial Act (1641) provided that no more than three years should pass between Parliaments. Another act provided that the current Parliament should not be dissolved without its own consent. Various hated laws, taxes, and institutions were abolished: the Star Chamber, the High Commission, and power of the Privy Council to deal with property rights. Ship money, a form of tax, was abolished, and tonnage duties were permitted only for a short time. The courts of common law were to remain supreme over the king's courts.

The Commons was ready to revoke the king's power over the Church of England, but there was disagreement over what form the state church would take: episcopal, presbyterian, or congregational. Puritans were in the majority.

The Grand Remonstrance listed 204 clauses of grievances against the king and demanded that all officers and ministers of the state be approved by Parliament.

In 1641 a rebellion began in Ireland. Irish Catholics murdered thousands of their Protestant neighbors. The Commons voted funds for an army, but it was unclear whether Parliament or the king would control the army.

Men began identifying themselves as Cavaliers if they supported the king, or Roundheads if they supported Parliament.

The king withdrew to Hampton Court and sent the queen to France for safety. In March 1642 Charles II went to York, and the English Civil War began.

Charles put together a sizeable force with a strong cavalry and moved on London, winning several skirmishes. He entered Oxford, but was beaten back from London. Oxford then became his headquarters for the rest of the war.

Oliver Cromwell (1599–1658), a gentleman farmer from Huntingdon, led the parliamentary troops to victory, first with his cavalry, which eventually numbered 1,100, and then as lieutenant general in command of the well-disciplined and well-trained New Model Army. He eventually forced the king to flee.

During the Civil War, under the authority of Parliament, the Westminster Assembly convened to write a statement of faith for the Church of England that was Reformed or Presbyterian in content. Ministers and laymen from both England and Scotland participated for six years and wrote the *Westminster Confession of Faith*, still a vital part of Presbyterian theology.

When the war ended, Parliament ordered the army to disband without receiving the pay due them. The army refused, and in 1647 Parliament sought to disperse them by force. The plan was to bring the Scottish army into England and use it against the men who had won the war.

The army refused to obey Parliament and arrested the king when he was brought across the border. In August the army occupied London and some of their leaders wrote an "Agreement of the People," to be presented to the House of Commons. It called for a democratic republic with a written constitution and elections every two years, equal electoral districts and universal manhood suffrage, freedom of conscience, freedom from impressment, equality before the law, and no office of king or House of Lords.

On the night of November 11, 1647, the king escaped from Hampton Court and went to the Isle of Wight. He had made a secret agreement with the Scots that he would establish Presbyterianism throughout England and Scotland if they would restore him to his throne.

The Second Civil War followed in 1648, but it consisted only of scattered local uprisings and the desertion of part of the English fleet.

The Scots invaded England, but were defeated by Cromwell at Preston, Wigan, and Warrington in the northwest of England. After these victories, the English army took control. London was again occupied. The army arrested 45 Presbyterian members of Parliament, excluded the rest, and admitted only about 60 Independents, who acted as the "Rump Parliament."

The army then tried Charles Stuart, formerly king of England, and sentenced him to death for treason. He was beheaded on January 30, 1649. The execution of the king particularly shocked the Scots, because the English had specifically promised not to take the king's life when the Scots delivered him into English hands.

After the execution of the king, Parliament abolished the office of king and the House of Lords. The new form of government was to be a Commonwealth, or Free State, governed by the representatives of the people in Parliament. Many large areas of the country had no representatives in Parliament. Parliament was more powerful than ever because there was neither king nor House of Lords to act as a check. This commonwealth lasted four years between 1649 and 1653.

Royalists and Presbyterians both opposed Parliament for its lack of broad representation and for regicide. The army was greatly dissatisfied that elections were not held, as one of the promises of the Civil War was popular representation.

Surrounded by foreign enemies, the Commonwealth became a military state with a standing army of 44,000. The North American and West Indian colonies were forced to accept the government of the Commonwealth.

When it became clear that Parliament intended to stay in office permanently, Cromwell agreed to serve as Lord Protector from 1653–1659, with a Council of State and a Parliament. Some degree of religious toleration, except for Catholics and Anglicans, was permitted by Cromwell's protectorate.

The new Parliament restored the monarchy from 1660–1688, but the Puritan Revolution clearly showed that the English constitutional system required a limited monarchy. Parliament in 1660 was in a far stronger position in its relationship to the king than it ever had been before.

Under the Convention Parliament of 1660, Royalists whose lands had been confiscated by the Puritans were allowed to recover them through the courts. Manorialism was largely abolished.

The leaders of Parliament were not willing to sacrifice the constitutional gains of the English Civil War and return to absolute monarchy. Two events in 1688 goaded them to action. In May James reissued the Declaration of Indulgence with the command that it be read on two successive Sundays in every parish church. On June 10, 1688, a son was born to the king and his queen, Mary of Modena. As long as James was childless by his second wife, the throne would go to one of his Protestant daughters, Mary or Anne. The birth of a son, who would be raised Roman Catholic, changed the picture completely.

A group of Whig and Tory leaders, speaking for both houses of Parliament, invited William and Mary to assume the throne of England. William III was stadtholder of Holland and Mary was the daughter of James II by his Protestant first wife, Anne Hyde. They were both in the Stuart dynasty.

On November 5, 1688, William and his army landed at Torbay in Devon. King James offered many concessions, but it was too late. He finally fled to France. William assumed temporary control of the government and summoned a free Parliament. In February 1689 William and Mary were declared joint sovereigns, with the administration given to William.

The English Declaration of Rights (1689) declared the following:

1) The king could not be a Roman Catholic.

2) A standing army in time of peace was illegal without Parliamentary approval.

3) Taxation was illegal without Parliamentary consent.

4) Excessive bail and cruel and unusual punishments were prohibited.

5) Right to trial by jury was guaranteed.

6) Free elections to Parliament would be held.

The Toleration Act (1689) granted the right of public worship to Protestant Nonconformists, but did not permit them to hold office. The Act did not extend liberty to Catholics or Unitarians, but normally they were left alone. The Trials for Treason Act (1696) stated that a person accused of treason should be shown the accusations against him and should have the advice of counsel. They also could not be convicted except upon the testimony of two independent witnesses. Freedom of the press was permitted, but with very strict libel laws.

Control of finances, including military appropriations, was to be in the hands of the Commons. There would no longer be uncontrolled grants to the king.

The Act of Settlement in 1701 provided that should William, or later Anne, die without children (Queen Mary had died in 1694) the throne should descend, not to the exiled Stuarts, but to Sophia, Electress Dowager of Hanover, a granddaughter of King James I, or to her Protestant heirs.

Judges were made independent of the Crown. Thus, England declared itself a limited monarchy and a Protestant nation.

Following the Act of Settlement in 1701, and Queen Anne's death in 1714, the House of Hanover inherited the English throne in order to ensure that a Protestant would rule the realm.

The Hanover dynasty order of reign was as follows: George I (1714–1727); George II (1727–1760); George III (1760–1820); George IV (1820–1830); William IV (1830–1837); and Queen Victoria (1837–1901).

Russia Under the Tsars

In 1480, Ivan III (1440–1505), "Ivan the Great," put an end to Mongol domination over Russia. In 1472, he married Sophie Paleologus, the niece of the last emperor of Constantinople. (The Byzantine Empire was conquered by the Ottoman Turks in 1453). Ivan took the title of Caesar (Tsar) as heir of the Eastern Roman Empire (Byzantine Empire). He encouraged the Eastern Orthodox Church and called Moscow the "Third Rome." Many Greek scholars, craftsmen, architects, and artists were brought to Russia.

Ivan IV (1530–1584), "Ivan the Terrible," grandson of Ivan III, began westernizing Russia. A contemporary of Queen Elizabeth, he welcomed both the English and Dutch, and opened new trade routes to Moscow and the Caspian Sea. English merchant-adventurers opened Archangel on the White Sea, which provided a link with the outer world free from Polish domination.

The ruling Muscovite family died out upon Ivan's death in 1584. The following "Time of Troubles" was a period of turmoil, famine, power struggles, and invasions from Poland.

The Romanov dynasty ruled Russia from 1613 to 1917. Stability returned to Russia in 1613 when the Zemsky Sobor (Estates General representing the Russian Orthodox church, landed gentry, townspeople, and a few peasants) elected Michael Romanov, who ruled as tsar from 1613 to 1645.

Russia, with a standing army of 70,000, was involved in a series of unsuccessful wars with Poland, Sweden, and Turkey. In 1654 Russia annexed the Ukraine with its rich farmlands.

Under Michael Romanov, Russia continued its expansion and extended its empire to the Pacific. Romanov continued westernization. By the end of the seventeenth century, 20,000 Europeans lived in Russia, developing trade and manufacturing, practicing medicine, and smoking tobacco, while Russians began trimming their beards and wearing western clothing.

Western books were translated into Russian. In 1649 three monks were appointed to translate the Bible for the first time into Russian. The Raskolniki (Old Believers) refused to accept any Western innovations or liturgy in the Russian Orthodox church and were severely persecuted as a result. In 20 years 20,000 of them were burned at the stake, but millions still called themselves Old Believers as late as 1917.

Peter I (reigned 1682–1725) was one of the most extraordinary people in Russian history. The driving ambitions of Peter the Great's life were to modernize Russia and to compete with the great powers of Europe on equal terms. Peter visited Western Europe in disguise in order to study the techniques and culture of the West. He worked as a carpenter in shipyards, attended gunnery school, and visited hospitals and factories. He sent back large numbers of European technicians and craftsmen to train Russians and to build factories. By the end of Peter's reign, Russia produced more iron than England.

Peter built up the army through conscription and a 25-year term of enlistment. He gave flintlocks and bayonets to his troops instead of the old muskets and pikes. Artillery was improved and discipline enforced. By the end of his reign, Russia had a standing army of 210,000, despite a population of only 13 million. Peter also developed the Russian navy. In 1696 Peter sailed his fleet of boats down the Don River and took Azov on the Black Sea from the Turks.

The tsar ruled by decree (*ukase*). Government officials and nobles acted under government authority, but there was no representative body.

All landowners owed lifetime service to the state, either in the army, the civil service, or at court. In return for government service, they received land and serfs to work their fields.

Conscription required each village to send recruits for the Russian army. By 1709 Russia manufactured most of its own weapons and had an effective artillery.

Catherine I, who ruled from 1725 to 1727, was the second wife of Peter the Great.

Peter II (1727–1730), the grandson of Peter the Great, died at age 15.

Anna (reigned 1730–1740) was dominated by German advisers. Under her rule the War of the Polish Succession (1733–1735) gave Russia firmer control over Polish affairs. War against the Turks (1736–1739) gave Azov to Russia once again. Russia agreed not to build a fleet on the Black Sea.

Ivan VI (reigned 1740–1741) was overthrown by a military coup.

Elizabeth (reigned 1741–1762) was the youngest daughter of Peter the Great. This was the Golden Age of the aristocracy, as they freed themselves from some of the obligations imposed on them by earlier tsars. Russia entered the Seven Years' War (1756–1763) during Elizabeth's reign.

Peter III (reigned 1762) was deposed and killed in a military revolt.

Catherine II "the Great," (reigned 1762–1796) continued the westernization process begun by Peter the Great. The three partitions of Poland, in 1772, 1793, and 1795 respectively, occurred under Catherine II's rule. Russia also annexed the Crimea and warred with Turkey during her reign.

Poland: Decline and Fall

In the early seventeenth century, Poland was an enormous country, with a rich cultural and political heritage. It encompassed diverse peoples and far-flung lands, and had developed an early form of modern democracy, whereby monarchs were elected by the noble assembly, or *Seym*. However, unrest among ethnic minorities, such as Ruthenes (Ukrainians), a series of weak and incompetent monarchs, and internal divisions between prominent noble families led to a slow and painful decline. Rebellions and hostile encroachments from neighbors throughout the seventeenth century left Poland a vulnerable and demoralized country in an era when other territories were assembling themselves into unified, powerful nation-states. In particular, Russia and Prussia began to eye Poland's ambitious series of programs designed to reinvigorate the nation, culturally, politically, and economically. Alarmed, Prussia and Russia began to devise a strategy to prevent Poland from reemerging as a major power.

In August 1772, following a brief and destructive civil war in Poland, Russia,

Prussia, and Austria took advantage of the resulting internal chaos to claim a portion of Polish territory, implementing the first partition. Poland was reduced in population and territory, and its link to the Baltic Sea was cut off. Poland continued attempts to produce reforms in order to fend off the destruction of the Polish state. On May 3, 1791, the Polish *Seym* ratified the first written constitution in Europe. British statesman and political philosopher Edmund Burke declared the constitution to be "...the most pure good...which ever has been conferred on mankind." Catherine of Russia, fearful of Poland's reemergence, sponsored a revolt against the constitution by several Polish nobles, supported by Russian troops. In 1793, a second partition was agreed upon between Prussia and Russia, reducing Poland to an unenviable skeleton of a country. A Polish campaign in 1795 to retake land from the partitioning powers resulted in the ultimate destruction of Poland; Russia, Prussia, and Austria collaborated to crush the rebellion, and the final partition was carried out, removing Poland from the map of Europe until 1918.

Italy and the Papacy

Italy in the seventeenth and eighteenth centuries remained merely a geographic expression divided into small kingdoms, most of which were under foreign domination. Unification of Italy into a national state did not occur until the mid-nineteenth century.

In the seventeenth century Spain controlled most of the Italian peninsula. Spain owned Lombardy (or Milan) in the north and Naples, Sicily, and Sardinia in the south. Lombardy's strategic location linked Spain with Austria and, through Franche-Comté, Flanders. It served as a barrier to a French invasion of Italy.

Savoy was the only state with a native Italian dynasty. In the early sixteenth century, Savoy was a battleground between the French and the Spanish. Emmanuel Philibert, Duke of Savoy (reigned 1553–1580), was rewarded by the Holy Roman Emperor with the restoration of the independence of Savoy. He built Savoy into a modern state.

Charles Emmanuel I (reigned 1580–1630) maintained his independence by playing France against Spain and vice versa.

Victor Amadeus (reigned 1630–1637) married Marie Christine, Louis XIII's sister, thus increasing French influence in Savoy. Charles Emmanuel II (reigned 1637–1675) was similarly dominated by France.

Victor Amadeus II (reigned 1675–1731) championed the Protestant Vaudois against Louis XIV.

In 1713 Victor Amadeus was awarded Sicily. In 1720 he gave Sicily to Austria in exchange for the island of Sardinia. Henceforth, he was known as the king of Sardinia.

Charles Emmanuel III (reigned 1731–1773) joined France and Spain in the War of the Polish Succession in an unsuccessful attempt to drive Austria out of Italy. Savoy sided with Austria in the War of the Austrian Succession and received part of Milan as a reward.

THE SCIENTIFIC REVOLUTION AND SCIENTIFIC SOCIETIES

Sir Isaac Newton (1642–1727) taught mathematics at Cambridge, was Master of the Royal Mint in London, and for 25 years was the president of the Royal Academy.

Science and religion were not in conflict in the seventeenth and eighteenth centuries. Scientists universally believed they were studying and analyzing God's creation, not an autonomous phenomenon known as "Nature." There was no attempt, as in the nineteenth and twentieth centuries, to secularize science. The question of the extent of the

Creator's involvement in Creation was an issue of the eighteenth century, but there was universal agreement among scientists and philosophers as to the supernatural origin of the universe.

For the first time in human history, the eighteenth century saw the appearance of a secular worldview. This became known as the age of the Enlightenment. In the past, some kind of a religious perspective had always been central to Western civilization. The philosophical starting point for the Enlightenment was the belief in the autonomy of man's intellect apart from God. The most basic assumption was faith in reason rather than faith in revelation. The "Enlightened" claimed for themselves, however, a rationality they were unwilling to concede to their opponents.

The Enlightenment believed in the existence of God as a rational explanation of the universe and its form; "God" was a deistic Creator who made the universe and then was no longer involved in its mechanistic operation. That mechanistic operation was governed by "natural law."

Rationalists stressed deductive reasoning or mathematical logic as the basis for their epistemology (source of knowledge). They started with "self-evident truths," or postulates, from which they constructed a coherent and logical system of thought.

René Descartes (1596–1650) sought a basis for logic and thought he found it in man's ability to think. "I think; therefore, I am" was his most famous statement. That statement cannot be denied without thinking. Therefore, it must be an absolute truth that man can think. His proof depends upon logic alone.

Benedict de Spinoza (1632–1677) developed a rational pantheism in which he equated God and nature. He denied all free will and ended up positing an impersonal, mechanical universe.

Gottfried Wilhelm Leibniz (1646–1716) worked on symbolic logic and calculus, and invented a calculating machine. He, too, had a mechanistic world- and lifeview and thought of God as a hypothetical abstraction rather than a persona.

Empiricists stressed inductive observation—the "scientific method"—as the basis for their epistemology.

John Locke (1632–1704) pioneered in the empiricist approach to knowledge and stressed the importance of environment in human development. He classified knowledge as 1) according to reason, 2) contrary to reason or, 3) above reason. Locke believed reason and revelation were not only complementary but also from God.

David Hume (1711–1776) was a Scottish historian and philosopher who began by emphasizing the limitations of human reasoning and later became a dogmatic skeptic.

The people of the Enlightenment believed in absolutes. They believed in absolute truth, absolute ethics, and absolute natural law. And they believed optimistically that these absolutes were discoverable by man's rationality. It wasn't long, of course, before one rationalist's "absolutes" clashed with another's.

The Enlightenment set forth a closed system of the universe in which the supernatural was not involved in human life, in contrast to the traditional view of an open system in which God, angels, and devils were very much a part of human life on earth.

The "Counter-Enlightenment" is a comprehensive term encompassing diverse and disparate groups who disagreed with the fundamental assumptions of the Enlightenment and pointed out its weaknesses.

Roman Catholic Jansenism in France argued against the idea of an uninvolved or impersonal God. Hasidism in Eastern European Jewish communities, especially in the 1730s, stressed a joyous religious fervor in direct communion with God.

CULTURE OF THE BAROQUE AND ROCOCO

The Baroque period (1550–1750) emphasized grandeur, spaciousness, unity, and emotional impact. The splendor of Versailles typifies the baroque form in architecture; gigantic frescoes unified around the emotional impact of a single theme is Baroque art; the glory of Bach's *Christmas Oratorio* expresses the baroque in music. Although the Baroque began in Catholic Counter-Reformation countries to teach in a concrete, emotional way, it soon spread to Protestant nations as well, and some of the greatest Baroque artists and composers were Protestant (e.g., Johann Sebastian Bach and George Frideric Handel).

Rococo, rooted in baroque, took hold in French art and architecture in the first half of the eighteenth century. This style was characterized by elaborate, often delicate, imitations of foliage, shellwork, scrolls, etc.

4. REVOLUTION AND THE NEW WORLD ORDER (1789–1848)

THE FRENCH REVOLUTION I (1789–1799)

Radical ideas about society and government were developed during the eighteenth century in response to the success of the "scientific" and "intellectual" revolutions of the preceding two centuries. Armed with new scientific knowledge of the physical universe, as well as new views of the human capacity to detect "truth," social critics assailed existing modes of thought governing political, social, religious, and economic life. Ten years of upheaval in France (1789–1799) further shaped modern ideas and practices.

Napoleon Bonaparte spread some of the revolutionary ideas about the administration of government as he conquered much of Europe. The modern world that came of age in the eighteenth century was characterized by rapid, revolutionary changes which paved the way for economic modernization and political centralization throughout Europe.

IMPACT OF THE SCIENTIFIC REVOLUTION (C. 1500–1700)

The "scientific method" involved identifying a problem or question, forming a hypothesis, making observations, conducting experiments, interpreting results with mathematics, and drawing conclusions.

INFLUENCE OF THE ENLIGHTENMENT (C. 1700–1800)

While they came from virtually every country in Europe, most of the famous social activists of the Enlightenment were French, and France was the center of this intellectual revolution. François Marie Arouet (1694–1778), better known as Voltaire, was one of the most famous *philosophes*.

Denis Diderot (1713–1784) served as editor of the *Encyclopedia*, the bible of the Enlightenment period. This 28-volume work was a compendium of all new learning.

Baron de Montesquieu (1689–1755) authored *The Spirit of the Laws* (1748), in which the separation of powers theory was found. Montesquieu believed such a separation would keep any individual (including the king) or group (including the nobles) from gaining total control of the government.

Jean Jacques Rousseau (1712–1778) wrote the *Social Contract* (1762) in an attempt to discover the origin of society, and to propose that the composition of the ideal society was based on a new kind of social contract.

The major assumptions of the Enlightenment were as follows:

Human progress was possible through changes in one's environment; i.e., better people, better societies, better standard of living.

Humans were free to use reason to reform the evils of society.

Material improvement would lead to moral improvement.

Natural science and human reason would discover the meaning of life.

Laws governing human society would be discovered through application of the scientific method of inquiry.

Inhuman practices and institutions would be removed from society in a spirit of humanitarianism.

Human liberty would ensue if individuals became free to choose what reason dictated was good.

Here is a summary of the Enlightenment's effect on society:

Religion: Deism, or "natural religion," rejected traditional Christianity by promoting an impersonal God who did not interfere in the daily lives of the people. The continued discussion of the role of God led to a general skepticism associated with Pierre Bayle (1647–1706), a type of religious skepticism pronounced by David Hume (1711–1776), and a theory of atheism or materialism advocated by Baron d'Holbach (1723–1789).

Political Theory: John Locke (1632–1704) and Jean Jacques Rousseau (1712–1778) believed that people were capable of governing themselves, either through a political (Locke) or social (Rousseau) contract forming the basis of society. However, most philosophes opposed democracy, preferring a limited monarchy that shared power with the nobility.

Economic Theory: The assault on mercantilist economic theory was begun by the physiocrats in France, who proposed a "laissez-faire" (nongovernmental interference) attitude toward land usage, and culminated in the theory of economic capitalism associated with Adam Smith (1723–1790) and his slogans of free trade, free enterprise, and the law of supply and demand.

Education: Attempting to break away from the strict control of education by the church and state, Jean Jacques Rousseau advanced the idea of progressive education, where children learn by doing and where self-expression is encouraged. This idea was carried forward by Johann Pestalozzi, Johann Basedow, and Friedrich Fröbel, and influenced a new view of childhood.

Psychological Theory: In the *Essay Concerning Human Understanding* (1690), John Locke offered the theory that all human knowledge was the result of sensory experience, without any preconceived notions. He believed that the mind at birth was a blank slate (tabula rasa) that registered the experience of the senses passively. According to Locke, since education was critical in determining human development, human progress was in the hands of society.

Most *philosophes* believed that human progress and liberty would ensue as absolute rulers became "enlightened." The rulers would still be absolute, but would use their power benevolently, as reason dictated. Most of the *philosophes* opposed democracy. According to Voltaire, the best form of government was a monarchy in which the rulers shared the ideas of the *philosophes* and respected the people's rights. Such an "enlightened" monarch would rule justly and introduce reforms. Voltaire's and other *philosophes'* influence on Europe's monarchs produced the "enlightened despots," who nonetheless failed to bring about lasting political change. Some famous "despots" included Frederick the Great of Prussia (reigned 1740–1786), Catherine the Great of Russia (reigned 1762–1796), and Joseph II of Austria (reigned 1765–1790).

CAUSES OF THE FRENCH REVOLUTION

The rising expectations of "enlightened" society were demonstrated by the increased criticism directed toward government inefficiency and corruption, and toward the privileged classes. The clergy (First Estate) and nobility (Second Estate), representing only two percent of the total population of 24 million, were the privileged classes and were essentially tax exempt. The remainder of the population (Third Estate) consisted of the middle class, urban workers, and the mass of peasants, who bore the entire burden of taxation and the imposition of feudal obligations. As economic conditions worsened in the eighteenth century, the French state became poorer, and totally dependent on the poorest and most depressed sections of the economy for support at the very time this tax base had become saturated.

The mode of absolute government practiced by the Bourbon dynasty was wed to the "Divine Right of Kings" philosophy. This in turn produced a government that was irresponsible and inefficient, with a tax system that was unjust and inequitable and without any means of redress because of the absence of any meaningful representative assembly. The legal system was chaotic, with no uniform or codified laws.

As France slid into bankruptcy, Louis XVI summoned an Assembly of Notables (1787) in the mistaken hope they would either approve his new tax program or consent to removing their exemption from payment of taxes. They refused to agree to either proposal.

Designed to represent the three estates of France, this ancient feudal body had only met twice, once at its creation in 1302 and again in 1614. When the French parlements insisted that any new taxes must be approved by this body, King Louis XVI reluctantly ordered it to assemble at Versailles by May 1789. Each estate was expected to elect its own representatives. As a gesture to the size of the Third Estate, the king doubled the number of its representatives. However, the Parlement of Paris decreed that voting in the Estates General would follow "custom and tradition," with each estate casting a vote as a unit. Therefore the First and Second Estates, with similar interests to protect, would control the meeting despite the increased size of the Third Estate.

Election fever swept over France for the very first time. The election campaign took place in the midst of the worst subsistence crisis in eighteenth-century France, with widespread grain shortages, poor harvests, and inflated bread prices. Finally, on May 5, 1789, the Estates General met and argued over whether to vote by estate or individual. Each estate was ordered to meet separately and vote as a unit. The Third Estate refused and insisted that the entire assembly stay together.

PHASES OF REVOLUTION

The National Assembly (1789–1791): After a six-week deadlock over voting methods, representatives of the Third Estate declared themselves the true National Assembly of France (June 17). They were immediately locked out of their meeting place by order of Louis XVI. Instead they assembled in an indoor tennis court, where they swore an oath never to disband until they had given France a constitution (Tennis Court Oath, June 20). Defections from the First and Second Estates then caused the king to recognize the National Assembly (June 27) after dissolving the Estates General. At the same time, Louis XVI ordered troops to surround Versailles.

The "Parisian" revolution began at this point. Angry because of food shortages, unemployment, high prices, and fear of military repression, the workers and tradespeople began to arm themselves.

The Legislative Assembly (1791–1792): While the National Assembly had been rather homogeneous in its composition, the new government began to fragment into competing political factions. The most important political clubs were republican groups such as the Jacobins (radical urban) and Girondins (moderate rural), while the sans-culottes (working-class, extremely radical) were a separate faction with an economic agenda.

The National Convention (1792–1795): Meeting for the first time in September 1792, the Convention abolished monarchy and installed republicanism. Louis XVI was charged with treason, found guilty, and executed on January 21, 1793. Later the same year, the queen, Marie Antoinette, would meet the same fate.

The most notorious event of the French Revolution was the famous "Reign of Terror" (1793–1794), the government's campaign against its internal enemies and counterrevolutionaries. Revolutionary Tribunals were created to hear the cases of accused enemies brought to "justice" under a new Law of Suspects. Approximately 25,000 people throughout France lost their lives. Execution by guillotine became a spectator sport.

The Directory (1795–1799): The Constitution of 1795 restricted voting and office holding to property owners. The middle class was in control. It wanted peace in order to gain more wealth and to establish a society in which money and property would become the only requirements for prestige and power. These goals confronted opposition groups such as the aristocracy, who in October 1795 attempted a royalist uprising. It might have succeeded were it not for the young Napoleon Bonaparte, who happened to be in Paris at the time, and loyally helped the government put down the rebellion. The Sans-culottes repeatedly attacked the government and its economic philosophy, but, leaderless and powerless, they were doomed to failure. Despite rising inflation and mass public dissatisfaction, the Directory government ignored a growing shift in public opinion. When elections in April 1797 produced a triumph for the royalist right, the results were annulled, and the Directory shed its last pretense of legitimacy.

Nonetheless, the weak and corrupt Directory government managed to hang on for two more years because of great military success. French armies annexed the Austrian Netherlands, the left bank of the Rhine, Nice, and Savoy. The Dutch republic was made a satellite state of France. The greatest military victories were won by Napoleon Bonaparte, who drove the Austrians out of northern Italy and forced them to sign the Treaty of Campo Formio (October 1797), in return for which the Directory government agreed to Bonaparte's scheme to conquer Egypt and threaten English interests in the East.

But a steady loss of support continued in the face of a government that was bankrupt, filled with corruption, and unwilling to halt an inflationary spiral that was aggravating the already-impoverished masses of French peasants.

THE FRENCH REVOLUTION II: THE ERA OF NAPOLEON (1799–1815)

The first 10 years of revolution did not prepare anyone in France for the dramatic changes that would distinguish this era. France was about to be mastered by a legendary "giant" and Europe overwhelmed by a mythical "titan."

Consulate Period, 1799–1804 (Enlightened Reform): The new government was installed on December 25, 1799, with a constitution which concentrated supreme power in the hands of Napoleon. Executive power was vested in three consuls, but the First Consul (Napoleon) behaved more as an enlightened despot than a revolutionary statesman. His aim was to govern France by demanding obedience, rewarding ability, and organizing everything in orderly hierarchical fashion. Napoleon's domestic reforms and policies affected every aspect of society.

Empire Period, 1804–1814 (War and Defeat): After being made Consul for Life (1801), Napoleon felt that only through an empire could France retain its strong position in Europe. On December 2, 1804, Napoleon crowned himself emperor of France in Notre Dame Cathedral.

Militarism and Empire Building: Beginning in 1805 Napoleon engaged in constant warfare that placed French troops in enemy capitals from Lisbon and Madrid to Berlin and Moscow, and temporarily gave Napoleon the largest empire since Roman times. Napoleon's Grand Empire consisted of an enlarged France, satellite kingdoms, and coerced allies.

The military campaigns of the Napoleonic Years included the War of the Second Coalition (1798–1801), the War of the Third Coalition (1805–1807), the Peninsular War (1808–1814), the "War of Liberation" (1809), the Russian Campaign (1812), the War of the Fourth Coalition (1813–1814), and the Hundred Days (March 20–June 22, 1815).

French-ruled peoples viewed Napoleon as a tyrant who repressed and exploited them for France's glory and advantage. Enlightened reformers believed Napoleon had betrayed the ideals of the Revolution. The downfall of Napoleon resulted from his inability to conquer England, economic distress caused by the Continental System (boycott of British goods), the Peninsular War with Spain, the German War of Liberation, and the invasion of Russia. The actual defeat of Napoleon was the result of the Fourth Coalition and the Battle of Leipzig ("Battle of Nations"). Napoleon was exiled to the island of Elba as a sovereign with an income from France.

After learning of allied disharmony at the Vienna peace talks, Napoleon left Elba and began the Hundred Days by seizing power from the restored French king, Louis XVIII. Napoleon's gamble ended at Waterloo in June 1815. He was exiled as a prisoner of war to the South Atlantic island of St. Helena, where he died in 1821.

THE POST-WAR SETTLEMENT: THE CONGRESS OF VIENNA (1814–1815)

The Congress of Vienna met in 1814 and 1815 to redraw the map of Europe after the Napoleonic era, and to provide some way of preserving the future peace of Europe. Europe was spared a general war throughout the remainder of the nineteenth century. But the failure of the statesmen who shaped the future in 1814–1815 to recognize the forces, such as nationalism and liberalism, unleashed by the French Revolution, only postponed the ultimate confrontation between two views of the world—change and accommodation, or maintaining the status quo.

The Vienna settlement was the work of the representatives of the four nations that had done the most to defeat Napoleon: England, Austria, Russia, and Prussia (The Big Four).

Prince Klemens von Metternich (1773–1859), who represented Austria, epitomized conservative reactionism. He resisted change and was generally unfavorable to ideas of liberals and reformers because of the impact such forces would have on the multinational Hapsburg Empire.

Lord Castlereagh (1769–1822) was England's representative. His principal objective was to achieve a balance of power on the Continent by surrounding France with larger and stronger states.

Karl von Hardenberg (1750–1822), as chancellor, represented Prussia. His goal was to recover Prussian territory lost to Napoleon in 1807 and to gain additional territory in northern Germany (Saxony).

Tsar Alexander I represented Russia. He was a mercurial figure who vacillated between liberal and reactionary views. The one specific "nonnegotiable" goal he advanced was a "free" and "independent" Poland, with himself as its king.

While Charles Maurice de Talleyrand Périgord (1754–1838), the French foreign minister, was not initially included in the early deliberations, he became a mediator when the interests of Prussia and Russia clashed with those of England and Austria. He thereby brought France into the ranks of the principal powers.

Arrangements to guarantee the enforcement of the status quo as defined by the Vienna settlement included two provisions: The "Holy Alliance" of Tsar Alexander I of Russia, an idealistic and unpractical plan, existed only on paper. No one except Alexander took it seriously. But the "Quadruple Alliance" of Russia, Prussia, Austria, and England provided for concerted action to arrest any threat to the peace or balance of power.

England defined concerted action as the great powers meeting in "congress" to solve each problem as it arose, so that no state would act unilaterally and independently of the other great powers. France was always believed to be the possible violator of the Vienna settlement.

Austria believed concerted action meant the great powers defending the status quo as established at Vienna against any change or threat to the system, including liberal or nationalist agitation.

From 1815 to 1822, European international relations were controlled by the series of meetings held by the great powers to monitor and defend the status quo: the Congress of Aix-la-Chapelle (1818), the Congress of Troppau (1820), the Congress of Laibach (1821), and the Congress of Verona (1822).

The principle of collective security required unanimity among members of the Quadruple Alliance. The history of the congress system points to the ultimate failure of this key provision in light of the serious challenges to the status quo after 1815.

THE INDUSTRIAL REVOLUTION

Twentieth-century English historian Arnold Toynbee began to refer to the period since 1750 as "the Industrial Revolution." The term was intended to describe a time of transition when machines began to significantly displace human and animal power in methods of producing and distributing goods, and an agricultural and commercial society converted into an industrial one.

These changes began slowly, almost imperceptibly, gaining momentum with each decade, so that by the middle of the nineteenth century, industrialism had swept across Europe west to east, from England to Eastern Europe. Few countries purposely avoided industrialization, because of its promised material improvement and national wealth. The economic changes that constitute the Industrial Revolution have done more than any other movement in Western civilization to revolutionize Western life.

Roots of the Industrial Revolution could be found in the following: 1) the Commercial Revolution (1500–1700), which spurred the great economic growth of Europe and brought about the Age of Discovery and Exploration, which in turn helped to solidify the economic doctrines of mercantilism; 2) the effect of the Scientific Revolution, which produced the first wave of mechanical inventions and technological advances; 3) the increase in population in Europe from 140 million people in 1750, to 266 million people by the mid-part of the nineteenth century (more producers, more consumers); and 4) the political and social revolutions of the nineteenth century, which began the rise to power of the "middle class," and provided leadership for the economic revolution.

England began the economic transformation by employing her unique assets:

1) A supply of cheap labor as the result of the Enclosure Movement, which created unemployment among the farmers; former agricultural laborers were now available for hire in the new industrial towns

2) A good supply of coal and iron, both indispensable for the technological and energy needs of the "revolution"

3) The availability of large supplies of capital amassed from profitable commercial activity in the preceding centuries and ready to be invested in new enterprises

4) A class of inventive people who possessed technological skill, and whose independence and nonconformity allowed them to take risks

5) England had access to the raw materials needed for the development of many industries through its colonial and maritime ventures

6) A government which was sympathetic to industrial development, and well-established financial institutions ready to make loans available

7) After a long series of successful wars, freedom to develop its new industries, which prospered because of the economic dislocations caused by the Napoleonic Wars.

The revolution occurred first in the cotton and metallurgical industries, because those industries lent themselves to mechanization. A series of mechanical inventions (1733–1793) would enable the cotton industry to mass-produce quality goods. The need to replace wood as an energy source led to the use of coal, which increased coal mining, and resulted ultimately in the invention of the steam engine and the locomotive. The development of steam power allowed the cotton industry to expand and transformed the iron industry. The factory system, which had been created in response to the new energy sources and machinery, was perfected to increase manufactured goods.

A transportation revolution ensued in order to distribute the productivity of machinery and deliver raw materials to the eager factories. This led to the growth of canal systems, the construction of hard-surfaced "macadam" roads, the commercial use of the steamboat (demonstrated by Robert Fulton, 1765–1815), and the railway locomotive (made commercially successful by George Stephenson, 1781–1848).

A subsequent revolution in agriculture made it possible for fewer people to feed the population, thus freeing people to work in factories, or in the new fields of communications, distribution of goods, or services like teaching, medicine, and entertainment.

In the wake of the Industrial Revolution, all modes of life would be challenged and transformed.

The Industrial Revolution created a unique new category of people who were dependent on their job alone for income, a job from which they might be dismissed without cause. The factory worker had no land, no home, no source of income but his labor. During the first century of the Industrial Revolution, the factory worker was completely at the mercy of the law of supply and demand for labor. Working in the factory meant more self-discipline and less personal freedom for workers. Contemporary social critics complained that industrialism brought misery to the workers, while others claimed that life was improving. Until 1850 workers as a whole did not share in the general wealth produced by the Industrial Revolution. Conditions would improve as the century wore on, as union action combined with general prosperity and a developing social conscience to improve the working conditions, wages, and hours first of skilled labor, and later of unskilled labor.

The most important sociological result of industrialism was urbanization. The new factories acted as magnets, pulling people away from their rural roots and beginning the most massive population transfer in history. Thus, the birth of factory towns and cities that grew into large industrial centers. The role of the cities changed in the nineteenth century from governmental and cultural centers to industrial centers. Workers in cities became aware of their numbers and their common problems. Cities made the working class a powerful force by raising consciousness and enabling people to unite for political action and to remedy economic dissatisfaction.

IMPACT OF THOUGHT SYSTEMS ("ISMS") ON THE EUROPEAN WORLD

The mindset of Western civilization was being challenged in the first half of the nineteenth century by the appearance of numerous new thought systems. Not since the eighteenth-century Enlightenment had humans sought to catalog, classify, and categorize their thoughts and beliefs. Several of these systems of thought acted as agents of change throughout the nineteenth century, while others would continue to define the modern world into the twentieth century.

Romanticism was a reaction against the rigid classicism, rationalism, and deism of the eighteenth century. Strongest between 1800 and 1850, the romantic movement differed from country to country and from romanticist to romanticist. Because it emphasized change, it was considered revolutionary in all aspects of life. It was an atmosphere in which events occurred and came to affect not only the way humans thought and expressed themselves, but also the way they lived socially and politically.

English Romantics like Wordsworth and Coleridge epitomized the romantic movement, along with Burns, Byron, Shelley, Keats, Tennyson, Browning, and Scott. The greatest German figures were Goethe, Schiller, Heine, and Herder. French romantics were Hugo, Balzac, Dumas, and Stendhal. The outstanding Russian exponents were Pushkin, Dostoyevsky, and Turgenev. Among the greatest American figures were Longfellow, Cooper, Irving, Emerson, Poe, Whitman, and Thoreau.

The leading Romantic painters in popular taste were the Frenchmen Millet and David, the Englishmen Turner and Constable, and the Spaniard Goya. The Gothic Revival Style marked the Romantic Era in architecture.

Music did not change as dramatically as did literature. Classical forms were still observed, but new ideas and innovations were increasing. Beethoven was a crossover, while straight romantics included Brahms, Schumann, Schubert, Berlioz, Chopin, and von Weber.

Romantic philosophy stimulated an interest in Idealism, the belief that reality consists of ideas, as opposed to materialism. This school of thought (Philosophical Idealism), founded by Plato, was developed through the writings of 1) Immanuel Kant whose work, *Critique of Pure Reason* (1781), advanced the theory that reality is twofold—physical and spiritual. Reason can discover what is true in the physical, but not in the spiritual, world 2) Johann Gottlieb Fichte, a disciple of Kant, and Friedrich Schelling, collaborator of Fichte, and 3) Georg Wilhelm Hegel, the greatest exponent of this school of thought. Hegel believed that an impersonal God rules the universe and guides humans along a progressive evolutionary course by means of a process called dialecticism; this is a historical process by which one thing is constantly reacting with its opposite (the thesis and antithesis), producing a result (synthesis) that automatically meets another opposite and continues the series of reactions. Hegel's philosophy exerted a great influence over Karl Marx, who turned the Hegelian dialectic upside down to demonstrate that the ultimate meaning of reality was a material end, not a higher or spiritual end, as Hegel suggested.

Conservatism arose in reaction to liberalism and became a popular alternative for those who were frightened by the violence, terror, and social disorder unleashed by the French Revolution. Early conservatism was allied to the restored monarchical governments of Austria, Russia, France, and England. Support for conservatism came from the traditional ruling classes as well as the peasants who still formed the majority of the population. Intellectual ammunition came from the pens of the Englishman Edmund Burke, the Frenchmen Joseph de Maistre and Louis de Bonald, the Austrian Friedrich Gentz, and many of the early romantics. In essence, conservatives believed in order, society, and the state; faith and tradition.

Conservatism was basically "anti-" in its propositions. It never had a feasible program of its own. The object of conservatives' hatred was a liberal society, which they claimed was antisocial and morally degrading. While their criticisms contained much justification, conservatives ignored the positive and promising features of liberal society. Conservative criticism poked holes in liberal ideology and pointed toward a new social tyranny of the aggressive middle class.

The theory of liberalism was the first major theory in the history of Western thought to teach that the individual is a self-sufficient being whose freedom and well-being are the sole reasons for the existence of society. Liberalism was more closely connected to the spirit and outlook of the Enlightenment than to any of the other "isms" of the early nineteenth century. While the general principles and attitudes associated with liberalism varied considerably from country to country, liberals tended to come from the middle class or bourgeoisie and to favor increased liberty for their class, and indirectly, for the masses of people, as long as the latter did not ask for so much freedom that they endangered the security of the middle class. Liberalism was reformist and political rather than revolutionary in character.

Individuals are entitled to seek their freedom in the face of arbitrary or tyrannical restrictions imposed upon them. Humans have certain natural rights and governments should protect them. These rights include the right to own property, freedom of speech, freedom from excessive punishment, freedom of worship, and freedom of assembly. These rights are best guaranteed by a written constitution with careful definition of the limits to which governmental actions may go. Examples include the American Declaration of Independence (1776) and the French Declaration of the Rights of Man (1789).

Liberals advocated economic individualism (i.e., laissez-faire capitalism), heralded by Adam Smith (1723–1790) in his 1776 economic masterpiece, *Wealth of Nations*. They regarded free enterprise as the most productive economy and the one that allowed for the greatest measure of individual choice. Economic inequality will exist and is acceptable, liberals held, because it does not detract from the individual's moral dignity, nor does it conflict with equality of opportunity and equality before the law.

In England advocates included the political economists, the utilitarians, and individuals like Thomas Babington Macaulay and John Stuart Mill; in France, Benjamin Constant de Rebecque, Victor Cousin, Jean Baptiste Say, and Alexis de Tocqueville; in Germany, Wilhelm von Humboldt, Friedrich List, Karl von Rotteck, and Karl Theodor Welcker.

The regenerative force of liberal thought in early nineteenth-century Europe was dramatically revealed in the explosive force of the power of nationalism. Raising the level of consciousness of people having a common language, soil, traditions, history, culture, and experience to seek political unity around an identity of what or who constitutes the nation, nationalism was aroused and made militant during the turbulent French Revolutionary era.

Nationalistic thinkers and writers examined the language, literature, and folkways of their people, thereby stimulating nationalist feelings. Emphasizing the history and culture of the various European peoples reinforced and glorified national sentiment.

Because of its inherently revolutionary implications, nationalism was suppressed by the established authorities. Yet it flourished in Germany, where conservative and reactionary nationalists competed with a somewhat more liberal form of nationalism associated with intellectuals like Fichte, Hegel, von Humboldt, and von Ranke. In eastern Europe conservative nationalists stressed the value of their own unique customs, culture, and folkways, while Western European nationalists demanded liberal political reforms. The influence of the Italian nationalist Mazzini and the Frenchman Michelet in stimulating nationalist feeling in the West was also key.

SOCIALISM

With the chief beneficiaries of industrialism being the new middle class, the increasing misery of the working classes disturbed the conscience of concerned liberal thinkers such as Bentham and Mill, who proposed a modification of the concept of laissez-faire economics. Other socially-concerned thinkers, observing the injustices and inefficiencies of capitalistic society, began to define social questions in terms of human equality and the means to be followed in order to secure this goal. As cures for the social evils of industrialism were laid out in elaborate detail, the emerging dogma came to be called socialism.

The Utopian Socialists (from *Utopia*, St. Thomas More's (1478–1535) book on a fictional ideal society) were the earliest writers to propose an equitable solution to improve the distribution of society's wealth. While they endorsed the productive capacity of industrialism, they denounced its mismanagement. Human society was to be organized as a community rather than a mixture of competing, selfish individuals. All the goods a person needed could be produced in one community.

The Anarchists rejected industrialism and the dominance of government. Auguste Blanqui (1805–1881) advocated terrorism as a means to end capitalism and the state. Pierre Joseph Proudhon (1809–1865) attacked the principle of private property because it denied justice to the common people.

"Scientific" Socialism, or Marxism, was the creation of Karl Marx (1818–1883), a German scholar who, with the help of Friedrich Engels (1820–1895), intended to replace utopian hopes and dreams with a militant blueprint for socialist working-class success. The principal works of this revolutionary school of socialism were *The Communist Manifesto* and *Das Kapital*.

The theory of dialectical materialism enabled Marx to explain the history of the world. By borrowing Hegel's dialectic, substituting materialism and realism in place of Hegel's idealism and inverting the methodological process, Marx was able to justify his theoretical conclusions. Marxism consisted of a number of key propositions: 1) An economic interpretation of history, i.e., all human history has been determined by economic factors (mainly who controls the means of production and distribution); 2) Class struggle, i.e., since the beginning of time there has been a class struggle between the rich and the poor or the exploiters and the exploited; 3) Theory of surplus value, i.e., the true value of a product was labor, and since the worker received a small portion of his just labor price, the difference was surplus value, "stolen" from him by the capitalist; and 4) Socialism was inevitable, i.e., capitalism contained the seeds of its own destruction (overproduction, unemployment, etc.); the rich would grow richer and the poor would grow poorer until the gap between each class (proletariat and bourgeoisie) is so great that the working classes would rise up in revolution and overthrow the elite bourgeoisie to install a "dictatorship of the proletariat." As modern capitalism was dismantled, the creation of a classless society guided by the principle "from each according to his abilities, to each according to his needs" would take place.

THE REVOLUTIONARY TRADITION

The era of reaction which had followed the collapse of the Napoleonic regime and the Congress of Vienna (1815) was followed by a wave of liberal and national agitation which was manifested in the revolutions of 1820, 1825, and 1830.

The year 1848 is considered the watershed of the nineteenth century. The revolutionary disturbances of the first half of the nineteenth century reached a climax in a new wave of revolutions that extended from Scandinavia to southern Italy, and from France to central Europe. Only England and Russia avoided violent upheaval.

The issues were substantially the same as they had been in 1789. What was new in 1848 was that these demands were far more widespread and irrepressible than ever. Whole classes and nations demanded to be fully included in society. The French Revolution of 1789 came at the end of a period ("Ancien Regime"), while the revolutions of 1848 signaled the beginning of a new age. Aggravated by rapid population growth and the social disruption caused by industrialism and urbanization, a massive tide of discontent swept across the Western world.

Generally speaking, the 1848 upheavals shared the strong influences of romanticism, nationalism, and liberalism, as well as a new factor of economic dislocation and instability. The increasingly radical political, economic, and social proposals advanced by the Utopian Socialists (Charles Fourier, Robert Owen), the Anarchists (Pierre Proudhon), and the Chartists in England also contributed to the revolutionary climate. Some authorities believe the absence of liberty was most responsible for the uprisings.

Specifically, a number of similar conditions existed in several countries: 1) Severe food shortages caused by poor harvests of grain and potatoes (e.g., Irish potato famine); 2) Financial crises caused by a downturn in the commercial and industrial economy; 3) Business failures; 4) Widespread unemployment; 5) A sense of frustration and discontent among urban artisan and working classes as wages diminished; 6) A system of poor relief which became overburdened; 7) Living conditions, which deteriorated in the cities; 8) The power of nationalism in the Germanys, Italian states, and in Eastern Europe to inspire the overthrow of existing governments. Middle-class predominance within the unregulated economy continued to drive liberals to push for more government reform and civil liberty. They enlisted the help of the working classes to put more pressure on the government to change.

In France, working-class discontent and liberals' unhappiness with the corrupt regime of King Louis Philippe (reigned 1830–1848)—especially his minister Guizot (1787–1874)—erupted in street riots in Paris on February 22–23, 1848. With the workers in control of Paris, King Louis Philippe abdicated on February 24, and a provisional government proclaimed the Second French Republic.

The "June Days" revolt was provoked when the government closed the national workshop. A general election in April resulted in a National Assembly dominated by the moderate republicans and conservatives under Lamartine who regarded socialist ideas as threats to private property. The Parisian workers, feeling that their revolution had been nullified, took to the streets.

This new revolution (June 23–26) was unlike previous uprisings in France. It marked the inauguration of genuine class warfare; it was a revolt against poverty and a cry for the redistribution of property. It foreshadowed the great social revolutions of the twentieth century. The revolt was extinguished after General Cavaignac was given dictatorial powers by the government. The June Days confirmed the political predominance of conservative property holders in French life.

The new Constitution of the Second French Republic provided for a unicameral legislature (with the National Assembly designating themselves as the first members) and executive power vested in a popularly elected president of the Republic. When the election returns were counted, the government's candidate was defeated by a "dark horse" candidate, Prince Louis Napoleon Bonaparte (1808–1873), a nephew of the great emperor. On December 20, 1848, Louis Napoleon was installed as president of the Republic.

In December 1852 Louis Napoleon became Emperor Napoleon III (reigned 1852–1870), and France retreated from republicanism again.

Italian nationalists and liberals wanted to end Hapsburg (Austrian), Bourbon (Naples and Sicily), and papal domination and unite these disparate Italian regions into a unified liberal nation. A revolt by liberals in Sicily in January 1848 was followed by the granting of liberal constitutions in Naples, Tuscany, Piedmont, and the Papal States. Milan and Venice expelled their Austrian rulers. In March 1848 upon hearing the news of the revolution in Vienna, a fresh outburst of revolution against Austrian rule occurred in Lombardy and Venetia, with Sardinia-Piedmont declaring war on Austria. Simultaneously, Italian patriots attacked the Papal States, forcing the pope, Pius IX (1792–1878), to flee to Naples for refuge.

The temporary nature of these initial successes was illustrated by the speed with which the conservative forces regained control. In the north Austrian Field Marshal Radetzky (1766–1858) swept aside all opposition, regaining Lombardy and Venetia and crushing Sardinia-Piedmont. In the Papal States the establishment of the Roman Republic (February 1849) under the leadership of Giuseppe Mazzini and the protection of Giuseppe Garibaldi (1807–1882), would fail when French troops took Rome in July 1849 after a heroic defense by Garibaldi. Pope Pius IX returned to Rome cured of his liberal leanings. In the south and in Sicily the revolts were suppressed by the former rulers.

Within 18 months the revolutions of 1848 had failed throughout Italy.

In the Italian peninsula revolutionary activity broke out in Milan in March 1848 and was directed primarily by nationalists who were interested in expelling the Austrians from Lombardy and Venetia. King Charles Albert of Sardinia-Piedmont (reigned 1831–1849) capitalized on the revolution by declaring war on Austria, but his army was twice defeated in battle (Custozza and Novara) by the Russian general Radetzky. In central Italy, Pope Pius IX expressed support for a unified Italian state. In the Kingdom of the Two Sicilies, an isolated revolt in Palermo which occurred earlier than the rebellion in Paris, resulted in the granting of a liberal constitution by the reactionary King Ferdinand II (reigned 1830–1859).

Throughout Italy the revolution emphasized the cause of Italian nationalism and the reemergence of Italian pride through the Risorgimento. There was no evidence that the revolution was seriously concerned with the economic and social problems which confronted the Italian peasants.

King Charles Albert abdicated in favor of his son, Victor Emmanuel II (1820–1878), who was destined to complete the unification of Italy in the second half of the nineteenth century.

The immediate effect of the 1848 Revolution in France was a series of liberal and nationalistic demonstrations in the German states (March 1848), with the rulers promising liberal concessions. The liberals' demand for constitutional government was coupled with another demand—some kind of union or federation of the German states. While popular demonstrations by students, workers, and the middle class produced the promise of a liberal future, the permanent success or failure of these "promises" rested on Prussian reaction.

GREAT BRITAIN AND THE VICTORIAN COMPROMISE

The Victorian Age (1837–1901) is associated with the long reign of Queen Victoria, who succeeded her uncle King William IV at the age of 18, and married her cousin, Prince Albert. The early years of her reign coincided with the continuation of liberal reform of the British government, accomplished through an arrangement known as the "Victorian Compromise." The Compromise was a political alliance of the middle class and aristocracy to exclude the working class from political power. The middle class gained control of the House of Commons, the aristocracy controlled the government, the army, and the Church of England. This process of accommodation worked successfully.

Parliamentary reforms continued after passage of the 1832 Reform Bill. Laws were enacted abolishing slavery throughout the Empire (1833). The Factory Act (1831) forbade the employment of children under the age of nine. The New Poor Law (1834) required the needy who were able and unemployed to live in workhouses. The Municipal Reform Law (1835) gave control of the cities to the middle class. The last remnants of the mercantilistic age fell with the abolition of the Corn Laws (1846) and repeal of the old navigation acts (1849).

After 1846 England was more and more dominated by the middle class; this was one of the factors that enabled it to escape the revolutions which shook Europe in 1848. The ability of the English to make meaningful industrial reforms gave the working class hope that its goals could be achieved without violent social upheaval.

The revolutions of 1848 began with much promise, but all ended in defeat for a number of reasons. They were spontaneous movements which lost their popular support as people lost their enthusiasm. Initial successes by the revolutionaries were due less to their strength than to the hesitancy of governments to use their superior force. Once this hesitancy was overcome, the revolutions were smashed. They were essentially urban movements, and the conservative landowners and peasants tended, in time, to nullify the spontaneous actions of the urban classes. The middle class, who led the revolutions, came to fear the radicalism of their working-class allies. While in favor of political reformation, the middle class drew the line at social engineering, much to the dismay of the laboring poor. Divisions among national groups, and the willingness of one nationality to deny rights to other nationalities, helped to destroy the revolutionary movements in central Europe.

In central Europe, revolutions, which had been led by the middle class, did not express any interest in addressing social and economic problems. When the workers and students demanded social and economic revolution, the middle class became alienated from the revolution which they had led earlier; they desired only political change through the establishment of a constitutional process. This breach within the revolutionary camp was detected and exploited by the old regime.

In eastern and southern Europe, the nationalist revolutions lacked organization, and above all, the military capacity to resist the professional armies of the Austrian Empire. However, the results of 1848–1849 were not entirely negative. Universal male suffrage was introduced in France; serfdom remained abolished in Austria and the German states; parliaments were established in Prussia and other German states, though dominated by princes and aristocrats; and Prussia and Sardinia-Piedmont emerged with new determination to succeed in their respective unification schemes.

The revolutions of 1848–1849 brought to a close the era of liberal revolutions that had begun in France in 1789. Reformers and revolutionists alike learned a lesson from the failures of 1848. They learned that planning and organization is necessary; that rational argument and revolution would not always assure success. With 1848, the Age of Revolution sputtered out. The Age of Romanticism was about to give way to an Age of Realism.

A new age followed the revolutions of 1848–1849, as Otto von Bismarck (1815–1898), one of the dominant political figures of the second half of the nineteenth century, was quick to realize. If the mistake of these years was to believe that great decisions could be brought about by speeches and parliamentary majorities, the sequel showed that in an industrial era new techniques involving ruthless force were all too readily available. The period of *Realpolitik*—of realistic, iron-fisted politics and diplomacy—followed.

5. REALISIM AND MATERIALISM (1848–1914)

REALPOLITIK AND THE TRIUMPH OF NATIONALISM

After the collapse of the revolutionary movements of 1848, the leadership of Italian nationalism was transferred to Sardinian leaders Victor Emmanuel II (1820–1878), Camillo de Cavour (1810–1861), and Giuseppe Garibaldi (1807–1882). They replaced the earlier leaders Giuseppe Mazzini (1805–1872) of the Young Italy movement, Charles Albert (1798–1849), the once liberal Pius IX (1792–1878), and Vincenzo Gioberti (1801–1852) and the Neo-Guelf movement, which promoted a unified Italian state centered on the Papacy. The new leaders did not entertain romantic illusions about the process of transforming Sardinia into a new Italian kingdom; they were practitioners of the politics of realism, *Realpolitik*.

Cavour was a Sardinian who served as editor of *Il Risorgimento*, a newspaper that argued that Sardinia should be the basis of a new Italy. Between 1852 and 1861, Cavour served as Victor Emmanuel II's Prime Minister. In that capacity Cavour transformed Sardinian society by implementing a series of liberal reforms designed to modernize the Sardinian state and attract the support of liberal states such as Great Britain and France.

In 1855, under Cavour's direction, Sardinia joined Britain and France in the Crimean War against Russia. At the Paris Peace Conference (1856), Cavour addressed the delegates on the need to eliminate the foreign (Austrian) presence in the Italian peninsula and attracted the attention and sympathy of the French Emperor, Napoleon III. Cavour and Napoleon III met at Plombières on July 20, 1858. The Plombières Agreement stated that in the event that Sardinia went to war with Austria—presumably after being attacked or provoked—France would provide military assistance to Sardinia, and with victory, Sardinia would annex Lombardy, Venetia, Parma, Modena, and a part of the Papal States. Additionally, the remainder of Italy would be organized into an Italian Confederation under the direction of the Pope, France would receive Nice and Savoy, and the alliance would be finalized by a marriage between the two royal families.

After being provoked, the Austrians declared war on Sardinia in 1859. French forces intervened and the Austrians were defeated in the battles of Magenta (June 4) and Solferino (June 24). Napoleon III's support then wavered for four reasons: 1) Prussia mobilized and expressed sympathy for Austria; 2) the outbreak of uncontrolled revolutions in several northern Italian states; 3) the forcefulness of the new Austrian military efforts; and 4) the lack of public support in France for his involvement and the mounting criticism being advanced by the French Catholic church, which opposed the war against Catholic Austria.

Napoleon III, without consulting Cavour, signed a secret peace (The Truce of Villafranca) on July 11, 1859. Sardinia received Lombardy but not Venetia; the other terms indicated that Sardinian influence would be restricted and that Austria would remain a power in Italian politics. The terms of Villafranca were clarified and finalized with the Treaty of Zurich (1859).

In 1860, Cavour arranged the annexation of Parma, Modena, Romagna, and Tuscany into Sardinia. These actions were recognized by the Treaty of Turin between Napoleon III and Victor Emmanuel II; Nice and Savoy were transferred to France. With these acquisitions, Cavour anticipated the need for a period of tranquility to incorporate these territories into Sardinia.

Giuseppe Garibaldi and his Red Shirts landed in Sicily in May 1860 and extended the nationalist activity to the south. Within three months, Sicily was taken and by September 7, Garibaldi was in Naples and the Kingdom of the Two Sicilies had fallen under Sardinian influence. Cavour distrusted Garibaldi, but Victor Emmanuel II encouraged him.

In February 1861, in Turin, Victor Emmanuel was declared King of Italy and presided over an Italian Parliament which represented the entire Italian peninsula with the exception of Venetia and the Patrimony of St. Peter (Rome). Cavour died in June 1861.

Venetia was incorporated into the Italian Kingdom in 1866 as a result of an alliance between Bismarck's Prussia and the Kingdom of Italy which preceded the German Civil War between Austria and Prussia. In return for opening a southern front against Austria, Prussia, upon its victory, arranged for Venetia to be transferred to Italy.

Bismarck was again instrumental in the acquisition of Rome into the Italian Kingdom in 1870. In 1870, the Franco-Prussian War broke out and the French garrison, which had been in Rome providing protection for the Pope, was withdrawn to serve on the front against Prussia. Italian troops seized Rome, and in 1871, as a result of a plebiscite, Rome became the capital of the Kingdom of Italy.

BISMARCK AND THE UNIFICATION OF GERMANY

In the period after 1815, Prussia emerged as an alternative to a Hapsburg-based Germany. During the early nineteenth century, Germany was politically decentralized and consisted of dozens of independent states. This multistate situation had been in place for centuries and had been sanctioned by the Peace of Westphalia in 1648. Prussia had absorbed many of the smaller states during the eighteenth and early nineteenth centuries.

Otto von Bismarck (1810–1898) entered the diplomatic service of Wilhelm I as the Revolutions of 1848 were being suppressed. By the early 1860s, Bismarck had emerged as the principal adviser and minister to the king. Bismarck was an advocate of a Prussian-based (Hohenzollern) Germany. During the 1850s and 1860s, he supported a series of military reforms which improved the Prussian army. In 1863, Bismarck joined the Russians in suppressing a Polish rebellion; this enterprise resulted in improved Russian-Prussian relations.

In 1863, the Schleswig-Holstein crisis broke. These provinces, which were occupied by Germans, were under the personal rule of Christian IX (1818–1906) of Denmark. The Danish government advanced a new constitution which specified that Schleswig and Holstein would be annexed into Denmark. German reaction was predictable and Bismarck arranged for joint Austro-Prussian military action. Denmark was defeated and agreed (Treaty of Vienna, 1864) to give up the provinces, and Schleswig and Holstein were to be jointly administered by Austria and Prussia.

Questions of jurisdiction provided the rationale for estranged relations between Austria and Prussia. In 1865, a temporary settlement was reached in the Gastein Convention, which stated that Prussia would administer Schleswig and Austria would manage Holstein. During 1865 and 1866, Bismarck made diplomatic preparations for the forthcoming struggle with Austria. Italy, France, and Russia would not interfere, and Great Britain was not expected to involve itself in a Central European war.

In 1870, deteriorating relations between France and Germany collapsed over the Ems Dispatch. Wilhelm I, while vacationing at Ems, was approached by representatives of the French government who requested a Prussian pledge not to interfere on the issue of the vacant Spanish throne. Wilhelm I refused to give such a pledge and informed Bismarck of these developments in a telegram from Ems.

Bismarck exploited the situation by initiating a propaganda campaign against the French. Subsequently, France declared war and the Franco-Prussian War (1870–1871) commenced. Prussian victories at Sedan and Metz proved decisive; Napoleon III and his leading general, Marshal MacMahon, were captured. Paris continued to resist but fell to the Prussians in January 1871. The Treaty of Frankfurt (May 1871) concluded the war and resulted in France ceding Alsace-Lorraine to Germany and a German occupation until an indemnity was paid.

The German Empire was proclaimed on January 18, 1871, with Wilhelm I becoming the Emperor of Germany. Bismarck became the Imperial Chancellor. Bavaria, Baden, Württemberg, and Saxony were incorporated into the new Germany.

THE CRIMEAN WAR

The Crimean War originated in the dispute between two differing groups of Christians and their protectors over privileges in the Holy Land. During the nineteenth century, Palestine was part of the Ottoman Turkish Empire. In 1852, the Turks negotiated an agreement with the French to provide enclaves in the Holy Land to Roman Catholic religious orders; this arrangement appeared to jeopardize already existing agreements which provided access to Greek Orthodox religious orders. Tsar Nicholas I (reigned 1825–1855), unaware of the impact of his action, ordered Russian troops to occupy several Danubian principalities; his strategy was to withdraw from these areas once the Turks agreed to clarify and guarantee the rights of the Greek Orthodox orders. The role of Britain in this developing crisis was critical; Nicholas mistakenly was convinced that the British Prime Minister, Lord Aberdeen, would be sympathetic to the Russian policy. Aberdeen, who headed a coalition cabinet, sought to use the Concert of Europe system to settle the question. However, Lord Palmerston, the Home Secretary, supported the Turks; he was suspicious of Russian intervention in the region. Consequently, misunderstandings about Britain's policy developed. In October 1853, the Turks demanded that the Russians withdraw from the occupied principalities. The Russians failed to respond, and the Turks declared war. In February 1854, Nicholas advanced a draft for a settlement of the Russo-Turkish War; it was rejected and Great Britain and France joined the Ottoman Turks and declared war on Russia.

With the exception of some naval encounters in the Gulf of Finland off the Aaland Islands, the war was conducted on the Crimean Peninsula in the Black Sea. In September 1854, more than 50,000 British and French troops landed in the Crimea, determined to take the Russian port city of Sebastopol. While this war has been remembered for the work of Florence Nightingale (1820–1910) and the "Charge of the Light Brigade," it was a conflict in which there were more casualties from disease and the weather than from combat. In December 1854, Austria reluctantly became a co-signatory of the Four Points of Vienna, a statement of British and French war aims. The Four Points specified that 1) Russia should renounce any claims to the occupied principalities; 2) the 1841 Straits Convention would be revised; 3) navigation in the mouth of the Danube River (on the Black Sea) should be internationalized; and 4) Russia should withdraw any claim to having a "special" protective role for Greek Orthodox residents in the Ottoman Empire. In 1855, Piedmont joined Britain and France in the war. In March 1855, Tsar Nicholas I died and was succeeded by Alexander II (reigned 1855–1881), who was opposed to continuing the war. In December 1855, the Austrians, under excessive pressure from the British, French, and Piedmontese, sent an ultimatum to Russia in which they threatened to renounce their neutrality. In response, Alexander II indicated that he would accept the Four Points.

Representatives convened in Paris between February and April 1856. The resulting Peace of Paris had the following major provisions: Russia had to acknowledge international commissions to regulate maritime traffic on the Danube, recognize Turkish control of the mouth of the Danube, renounce all claims to the Danubian Principalities of Moldavia and Wallachia (which later led to the establishment of Rumania), agree not to fortify the Aaland Islands, renounce its previously espoused position of protector of the Greek Orthodox residents of the Ottoman Empire, and return all occupied territories to the Ottoman Empire. The Straits Convention of 1841 was revised by neutralizing the Black Sea. The Declaration of Paris specified rules to regulate commerce during periods of war. Lastly, the independence and integrity of the Ottoman Empire were recognized and guaranteed by the signatories.

THE EASTERN QUESTION AND THE CONGRESS OF BERLIN

Another challenge to the Concert of Europe developed in the 1870s with a seemingly endless number of Balkan crises. Once again, the conflict initially involved Russia and Ottoman Turks, but Britain and Russia quickly became the principal protagonists.

In 1876, Turkish forces under the leadership of Osman Pasha soundly defeated Serbian armies. Serbia requested assistance from the great powers and, as a consequence of the political pressures exercised by the great powers, the Turks agreed to participate in a conference in Constantinople. The meeting resulted in a draft agreement between the Serbs and the Turks. However, Britain quietly advised the Sultan, Abdülhamid II (reigned 1876–1909), to scuttle the agreement, which he did. In June 1877, Russia dispatched forces across the Danube. During the next month, Osman Pasha took up a defensive position in Plevna. During the period of the siege, sympathy in the West shifted toward the Turks, and Britain and Austria became alarmed over the extent of Russian influence in the region. In March 1878, the Russians and the Turks signed the Peace of San Stephano; implementation of its provisions would have resulted in Russian hegemony in the Balkans and dramatically altered the balance of power in the eastern Mediterranean. The treaty provided for the establishment of a large Bulgarian state which would be under Russian influence; the transfer of Dobrudja, Kars, Ardahan, Bayazid, and Batum to Russia; the expansion of Serbia and Montenegro; and the establishment of an autonomous Bosnia-Herzegovina which would be under Russian control.

Britain, under the leadership of Prime Minister Benjamin Disraeli (1804–1881), denounced the San Stephano Accord, dispatched a naval squadron to Turkish waters, and demanded that the San Stephano agreement be scrapped. The German Chancellor, Otto von Bismarck, intervened and offered his services as mediator.

The delegates of the major powers convened in June and July 1878 to negotiate a settlement. Prior to the meeting, Disraeli had concluded a series of secret arrangements with Austria, Russia, and Turkey. The combined impact of these accommodations was to restrict Russian expansion in the region, reaffirm the independence of Turkey, and maintain British control of the Mediterranean. The specific terms of the Treaty of Berlin resulted in the following: 1) recognition of Rumania, Serbia, and Montenegro as independent states 2) the establishment of the autonomous principality of Bulgaria 3) Austrian acquisition of Bosnia and Herzegovina and 4) the transfer of Cyprus to Great Britain.

The Russians, who had won the war against Turkey and had imposed the harsh terms of the San Stephano Treaty, found that they left the conference with very little (Kars, Batum, etc.) for their effort. Although Disraeli was the primary agent of this anti-Russian settlement, the Russians blamed Bismarck for their dismal results. Their hostility toward Germany led Bismarck (1879) to embark upon a new system of alliances which transformed European diplomacy and rendered any additional efforts of the Concert of Europe futile.

CAPITALISM AND THE EMERGENCE OF THE NEW LEFT (1848–1914)

During the nineteenth century, Europe experienced the full impact of the Industrial Revolution. The Industrial Revolution resulted in improving aspects of the physical lives of a greater number of Europeans; at the same time, it led to a factory system with undesirable working and living conditions and the abuses of child labor.

As the century progressed, the inequities of the system became increasingly evident. Trade-unionism and socialist political parties emerged which attempted to address these problems and improve the lives of the working class. In most of these expressions of discontent, the influences of Utopian Socialism or Marxism were evident. Socialism was steeped in economic materialism, which had emerged in the eighteenth century and came to dominate the nineteenth and twentieth centuries. Economics was a component in the rise of scientism; by its very nature, it advanced the values of material culture.

During the period from 1815 to 1848, Utopian Socialists such as Robert Owen (1771–1858), St. Simon, and Charles Fourier advocated the establishment of a political-economic system which was based on romantic concepts of the ideal society. The failure of the Revolutions of 1848 and 1849 discredited the Utopian Socialists, and the new "Scientific Socialism" advanced by Karl Marx (1818–1883) became the primary ideology of protest and revolution. Marx believed that the history of humanity was the history of class struggle and that the process of the struggle (the dialectic) would continue until a classless society was realized. The Marxian dialectic was driven by the dynamics of materialism. Marx contended that the age of the bourgeois domination of the working class was the most severe and oppressive phase of the struggle. The proletariat, or the industrial working class, needed to be educated and led towards a violent revolution which would destroy the institutions which perpetuated the struggle and the suppression of the majority. After the revolution, the people would experience the dictatorship of the proletariat, during which the Communist party would provide leadership. Marx advanced these concepts in a series of tracts and books including *The Communist Manifesto* (1848), *Critique of Political Economy* (1859), and *Capital* (1863–1864). In most instances, his arguments were put forth in scientific form; Marx accumulated extensive data and developed a persuasive rhetorical style. In the 1860s, Marxism was being accepted by many reformers. Marx lived most of his adult life in London, where he died in 1883.

Britain and France

During the second half of the nineteenth century, Britain and France enjoyed considerable economic prosperity, experienced periods of jingoistic nationalism, and were confronted with demands for expanding democracy. Great Britain, under the leadership of Lord Palmerston, William Gladstone, and Benjamin Disraeli, represented a dichotomy of values and political agendas. On one hand, Britain led Europe into an age of revitalized imperialism and almost unbridled capitalism; on the other hand, Gladstone and the Liberal party advocated democratic reforms, an anti-imperialist stance, and a program to eliminate or restrict unacceptable working and social conditions. In France, the evolution of a more democratic political order was slowed by the collapse of the Second French Republic and the development of the Second Empire. However, in 1871, the Third Republic was established and the French moved closer to realizing democracy.

In 1865, Palmerston died, and during the next two decades significant domestic developments occurred which expanded democracy in Great Britain. The dominant leaders of this period were William Gladstone (1809–1898) and Benjamin Disraeli (1804–1881). Gladstone, who was initially a Conservative, emerged as a severe critic of the Corn Laws and, as a budgetary expert, became Chancellor of the Exchequer under Palmerston. As the leader of the Liberal party (until 1895), Gladstone supported Irish Home Rule, fiscal responsibility, free trade, and the extension of democratic principles. He was opposed to imperialism, the involvement of Britain in European affairs, and the further centralization of the British government. Disraeli argued for an aggressive foreign policy, the expansion of the British Empire, and, after opposing democratic reforms, the extension of the franchise.

After defeating Gladstone's effort to extend the vote in 1866, Disraeli advanced the Reform Bill of 1867. This bill, which expanded on the Reform Bill of 1832, was enacted and specified two reforms: 1) There would be a redistribution (similar to reapportionment) of seats which would provide a more equitable representation in the House of Commons; the industrial cities and boroughs gained seats at the expense of some depopulated areas in the north and west. 2) The right to vote was extended to include all adult male citizens of boroughs who paid £10 or more rent annually, and all adult male citizens of the counties who were £12 tenants or £5 leaseholders.

The Second French Republic and the Second Empire

Louis Napoleon became the president of the Second French Republic in December 1848. It was evident that he was not committed to the Republic and in May 1849, elections for the Legislative Assembly clearly indicated that the people were not bound to its continuance either. In this election, the Conservatives and Monarchists scored significant gains, and the Republicans and Radicals lost power in the Assembly. During the three-year life of the Second Republic, Louis Napoleon demonstrated his skills as a gifted politician through the manipulation of the various factions in French politics. His deployment of troops in Italy to rescue and restore Pope Pius IX was condemned by the republicans, but strongly supported by the monarchists and moderates. As a consequence of the French military intervention, a French garrison under General Oudinot was stationed in Rome until the fall of 1870, when it was recalled during the Franco-Prussian War.

Louis Napoleon minimized the importance of the Legislative Assembly, capitalized on the developing Napoleonic Legend, and courted the support of the army, the Catholic church, and a range of conservative political groups. The Falloux Law returned control of education to the church. Further, Louis Napoleon was confronted with Article 45 of the constitution, which stipulated that the president was limited to one four-year term; he had no intention of relinquishing power. With the assistance of a core of dedicated supporters, Louis Napoleon arranged for a coup d'état on the night of December 1–2, 1851. The Second Republic fell and was soon replaced by the Second French Empire.

Louis Napoleon drafted a new constitution which resulted in a highly centralized government. He was to have a 10–year term, power to declare war, lead the armed forces, conduct foreign policy, initiate and pronounce all laws, and control the new Legislative Assembly. On December 2, 1852, he announced that he was Napoleon III, Emperor of the French.

The Second Empire collapsed after the capture of Napoleon III during the Franco-Prussian War (1870–1871). After a regrettable Parisian experience with a communist type of government, the Third French Republic was established; it would survive until 1940.

Imperial Russia

The autocracy of Nicholas I's (reigned 1825–1855) regime was not threatened by the revolutionary movements of 1848. The consequences of the European revolutionary experience of 1848 to 1849 reinforced the conservative ideology which was the basis of the Romanov regime. In 1848 and 1849, Russian troops suppressed disorganized Polish attempts to reassert Polish nationalism.

Russian involvement in the Crimean War met with defeat. Russian ambitions in the eastern Mediterranean had been thwarted by a coalition of Western European states. In 1855 Nicholas I died and was succeeded by Alexander II (reigned 1855–1881) who feared the forces of change and introduced reforms in order to remain in power.

Fearing the transformation of Russian society from below, Alexander II instituted a series of reforms which altered the nature of the social contract in Russia. In 1861, Alexander II declared that serfdom was abolished. Further, he issued the following reforms: 1) The serf (peasant) would no longer be dependent upon the lord; 2) all people were to have freedom of movement and were free to change their means of livelihood; and 3) the serf could enter into contracts and could own property.

The last years of the reign of Alexander II witnessed increased political opposition, manifested in demands for reforms from an ever more hostile group of intellectuals, the emergence of a Russian populist movement, and attempts to assassinate the tsar. Some of the demands for extending reforms came from within the government from such dedicated and talented ministers as D.A. Miliutin, a Minister of War, who reorganized the Russian military system during the 1870s. However, reactionary ministers such as Count Dimitri Tolstoy, Minister of Education, did much to discredit any progressive policies emanating from the regime; Tolstoy repudiated academic freedom and advanced anti-scientism. As the regime matured, greater importance was placed on traditional values. This attitude developed at the same time that nihilism, which rejected romantic illusions of the past in favor of a rugged realism, was being advanced by such writers as Ivan Turgenev in his *Fathers and Sons*.

The notion of the inevitability and desirability of a social and economic revolution was promoted through the Russian populist movement. Originally, the populists were interested in an agrarian utopian order. The populists had no national support. Government persecution of the populists resulted in the radicalization of the movement. In the late 1870s and early 1880s, leaders such as Andrei Zheleabov and Sophie Perovsky became obsessed with the need to assassinate Alexander II. In March 1881, the tsar was killed in St. Petersburg when his carriage was bombed. He was succeeded by Alexander III (reigned 1881–1894), who advocated a national policy based on "Orthodoxy, Autocracy, and Nationalism." Alexander III selected as his primary aides conservatives such as Count Dimitri Tolstoy, now Minister of the Interior, Count Delianov, Minister of Education, and Constantine Pobedonostev, who headed the Russian Orthodox Church. Alexander III died in 1894 and was succeeded by the last of the Romanovs to hold power, Nicholas II (reigned 1894–1917). Nicholas II displayed lack of intelligence, wit, political acumen, and the absence of a firm will throughout his reign. From his ministers to his wife, Alexandra, to Rasputin (1872–1916), Nicholas was influenced by stronger personalities.

The opposition to the tsarist government became more focused and thus, more threatening, with the emergence of the Russian Social Democrats and the Russian Social Revolutionaries. Both groups were Marxist. Vladimir Ilyich Ulyanov, also known as Lenin, became the leader of the Bolsheviks, a splinter group of the Social Democrats. Until the impact of the 1899 depression and the horrors associated with the Russo-Japanese War were realized, groups advocating revolutions commanded little support. By winter (1904–1905), the accumulated consequences of inept management of the economy and the prosecution of the Russo-Japanese War reached a critical stage. A group under the leadership of the radical priest Gapon marched on the Winter Palace in St. Petersburg (January 9, 1905) to submit a list of grievances to the tsar. Troops fired on the demonstrators and many casualties resulted on this "Bloody Sunday." In response to the massacre, a general strike was called followed by a series of peasant revolts through the spring. During these same months, the Russian armed forces were being defeated by the Japanese and a lack of confidence in the regime became widespread. In June 1905, naval personnel on the battleship *Potemkin* mutinied while the ship was in Odessa. With this startling development, Nicholas II's government lost its nerve. In October 1905, Nicholas II issued the October Manifesto calling for the convocation of a Duma, or assembly of state, which would serve as an advisory body to the tsar, extending civil liberties to include freedom of speech, assembly, and press, and announcing that Nicholas II would reorganize his government.

The leading revolutionary forces differed in their responses to the manifesto. The Octobrists indicated that they were satisfied with the arrangements; the Constitutional Democrats, also known as the Kadets, demanded a more liberal representative system. The Duma convened in 1906 and, from its outset to the outbreak of the First World War, was paralyzed by factionalism which was exploited by the tsar's ministers. By 1907, Nicholas II's ministers had recovered the real power of government. Russia experienced a general though fragile economic recovery by 1909, which lasted until the war.

ORIGINS, MOTIVES, AND IMPLICATIONS OF THE NEW IMPERIALISM (1870–1914)

During the first seven decades of the nineteenth century, the European powers did not pursue active imperial expansion. Internal European development preoccupied the powers; colonies were viewed as liabilities because of the direct costs associated with their administration. However, by the 1870s, the European industrial economies required external markets to distribute products which could not be absorbed within their domestic economies. Further, excess capital was available and foreign investment, while risky, appeared to offer high returns. Finally, the need for additional sources of raw materials served as a rationale and stimulant for imperialism. Politicians were also influenced by the numerous missionary societies which sought government protection, in extending Christianity throughout the world. (British and French missionary societies were vehemently anti-slavery.) European statesmen, were also interested in asserting their national power overseas through the acquisition of strategic (and many not so strategic) colonies.

The focus of most of the European imperial activities during the late nineteenth century was Africa. Since the 1850s, Africa had commanded the attention of European explorers such as Richard Burton, Carl Peters, David Livingstone, and many others, who were interested in charting the unknown interior of the continent, and, in particular, in locating the headwaters of the Nile. Initially, European interest in these activities was romantic. With John Hanning Speke's discovery of Lake Victoria (1858), Livingstone's surveying of the Zambezi, and Stanley's work on the Congo River, Europeans became enraptured with the greatness and novelty of Africa south of the Sahara.

Disraeli was involved in the intrigue which would result in the British acquisition of the Suez Canal (1875), and during the 1870s and 1880s Britain was involved in a Zulu War and announced the annexation of the Transvaal, which the Boers regained after their great victory of Majuba Hill (1881). At about the same time, Belgium established its interest in the Congo; France, in addition to seizing Tunisia, extended its influence into French Equitorial Africa, and Italy established small colonies in East Africa. During the 1880s Germany acquired several African colonies including German East Africa, the Cameroons, Togoland, and German South West Africa. All of these imperial activities heightened tensions among the European powers. Consequently, the Berlin Conference (1884–1885) was convened. The conference resulted in an agreement which specified the following: 1) The Congo would be under the control of Belgium through an International Association; 2) More liberal use of the Niger and Congo river; 3) European powers could acquire African territory through first occupation and second notifying the other European states of their occupation and claim.

British movement north of the Cape of Good Hope resulted in a different type of struggle—one that involved Europeans fighting one another rather than a native African force. The Boers had lived in South Africa since the beginning of the nineteenth century. With the discovery of gold (1882) in the Transvaal, many English Cape settlers moved into the region. The Boers, under the leadership of Paul Kruger, restricted the political and economic rights of the British settlers and developed alternative railroads through Mozambique which would lessen the Boer dependency on the Cape colony. Relations between the British and Boers steadily deteriorated; in 1895, the Jameson Raid, an ill-conceived action not approved by Britain, failed to result in restoring the status of British citizens. The crisis mounted and, in 1899, the Boer War began. Until 1902, the British and Boers fought a war which was costly to both sides. Britain prevailed and by 1909, the Transvaal, Orange Free State, Natal, and the Cape of Good Hope were united into the Union of South Africa.

Another area of increased imperialist activity was the Pacific. In 1890, the American naval Captain Alfred Mahan published *The Influence of Sea Power Upon History*; in this book he argued that history demonstrated that nations which controlled the seas prevailed. During the 1880s and 1890s naval ships required coaling stations. While Britain, the Netherlands, and France demonstrated that they were interested in Pacific islands, the most active states in this region during the last 20 years of the nineteenth century were Germany and the United States. Britain's Pacific interests were motivated primarily in sustaining its control of Australia. The French were interested in Tahiti; after a dispute with France over the Samoan Islands, the islands were split with France, Germany, and the United States. The United States acquired the Philippines in 1898. Germany gained part of New Guinea, and the Marshall, Caroline, and Mariana island chains. The European powers were also interested in the Asian mainland. In 1900, the Boxer Rebellion broke in Peking; it was a native reaction against Western influence in China. An international force was organized to break the siege of the Western legations. Most powers agreed with the American Open Door Policy which recognized the independence and integrity of China and provided economic access for all the powers. Rivalry over China (Manchuria) was a principal cause for the outbreak of the Russo-Japanese War in 1904.

THE AGE OF BISMARCK (1871–1890)

During the period from the establishment of the German Empire in January 1871 to his dismissal as chancellor of Germany in March 1890, Otto von Bismarck dominated European diplomacy and established an integrated political and economic structure for the new German state. Bismarck established a statist system which was reactionary in political philosophy and based upon industrialism, militarism, and innovative social legislation. German adaptation during the *Grundjahre* (the founding years of the new industrial order, 1870–1875) was staggering and remarkable increases in productivity and the expansion of industrialization took place from 1870–1890.

Until the mid-nineteenth century, Germany consisted of numerous independent states which identified with regional rather than national concerns. This condition reflected the continuing impact of the Peace of Westphalia (1648). With the unification of Germany, a German state became a reality, but the process of integration of regional economic, social, political, and cultural interests had not yet occurred. Bismarck, with the consent and approval of Wilhelm I (1797–1888), the German emperor, developed a constitution for the new nation which provided for the following:

1) The emperor would be the executor of state and, as such, establish the domestic and foreign policies; he was also the commander of the armed forces. The chancellor (similar to prime minister) held office at the discretion of the Emperor.

2) A bicameral legislature was established. It consisted of the *Reichstag*; a lower body which represented the people (the *Volk*); and the *Bundesrat*, an upper body which represented the various German states. During Bismarck's tenure, the *Bundesrat* identified with a progressive social agenda—though not one that encouraged or developed civil and political liberties—and served to check any populism in the *Reichstag*.

During the 1870s and 1880s, Bismarck's domestic policies were directed at the establishment of a strong united German state which would be capable of defending itself from a French war of revenge designed to restore Alsace-Lorraine to France. Laws were enacted which unified the monetary system, established an Imperial Bank and strengthened existing banks, developed universal German civil and criminal codes, and required compulsory military service. All of these measures contributed to the integration of the German state.

Bismarck's social programs were part of a nationalist program to unify Germany and create a strong, modern state. He recognized that by improving the condition and education of the people, the nation itself would become stronger. On the economic front, Bismarck instituted a protective tariff, to maintain domestic production, and introduced many social and economic laws to provide social security, regulate child labor, and improve working conditions for all Germans.

Bismarck's foreign policy was centered on maintaining the diplomatic isolation of France. After a few years of recovery from their defeat in the Franco-Prussian War, the French were regaining their confidence and publicly discussing the feasibility of a war of revenge to regain Alsace-Lorraine. In 1875, the War-In-Sight-Crisis occurred between the French and Germans. While war was avoided, the crisis clearly indicated the delicate state of the Franco-German relationship. In the crisis stemming from the Russo-Turkish War (1877–1878), Bismarck tried to serve as the "Honest Broker" at the Congress of

Berlin. Russia did not succeed at the conference and incorrectly blamed Bismarck for its failure. Early in the next year, a cholera epidemic affected Russian cattle herds, and Germany placed an embargo on the importation of Russian beef. The Russians were outraged by the German action and launched an anti-German propaganda campaign in the Russian press. Bismarck, desiring to maintain the peace and a predictable diplomatic environment, concluded a secret defensive treaty with Austria-Hungary in 1879. The Dual Alliance was very significant because it was the first "hard" diplomatic alliance of the era. A "hard" alliance involved the specific commitment of military support; traditional or "soft" alliances involved pledges of neutrality or to hold military conversations in the event of a war. The Dual Alliance, which had a five-year term and was renewable, directed that one signatory would assist the other in the event that one power was attacked by two or more states.

In 1882, another agreement, the Triple Alliance, was signed between Germany, Austria-Hungary, and Italy. In the 1880s, relations between Austria-Hungary and Russia became estranged over Balkan issues. Bismarck, fearing a war, intervened and by 1887, had negotiated the secret Reinsurance Treaty with Russia. This was a "hard" defensive alliance with a three-year term, that was renewable. Since these were "defensive" arrangements, Bismarck was confident that through German policy, the general European peace would be maintained and the security of Germany ensured by sustaining the diplomatic isolation of France. Bismarck also acted to neutralize the role of Great Britain in European affairs through a policy which in most instances was supportive of British interests.

In 1888, Wilhelm I died and was succeeded by his son Friedrich III, who also died within a few months. Friedrich's son, Wilhelm II (reigned 1888–1918), came to power and soon found himself in conflict with Bismarck. Wilhelm II was intent upon administering the government personally and viewed Bismarck as an archaic personality. Early in 1890, two issues developed which led ultimately to Bismarck's dismissal. First, Bismarck had evolved a scheme for a fabricated attempted coup by the Social Democratic Party; his intent was to use this situation to create a national hysteria through which he could restrict the SPD through legal action. Second, Bismarck intended to renew the Reinsurance Treaty with Russia to maintain his policy of French diplomatic isolation. Wilhelm II opposed both of these plans; in March 1890, Bismarck, who had used the threat of resignation so skillfully in the past, suggested that he would resign if Wilhelm II would not approve of these actions. Wilhelm II accepted his resignation; in fact, Bismarck was dismissed. The diplomatic developments after 1890 radically altered the alignment of power in Europe. The position of Chancellor of Germany was filled by a series of less talented statesmen including Count von Caprivi (1890–1894), Prince Hohenlohe (1894–1900), Prince Bernhard von Bulow (1900–1909), and Chancellor Bethmann-Hollweg.

THE MOVEMENT TOWARD DEMOCRACY IN WESTERN EUROPE TO 1914

Even after the reform measures of 1867 and 1884 to 1885, the movement toward democratic reforms in Great Britain continued unabated. Unlike other European nations where the focus on democracy was limited to gaining the vote, British reform efforts were much more complex and sophisticated and involved social and economic reforms as well as continuing changes in the political process; participation in the system as well as representation was desired by many.

The most significant political reform of this long-lived Liberal government was the Parliament Act of 1911, which eliminated the powers of the House of Lords and resulted in the House of Commons becoming the unquestioned center of national power. All revenue bills approved by the House of Commons would automatically become law 30 days after being sent to the House of Lords. If the Lords voted favorably, the law would be enacted earlier. The Lords had no veto power.

The most recurring and serious problem which Great Britain experienced during the period from 1890 to 1914 was the "Irish Question." Gladstone, in his final ministry, argued unsuccessfully for Irish Home Rule. In Ireland opposition to British rule and the abuses of British power was advanced by the National Land League established in 1879. This organization stimulated and coordinated Irish opposition to British and Irish landlords. During the 1880s Charles Stewart Parnell led the Irish delegation to the House of Commons. Parnell, through the support of Gladstone, attained some gains for the Irish such as the Land Reform Act and the Arrears Act. In 1890 Parnell became involved in a divorce case and the scandal ruined his career; he died the next year. In 1893, Gladstone devised the Irish Home Rule bill, which was passed by the House of Commons but rejected by the House of Lords. The Irish situation became more complicated when the Protestant counties of the north started to enjoy remarkable economic growth from the mid-1890s; they were adamant in their rejection of all measures of Irish Home Rule. In 1914, an Irish Home Rule Act was passed by both the Commons and the Lords, but the Protestants refused to accept it. Implementation was deferred until after the war.

The Third French Republic

In the fall of 1870, Napoleon III's Second Empire collapsed when it was defeated by the Prussian armies. Napoleon III and his principal aides were captured; later, he abdicated and fled to England. A National Assembly (1871–1875) was created and Adolphe Thiers was recognized as its chief executive. At the same time, a more radical political entity, the Paris Commune (1870–1871), came into existence and exercised extraordinary power during the siege of Paris. After the siege and the peace agreement with Prussia, the Commune refused to recognize the authority of the National Assembly. Led by radical Marxists, anarchists, and republicans, the Paris Commune repudiated the conservative and monarchist leadership of the National Assembly. From March to May 1871, the Commune fought a bloody struggle with the troops of the National Assembly. Thousands died and when Paris surrendered, there were thousands of executions—accepted estimates place the number at 20,000 during the first week after Paris fell on May 28, 1871. France began a program of recovery which led to the formulation of the Third French Republic in 1875. The National Assembly sought to 1) put the French political house in order; 2) establish a new constitutional government; 3) pay off an imposed indemnity and, in doing so, remove German troops from French territory; and 4) restore the honor and glory of France. In 1875 a constitution was adopted which provided for a republican government of a president (with little power), a Senate, and a Chamber of Deputies, which was the center of political power. The overwhelming influence of the French bourgeoisie (middle class), which was intent upon establishing and sustaining a French republican government; the mounting hostility between the Catholic church and the French government; the unpredictability which accompanied multi-party politics; and finally, the extreme nationalism which gripped France during these decades and resulted in continuing calls for a war of revenge against Germany in order to regain Alsace-Lorraine, were the chief challenges to the new Republic.

During the early years of the Republic, Leon Gambetta (1838–1882) led the republicans. Beginning in the 1880s the Third French Republic was challenged by a series of crises which threatened its continuity. The Boulanger Crisis (1887–1889), the Panama

Scandal (1894), and the Dreyfus Affair (1894–1906) were serious domestic problems; in all of these developments, the challenge to republicanism came from the right.

The most serious threat to the Republic came through the Dreyfus Affair. In 1894, Captain Alfred Dreyfus (1859–1935) was assigned to the French General Staff. A scandal broke when it was revealed that classified information had been provided to German spies. Dreyfus, a Jew, was charged, tried, and convicted. Later, it was determined that the actual spy was Commandant Marie Charles Esterhazy (1847–1923), who was acquitted in order to save the pride and reputation of the army. The monarchists used this incident to criticize republicanism; the republicans countered when Emile Zola (1840–1902) took up Dreyfus's cause and wrote an open letter entitled *J'accuse*, condemning the General Staff's actions and pronouncing Dreyfus's innocence. Leftists supported the Republic and in 1906, the case was closed when Dreyfus was declared innocent and returned to the ranks. Rather than lead to the collapse of the Republic, the Dreyfus Affair demonstrated the intensity of anti-Semitism in French society, the level of corruption in the French army, and the willingness of the Catholic church and the monarchists to join in a conspiracy against an innocent man. The republicans launched an anti-clerical campaign which included the Association Act (1901) and the separation of church and state (1905).

From 1905 to 1914 the socialists under Jean Jaurès gained seats in the Chamber of Deputies. The Third French Republic endured the crises which confronted it and, in 1914, enjoyed the support of the vast majority of French citizens.

EUROPEAN CULTURAL DEVELOPMENTS (1848–1914)

The great political and economic changes of this period were accompanied by cultural achievements which included the development of a literate citizenry and substantive innovations in science, literature, art, music, and other areas of intellectual activity. In large part, these developments occurred as a reaction against the mechanistic sterility of the scientism and positivism of the age; however, some of the initial achievements, such as Darwin's theories of evolution and natural selection, resulted in extending the exaggerated claims of scientism. From Charles Darwin (1809–1882), Richard Wagner, (1813–1883), Friedrich Nietzche (1844–1900), and Sigmund Freud (1856–1939) to Claude Monet (1840–1926), Richard Strauss (1864–1949), Igor Stravinsky (1882–1971), Oscar Wilde (1854–1900), Thomas Mann (1875–1955), and James Joyce (1882–1941), intelligent Europeans of the era pursued many different approaches in the quest for truth and understanding. Many philosophers were critical of the movement toward democracy, which they identified with mass culture and political ineptitude.

Austro-Serbian Relations

Serbia, a small, fiercely independent and proud nation, was economically and politically subservient to Austria in the latter part of the nineteenth and early twentieth centuries. In 1905, Serbia sought to diversify its economic trading relationships by exporting its main product, livestock, to nations besides Austria. The so-called "Pig War" erupted when Austria, in retaliation, banned the import of Serbian livestock. Austria hoped to force the Serbs into ceasing their efforts to develop an economy that would be independent of the Hapsburg empire. Serbia responded by vigorously working to develop alternate trading partners, an effort that proved surprisingly successful—much to the annoyance of the Austrians. The affair, although perhaps a minor incident in itself, points up the growing tensions between tiny Serbia and the vast Hapsburg empire. The Austrians were sensitive to any perceived display of Serbian independence or Slavic nationalism, while the Serbs and other ethnic minorities within the Austrian empire and under its influence became increasingly hostile to Hapsburg control.

6. WORLD WAR I AND EUROPE IN CRISIS (1914–1935)

THE ROOT CAUSES OF THE WAR

In August 1914, most of the world's major powers became engaged in a conflict that most people welcomed romantically and felt would last only a few months. Instead, a war of world dimensions evolved that saw the clash of outdated military values with modern technological warfare. A war that no one seemed to be able to win lasted more than four years, and resulted in 12 million deaths.

The long-range roots of the origins of World War I can be traced to numerous factors, beginning with the creation of modern Germany in 1871. Achieved through a series of wars, the emergence of this new German state completely destroyed Europe's traditional balance of power, and forced its diplomatic and military planners back to their drawing boards to rethink their collective strategies. In the period between 1871 and 1914, a number of developments took place that increased tensions between the major powers.

From 1871 to 1890, balance of power was maintained through the network of alliances created by the German Chancellor, Otto von Bismarck, and centered around his *Dreikaiserbund* (League of the Three Emperors) that isolated France, and the Dual (Germany, Austria) and Triple (Germany, Austria, Italy) Alliances. Bismarck's fall in 1890 resulted in new policies that saw Germany move closer to Austria, while England and France (Entente Cordiale, 1904), and later Russia (Triple Entente, 1907), drew closer.

Germany's dramatic defeat of France in 1870–1871 coupled with Kaiser Wilhelm II's decision in 1890 to build up a navy comparable to that of Great Britain created a reactive arms race. This, blended with European efforts to carve out colonial empires in Africa and Asia—plus a new spirit of nationalism and the growing romanticization of war—helped create an unstable international environment in the years before the outbreak of World War I.

The Balkans, the area of Europe that now comprises the former Yugoslavia, Albania, Greece, Bulgaria, and Rumania, was Europe's most unstable area. Part of the rapidly decaying Ottoman (Turkish) Empire, it was torn by ethnic nationalism among the various small groups that lived there, and competition between Austria-Hungary and Russia over spheres of influence in the region. Friction was intense in the region between Austria and Serbia, particularly after the former annexed Bosnia and Herzegovina in 1908. In 1912, with Russian encouragement, a Balkan League which included Serbia, Montenegro, Greece, and Bulgaria went to war with Turkey. Serbia, which wanted a spot on the Adriatic, was rebuffed when Austria created Albania in an attempt to deter Serbia. This intensified bitterness between both countries and prompted Russia to take a more protective attitude toward its southern Slavic cousins.

THE OUTBREAK OF WORLD WAR

On June 28, 1914, the Archduke Franz Ferdinand (1863–1914), heir to the Austrian throne, was assassinated by Gavrilo Princip, a young Serbian nationalist. Princip was working for the Serbian Army Intelligence in Sarajevo, then the capital of Bosnia. Austria's rulers felt the murder provided them with an opportunity to move against Serbia and end anti-Austrian unrest in the Balkans. Austria consulted with the German government on July 6 and received a "blank check" to take whatever steps necessary to punish Serbia. On July 23, 1914, the Austrian government presented Serbia with a 10-point ultimatum. It required Serbia to suppress and punish all forms of anti-Austrian sentiment there with the help of Austrian officials. On July 25, 1914, three hours after mobilizing its army, Serbia accepted most of Austria's terms; it requested only that Austria's demand to participate in Serbian judicial proceedings—a demand that Serbia characterized as unprecedented in the affairs of sovereign states—be adjudicated by the International Tribunal at The Hague.

Austria immediately broke official relations with Serbia and mobilized its army. Meanwhile, between July 18 and July 24, Russia let the Austrians and the Germans know that it intended to back Serbia fully in the dispute. France, Russia's ally, voiced support of Russia's moves. On July 28, 1914, Austria went to war against Serbia, and began to bombard Belgrade the following day. At the same time, Russia gradually prepared for war against Austria and Germany, declaring full mobilization on July 30.

German military strategy, based in part on the plan of the Chief of the General Staff Count Alfred von Schlieffen, viewed Russian mobilization as an act of war. The Schlieffen Plan was based on a two-front war with Russia and France. It was predicated on a swift, decisive blow against France while maintaining a defensive position against slowly mobilizing Russia, which would be dealt with after France. Attacking France required the Germans to march through neutral Belgium, which would later bring England into the war as a protector of Belgian neutrality.

Germany demanded that Russia demobilize in 12 hours and appealed to the Russian ambassador in Berlin. Russia's offer to negotiate the matter was rejected, and Germany declared war on Russia on August 1, 1914. Germany asked France its intentions and Paris replied that it would respond according to its own interests. On August 3, Germany declared war on France. Berlin asked Belgium for permission to send its troops through its territory to attack France, which Belgium refused. On August 4, England, which agreed in 1839 to protect Belgian neutrality, declared war on Germany; Belgium followed suit. Between 1914 and 1915, the alliance of the Central Powers (Germany, Austria-Hungary, Bulgaria, and Turkey) faced the Allied Powers of England, France, Russia, Japan, and in 1917, the United States. A number of smaller countries were also part of the Allied coalition.

The War in 1914

The Western Front: After entering Belgium, the Germans attacked France on five fronts in an effort to encircle Paris rapidly. France was defeated in the Battle of the Frontier (August 14–24) in Lorraine, the Ardennes, and in the Charleroi-Mons area. However, the unexpected Russian attack in East Prussia and Galicia from August 17 to 20 forced Germany to transfer important forces eastward to halt the Russian drive.

To halt a further German advance, the French army, aided by Belgian and English forces, counterattacked. In the Battle of the Marne (September 5–9), they stopped the German drive and forced small retreats. Mutual outflanking maneuvers by France and Germany created a battlefront that would determine the demarcation of the Western Front for the next four years. It ran, in uneven fashion, from the North Sea to Belgium and from northern France to Switzerland.

The Eastern Front: The Germans retreated after their assault against Warsaw in late September. Hindenburg's attack on Lodz, 10 days after he was appointed Commander-in-Chief of the Eastern Front (Nov. 1), was a more successful venture; by the end of 1914 this important textile center was in German hands.

The War in 1915

The Western Front: With Germany concentrating on the East, France and England launched a series of small attacks throughout the year that resulted in a few gains and extremely heavy casualties. Wooed by both sides, Italy joined the Allies and declared war on the Central Powers on May 23 after signing the secret Treaty of London (April 26). This treaty gave Italy Austrian provinces in the north and some Turkish territory. Italian attacks against Austria near Trieste were unsuccessful because of difficult terrain, and failed to lessen pressure on the Russians in the East.

The Eastern Front: On January 23, 1915, Austro-German forces began a coordinated offensive in East Russia and in the Carpathians. The two-pronged German assault in the north was stopped on February 27, while Austrian efforts to relieve their besieged defensive network at Przemysl failed when it fell into Russian hands on March 22. In early March, Russian forces under Nikolai Ivanov drove deeper into the Carpathians with inadequate material support.

German forces, strengthened by troops from the Western Front under August von Mackensen, began a move on May 2 to strike at the heart of the Russian Front. They used the greatest artillery concentration of the war at that time as part of their strategy. In June, Mackensen shifted his assault towards Lublin and Brest-Litovsk, while the German XII, X, and Niemen armies moved toward Kovno in the Baltic. By August 1915, much of Russian Poland was in German hands.

In an effort to provide direct access to the Turks defending Gallipoli, Germany and Austria invaded Serbia in the early fall, aided by their new ally, Bulgaria. On October 7, the defeated Serbian army retreated to Corfu. Belated Allied efforts to ship troops from Gallipoli to help Serbia failed.

Allied frustration resulted in the appointment of Marshal Joseph Joffre (1852–1931) as French Commander-in-Chief and Field Marshal Sir Douglas Haig (1861–1928) as British Commander in December 1915.

The Eastern Mediterranean

Turkey entered the war on the Central Power side on October 28, 1914, which prevented the shipment of Anglo-French aid to Russians through the Straits.

The Western stalemate caused Allied strategists to look to the eastern Mediterranean for a way to break the military deadlock. Winston Churchill, Britain's First Lord of the Admiralty, devised a plan to seize the Straits of the Dardanelles to open lines to Russia, take Constantinople, and isolate Turkey. These unsuccessful efforts occurred between February 19 and March 18, 1915.

On April 25, Allied forces invaded Gallipoli Peninsula in a different attempt to capture the Straits. Turkish troops offered strong resistance and forced the Allies (after suffering 252,000 casualties) to begin a three week evacuation that began on December 20, 1915.

The War in 1916

The Western Front: In order to break the stalemate on the Western Front and drain French forces in the effort, the Germans decided to attack the French fortress town of Verdun. The Battle for Verdun lasted from February 21 to December 18, 1916. From

February until June, German forces, aided by closely coordinated heavy artillery barrages, assaulted the forts around Verdun. The Germans suffered 281,000 casualties while the French, under Marshal Henri Pétain (1856–1951), lost 315,000 while successfully defending their position.

To take pressure off the French, an Anglo-French force mounted three attacks on the Germans to the left of Verdun in July, September, and November. After the Battle of the Somme (July 1–November 18), German pressure was reduced, but at great loss. Anglo-French casualties totaled 600,000.

The Eastern Front: Initially, the Allies had hoped for a general coordinated attack on all fronts against the Central Powers. Now efforts centered on relieving pressure at Verdun and on the Italians at Trentino.

Orchestrated by Aleksei Brusilov (1853–1926), The Brusilov Offensive (June 4–September 20) envisioned a series of unexpected attacks along a lengthy front to confuse the enemy. By late August, he had advanced into Galicia and the Carpathians. The number of enemy troops dead, wounded, or captured numbered 1.5 million. Russian losses numbered 500,000.

Rumania entered the war on the Allied side as a result of Russian successes and the secret Treaty of Bucharest (August 17). This treaty specified that Rumania would get Transylvania, Bukovina, the Banat, and part of the Hungarian Plain if the Allies won. The ensuing Rumanian thrust into Transylvania was pushed back, and on December 6, a German-Bulgarian army occupied Bucharest as well as the bulk of Rumania.

The death of Austrian Emperor Franz Joseph (reigned 1848–1916) on November 21 prompted his successor, Charles I (1887–1922), to discuss the prospect of peace terms with his allies. On December 12, the four Central Powers, strengthened by the fall of Bucharest, offered four separate peace proposals based on their recent military achievements. The Allies rejected them on December 30 because they felt them to be insincere.

Britain's naval strategy in the first year of the war was to disrupt German shipping worldwide with the aid of the French and the Japanese. Germany sought ways to defend itself and weaken Allied naval strength. By the end of 1914, Allied fleets had gained control of the high seas, which caused Germany to lose control of its colonial empire.

Germany's failure in 1914 to weaken British naval strength prompted German naval leaders to begin using the submarine as an offensive weapon to weaken the British. On February 4, Germany announced a war zone around the British Isles, and advised neutral powers to sail there at their own risk. On May 7, 1915, a German submarine sank the *Lusitania*, a British passenger vessel because it was secretly carrying arms. There were 1,201 casualties, including 139 Americans.

NEW MILITARY TECHNOLOGY

Germany, Russia, and Great Britain all had submarines, but the German U-boats were the most effective. Designed principally for coastal protection, they increasingly used them to reduce British naval superiority through tactical and psychological means.

By the spring of 1915, British war planners finally awoke to the fact that the machine gun had become the mistress of defensive trench warfare. In a search for a weapon to counter trench defenses, the British developed tanks as an armored "land ship," and first used them on September 15, 1916, in the battle of the Somme. Their value was not immediately realized because there were too few of them to be effective, and interest in them waned. Renewed interest came in 1917.

Airplanes were initially used for observation purposes in the early months of the war. As their numbers grew, mid-air struggles using pistols and rifles took place, until the

Germans devised a synchronized propeller and machine gun on its Fokker aircraft in May 1915. The Allies responded with similar equipment and new squadron tactics during the early days of the Verdun campaign in February 1916, and briefly gained control of the skies. They also began to use their aircraft for bombing raids against Zeppelin bases in Germany. Air supremacy shifted to the Germans in 1917.

During the first year of the war, the Germans began to use Zeppelin airships to bomb civilian targets in England. Though their significance was neutralized with the development of the explosive shell in 1916, Zeppelins played an important role as a psychological weapon in the first two years of the war.

In the constant search for methods to counter trench warfare, the Germans and the Allied forces experimented with various forms of internationally outlawed gas. On October 27, 1914, the Germans tried a nose/eye irritant gas at Neuve-Chapelle, and by the spring of 1915 had developed an asphyxiating lachrymatory chlorine gas used in the Battles of Ypres. This marked the first time poison gas was used in warfare. The British countered with a similar chemical at the battles of Champagne and Loos that fall. Military strategists initially had little faith in gas since its use depended heavily on wind conditions, which could change the direction of the gas at any moment. However, as they desperately struggled to find ways to break the deadlock on the Western Front, they devised tactics and protection methods that enabled them to integrate the use of gas into their strategy.

THE LAST YEARS OF THE TSARS

Two events that would have a dramatic impact on the war and the world were the February and October Revolutions in 1917. The former toppled the Romanov dynasty and spawned that country's brief flirtation with democracy under the temporary Provisional Government. It collapsed later that year as a result of the October Revolution, which brought Lenin and his Bolshevik faction to power.

Plagued for centuries by a backward autocratic government and a rural serf economy, Russia seemed on the verge of dramatic change after Tsar Alexander II (1855–1881) freed the serfs in 1861. Emancipation, coupled with other important government and social reforms, created chaos nationwide and helped stimulate a new class of violent revolutionaries bent on destroying the tsarist system. Terrorists murdered Alexander II, which prompted the country's last two rulers, Alexander III (reigned 1881–1894) and Nicholas II (reigned 1894–1917), to turn the clock backward politically.

The Russo-Japanese War and the 1905 Revolution: In February 1904, war broke out between Russia and Japan over spheres-of-influence in Korea and Manchuria. Russia's inability to adequately support its military forces in Asia, coupled with growing battlefield losses, prompted a nationwide revolution after police fired on peaceful demonstrators in January 1905. A groundswell of strikes and demonstrations swept the country and neutralized the government, which was on the verge of collapse. Nicholas II survived because he agreed in his October Manifesto (October 30, 1905) to create a constitution, share power with a legislature (Duma), and grant civil rights. This decree defused the crisis and enabled the government to survive and rebuild its political base.

Era of Reaction and Reforms (1906–1912): Once the tsar lessened the threat to his throne, he issued the Fundamental Laws (May 6, 1906), which severely limited the power of the Duma. Over the next 11 years, however, four increasingly conservative Dumas met, providing a tradition of constitutional government for the country. Workers' and soldiers' *soviets* (councils) and political parties (Kadets, Constitutional Democrats, Octobrists) emerged to challenge the government. To counter this mood, the tsar appointed Peter Stolypin prime minister (1906–1911). Stolypin initiated mollifying reforms for the peasants and sought to develop a private agricultural system throughout the country. These efforts, together with a fortuitous industrial boom, proved a boon to Russia's economy.

Rasputin and the Upheaval (1912-1914): The death of Stolypin in 1911, coupled with a government that had proved incapable of dealing with new labor unrest, brought to power a semi-literate, self-styled holy man, Grigory Rasputin (1872–1916). Rasputin was credited with possessing the power to control, through hypnosis, the bleeding of the tsar's hemophiliac son, Alexei. This opened the door to tremendous influence over the royal family.

RUSSIA AT WAR: THE HOME FRONT (1914–1917)

Russia's entrance into World War I was met with broad public acceptance and support. Serious problems, however, plagued the government, the military, and the economy, and threatened to undermine a military effort most expected would win the war in a matter of months.

The Military: The draft caused Russia's armed forces to grow from 1.3 million to 6.5 million during the war, though the government was able to equip fully only a small percentage of the troops. In addition, the country's military leaders differed on whether to concentrate their efforts on the Austrians or the Germans. While in the field, commanders were handicapped by inadequate communication and maps. As a result, German drives in the spring and summer of 1915 saw Russian morale collapse as defensive efforts proved ineffective. By the end of the year, however, High Command personnel changes, aided by new industrial output, enabled the Russians briefly to turn the tide of battle.

Government and the Bureaucracy: As the country's problems mounted, the tsar responded by assuming direct command of his army on the front in September 1915, leaving the reins of government in the hands of his wife, Alexandra, and Rasputin. Critics of the tsar's policies were dismissed, and, as a result, Russia lost its most effective leaders. The Duma, which was forced to assume more responsibilities, formed the Progressive Bloc, a coalition mainly of Kadets and Octobrists, in an effort to try to force the tsar to appoint more competent officials. The tsar's refusal to accept the group's proposals led to increasing criticism of his policies. In November 1916, a member of the Duma and distant relatives of the tsar collaborated in the secret murder of Rasputin.

The February Revolution

The government's handling of the war prompted a new wave of civilian unrest. Estimates are that 1,140 riots and strikes swept Russia in January and February of 1917. Military and police units ordered to move against the mobs either remained at their posts or joined them.

Though ordered by the tsar not to meet until April, Duma leaders demanded dramatic solutions to the country's problems. Though dissolved on March 11, the Duma met in special session on March 13 and created a Provisional Committee of Elders to deal with the civil war. Two days later, it decided that the tsar must relinquish the throne, and on March 15, 1917, President Michael Rodzianko and Aleksandr Ivanovich Guchkov, leader of the Octobrist Party, persuaded the tsar to abdicate. He agreed, turning the throne over to his brother, the Grand Duke Michael, who himself abdicated the following day.

The Bolshevik October Revolution

The Kornilov affair and Kerensky's failure to rebuild support for the Provisional

Government convinced the Bolshevik's two leaders, Lenin and Leon Trotsky (1879–1940), that now was the time for them to attempt to seize power.

On October 23–24, Lenin returned from Finland to meet with the party's Central Committee to plan the coup. Though he met with strong resistance, the Committee agreed to create a Political Bureau (Politburo) to oversee the revolution.

Leon Trotsky, head of the Petrograd Soviet and its Military Revolutionary Committee, convinced troops in Petrograd to support Bolshevik moves. While Trotsky gained control of important strategic points around the city, Kerensky, well-informed of Lenin's plans, finally decided on November 6 to move against the plotters.

In response, Lenin and Trotsky ordered their supporters to seize the city's transportation and communication centers. The Winter Palace was captured later that evening, along with most of Kerensky's government.

The Second Congress opened at 11 p.m. on November 7, with Lev Kamenev (1883–1936), a member of Lenin's Politburo, as its head. Over half (390) of the 650 delegates were Bolshevik supporters, and its newly selected 22–member Presidium had 14 Bolsheviks on it. Soon after the Second Congress opened, many of the moderate socialists walked out in opposition to Lenin's coup, leaving the Bolsheviks and the Left Socialist Revolutionaries in control of the gathering. Lenin now used the rump Congress as the vehicle to announce his regime.

At the Congress, it was announced that the government's new Cabinet, officially called the Council of People's Commissars (Sovnarkom), and responsible to a Central Executive Committee, would include Lenin as Chairman or head of government, Trotsky as Foreign Commissar, and Josef Stalin as Commissar of Nationalities. The Second Congress issued two decrees on peace and land. The first called for immediate peace without any consideration of indemnities or annexations, while the second adopted the Socialist Revolutionary land program that abolished private ownership of land and decreed that a peasant could only have as much land as he could farm. Village councils would oversee distribution.

The Constituent Assembly

The Constituent Assembly, long promised by the Provisional Government as the country's first legally elected legislature, presented serious problems for Lenin, since he knew the Bolsheviks could not win a majority of seats in it. Regardless, Lenin allowed elections for it to be held on November 25 under universal suffrage. More than 41 million Russians voted. The SR's got 58 percent of the vote, the Bolsheviks 25 percent, and the Kadets and other parties, 17 percent. When the assembly convened on January 18 in the Tauride Palace, the building was surrounded by Red Guards and others. The Assembly voted down Bolshevik proposals and elected Victor Chernov, a Socialist Revolutionary, as president, and declared the country a democratic federal republic. The Bolsheviks walked out. The next day, troops dissolved the Assembly.

WORLD WAR I: THE FINAL PHASE (1917–1918)

Marshall Henri Pétain (1856–1951) became French Commander in May 1917 after a failed French offensive in Champagne (second Battle of the Aisne) resulted in large-scale mutinies. Against French wishes, Haig began a new series of unsuccessful assaults (Third Battle of Ypres from July 31 to November 4).

On October 24, a Central Power campaign began at Caporetto, which resulted in an Italian retreat through November 12 and the capture of 250,000 Italians. The loss convinced the Allies to form a Supreme War Council at Versailles to enhance Allied cooperation.

Russia Leaves the War

One of the cornerstones of Bolshevik propaganda throughout 1917 was a promise to end the war after they had seized power. Once in control, Soviet authorities issued a decree that called for immediate peace "with no indemnities or annexations" at the Second Congress of Soviets on November 8, 1917.

As order collapsed among Russian units along the Eastern Front, the Soviet government began to explore cease fire talks with the Central Powers. Leon Trotsky, the Commissar of Foreign Affairs, offered general negotiations to all sides, and signed an initial armistice as a prelude to peace discussions with Germany at Brest-Litovsk on December 5, 1917.

Trotsky was shocked by German demands for Poland, Lithuania, and Kurland when negotiations opened on December 22, 1917. This prompted him to return to Moscow for consultations with the Bolshevik leadership.

Three different perspectives emerged over the German peace terms among the Soviet leadership. One group, led by Nikolay Bukharin (1888–1938), wanted the conflict to continue as a revolutionary war designed to spread Bolshevism. Lenin, however, felt the country needed peace for his government to survive. Western revolution would take place later.

On the day the German offensive began, Lenin barely convinced Party leaders to accept Germany's earlier offer. Berlin responded with harsher ones, which the Soviets grudgingly accepted, and were integrated into the Treaty of Brest-Litovsk of March 3, 1918. According to its terms, in return for peace, Soviet Russia lost its Baltic provinces, the Ukraine, Finland, Byelorussia, and part of Transcaucasia. The area lost totaled 1.3 million square miles and included 62 million people.

The U.S. Presence: Naval and Economic Support

The United States, which had originally hoped that it could simply supply the Allies with naval and economic support, made its naval presence known immediately and helped Great Britain mount an extremely effective blockade of Germany and, through a convoy system, strengthened the shipment of goods across the Atlantic.

Despite the difficulties of building a military system from scratch, the United States was slowly able to transform its peacetime army of 219,665 men and officers into a force of 2 million. An initial token group, the American Expeditionary Force under General John J. Pershing (1860–1948), arrived in France on June 25, 1917, while by the end of April 1918, 300,000 Americans a month were placed as complete divisions alongside British and French units.

Stirred by the successes on the Marne, the Allies began their offensive against the Germans at Amiens on August 8, 1918. Ludendorff, who called this Germany's "dark day," soon began to think of ways to end the fighting. By September 3, the Germans retreated to the Hindenburg Line. On September 26, Foch began his final offensive, and took the Hindenburg Line the following day. Two days later, Ludendorff advised his government to seek a peace settlement. Over the next month, the French took St. Quetin (October 1), while the British occupied Cambrai, Le Cateau, and Ostend.

On September 14, Allied forces attacked in the Salonika area of Macedonia and forced Bulgaria to sue for peace on September 29. On September 19, General Allenby began an attack on Turkish forces at Megiddo in Palestine and quickly defeated them. In a rapid collapse of Turkish resistance, the British took Damascus, Aleppo, and finally forced Turkey from the war at the end of October. On October 24, the Italians began an assault against Austria-Hungary at Vitto Veneto and forced Vienna to sign armistice terms on November 3. Kaiser Wilhelm II, pressured to abdicate, fled the country on November 9, and a republic was declared. On November 11, at 11 a.m., the war ended, with Germany accepting a harsh armistice.

THE PARIS PEACE CONFERENCE OF 1919–1920

To a very great extent, the direction and thrust of the discussions at the Paris Peace Conference were determined by the destructive nature of the war itself and the political responsibilities, ideals, and personalities of the principal architects of the settlements at Paris: President Woodrow Wilson (1856–1924) of the United States, Prime Minister David Lloyd George (1863–1945) of Great Britain, Prime Minister/Minister of War Georges Clemenceau (1841–1929) of France, and Prime Minister Vittorio Orlando (1860–1952) of Italy.

The "Big Four" Convene

The sudden, unexpected end of the war, combined with the growing threat of communist revolution throughout Europe created an unsettling atmosphere at the conference. The "Big Four" of Wilson (U.S.), Clemenceau (France), Lloyd-George (England), and Orlando (Italy) took over the peace discussions. Initially, the Allied Powers had hoped for a negotiated settlement with the defeated powers, which necessitated hard terms that would be negotiated down. However, the delays caused by uncertainty over direction at the beginning of the conference, Wilson's insistence that the League of Nations be included in the settlement, and fear of European-wide revolution resulted in a hastily prepared, dictated peace settlement.

Woodrow Wilson and the Fourteen Points

Not handicapped by significant financial or territorial concerns, Wilson idealistically promoted his Fourteen Points—particularly the last, which called for the establishment of the League of Nations (which was created on January 10, 1920, by the Treaty of Versailles)—as the basis of the armistice and the peace settlement.

Secret Allied Agreements

Throughout the war, the Allied powers had concluded a number of secret agreements designed to encourage countries to join their side or as compensation for war efforts. In March 1915, England and France had promised Russia Constantinople, the Straits, and the bordering areas as long as they were openly accessible. In April of the following year, England and France had promised one another, respectively, spheres in Mesopotamia and Palestine, as well as Syria, Adana, Cilia, and southern Kurdistan. The Sykes-Picot Treaty in May 1916 better defined both countries' Arabian spheres. Russia was to have similar rights in Armenia, portions of Kurdistan, and northeastern Anatolia. The Allies gave Italy and Rumania significant territories to encourage them in their war effort in April 1915 and August 1916, while the English promised to support Japan's desire for Germany's Asian possessions. France and Russia agreed to promote one another's claims at a future peace conference, while Arab independence and the creation of a Jewish homeland were also promised to others.

THE TREATY OF VERSAILLES

The treaty's war guilt statements were the justification for its harsh penalties. The former German king, Wilhelm II, was accused of crimes against "international morality and the sanctity of treaties," while Germany took responsibility for itself and for its allies for all losses suffered by the Allied Powers and their supporters as a result of German and Central Power aggression.

Germany had to return Alsace and Lorraine to France and Eupen-Malmedy to Belgium. France got Germany's Saar coal mines as reparations, while the Saar Basin was to be occupied by the major powers for 15 years, after which a plebiscite would decide its ultimate fate. Poland got a number of German provinces and Danzig, now a free city, as its outlet to the sea. Additionally, Germany lost all of its colonies in Asia and Africa.

The German Army was limited to 100,000 men and officers with 12 year enlistments for the former and 25 for the latter. The General Staff was also abolished. The Navy lost its submarines and most offensive naval forces, and was limited to 15,000 men and officers with the same enlistment periods as the army. Aircraft and blimps were outlawed. A Reparations Commission was created to determine Germany's war debt to the Allies, which it figured in 1921 to be $32.4 billion, to be paid over an extended period of time. In the meantime, Germany was to begin immediate payments in goods and raw materials.

The Allies presented the treaty to the Germans on May 7, 1919, but the Germans stated that its terms were too much for the German people, and that it violated the spirit of Wilson's Fourteen Points. After some minor changes were made, the Germans were told to sign the document or face an Allied advance into Germany. The treaty was signed on June 28, 1919, at Versailles.

TREATIES WITH GERMANY'S ALLIES

The Allied treaty with Austria legitimized the breakup of the Austrian Empire in the latter days of the war and saw Austrian territory ceded to Italy and the new states of Czechoslovakia, Poland, and Yugoslavia. The agreement included military restrictions and debt payments.

PROBLEMS OF ALLIED UNITY: JAPAN, ITALY, AND THE U.S.

During and after the meetings in Paris that resulted in the Treaty of Versailles, disputes arose among the Allies that caused friction among them later.

During the treaty talks, Japan asked for Germany's Shantung Province in China, its Pacific colonies, and a statement on racial equality in the League Covenant. Japan got what it essentially wanted on the first two requests, despite protests from China on Shantung. However, Japan's request for a racial equality clause met strong opposition from the United States and some members of the British Commonwealth, who feared the impact of the statement on immigration. The proposal was denied, principally at the instigation of President Wilson.

Italy got the Tyrol, as well as Istria and some Adriatic islands in the Treaty of Rapallo (December 12, 1920). Dalmatia, however, went to Yugoslavia, while Fiume was seized by the Italian patriot/poet Gabriele D'Annunzio, on September 12, 1919. After a 14-month occupation he departed, leaving its destiny to Italy and Yugoslavia. The Treaty of Rome (January 27, 1924) divided the city between the two, with Italy getting the lion's share of the area.

Weimar Germany (1918–1929)

The dramatic collapse of the German war effort in the second half of 1918 ultimately created a political crisis that forced the abdication of the kaiser and the creation of a German Republic on November 9.

From the outset, the Provisional Government, formed of a coalition of Majority and Independent Social Democrats Socialists, was beset by divisions from within and threats of revolution throughout Germany. The first chancellor was Friedrich Ebert, the Majority Socialist leader. On November 22, state leaders agreed to support a temporary government until elections could be held for a nationally elected legislature, which would draw up a constitution for the new republic.

Elections for the new National Constituent Assembly, which was to be based on proportional representation, gave no party a clear majority. A coalition of the Majority Socialists, the Catholic Center party, and the German Democratic party (DDP) dominated the new assembly. On February 11, 1919, the assembly met in the historic town of Weimar and selected Friedrich Ebert President of Germany. Two days later, Phillip Scheidemann (1865–1939) formed the first Weimar Cabinet and became its first Chancellor.

On August 11, 1919, a new constitution was promulgated, which provided for a bicameral legislature. The upper chamber, the Reichsrat, represented the Federal states, while the lower house, the Reichstag, with 647 delegates elected by universal suffrage, supplied the country's chancellor and cabinet. A president was also to be elected separately for a seven-year term. As a result of Article 48 of the Constitution, he could rule through emergency decree, though the Reichstag could take this authority from him.

Problems of the Weimar Republic (1919–1923): The new government faced a number of serious domestic problems that severely challenged or undercut its authority. Its forced acceptance of the hated Friedensdiktat ("the dictated peace") seriously undermined its prestige, while the unsuccessful, though violent Communist Spartikist Rebellion (January 5–11, 1919) in Berlin created a climate of instability. This was followed three months later by the brief communist takeover of Bavaria, and the rightist Kapp Putsch (March 13–17, 1920) in the capital the following year.

The territorial, manpower, and economic losses suffered during and after the war, coupled with a $32.4 billion reparations debt, had a severe impact on the German economy and society, and severely handicapped the new government's efforts to establish a stable governing environment.

In an effort of good faith based on hopes of future reparation payment reductions, Germany borrowed heavily and made payments in kind to fulfill its early debt obligations. The result was a spiral of inflation later promoted by the Weimar government to underline Allied insensitivity to Germany's plight, that saw the mark go from 8.4 to the dollar in 1919 to 7,000 marks to the dollar by December 1922. After the Allied Reparations Commission declared Germany in default on its debt, the French and the Belgians occupied the Ruhr on January 11, 1923.

Chancellor Wilhelm Cuno (1876–1933) encouraged the Ruhr's Germans passively to resist the occupation, and printed worthless marks which dropped from 40,000 to the dollar in January 1923 to 4.2 trillion to the dollar eleven months later. The occupation ended on September 26, and helped prompt stronger Allied sympathy to Germany's payment difficulties, though the inflationary spiral had severe economic, social, and political consequences.

Weimar Politics (1919–1923): Germany's economic and social difficulties deeply affected its infant democracy. From February 1919 to August 1923, the country had six chancellors. In the aftermath of the Kapp Putsch, conservative demands for new elections resulted in a June defeat for the ruling coalition that saw the Democrats (DDP) lose seats to the German National People's party (DVP) headed by Gustav Stresemann (1878–1929), and the Majority Socialists lose seats to the more reactionary Independent socialists. Conservative Germans blamed the Weimar Coalition for the hated Versailles "Diktat" with its war guilt and reparations terms, while leftist voters felt the government had forgotten its social and revolutionary ideals.

Growing right-wing discontent with the Weimar Government resulted in the assassination of the gifted head of the Catholic Center Party, Matthias Erzberger (1875–1921), on August 29, 1921, and the murder of Foreign Minister Walter Rathenau (1867–1922) on June 24, 1922. These were two of the most serious of over 350 political murders in Germany since the end of the war.

Weimar Politics (1924–1928): Reichstag elections were held twice in 1924. The May 4 contest reflected a backlash against the country's economic difficulties, and saw the Communists win 3,700,000 votes and the Nazis almost 2 million, at the expense of the moderate parties. The December 7 elections were something of a vote on the Dawes Plan and economic revival, and saw the Nazis and the Communists lose almost a million votes apiece.

Following the death of President Ebert on February 28, 1925, two ballots were held for a new president, since none of the candidates won a majority on the first vote. On the second ballot on April 26, the Reichsblock, a coalition of Conservative parties, was able to get its candidate elected. War hero Paul von Hindenburg was narrowly elected. Hindenburg, who some conservatives hoped would turn the clock back, vowed to uphold Weimar's Constitution.

The elections of May 20, 1928, saw the Social Democrats get almost one-third of the popular vote which, blended with other moderate groups, created a stable, moderate majority in the Reichstag, which chose Hermann Müller (1876–1931) as chancellor. The Nazis, who held 14 Reichstag seats at the end of 1924, lost one, while Communist strength increased.

Italy

Like other countries that had fought in World War I, Italy had suffered greatly and gained little. Its economy, very weak even before the war broke out, relied heavily upon small-family agriculture, which contributed 40 percent of the country's GNP in 1920. Consequently, many of the social, political, and economic problems that plagued the country after the war could not be blamed solely on the conflict itself.

Benito Mussolini, named by his Socialist blacksmith father after the Mexican revolutionary, Benito Juarez, was born in 1883. After a brief teaching stint, he went to Switzerland to avoid military service but returned and became active in Socialist politics. In 1912, he became editor of the party's newspaper, *Avanti*. Several months after the outbreak of the World War, he broke with the party over involvement in the war, and began to espouse nationalistic ideas that became the nucleus of his fascist movement. He then opened his own newspaper, *Il Popolo d'Italia* (The People of Italy) to voice his ideas. Mussolini was drafted into military service in 1915 and was badly wounded two years later. After recuperating, he returned to his newspaper, where he blended his feelings about socialism and nationalism with an instinct for violence.

Mussolini, capitalizing on the sympathy of unfulfilled war veterans, disaffected nationalists, and those fearful of communism, formed the Fascio Italiano di Combattimento (Union of Combat) in Milan on March 23, 1919. Initially, Mussolini's movement had few followers, and it did badly in the November 1919 elections. However, Socialist strikes and unrest enabled him to convince Italians that he alone could bring stability and prosperity to their troubled country.

Fascism's most significant growth came in the midst of the Socialist unrest in 1920. Strengthened by large contributions from wealthy industrialists, Mussolini's black-suited Squadristi attacked Socialists, Communists, and ultimately, the government itself. Mussolini's followers won 35 seats in the legislative elections in May 1921, which also toppled the Giolitti cabinet.

The resignation of the Bonomi Cabinet on February 9, 1922, underlined the government's inability to maintain stability. In the meantime, the Fascists seized control of Bologna in May, and Milan in August. In response, Socialist leaders called for a nationwide strike on August 1, 1922; it was stopped by Fascist street violence within 24 hours. On October 24, 1922, Mussolini told followers that if he was not given power, he would "March on Rome." Three days later, Fascists began to seize control of other cities, while 26,000 began to move towards the capital. The government responded with a declaration of martial law, which the king, Victor Emmanuel III (1869–1947), refused to approve. On October 29, the king asked Mussolini to form a new government as Premier of Italy.

Beginning in 1925, Mussolini arrested opponents, closed newspapers, and eliminated civil liberties in a new reign of terror. On December 24, 1925, the legislature's powers were greatly limited, while those of Mussolini were increased as the new Head of State. Throughout 1926, Mussolini intensified his control over the country with legislation that outlawed strikes and created the syndicalist corporate system. A failed assassination attempt prompted the "Law for the Defense of the State" of November 25, 1926, that created a Special Court to deal with political crimes and introduced the death penalty for threats against the king, his family, or the Head of State.

The Syndicalist-Corporate System: On April 3, 1926, the Rocco Labor Law created syndicates, or organizations, for all workers and employers in Italy. It also outlawed strikes and walkouts. Later altered, it created nine syndicate corporations: four for workers and four for employers in each of the major segments of the economy and a ninth for professionals and artists.

On July 1, 1926, Corporations were created to coordinate activities between the worker-employer syndicates, while later that year a Ministry of Corporations came into existence. On February 5, 1934, a Law on Corporations created 22 such bodies that oversaw every facet of the economy, coordinated management-labor relations and economic production and shipment in every segment of the economy. Each Corporation was overseen by a Minister or other important government or party official, who sat on the National Council of Corporations that was headed by Mussolini.

The nation's wish for post-war peace and stability saw Italy participate in all of the international developments in the 1920s aimed at securing normalcy in relations with its neighbors. Because Italy did not receive its desired portions of Dalmatia at the Paris Peace Conference, Italian nationalist Gabriele D'Annunzio seized Fiume on the Adriatic in the fall of 1919. D'Annunzio's daring gesture as well as his deep sense of Italian national pride deeply affected Mussolini. However, in the atmosphere of detente prevalent in Europe at the time, he agreed to settle the dispute with Yugoslavia in a treaty on January 27, 1924, which ceded most of the port to Italy, and the surrounding area to Yugoslavia.

In the fall of 1923, Mussolini used the assassination of Italian officials, who were working to resolve a Greek-Albanian border dispute, to seize the island of Corfu. Within a month, however, the British and the French convinced him to return the island for an indemnity.

Soviet Russia

Soon after the Bolshevik seizure of power, opposition forces began to gather throughout Russia that sought to challenge Soviet authority or use the occasion to break up the Russian Empire.

The Civil War and "War Communism" had brought economic disaster and social upheaval throughout the country. On March 1, 1921, as the Soviet leadership met to decide on policies to guide the country in peace, a naval rebellion broke out at the Kronstadt naval base. The Soviet leadership sent Trotsky to put down the rebellion, which he did brutally by March 18.

Vladimir Ilyich Lenin, the founder of the Soviet State, suffered a serious stroke on May 26, 1922, and a second in December of that year. As he faced possible forced retirement or death, he composed a secret "testament" that surveyed the strengths and weaknesses of his possible successor, Stalin, who he feared would abuse power. Unfortunately, his third stroke prevented him from removing Stalin from his position as General Secretary. Lenin died on January 21, 1924.

Iosef Vissarionovich Dzugashvili (Joseph Stalin, 1879–1953) was born in the Georgian village of Gori. He became involved in Lenin's Bolshevik movement in his 20s and became Lenin's expert on minorities. Intimidated by the party's intellectuals, he took over numerous, and in some cases, seemingly unimportant party organizations after the Revolution and transformed them into important bases of power. Among them were Politburo (Political Bureau), which ran the country; the Orgburo (Organizational Bureau), which Stalin headed, and which appointed people to positions in groups that implemented Politiburo decisions, the Inspectorate (Rabkrin, Commissariat of the Workers' and Peasants' Inspectorate) which tried to eliminate party corruption, and the Secretariat, which worked with all party organs and set the Politburo's agenda. Stalin served as the party's General Secretary after 1921.

Lev Davidovich Bronstein (Trotsky, 1879–1940) was a Jewish intellectual active in Menshevik revolutionary work, particularly in the 1905 Revolution. He joined Lenin's movement in 1917, and soon became his right-hand man. He was Chairman of the Petrograd Soviet, headed the early Brest-Litovsk negotiating team, served as Foreign Commissar, and was father of the Red Army. A brilliant organizer and theorist, Trotsky was also brusque and, some felt, overbearing.

In China the Soviets helped found a young Chinese Communist party (CCP) in 1921. However, when it became apparent that Sun Yat-sen's (1866–1925) revolutionary Kuomintang (KMT) was more mature than the infant CCP, the Soviets encouraged an alliance between its party and this movement. Sun's successor, Chiang Kai-shek (1887–1975), was deeply suspicious of the Communists and made their destruction part of his effort to militarily unite China.

Founded in 1919, the Soviet-controlled Comintern (Third International or Communist International) sought to coordinate the revolutionary activities of Communist parties abroad, though it often conflicted with Soviet diplomatic interests. It became an effectively organized body by 1924, and was completely Stalinized by 1928.

EUROPE IN CRISIS: DEPRESSION AND DICTATORSHIP (1929–1935)

Required by law to hold elections in 1929, the May 30 contest in Great Britain saw the

Conservatives drop to 260 seats, Labour rise to 287, and the Liberals to 59. Ramsay MacDonald formed a minority Labour government that would last until 1931. The most serious problem facing the country was the Depression, which caused unemployment to reach 1,700,000 by 1930 and over 3 million, or 25 percent of the labor force, by 1932. To meet growing budget deficits caused by heavy subsidies to the unemployed, a special government commission recommended budget cuts and tax increases. Cabinet and labor union opposition helped reduce the total for the cuts (from 78 million to 22 million), but this could not help restore confidence in the government, which fell on August 24, 1931.

The "National Government" (1931–1935)

The following day, August 25, King George VI (1895–1952) helped persuade MacDonald to return to office as head of a National Coalition cabinet made up of four Conservatives, four Labourites, and two Liberals. The Labour party refused to recognize the new government and ejected MacDonald and Philip Snowden (1864–1937) from the party. MacDonald's coalition swept the November 1931 general elections winning 554 of 615 seats.

The British government abandoned the gold standard on September 21, 1931, and adopted a series of high tariffs on imports. Unemployment peaked at 3 million in 1932 and dropped to 2 million two years later.

In 1931, the British government implemented the Statute of Westminster, which created the British Commonwealth of Nations, granting its members political equality and freedom to reject any act passed by Parliament that related to a Dominion state.

MacDonald resigned his position in June 1935 because of ill health and was succeeded by Stanley Baldwin, whose conservative coalition won 428 seats in new elections in November.

France: Return of the Cartel des Gauches (1932–1934)

The defeat of the Moderates and the return of the leftists in the elections of May 1, 1932, reflected growing concern over the economy and the failed efforts of the government to respond to the country's problems.

France remained plagued by differences over economic reform between the Radicals and the Socialists. The latter advocated nationalization of major factories, expanded social reforms, and public works programs for the unemployed, while the Radicals sought a reduction in government spending. This instability was also reflected in the fact that there were six Cabinets between June 1932 and February 1934.

The government's inability to deal with the country's economic and political problems saw the emergence of a number of radical groups from across the political spectrum. Some of the more prominent were the Fascist Francistes, the Solidarite Française, the "Cagoulards" (Comite Secret d'Action Révolutionnaire), the Parti Populaire Française (PPF), and the Jeunesses Patriotes. Not as radical, though still on the right were the Croix de Feu and the Action Française. At the other extreme was the French Communist party.

Germany: The Depression

The Depression had a dramatic effect on the German economy and politics. German exports, which had peaked at 13.5 billion marks in 1929, fell to 12 billion marks in 1930, and to 5.7 billion marks two years later. Imports suffered the same fate, going from 14 billion marks in 1928 to 4.7 billion marks in 1932. The country's national income dropped 20 percent during this period, while unemployment rose from 1.32 million in

1929 to 6 million by January 1932. This meant that 43 percent of the German work force were without jobs (compared to one-quarter of the work force in the U.S.).

The history of nazism is deeply intertwined with that of its leader, Adolf Hitler. Adolf Hitler was born on April 20, 1889, in the Austrian village of Braunau am Inn. A frustrated artist, he moved to Vienna where he unsuccessfully tried to become a student in the Vienna Academy of Fine Arts. He then became an itinerant artist, living in hovels, until the advent of the World War, which he welcomed. He served four years and emerged a decorated corporal with a mission to enter politics.

In 1919, Hitler joined the German Workers party (DAP), which he soon took over and renamed the National Socialist German Workers party (NAZI). In 1920, the party adopted a 25–point program that included treaty revision, anti-Semitism, economic, and other social changes. They also created a defense cadre of the *Sturm-abteilung* (SA)— "Storm Troopers," or "brown shirts"—which was to help the party seize power.

The Beer Hall Putsch (1923): In the midst of the country's severe economic crisis in 1923, the party, which now had 55,000 members, tried to seize power, first by a march on Berlin, and then, when this seemed impossible, on Munich. The march was stopped by police, and Hitler and his supporters were arrested. Their trial, which Hitler used to voice Nazi ideals, gained him a national reputation. Though sentenced to five years imprisonment, he was released after eight months. While incarcerated, he dictated *Mein Kampf* to Rudolf Hess.

Hitler's failed coup and imprisonment convinced him to seek power through legitimate political channels, which would require transforming the Nazi party. To do this, he reasserted singular control over the movement from 1924 to 1926. Party districts were set up throughout Germany, overseen by *gauleiters* personally appointed by Hitler.

Hindenburg's seven-year presidential term expired in 1932, and he was convinced to run for reelection to stop Hitler from becoming president in the first ballot of March 13. Hitler got only 30 percent of the vote (11.3 million) to Hindenburg's 49.45 percent (18.6 million).

On June 1, chancellor Bruenig was replaced by Franz von Papen (1879–1969), who formed a government made up of aristocratic conservatives and others that he and Hindenburg hoped would keep Hitler from power. He held new elections on July 31 that saw the Nazis win 230 Reichstag seats with 37 percent of the vote (13.7 million), and the Communists 89 seats. Offered the Vice-Chancellorship and an opportunity to join a coalition government, Hitler refused. Von Papen, paralyzed politically, ruled by presidential decree. Von Papen dissolved the Reichstag on September 12 and held new elections on November 6. The Nazis only got 30 percent of the vote and 196 Reichstag seats, while the Communists made substantial gains (120 seats from 89). Von Papen resigned the chancellorship in favor of Kurt von Schleicher (1882–1934), one of the president's closest advisers.

Von Papen joined with Hitler to undermine Schleicher, and convinced Hindenburg to appoint Hitler as chancellor and head of a new coalition cabinet with three seats for the Nazis. Hitler dissolved the Reichstag and called for new elections on March 5. Using presidential decree powers, he initiated a violent anti-Communist campaign that included the lifting of certain press and civil freedoms. On February 27, the Reichstag burned, which enabled Hitler to get Hindenburg to issue the "Ordinances for the Protection of the German State and Nation," that removed all civil and press liberties as part of a "revolution" against communism. In the Reichstag elections of March 5, the Nazis only got 43.9 percent of the vote and 288 Reichstag seats but, through an alliance with the Nationalists, got majority control of the legislature.

Once Hitler had full legislative power, he began a policy of *Gleichschaltung* (coordination) to bring all independent organizations and agencies throughout Germany under his control. All political parties were outlawed or forced to dissolve, and on July 14, 1933, the Nazi party became the only legal party in Germany. In addition, German state authority was reduced and placed under Nazi-appointed *Statthallter* (governors), while the party throughout Germany was divided into *Gaue* (districts) under a Nazi-selected *Gauleiter*. In addition, non-Aryans and Nazi opponents were removed from the civil service, the court system, and higher education. On May 2, 1933, the government declared strikes illegal, abolished labor unions, and later forced all workers to join the German Labor Front (DAF) under Robert Ley. In 1934 the Reichsrat was abolished and a special People's Court was created to handle cases of treason. Finally, the secret police or Gestapo (*Geheime Staatspolizei*) was created on April 24, 1933, under Hermann Göring to deal with opponents and operate concentration camps. The party had its own security branch, the SD (*Sicherheitsdienst*) under Reinhard Heydrich.

From the inception of the Nazi state in 1933, anti-Semitism was a constant theme and practice in all *Gleichschaltung* and nazification efforts. Illegal intimidation and harassment of Jews was coupled with rigid enforcement of civil service regulations that forbade employment of non-Aryans. This first wave of anti-Semitic activity culminated with the passage of the Nuremburg Laws on September 15, 1935, that deprived Jews of German citizenship and outlawed sexual or marital relations between Jews and other Germans, thus effectively isolating them from the mainstream of German society.

Hitler's international policies were closely linked to his rebuilding efforts to give him a strong economic and military base for an active, aggressive, independent foreign policy. On October 14, 1933, Hitler had his delegates walk out of the Disarmament Conference because he felt the Allied powers had reneged on an earlier promise to grant Germany arms equality. The Reich simultaneously quit the League of Nations. On January 26, 1934, Germany signed a non-aggression pact with Poland, which ended Germany's traditional anti-Polish foreign policy and broke France's encirclement of Germany via the Little Entente. This was followed by the Saarland's overwhelming decision to return to Germany. The culmination of Hitler's foreign policy moves, though, came with his March 15, 1935, announcement that Germany would no longer be bound by the military restrictions of the Treaty of Versailles, that it had already created an air force (Luftwaffe), and that the Reich would institute a draft to create an army of 500,000 men. Allied opposition to this move was compromised by England's decision to conclude a naval pact with Hitler on June 18, 1935, that restricted German naval tonnage (excluding submarines) to 35 percent of that for England.

Italy

Until Mussolini's accession to power, the pope had considered himself a prisoner in the Vatican. In 1926, Mussolini's government began talks to resolve this issue, which resulted in the Lateran Accords of February 11, 1929. Italy recognized the Vatican as an independent state, with the pope as its head, while the papacy recognized Italian independence. Catholicism was made the official state religion of Italy, and religious teaching was required in all secondary schools. Church marriages were now fully legal, while the state could veto papal appointments of bishops. In addition, the clergy would declare loyalty to the Italian state. Additionally, the government agreed to pay the Church a financial settlement of 1.75 billion lira for the seizure of Church territory in 1860–1870.

A conflict soon broke out over youth education and in May 1931 Mussolini dissolved the Catholic Action's youth groups. The pope responded with an encyclical, *Non abbianio bisogno*, which defended these groups, and criticized the Fascist deification of the state. Mussolini agreed later that year to allow Catholic Action to resume limited youth work.

Since the late 1920s, Mussolini began to support German claims for revision of the Treaty of Versailles to strengthen ties with that country and to counterbalance France, a nation he strongly disliked. These goals were current in his Four Power Pact proposal of March 1933 that envisioned a concert of powers—England, France, Italy, and Germany—that included arms parity for the Reich. French opposition to arms equality and treaty revision, plus concerns that the new consortium would replace the League of Nations, saw an extremely weakened agreement signed in June that was ultimately accepted only by Italy and Germany.

In an effort to counter the significance of France's Little Entente with Czechoslovakia, Yugoslavia, and Rumania, Mussolini concluded the Rome Protocols with Austria and Hungary which created a protective bond of friendship between the three countries. The first test of the new alliance between Italy and Austria came in July 1934, when German-directed Nazis tried to seize control of the Austrian government. Mussolini, opposed to any German *Anschluss* with Austria, mobilized Italian forces along the northern Renner Pass as a warning to Hitler. The coup collapsed from lack of direct German aid.

In response to Hitler's announcement of German rearmament in violation of the Treaty of Versailles on March 16, 1935, France, England, and Italy met at Stresa in northern Italy on April 11–14, and concluded agreements that pledged joint military collaboration if Germany moved against Austria or along the Rhine. The three states criticized Germany's recent decision to remilitarize and appealed to the Council of the League of Nations on the matter.

Ethiopia (Abyssinia) became an area of strong Italian interest in the 1880s. The coastal region was slowly brought under Italian control until the Italian defeat at Ethiopian hands at Adowa in 1894. In 1906, the country's autonomy was recognized and in 1923 it joined the League of Nations. Mussolini, driven by a strong patriotic desire to avenge the humiliation at Adowa and to create an empire to thwart domestic concerns over the country's economic problems, searched for the proper moment to seize the country. Acquisition of Ethiopia would enable him to join Italy's two colonies of Eritrea and Somalia, which could become a new area of Italian colonization.

Mussolini, who had been preparing for war with Ethiopia since 1932, established a military base at Wal Wal in Ethiopian territory. Beginning in December 1934, a series of minor conflicts took place between the two countries, which gave Mussolini an excuse to plan for the full takeover of the country in the near future.

Mussolini refused to accept arbitration over Ethiopia and used Europe's growing concern over Hitler's moves there to cover his own secret designs. On October 2, 1935, Italy invaded Ethiopia, while the League of Nations, which had received four appeals from Ethiopia since January about Italian territorial transgressions, finally voted to adopt economic sanctions against Mussolini. Mussolini was convinced he could act with impunity when he realized the League was reluctant to do more than make verbal objections to Italian actions. Unfortunately, the League failed to stop shipments of oil to Italy and continued to allow it to use the Suez Canal. On May 9, 1936, Italy formally annexed the country and joined it to Somalia and Eritrea, which now became known as Italian East Africa.

Soviet Russia

The period from 1929 to 1935 was a time of tremendous upheaval for the U.S.S.R.

as Stalin tried to initiate major programs of collectivization of agriculture and massive industrial development.

The Second Five Year Plan (1933–1937) was adopted by the Seventeenth Party Congress in early 1934. Its economic and production targets were less severe than the First Plan, and thus more was achieved. By the end of the Second Plan, Soviet Russia had emerged as a leading world industrial power, though at great costs. It gave up quality for quantity, and created tremendous social and economic discord. The tactics used by Stalin to institute his economic reforms formed the nucleus of his totalitarian system, while reaction to them within the party led to the Purges.

In the spring of 1935, the recently renamed and organized secret police, the NKVD, oversaw the beginnings of a new, violent Purge that eradicated 70 percent of the 1934 Central Committee, and a large percentage of the upper military ranks. Stalin sent between 8 and 9 million to camps and prisons, and caused untold deaths before the Purges ended in 1938.

The period from 1929 to 1933 saw the U.S.S.R. retreat inward as the bulk of its energies were put into domestic economic growth. Regardless, Stalin remained sensitive to growing aggression and ideological threats abroad such as the Japanese invasion of Manchuria in 1931 and Hitler's appointment as Chancellor in 1933. As a result, Russia left its cocoon in 1934, joined the League of Nations, and became an advocate of "collective security" while the Comintern adopted Popular Front tactics, allying with other parties against fascism, to strengthen the U.S.S.R.'s international posture. Diplomatically, in addition to League membership, the Soviet Union completed a military pact with France.

INTERNATIONAL DEVELOPMENTS (1918–1935)

Efforts to create an international body to arbitrate international conflicts gained credence with the creation of a Permanent Court of International Justice to handle such matters at the First Hague Conference (1899). But no major efforts towards this goal were initiated until 1915, when pro-League of Nations organizations arose in the United States and Great Britain. Support for such a body grew as the war lengthened, and creation of such an organization became the cornerstone of President Woodrow Wilson's post-war policy, enunciated in his "Fourteen Points" speech before Congress on January 8, 1918.

The Preamble of the League's Covenant defined the League's purposes, which were to work for international friendship, peace, and security. To attain this, its members agreed to avoid war, maintain peaceful relations with other countries, and honor international law and accords.

Headquartered in Geneva, the League came into existence as the result of an Allied resolution on January 25, 1919, and the signing of the Treaty of Versailles on June 28, 1919. The League's Council originally consisted of five permanent members (France, Italy, England, Japan, and the U.S.), though the U.S. seat was left vacant because the U.S. Senate refused to ratify the Treaty of Versailles. Germany filled the vacancy in 1926. It also had four one-year rotating seats (increased to six in 1922, and raised to nine seats in 1926). The Council, with each member having one vote, could discuss any matter that threatened international stability, and could recommend action to member states. It also had the right, according to Article 8 of the League Covenant, to seek ways to reduce arms strength, while Articles 10 through 17 gave it the authority to search for means to stop war. It could recommend through a unanimous vote ways to stop aggression, and could suggest economic sanctions and other tactics to enforce its decisions, though its military ability to enforce its decisions was vague. It met four times a year from 1923 to 1929, and then three times annually afterwards.

The League's legislative body had similar debating and discussion authority, though it had no legislative powers. It initially had 43 members, which rose to 49 by the mid-1930s, though six others, including Italy, Germany, and Japan, withdrew their membership during the same period. The U.S.S.R., which joined in 1934, was expelled six years later.

The Locarno Pact (1925)

Failure of the European powers to create some type of international system to prevent aggression was followed by regional efforts prompted by Germany's visionary Foreign Minister, Gustav Stresemann, who in early 1925 approached England and France about an accord whereby Germany would accept its western borders in return for early Allied withdrawal from the demilitarized Rhine area. Stresemann also wanted League membership for his country. While England responded with guarded regional interest, France hesitated. Six months after consultation with its eastern allies, Paris countered with a proposal that would include similar provisions for Germany's eastern borders, secured by a mutual assistance pact between Italy, Great Britain, and France. These countries, along with Belgium, Czechoslovakia, and Poland, met for two months in Locarno, Switzerland, and concluded a number of separate agreements. The sum and substance of these agreements was to promote peace in Europe by having all nations respect existing borders.

Treaty of Mutual Guarantees (Rhineland Pact)

Signed on October 16, 1925, by England, France, Italy, Germany, and Belgium, they guaranteed Germany's western boundaries and accepted the Versailles settlement's demilitarized zones. Italy and Great Britain agreed militarily to defend these lines if flagrantly violated.

In the same spirit, Germany signed arbitration dispute accords that mirrored the Geneva Protocol with France, Belgium, Poland, and Czechoslovakia, and required acceptance of League-determined settlements.

Since Germany would only agree to arbitration and not finalize its eastern border, France separately signed guarantees with Poland and Czechoslovakia to defend their frontiers.

The Locarno Pact went into force when Germany joined the League on September 10, 1926, acquiring, after some dispute, the U.S.'s permanent seat on the Council. France and Belgium began to withdraw from the Rhineland, though they left a token force there until 1930.

The Pact of Paris (The Kellogg-Briand Pact)

The Locarno Pact heralded a new period in European relations known as the "Era of Locarno" that marked the end of post-war conflict and the beginning of a more normal period of diplomatic friendship and cooperation. It reached its peak, idealistically, with the Franco-American effort in 1928 to seek an international statement to outlaw war. In December 1927, Frank Kellogg, the American Secretary of State, proposed that this policy be offered to all nations in the form of a treaty. On August 27, 1928, 15 countries, including the U.S., Germany, France, Italy, and Japan, signed this accord with some minor limitations, which renounced war as a means of solving differences and as a tool of national policy. Within five years, 50 other countries signed the agreement. Unfortunately, without something more than idealism to back it up, the Kellogg-Briand Pact had little practical meaning.

The Waning Search for Disarmament

In March 1930, Great Britain and the United States sought to expand the naval limitation terms of the Five Power Treaty of 1922. France and Italy could not agree on terms, while the U.S., England, and Japan accepted mild reductions in cruiser and destroyer strength.

Attended by 60 countries, the World Disarmament Conference opened in 1932. Germany withdrew in 1933 after Hitler took power, and the conference closed in failure in 1934.

League and Allied Response to Aggression

By 1931, international attention increasingly turned to growing acts or threats of aggression in Europe and Asia, and transformed Europe from a world that hoped for eternal peace to a continent searching desperately for ways to contain growing aggression.

On September 19, 1931, the Japanese Kwantung Army, acting independently of the government in Tokyo, began the gradual conquest of Manchuria after fabricating an incident at Mukden to justify their actions. Ultimately, they created a puppet state, Manchukuo, under the last Chinese emperor, Henry P'u-i. China's League protest resulted in the creation of an investigatory commission under the Earl of Lytton that criticized Japan's actions and recommended a negotiated settlement that would have allowed Japan to retain most of its conquest. Japan responded by resigning from the League on January 24, 1933.

Hitler's announcement on March 15, 1935, of Germany's decisions to rearm and to introduce conscription in violation of the Treaty of Versailles prompted the leaders of England, France, and Italy to meet in Stresa, Italy (April 11–14). They condemned Germany's actions, underlined their commitment to the Locarno Pact, and reaffirmed the support they collectively gave for Austria's independence in early 1934. The League Council also rebuked Germany and created an investigatory committee to search for economic means to punish the Reich. Great Britain's decision, however, to separately protect its naval strength vis-à-vis a German buildup in the Anglo-German Naval Treaty of June 18, 1935, effectively compromised the significance of the Stresa Front.

7. FROM WORLD WAR II TO THE DEMISE OF COMMUNISM (1935–1996)

CULTURE IN THE LATE 1930s: ENGAGEMENT

The twentieth century generally has been one in which there has been a feeling of fragmentation and uncertainty in European thought and the arts. Much of this was due to the discoveries of Freud and Einstein: one emphasizing that much of human behavior is irrational and the other undermining in his theories of relativity the long-held certainties of Newtonian science.

Existentialism is the philosophy that best exemplified European feelings in the era of the World Wars. Three nineteenth-century figures greatly influenced this movement: Kierkegaard, Dostoyevski, and Nietzsche. Martin Heidegger (1889–1976) (though he rejected the term), Karl Jaspers (1883–1969), Jean-Paul Sartre (1905–1980), and Simone de Beauvoir (1908–1986) are four noted figures in twentieth-century existentialism, which sought to come to grip with life's central experiences and the traumas of war, death, and evil.

INTERNATIONAL RELATIONS: THE ROAD TO WAR

Germany, Italy, Japan, and the U.S.S.R. were not satisfied with the peace settlement of 1919. They used force to achieve change, from the Japanese invasion of Manchuria in 1931 to the outbreak of war in 1939 over Poland. Hitler, bit by bit, dismantled the Versailles Treaty in Central and Eastern Europe.

The U.S.S.R. was a revisionist power profoundly distrustful of Germany, Italy, and Japan. It pursued a policy of collective security through the League of Nations (which they joined in 1934). Only after evidence of Anglo-French weakness did Stalin in 1939 enter an agreement with Hitler. This event, like the Great Purges, only heightened suspicion of Soviet motives and was later to become the subject of debate and recrimination in the Cold War that followed World War II.

Finally, Neville Chamberlain's policy of appeasement was not based on any liking for Hitler, whom he considered "half-crazed," but on a genuine desire to remove causes of discontent inherent in the Versailles settlement and thus create conditions where peace could be maintained. His error lay in his belief that Hitler was open to reason, preferred peace to war, and would respect agreements.

Britain and France, as well as other democratic states, were influenced in their policy by a profound pacifism based on their experience with the loss of life and devastation in World War I and by a dislike of the Stalinist regime in Russia.

THE COURSE OF EVENTS

Using a Franco-Soviet agreement of the preceding year as an excuse, Hitler, on March 7, 1936, repudiated the Locarno agreements and reoccupied the Rhineland (an area demilitarized by the Versailles Treaty). Neither France (which possessed military superiority at the time) nor Britain was willing to oppose these moves.

The Spanish Civil War (1936–1939) is usually seen as a rehearsal for World War II because of outside intervention. The government of the Spanish Republic (established in 1931) caused resentment among conservatives by its programs, including land reform and anti-clerical legislation aimed at the Catholic church. Labor discontent led to disturbances in industrial Barcelona and the surrounding province of Catalonia. Following an election victory by a popular front of republican and radical parties, right-wing generals in July began a military insurrection. Francisco Franco, stationed at the time in Spanish Morocco, emerged as the leader of this revolt, which became a devastating civil war lasting nearly three years.

The democracies, including the United States, followed a course of neutrality. Nazi Germany, Italy, and the U.S.S.R. did intervene despite non-intervention agreements negotiated by Britain and France. German air force units were sent to aid the fascist forces of Franco and participated in bombardments of Madrid, Barcelona, and Guernica (the latter incident being the inspiration for Picasso's famous painting which became an anti-fascist symbol known far beyond the world of art). Italy sent troops, tanks, and other material. The U.S.S.R. sent advisers and recruited soldiers from among anti-fascists in the United States and other countries to fight in the international brigades with the republican forces. Spain became a battlefield for fascist and anti-fascist forces with

Franco winning by 1939 in what was seen as a serious defeat for anti-fascist forces everywhere.

The Spanish Civil War was a factor in bringing together Mussolini and Hitler in a Rome-Berlin Axis. Already Germany and Japan had signed the Anti-Comintern Pact in 1936. Ostensibly directed against international communism, this was the basis for a diplomatic alliance between those countries, and Italy soon adhered to this agreement, becoming Germany's ally in World War II.

In 1937 there was Nazi-inspired agitation in the Baltic port of Danzig, a city basically German in its population, but which had been made a free city under the terms of the Versailles Treaty.

In 1938 Hitler pressured the Austrian chancellor to make concessions and when this did not work, German troops annexed Austria (the *Anschluss*). Again Britain and France took no effective action, and about six million Austrians were added to Germany.

Hitler turned next to Czechoslovakia. Three million persons of German origin lived in the Sudetenland, a borderland between Germany and Czechoslovakia given to Czechoslovakia in order to provide it with a more defensible boundary. These ethnic Germans (and other minorities of Poles, Ruthenians, and Hungarians) agitated against the democratic government (the only one in Eastern Europe in 1938) despite its enlightened minority policy. Hitler used the Sudeten Nazi party to deliberately provoke a crisis by making demands for a degree of independence unacceptable to the Czech authorities. He then claimed to interfere as the protector of a persecuted minority. In May 1938, rumors of invasion led to warnings from Britain and France followed by assurances from Hitler. Nevertheless, in the fall, the crisis came to a head with renewed demands from Hitler. Chamberlain twice flew to Germany in person to get German terms. The second time, Hitler's increased demands led to mobilization and other measures towards war. At the last minute a four-power conference was held in Munich with Hitler, Mussolini, Chamberlain, and Daladier in attendance. At Munich, Hitler's terms were accepted in the Munich Agreement. Neither Czechoslovakia nor the U.S.S.R. was in attendance. Britain and France, despite the French alliance with Czechoslovakia, put pressure on the Czech government to force it to comply with German demands. Hitler signed a treaty agreeing to this settlement as the limit of his ambitions. At the same time the Poles seized control of Teschen, and Hungary (with the support of Italy and Germany and over the protests of the British and French) seized 7,500 square miles of Slovakia. By the concessions forced on her at Munich, Czechoslovakia lost its frontier defenses and was totally unprotected against any further German encroachments.

In March 1939, Hitler annexed most of the rump Czech state while Hungary conquered Ruthenia. At almost the same time Germany annexed Memel from Lithuania. In April, Mussolini, taking advantage of distractions created by Germany, landed an army in Albania and seized that Balkan state in a campaign lasting about one week.

Disillusioned by these continued aggressions, Britain and France made military preparations. Guarantees were given to Poland, Rumania, and Greece. The two democracies also opened negotiations with the U.S.S.R. for an arrangement to obtain that country's aid against further German aggression. Hitler, with Poland next on his timetable, also began a cautious rapprochement with the U.S.S.R. Probably Russian suspicion that the Western powers wanted the U.S.S.R. to bear the brunt of any German attack led Stalin to respond to Hitler's overtures. Negotiations which began very quietly in the spring of 1939 were continued with increasing urgency as summer approached and with it, the time of Hitler's planned attack on Poland. On August 23, 1939, the world was stunned by the announcement of a Nazi-Soviet Treaty of friendship. A secret protocol provided that in the event of a "territorial rearrangement" in Eastern Europe the two powers would divide Poland. In addition, Russia would have the Baltic states (Latvia, Lithuania, and Estonia) and Bessarabia (lost to Rumania in 1918) as part of her sphere. Stalin agreed to remain neutral in any German war with Britain or France. World War II began with the German invasion of Poland on September 1, 1939, followed by British and French declarations of war against Germany on September 3.

WORLD WAR II BEGINS

The German attack (known as the "blitzkrieg" or "lightning war") overwhelmed the poorly equipped Polish army, which could not resist German tanks and airplanes. The outcome was clear after the first few days of fighting, and organized resistance ceased within a month.

In accordance with the secret provisions of the Nazi-Soviet Treaty of August 1939, Russia and Germany shared the Polish spoils. On September 17 the Russian armies attacked the Poles from the east. They met the Germans two days later. Stalin's share of Poland extended approximately to the Curzon Line. Russia also made demands on Finland. Later, in June 1940, while Germany was attacking France, Stalin occupied the Baltic states of Latvia, Lithuania, and Estonia.

Nazi Germany formally annexed the port of Danzig and the Polish Corridor and some territory along the western Polish border. Central Poland was turned into a German protectorate called the Government-General.

Following the successful completion of the Polish campaign, the war settled into a period of inaction on the part of both the Germans and the British and French known as the "phony war" or "sitzkrieg." The British and French prepared for a German attack on France and Belgium.

The only military action of any consequence during the winter of 1939–1940 resulted from Russian demands made on Finland, especially for territory adjacent to Leningrad (then only 20 miles from the border). Finnish refusal led to a Russian attack in November 1939. The Finns resisted with considerable vigor, receiving some supplies from Sweden, Britain, and France, but eventually by March they had to give in to the superior Russian forces. Finland was forced to cede the Karelian Isthmus, Viipuri, and a naval base at Hangoe. Britain and France prepared forces to aid the Finns, but by the time they were ready to act the Finns had been defeated.

On May 10, the main German offensive was launched against France. Belgium and the Netherlands were simultaneously attacked. According to plan, British and French forces advanced to aid the Belgians. At this point the Germans departed from their World War I strategy by launching a surprise armored attack through Luxembourg and the Ardennes Forest (considered by the British and French to be impassable for tanks). As these forces moved towards the Channel coast, they divided the Allied armies leaving the Belgians, the British Expeditionary Force, and some French forces virtually encircled. The Dutch could offer no real resistance and collapsed in four days after the May 13 German bombing of Rotterdam.

Hitler concentrated on occupying Paris. This provided just enough time for the British to affect an emergency evacuation of some 230,000 of their own men as well as about 120,000 French from the port of Dunkirk and the adjacent coast.

Paris fell to the Germans in mid-June. In this crisis Paul Reynaud (1878–1966) succeeded Edouard Daladier as premier but was unable to deal with the defeatism of some of his cabinet. On June 16 Reynaud resigned in favor of a government headed by aged Marshal Pétain, one of the heroes of World War I. The Pétain government quickly made peace with Hitler, who added to French humiliation by dictating the terms of the armistice to the French at Compiégne in the same railroad car used by Marshal Foch when he gave terms to the Germans at the end of the First World War. The complete collapse of France quickly came as a tremendous shock to the British and Americans.

Mussolini declared war on both France and Britain on June 10. He gained little by this action, and Hitler largely ignored the Italian dictator in making peace with France. Hitler's forces remained in occupation of the northern part of France, including Paris. He allowed the French to keep their fleet and overseas territories probably in the hope of making them reliable allies. Pétain and his chief minister Pierre Laval established their capital at Vichy and followed a policy of collaboration with their former enemies. A few Frenchmen, however, joined the Free French movement started in London by the then relatively unknown General Charles de Gaulle (1890–1970).

FROM THE FRENCH DEFEAT TO THE INVASION OF RUSSIA

By midsummer 1940, Germany, together with its Italian ally, dominated most of Western and Central Europe. Germany began with no real plans for a long war, but continued resistance by the British made necessary the belated mobilization of German resources. Hitler's policy included exploiting areas Germany conquered. Collaborators were used to establish governments subservient to German policy. These received the name "Quislings" after the Norwegian traitor Vidkun Quisling (1887–1945), who was made premier of Norway during the German occupation. Germany began the policy of forcibly transporting large numbers of conquered Europeans to work in German war industries. Jews especially were forced into slave labor for the German war effort, and increasingly large numbers were rounded up and sent to concentration camps, where they were systematically murdered as the Nazis carried out Hitler's "final solution" of genocide against European Jewry. Although much was known about this during the war, the full horror of these atrocities was not revealed until Allied troops entered Germany in 1945.

"Operation Sea Lion"

With the fall of France, Britain remained the only power of consequence at war with the Axis. Hitler began preparations for invading Britain ("Operation Sea Lion"). Air control over the Channel was vital if an invasion force was to be transported safely to the English Coast. The German Air Force (Luftwaffe) under Herman Göring began its air offensive against the British in the summer of 1940. The British, however, had used the year between Munich and the outbreak of war to good advantage, increasing their production of aircraft to 600 per month, almost equal to German production. Their Spitfire and Hurricane fighters proved superior. The British had also developed the first radar just in time to be used to give early warning of German attacks. British intelligence was also effective in deciphering German military communications and in providing ways to interfere with the navigational devices used by the German bombers. The Germans concentrated first on British air defenses, then on ports and shipping, and finally, in early September, they began an attack on London. The Battle of Britain was eventually a defeat for the Germans, who were unable to gain decisive superiority over the British, although they inflicted great damage on both British air defenses and major cities such as London. Despite the damage and loss of life, British morale remained high and necessary war production continued. German losses determined that bombing alone could not defeat

Britain. "Operation Sea Lion" was postponed October 12 and never seriously taken up again, although the British did not know this and had to continue for some time to give priority to their coastal and air defenses.

During the winter of 1940–1941, having given up "Operation Sea Lion," Hitler began to shift his forces to the east for an invasion of Russia ("Operation Barbarossa"). The alliance of August 1939 was never harmonious, and German fears were aroused by Russia's annexation of the three Baltic states in June 1940, by the attack on Finland, and by Russian seizure of the province of Bessarabia from Rumania. Russian expansion towards the Balkans dismayed the Germans, who hoped for more influence there themselves. In addition, on October 28, 1940, Mussolini began an ill-advised invasion of Greece from Italian bases in Albania. Within a few weeks, the Greeks repulsed the Italians and drove them back into Albania.

The German invasion of Russia began June 22, 1941. The invasion force of three million included Finnish, Rumanian, Hungarian, and Italian contingents along with the Germans and advanced on a broad front of about 2,000 miles. In this first season of fighting, the Germans seized White Russia and most of the Ukraine, advancing to the Crimean Peninsula in the south. They surrounded the city of Leningrad (although they never managed to actually capture it) and came within about 25 miles of Moscow. In November the enemy actually entered the suburbs, but then the long supply lines, early winter, and Russian resistance (strong despite heavy losses) brought the invasion to a halt. During the winter a Russian counterattack pushed the Germans back from Moscow and saved the capital.

Sino-Japanese War

With the coming of the Great Depression and severe economic difficulties, Japanese militarists gained more and more influence over the civilian government. On September 18, 1931, the Japanese occupied all of Manchuria. On July 7, 1937, a full-scale Sino-Japanese war began with a clash between Japanese and Chinese at the Marco Polo Bridge in Peking (now Beijing). An indication of ultimate Japanese aims came on November 3, 1938, when Prince Fumimaro Konoye's (1891–1946) government issued a statement on "A New Order in East Asia." This statement envisaged the integration of Japan, Manchuria (now the puppet state of Manchukuo), and China into one "Greater East Asia Co-Prosperity Sphere" under Japanese leadership. In July 1940, the Konoye government was re-formed with General Hideki Tojo (1884–1948) (Japan's principal leader in World War I) as minister of war. Japan's policy of friendship with Nazi Germany and Fascist Italy was consolidated with the signing of a formal alliance in September 1940. The war in Europe gave Japan further opportunities for expansion. Concessions were obtained from the Vichy government in French Indochina and Japanese bases were established there.

All of these events led to worsening relations between Japan and the two states in a position to oppose her expansion—the Soviet Union and the United States. Despite border clashes with the Russians, Japan avoided any conflict with that state, and Stalin wanted no war with Japan after he became fully occupied with the German invasion. In the few weeks after attacking the U.S. at Pearl Harbor, Japanese forces were able to occupy strategically important islands (including the Philippines and Dutch East Indies) and territory on the Asian mainland (Malaya, with the British naval base at Singapore, and all of Burma to the border of India).

The U.S. Enters the War

The Japanese attack brought the United States not only into war in the Pacific, but resulted in German and Italian declarations of war which meant the total involvement of the United States in World War II.

U.S. strategists decided—with British concurrence—that priority should be given to the war in Europe (a "Germany first" policy), because the danger to both Britain and the U.S.S.R. seemed more immediate than the threat from Japan. As it turned out, the United States mobilized such great resources that sufficient forces were available to go over to the offensive in the Pacific, while at the same time meeting European theater requirements.

American involvement in the war was ultimately decisive, for it meant that the greatest industrial power of that time was now arrayed against the Axis powers. American aid was crucial to the immense effort of the Soviet Union. Lend-Lease aid was extended to Russia. By 1943 supplies and equipment were reaching Russia in considerable quantities.

The German forces launched a second offensive in the summer of 1942. This attack concentrated on the southern part of the front, aiming at the Caucasus and vital oil fields around the Caspian Sea. At Stalingrad on the Volga River the Germans were stopped. There were weeks of bitter fighting in the streets of the city itself. With the onset of winter, Hitler refused to allow the strategic retreat urged by his generals. As a result, the Russian forces crossed the river north and south of the city and surrounded 22 German divisions. On January 31, 1943, following the failure of relief efforts, the German commander Friedrich Paulus (1890–1957) surrendered the remnants of his army. From then on the Russians were almost always on the offensive.

After entering the war in 1940, the Italians invaded British-held Egypt. In December 1940, the British General Archibald Wavell (1883–1950) launched a surprise attack. The Italian forces were driven back about 500 miles and 130,000 were captured. Then Hitler intervened, sending General Erwin Rommel with a small German force (the Afrika Korps) to reinforce the Italians. Rommel took command and launched a counter-offensive which put his forces on the border of Egypt. By mid-1942 Rommel had driven to El Alamein, only 70 miles from Alexandria.

A change in the British high command now placed General Harold Alexander (1891–1969) in charge of Middle Eastern forces, with General Bernard Montgomery (1887–1976) in immediate command of the British Eighth Army. Montgomery attacked at El Alamein, breaking Rommel's lines and starting a British advance which was not stopped until the armies reached the border of Tunisia.

Meanwhile, the British and American leaders decided that they could launch a second offensive in North Africa ("Operation Torch") which would clear the enemy from the entire coast and make the Mediterranean once again safe for Allied shipping. To avoid fighting the French forces which garrisoned the main landing areas (at Casablanca, Oran, and Algiers), the Allied command under the American General Dwight Eisenhower (1890–1969) made an agreement with the French commander Admiral Jean Darlan (1881–1942).

The landings resulted in little conflict with the French, and the French forces soon joined the war against the Axis. It was only a matter of time before German troops were forced into northern Tunisia and surrendered. American forces, unused to combat, suffered some reverses at the Battle of the Kasserine Pass, but gained valuable experience. The final victory came in May 1943, about the same time as the Russian victory at Stalingrad.

Relatively safe shipping routes across the North Atlantic to Britain were essential to the survival of Britain and absolutely necessary if a force was to be assembled to invade France and strike at Germany proper. New types of aircraft, small aircraft carriers, more numerous and better-equipped escort vessels, new radar and sonar (for underwater detection), extremely efficient radio direction finding, decipherment of German signals plus the building of more ships turned the balance against the Germans despite their development of improved submarines by early 1943, and the Atlantic became increasingly dangerous for German submarines.

A Turning Point

Success in these three campaigns—Stalingrad, North Africa, and the Battle of the Atlantic—gave new hope to the Allied cause and set the stage for Allied victory. With the stage set with the beginning of an offensive in late 1942 in the Solomon Islands against the Japanese, 1943 became the turning point of the war.

At their conference at Casablanca in January 1943, Roosevelt and Churchill developed a detailed strategy for the further conduct of the war. Sicily was to be invaded, then Italy proper. Historians differ as to the significance of the Casablanca decisions. The Italian campaign did knock Italy out of the war and cause Hitler to send forces to Italy that might otherwise have opposed the 1944 landing in Normandy, and it did bring about the downfall of Mussolini and Italian surrender. It also ensured, by using up limited resources such as landing craft, that no second front in France could be opened in 1943—a fact most unpalatable to Stalin, whose Russian armies were fighting desperately against the bulk of the German army and air force. But the drawing off of forces from Italy to ensure a successful landing in France made it extremely difficult to achieve decisive victory in Italy and meant a long and costly campaign against skillful and stubborn resistance by the Germans under Marshal Albert Kesselring (1885–1960). Rome was not captured by the Allied forces until June 4, 1944. With a new Italian government now supporting the Allied cause, Italian resistance movements in northern Italy became a major force in helping to liberate that area from the Germans.

At the Teheran Conference, held in November 1943 and attended by all three major Allied leaders, the final decision reached by Roosevelt and Churchill some six months earlier to invade France in May 1944 was communicated to the Russians. Stalin promised to open a simultaneous Russian offensive.

The Normandy invasion (Operation "Overlord") was the largest amphibious operation in history. Plans included an air offensive with a force of 10,000 aircraft of all types, a large naval contingent and pre-invasion naval bombardment of the very strong German defenses, a transport force of some 4,000 ships, artificial harbors to receive supplies after the initial landings, and several divisions of airborne troops to be landed behind enemy coastal defenses the night preceding the sea-borne invasion. The landings actually took place beginning June 6, 1944. The first day, 130,000 men were successfully landed. Strong German resistance hemmed in the Allied forces for about a month. Then the Allies, now numbering about 1,000,000, managed a spectacular breakthrough. By the end of 1944, all of France had been seized. A second invasion force landed on the Mediterranean coast in August, freed southern France, and linked up with Eisenhower's forces. By the end of 1944, the Allied armies stood on the borders of Germany ready to invade from both east and west.

Russian successes brought their forces to the border of Poland by July 1944. Russian relations with the Polish government in exile in London, however, had by that time been broken off after the Poles had voiced their suspicions that the Russians and not the

Germans might have caused the mass executions of a large number of Polish officers in the Katyn Forest early in the war.

Stalin's armies crossed into Poland July 23, 1944, and three days later the Russian dictator officially recognized a group of Polish Communists (the so-called Lublin Committee) as the government of Poland. As the Russian armies drew near the eastern suburbs of Warsaw, the London Poles, a resistance group, launched an attack. Stalin's forces waited outside the city while the Germans brought in reinforcements and slowly wiped out the Polish underground army in several weeks of heavy street fighting. The offensive then resumed and the city was liberated by the Red Army, but the influence of the London Poles was now virtually nil. Needless to say, this incident aroused considerable suspicion concerning Stalin's motives and led both Churchill and Roosevelt to begin to think through the political implications of their alliance with Stalin.

By late summer of 1944, the German position in the Balkans began to collapse. The Red Army crossed the border into Rumania, leading King Michael (1921–) to seize the opportunity to take his country out of its alliance with Germany and to open the way to the advancing Russians. German troops were forced to make a hasty retreat. At this point Bulgaria changed sides. The German forces in Greece withdrew in October.

Churchill Visits Moscow

From October 9–18, Winston Churchill visited Moscow to try to work out a political arrangement regarding the Balkans and Eastern Europe. (Roosevelt was busy with his campaign for election to a fourth term.) In Moscow, Churchill worked out the famous agreement that he describes in his book on World War II. Dealing from a position of weakness, he simply wrote out some figures on a sheet of paper: Russia to have the preponderance of influence in countries like Bulgaria and Rumania, Britain to have the major say in Greece, and a fifty-fifty division in Yugoslavia and Hungary. Stalin agreed. The Americans refused to have anything to do with this "spheres of influence" arrangement.

In Greece, Stalin maintained a hands-off policy when the British used military force to suppress the Communist resistance movement and install a regent for the exiled government.

In early spring of 1945 the Allied armies crossed the Rhine. As the Americans and British and other Allied forces advanced into Germany, the Russians attacked from the east. While the Russian armies were fighting their way into Berlin, Hitler committed suicide in the ruins of the bunker where he had spent the last days of the war. Power was handed over to a government headed by Admiral Karl Dönitz (1891–1980). On May 7, General Alfred Jodl (1890–1946), acting for the German government, made the final unconditional surrender at General Eisenhower's headquarters near Reims.

The future treatment of Germany, and Europe in general, was determined by decisions of the "Big Three" (Churchill, Stalin, and Roosevelt). There were two summit meetings attended by all three leaders. Even before the first of these was held at Teheran, Churchill and Roosevelt had met at Casablanca and laid down a basic policy of demanding the unconditional surrender of their enemies. Stalin was agreeable to this.

The first major conference convened at Teheran on November 28, 1943, and lasted until December 1st. Here the two Western allies told Stalin of the May 1944 date for the planned invasion of Normandy. In turn, Stalin confirmed a pledge made earlier that Russia would enter the war against Japan after the war with Germany was concluded.

The Yalta Conference was the second attended personally by Stalin, Churchill, and Roosevelt. It lasted from the 4th to the 11th of February 1945. A plan to divide Germany into zones of occupation, which had been devised in 1943 by a committee under British Deputy Prime Minister Clement Attlee, was formally accepted with the addition of a fourth zone taken from the British and American zones for the French to occupy. Berlin, which lay within the Russian Zone, was divided into four zones of occupation also.

Such lack of precision was characteristic of other parts of the Yalta agreements, such as those governing borders and reparations leading to future disputes and recriminations between the Western powers and the Russians. A Declaration on Liberated Europe promised to assist liberated nations in solving problems through elections and by "democratic" means.

Advent of the Atomic Bomb

The third summit meeting of the Big Three took place at Potsdam outside Berlin after the end of the European war but while the Pacific war was still going on. The conference began July 17, 1945, with Stalin, Churchill, and the new American President Harry Truman attending. (Roosevelt had died suddenly, shortly after the conclusion of the Yalta meeting.) While the conference was in session, the results of the British general election became known: Churchill was defeated, his place taken by his wartime deputy prime minister, the Labour leader Clement Attlee. The meeting confirmed, in detail, arrangements regarding Germany. A Potsdam Declaration, aimed at Japan, called for immediate Japanese surrender and hinted at the consequences that would ensue if it were not forthcoming. While at the conference, American leaders received the news of the successful testing of the first atomic bomb in the New Mexico desert, but the Japanese were given no clear warning that such a destructive weapon might be used against them.

President Truman established a committee of prominent scientists and leaders to determine how best to utilize the bomb. They advised the president that they could not devise any practical way of demonstrating the bomb. If it was to be used, it had to be dropped on Japan; President Truman then made the decision to do so. On August 6, 1945, the bomb was dropped by a single plane on Hiroshima and an entire city disappeared, with the instantaneous loss of 70,000 lives. In time many other persons died from radiation poisoning and other effects. Since no surrender was received, a second bomb was dropped on Nagasaki, obliterating it. Even the most fanatical of the Japanese leaders saw what was happening and surrender came quickly. The only departure from unconditional surrender was to allow the Japanese to retain their emperor (Hirohito, 1901–1989), but only with the proviso that he would be subject in every respect to the orders of the occupation commander. The formal surrender took place September 2, 1945, in Tokyo Bay on the deck of the battleship *Missouri*, and the occupation of Japan began under the immediate control of the American commander General Douglas MacArthur (1880–1964).

EUROPE AFTER WORLD WAR II: 1945 TO 1953

After World War II there was no clear-cut settlement in treaty form as there was after World War I. Planning had been done at the major wartime conferences and in the years immediately following the German surrender, a series of de facto arrangements were made, shaped by the course of events during the occupation of Germany and the opening years of the so-called Cold War which followed the breakdown of the wartime alliance between the Western powers (Britain, France, and the United States) and the Soviet Union.

Anglo-American ideas about what the postwar world should be like were expressed by Roosevelt and Churchill at their meeting off the coast of Newfoundland in August

1941. The Atlantic Charter was a general statement of goals: restoration of the sovereignty and self-government of nations conquered by Hitler, free access to world trade and resources, cooperation to improve living standards and economic security, and a peace that would ensure freedom from fear and want and stop the use of force and aggression as instruments of national policy, what Roosevelt had earlier called "The Four Freedoms."

At the Casablanca Conference, the policy of requiring unconditional surrender by the Axis powers was announced. This ensured that at the end of the war, all responsibility for government of the defeated nations would fall on the victors, and they would have a free hand in rebuilding government in those countries. No real planning was done in detail before the time arrived to meet this responsibility. It was done for the most part as the need arose.

At Teheran, the Big Three did discuss in a general way the occupation and demilitarization of Germany. They also laid the foundation for a post-war organization—the United Nations Organization—which like the earlier League of Nations was supposed to help regulate international relations and keep the peace and ensure friendly cooperation between the nations of the world.

At Potsdam, agreement was reached to sign peace treaties as soon as possible with former German allies. A Council of Foreign Ministers was established to draft the treaties. Several meetings were held in 1946 and 1947 and treaties were signed with Italy, Rumania, Hungary, Bulgaria, and Finland. These states paid reparations and agreed to some territorial readjustments as a price for peace. No agreement could be reached on Japan or Germany. In 1951, the Western powers led by the U.S. concluded a treaty with Japan without Russian participation. The latter made their own treaty in 1956. A final meeting of the Council of Foreign Ministers broke up in 1947 over Germany, and no peace treaty was ever signed with that country. The division of Germany for purposes of occupation and military government became permanent, with the three Western zones joining and eventually becoming the Federal Republic of Germany and the Russian zone becoming the German Democratic Republic.

Arrangements for the United Nations were confirmed at the Yalta Conference: the large powers would predominate in a Security Council, where they would have permanent seats together with several other powers elected from time to time from among the other members of the U.N. Consent of all the permanent members was necessary for any action to be taken by the Security Council (thus giving the large powers a veto). The General Assembly was to include all members.

Eastern Europe: 1945–1953

Much of European Russia had been devastated, and about 25 million people made homeless. Recovery was achieved using the same drastic, dictatorial methods used by the Communists during the 1930s. Stalin's dictatorship became more firmly entrenched than ever. Any potential opposition was purged. In March 1946 a fourth five-year plan was adopted by the Supreme Soviet intended to increase industrial output to a level 50 percent higher than before the war. A bad harvest and food shortage in 1946 had been relieved by a good harvest in 1947, and in December 1947, the government announced the end of food rationing. At the same time a drastic currency devaluation was put through, which brought immediate hardship to many people but strengthened the Soviet economy in the long run. As a result of these and other forceful and energetic measures, the Soviet Union was able within a few years to make good most of the wartime damage and to surpass pre-war levels of production. While this was being done at home, Stalin pursued an aggressive foreign policy and established a series of Soviet satellite states in Eastern Europe.

The fate of Eastern Europe (including Poland, Hungary, Rumania, Bulgaria, Czechoslovakia, and the Russian zone of Germany) from 1945 on was determined by the presence of Russian armies in that area. Stalin undoubtedly wanted a group of friendly nations on his western border from which invasion had come twice during his lifetime. The Russian Communists were also determined to support the advance of a communist system similar to that developed in Russia into the countries of Eastern Europe.

Communization of Eastern Europe and the establishment of regimes in the satellite areas of the Soviet Union occurred in stages over a three-year period following the end of the war. The timetable of events varied in each country.

During the Nazi period, a number of German Communists fled to Moscow. When the Red Army invaded Germany, these exiles returned under the leadership of Wilhelm Pieck and Otto Grotewohl. As relations broke down between the four occupying powers, the Soviet authorities gradually created a Communist state in their zone. On October 7, 1948, a German Democratic Republic was established. Pieck became president and Grotewohl head of a predominantly Communist cabinet. In June 1950, an agreement with Poland granted formal recognition of the Oder-Neisse Line as the boundary between the two states. Economic progress was unsatisfactory for most of the population, and on June 16–17, 1953, riots occurred in East Berlin which were suppressed by Soviet forces using tanks. In East Germany, a program of economic reform was announced which eventually brought some improvement.

In Yugoslavia, Marshal Tito (1892–1980) and his Communist partisan movement emerged from the war in a strong position because of their effective campaign against the German occupation. Tito was able to establish a Communist government despite considerable pressure from Stalin, and pursue a course independent of the Soviet Union unique among the countries of Eastern Europe.

Elections held November 11, 1945, gave victory to Tito's Communist-dominated National Front. A few days later the Yugoslav monarchy was abolished and the country declared to be the Federal People's Republic of Yugoslavia.

Western Europe: 1945–1953

In Italy, following the end of hostilities with Germany, the leaders of the Resistance in the north ousted Premier Ivan Bonomi and placed one of their own top leaders, Ferruccio Parri, in power. Parri was the leader of a faction—the Party of Action—which was socialist in its program. Although he was a man of great moral stature, he was a poor administrator and did not appeal to the public. He was left politically isolated when the Socialist leader Pietro Nenni (1890–1980) made an alliance with the Communists. Meanwhile, more conservative forces had been gathering strength, and in November 1945, Parri was forced to resign.

The monarchy which had governed Italy since the time of unification in the mid-nineteenth century was now discarded in favor of a republic. King Victor Emmanuel III (1869–1947), compromised by his association with Mussolini, resigned in favor of his son, but a referendum in June 1946 established a republic. In simultaneous elections for a constituent assembly, three parties predominated: the Social Democrats, the Communists, and the Christian Democrats. Under the new regime Enrico de Nicola was chosen president and Alcide de Gasperi (1881–1954) formed a new coalition cabinet.

In the last two years of the war, France recovered sufficiently under the leadership of General Charles de Gaulle to begin playing a significant military and political role once again. In July 1944, the United States recognized de Gaulle's Committee of National Liberation as the de facto government of areas liberated from the German occupation. As the war ended, this provisional government purged collaborators, including Marshal Pétain and Pierre Laval, who had headed the Vichy regime during the war.

In foreign affairs, France occupied Germany. In addition, the Fourth Republic was faced with two major problems abroad when it attempted to assert its authority over Indochina and Algeria. The Indochina situation resulted in a long and costly war against nationalists and Communists under Ho Chi Minh (1890–1969). French involvement ended with the Geneva Accords of 1954 and French withdrawal. The Algerian struggle reached a crisis in 1958 resulting in General de Gaulle's return to power and the creation of a new Fifth Republic.

Germany in Ruins

In May 1945, when Germany surrendered unconditionally, the country lay in ruins. About three-quarters of city houses had been gutted by air raids, industry was in a shambles, and the country was divided into zones of occupation ruled by foreign military governors. Economic chaos was the rule, currency was virtually worthless, food was in short supply, and the black market flourished for those who could afford to buy in it. By the Potsdam agreements, Germany lost about one-quarter of its pre-war territory. In addition, some 12 million people of German origin driven from their homes in countries like Poland and Czechoslovakia had to be fed, housed, and clothed along with the indigenous population.

Demilitarization, denazification, and democratization were the initial goals of the occupation forces. All four wartime allies agreed on the trial of leading Nazis for a variety of war crimes and "crimes against humanity." An International Military Tribunal was established at Nuremburg to try 22 major war criminals, and lesser courts tried many others. Most of the defendants were executed, although a few like Rudolf Hess were given life imprisonment.

The reestablishment of German government in the Western zones met with more success. As relations between the three Western powers and the Soviets gradually broke down in Germany, East and West became separate states. In the West, the British and American zones were fused into one in 1946, with the French joining in 1948. Political parties were gradually re-established.

During 1947 there were two meetings of the Council of Foreign Ministers to work out a peace treaty for Germany. Both failed and the occupying powers began to go their own ways in their own zones—the Russians to create a Communist satellite state in East Germany and the British, Americans, and French to create a West German Federal Republic.

In February 1948, a charter granted further powers of government to the Germans in the American and British zones. Later that year, the Russians and East Germans, in an effort to force the Western powers out of their zones in Berlin, began a blockade of the city which was located within the Russian zone. The response was an allied airlift to supply the city, and eventually, after some months, the blockade was called off.

In 1951 a Conservative majority was returned, and Winston Churchill became prime minister again. The new regime immediately reversed the nationalization of iron and steel. Other measures survived, however, especially the universal health care program which proved to be one of the most popular parts of the Labour achievement. In April 1955, Churchill resigned for reasons of age and health and turned over the prime minister's office to Anthony Eden (1897–1977).

The Marshall Plan

European recovery from the effects of the war was slow for the first two or three years after 1945. The European Recovery Program (Marshall Plan, named after the secretary of state and World War II army chief of staff) began in 1948 and showed substantial results in all the Western European countries that took part. The most remarkable gains were in West Germany. The country soon experienced gains so great as to constitute what many called an "economic miracle." During the first two years of the Marshall Plan about $8 billion of American aid is estimated to have resulted in an overall expansion of some $30 billion annual output of goods and services. The Plan aimed to strengthen Western Europe's resistance to communism.

THE COLD WAR

World War II was an exception to the rule of general hostility between capitalism and communism. Powerful though the alliance between the two was, it turned out to be one only of expedience, and, thus, broke down when a common enemy no longer loomed as a threat. This era of tension and hostility came to be known as the "Cold War," to characterize the post–World War II relationship between the Soviet Union and the powerful non-communist nations of the West, led by the United States. The next generation would see the two sides engage in harsh economic and political attacks on each other—creating severe crises at times—but stopping short of a so-called hot, or shooting war. A thaw in relations was brought about by the Nixon administration's pursuit of détente with the Soviet Union in the 1970s; this led to significant arms control agreements. But the Cold War continued in some form until the breakup of the U.S.S.R. in 1990.

Strengthening of NATO

One result of the Korean War was the strengthening of the NATO alliance begun in 1949. A mood approaching panic set in after the North Korean invasion began. The U.S. expressed its fear that NATO would be too weak to resist a possible Russian attack which might come while American forces were engaged in the Far East. The U.S. insisted on a policy of rearming West Germany. Eventually Western European nations accepted West German rearmament but only after agreement to make German forces part of a European defense under NATO control. This policy of military buildup changed the emphasis of foreign aid under the Marshall Plan. In the first two years the aid was primarily economic, with few strings attached. Later it became increasingly military aid.

BRITISH OVERSEAS WITHDRAWAL

Britain received a mandate from the League of Nations following World War I to govern Palestine. Britain indicated in the Balfour Declaration of November 2, 1917, that it favored the creation of a Jewish "national home" in Palestine. The British position there was complicated by its involvement in the creation of Arab states such as Saudi Arabia and Transjordan, which were adamantly opposed to any Jewish state in Palestine.

Following World War II, there was a considerable migration of Jews who had survived the Nazi Holocaust to Palestine to join Jews who had settled there earlier. Conflicts broke out with the Arabs. The British occupying forces tried to suppress the violence and to negotiate a settlement between the factions. In 1948, after negotiations failed, the British, feeling they could no longer support the cost of occupation, announced their withdrawal. Zionist leaders then proclaimed the independent state of Israel and took up arms to fight the armies of Egypt, Syria, and other Arab states which invaded the Jewish-held area. The new Israeli state quickly proved its technological and military superiority by defeating the invaders. Over 500,000 Arabs were displaced from their homes by the establishment of Israel. Efforts to permanently relocate them failed, and they became a factor in the continued violence in the Middle East.

The Jews of Israel created a modern parliamentary state on the European model with an economy and technology superior to their Arab neighbors. The new state was thought by many Arabs to be simply another manifestation of European imperialism made worse by religious antagonisms.

In 1956, the Israelis chose the opportunity created by the ill-fated Anglo-French attempt to retake the Suez Canal to launch their own attack on Egypt. Public opinion eventually forced the withdrawal of the British and French, and although the Israelis had achieved military successes, they found themselves barred from use of the Canal by Egypt, which was now in control.

In 1967, Israel defeated Egypt, Syria, and Jordan in a six-day war, and the Israelis occupied additional territory including the Jordanian sector of the city of Jerusalem. An additional million Arabs came under Israeli rule as a result of this campaign.

Although defeated, the Arabs refused to sign any treaty or to come to terms with Israel. Palestinian refugees living in camps in states bordering Israel created grave problems. The Palestine Liberation Organization (PLO) was formed to eliminate the Jewish state in Palestine. The PLO resorted to terrorist tactics both against Israel and other states in support of their cause.

Yom Kippur War: In October 1973, the Egyptians and Syrians launched an attack on Israel known as the Yom Kippur War. With some difficulty the attacks were repulsed. A settlement was mediated by American Secretary of State Henry Kissinger. The situation has remained unstable, however, with both sides resorting to limited military actions, the Israeli invasion of Lebanon, and terrorist attacks on Israel.

The British exercised control over Egypt from the end of the nineteenth century and declared it a British protectorate in December 1914. In 1922 Egypt became nominally independent.

The government under King Farouk I (1920–1965) did little to alleviate the overriding problem of poverty after the war. In 1952, a group of army officers, including Gamal Abdel Nasser (1918–1970) and Anwar Sadat (1918–1981), plotted against the government, and on July 23 the king was overthrown. Colonel Nasser became premier in April 1954. A treaty with Britain later that year resulted in the withdrawal of all British troops from the Canal Zone.

The United States had agreed to lend money to Egypt, under the leadership of Colonel Nasser, to build the Aswan Dam, but refused to give arms. Nasser then drifted toward the Soviet Union and in 1956 established diplomatic relations with the People's Republic of China. In July 1956 the U.S. withdrew its loan to Egypt. In response, Nasser nationalized the Suez Canal. France, Great Britain, and Israel then attacked Egypt but Eisenhower demanded that they pull out. On November 6, a cease fire was announced.

India under Jawaharlal Nehru (1889–1964) and the Congress Party became a parliamentary democracy. Nehru died in 1964. His daughter, Indira Gandhi (1917–1984), became prime minister in 1966. The country made economic progress, but gains were largely negated by a population increase to 600 million from 350 million. In 1975, Indira Gandhi was found guilty of electoral fraud. She resorted to force to keep herself in power. When elections were permitted in 1977, she was ousted by the opposition. Eventually her son, Rajiv Ghandi (1944–1991), became prime minister.

THE FRENCH IN INDOCHINA AND ALGERIA

Following World War II, the French returned to Indochina and attempted to restore their rule there. The opposition nationalist movement was led by the veteran Communist Ho Chi Minh. War broke out between the nationalists and the French forces. Despite aid from the U.S., the French were unable to maintain their position in the north of Vietnam. In 1954 their army was surrounded at Dienbienphu and forced to surrender. This military disaster prompted a change of government in France.

This new government under Premier Pierre Mendès-France (1907–1982) negotiated French withdrawal at a conference held at Geneva, Switzerland in 1954. Cambodia and Laos became independent and Vietnam was partitioned at the 17th parallel. The North, with its capital at Hanoi, became a Communist state under Ho Chi Minh. The South remained non-Communist. Under the Geneva Accords, elections were to be held in the South to determine the fate of that area. However, the United States chose to intervene and support the regime of Ngo Dinh Diem (1901–1963), and elections were never held. Eventually a second Vietnamese war resulted, with the United States playing the role earlier played by France.

In a referendum, on January 8, 1961, the French people approved of eventual Algerian self-determination. In July 1962 French rule ended in Algeria. There was a mass exodus of Europeans from Algeria, but most Frenchmen were grateful to de Gaulle for ending the long Algerian conflict.

THE DUTCH AND INDONESIA

During World War II, the Japanese conquered the Dutch East Indies. At the end of the war, they recognized the independence of the area as Indonesia. When the Dutch attempted to return, four years of bloody fighting ensued against the nationalist forces of Achmed Sukarno (1901–1970). In 1949, the Dutch recognized Indonesian independence. In 1954, the Indonesians dissolved all ties with the Netherlands. Sukarno's regime became one of increasing dictatorship. In 1966, Sukarno was overthrown and replaced by a more stable administration under General Suharto.

THE COLD WAR AFTER THE DEATH OF STALIN

Following Stalin's death, Russian leaders—while maintaining an atmosphere first of tension and then of relaxation in international affairs—appeared more willing than Stalin to be conciliatory and to consider peaceful coexistence.

In the U.S. the atmosphere also changed with the election of President Dwight Eisenhower; and despite the belligerent rhetoric of Secretary of State John Foster Dulles (1888–1959), conciliatory gestures were not always automatically considered appeasement of the Communists. In 1955 a summit conference of Eisenhower, the British and French leaders, and Khrushchev (1894–1971) met at Geneva in an atmosphere more cordial than any since World War II. The "spirit of Geneva" did not last long, however.

After his return to power in France in 1958, General de Gaulle endeavored to make France a leader in European affairs with himself as spokesman for a Europe that he hoped would be a counter to the "dual hegemony" of the U.S. and U.S.S.R. His policies at times were anti-British or anti-American. He vetoed British entry into the Common Market, developed an independent French nuclear force, and tried to bridge the gap between East and West Europe. Despite his prestige as the last great wartime leader, he did not have great success. Nevertheless, Western Europe came into its own as a factor in international affairs.

A NEW ERA BEGINS

Joseph Stalin died in March 1953. His ruthlessness and paranoid suspicions grew worse towards the end of his life. Postwar economic reconstruction was accompanied by ideological intolerance and a regime of terror and persecution with overtones of anti-Semitism. There were indications of a new series of purges coming when Stalin died.

A so-called "troika" consisting of Georgy Malenkov (1902–1988) (Chairman of the Council of Ministers), Lavrenti Beria (1899–1953) (Stalin's chief of police), and Vyacheslav Molotov (1890–1986) (foreign minister) took over the government. A power struggle took place in which the first event was the secret trial and execution of Beria. Eventually a little-known party functionary, Nikita Khrushchev, became Communist Party General Secretary in 1954. Malenkov and Molotov were demoted to lesser positions and eventually disappeared from public view.

Khrushchev in 1956 delivered a "secret speech" to the twentieth Congress of the Communist party of the Soviet Union. It soon became public knowledge that he had accused Stalin of wholesale "violations of socialist legality" and of creating a "cult of personality." Khrushchev's policy of relaxing the regime of terror and oppression of the Stalin years became known as "The Thaw," after the title of a novel by Ilya Ehrenburg (1891–1967).

Change occurred in foreign affairs also. Khrushchev visited Belgrade and re-established relations with Tito, admitting that there was more than one road to socialism. He also visited the United States, met with President Eisenhower, and toured the country. Later, relations became more tense after the U-2 spy plane incident.

Following the loss of face sustained by Russia as a result of the Cuban Missile Crisis and the failure of Khrushchev's domestic agricultural policies, he was forced out of the party leadership and lived in retirement in Moscow until his death in 1971.

After Khrushchev's ouster, the leadership in the Central Committee divided power, making Leonid Brezhnev (1906–1982) party secretary and Aleksei Kosygin chairman of the council of ministers, or premier. Brezhnev's party position ensured his dominance by the 1970s. In 1977, he presided over the adoption of a new constitution which altered the structure of the regime very little. The same year he was elected president by the Supreme Soviet.

Stalin's successors rehabilitated many of Stalin's victims. They also permitted somewhat greater freedom in literary and artistic matters and even allowed some political criticism. Controls were maintained, however, and sometimes were tightened. Anti-semitism was also still present, and Soviet Jews were long denied permission to emigrate to Israel. American pressure may have helped to relax this policy in the 1970s, when about 150,000 Jews were allowed to leave Russia. Other evidences of continued tight control were the 1974 arrest for treason and forcible deportation of the writer Alexander Solzhenitsyn and the arrest and internal exile for many years of the physicist Andrei Sakharov, who was an outspoken critic of the regime and its violations of human rights.

Brezhnev occupied the top position of power until his death in 1982. He was briefly succeeded by Yuri Andropov (1914–1984) (a former secret police chief) and then by Mikhail Gorbachev, who carried out a further relaxation of the internal regime. Gorbachev pushed disarmament and detente in foreign relations, and attempted a wide range of internal reforms known as *perestroika* ("restructuring"). In August 1991, conservatives and hard liners attempted a coup. The revolt was put down thanks to the determined stand taken by Boris Yeltsin, who headed popular resistance. Gorbachev's reforms came to take on a life of their own, leading to Yeltsin's ascendancy. Gorbachev's hold on power began to slip away until, in December, with the dissolution of the U.S.S.R., he resigned and Yeltsin took his place.

The old Soviet Union broke apart once the controls were removed. The Baltic provinces of Latvia, Lithuania, and Estonia opted for independence, as did the Ukraine and other provinces of the union dominated for so long by the huge Russian Republic. A loose confederation known as the Commonwealth of Independent States emerged containing 11 of the former Soviet republics. Four—the Baltic provinces of Latvia, Lithuania and Estonia, and Georgia—refused to join.

Economic difficulties associated with a transition to a free economy, the mishandled repression of the Chechnya independence movement, and the forceful dispersal of Yeltsin's parliamentary opponents in 1993 gave ammunition to Yeltsin's opponents. In the 1996 elections, Yeltsin retained office as president, but the poor state of his health, despite successful heart bypass surgery in the fall of 1996, made his future leadership uncertain.

CHANGE IN EASTERN EUROPE

In the 1980s, the trade union movement known as Solidarity and its leader, Lech Walesa, emerged as a political force, organizing mass protests in 1980–1981 and maintaining almost continuous pressure on the government headed by General Wojciech Jaruzelski. Despite government efforts to maintain strong central control and suppress the opposition, the ruling Communists were forced to recognize the opposition and make concessions. In June 1989, after power had passed to the Polish Parliament, a national election gave Solidarity an overwhelming majority, and Walesa assumed the presidency. By 1993-94, economic problems resulted in a Communist majority and a change of administration, but there was no return to the old Communist dictatorship.

CHANGE IN WESTERN EUROPE

In March 1957, inspired chiefly by Belgian Foreign Minister Paul-Henri Spaak, two treaties were signed in Rome creating a European Atomic Energy Commission (Euratom) and a European Economic Community (the Common Market)—which eventually absorbed Euratom. The EEC was to be a customs union creating a free market area with a common external tariff for member nations. Toward the outside world, the EEC acted as a single bargaining agent for its members in commercial transactions, and it reached a number of agreements with other European and Third World states.

In 1973, the original six were joined by three new members: Britain, Ireland, and Denmark. The name was changed to "European Community." In 1979, there were three more applicants: Spain, Portugal, and Greece. These latter states were less well off and created problems of cheap labor, agricultural products, etc., which delayed their reception as members until 1986.

Relations with Northern Ireland proved a burden to successive British governments. The 1922 settlement had left Northern Ireland as a self-governing part of the United Kingdom. Of 1.5 million inhabitants, one-third were Roman Catholic and two-thirds were Protestant. Catholics claimed they were discriminated against and pressed for annexation by the Republic of Ireland. Activity by the Irish Republican Army brought retaliation by Protestant extremists. From 1969 on, there was considerable violence, causing the British to bring in troops to maintain order. Over 1,500 were killed in the next several years in sporadic outbreaks of violence.

Under Prime Minister Margaret Thatcher in the 1980s, the British economy improved somewhat. London regained some of its former power as a financial center. In recent years, an influx of people from former colonies in Asia, Africa, and the West Indies has caused some racial tensions.

Prime Minister Thatcher was a partisan of free enterprise. She fought inflation with austerity and let economic problems spur British employers and unions to change for greater efficiency. She received a boost in popularity when Britain fought a brief war with Argentina over the Falkland Islands and emerged victorious. She stressed close ties with the Republican administration of Ronald Reagan in the U.S. A Conservative victory in the 1987 elections made Thatcher the longest-serving prime minister in modern British history.

In 1990, having lost the support of Conservatives in Parliament, Thatcher resigned and was replaced by Chancellor of the Exchequer John Major. Under Major's leadership, Conservatives have had to deal with slow economic growth, unemployment, and racial tensions caused by resentment over the influx of immigrants from the Commonwealth. And there remains the seemingly intractable religious strife in Northern Ireland, with its Protestant-Catholic animosities.

France under de Gaulle saw a new constitution drafted and approved establishing the Fifth Republic with a much strengthened executive in the form of a president with power to dissolve the legislature and call for elections, to submit important questions to popular referendum, and if necessary to assume emergency powers. De Gaulle used all these powers in his 11 years as president.

In domestic politics, de Gaulle strengthened the power of the president by often using the referendum and bypassing the Assembly. De Gaulle was re-elected in 1965, but people became restless with what amounted to a republican monarch. Labor became restive over inflation and housing while students objected to expenditures on nuclear forces rather than education. In May 1968, student grievances over conditions in the universities caused hundreds of thousands to revolt. They were soon joined by some 10 million workers, who paralyzed the economy. De Gaulle survived by promising educational reform and wage increases. New elections were held June 1968, and de Gaulle was returned to power. Promised reforms were begun, but in April 1969, he resigned and died about a year later.

De Gaulle's immediate successors were Georges Pompidou (1969–1974) and Valéry Giscard d'Estaing (1974–1981). Both provided France with firm leadership, and continued to follow an independent foreign policy.

In 1981 François Mitterand succeeded Giscard d'Estaing. He inherited a troubled economy. During his first year Mitterand tried to revitalize economic growth, granted wage hikes, reduced the work week, expanded paid vacations, and nationalized 11 large private companies and banks. The aim was to stimulate the economy by expanding worker purchasing power and confiscating the profits of large corporations for public investment. Loans were made abroad to finance this program. When results were poor, these foreign investors were reluctant to grant more credit. Mitterand then reversed his policy and began to cut taxes and social expenditures. By 1984, this had brought down inflation but increased unemployment.

Mitterand lost his Socialist majority in Parliament in 1986, but regained it in 1988. In 1995, an ailing Mitterand indicated he would retire at the end of his term. He died in January 1996. Out of the election of April 1995 emerged a fractured right-of-center bloc that came to coalesce around Jacques Chirac, the major of Paris and former two-time prime minister. Following a second-round runoff, Chirac won 52 percent of the vote.

In Germany in November 1966, the Christian Democrats formed a so-called "great coalition" with the Social Democrats under Willy Brandt. Kurt Georg Kiesinger (1904–1988) became chancellor, and Brandt the Socialist took over as foreign minister. Brandt announced his intention to work step by step for better relations with East Germany, but found that in a coalition of two very dissimilar parties he could make no substantial progress.

Problems with the economy and the environment brought an end to Kessinger's chancellorship and the rule of the Socialists in 1982. An organization called the Greens, which was a loosely organized coalition of environmentalists alienated from society, detracted from Socialist power. In 1982, the German voters turned to the more conservative Christian Democrats again, and Helmut Kohl became chancellor.

In Italy, the Christian Democrats, who were closely allied with the Roman Catholic Church, dominated the national scene. Their organization, though plagued by corruption, did provide some unity to Italian politics by supplying the prime ministers for numerous coalitions.

Italy advanced economically. Natural gas and some oil was discovered in the north and the Po valley area especially benefited. Unfortunately, business efficiency found no parallel in the government or civil service. Italy suffered from terrorism, kidnappings, and assassinations by extreme radical groups such as the Red Brigades. These agitators hoped to create conditions favorable to the overthrow of the democratic constitution. The most notorious terrorist act was the assassination in 1978 of Aldo Moro (1916–1978), a respected Christian Democratic leader.

In 1983, Bettino Craxi (Socialist) became prime minister at the head of an uneasy coalition which lasted four years—the longest single government in postwar Italian history. By the 1990s Italian industry and its economy generally had advanced to a point where Italy was a leading center in high-tech industry, fashion, design, and banking. But instability continued to mark Italian politics as it had since the end of World War II. Corruption within a system dominated by the Christian Democrats resulted in criminal trials in the 1990s that sent a number of high government officials to prison. In 1993 the electoral system for the Senate was changed from proportional representation to one that gives power to the majority vote-getting party. The 1994 elections for Parliament brought to power the charismatic, conservative Silvio Berlusconi and his *Forzia Italia* ("Let's go, Italy") movement.

In Portugal, Europe's longest right-wing dictatorship came to an end in September 1968, when a stroke incapacitated Antonio Salazar, who died two years later. A former collaborator, Marcelo Caetano (1906–1980), became prime minister, and an era of change began. Censorship was relaxed and some freedom was given to political parties.

In April 1974, the Caetano regime was overthrown and a "junta of national salvation" took over, headed by General Spinola, who later retired and went into exile. Portugal went through a succession of governments. Its African colonies of Mozambique and Angola were finally granted independence in 1975. Portugal joined the Common Market in 1986.

Spain's Francisco Franco, who had been ruler of a fascist regime since the end of the Civil War in 1939, held on until he was close to 70. He then designated the Bourbon prince, Juan Carlos, to be his successor. In 1975, Franco relinquished power and died three weeks later. Juan Carlos proved a popular and able leader and over the next several years took the country from dictatorship to constitutional monarchy. Basque and Catalan separatist movements, which had caused trouble for so long, were appeased by the granting of local autonomy. Spain also entered the European Community in 1986.

Under the Maastricht Treaties of 1991, all members of the EC began measured steps toward an economic and political union that would ultimately have its own common currency. In 1996, the 12 member nations of the EC accounted for one-fifth of world trade.

8. AMERICAN HISTORY: THE COLONIAL PERIOD (1500–1763)

THE AGE OF EXPLORATION

The Treaty of Tordesillas (1493) drew a line dividing the land in the New World between Spain and Portugal. Lands east of the line were Portuguese. As a result, Brazil eventually became a Portuguese colony, while Spain maintained claims to the rest of the Americas. As other European nations joined the hunt for colonies, they tended to ignore the Treaty of Tordesillas.

To conquer the Americas, the Spanish monarchs used their powerful army, led by independent Spanish adventurers known as conquistadores. The European diseases they unwittingly carried with them devastated the local Native American populations, who had no immunities against such diseases.

In 1513, Vasco Núñez de Balboa crossed the isthmus of Panama and became the first European to see the Pacific Ocean. The same year, Juan Ponce de León explored Florida in search of gold and a fabled fountain of youth. He found neither, but claimed Florida for Spain. In 1519, Hernando (Hernán) Cortes led his dramatic expedition against the Aztecs of Mexico. Aided by the fact that the Aztecs at first mistook him for a god, as well as by firearms, armor, horses, and (unknown to him) smallpox germs, all previously unknown in America, Cortes destroyed the Aztec Empire and won enormous riches. By the 1550s, other such fortune seekers had conquered much of South America.

Hernando de Soto (ca. 1496–1542) led 600 men (1539–1541) through what is now the southeastern United States, penetrating as far west as Oklahoma and encountering the Mississippi River, on whose banks de Soto was buried. Francisco Vasquez de Coronado led an expedition (1540–1542) from Mexico north across the Rio Grande and through New Mexico, Arizona, Texas, Oklahoma, and Kansas. Some of Coronado's men were the first Europeans to see the Grand Canyon.

Spain administered its new holdings as an autocratic, rigidly controlled empire in which everything was to benefit the parent country. The Spaniards developed a system of large manors or estates (encomiendas), with Indian slaves ruthlessly managed for the benefit of the conquistadores. The encomienda system was later replaced by the similar but somewhat milder hacienda system. As the Indian population died from overwork and European diseases, Spaniards began importing African slaves to supply their labor needs.

ENGLISH AND FRENCH BEGINNINGS

In 1497, the Italian John Cabot (Giovanni Caboto, ca. 1450–1499), sailing under the sponsorship of the king of England in search of a Northwest Passage (a water route to the Orient through or around the North American continent), became the first European since the Vikings more than four centuries earlier to reach the mainland of North America, which he claimed for England.

In 1524, the king of France authorized another Italian, Giovanni da Verrazzano (ca. 1485–1528), to undertake a mission similar to Cabot's. Endeavoring to duplicate the achievement of the Spaniard Ferdinand Magellan, who had five years earlier found a way around the southern tip of South America, Verrazzano followed the American coast from present-day North Carolina to Maine.

Beginning in 1534, Jacques Cartier (1491–1557), also authorized by the king of France, mounted three expeditions to the area of the St. Lawrence River, which he believed might be the hoped for Northwest Passage. He explored up the river as far as the site of Montreal.

When the English finally began colonization, commercial capitalism in England had advanced to the point that the English efforts were supported by private rather than government funds, allowing English colonists to enjoy greater freedom from government interference.

Fearing encroachment from Huguenot settlers, the Spaniards built a fort at St. Augustine, the oldest city in North America.

Francis Drake (ca. 1540–1596), an Englishman, sailed around South America and raided the Spanish settlements on the Pacific coast of Central America before continuing on to California, which he claimed for England and named Nova Albion. Drake then returned to England by sailing around the world.

English nobleman Sir Humphrey Gilbert (1537–1583) believed England should found colonies and find a Northwest Passage. In 1576, he sent English sea captain Martin Frobisher (ca. 1535–1594) to look for such a passage. Gilbert's attempts to found a colony in Newfoundland failed, and while pursuing these endeavors he was lost at sea.

Gilbert's half-brother, Sir Walter Raleigh (1554–1618), turned his attention to a more southerly portion of the North American coastline, which he named Virginia, in honor of England's unmarried queen. He selected as a site for the first settlement Roanoke Island, just off the coast of present-day North Carolina.

After one abortive attempt, a group of 114 settlers—men, women, and children—were landed in July 1587. Shortly thereafter, Virginia Dare became the first English child born in America. Later that year the expedition's leader, John White, returned to England to secure additional supplies. Delayed by the war with Spain, he did not return until 1590, when he found the colony deserted. It is not known what became of the Roanoke settlers. After this failure, Raleigh was forced by financial constraints to abandon his attempts to colonize Virginia. Hampered by unrealistic expectations, inadequate financial resources, and the ongoing war with Spain, English interest in American colonization was submerged for 15 years.

THE BEGINNINGS OF COLONIZATION

Two groups of merchants gained charters from James I, Queen Elizabeth's successor. One group of merchants was based in London and received a charter to North America between what are now the Hudson and the Cape Fear rivers. The other was based in Plymouth and was granted the right to colonize in North America from the Potomac to the northern border of present-day Maine. They were called the Virginia Company of London and the Virginia Company of Plymouth, respectively. They were joint-stock companies that raised their capital by the sale of shares of stock. Companies of this sort had already been used to finance and carry on English trade with Russia, Africa, and the Middle East.

The Plymouth Company, in 1607, attempted to plant a colony in Maine, but after one winter the colonists became discouraged and returned to Britain. Thereafter, the Plymouth Company folded.

The Virginia Company of London settled Jamestown in 1607. It became the first permanent English settlement in North America. During the early years of Jamestown, the majority of the settlers died of starvation, various diseases, or hostile actions by Native Americans. The colony's survival remained in doubt for a number of years.

Impressed by the potential profits from tobacco growing, King James I determined to have Virginia for himself. In 1624, he revoked the London Company's charter and made Virginia a royal colony. This pattern was followed throughout colonial history; both company colonies and proprietary colonies tended eventually to become royal colonies. Upon taking over Virginia, James revoked all political rights and the representative assembly (15 years later his son, Charles I, was forced, by constant pressure from the Virginians and the continuing need to attract more settlers, to restore these rights).

The French opened a lucrative trade in fur with the Native Americans. In 1608, Samuel de Champlain established a trading post in Quebec, from which the rest of what became New France eventually spread.

French exploration and settlement spread through the Great Lakes region and the valleys of the Mississippi and Ohio rivers. In 1673, Jacques Marquette explored the Mississippi Valley, and in 1682, Sieur de la Salle followed the river to its mouth. French settlements in the Midwest were generally forts and trading posts serving the fur trade.

Throughout its history, New France was handicapped by an inadequate population and a lack of support by the parent country.

In 1609, Holland sent an Englishman named Henry Hudson (d. 1611) to search for a Northwest Passage. In this endeavor, Hudson discovered the river that bears his name.

Arrangements were made to trade with the Iroquois for furs. In 1624, Dutch trading outposts were established on Manhattan Island (New Amsterdam) and at the site of present-day Albany (Fort Orange). A profitable fur trade was carried on and became the main source of revenue for the Dutch West India Company, the joint-stock company that ran the colony.

Many Englishmen came from England for religious reasons. For the most part, these fell into two groups, Puritans and Separatists. Though similar in many respects to the Puritans, the Separatists believed the Church of England was beyond saving and so felt they must separate from it.

One group of Separatists, suffering government harassment, fled to Holland. Dissatisfied there, they went to America and later became the famous Pilgrims.

Led by William Bradford (1590–1657), they departed in 1620, having obtained from the London Company a charter to settle just south of the Hudson River. Driven by storms, their ship, the *Mayflower*, made landfall at Cape Cod in Massachusetts. They decided it was God's will for them to settle in that area. This, however, put them outside the jurisdiction of any established government; and so before going ashore they drew up and signed the Mayflower Compact, establishing a foundation for orderly government based on the consent of the governed. After a difficult first winter that saw many die, the Pilgrims went on to establish a quiet and modestly prosperous colony. After a number of years of hard work, they were able to buy out the investors who had originally financed their voyage, and thus gain greater autonomy.

The Puritans were far more numerous than the Separatists. Charles I determined in 1629 to persecute the Puritans aggressively and to rule without the Puritan-dominated Parliament.

In 1629, they chartered a joint-stock company called the Massachusetts Bay Company. The charter neglected to specify where the company's headquarters should be located. Taking advantage of this unusual omission, the Puritans determined to make their headquarters in the colony itself, 3,000 miles from meddlesome royal officials.

Puritans saw their colony not as a place to do whatever might strike one's fancy, but as a place to serve God and build His kingdom. Dissidents would only be tolerated insofar as they did not interfere with the colony's mission.

One such dissident was Roger Williams (ca. 1603–1683). When his activities became disruptive he was asked to leave the colony. He fled to the wilderness around

Narragansett Bay, bought land from the Indians, and founded the settlement of Providence (1636). It was soon populated by his many followers.

Another dissident was Anne Hutchinson (1591–1643), who openly taught things contrary to Puritan doctrine. She was banished from the colony. She also migrated to the area around Narragansett Bay and with her followers founded Portsmouth (1638). She later migrated still farther west and was killed by Indians.

In 1663, Charles II, having recently been restored to the throne after a 20–year Puritan revolution which had seen his father beheaded, moved to reward eight of the noblemen who had helped him regain the crown by granting them a charter for all the lands lying south of Virginia and north of Spanish Florida.

The new colony was called Carolina, after the king. In hopes of attracting settlers, the proprietors came up with an elaborate plan for a hierarchical, almost feudal, society. Not surprisingly, this proved unworkable, and despite offers of generous land grants to settlers, the Carolinas grew slowly.

In 1664, Charles gave his brother James, Duke of York, title to all the Dutch lands in America, provided James conquered them first. To do this, James sent an invasion fleet under the command of Colonel Richard Nicols. New Amsterdam fell almost without a shot and became New York.

THE COLONIAL WORLD

New England enjoyed a much more stable and well-ordered society than did the Chesapeake colonies. Puritans placed great importance on the family, which in their society was highly patriarchal. Puritans also placed great importance on the ability to read, since they believed everyone should be able to read the Bible. As a result, New England was ahead of the other colonies educationally and enjoyed extremely widespread literacy. Since New England's climate and soil were unsuited to large-scale farming, the region developed a prosperous economy based on small farming, home industry, fishing, and especially trade and a large shipbuilding industry. Boston became a major international port.

The typical Chesapeake colonist lived a shorter, less healthy life than his New England counterpart, and was survived by fewer children. As a result, the Chesapeake's population steadily declined despite a constant influx of settlers. Nor was Chesapeake society as stable as that of New England. Most Chesapeake settlers came as indentured servants; since planters desired primarily male servants for work in the tobacco fields, men largely outnumbered women in Virginia and Maryland. This disparity hindered the development of family life.

The system of indentured servitude was open to serious abuse, with masters sometimes treating their servants brutally or contriving through some technicality to lengthen their terms of indenture. In any case, 40 percent of indentured servants in the Chesapeake region failed to survive long enough to gain their freedom.

On the bottom rung of Southern society were the black slaves. During the first half of the 17th century, blacks in the Chesapeake made up only a small percentage of the population, and were treated more or less as indentured servants. Between 1640 and 1670 this gradually changed, and blacks came to be seen and treated as lifelong chattel slaves whose status would be inherited by their children. By 1750, they composed 30 to 40 percent of the Chesapeake population.

While North Carolina tended to follow Virginia in its economic and social development (although with fewer great planters and more small farmers), South Carolina developed a society even more dominated by large plantations and chattel slavery. By the early decades of the eighteenth century, blacks had come to outnumber whites in that colony. South Carolina's economy remained dependent on the cultivation of its two staple crops—rice and, to a lesser extent, indigo.

Stepped-up Regulation: Beginning around 1650, British authorities began to take more interest in regulating American trade for the benefit of the mother country. A key idea that underlay this policy was the concept of mercantilism. Each nation's goal was to export more than it imported (i.e., to have a "favorable balance of trade"). The difference would be made up in gold and silver. To achieve their goals, mercantilists believed economic activity should be regulated by the government. Colonies could fit into England's mercantilist scheme by providing staple crops, such as rice, tobacco, sugar, and indigo, and raw materials, such as timber, that England would otherwise have been forced to import from other countries.

Parliament passed a series of Navigation Acts (1651, 1660, 1663, and 1673). The Navigation Acts stipulated that trade with the colonies was to be carried on only in ships made in Britain or America, that had at least 75 percent British or American crews. Additionally, when certain "enumerated" goods were shipped from an American port, they were to go only to Britain or to another American port. Finally, almost nothing could be imported to the colonies without going through Britain first.

In 1676, Bacon's Rebellion occurred when a nobleman's followers burned Jamestown because of disagreement over policy toward Native Americans. The British removed the governor, who Virginians felt was running the colony for his friends' benefit, and thenceforth Virginia's royal governors had strict instructions to run the colony for the benefit of the mother country. In response, Virginia's gentry, who had been divided over Bacon's Rebellion, united to face this new threat to their local autonomy. By political means they consistently obstructed the governors' efforts to increase royal control.

In 1692, several young girls in Salem Village (now Danvers) claimed to be tormented by the occult activities of certain of their neighbors. Before the resulting Salem witch trials could be stopped by the intervention of Puritan ministers such as Cotton Mather (1663–1728), some 20 persons had been executed.

Pennsylvania was founded as a refuge for Quakers. One of a number of radical religious sects that had sprung up about the time of the English Civil War, the Quakers held many controversial beliefs. They believed all persons had an "inner light" that allowed them to commune directly with God, thus deemphasizing the notion of church hierarchy. They were also pacifists and declined to show customary deference to those who were considered to be their social superiors.

Delaware, though at first part of Pennsylvania, was granted a separate legislature by Penn, but until the American Revolution, Pennsylvania's proprietary governors also functioned as governors of Delaware.

THE EIGHTEENTH CENTURY

America's population continued to grow rapidly, both from natural increases due to prosperity and a healthy environment and from large-scale immigration, not only of English but also of other groups such as Scots-Irish and Germans.

The Germans were prompted to migrate by wars, poverty, and religious persecution in their homeland. They found Pennsylvania especially attractive and settled fairly close to the frontier, where land was more readily available. They eventually came to be called the "Pennsylvania Dutch."

The Scots-Irish, Scottish Presbyterians who had been living in northern Ireland for several generations, settled on or beyond the frontier in the Appalachians and spread southward into the mountain valleys of Virginia and North Carolina.

It was decided to found a colony as a buffer between South Carolina and Spanish-held Florida. In 1732, a group of British philanthropists, led by General James Oglethorpe (1696–1785), obtained a charter for such a colony, to be located between the Savannah and Altamaha rivers, and to be populated by such poor as could not manage to make a living in Great Britain.

England and France continued on a collision course, as France determined to take complete control of the Ohio Valley and western Pennsylvania.

British authorities ordered colonial governors to resist this; and Virginia's Robert Dinwiddie, already involved in speculation on the Ohio Valley lands, was eager to comply. George Washington (1732–1799), a young major of the Virginia militia, was sent to western Pennsylvania to request the French to leave. When the French declined in 1754, Washington was sent with 200 Virginia militiamen to expel them. After success in a small skirmish, Washington was forced by superior numbers to fall back on his hastily built Fort Necessity and then to surrender.

While Washington skirmished with the French in western Pennsylvania, delegates of seven colonies met in Albany, New York, to discuss common plans for defense. Delegate Benjamin Franklin proposed a plan for an intercolonial government. While the other colonies showed no support for the idea, it was an important precedent for the concept of uniting in the face of a common enemy.

The British dispatched Major General Edward Braddock (1695–1755) with several regiments of British regular troops. Braddock marched overland toward the French outpost of Fort Duquesne, which was at the place where the Monongahela and Allegheny rivers join to form the Ohio. About eight miles short of his goal, he was ambushed by a small force of French and Indians. Two-thirds of the British regulars, including Braddock himself, were killed. However, under the leadership of its capable and energetic prime minister, William Pitt, England by 1760 had taken Quebec and Montreal and virtually liquidated the French empire in North America.

By the Treaty of Paris of 1763, Britain gained all of Canada and all of what is now the United States east of the Mississippi River. France lost all of its North American holdings.

9. THE AMERICAN REVOLUTION (1763–1787)

THE COMING OF THE AMERICAN REVOLUTION

A drive to gain new authority over the colonies, beginning in 1763, led directly to American independence.

In 1763, George Grenville (1712–1770) became prime minister and set out to solve some of the empire's more pressing problems. Chief among these was the large national debt incurred in the recent war.

In 1764, Grenville pushed through Parliament the Sugar Act (also known as the Revenue Act), which aimed at raising revenue by taxing goods imported by the Americans. It was stringently enforced, with accused violators facing trial in admiralty courts without benefit of jury or the normal protections of due process.

Grenville secured passage of the Quartering Act, which required the colonies in which British troops were stationed to pay for their maintenance. Americans had never before been required to support a standing army in their midst.

Grenville also saw the passage of his Currency Act of 1764, which forbade once and for all any colonial attempts to issue currency not redeemable in gold or silver, and made it more difficult for Americans to avoid the constant drain of money that Britain's mercantilist policies were designed to create in the colonies.

The Stamp Act (1765) imposed a direct tax on Americans for the first time. It required Americans to purchase revenue stamps on everything from newspapers to legal documents, and would have created an impossible drain on hard currency in the colonies.

Americans reacted first with restrained and respectful petitions and pamphlets in which they pointed out that "taxation without representation is tyranny." From there, resistance progressed to stronger protests that eventually became violent.

In October 1765, delegates from nine colonies met as the Stamp Act Congress. Called by the Massachusetts legislature at the instigation of James Otis, the Stamp Act Congress passed moderate resolutions against the act, asserting that Americans could not be taxed without the consent of their representatives. They pointed out that Americans were not represented in Parliament, and called for the repeal of both the Stamp and Sugar Acts. The Stamp Act Congress showed that representatives of the colonies could work together, and gave political leaders in the various colonies a chance to become acquainted with each other.

Colonial merchants' boycott of British goods spread throughout the colonies and had a powerful effect on British merchants and manufacturers, who began clamoring for the act's repeal.

Meanwhile, the fickle King George III had dismissed Grenville over an unrelated disagreement and replaced him with a cabinet headed by Charles Lord Rockingham (1730–1782). In March 1766, under the leadership of the new ministry, Parliament repealed the Stamp Act. At the same time, however, it passed the Declaratory Act, which claimed the power to tax or make laws for the Americans "in all cases whatsoever."

Though the Declaratory Act denied the exact principle they had just been at such pains to assert—that of no taxation without representation—the Americans generally ignored it in their exuberant celebration of the repeal of the Stamp Act. Americans eagerly proclaimed their loyalty to Great Britain.

The Rockingham ministry was replaced with a cabinet dominated by Chancellor of the Exchequer Charles Townshend (1725–1767). In 1766, Parliament passed his program of taxes on items imported into the colonies. These taxes came to be known as the Townshend duties. Townshend mistakenly believed the Americans would accept this method, while rejecting the use of direct internal taxes.

The Townshend Acts also included the use of admiralty courts to try those accused of violations, the use of writs of assistance, and the paying of customs officials out of the fines they levied. Townshend also had the New York legislature suspended for noncompliance with the Quartering Act.

American reaction was at first slow.

Philadelphia lawyer John Dickinson (1732–1808) wrote an anonymous pamphlet entitled "Letters from a Farmer in Pennsylvania," in which he pointed out in moderate terms that the Townshend Acts violated the principle of no taxation without representation, and that if Parlimaent could suspend the New York legislature, it could do the same to others. At the same time, he urged a restrained response on the part of his fellow Americans.

The sending of troops aroused the Americans to resistance. Nonimportation was again instituted, and soon British merchants were calling on Parliament to repeal the acts. In March 1770, Parliament, under the new prime minister, Frederick Lord North (1737–1792), repealed all of the taxes except that on tea, which was retained to prove Parliament had the right to tax the colonies if it so desired.

By the time of the repeal, however, friction between British soldiers and Boston citizens had led to an incident in which five Bostonians were killed. Although the British soldiers had acted more or less in self-defense, Samuel Adams labeled the incident the "Boston Massacre" and publicized it widely. At their trial, the British soldiers were defended by prominent Massachusetts lawyer John Adams (1735–1826) and were acquitted on the charge of murder.

In the years that followed, American orators desiring to stir up anti-British feeling often alluded to the Boston Massacre. Following the repeal of the Townshend duties, a period of relative peace set in.

The relative peace was brought to an end by the Tea Act of 1773. In desperate financial condition—partially because the Americans were buying smuggled Dutch tea rather than the taxed British product—the British East India Company sought and obtained from Parliament concessions that allowed it to ship tea directly to the colonies rather than only by way of Britain. The result would be that East India Company tea, even with the tax, would be cheaper than smuggled Dutch tea. The colonists would thus, it was hoped, buy the tea, tax and all. The East India Company would be saved, and the Americans would be tacitly accepting Parliament's right to tax them.

The Americans, however, proved resistant to this approach; rather than seem to admit Parliament's right to tax, they vigorously resisted the cheaper tea. Various methods, including tar and feathers, were used to prevent the collection of the tax on tea. In most ports, Americans did not allow the tea to be landed.

In Boston, however, pro-British Governor Thomas Hutchinson (1711–1780) forced a confrontation by ordering Royal Navy vessels to prevent the tea ships from leaving the harbor. After 20 days, this would, by law, result in the cargoes being sold at auction and the tax paid. The night before the time was to expire, December 16, 1773, Bostonians thinly disguised as Native Americans boarded the ships and threw the tea into the harbor. Many Americans felt this was going too far, but the reaction of Lord North and Parliament quickly united Americans in support of Boston and in opposition to Britain.

The British responded with four acts collectively titled the Coercive Acts. First, the Boston Port Act closed the port of Boston to all trade until local citizens would agree to pay for the lost tea (they would not). Secondly, the Massachusetts Government Act greatly increased the power of Massachusetts's royal governor at the expense of the legislature. Thirdly, the Administration of Justice Act provided that royal officials accused of crimes in Massachusetts could be tried elsewhere, where chances of acquittal might be greater. Finally, a strengthened Quartering Act allowed the new governor, General Thomas Gage (1721–1787), to quarter his troops anywhere, including unoccupied private homes.

THE WAR FOR INDEPENDENCE

The British government paid little attention to the First Continental Congress, having decided to teach the Americans a military lesson. More troops were sent to Massachusetts, which was officially declared to be in a state of rebellion. Orders were sent to General Gage to arrest the leaders of the resistance, or failing that, to provoke any sort of confrontation that would allow him to turn British military might loose on the Americans.

Gage decided on a reconnaissance-in-force to find and destroy a reported stockpile of colonial arms and ammunition at Concord. Seven hundred British troops set out on this mission on the night of April 18, 1775. Their movement was detected by American surveillance, and news was spread throughout the countryside by dispatch riders Paul Revere (1735–1818) and William Dawes (1745–1799).

At the little village of Lexington, Captain John Parker and some 70 Minutemen (militiamen trained to respond at a moment's notice) awaited the British on the village green. As the British approached, a British officer shouted at the Minutemen to lay down their arms and disperse. The Minutemen did not lay down their arms, but did turn to file off the green. A shot was fired, and then the British opened fire and charged. Eight Americans were killed and several others wounded, most shot in the back.

The British continued to Concord only to find that nearly all of the military supplies they had expected to find had already been moved. Attacked by growing numbers of Minutemen, they began to retreat toward Boston. As the British retreated, Minutemen swarmed from every village for miles around and fired on the column from behind rocks, trees, and stone fences. Only a relief force of additional British troops saved the first column from destruction.

Open warfare had begun, and the myth of British invincibility was destroyed. Militia came in large numbers from all the New England colonies to join the force besieging Gage and his army in Boston.

In May 1775, three more British generals, William Howe (1729–1814), Henry Clinton (1738–1795), and John Burgoyne (1722–1792), arrived in Boston. The following month the Americans tightened the noose around Boston by fortifying Breed's Hill (a spur of Bunker Hill).

The British determined to remove them by a frontal attack. Twice the British were thrown back, but they finally succeeded when the Americans ran out of ammunition. Over a thousand British soldiers were killed or wounded in what turned out to be the bloodiest battle of the war (June 17, 1775). Yet the British had gained very little and remained bottled up in Boston.

Meanwhile in May 1775, American forces under Ethan Allen (1738–1789) and Benedict Arnold (1741–1801) took Fort Ticonderoga on Lake Champlain.

Congress, hoping Canada would join in resistance against Britain, authorized two expeditions into Quebec. One, under General Richard Montgomery (1736–1775), took Montreal and then turned toward the city of Quebec. It was met there by the second expedition under Benedict Arnold. The attack on Quebec (December 31, 1775) failed; Montgomery was killed, Arnold wounded, and American hopes for Canada ended.

While these events were taking place in New England and Canada, the Second Continental Congress met in Philadelphia in May 1775. Congress was divided into two main factions. One was composed mostly of New Englanders and leaned toward declaring independence from Britain. The other drew its strength primarily from the Middle Colonies and was not yet ready to go that far. It was led by John Dickinson of Pennsylvania.

The Declaration of Independence was primarily the work of Thomas Jefferson (1743–1826) of Virginia. It was a restatement of political ideas by then commonplace in America and showed why the former colonists felt justified in separating from Great Britain. It was formally adopted by Congress on July 4, 1776.

Britain, meanwhile, was preparing a massive effort to conquer the United States. Gage was removed for being too timid, and top command went to Howe. To supplement the British army, large numbers of troops were hired from various German principalities. Since many of these Germans came from the state of Hesse-Cassel, Americans referred to all such troops as Hessians.

The British landed that summer at New York City, where they hoped to find many loyalists. Washington anticipated the move and was waiting at New York. However, the undertrained, underequipped, and badly outnumbered American army was no match for the powerful forces under General Howe and his brother, Admiral Lord Richard Howe

(1726–1799). Defeated at the Battle of Long Island (August 27, 1776), Washington narrowly avoided being trapped there (an escape partially due to the Howes' slowness). Defeated again at the Battle of Washington Heights (August 29–30, 1776) in Manhattan, Washington was forced to retreat across New Jersey with the aggressive British General Lord Charles Cornwallis (1738–1805) in pursuit. By December, what was left of Washington's army had made it into Pennsylvania.

With his victory almost complete, General Howe decided to wait till spring to finish annihilating Washington's army. Scattering his troops in small detachments so as to hold all of New Jersey, he went into winter quarters.

Washington, with his small army melting away as demoralized soldiers deserted, decided on a bold stroke. On Christmas night 1776, his army crossed the Delaware River and struck the Hessians at Trenton. The Hessians, still groggy from their hard-drinking Christmas party, were easily defeated. A few days later, Washington defeated a British force at Princeton (January 3, 1777). Much of New Jersey was regained, and Washington's army was saved from disintegration.

Hoping to weaken Britain, France began making covert shipments of arms to the Americans early in the war. Shipments from France were vital for the Americans.

For the summer of 1777, the British home authorities adopted an elaborate plan of campaign urged on them by General Burgoyne. According to the plan, Burgoyne would lead an army southward from Canada along the Lake Champlain corridor, while another army under Howe moved up the Hudson River to join Burgoyne at Albany. This, it was hoped, would cut off New England, which they considered the hotbed of the "rebellion."

The American victory at Saratoga convinced the French to join openly in the war against England. Eventually the Spanish (1779) and the Dutch (1780) joined as well.

The new circumstances brought a change in British strategy. With fewer troops available for service in America, the British would have to depend more on loyalists, and since they imagined that larger numbers of these existed in the South than elsewhere, it was there they turned their attention.

Howe was replaced by General Henry Clinton (1738–1795), who was ordered to abandon Philadelphia and march to New York. In doing so, he narrowly avoided defeat at the hands of Washington's army—much improved after a winter's drilling at Valley Forge under the spry direction of Prussian nobleman Baron von Steuben, a gifted mercenary—at the Battle of Monmouth, New Jersey (June 28, 1778).

Clinton maintained New York as Britain's main base. In November 1778, the British easily conquered Georgia. Late the following year, Clinton moved on South Carolina and in May 1780 Charleston surrendered. Clinton then returned to New York, leaving Cornwallis to continue the Southern campaign.

Congress, alarmed at the British successes, sent General Horatio Gates to lead the forces opposing Cornwallis. Gates was soundly defeated at the Battle of Camden in South Carolina (August 16, 1780).

The outlook seemed bad for America. Washington's officers grumbled about not getting paid. The army was understrength and then suffered successive mutinies among the Pennsylvania and New Jersey troops. Benedict Arnold went over to the British.

In the west, George Rogers Clark (1752–1818), led an expedition down the Ohio River and into the area of present-day Illinois and Indiana, defeating a British force at Vincennes, Indiana, and securing the area north of the Ohio River for the United States.

In the south, Cornwallis began to move northward toward North Carolina, but on October 7, 1780, a detachment of his force under Major Patrick Ferguson (1744–1780), the inventor of the breech-loading rifle, was defeated by American frontiersmen at the

Battle of Kings Mountain in northern South Carolina. Cornwallis unwisely moved north without bothering to secure South Carolina first. The result was that the British would no sooner leave an area than American militia or guerilla bands, such as that under Francis Marion "the Swamp Fox" (ca. 1732–1795), were once again in control.

American commander Nathaniel Greene's (1742–1786) brilliant southern strategy led to a crushing victory at Cowpens, South Carolina (January 17, 1781), by troops under Greene's subordinate, General Daniel Morgan (1736–1802) of Virginia. It also led to a near victory by Greene's own force at Guilford Court House, North Carolina (March 15, 1781).

The frustrated and impetuous Cornwallis now abandoned the southern strategy and moved north into Virginia, taking a defensive position at Yorktown. With the aid of a French fleet which took control of Chesapeake Bay and a French army which joined him in sealing off the land approaches to Yorktown, Washington succeeded in trapping Cornwallis. After three weeks of siege, Cornwallis surrendered (October 17, 1781).

Ships of the small but daring United States Navy, as well as privateers, preyed on the British merchant marine. John Paul Jones (1747–1792), the most famous of American naval leaders, captured ships and carried out raids along the coast of Britain itself. French and Spanish naval forces also struck various outposts of the British Empire.

News of the debacle at Yorktown brought the collapse of Lord North's ministry, and the new cabinet opened peace negotiations. The American negotiating team was composed of Benjamin Franklin, John Adams, and John Jay (1745–1829). The negotiations continued for some time, delayed by French and Spanish maneuvering. When it became apparent that France and Spain were planning to achieve an agreement unfavorable to the United States, the American envoys negotiated a separate treaty with Britain.

The final agreement became known as the Treaty of Paris of 1783. Its terms stipulated the following: 1) The United States was recognized as an independent nation by the major European powers, including Britain 2) Its western boundary was set at the Mississippi River 3) Its southern boundary was set at 31° north latitude (the northern boundary of Florida) 4) Britain retained Canada, but had to surrender Florida to Spain 5) Private British creditors would be free to collect any debts owed by United States citizens and 6) Congress was to recommend that the states restore confiscated loyalist property.

THE CREATION OF NEW GOVERNMENTS

After the collapse of British authority in 1775, it became necessary to form new state governments. By the end of 1777, 10 new state constitutions had been formed. Most state constitutions included bills of rights—lists of things the government was not supposed to do to the people.

In the summer of 1776, Congress appointed a committee to begin devising a framework for a national government. John Dickinson, who had played a leading role in writing the articles, felt a strong national government was needed; but by the time Congress finished revising them, the articles went to the opposite extreme of preserving the sovereignty of the states and creating a very weak national government.

The Articles of Confederation provided for a unicameral Congress in which each state would have one vote, as had been the case in the Continental Congress. Executive authority under the articles would be vested in a committee of 13, with one member from each state. In order to amend the articles, the unanimous consent of all the states was required.

The Articles of Confederation government was empowered to make war, make treaties, determine the amount of troops and money each state should contribute to the war effort, settle disputes between states, admit new states to the Union, and borrow money. But it was not empowered to levy taxes, raise troops, or regulate commerce.

Ratification of the Articles of Confederation was delayed by disagreements over the future status of the lands that lay to the west of the original 13 states. Some states, notably Virginia, held extensive claims to these lands based on their original colonial charters. Maryland, which had no such claim, withheld ratification until, in 1781, Virginia agreed to surrender its western claims to the new national government.

10. THE UNITED STATES CONSTITUTION (1787–1789)

DEVELOPMENT AND RATIFICATION

As time went on, the inadequacy of the Articles of Confederation became increasingly apparent. Congress could not compel the states to comply with the terms of the Treaty of Paris of 1783 in regard to debts and loyalists' property. The British used this as an excuse for not evacuating their northwestern posts, hoping to be on hand to make the most of the situation when, as they not unreasonably expected, the new government fell to pieces. In any case, Congress could do nothing to force them out of the posts, nor to solve any of the nation's other increasingly pressing problems.

In these dismal straits, some called for disunion, others for monarchy. Still others felt that republican government could still work if given a better constitution, and they made it their goal to achieve this.

The Annapolis Convention met in September 1786 to discuss a new constitution, but only five states were represented. With so few states represented, it was decided instead to call for a convention of all the states to meet the following summer in Philadelphia for the purpose of revising the Articles of Confederation.

The men who met in Philadelphia in 1787 were remarkably able, highly educated, and exceptionally accomplished. For the most part they were lawyers, merchants, and planters. Though representing individual states, most thought in national terms. Prominent among them were James Madison (1751–1836), Alexander Hamilton (1755–1804), Gouverneur Morris (1752–1816), Robert Morris (1734–1806), John Dickinson, and Benjamin Franklin.

George Washington was unanimously elected to preside, and the enormous respect that he commanded helped hold the convention together through difficult times.

While most delegates believed that human beings need government to keep their more selfish instincts at bay, they also were intent on structuring government in such a way as to prevent the possibility for corruption. With this in mind, the document that they crafted contained many checks and balances, designed to prevent the government, or any one branch of the government, from gaining too much power.

Madison, who has been called the "father of the Constitution," devised a plan of national government and persuaded fellow Virginian Edmund Randolph (1753–1813), who was more skilled at public speaking, to introduce it. Known as the "Virginia Plan," it called for an executive branch and two houses of Congress, each based on population.

Smaller states, who would thus have seen their influence decreased, objected and countered with William Paterson's (1745–1806) "New Jersey Plan," which called for the continuation of a unicameral legislature with equal representation for the states as well as sharply increased powers for the national government.

Benjamin Franklin played an important role in reconciling the often heated delegates and in making various suggestions that eventually helped the convention arrive at the "Great Compromise," proposed by Roger Sherman (1721–1793) and Oliver Ellsworth (1745–1807). The Great (or Connecticut) Compromise provided for a presidency, a Senate with all states represented equally (by two senators each), and a House of Representatives with representation according to population.

Another crisis involved North-South disagreement over the issue of slavery. Here also a compromise was reached. Slavery was neither endorsed nor condemned by the Constitution. Each slave was to count as three-fifths of a person for purposes of apportioning representation and direct taxation on the states (the Three-Fifths Compromise). The federal government was prohibited from stopping the importation of slaves prior to 1808.

The third major area of compromise was the nature of the presidency. This was made easier by the virtual certainty that George Washington would be the first president, and the universal trust that he would not abuse the powers of the office or set a bad example for his successors. The result was a strong presidency with control of foreign policy and the power to veto Congress's legislation. Should the president commit an actual crime, Congress would have the power to impeach him. Otherwise, the president would serve for a term of four years and be reelectable without limit. As a check to the possible excesses of democracy, the president was to be elected by an electoral college, in which each state would have the same number of electors as it did senators and representatives combined. The person with the second highest total in the electoral college would be vice president. If no one gained a majority in the electoral college, the president would be chosen by the House of Representatives.

The new Constitution was to take effect when nine states, through special state conventions, had ratified it.

As the struggle over ratification got under way, those favoring the Constitution astutely named themselves Federalists (i.e., advocates of centralized power) and labeled their opponents Antifederalists. The Federalists were effective in explaining the convention and the document it had produced. The *Federalist Papers*, written as a series of 85 newspaper articles by Alexander Hamilton, James Madison, and John Jay, brilliantly expounded the Constitution and demonstrated how it was designed to prevent the abuse of power. These essays are considered to be the best commentary on the Constitution by those who helped write it.

At first, ratification progressed smoothly, with five states approving in quick succession. In Massachusetts, however, a tough fight developed. By skillful maneuvering, the Federalists were able to win over to their side such popular opponents of the Constitution as Samuel Adams and John Hancock. Others were won over by the promise that a bill of rights would be added to the Constitution, limiting the federal government just as state governments were limited by their bills of rights. With such promises, Massachusetts ratified by a narrow margin.

By June 21, 1788, the required nine states had ratified, but the crucial states of New York and Virginia still held out. In Virginia, where George Mason (1725–1792) and Patrick Henry opposed the Constitution, the influence of George Washington and the promise of a bill of rights finally prevailed and ratification was achieved. In New York, where Alexander Hamilton led the fight for ratification, *The Federalist Papers*, the promise of a bill of rights, and the news of Virginia's ratification were enough to carry the day.

Only North Carolina and Rhode Island still held out, but they both ratified within the next 15 months. In March 1789, George Washington was inaugurated as the nation's first president.

OUTLINE OF THE UNITED STATES CONSTITUTION

Preamble

"We the People of the United States, in order to form a more perfect Union, establish justice, insure domestic tranquility, provide for the common defense, promote the general welfare, and secure the blessings of liberty to ourselves and our posterity, do ordain and establish this Constitution for the United States of America."

Article I—Legislature

The legislature is divided into two parts—the House of Representatives (435 members currently; determined by proportional representation of the population) and the Senate (100 members currently; two from each state).

The House of Representatives may bring impeachment charges. All bills which concern money must originate in the House. Because of the size of the body, debate is limited except in special cases, where all representatives may meet as the Committee of the Whole. The Speaker of the House presides over the proceedings. Terms of representatives are two years, reelectable without limit, to persons who are at least 25 years of age.

The Senate, originally elected by state legislatures but now by direct election (Seventeenth Amendment), approves or rejects presidential nominations and treaties, and serves as the court and jury in impeachment proceedings. Debate within the Senate is unlimited. The president pro tempore usually presides, but the vice-president of the United States is the presiding officer, and may vote to break a tie. Senate terms are for six years, reelectable without limit, to persons who are at least 30 years of age.

Article II—Executive

The president of the United States is elected for a four-year term, originally electable without limit (the Twenty-Second Amendment limits election to two terms), and must be at least 35 years old.

Responsibilities for the president outlined in the Constitution include acting as chief of state, chief executive, commander-in-chief of the armed forces, chief diplomat, and chief legislator.

Article III—Judiciary

While the Constitution describes the Supreme Court in Article III, the actual construction of the court system was accomplished by the Judiciary Act of 1789. The Supreme Court has jurisdiction for federal courts and appellate cases on appeal from lower courts.

Article IV—Interstate Relations

This article guarantees that court decisions and other legal actions (marriage, incorporation, etc.) valid in one state are valid in another. Expedition of criminals (and, originally, runaway slaves), and the exchange of citizenship benefits are likewise guaranteed. Article IV also provides for the admission of new states.

Article V—Amendment Process

Amendments are proposed by a two-thirds vote of each House of Congress, or by a special convention called by Congress upon the request of two-thirds of the state legislatures. Amendments are ratified by three-fourths of the state legislatures or state conventions.

Article VI—Supremacy Clause

Article VI sets up the hierarchy of laws in the United States. The Constitution is the "supreme law of the land," and supersedes treaties. Treaties supersede federal laws, federal laws (later to include federal regulatory agency directives) supersede state constitutions, state laws, and local laws, respectively. All federal and state officials, including judges, must take an oath to support and defend the Constitution.

Article VII—Ratification

This article specified the ratification process necessary for the Constitution to take effect. Nine of the original 13 states had to ratify the Constitution before it became operative.

Amendments to the Constitution

The amendments to the Constitution guarantee certain individual rights and amend original dictates of the Constitution. The first 10 amendments are known as the Bill of Rights, for which Thomas Jefferson provided the impetus.

1—freedom of religion, speech, press, assembly, as well as the right to petition the government for redress of grievances (1791)

2—right to bear arms in a regulated militia (on a state basis; it was not intended to guarantee an individual's rights) (1791)

3—troops will not be quartered (housed) in private citizens' homes (1791)

4—protects against unreasonable search and seizure (need for search warrant) (1791)

5—protects the rights of the accused, including required indictments, double jeopardy, self-incrimination, due process, and just compensation (1791)

6—guarantees a speedy and public trial, the confrontation of witnesses, and the right to call witnesses on one's own behalf (1791)

7—guarantees a jury trial (1791)

8—protects against excessive bail and cruel and unusual punishment (1791)

9—states that all rights not enumerated are nonetheless retained by the people (1791)

10—states that all powers not specifically delegated to the federal government are retained by the states (1791)

11—states may not be sued by individuals (1798)

12—dictates that electors will cast separate ballots for president and vice-president; in the event of no clear winner, the House will select the president and the Senate the vice-president (1804)

13—abolished slavery (1865)

14—extended citizenship to all persons; made Confederate debt void and Confederate leaders ineligible for public office; states which denied voting rights to qualified citizens (blacks) would have their representation in Congress reduced; conferred "dual" citizenship (both of the United States and of a specific state) on all citizens (1868)

15—extended voting rights to blacks (1870)

16—legalized the income tax (1913)

17—provided for the direct election of senators (1913)

18—prohibited the general manufacture, sale, and use of alcoholic beverages (1919)

19—extended voting rights to women (1920)

20—changed inauguration date from March 4 to January 20; eliminated the "lame-duck" session of Congress (after the November elections) (1933)

21—repealed the Eighteenth Amendment (1933)

22—limited presidents to two terms (1951)

23—gave presidential electoral votes to the District of Columbia (1961)

24—prohibited poll taxes (1964)

25—changed the order of the presidential line of succession and provided guidelines for presidential disability (1967)

26—extended voting rights to 18-year-olds (1971)

SEPARATION AND LIMITATION OF POWERS
Powers Reserved for the Federal Government Only

- Regulate foreign commerce
- Regulate interstate commerce
- Mint money
- Create and establish post offices
- Regulate naturalization and immigration
- Grant copyrights and patents
- Declare and wage war, declare peace
- Admit new states
- Fix standards for weights and measures
- Raise and maintain an army and navy
- Govern the federal city (Washington, D.C.)
- Conduct relations with foreign powers
- Universalize bankruptcy laws

Powers Reserved for the State Governments Only

- Conduct and monitor elections
- Establish voter qualifications
- Provide for local governments
- Ratify proposed amendments to the Constitution
- Regulate contracts and wills
- Regulate intrastate commerce
- Provide education for its citizens
- Levy direct taxes
- Maintain police power over public health, safety, and morals
- Maintain integrity of state borders

Powers Shared by Federal and State Governments

- Taxing, borrowing, and spending money
- Controlling the militia
- Acting directly on individuals

Restrictions on the Federal Government

- No ex post facto laws
- No bills of attainder
- Two-year limit on appropriation for the military
- No suspension of habeus corpus (except in a crisis)
- One port may not be favored over another
- All guarantees as stated in the Bill of Rights

Restrictions on State Governments

- Treaties, alliances, or confederations may not be entered into
- Letters of marque and reprisal may not be granted
- Contracts may not be impaired
- Money may not be printed or bills of credit emitted
- No import or export taxes
- May not wage war (unless invaded)

Actions which require a simple majority include raising taxes, requesting appropriations, declaring war, increasing the national debt, instituting a draft, and introducing impeachment charge (House).

Actions which require a two-thirds majority include overriding a presidential veto, proposing amendments to the Constitution, expelling a member of Congress (in the individual house only), ratifying treaties (Senate), acting as a jury for impeachment (Senate), ratifying presidential appointments (Senate).

Approving a proposed constitutional amendment requires a three-fourths majority of states.

11. THE NEW NATION (1789–1824)

THE FEDERALIST ERA

Few Antifederalists were elected to Congress, and many of the new legislators had served as delegates to the Philadelphia Convention two years before.

George Washington received virtually all the votes of the presidential electors, and John Adams received the next highest number, thus becoming the vice-president. After a triumphal journey from Mount Vernon, Washington was inaugurated in New York City, the temporary seat of government (April 30, 1789).

Ten amendments were ratified by the states by the end of 1791 and became the Bill of Rights. The first nine spelled out specific guarantees of personal freedoms, and the Tenth Amendment reserved to the states all those powers not specifically withheld or granted to the federal government. This last was a concession to those who feared the potential of the central government to usurp the sovereignty of the individual states.

The Judiciary Act of 1789 provided for a Supreme Court with six justices, and invested it with the power to rule on the constitutional validity of state laws. It was to be the interpreter of the "supreme law of the land." A system of district courts was set up to serve as courts of original jurisdiction, and three courts of appeal were established.

THE ESTABLISHMENT OF THE EXECUTIVE DEPARTMENTS

Congress established three departments of the executive branch—state, treasury, and war—as well as the offices of attorney general and postmaster general. President Washington immediately appointed Thomas Jefferson, Alexander Hamilton, and Henry Knox (1750–1806), respectively, to fill the executive posts, and Edmund Randolph became attorney general.

WASHINGTON'S ADMINISTRATION (1789–1797)

Treasury Secretary Alexander Hamilton, in his "Report on the Public Credit," proposed the funding of the national debt at face value, federal assumption of state debts, and the establishment of a national bank. In his "Report on Manufactures," Hamilton proposed an extensive program for federal stimulation of industrial development through subsidies and tax incentives. The money needed to fund these programs would come from an excise tax on distillers and from tariffs on imports.

Jefferson and others objected to the funding proposal because it would benefit speculators who had bought up state and confederation obligations at depressed prices, and who would profit handsomely by their redemption at face value. They opposed the tax program because it would fall primarily on the small farmers. They saw Hamilton's entire program as enriching a small elite group at the expense of the more worthy common citizen.

The Constitution omitted mention of political parties, which were seen as a detrimental force by the founding fathers. But differences in philosophy very quickly began to drive the leaders of government into opposing camps—the Federalists and the Republicans.

Hamilton interpreted the Constitution as having vested extensive powers in the federal government. This "implied powers" stance claimed that the government was given all powers that were not expressly denied to it. This is the "broad" interpretation.

Jefferson and Madison held the view that any action not specifically permitted in the Constitution was thereby prohibited. This is the "strict" interpretation, and the Republicans opposed the establishment of Hamilton's national bank based on this view of government. The Jeffersonian supporters, primarily under the guidance of James Madison, began to organize political groups in opposition to the Federalist program. They called themselves Republicans.

The Federalists received their strongest support from the business and financial groups in the commercial centers of the Northeast and from the port cities of the South. The strength of the Republicans lay primarily in the rural and frontier areas of the South and West.

Foreign and Frontier Affairs

The U.S. proclaimed neutrality when France went to war with Britain in 1792, and American merchants traded with both sides. In retaliation, the British began to seize American merchant ships and force their crews into service with the British navy.

John Jay negotiated a treaty with the British that attempted to settle the conflict at sea, as well as to curtail English agitation of their Native American allies on the western borders in 1794. The agreement actually settled few of the issues and merely bought time for the new nation in the worsening international conflict. Jay was severely criticized for his efforts.

In the Pinckney Treaty, ratified by the Senate in 1796, the Spanish opened the Mississippi River to American traffic and recognized the 31st parallel as the northern boundary of Florida.

Internal Problems

In 1794, western farmers refused to pay the excise tax on whiskey which formed the backbone of Hamilton's revenue program. When a group of Pennsylvania farmers terrorized the tax collectors, President Washington sent out a federalized militia force of some 15,000 men and the rebellion evaporated, thus strengthening the credibility of the young government.

The Election of 1796

In the election of 1796 John Adams was the Federalist candidate, Thomas Jefferson the Republican. John Adams was elected president. Jefferson received the second highest number of electoral votes and became vice president.

JOHN ADAMS'S ADMINISTRATION (1797–1801)

Adams was a brilliant lawyer and statesman, but too dogmatic and uncompromising to be an effective politician; he endured a very frustrating and unproductive term in office. Nonetheless, he did send a three-man delegation to France in 1798 to persuade the French to stop harassing American shipping. When they were solicited for a bribe, by three subordinates of French Minister Talleyrand, the Americans indignantly refused. Their report of this insult produced outrage at home. The cry, "millions for defense, but not one cent for tribute," was raised, and public feelings against the French ran high. Since Talleyrand's officials were unnamed in the dispatches, the incident became known as the "XYZ affair."

Repression and Protest

The elections in 1798 increased the Federalist's majorities in both houses of Congress and they used their "mandate" to enact legislation to stifle foreign influences. The Alien Act raised new hurdles in the path of immigrants trying to obtain citizenship, and the Sedition Act widened the powers of the Adams administration to muzzle its newspaper critics. Both bills were aimed at actual or potential Republican opposition, and a number of editors were actually jailed for printing critical editorials.

Republican leaders were convinced that the Alien and Sedition Acts were unconstitutional, but the process of deciding on the constitutionality of federal laws was as yet undefined. Jefferson and Madison decided that state legislatures should have that power, and they drew up a series of resolutions which were presented to the Kentucky and Virginia legislatures. They proposed that state bodies could "nullify" federal laws within those states. These resolutions were adopted only in these two states, and so the issue died, but the principle of states' rights would have great force in later years.

The Election of 1800

Thomas Jefferson and Aaron Burr (1756–1836) ran on the Republican ticket against John Adams and Charles Pinckney (1746–1825) for the Federalists. The Republican candidates won handily, but both received the same number of electoral votes, thus throwing the selection of the president into the House of Representatives. After a lengthy deadlock, Alexander Hamilton threw his support to Jefferson and Burr had to accept the vice-presidency, the result obviously intended by the electorate. This increased the ill-will between Hamilton and Burr and contributed to their famous duel in 1804. Jefferson appointed James Madison as secretary of state and Albert Gallatin (1761–1849) secretary of the Treasury.

The Federalist Congress passed a new Judiciary Act early in 1801, and President Adams filled the newly created vacancies with party supporters, many of them with last-minute commissions. John Marshall (1755–1835) was then appointed chief justice of the United States Supreme Court, thus guaranteeing continuation of Federalist policies from the bench of the high court.

THE JEFFERSONIAN ERA

Thomas Jefferson and his Republican followers envisioned a nation of independent farmers living under a central government that exercised a minimum of control and served merely to protect the individual liberties guaranteed by the Constitution. This agrarian paradise would be free from the industrial smoke and urban blight of Europe, and would serve as a beacon light of Enlightenment rationalism to a world searching for direction. But Jefferson presided over a nation that was growing more industrialized and urban, and which seemed to need an ever-stronger president.

The city of Washington was designed by Pierre-Charles L'Enfant (1754–1825), and was briefly occupied by the Adams administration. Most of its inhabitants moved out when Congress was not in session.

Conflict with the Judges

Marbury vs. Madison: Judge William Marbury, one of Adams's last-minute appointments, sued Madison to force delivery of his commission as a justice of the peace in the federal district. Chief Justice John Marshall ruled that the law giving the Supreme Court jurisdiction of the case was unconstitutional, and thus asserted the power of judicial review over federal legislation, a power which has become the foundation of the Supreme Court's check on the other two branches of government.

Domestic Affairs

Enforcement of the Alien and Sedition Acts was immediately suspended, and the men convicted under those laws were released.

The Twelfth Amendment was adopted and ratified in 1804, ensuring that a tie vote between candidates of the same party could not again cause the confusion of the Jefferson-Burr affair.

Following the Constitutional mandate, the importation of slaves was stopped by law in 1808.

The Louisiana Purchase: An American delegation purchased the trans-Mississippi territory from Napoleon for $15 million in April 1803, even though they had no authority to buy more than the city of New Orleans.

The Constitutional Dilemma: Jefferson's stand on the strict interpretation of the Constitution would not permit him to purchase land without congressional approval. But he accepted his advisors' counsel that his treaty-making powers included the authority to buy the land. Congress concurred, after the fact, and the purchase price was appropriated, thus doubling the territory of the nation overnight.

Exploring the West: Meriwether Lewis (1774–1809) and William Clark's (1770–1838) group left St. Louis in 1804 and returned two years later with a wealth of scientific and anthropological information. At the same time, Zebulon Pike and others had been traversing the middle parts of Louisiana and mapping the land.

MADISON'S ADMINISTRATION (1809–1817)

The Election of 1808: Republican James Madison won the election over Federalist Charles Pinckney, but the Federalists gained seats in both houses of the Congress.

The War of 1812: Congress passed a modified embargo just before Madison's inauguration, known as the Non-Intercourse Act, which opened trade to all nations except France and Britain. When it expired in 1810, it was replaced by Macon's Bill No. 2, which gave the president power to prohibit trade with any nation when they violated United States neutrality.

The Native American tribes of the Northwest and the Mississippi Valley were resentful of the government's policy of pressured removal to the West, and the British authorities in Canada exploited their discontent by encouraging border raids against the American settlements.

The Shawnee chief Tecumseh (1768–1813) set out to unite the Mississippi Valley tribes and reestablish Native American dominance in the old Northwest. On November 11, 1811, General William Henry Harrison (1773–1841) destroyed Tecumseh's village on Tippecanoe Creek and dashed his hopes for an North American confederacy.

The Congress in 1811 contained a strong prowar group called the War Hawks led by Henry Clay (1777–1852) and John C. Calhoun (1782–1850). They gained control of both houses and began agitating for war with the British. On June 1, 1812, President Madison asked for a declaration of war and Congress complied.

A three-pronged invasion of Canada met with disaster on all three fronts, and the Americans fell back to their own borders. At sea, American privateers and frigates, including "Old Ironsides," (the U.S.S. *Constitution*) scored early victories over British warships, but were soon driven back into their home ports and blockaded by the powerful British ships-of-the-line.

On September 10, 1813, Admiral Oliver Hazard Perry (1785–1819) defeated a British force at Put-in-Bay on Lake Erie. His flagship flew the banner, "Don't Give Up the Ship." This victory opened the way for William Henry Harrison to invade Canada in October and defeat a combination British and Native American forces at the Battle of the Thames.

Andrew Jackson (1767–1845) led a force of frontier militia into Alabama in pursuit of Creek Native Americans who had massacred the white inhabitants of Fort Mims. On March 27, 1814, he crushed the Native Americans at Horseshoe Bend, and seized the Spanish garrison at Pensacola.

A British force came down Lake Champlain and met defeat at Plattsburgh, New York, in September. A British armada sailed up the Chesapeake Bay and sacked and burned Washington, D.C. They then proceeded up the bay toward Baltimore, which was guarded by Fort McHenry. That fort held firm through the British bombardment, inspiring Francis Scott Key's (1779–1843) "Star Spangled Banner."

A powerful British invasion force was sent to New Orleans to close the mouth of the Mississippi River, but Andrew Jackson decisively defeated it. The battle was fought on January 8, 1815, two weeks after a peace treaty had been signed at the city of Ghent in Belgium.

The Treaty of Ghent provided for the acceptance of the status quo that had existed at the beginning of hostilities, and both sides restored their wartime conquests to the other.

The Federalists had increasingly become a minority party. They vehemently op-posed the war, and Daniel Webster (1782–1852) and other New England congressmen consistently blocked the Administration's efforts to prosecute the war effort. On December 15, 1814, delegates from the New England states met in Hartford, Connecticut, and drafted a set of resolutions suggesting nullification—and even secession—if their interests were not protected against the growing influence of the South and the West.

Soon after the convention adjourned, the news of the victory at New Orleans was announced and their actions were discredited. The Federalist party ceased to be a political force from this point on.

Post-War Developments

Protective Tariff (1816): The first protective tariff in the nation's history was passed in 1816 to slow the flood of cheap British manufactures into the country.

Rush-Bagot Treaty (1817): An agreement was reached in 1817 between Britain and the United States to stop maintaining armed fleets on the Great Lakes. This first "disarmament" agreement is still in effect.

Native American Policy

The government began to systematically pressure all the Native American tribes remaining in the East to cede their lands and accept new homes west of the Mississippi. Most declined the offer.

The Adams-Onis Treaty (1819): Spain had decided to sell the remainder of the Florida territory to the Americans before they took it anyway. Under this agreement, the Spanish surrendered all their claims to Florida. The United States agreed to assume $5 million in debts owed to American merchants.

THE MONROE DOCTRINE

Around 1810, national revolutions had begun in Latin America, as the colonial populations there refused to accept the rule of the new Napoleonic governments in Europe. Leaders like San Martín and Bolívar declared independence for their countries and after Napoleon's fall in 1814, were in defiance of the restored Hapsburg and Bourbon rulers of Europe.

British and American leaders feared that the new European governments would try to restore the former New World colonies to their erstwhile royal owners.

In December 1823, President James Monroe (1758–1831) included in his annual message to Congress a statement that the peoples of the American hemisphere were "henceforth not to be considered as subjects for future colonization by any European powers." Thus began a 30-year period of freedom from serious foreign involvement for the United States.

INTERNAL DEVELOPMENT (1820–1830)

The years following the War of 1812 were years of rapid economic and social development, followed by a severe depression in 1819. But this slump was temporary, and it became obvious that the country was moving rapidly from its agrarian origins toward an industrial, urban future. Westward expansion accelerated, and the mood of the people became very positive. In fact, these years were referred to as the "Era of Good Feelings."

The Monroe Presidency (1817–1823): James Monroe, the last of the "Virginia dynasty," had been handpicked by the retiring Madison and he was elected with only one electoral vote opposed—a symbol of national unity.

THE MARSHALL COURT

John Marshall delivered the majority opinions in a number of critical decisions in these formative years, all of which served to strengthen the power of the federal government and restrict the powers of state governments.

Marbury vs. Madison (1803): This decision established the Supreme Court's power of judicial review over federal legislation.

Dartmouth College vs. Woodward (1819): This decision was to limit severely the power of state governments to control corporations, the emerging form of business organization.

McCulloch vs. Maryland (1819): The state of Maryland had tried to levy a tax on the Baltimore branch of the Bank of the United States in order to protect the competitive position of its own state banks. Marshall said that no state has the right to control an agency of the federal government. Since "...the power to tax is the power to destroy...," such state action violates Congress's "implied powers" to establish and run a national bank.

Gibbons vs. Ogden (1824): In a case involving competing steamboat companies, Marshall ruled that commerce included navigation, and that only Congress has the right to regulate commerce among states. Thus, the state-granted monopoly was voided.

STATEHOOD: A BALANCING ACT

The Missouri Compromise (1820): The Missouri Territory, the first to be organized from the Louisiana Purchase, applied for statehood in 1819. Since the Senate membership was evenly divided between slaveholding and free states at that time, the admission of a new state would give the voting advantage either to the North or to the South. Slavery was already well-established in the new territory, so the southern states were confident in their advantage, until Representative Tallmadge of New York proposed an amendment to the bill which would prohibit slavery in Missouri. The southern outcry was immediate, and the ensuing debate grew hot.

As the debate dragged on, the northern territory of Massachusetts applied for admission as the state of Maine. This offered a way out of the dilemma, and House Speaker Clay formulated a package that both sides could accept. The two admission bills were combined, with Maine coming in free and Missouri coming in as a slave state. To make the package palatable for the House, a provision was added that prohibited slavery in the remainder of the Louisiana Territory north of the southern boundary of Missouri (latitude 36 degrees 30').

12. JACKSONIAN DEMOCRACY AND WESTWARD EXPANSION (1824–1850)

JACKSONIAN DEMOCRACY (1829–1841)

The "Age of Jackson" marked a transformation in the political life of the nation which attracted the notice of European travelers and observers. Alexis de Tocqueville observed an "equality of condition" here that existed nowhere else in the world, and an egalitarian spirit among the people that was unique.

The Election of 1824: Secretary of the Treasury William H. Crawford of Georgia was the pick of the congressional caucus. Secretary of State John Quincy Adams (1767–1848) held the job that traditionally had been the stepping-stone to the executive office. Speaker of the House Henry Clay presented the only coherent program to the voters, the "American System," which provided a high tariff on imports to finance an extensive internal improvement package. Andrew Jackson of Tennessee presented himself as a war hero from the 1812 conflict. All four candidates claimed to be Republicans.

Jackson won 43 percent of the popular vote, but the four-way split meant that he only received 38 percent of the electoral votes. Under the provisions of the twelfth Amendment, the top three candidates were voted on by the House of Representatives. This left Henry Clay out of the running, and he threw his support to Adams. The votes had no sooner been counted, when the new president, Adams, appointed Henry Clay as secretary of state.

Andrew Jackson and his supporters immediately cried "foul!" and accused Clay of making a deal for his vote. The rallying cry of "corrupt bargain" became the impetus for their immediate initiation of the campaign for the 1828 election.

The new president pushed for an active federal government in areas like internal improvements and Native American affairs. These policies proved unpopular in an age of increasing sectional jealousies and conflicts over states' rights.

Adams was frustrated at every turn by his Jacksonian opposition, and his unwillingness, or inability, to compromise further antagonized his political enemies.

Jackson was popular with the common man. He seemed to be the prototype of the self-made westerner: rough-hewn, violent, vindictive, with few ideas but strong convictions. He ignored his appointed cabinet officers and relied instead on the counsel of his "Kitchen Cabinet," a group of partisan supporters.

Jackson expressed the conviction that government operations could be performed by untrained, common folk, and he threatened to dismiss large numbers of government employees and replace them with his supporters. Actually, he talked more about this "spoils system" than he acted on it.

He exercised his veto power more than any other president before him.

JOHN C. CALHOUN AND NULLIFICATION

In 1828, Congress passed a new tariff bill that included higher import duties for many goods which were bought by southern planters. Southerners bitterly denounced the law as the "Tariff of Abominations."

John C. Calhoun, Adams's vice-president, anonymously published the "South Carolina Exposition and Protest," which outlined this theory of the "concurrent majority"—that a federal law which was deemed harmful to the interests of an individual state could be declared null and void within that state by a convention of the people. Thus, a state holding a minority position could ignore a law enacted by the majority which its citizens considered unconstitutional.

The Election of 1828: Adams's supporters now called themselves the National Republicans, and Jackson's party ran as the Democratic Republicans.

It was a dirty campaign. Adams's people accused Jackson of adultery and of the murder of several militiamen who had been executed for desertion during the War of 1812. Jackson's followers accused Adams of extravagance with public funds.

When the votes were counted, Jackson had won 56 percent of the popular vote and swept 178 of the 261 electoral votes. John C. Calhoun was elected vice-president.

THE WAR ON THE BANK

The Bank of the United States had operated under the direction of Nicholas Biddle (1786–1844) since 1823. He was a cautious man, and his conservative economic policy enforced conservatism among the state and private banks—which many bankers resented. Many of the bank's enemies opposed it simply because it was big and powerful. Many still disputed its constitutionality.

Jackson had handpicked his Democratic successor, Martin Van Buren (1782–1862) of New York. The Whigs ran three regional candidates in hopes of upsetting the Jacksonians. The Whig party had emerged from the ruins of the National Republicans and other groups who opposed Jackson's policies. The name was taken from the British Whig tradition, which simply refers to the "opposition."

Van Buren, known as Old Kinderhook (O.K.), inherited all the problems and resentments generated by his mentor. He spent most of his term in office dealing with the financial chaos left by the death of the Second Bank. The best he could do was to eventually persuade Congress to establish an Independent Treasury to handle government funds. It began functioning in 1840.

The Election of 1840: The Whigs nominated William Henry Harrison, "Old Tippecanoe," a western fighter against the Native Americans. Their choice for vice-president was John Tyler (1790–1862), a former Democrat from Virginia. The Democrats put up Van Buren again, but they could not agree on a vice-presidential candidate, so they ran no one.

Harrison won a narrow popular victory, but swept 80 percent of the electoral vote. Unfortunately for the Whigs, President Harrison died only a month after the inauguration, having served the shortest term in presidential history.

THE MEANING OF JACKSONIAN POLITICS

The Age of Jackson was the beginning of the modern party system. Popular politics, based on emotional appeal, became the accepted style. The practice of meeting in mass conventions to nominate national candidates for office was established during these years.

The Democrats opposed big government and the requirements of modernization: urbanization and industrialization. Their support came from the working classes, small merchants, and small farmers.

The Whigs promoted government participation in commercial and industrial development, the encouragement of banking and corporations, and a cautious approach to westward expansion. Their support came largely from northern business and manufacturing interests and large southern planters. Calhoun, Clay, and Webster dominated the Whig party during the early decades of the nineteenth century.

ANTEBELLUM CULTURE: AN AGE OF REFORM

The American people in 1840 found themselves living in an era of transition and instability. The responses to this uncertainty were twofold: a movement toward reform and a rising desire for order and control. Both of these major streams of reform activity were centered in the Northeast, especially in New England.

REMAKING SOCIETY: ORGANIZED REFORM

The early antislavery movement advocated only the purchase and transport of slaves to free states in Africa. The American Colonization Society was organized in 1817, and established the colony of Liberia in 1830, but by that time the movement had reached a dead end.

In 1831, William Lloyd Garrison (1805–1879) started his paper, *The Liberator*, and began to advocate total and immediate emancipation. He founded the New England Anti-slavery Society in 1832 and the American Anti-slavery Society in 1833. Theodore Weld (1803–1895) pursued the same goals, but advocated more gradual means.

Frederick Douglass (1817–1895) escaped from his Maryland owner and became a fiery orator for the movement. He published his own newspaper, the *North Star*.

There were frequent outbursts of antiabolition violence in the 1830s. Abolitionist editor Elijah Lovejoy (1802–1837) was killed by a mob in Illinois.

The movement split into two wings: Garrison's radical followers, and the moderates who favored "moral suasion" and petitions to Congress. In 1840, the Liberty party, the first national antislavery party, fielded a presidential candidate on the platform of "free soil" (nonexpansion of slavery into the new western territories).

The literary crusade continued, with Harriet Beecher Stowe's *Uncle Tom's Cabin* being the most influential among the many books that presented the abolitionist message.

DIVERGING SOCIETIES—LIFE IN THE NORTH

As the nineteenth century progressed, the states seemed to polarize more into the two sections we call the North and the South, with the expanding West becoming ever more identified with the North.

The influx of immigrants had slowed during the conflicts with France and England, but the flow increased between 1815 and 1837. Then the economic downturn again sharply reduced their numbers. Thus, the overall rise in population during these years was due more to incoming foreigners than to natural increase. Most of the newcomers were from Britain, Germany, and southern Ireland. Discrimination was common in the job market and was primarily directed against the Catholics. "Irish Need Not Apply" signs were common. However, the persistent labor shortage prevented the natives from totally excluding the foreign elements.

The Role of Minorities and Women

Women were treated as minors by the law. In most states, a woman's property became her husband's with marriage. Political activity was limited to the formation of associations in support of various pious causes such as abolition. Professional employment was largely limited to schoolteaching. The women's rights movement focused on social and legal discrimination, and women like Lucretia Mott (1793–1880) and Sojourner Truth (ca. 1797–1883) became well-known figures on the speakers' circuit.

By 1850, 200,000 free blacks lived in the North and West. Their lives were restricted everywhere by prejudice, and "Jim Crow" laws separated the races. Black citizens organized separate churches and fraternal orders. The African Methodist Episcopal Church, for example, had been organized in 1794 in Philadelphia and flourished in the major Northern cities. Black Masonic and Odd Fellows lodges were likewise established. The economic security of the free blacks was constantly threatened by the newly arrived immigrants, who were willing to work at the least desirable jobs for lower wages. Racial violence was a daily threat.

The Growth of Industry

By 1850, the value of industrial output had surpassed that of agricultural production. The Northeast produced more than two-thirds of the manufactured goods.

Between 1830 and 1850, the number of patents issued for industrial inventions almost doubled. Charles Goodyear's (1800–1860) process of vulcanizing rubber was put to 500 different uses and formed the basis for an entire new industry. Elias Howe's (1819–1867) sewing machine was to revolutionize the clothing industry. The mass production of iron created an array of businesses, of which the new railroad industry was the largest consumer. Samuel B. Morse's (1791–1872) electric telegraph was first used in 1840 to transmit business news and information.

DIVERGING SOCIETIES—LIFE IN THE SOUTH

The southern states experienced dramatic growth in the second quarter of the nineteenth century. The economy grew more productive and more prosperous, but still the section called the South was basically agrarian, with few important cities and only scattered industry. The plantation system, with its cash-crop production driven by the use of slave labor, remained the dominant institution. The South grew more unlike the North and became more defensive of its distinctive way of life.

The most important economic phenomenon of the early decades of the nineteenth century was the shift in population and production from the old "upper South" of Virginia and the Carolinas to the "lower South" of the newly opened Gulf states of Alabama, Mississippi, and Louisiana. This shift was the direct result of the increasing importance of cotton. In the older Atlantic states, tobacco retained its importance, but shifted westward to the Piedmont. It was replaced in the East by food grains. The southern Atlantic coast continued to produce rice, and southern Louisiana and east Texas retained their emphasis on sugar cane. But the rich black soil of the new Gulf states proved ideal for the production of short-staple cotton, especially after the invention of the "gin." Cotton soon became the center of the southern economy.

By 1860, cotton was to account for two-thirds of the value of United States exports. In the words of a Southern legislator of that era, "Cotton is King!"

Classes in the South

The utilization of slave labor varied according to the region and the size of the growing unit. The large plantations growing cotton, sugar, or tobacco used the gang system, in which white overseers directed black drivers who supervised large groups of workers in the fields, all performing the same operation. In the culture of rice, and on the smaller farms, slaves were assigned specific tasks, and when those tasks were finished, the worker had the remainder of the day to himself.

House servants usually were considered the most favored since they were spared the hardest physical labor and enjoyed the most intimate relationship with the owner's family. This could be considered a drawback, as they were frequently deprived of the social communion of the other slaves, enjoyed less privacy, and were more likely to suffer the direct wrath of a dissatisfied master or mistress.

Commerce and Industry

The lack of manufacturing and business development has frequently been blamed for the South's losing its bid for independence in 1861–1865. Actually, the South was highly industrialized for its day and compared favorably with most European nations in the development of manufacturing capacity. However, it trailed far behind the North, so much so that when war erupted in 1861, the northern states owned 81 percent of the factory capacity in the United States.

The southern states saw considerable development in the 1820s and 1830s in textiles and iron production and in flour milling. Even so, most of the goods manufactured in these plants were for plantation consumption rather than for export, and they never exceeded two percent of the value of the cotton crop.

MANIFEST DESTINY AND WESTWARD EXPANSION

Although the term "Manifest Destiny" was not actually coined until 1844, the belief that the American nation was destined to eventually expand all the way to the Pacific Ocean, and to possibly embrace Canada and Mexico, had been voiced for years by many who believed that American liberty and ideals should be shared with everyone possible, by force if necessary. The rising sense of nationalism which followed the War of 1812 was fed by the rapidly expanding population, the reform impulse of the 1830s, and the desire to acquire new markets and resources for the burgeoning economy of "Young America."

A variety of adventurers explored the newly acquired territory of Louisiana and the lands beyond. John Jacob Astor established a fur post at the mouth of the Columbia River, which he named Astoria. This challenged the British claim to the northwest. Though he was forced to sell out his establishment to the British, he lobbied Congress to pass trade restrictions against British furs, and eventually became the first American millionaire from the profits of the American Fur Company. The growing trade with the Orient in furs and other specialty goods was sharpening the desire of many businessmen for American ports on the Pacific coast.

The Adams-Onis Treaty of 1819 had set the northern boundary of Spanish possessions near the present northern border of California. The territory north of that line and west of the vague boundaries of the Louisiana Territory had been claimed over the years by Spain, England, Russia, France, and the United States. By the 1820s, all these claims had been yielded to Britain and the United States. The Hudson's Bay Company had established a fur trading station at Fort Vancouver, and claimed control south to the Columbia. The United States claimed all the way north to the 54°40' parallel. Unable to settle the dispute, they had agreed on a joint occupation of the disputed land.

In the 1830s, American missionaries followed the traders and trappers to the Oregon country. They began to publicize the richness and beauty of the land, sending back official reports on their work, which were published in the new inexpensive "penny press" papers. The result was the "Oregon Fever" of the 1840s, as thousands of settlers trekked across the Great Plains and the Rocky Mountains to settle the new Shangri-la.

Texas had been a state in the Republic of Mexico since 1822, following the Mexican revolution against Spanish control. The United States had offered to buy the territory at the time, since it had renounced its claim to the area in the Adams-Onis agreement of 1819. The new Mexican government refused to sell, but invited immigration from the north by offering land grants to Stephen Austin (1793–1836) and other Americans. They wanted to increase the population of the area and to produce revenue for their infant government. By 1835, approximately 35,000 "gringos" were homesteading on Texas land.

The Mexican officials saw their power base eroding as the foreigners flooded in, so they moved to tighten control through restrictions on immigration and through tax increases. The Texans responded in 1836 by proclaiming independence and establishing a new republic. The ensuing war was short-lived. The Mexican dictator, Antonia López de Santa Anna (1794–1876), advanced north and annihilated the Texan garrisons at the Alamo and at Goliad. On April 23, 1836, Sam Houston (1793–1863) defeated him at San Jacinto, and the Mexicans were forced to let Texas go its way.

Houston immediately asked the American government for recognition and annexation, but President Andrew Jackson feared the revival of the slavery issue, as the new state would come in on the slaveholding side of the political balance. He also feared war with Mexico and so did nothing. When Van Buren followed suit, the new republic sought foreign recognition and support, which the European nations eagerly provided, hoping thereby to create a counterbalance to rising American power and influence in the Southwest. France and England both quickly concluded trade agreements with the Texans.

The district of New Mexico had, like Texas, encouraged American immigration. Soon that state was more American than Mexican. The Santa Fe Trail, running from Independence, Missouri, to the town of Santa Fe, created a prosperous trade in mules, gold, silver, and furs, which moved north in exchange for manufactured goods. American settlements sprung up all along the route.

Though the Mexican officials in California had not encouraged it, American immigration nevertheless had been substantial. Since the Missouri Compromise had established the northern limits for slavery at the 36°30' parallel, most of this Mexican territory lay in the potential slaveholding domain, and many of the settlers carried their bondsmen with them.

The Democrats generally favored the use of force, if necessary, to extend American borders. The Whigs favored more peaceful means like diplomacy. Some Whigs, like Henry Clay, feared expansion under any circumstances, because of its potential for aggravating the slavery issue.

TYLER, POLK, AND CONTINUED WESTWARD EXPANSION

When William Henry Harrison became president, he immediately began to rely on Whig leader Henry Clay for advice and direction. He appointed to his cabinet those whom Clay suggested, and at Clay's behest he called a special session of Congress to vote the Whig legislative program into action. To the Whigs' dismay, Harrison died of pneumonia just one month into his term and was replaced by Vice President John Tyler.

A states' rights southerner and a strict constitutionalist who had been placed on the Whig ticket to draw Southern votes, Tyler rejected the entire Whig program of a national bank, high protective tariffs, and federally funded internal improvements (roads, canals, etc.). In the resulting legislative confrontations, Tyler vetoed a number of Whig-sponsored bills.

The Whigs were furious. Every cabinet member but one resigned in protest. Tyler was officially expelled from the party and made the target of the first serious impeachment attempt—which failed. In opposition to Tyler over the next few years, the Whigs, under the leadership of Clay, transformed themselves from a loose grouping of diverse factions to a coherent political party with an elaborate organization.

One piece of important legislation that did get passed during Tyler's administration was the Preemption Act (1841), which gave settlers who had squatted on unsurveyed federal lands first chance to buy the land (up to 160 acres at low prices) once it was put on the market.

Scorned by the Whigs and without ties to the Democrats, Tyler was a politician without a party. Hoping to gather a political following of his own, he sought an issue with powerful appeal and believed he had found it in the question of Texas annexation.

Texas President Sam Houston made much show of negotiating for closer relations with Great Britain. Southerners feared that Britain, which opposed slavery, might bring about its abolition in Texas and then use Texas as a base to undermine slavery in the American South. Other Americans were disturbed at the possibility of a British presence in Texas because of the obstacle it would present to what many Americans were coming to believe was, in the words of New York journalist John L. O'Sullivan, America's "manifest destiny to overspread the continent."

Tyler's new secretary of state, John C. Calhoun, negotiated an annexation treaty with Texas. Calhoun's identification with extreme proslavery forces and his insertion in the treaty of proslavery statements caused the treaty's rejection by the Senate (1844).

The Election of 1844: Democratic front-runner Martin Van Buren and Whig front-runner Henry Clay agreed privately that neither would endorse Texas annexation, and that it would not become a campaign issue, but expansionists at the Democratic convention succeeded in dumping Van Buren in favor of James K. Polk (1795–1849). Polk, called "Young Hickory" by his supporters, was a staunch Jacksonian who opposed protective tariffs and a national bank, but favored territorial expansion, including not only annexation of Texas but also occupation of all the Oregon country (up to latitude 54° 40') hitherto jointly occupied by the United States and Britain. The latter claim was expressed in his campaign slogan, "Fifty-four forty or fight."

Tyler, despite his introduction of the issue that was to decide that year's presidential campaign, was unable to build a party of his own and withdrew from the race.

The Whigs nominated Clay, who continued to oppose Texas annexation. Later, sensing the mood of the country was against him, he began to equivocate.

The antislavery Liberty party nominated James G. Birney. Apparently because of Clay's wavering on the Texas issue, Birney was able to take enough votes away from Clay in New York to give that state, and thus the election, to Polk.

Tyler, as a lame-duck president, made one more attempt to achieve Texas annexation before leaving office. By means of a joint resolution, which unlike a treaty required only a simple majority rather than a two-thirds vote, he was successful in getting the measure through Congress. Texas was finally admitted to the Union in 1845.

Though a relatively unknown "dark horse" at the time of his nomination for the presidency, Polk had considerable political experience within his home state of Tennessee and was an adept politician. He turned out to be a skillful and effective president.

As a good Jacksonian, Polk favored a low, revenue-only tariff rather than a high, protective tariff. This he obtained in the Walker Tariff (1846). He also opposed a national debt and a national bank and reestablished Van Buren's Independent Sub-Treasury system, which remained in effect until 1920.

A major issue in the election campaign of 1844, Oregon at this time comprised all the land bounded on the east by the Rockies, the west by the Pacific, the south by latitude 42°, and the north by the boundary of Russian-held Alaska at 54° 40'.

By the terms of the Oregon Treaty (1846), a compromise solution was reached. The current United States-Canada boundary east of the Rockies (49°) was extended westward to the Pacific, thus securing Puget Sound and shared use of the Strait of Juan de Fuca for the United States. Some northern Democrats were angered and felt betrayed by Polk's failure to insist on all of Oregon, but the Senate readily accepted the treaty.

Though Mexico broke diplomatic relations with the United States immediately upon Texas's admission to the Union, there was still hope of a peaceful settlement. In the fall of 1845, Polk sent John Slidell (1793–1871) to Mexico City with a proposal for a peaceful settlement. Slidell was empowered to cancel the damage claims and pay $5,000,000 for the disputed land in southern Texas. He was also authorized to offer $25,000,000 for California and $5,000,000 for other Mexican territory in the Far West. Polk was especially anxious to obtain California because he feared the British would snatch it from Mexico's extremely weak grasp.

Nothing came of these attempts at negotiation. Racked by coup and counter-coup, the Mexican government refused even to receive Slidell.

Polk thereupon sent United States troops into the disputed territory in southern Texas. A force under General Zachary Taylor (1784–1850) (who was nicknamed "Old Rough and Ready") took up a position just north of the Rio Grande. Eight days later, April 5, 1846, Mexican troops attacked an American patrol. When news of the clash reached Washington, Polk sought and received from Congress a declaration of war against Mexico on May 13, 1846.

Some criticized the war, among them Henry David Thoreau, who, to display his protest, went to live at Walden Pond and refused to pay his taxes. Jailed for this, he wrote "Civil Disobedience."

Americans were sharply divided about the war. Some favored it because they felt Mexico had provoked the war, or because they felt it was the destiny of America to spread the blessings of freedom to oppressed peoples. Others, generally northern abolitionists, saw in the war the work of a vast conspiracy of southern slaveholders greedy for more slave territory.

Negotiated peace finally came about when the State Department clerk Nicholas Trist, though his authority had been revoked and he had been ordered back to Washington two months earlier, negotiated and signed the Treaty of Guadalupe-Hidalgo (February 2, 1848), ending the Mexican War. Under the terms of the treaty, Mexico ceded to the United States the territory Polk had originally sought to buy, this time in exchange for a payment of $15,000,000 and the assumption of $3,250,000 in American citizens' claims against the Mexican government. This territory, the Mexican Cession, included the natural harbors at San Francisco and San Diego, thus giving the United States all three of the major West coast natural harbors.

Despite the appropriation of vast territories, many, including Polk, felt the treaty was far too generous. There had been talk of annexing all of Mexico or of forcing Mexico to pay an indemnity for the cost of the war. Still, Polk felt compelled to accept the treaty as it was, and the Senate subsequently ratified it.

Although the Mexican War increased the nation's territory by one-third, it also brought to the surface serious political issues that threatened to divide the country, particularly the question of slavery in the new territories.

13. SECTIONAL CONFLICT AND THE CAUSES OF THE CIVIL WAR (1850–1860)

THE CRISIS OF 1850 AND AMERICA AT MID-CENTURY

The Mexican War had no more than started when, on August 8, 1846, freshman Democratic Congressman David Wilmot (1814–1868) of Pennsylvania introduced his Wilmot Proviso as a proposed amendment to a war appropriations bill. It stipulated that "neither slavery nor involuntary servitude shall ever exist" in any territory to be acquired from Mexico. It was passed by the House, and though rejected by the Senate, it was reintroduced again and again amid increasingly acrimonious debate.

The Wilmot Proviso aroused intense sectional feelings. Southerners, who had supported the war enthusiastically, felt they were being treated unfairly. There came to be four views regarding the status of slavery in the newly acquired territories.

The southern position was expressed by John C. Calhoun, now serving as senator from South Carolina. He argued that the territories were the property not of the United

States federal government, but of all the states together, and therefore Congress had no right to prohibit in any territory any type of "property" (by which he meant slaves) that was legal in any of the states.

Antislavery northerners, pointing to the Northwest Ordinance of 1787 and the Missouri Compromise of 1820 as precedents, argued that Congress had the right to make what laws it saw fit for the territories, including, if it so chose, laws prohibiting slavery.

A compromise proposal favored by President Polk and many moderate southerners called for the extension of the 36° 30' line of the Missouri Compromise westward through the Mexican Cession to the Pacific, with territory north of the line to be closed to slavery.

Another compromise solution, favored by northern Democrats such as Lewis Cass (1782–1866) of Michigan and Stephen A. Douglas (1813–1861) of Illinois, was known as "squatter sovereignty" and later as "popular sovereignty." It held that the residents of each territory should be permitted to decide for themselves whether to allow slavery.

The Election of 1848: The Democrats nominated Lewis Cass, and their platform endorsed his middle-of-the-road popular sovereignty position with regard to slavery in the territories.

The Whigs dodged the issue even more effectively by nominating General Zachary Taylor, whose fame in the Mexican War made him a strong candidate. Taylor knew nothing of politics, had never voted, and liked to think of himself as above politics. He took no position at all with respect to slavery in the territories.

Some antislavery northern Whigs and Democrats, disgusted with their parties' failure to take a clear stand against the spread of slavery, deserted the party ranks to form an antislavery third party. Their party was called the Free Soil party, since it stood for keeping the soil of new western territories free of slavery. Its candidate was Martin Van Buren.

The election excited relatively little public interest. Taylor won a narrow victory.

The California Gold Rush

The question of slavery's status in the western territories was made more immediate when, on January 24, 1848, gold was discovered at Sutter's Mill, not far from Sacramento, California. The next year, gold seekers from the eastern United States and from many foreign countries swelled California's population from 14,000 to 100,000.

California was a wild and lawless place. No territorial government had been organized since the United States had received the land as part of the Mexican Cession, and all that existed was an inadequate military government. In September 1849, having more than the requisite population and being in need of better government, California petitioned for admission to the Union as a state.

Since few slaveholders had chosen to risk their valuable investments in human property in the turbulent atmosphere of California, the people of the area sought admission as a free state, touching off a serious sectional crisis back East.

The Compromise of 1850

President Zachary Taylor, though himself a Louisiana slaveholder, opposed the further spread of slavery. Hoping to sidestep the dangerously divisive issue of slavery in the territories, he encouraged California as well as the rest of the Mexican Cession to organize and seek admission directly as states, thus completely bypassing the territorial stage.

Southerners were furious. Long outnumbered in the House of Representatives, the

South would now find itself, should California be admitted as a free state, also outvoted in the Senate.

At this point, the aged Henry Clay attempted to compromise the various matters of contention between North and South. He proposed an eight-part package. For the North, California would be admitted as a free state; the land in dispute between Texas and New Mexico would go to New Mexico; the New Mexico and Utah territories (all of the Mexican Cession outside of California) would not be specifically reserved for slavery, the status there would be decided by popular sovereignty; and the slave trade would be abolished in the District of Columbia.

For the South, a tougher Fugitive Slave Law would be enacted; the federal government would pay Texas's $10,000,000 preannexation debt; Congress would declare that it did not have jurisdiction over the interstate slave trade and would promise not to abolish slavery itself in the District of Columbia.

The opponents of the Compromise were many and powerful and ranged from President Taylor, who demanded admission of California without reference to slavery, to northern extremists such as Senator William Seward (1801–1872) of New York, who spoke of a "higher law" than the Constitution which forbade the spread of slavery, to southern extremists such as Calhoun or Senator Jefferson Davis (1808–1889) of Mississippi. By midsummer all seemed lost for the Compromise, and Clay left Washington exhausted and discouraged.

Then the situation changed dramatically. President Taylor died (apparently of gastroenteritis) on July 9, 1850, and was succeeded by Vice-President Millard Fillmore (1800–1874), a quiet but efficient politician, and a strong supporter of compromise. In Congress, the fight for the Compromise was taken up by Senator Stephen A. Douglas of Illinois. Called the "Little Giant" for his small stature and large political skills, Douglas broke Clay's proposal into its component parts so that he could use varying coalitions to push each part through Congress. The Compromise was adopted.

The Compromise of 1850 was received with joy by most of the nation. The issue of slavery in the territories seemed to have been permanently settled.

The 1852 Democratic convention deadlocked between Cass and Douglas and so settled on dark horse Franklin Pierce (1804–1869) of New Hampshire. The Whigs chose General Winfield Scott, a war hero with no political background.

The result was an easy victory for Pierce, largely because the Whig party, badly divided along North-South lines as a result of the battle over the Compromise of 1850, was beginning to come apart. The Free Soil party's candidate, John P. Hale of New Hampshire, fared poorly, demonstrating the electorate's weariness with the slavery issue.

President Pierce expressed the nation's hope that a new era of sectional peace was beginning. He sought to distract the nation's attention from the slavery issue to an aggressive program of foreign economic and territorial expansion known as "Young America."

In 1853, Commodore Matthew Perry (1794–1858) led a United States naval force into Tokyo Bay on a mission to open Japan—previously closed to the outside world—to American diplomacy and commerce.

By means of the Reciprocity Treaty (1854), Pierce succeeded in opening Canada to greater United States trade. He also sought to annex Hawaii, increase United States interest in Central America, and acquire territories from Mexico and Spain.

From Mexico he acquired in 1853 the Gadsden Purchase, a strip of land in what is now southern New Mexico and Arizona along the Gila River. The purpose of this purchase was to provide a good route for a transcontinental railroad across the southern part of the country.

The chief factor in the economic transformation of America during the 1840s and 1850s was the dynamic rise of the railroads. They helped link the Midwest to the Northeast rather than just the South, as would have been the case had only water transportation been available.

The 1850s was the heyday of the steamboat on inland rivers, and the clipper ship on the high seas. The period also saw rapid and sustained industrial growth. The factory system began in the textile industry, with Elias Howe's invention of the sewing machine (1846). Isaac Singer's improved model (1851) aided the process of mechanization, which spread to other industries.

In the North, the main centers of agricultural production shifted from the Mid-Atlantic states to the more fertile lands of the Midwest. Unlike the South, where 3,500,000 slaves provided abundant labor, the North faced incentives to introduce labor-saving machines. Mechanical reapers and threshers came into wide use.

America's second two-party system, which had developed during the 1830s, was in the process of breaking down. The Whig party was now in the process of complete disintegration. This was partially the result of the slavery issue, which divided the party along North-South lines, and partially the result of the nativist movement.

The nativist movement and its political party, the American, or, as it was called, the Know-Nothing party, grew out of alarm on the part of native-born Americans at the rising tide of German and Irish immigration during the late 1840s and early 1850s.

The collapse of a viable two-party system made it much more difficult for the nation's political process to contain the explosive issue of slavery.

THE RETURN OF SECTIONAL CONFLICT

The strengthened Fugitive Slave Law enraged northerners. Under its provisions, blacks living in the North who were claimed by slave catchers were denied trial by jury and many of the other protections of due process. Even more distasteful to antislavery northerners was the provision that required all United States citizens to aid, when called upon, in the capture and return of alleged fugitives. So violent was northern feeling against the law that several riots erupted as a result of attempts to enforce it. Some northern states passed personal liberty laws in an attempt to prevent the enforcement of the Fugitive Slave Law.

Many northerners who had not previously taken an interest in the slavery issue now became opponents of slavery as a result of having its injustices forcibly brought home to them by the Fugitive Slave Law.

One northerner who was outraged by the Fugitive Slave Act was Harriet Beecher Stowe. She wrote *Uncle Tom's Cabin*, a fictional book depicting what she perceived as the evils of slavery. Furiously denounced in the South, the book became an overnight bestseller in the North, where it turned many toward active opposition to slavery.

All illusion of sectional peace ended abruptly in 1854 when Senator Stephen A. Douglas of Illinois introduced a bill in Congress to organize the area west of Missouri and Iowa as the territories of Kansas and Nebraska.

Though he sought to avoid directly addressing the touchy issue of slavery, Douglas was compelled by pressure from southern senators such as David Atchison of Missouri to include in the bill an explicit repeal of the Missouri Compromise (which banned slavery in the areas in question) and a provision that the status of slavery in the newly organized territories be decided by popular sovereignty.

The bill was opposed by most northern Democrats and a majority of the remaining Whigs, but with the support of the southern-dominated Pierce administration it was passed and signed into law.

The Kansas-Nebraska Act aroused a storm of outrage in the North, where the repeal of the Missouri Compromise was seen as the breaking of a solemn agreement. It hastened the disintegration of the Whig party and divided the Democratic party along North-South lines.

In the North, many Democrats left the party and were joined by former Whigs and Know-Nothings in the newly created Republican party. Springing to life almost overnight as a result of northern fury at the Kansas-Nebraska Act, the Republican party included diverse elements whose sole unifying principle was the firm belief that slavery should be banned from all the nation's territories, confined to the states where it already existed, and allowed to spread no further.

Though its popularity was confined almost entirely to the North, the Republican party quickly became a major power in national politics.

With the status of Kansas (Nebraska was never in much doubt) to be decided by the voters there, North and South began competing to see which could send the greatest number of settlers. Northerners formed the New England Emigrant Aid Company to promote the settling of antislavery men in Kansas, and southerners responded in kind. The majority of Kansas settlers were opposed to the spread of slavery. But large-scale election fraud, especially on the part of heavily armed Missouri "border ruffians" who crossed into Kansas on election day to vote their proslavery principles early and often, led to the creation of a virulently proslavery territorial government. When the presidentially appointed territorial governor protested this gross fraud, Pierce removed him from office.

Free-soil Kansans responded by denouncing the pro-slavery government as illegitimate and forming their own free-soil government in an election which the pro slavery faction boycotted. Kansas now had two rival governments, each claiming to be the only lawful one.

Both sides began arming themselves, and soon the territory was being referred to in the northern press as "Bleeding Kansas" because full-scale guerilla war erupted. In May 1856, Missouri border ruffians sacked the free-soil town of Lawrence, killing two, and destroying homes, businesses, and printing presses. Two days later, a small band of antislavery zealots under the leadership of fanatical abolitionist John Brown (1800–1859) retaliated by killing and mutilating five unarmed men and boys at a proslavery settlement on Pottawatomie Creek. In all, some 200 died in the months of guerilla fighting that followed.

In *Dred Scott vs. Sanford*, the Supreme Court attempted to finally settle the slavery question. The case involved a Missouri slave, Dred Scott (ca. 1795–1858), who had been encouraged by abolitionists to sue for his freedom on the basis that his owner had taken him for several years to a free state, Illinois, and then to a free territory, Wisconsin.

Under the domination of aging pro-southern Chief Justice Roger B. Taney of Maryland, the Court attempted to read the extreme southern position on slavery into the Constitution, ruling not only that Scott had no standing to sue in federal court, but also that temporary residence in a free state, even for several years, did not make a slave free, and that the Missouri Compromise (already a dead letter by that time) had been unconstitutional all along because Congress did not have the authority to exclude slavery from a territory. Nor did territorial governments have the right to prohibit slavery. Far from settling the sectional controversy, the Dred Scott case only made it worse.

Later in 1857, the proslavery government in Kansas, through largely fraudulent means, arranged for a heavily proslavery constitutional convention to meet at the town of Lecompton. The result was a state constitution that allowed slavery. To obtain a pretense of popular approval for this constitution, the convention provided for a referendum in which the voters were to be given a choice only to prohibit the entry of additional slaves into the state.

Disgusted free-soilers boycotted the referendum, and the result was a constitution that put no restrictions at all on slavery. Touting this Lecompton constitution, the proslavery territorial government petitioned Congress for admission to the Union as a slave state. Meanwhile, the free-soilers drafted a constitution of their own and submitted it to Congress as the legitimate one for the prospective state of Kansas.

Eager to appease the South, which had started talking of secession again, and equally eager to suppress antislavery agitation in the North, Buchanan vigorously backed the Lecompton constitution. Douglas, appalled at this travesty of popular sovereignty, broke with the administration to oppose it. He and Buchanan became bitter political enemies, with the president determined to use all the power of the Democratic organization to crush Douglas politically.

After extremely bitter debate, the Senate approved the Lecompton constitution, but the House insisted that Kansans be given a chance to vote on the entire document. Southern congressmen pressured Kansas voters by adding the stipulation that should the Lecompton constitution be approved, Kansas would receive a generous grant of federal land, but should it be voted down, Kansas would remain a territory.

Nevertheless, Kansas voters, when given a chance to express themselves in a fair election, turned down the Lecompton constitution by an overwhelming margin, choosing to remain a territory rather than become a slave state. Kansas was finally admitted as a free state in 1861.

The 1858 Illinois senatorial campaign produced a series of debates that got to the heart of the issues that were threatening to divide the nation. Incumbent Democratic senator and front-runner for the 1860 presidential nomination Stephen A. Douglas was opposed by a Springfield lawyer, little known outside the state, by the name of Abraham Lincoln.

Though Douglas had been hailed in some free-soil circles for his opposition to the Lecompton constitution, Lincoln, in a series of seven debates that the candidates agreed to hold during the course of the campaign, stressed that Douglas's doctrine of popular sovereignty failed to recognize slavery for the moral wrong it was.

Douglas, for his part, maintained that his guiding principle was democracy, not any moral standard of right or wrong with respect to slavery. The people could, as far as he was concerned, "vote it up or vote it down." At the same time, he strove to depict Lincoln as a radical and an abolitionist who believed in racial equality and race mixing.

At the debate held in Freeport, Illinois, Lincoln pressed Douglas to reconcile the principle of popular sovereignty to the Supreme Court's decision in the Dred Scott case. How could the people "vote it up or vote it down," if, as the Supreme Court alleged, no territorial government could prohibit slavery? Douglas, in what came to be called his "Freeport Doctrine," replied that the people of any territory could exclude slavery simply by declining to pass any of the special laws that slave jurisdictions usually passed for their protection.

Douglas's answer was good enough to win him reelection to the Senate, although by the narrowest of margins, but hurt him in the coming presidential campaign. His Freeport Doctrine hardened the opposition of southerners already angered by his anti-Lecompton stand.

For Lincoln, despite the failure to win the Senate seat, the debates were a major success, propelling him into the national spotlight, and strengthening the resolve of the Republican party to resist compromise on the free-soil issue.

THE COMING OF THE CIVIL WAR

On the night of October 16, 1859, John Brown, the Pottawatomie Creek murderer, led 18 followers in seizing the federal arsenal at Harpers Ferry, Virginia (now West Virginia), taking hostages, and endeavoring to incite a slave uprising. Brown, supported and bankrolled by several prominent northern abolitionists (later referred to as "the Secret Six"), planned to arm local slaves and then spread his uprising across the South. His scheme was ill conceived and had little chance of success. Quickly cornered by Virginia militia, he was eventually captured by a force of United States Marines under the command of army Colonel Robert E. Lee (1807–1870). Ten of Brown's 18 men were killed in the fight, and Brown himself was wounded.

Charged under Virginia law with treason and various other crimes, Brown was quickly tried, convicted, sentenced, and on December 2, 1859, hanged. His death was marked in the North by signs of public mourning. Many northerners looked upon Brown as a martyr.

Though responsible northerners such as Lincoln denounced Brown's raid as a criminal act which deserved to be punished by death, many southerners became convinced that the entire northern public approved of Brown's action and that the only safety for the South lay in a separate southern confederacy. This was all the more so because Brown, in threatening to create a slave revolt, had touched on the foremost fear of white southerners.

In this mood, the country approached the election of 1860, a campaign that eventually became a four-man contest.

Two Democratic conventions failed to reach consensus, and the sundered halves of the party nominated separate candidates. The southern wing of the party nominated Buchanan's vice president, John C. Breckinridge of Kentucky, on a platform calling for a federal slave code in all the territories. What was left of the national Democratic party nominated Douglas on a platform of popular sovereignty.

A third presidential candidate was added by the Constitutional Union party, a collection of aging former Whigs and Know-Nothings from the southern and border states, plus a handful of moderate southern Democrats. It nominated John Bell of Tennessee on a platform that sidestepped the issues and called simply for the Constitution, the Union, and the enforcement of the laws.

The Republicans met in Chicago, confident of victory and determined to do nothing to jeopardize their favorable position. Accordingly, they rejected as too radical front-running New York Senator William H. Seward in favor of Illinois favorite son Abraham Lincoln. The platform called for federal support of a transcontinental railroad and for the containment of slavery.

Douglas, believing only his victory could reconcile North and South, became the first United States presidential candidate to make a vigorous nationwide speaking tour.

On election day, the voting went along strictly sectional lines. Breckinridge carried the Deep South; Bell, the border states; and Lincoln, the North. Douglas, although second in popular votes, carried only a single state and part of another. Lincoln led in popular votes, and though he was short of a majority in that category, he did have the needed majority in electoral votes and was elected.

THE SECESSION CRISIS

Lincoln had declared he had no intention of disturbing slavery where it already existed, but many southerners thought otherwise. They also feared further raids of the sort John Brown had attempted, and felt their pride injured by the election of a president for whom no southerner had voted.

On December 20, 1860, South Carolina, by vote of a special convention, declared itself out of the Union. By February 1, 1861, six more states (Alabama, Georgia, Florida, Mississippi, Louisiana, and Texas) had followed suit.

Representatives of the seceded states met in Montgomery, Alabama, in February 1861 and declared themselves to be the Confederate States of America. They elected former Secretary of War and United States Senator Jefferson Davis of Mississippi as president, and Alexander Stephens (1812–1883) of Georgia as vice president. They also adopted a constitution for the Confederate states which, while similar to the United States Constitution in many ways, contained several important differences:

1) Slavery was specifically recognized, and the right to move slaves from one state to another was guaranteed.

2) Protective tariffs were prohibited.

3) The president was to serve for a single nonrenewable six-year term.

4) The president was given the right to veto individual items within an appropriations bill.

5) State sovereignty was specifically recognized.

In the North, reaction was mixed. President Buchanan, now a lame duck, declared secession to be unconstitutional, but at the same time stated his belief that it was unconstitutional for the federal government to do anything to stop states from seceding. Taking his own advice, he did nothing.

Others, led by Senator John J. Crittenden of Kentucky, strove for a compromise that would preserve the Union. As the southern states one by one declared their secession, Crittenden worked desperately with a congressional compromise committee in hopes of working out some form of agreement.

The compromise proposals centered on the passage of a constitutional amendment forever prohibiting federal meddling with slavery in the states where it existed, as well as the extension of the Missouri Compromise line (36° 30') to the Pacific, with slavery specifically protected in all the territories south of it.

Some congressional Republicans were inclined to accept this compromise, but President-elect Lincoln urged them to stand firm for no further spread of slavery. Southerners would consider no compromise that did not provide for the spread of slavery, and talks broke down.

14. THE CIVIL WAR AND RECONSTRUCTION (1860–1877)

HOSTILITIES BEGIN

Lincoln did his best to avoid angering the slave states that had not yet seceded. In his inaugural address, he urged southerners to reconsider their actions, but warned that the Union was perpetual, that states could not secede, and that he would therefore hold the federal forts and installations in the South.

Only two remained in federal hands: Fort Pickens, off Pensacola, Florida; and Fort

Sumter, in the harbor of Charleston, South Carolina. Lincoln soon received word from Major Robert Anderson, commander of the small garrison at Sumter, that supplies were running low. Desiring to send in the needed supplies, Lincoln informed the governor of South Carolina of his intention, but promised that no attempt would be made to send arms, ammunition, or reinforcements unless southerners initiated hostilities.

Not satisfied, southerners determined to take the fort. Confederate General P.G.T. Beauregard (1818–1893), acting on orders from President Davis, demanded Anderson's surrender. Anderson said he would surrender if not resupplied. Knowing supplies were on the way, the Confederates opened fire at 4:30 a.m. on April 12, 1861. The next day, the fort surrendered.

The day following Sumter's surrender, Lincoln declared an insurrection and called for the states to provide 75,000 volunteers to put it down. In response to this, Virginia, Tennessee, North Carolina, and Arkansas declared their secession.

The remaining slave states, Delaware, Kentucky, Maryland, and Missouri, wavered, but stayed with the Union. Delaware, which had few slaves, gave little serious consideration to the idea of secession. Kentucky declared itself neutral, and then sided with the North when the South failed to respect this neutrality. Maryland's incipient secession movement was crushed by Lincoln's timely imposition of martial law. Missouri was saved for the Union by the quick and decisive use of federal troops, as well as the sizable population of pro-Union, antislavery German immigrants living in St. Louis.

The North enjoyed at least five major advantages over the South. It had overwhelming preponderance in wealth and was vastly superior in industry.

The North also had an advantage of almost three to one in manpower; and over one-third of the South's population was composed of slaves, whom Southerners would not use as soldiers. Unlike the South, the North received large numbers of immigrants during the war. The North retained control of the United States Navy, and thus would command the sea and be able to blockade the South. Finally, the North enjoyed a much superior system of railroads.

The South did, however, have several advantages. It was vast in size, making it difficult to conquer. Its troops would be fighting on their own ground, a fact that would give them the advantage of familiarity with the terrain, as well as the added motivation of defending their homes and families. Its armies would often have the opportunity of fighting on the defensive, a major advantage in the warfare of that day.

At the outset of the war, the South drew a number of highly qualified senior officers, men like Robert E. Lee, Joseph E. Johnston (1807–1891), and Albert Sidney Johnston (1803–1862), from the U.S. Army. By contrast, the Union command structure was already set when the war began, with the aged Winfield Scott, of Mexican War fame, at the top. It took young and talented officers such as Ulysses S. Grant (1822–1885) and William T. Sherman (1820–1891) time to work up to high rank. Meanwhile, Union armies were often led by inferior commanders as Lincoln experimented in search of good generals.

Though Jefferson Davis had extensive military and political experience, Lincoln was much superior to Davis as a war leader, showing firmness, flexibility, mental toughness, great political skill, and, eventually an excellent grasp of strategy.

At a creek called Bull Run near the town of Manassas Junction, Virginia, just southwest of Washington, D.C., the Union Army met a Confederate force under generals P.G.T. Beauregard and Joseph E. Johnston, July 21, 1861. In the First Battle of Bull Run (called First Battle of Manassas in the South), the Union army was forced to retreat in confusion back to Washington.

Bull Run demonstrated the unpreparedness and inexperience of both sides. It also demonstrated that the war would be long and hard.

THE UNION PRESERVED

To replace the discredited McDowell, Lincoln chose General George B. McClellan (1826–1885). McClellan was a good trainer and organizer and was loved by the troops, but he was unable to effectively use the powerful army (now called the Army of the Potomac) he had built up.

Lee summoned General Thomas J. "Stonewall" Jackson (1824–1863) and his army from the Shenandoah Valley (where Jackson had just finished defeating several superior federal forces), and with the combined forces attacked McClellan.

After two days of bloody but inconclusive fighting, McClellan lost his nerve and began to retreat. In the remainder of what came to be called the Battle of the Seven Days, Lee continued to attack McClellan, forcing him back to his base, though at great cost in lives. McClellan's army was loaded back onto its ships and taken back to Washington.

Before McClellan's army could reach Washington, Lee took the opportunity to thrash Union General John Pope (1822–1892), who was in northern Virginia with another northern army, at the Second Battle of Bull Run.

West of the Appalachian Mountains, matters were proceeding differently. The northern commanders there, Henry W. Halleck (1815–1872) and Don Carlos Buell (1818–1898), were no more enterprising than McClellan, but Halleck's subordinate, Ulysses S. Grant, was.

With permission from Halleck, Grant mounted a combined operation—army troops and navy gunboats—against two vital Confederate strongholds, forts Henry and Donelson, which guarded the Tennessee and Cumberland rivers in northern Tennessee. When Grant captured the forts in February 1862, Johnston was forced to retreat to Corinth in northern Mississippi.

Grant pursued, but ordered by Halleck to wait until all was in readiness before proceeding, halted his troops at Pittsburg Landing on the Tennessee River, 25 miles north of Corinth. On April 6, 1862, General Albert Sidney Johnston, who had received reinforcements and been joined by General P.G.T. Beauregard, surprised Grant there, but in the two-day battle that followed (Shiloh) failed to defeat him. Johnston was among the many killed in what was, up to this point, the bloodiest battle in American history.

Grant was severely criticized in the North for having been taken by surprise. Yet with other Union victories and Farragut's capture of New Orleans, the North had taken all of the Mississippi River except for a 110-mile stretch between the Confederate fortresses of Vicksburg, Mississippi, and Port Hudson, Louisiana.

Many southerners believed Britain and France would rejoice in seeing a divided and weakened America. They also believed the two countries would likewise be driven by the need of their factories for cotton and thus intervene on the Confederacy's behalf. So strongly was this view held that during the early days of the war, when the Union blockade was still too weak to be very effective, the Confederate government itself prohibited the export of cotton in order to hasten British and French intervention.

This view proved mistaken. Britain already had a large supply of cotton, and had other sources besides the U.S. British leaders may also have weighed their country's need to import wheat from the northern United States against its desire for cotton from the southern states. Finally, British public opinion opposed slavery.

Skillful northern diplomacy had a great impact. In this, Lincoln had the extremely able assistance of Secretary of State William Seward, who took a hard line in warning

Europeans not to interfere, and of ambassador to Great Britain Charles Francis Adams (1807–1886). Britain remained neutral, and other European countries, including France followed its lead.

The Confederacy's major bid to challenge the Union's naval superiority was based on a technological innovation—the ironclad ship. The first and most successful of the Confederate ironclads was the C.S.S. *Virginia*. Built on the hull of the abandoned Union frigate *Merrimac*, the *Virginia* was protected from cannon fire by iron plates bolted over her sloping wooden sides. In May 1862, she destroyed two wooden warships of the Union naval force at Hampton Roads, Virginia, and was seriously threatening to destroy the rest of the squadron before being met and fought to a standstill by the Union ironclad U.S.S. *Monitor*.

Congress in 1862 passed two highly important acts dealing with domestic affairs in the North. The Homestead Act granted 160 acres of government land free of charge to any person who would farm it for at least five years. Much of the West was eventually settled under the provisions of this act. The Morrill Land Grant Act offered large amounts of the federal government's land to states that would establish "agricultural and mechanical" colleges. Many of the nation's large state universities were later founded under the provisions of this act.

THE EMANCIPATION PROCLAMATION

By mid-1862, Lincoln, under pressure from radical elements of his own party and hoping to create a favorable impression on foreign public opinion, determined to issue the Emancipation Proclamation, which declared free all slaves in areas still in rebellion as of January 1, 1863. At Seward's recommendation, Lincoln waited to announce the proclamation until the North should win some sort of victory. This was provided by the Battle of Antietam (September 17, 1863).

Though the Radical Republicans, prewar abolitionists for the most part, had for some time been urging Lincoln to take such a step, northern public opinion as a whole was less enthusiastic. The Republicans suffered major losses in the November 1862 congressional elections.

After his victory at the Second Battle of Bull Run, Lee moved north and crossed into Maryland, where he hoped to win a decisive victory that would force the North to recognize southern independence.

McClellan got hold of Lee's plans, but by extreme caution and slowness, threw away this incomparable chance to annihilate Lee and win—or at least shorten—the war.

The armies finally met along Antietam Creek, just east of the town of Sharpsburg in western Maryland. In a bloody but inconclusive day-long battle, known as Antietam in the North and Sharpsburg in the South, McClellan's timidity led him to miss another excellent chance to destroy Lee's cornered and badly outnumbered army. After the battle, Lee retreated to Virginia, and Lincoln removed McClellan from command.

To replace him, Lincoln chose General Ambrose E. Burnside (1824–1881), who promptly demonstrated his unfitness by blundering into a lopsided defeat at Fredericksburg, Virginia (December 13, 1862).

Lincoln then replaced Burnside with General Joseph "Fighting Joe" Hooker (1814–1879). Handsome and hard-drinking, Hooker had bragged of what he would do to "Bobby Lee" when he got at him; but when he took his army south, "Fighting Joe" quickly lost his nerve. He was soundly beaten at the Battle of Chancellorsville (May 5–6, 1863). At this battle, the brilliant Southern General "Stonewall" Jackson was accidentally shot by his own men and died several days later.

Lee received permission from President Davis to invade Pennsylvania. He was pursued by the Army of the Potomac, now under the command of General George G. Meade (1815–1872), who had replaced the discredited Hooker. They met at Gettysburg in a three-day battle (July 1–3, 1863) that was the bloodiest of the war. Lee, who sorely missed the services of Jackson and whose cavalry leader, the normally reliable J.E.B. Stuart (1833–1864), failed to provide him with timely reconnaissance, was defeated. However, he was allowed by the victorious Meade to retreat to Virginia with his army intact if battered, much to Lincoln's disgust. Still, Lee would never again have the strength to mount such an invasion.

Meanwhile, Grant moved on Vicksburg, one of the two last Confederate bastions on the Mississippi River. In a brilliant campaign, he bottled up the Confederate forces of General John C. Pemberton (1814–1881) inside the city and placed them under siege. After six weeks, the defenders surrendered on July 4, 1863. Five days later, Port Hudson surrendered, giving the Union complete control of the Mississippi.

After Union forces under General William Rosecrans (1819–1898) suffered an embarrassing defeat at the Battle of Chickamauga in northwestern Georgia (September 19–20, 1863), Lincoln named Grant overall commander of Union forces in the West.

Grant went to Chattanooga, Tennessee, where Confederate forces under General Braxton Bragg (1817–1876) were virtually besieging Rosecrans, and immediately took control of the situation. Gathering Union forces from other portions of the western theater and combining them with reinforcements from the East, Grant won a resounding victory at the Battle of Chattanooga (November 23–25, 1863), in which federal forces stormed seemingly impregnable Confederate positions on Lookout Mountain and Missionary Ridge. This victory put Union forces in position for a drive into Georgia, which began the following spring.

Early in 1864, Lincoln made Grant commander of all Union armies. Grant devised a coordinated plan for constant pressure on the Confederacy. General William T. Sherman would lead a drive toward Atlanta, Georgia, with the goal of destroying the Confederate army under General Joseph E. Johnston (who had replaced Bragg). Grant would accompany Meade and the Army of the Potomac in advancing toward Richmond with the goal of destroying Lee's Confederate army.

In a series of bloody battles (the Wilderness, Spotsylvania, Cold Harbor) in May and June of 1864, Grant drove Lee to the outskirts of Richmond. Still unable to take the city or get Lee at a disadvantage, Grant circled around, attacking Petersburg, Virginia, an important railroad junction just south of Richmond and the key to that city's—and Lee's—supply lines. Once again turned back by entrenched Confederate troops, Grant settled down to besiege Petersburg and Richmond in a stalemate that lasted some nine months.

Sherman had been advancing simultaneously in Georgia. He maneuvered Johnston back to the outskirts of Atlanta with relatively little fighting. At that point, Confederate President Davis lost patience with Johnston and replaced him with the aggressive General John B. Hood (1831–1879). Hood and Sherman fought three fierce but inconclusive battles around Atlanta in late July, and then settled down to a siege of their own during the month of August.

The Election of 1864 and Northern Victory: In the North, discontentment grew with the long casualty lists and seeming lack of results. Yet, the South could stand the grinding war even less. By late 1864, Jefferson Davis had reached the point of calling for the use of slaves in the Confederate armies, though the war ended before black troops could fight for the Confederacy. The South's best hope was that northern war-weariness would bring the defeat of Lincoln and the victory of a peace candidate in the election of 1864.

Lincoln ran on the ticket of the National Union party, essentially the Republican party with loyal or "War" Democrats. His vice-presidential candidate was Andrew Johnson (1808–1875), a loyal Democrat from Tennessee.

The Democratic party's presidential candidate was General George B. McClellan, who, with some misgivings, ran on a platform labeling the war a failure, and calling for a negotiated peace settlement even if that meant independence for the South.

Even Lincoln believed that he would be defeated. Then in September 1864, word came that Sherman had taken Atlanta. The capture of this vital southern rail and manu-facturing center brought an enormous boost to northern morale. Along with other north-ern victories that summer and fall, it ensured a resounding election victory for Lincoln and the continuation of the war to complete victory for the North.

To speed that victory, Sherman marched through Georgia from Atlanta to the sea, arriving at Savannah in December 1864 and turning north into the Carolinas, leaving behind a 60–mile-wide swath of destruction. His goal was to impress on southerners that continuation of the war could only mean ruin for all of them. He and Grant planned that his army should press on through the Carolinas and into Virginia to join Grant in finish-ing off Lee.

Before Sherman's troops could arrive, Lee abandoned Richmond (April 3, 1865) and attempted to escape with what was left of his army. Pursued by Grant, he was cornered and forced to surrender at Appomattox, Virginia (April 9, 1865). Other Con-federate armies still holding out in various parts of the South surrendered over the next few weeks.

Lincoln did not live to receive news of the final surrenders. On April 14, 1865, he was shot in the back of the head while watching a play in Ford's Theater in Washington. His assassin, pro-southern actor John Wilkes Booth (1838–1865), injured his ankle in making his escape. Hunted down by Union cavalry several days later, he died of a gunshot wound, apparently self-inflicted. Several other individuals were tried, convicted, and hanged by a military tribunal for participating with Booth in a conspiracy to assassi-nate not only Lincoln, but also Vice-President Johnson and Secretary of State Seward.

THE ORDEAL OF RECONSTRUCTION

Reconstruction began well before the fighting of the Civil War came to an end. It brought a time of difficult adjustments in the South.

Among those who faced such adjustments were the recently freed slaves, who flocked into Union lines or followed advancing Union armies or whose plantations were part of the growing area of the South that came under Union military control. Some slaves had left their plantations, and thus their only means of livelihood, in order to obtain freedom within Union lines.

To ease the adjustment for these recently freed slaves, Congress in 1865 created the Freedman's Bureau to provide food, clothing, and education, and generally look after the interests of former slaves.

To restore legal governments in the seceded states, Lincoln's policy, known as the Ten Percent Plan, stipulated that southerners, except for high-ranking rebel officials, could take an oath promising future loyalty to the Union and acceptance of the end of slavery. When the number of those who had taken this oath within any one state reached 10 percent of the number who had been registered to vote in that state in 1860, a loyal state government could be formed. Only those who had taken the oath could vote or participate in the new government.

Tennessee, Arkansas, and Louisiana met the requirements and formed loyal governments, but were refused recognition by a Congress dominated by Radical Republicans.

Radical Republicans such as Thaddeus Stevens (1792–1868) of Pennsylvania believed Lincoln's plan did not adequately punish the South, restructure southern society, or boost the political prospects of the Republican party. The loyal southern states were denied representation in Congress and electoral votes in the election of 1864.

Instead, the radicals in Congress drew up the Wade-Davis Bill. Under its stringent terms, a majority of the number who had been alive and registered to vote in 1860 would have to swear an "ironclad" oath stating that they were now loyal and had never been disloyal. This was obviously impossible in any former Confederate state unless blacks were given the vote, something Radical Republicans desired but southerners definitely did not. Unless the requisite number swore the "ironclad" oath, Congress would not allow the state to have a government.

Lincoln killed the Wade-Davis Bill with a "pocket veto," and the radicals were furious. When Lincoln was assassinated the radicals rejoiced, believing Vice President Andrew Johnson would be less generous to the South, or at least easier to control.

In 1866, the Russian minister approached Seward with an offer to sell Alaska to the United States. Seward, who was an ardent expansionist, pushed hard for the purchase of Alaska, known as "Seward's Folly" by its critics. In 1867, the sale went through and Alaska was purchased for $7,200,000.

Congressional Reconstruction

Determined to reconstruct the South as it saw fit, Congress passed a Civil Rights Act and extended the authority of the Freedman's Bureau, giving it both quasi-judicial and quasi-executive powers.

Johnson vetoed both bills, claiming they were unconstitutional; but Congress overrode the vetoes. Fearing that the Supreme Court would agree with Johnson and overturn the laws, Congress approved and sent on to the states for ratification (June 1866) the fourteenth Amendment, making constitutional the laws Congress had just passed. The fourteenth Amendment defined citizenship and forbade states to deny various rights to citizens, reduced the representation in Congress of states that did not allow blacks to vote, forbade the paying of the Confederate debt, and made former Confederates ineligible to hold public office.

To control the president, Congress passed the Army Act, reducing the president's control over the army. In obtaining the cooperation of the army, the Radicals had the aid of General Grant, who already had his eye on the 1868 Republican presidential nomination. Congress also passed the Tenure of Office Act, forbidding Johnson to dismiss cabinet members without the Senate's permission. In passing the latter act, Congress was especially thinking of radical Secretary of War Edwin M. Stanton (1814–1869), a Lincoln holdover whom Johnson desired to dismiss.

Johnson obeyed the letter but not the spirit of the Reconstruction acts, and Congress, angry at his refusal to cooperate, sought in vain for grounds to impeach him, until in August 1867 Johnson violated the Tenure of Office Act (by dismissing Stanton) in order to test its constitutionality. The matter was not tested in the courts, however, but in Congress, where Johnson was impeached by the House of Representatives and came within one vote of being removed by the Senate. For the remaining months of his term, he offered little resistance to the radicals.

The Election of 1868 and the 15th Amendment: In 1868, the Republican convention, dominated by the radicals, drew up a platform endorsing Radical Reconstruction. For president, the Republicans nominated Ulysses S. Grant, who had no political record and whose views—if any—on national issues were unknown. The vice-presidential nominee was Schuyler Colfax.

The narrow victory of even such a strong candidate as Grant prompted Republican leaders to decide that it would be politically expedient to give the vote to all blacks, North as well as South. For this purpose, the 15th Amendment was drawn up and submitted to the states. Ironically, the idea was so unpopular in the North that it won the necessary three-fourths approval only with its ratification by southern states required to do so by Congress.

Though of unquestioned personal integrity, Grant naively placed his faith in a number of thoroughly dishonest men. His administration was rocked by one scandalous revelation of government corruption after another.

A faction of the Republican party separated and called itself the Liberal Republicans. Besides opposing corruption and favoring sectional harmony, the Liberal Republicans favored hard money and a laissez-faire approach to economic issues. For the election of 1872, they nominated *New York Tribune* editor Horace Greeley (1811–1872) for president. Greeley was easily defeated by Grant, who was again the nominee of the radicals.

Many of the economic difficulties the country faced during Grant's administration were caused by the necessary readjustments from a wartime economy back to a peacetime economy. The central economic question was deflation versus inflation, or more specifically, whether to retire the unbacked paper money, greenbacks, printed to meet the wartime emergency, or to print more.

Economic conservatives, creditors, and business interests usually favored retirement of the greenbacks and an early return to the gold standard.

Early in Grant's second term, the country was hit by an economic depression known as the Panic of 1873. Brought on by the overexpansive tendencies of railroad builders and businessmen during the immediate postwar boom, the Panic was triggered by economic downturns in Europe, and more immediately, by the failure of Jay Cooke and Company, a major American financial firm.

The Panic led to clamor for the printing of more greenbacks. In 1874, Congress authorized a small new issue of greenbacks, but it was vetoed by Grant. Pro-inflation forces were further enraged when Congress in 1873 demonetized silver, going to a straight gold standard. Silver was becoming more plentiful due to western mining and was seen by some as a potential source of inflation. Pro-inflation forces referred to the demonetization of silver as the "Crime of '73."

In 1875, Congress took a further step toward retirement of the greenbacks and return to a working gold standard when, under the leadership of John Sherman, it passed the Specie Resumption Act, calling for the resumption of specie payments (i.e., the redeemability of the nation's paper money in gold) by January 1, 1879.

Disgruntled proponents of inflation formed the Greenback party and nominated Peter Cooper (1791–1883) for president in 1876. However, they gained only an insignificant number of votes.

In the election of 1876, the Democrats campaigned against corruption and nominated New York Governor Samuel J. Tilden (1814–1886), who had broken the Tweed political machine of New York City.

The Republicans passed over Grant and turned to Governor Rutherford B. Hayes (1822–1893) of Ohio. Like Tilden, Hayes was decent, honest, in favor of hard money and civil service reform, and opposed to government regulation of the economy.

Tilden won the popular vote and led in the electoral vote 184 to 165. However, 185 electoral votes were needed for election, and 20 votes, from the three Southern states still occupied by federal troops and run by Republican governments, were disputed.

Reconstruction would probably have ended anyway, since the North had already lost interest in it.

15. INDUSTRIALISM, WAR, AND THE PROGRESSIVE ERA (1877–1912)

THE NEW INDUSTRIAL ERA (1877–1882)

Between the 1870s and 1890s, "Gilded Age" America emerged as the world's leading industrial and agricultural producer.

Politics of the Period (1877–1882)

The presidencies of Abraham Lincoln and Theodore Roosevelt (1858–1919) mark the boundaries of a half century of relatively weak executive leadership and legislative domination by Congress and the Republican party.

With the withdrawal of Union troops from the South, the country was at last reunified as a modern nation-state led by corporate and industrial interests.

"Stalwarts," led by New York Senator Roscoe Conkling (1829–1888) favored the old spoils system of political patronage. "Half-Breeds," headed by Maine Senator James G. Blaine (1830–1893), pushed for civil service reform and merit appointments to government posts.

Election of 1880: James A. Garfield (1831–1881) of Ohio, a Half-Breed, and his vice-presidential running mate, Chester A. Arthur (1829–1886) of New York, a Stalwart, defeated the Democratic candidate, General Winfield S. Hancock (1824–1886) of Pennsylvania and former Indiana Congressman William English. Tragically, the president was assassinated in 1881 by Charles Guiteau, a mentally disturbed patronage seeker. Arthur had the courage to endorse reform of the political spoils system by supporting passage of the Pendleton Act (1883), which established open competitive examinations for civil service positions.

The Greenback-Labor Party polled more than one million votes in 1878, and elected 14 members to Congress as part of an effort to promote inflation of farm prices and the cooperative marketing of agricultural produce. In 1880, the party's presidential candidate, James Weaver of Iowa, advocated public control and regulation of private enterprises such as railroads, in the common interest of more equitable competition. Weaver polled only 3 percent of the vote.

The Economy (1877–1882)

Between 1860 and 1894, the United States moved from the fourth-largest manufacturing nation to the world's leader through capital accumulation, natural resources, especially in iron, oil, and coal, an abundance of labor helped by massive immigration, railway transportation, and communications [the telephone was introduced by Alexander Graham Bell (1847–1922) in 1876], and major technical innovations such as the development of the modern steel industry by Andrew Carnegie (1835–1919) and electrical energy by Thomas Edison (1847–1931). In the petroleum industry, John D. Rockefeller (1839–1937) controlled 95 percent of U.S. oil refineries by 1877.

By 1880, northern capital erected the modern textile industry in the New South by bringing factories to the cotton fields. Birmingham, Alabama, emerged as the South's leading steel producer, and the introduction of machine-made cigarettes propelled the Duke family to prominence as tobacco producers.

Social and Cultural Developments (1877–1882)

In time, advocates of the "social gospel" such as Jane Addams (1860–1939) and Washington Gladden (1836–1918) urged the creation of settlement houses and better health and education services to accommodate the new immigrants. New religions also appeared, including the Salvation Army and Mary Baker Eddy's (1821–1910) Church of Christian Science in 1879.

In 1881, Booker T. Washington (1856–1915) became president of Tuskegee Institute in Alabama, a school devoted to teaching and vocational education for African Americans. Among those educated there was George Washington Carver (1864–1943) an agricultural chemist who did much to find industrial applications for agricultural products.

Foreign Relations (1877–1882)

In 1876, the Interoceanic Canal Commission recommended a Nicaraguan route for a canal to link the Atlantic and Pacific oceans. In the 1880s, the United States officially took a hostile position against the French Panama Canal project.

The Economy (1882–1887)

Captains of industry, or robber barons, such as John D. Rockefeller in oil, J. P. Morgan (1837–1919) in banking, Gustavus Swift (1839–1903) in meat processing, Andrew Carnegie in steel, and E. H. Harriman (1848–1909) in railroads, put together major industrial empires.

The concentration of wealth and power in the hands of a relatively small number of giant firms led to a monopoly capitalism that minimized competition. This led to a demand by smaller businessmen, farmers, and laborers for government regulation of the economy in order to promote competition.

The Interstate Commerce Act (1887): Popular resentment of railroad abuses such as price-fixing, kickbacks, and discriminatory freight rates created demands for state regulation of the railway industry. When the Supreme Court ruled individual state laws unconstitutional (*Wabash, St. Louis and Pacific Railroad Company* vs. *Illinois* (1886)) because only Congress had the right to control interstate commerce, the Interstate Commerce Act was passed providing that a commission be established to oversee fair and just railway rates, prohibit rebates, end discriminatory practices, and require annual reports and financial statements. The Supreme Court, however, remained a friend of special interests, and often undermined the work of the I.C.C.

American Federation of Labor (1886): Samuel Gompers (1850–1924) and Adolph Strasser put together a combination of national craft unions to represent labor's concerns with wages, hours, and safety conditions. The A.F. of L. philosophy was pragmatic and not directly influenced by the dogmatic Marxism of some European labor movements. Although militant in its use of the strike and in its demand for collective bargaining in labor contracts with large corporations, it did not promote violence or radicalism.

After graduating from Stevens Institute of Technology in 1883, Frederick W. Taylor (1856–1915), the father of scientific management, introduced modern concepts of industrial engineering, plant management, time and motion studies, efficiency experts, and a separate class of managers in industrial manufacturing.

Social and Cultural Developments (1882–1887)

Colleges and universities expanded and introduced more modern curriculums. Graduate study emphasized meticulous research and the seminar method as pioneered in the United States at Johns Hopkins University. A complex society required a more professional and specialized education.

Bryn Mawr (1885) was established and soon found a place among such schools as Vassar, Wellesley, and Mount Holyoke in advancing education for women.

Foreign Relations (1882–1887)

In 1882, Congress passed a law suspending Chinese immigration to the United States for 10 years. The act reflected racist attitudes and created friction with China.

In 1886, the United States obtained the Pearl Harbor Naval Base by way of a treaty with Hawaii.

THE EMERGENCE OF A REGIONAL EMPIRE (1887–1892)

Despite a protective tariff policy, the United States became increasingly international as it sought to export surplus manufactured and agricultural goods. Foreign markets were viewed as a safety valve for labor employment problems and agrarian unrest. The return of Secretary of State James G. Blaine in 1889 marked a major attempt by the United States to promote a regional empire in the Western Hemisphere and reciprocal trade programs.

The Economy (1887–1892)

Antimonopoly measures, protective tariffs and reciprocal trade, and a billion-dollar budget became the order of the day.

Corporate monopolies (trusts) which controlled whole industries were subject to federal prosecution if they were found to be combinations or conspiracies in restraint of trade. Although supported by smaller businesses, labor unions, and farm associations, the Sherman Antitrust Act of 1890 was in time interpreted by the Supreme Court to apply to labor unions and farmers' cooperatives as much as to large corporate combinations.

Foreign Relations (1887–1892)

As secretary of state, James G. Blaine was concerned with international trade, political stability, and excessive militarism in Latin America. His international Bureau of American Republics was designed to promote a Pan-American customs union and peaceful conflict resolution. To achieve his aims, Blaine opposed U.S. military intervention in the hemisphere.

Economic Depression and Social Crisis (1892–1897)

The economic depression that began in 1893 brought about a collective response from organized labor, militant agriculture, and the business community. Each group called for economic safeguards and a more humane free-enterprise system which would expand economic opportunities in an equitable manner.

Politics of the Period (1892–1897)

The most marked development in American politics in the mid-1890s was the emergence of a viable third-party movement in the form of the essentially agrarian Populist party.

Democrat Grover Cleveland (New York) and his vice-presidential running mate Adlai E. Stevenson (1835–1914) (Illinois) regained the White House by defeating Republican president Benjamin Harrison (Indiana) and Vice President Whitelaw Reid (1837–1912) (New York). Voters reacted against the inflationary McKinley Tariff. Cleveland's conservative economic stand in favor of the gold standard brought him the support of various business interests. The Democrats won control of both houses of Congress.

The People's Party (Populist) nominated James Weaver (Iowa) for president and James Field (Virginia) for vice president in 1892. The party platform put together by such Populist leaders as Ignatius Donnelly (Minnesota), Thomas Watson (Georgia), Mary Lease (Kansas), and "Sockless" Jerry Simpson (Kansas) called for the enactment of a program espoused by agrarians, but also for a coalition with urban workers and the middle class. Specific goals were the coinage of silver to gold at a ratio of 16 to 1; federal loans to farmers; a graduated income tax; postal savings banks; public ownership of railroads and telephone and telegraph systems; prohibition of alien land ownership; immigration restriction; a ban on private armies used by corporations to break up strikes; an eight-hour working day; a single six-year term for president and direct election of senators; the right of initiative and referendum; and the use of the secret ballot.

Although the Populists were considered radical by some, they actually wanted to reform the system from within and allow for a fairer distribution of wealth. In a society in which 10 percent of the population controlled 90 percent of the nation's wealth, the Populists were able to garner about one million votes (out of 11 million votes cast) and 22 electoral votes. By 1894, Populists had elected 4 senators, 4 congressmen, 21 state executive officials, 150 state senators, and 315 state representatives, primarily in the West and South. After the 1893 depression, the Populists planned a serious bid for national power in the 1896 election.

After the economic panic of 1893, Cleveland tried to limit the outflow of gold reserves by asking Congress to repeal the Sherman Silver Purchase Act in 1893, which had provided for notes redemptive in either gold or silver. Congress did repeal the act, but the Democratic party split over the issue.

Election of 1896: In the election of 1896, the Republicans nominated William McKinley (Ohio) for president and Garrett Hobart (1844–1899) (New Jersey) for vice president on a platform which promised to maintain the gold standard and protective tariffs. The Democratic party repudiated Cleveland's conservative economics and nominated William Jennings Bryan (1860–1925) (Nebraska) and Arthur Sewell (Maine) for president and vice president on a platform similar to the Populists. Bryan delivered one of the most famous speeches in American history when he declared that the people must not be "crucified upon a cross of gold."

The Populist party also nominated Bryan, but chose Thomas Watson (Georgia) for vice president. Having been outmaneuvered by the Silver Democrats, the Populists lost the opportunity to become a permanent political force.

McKinley won a hard-fought election by only about one-half million votes, as Republicans succeeded in creating the fear among business groups and middle-class voters that Bryan represented a revolutionary challenge to the American system. A warning to labor unions that they would face unemployment if Bryan won the election also helped McKinley. An often forgotten issue in 1896 was the Republican promise to stabilize the ongoing Cuban revolution. This pledge would eventually lead the United States into war with Spain (1898) for Cuban independence. The Republicans retained control over Congress, which they had gained in 1894.

The Economy (1892–1897)

The 1890s was a period of economic depression and labor agitation.

Homestead Strike (1892): Iron and steel workers went on strike in Pennsylvania against the Carnegie Steel Company to protest salary reductions. Carnegie employed strikebreaking Pinkerton security guards. Management-labor warfare led to a number of deaths on both sides.

The primary causes for the depression of 1893 were dramatic growth of the federal deficit, withdrawal of British investments from the American market and the outward transfer of gold, and loss of business confidence. The bankruptcy of the National Cordage Company was the first among thousands of U.S. corporations. Twenty percent of the work force was eventually unemployed. The depression would last four years. Recovery would be helped by war preparation.

March of Unemployed (1894): The Populist businessman Jacob Coxey (1854–1951) led a march of hundreds of unemployed workers on Washington asking for a government work-relief program. The government met the marchers with force and arrested their leaders.

Pullman Strike (1894): Eugene V. Debs's (1855–1926) American Railway Union struck the Pullman Palace Car Co. in Chicago over wage cuts and job losses. President Cleveland broke the violent strike with federal troops.

Wilson-Gorman Tariff (1894): This protective tariff did little to promote overseas trade as a way to ease the depression. A provision amended to create a graduated income tax was stricken by the Supreme Court as unconstitutional (*Pollack v. Farmers' Loan and Trust Co.*, 1895).

Dingley Tariff (1897:): The Dingley Tariff raised protection to new highs for certain commodities.

Social and Cultural Developments (1892–1897)

Economic depression and war dominated thought and literature in the 1890s.

The Anti-Saloon League was formed in 1893. Women were especially concerned about the increase of drunkenness during the depression.

Immigration declined by almost 400,000 during the depression. Jane Addams's Hull House in Chicago continued to settle poor immigrants into American society. Lillian Wald's (1867–1940) Henry Street Settlement in New York and Robert Wood's South End House in Boston performed similar functions. Such institutions also lobbied against sweatshop labor conditions, and for bans on child labor.

Home study courses growing out of the Chautauqua Movement in New York State became popular.

Foreign Relations (1892–1897)

The Cuban revolt against Spain in 1895 threatened American businessmen's $100 million worth of annual business activity and $50 million in investments in Cuba. During the election of 1896, McKinley promised to stabilize the situation and work for an end to hostilities. Sensational "yellow" journalism, and nationalistic statements from officials such as Assistant Secretary of the Navy Theodore Roosevelt (1858–1919), encouraged popular support for direct American military intervention on behalf of Cuban independence. President McKinley, however, proceeded cautiously through 1897.

The Sino-Japanese War (1894–1895)

Japan's easy victory over China signaled to the United States and other nations trading in Asia that China's weakness might result in its colonization by industrial powers, and thus in the closing of the China market. The United States resolved to seek a naval base in the Pacific to protect its interests. The decision to annex the Philippines after the war with Spain was partly motivated by the desire to protect America's trade in Asia. This concern would also lead the United States to announce the Open Door policy with China, designed to protect equal opportunity of trade and China's political independence (1899 and 1900).

Politics of the Period (1897–1902)

The death of Vice President Garrett Hobart led the Republican party to choose the war hero and reform governor of New York, Theodore Roosevelt, as President William McKinley's vice-presidential running mate. Riding the crest of victory against Spain, the G.O.P. platform called for upholding the gold standard for full economic recovery, promoting economic expansion and power in the Caribbean and the Pacific, and building a canal in Central America. The Democrats once again nominated William Jennings Bryan and Adlai Stevenson on a platform condemning imperialism and the gold standard. McKinley easily won reelection by about 1 million votes (7.2 million to 6.3 million), and the Republicans retained control of both houses of Congress.

While attending the Pan American Exposition in Buffalo, New York, the president was shot on September 6 by Leon Czolgosz, an anarchist sworn to destroy all governments. The president died on September 14, after many officials thought he would recover. Theodore Roosevelt became the nation's 25th president, and at age 42, its youngest to date.

Foreign Policy (1897–1902)

On March 27, President McKinley asked Spain to call an armistice, accept American mediation to end the war, and end the use of concentration camps in Cuba. Spain refused to comply. On April 21, Congress declared war on Spain with the objective of establishing Cuban independence (Teller Amendment).

After the first U.S. forces landed in Cuba on June 22, 1898, the United States proceeded to victories at El Caney and San Juan Hill. By July 17, Admiral Sampson's North Atlantic Squadron destroyed the Spanish fleet, Santiago surrendered, and American troops quickly captured Puerto Rico.

As early as December 1897, Commodore George Dewey's (1837–1917) Asiatic Squadron was alerted to possible war with Spain. On May 1, 1898, the Spanish fleet in the Philippines was destroyed, and Manila surrendered on August 13. Spain agreed to a peace conference to be held in Paris in October 1898.

Secretary of State William Day (1849–1923) led the American negotiating team, which secured Cuban independence, the ceding of the Philippines, Puerto Rico, and Guam to the United States, and the payment of $20 million to Spain for the Philippines. The Treaty of Paris was ratified by the Senate on February 6, 1900.

Filipino nationalists under Emilio Aguinaldo (1869–1964) rebelled against the United

States (February 1899) when they learned the Philippines would not be given independence. The United States used 70,000 men to suppress the revolutionaries by June 1902. A special U.S. commission recommended eventual self-government for the Philippines.

During the war with Spain, the United States annexed Hawaii on July 7, 1898. In 1900, the United States claimed Wake Island, 2,000 miles west of Hawaii.

Fearing the breakup of China into separate spheres of influence, Secretary of State John Hay (1838–1905) called for acceptance of the Open Door Notes by all nations trading in the China market. He wanted to guarantee equal opportunity of trade (1899) and the sovereignty of the Manchu government of China (1900).

Boxer Rebellion (1900): Chinese nationalists ("Boxers") struck at foreign settlements in China, and at the Ch'ing dynasty's Manchu government in Beijing, for allowing foreign industrial nations large concessions within Chinese borders. An international army helped to put down the rebellion and aided the Chinese government to remain in power.

Although Cuba was granted its independence, the Platt Amendment of 1901 guaranteed that it would become a virtual protectorate of the United States. Cuba could not: 1) make a treaty with a foreign state impairing its independence, or 2) contract an excessive public debt. Cuba was required to: 1) allow the United States to preserve order on the island, and 2) lease a naval base for 99 years to the United States at Guantanamo Bay.

The Supreme Court decided that constitutional rights did not extend to territorial possessions; thus, the Constitution did not follow the flag.

THEODORE ROOSEVELT AND PROGRESSIVE REFORMS (1902–1907)

Theodore Roosevelt restored the presidency to the high eminence it had held through the Civil War era, and redressed the balance of power with old guard leaders in Congress.

Politics of the Period (1902–1907)

President Roosevelt did much to create a bipartisan coalition of liberal reformers whose objective was to restrain corporate monopoly and promote economic competition at home and abroad.

The president pledged strict enforcement of the Sherman Antitrust Act (1890), which was designed to break up illegal monopolies and regulate large corporations for the public good.

Significant state reformers in this period were Robert LaFollette (1855–1925) of Wisconsin, Albert Cummins of Iowa, Charles Evans Hughes (1862–1948) of New York, James M. Cox of Ohio, Hiram Johnson of California, William S. U'ren of Oregon, Albert Beveridge of Indiana, and Woodrow Wilson of New Jersey.

Hepburn Act (1906): Membership of the Interstate Commerce Commission was increased from five to seven. The I.C.C. could set its own fair freight rates, had its regulatory power extended over pipelines, bridges, and express companies, and was empowered to require a uniform system of accounting by regulated transportation companies. This act and the Elkins Act (1903—reiterated illegality of railroad rebates) gave teeth to the original Interstate Commerce Act of 1887.

Pure Food and Drug Act (1906): This prohibited the manufacture, sale, and transportation of adulterated or fraudulently labeled foods and drugs in accordance with consumer demands.

Meat Inspection Act (1906): This provided for federal and sanitary regulations and inspections in meat packing facilities. Wartime scandals in 1898 involving spoiled canned meats were a powerful force for reform.

Immunity of Witness Act (1906): Corporate officials could no longer make a plea of immunity to avoid testifying in cases dealing with their corporation's illegal activities.

The Economy (1902–1907)

Antitrust Policy (1902): Roosevelt ordered the Justice Department to prosecute corporations pursuing monopolistic practices. Attorney General P. C. Knox (1853–1921) first brought suit against the Northern Securities Company, a railroad holding corporation put together by J. P. Morgan (1837–1913), and then moved against Rockefeller's Standard Oil Company. By the time he left office in 1909, Roosevelt had indictments against 25 monopolies.

Department of Commerce and Labor (1903): A new cabinet position was created to address the concerns of business and labor. Within the department, the Bureau of Corporations was empowered to investigate and report on the illegal activities of corporations.

Coal Strike (1902): Roosevelt interceded with government mediation to bring about negotiations between the United Mine Workers union and the anthracite mine owners after a bitter strike over wages, safety conditions, and union recognition. This was the first time that the government intervened in a labor dispute without automatically siding with management.

A brief economic recession and panic occurred in 1907 as a result, in part, of questionable bank speculations, a lack of flexible monetary and credit policies, and a conservative gold standard. This event called attention to the need for banking reform which would lead to the Federal Reserve System in 1913. Although Roosevelt temporarily eased the pressure on antitrust activity, he made it clear that reform of the economic system to promote free-enterprise capitalism would continue.

Social and Cultural Developments (1902–1907)

Debate and discussion over the expanding role of the federal government commanded the attention of the nation.

There was not one unified progressive movement, but a series of reform causes designed to address specific social, economic, and political problems. Progressive reforms might best be described as evolutionary change from above rather than revolutionary upheaval from below.

Muckrakers (a term coined by Roosevelt) were investigative journalists and authors who were often the publicity agents for reforms. Popular magazines included *McClure's*, *Collier's, Cosmopolitan,* and *Everybody's*. Famous articles that led to reforms included "The Shame of the Cities" by Lincoln Steffens (1866–1936), "History of Standard Oil Company" by Ida Tarbell (1857–1944), "The Treason of the Senate" by David Phillips, and "Frenzied Finance" by Thomas Lawson.

Works of literature with a social message included *Following the Color Line* by Ray Stannard Baker (1870–1946), *The Bitter Cry of the Children* by John Spargo, *Poverty* by Robert Hunter, *The Story of Life Insurance* by Burton Hendrick, *The Financier* by Theodore Dreiser (1871–1945), *The Jungle* by Upton Sinclair (1878–1968), *The Boss* by Henry Lewis, *The Call of the Wild, The Iron Heel,* and *The War of the Classes* by Jack London (1876–1916), *A Certain Rich Man* by William Allen White (1868–1944), and *The Promise of American Life* by Herbert Croly.

Foreign Relations (1902–1907)

Panama Canal: Roosevelt engineered the separation of Panama from Colombia and the recognition of Panama as an independent country. The Hay-Bunau-Varilla Treaty of 1903 granted the United States control of the canal zone in Panama for $10 million and an annual fee of $250,000, beginning nine years after ratification of the treaty by both parties. Construction of the canal began in 1904 and was completed in 1914.

Roosevelt Corollary to the Monroe Doctrine: The United States reserved the right to intervene in the internal affairs of Latin American nations to keep European powers from using military force to collect debts in the Western Hemisphere. The United States, brandishing the "big stick" against Europeans and Latin Americans, by 1905, had intervened in the affairs of Venezuela, Haiti, the Dominican Republic, Nicaragua, and Cuba.

Russo-Japanese War (1904–1905): With American encouragement and financial loans, Japan pursued and won a war against tsarist Russia. Roosevelt negotiated the Treaty of Portsmouth, New Hampshire, which ended the war, and which ironically won the president the Nobel Peace Prize in 1906. Japan, however, was disappointed at not receiving more territory and financial compensation from Russia and blamed the U.S.

Taft-Katsura Memo (1905): The United States and Japan pledged to maintain the Open Door principles in China. Japan recognized American control over the Philippines, and the United States granted a Japanese protectorate over Korea.

Gentleman's Agreement with Japan (1907): After numerous incidents of racial discrimination against Japanese in California, Japan agreed to restrict the emigration of unskilled Japanese workers to the United States.

THE REGULATORY STATE AND THE ORDERED SOCIETY (1907–1912)

The nation increasingly looked to Washington to protect the less powerful segments of the republic from the special interests that had grown up in the late nineteenth century. A persistent problem for the federal government was how best to preserve order and standards in a complex technological society without interfering with the basic liberties Americans had come to cherish. The strain of World War I after 1914 would further complicate the problem.

Deciding not to run for reelection, Theodore Roosevelt opened the way for William H. Taft (1857–1930) (Ohio) and James S. Sherman (1855–1912) (New York) to run on a Republican platform calling for a continuation of antitrust enforcement, environmental conservation, and a lower tariff policy to promote international trade. The Democrats nominated William Jennings Bryan for a third time, with John Kern (Indiana) for vice president, on an antimonopoly and low tariff platform. The Socialists once again nominated Eugene Debs. Taft easily won by over a million votes, and the Republicans retained control of both houses of Congress. For the first time, the American Federation of Labor entered national politics officially with an endorsement of Bryan. This decision began a long alliance between organized labor and the Democratic party in the twentieth century.

Antitrust Policy: In pursuing anti-monopoly law enforcement, Taft chose as his attorney general George Wickersham (1858–1936), who brought 44 indictments in antitrust suits.

Taft was less successful in healing the Republican split between conservatives and progressives over such issues as tariff reform, conservation, and the almost dictatorial power held by the reactionary Republican Speaker of the House, Joseph Cannon (Illinois). Taft's inability to bring both wings of the party together led to the hardened division which would bring about a complete Democratic victory in the 1912 elections.

This election was one of the most dramatic in American history. President Taft's inability to maintain party harmony led Theodore Roosevelt to return to national politics. When denied the Republican nomination, Roosevelt and his supporters formed the Progressive (Bull Moose) party and nominated Roosevelt for president and Hiram Johnson (California) for vice president on a political platform nicknamed "The New Nationalism." It called for stricter regulation on large corporations, creation of a tariff commission, women's suffrage, minimum wages and benefits, direct election of senators, initiative, referendum and recall, presidential primaries, and prohibition of child labor. Roosevelt also called for a Federal Trade Commission to regulate the economy, a stronger executive, and more government planning. Theodore Roosevelt did not see big business as evil, but as a permanent development that was necessary in a modern economy.

The Republicans: President Taft and Vice President Sherman were nominated on a platform of "Quiet Confidence," which called for a continuation of the progressive programs pursued by Taft.

The Democrats: A compromise nominated New Jersey governor Woodrow Wilson for president. Thomas Marshall (1854–1925) of Indiana was selected as vice president. Wilson called his campaign the "New Freedom"; it was similar to programs in the Progressive and Republican parties. Wilson, however, did not agree with Roosevelt on the issue of big business, which Wilson saw as morally evil. Therefore, Wilson called for breaking up large corporations rather than just regulating them. He differed from the other two party candidates by favoring independence for the Philippines, and by advocating the exemption from prosecution of labor unions under the Sherman Antitrust Act. Wilson also supported such measures as lower tariffs, a graduated income tax, banking reform, and direct election of senators. Philosophically, Wilson was skeptical of big business and big government. In some respects, he hoped to return to an earlier and simpler concept of a free-enterprise republic. After his selection, however, he would modify his views to conform more with those of Theodore Roosevelt.

The Republican split paved the way for Wilson's victory. Wilson received 6.2 million votes, Roosevelt 4.1 million, Taft 3.5 million, and the Socialist Debs 900,000 votes. In the electoral college, Wilson received 435 votes, Roosevelt 88, and Taft 8. Although a minority president, Wilson garnered the largest electoral majority in American history up to that time. Democrats won control of both houses of Congress.

Foreign Relations (1907–1915)

President Taft sought to avoid military intervention, especially in Latin America, by replacing "big stick" policies with "dollar diplomacy" in the expectation that American financial investments would encourage economic, social, and political stability. This idea proved an illusion as investments never really filtered through all levels of Latin American societies, nor did such investments generate democratic reforms.

Francisco I. Madero overthrew the dictator Porfirio Diaz (1911), declaring himself a progressive revolutionary akin to reformers in the United States. American and European corporate interests (especially oil and mining) feared interference with their investments in Mexico. President Taft recognized Madero's government, but stationed 10,000 troops on the Texas border (1912) to protect Americans from the continuing fighting. In 1913, Madero was assassinated by General Victoriano Huerta. Wilson urged Huerta to hold democratic elections and adopt a constitutional government. When Huerta refused his advice, Wilson invaded Mexico with troops at Veracruz in 1914. A second U.S. invasion came in northern Mexico in 1916. War between the United States and Mexico might have occurred had not World War I intervened.

Although Taft and Secretary of State P.C. Knox created the Latin American division of the State Department in 1909 to promote better relations, the United States kept a military presence in the Dominican Republic and Haiti, and intervened militarily in Nicaragua (1911) to quiet fears of revolution and help manage foreign financial problems.

Lodge Corollary to the Monroe Doctrine (1911): When a Japanese syndicate moved to purchase a large tract of land in Mexico's Lower California, Senator Lodge introduced a resolution to block the investment. The corollary excluded non-European powers from the Western Hemisphere under the Monroe Doctrine.

16. WILSON AND WORLD WAR I (1912–1920)

IMPLEMENTING THE NEW FREEDOM: THE EARLY YEARS OF THE WILSON ADMINISTRATION

Wilson was only the second Democrat (Cleveland was the first) elected president since the Civil War. He was born in Virginia in 1856, the son of a Presbyterian minister, and was reared and educated in the South. After earning a doctorate at Johns Hopkins University, he taught history and political science at Princeton, and in 1902 became president of that university. In 1910, he was elected governor of New Jersey as a reform, or progressive, Democrat.

Key appointments to the cabinet were William Jennings Bryan as secretary of state and William Gibbs McAdoo (1863–1941) as secretary of the Treasury.

The Federal Reserve Act of 1913: The law divided the nation into 12 regions, with a Federal Reserve bank in each region. Commercial banks in the region owned the Federal Reserve bank by purchasing stock equal to six percent of their capital and surplus. They also elected the directors of the bank. National banks were required to join the system, and state banks were invited to join. The Federal Reserve banks held the gold reserves of their members. Federal Reserve banks loaned money to member banks by rediscounting their commercial and agricultural paper; that is, the money was loaned at interest less than the public paid to the member banks, and the notes of indebtedness of businesses and farmers to the member banks were held as collateral. This allowed the Federal Reserve to control interest rates by raising or lowering the discount rate.

The money loaned to the member banks was in the form of a new currency, Federal Reserve notes, which were backed 60 percent by commercial paper and 40 percent by gold. This currency was designed to expand and contract with the volume of business activity and borrowing. Checks on member banks were cleared through the Federal Reserve system.

The Federal Reserve System serviced the financial needs of the federal government. The system was supervised and policy was set by a national Federal Reserve Board composed of the secretary of the Treasury, the comptroller of the currency, and five other members appointed by the president of the United States.

The Clayton Antitrust Act of 1914: This law supplemented and interpreted the Sherman Antitrust Act of 1890. Under its provisions, stock ownership by a corporation in a competing corporation was prohibited, and the same persons were prohibited from managing competing corporations. Price discrimination (charging less in some regions than in others to undercut the competition) and exclusive contracts which reduced competition were prohibited. Officers of corporations could be held personally responsible for violations of antitrust laws. Lastly, labor unions and agricultural organizations were not to be considered "combinations or conspiracies in restraint of trade" as defined by the Sherman Antitrust Act.

The Election of 1916: The minority party nationally in terms of voter registration, the Democrats nominated Wilson and adopted his platform calling for continued progressive reforms and neutrality in the European war. "He kept us out of war" became the principal campaign slogan of Democratic politicians.

The convention bypassed Theodore Roosevelt and chose Charles Evans Hughes (1862–1948), an associate justice of the Supreme Court and formerly a progressive Republican governor of New York.

Wilson won the election with 277 electoral votes and 9,129,000 popular votes, almost three million more than he received in 1912.

SOCIAL ISSUES IN THE FIRST WILSON ADMINISTRATION

In 1913, Treasury Secretary William G. McAdoo and Postmaster General Albert S. Burleson segregated workers in some parts of their departments with no objection from Wilson. Many northern blacks and whites protested, especially black leader W.E.B. DuBois (1868–1963), who had supported Wilson in 1912. No further segregation in government agencies was initiated, but Wilson had gained a reputation for being inimical to civil rights.

The movement for women's suffrage, led by the National American Woman Suffrage Association, was increasing in momentum at the time Wilson became president, and several states had granted the vote to women. Wilson opposed a federal women's suffrage amendment, maintaining that the franchise should be controlled by the states. Later, he changed his view and supported the nineteenth Amendment.

Wilson opposed immigration restrictions and vetoed a literacy test for immigrants in 1915, but in 1917, Congress overrode a similar veto.

WILSON'S FOREIGN POLICY

New Freedom Policy: Wilson promised a more moral foreign policy than that of his predecessors, denouncing imperialism and dollar diplomacy, and advocating the advancement of democratic capitalist governments throughout the world.

Wilson signaled his repudiation of Taft's dollar diplomacy by withdrawing American involvement from the six-power loan consortium of China.

Like his predecessors, Wilson sought to protect the Panama Canal, which opened in 1914, by maintaining stability in the area. He also wanted to encourage diplomacy and economic growth in the underdeveloped nations of the region. In applying his policy, he became as interventionist as Roosevelt and Taft.

In 1912, American marines had landed in Nicaragua to maintain order, and an American financial expert had taken control of the customs station. The Wilson administration kept the marines in Nicaragua and negotiated the Bryan-Chamorro Treaty of 1914, which gave the United States an option to build a canal through the country. In effect, Nicaragua became an American protectorate, although treaty provisions authorizing such action were not ratified by the Senate.

Claiming that political anarchy existed in Haiti, Wilson sent marines in 1915 and imposed a treaty making the country a protectorate, with American control of its finances and constabulary. The marines remained until 1934.

In 1916, Wilson sent marines to the Dominican Republic to stop a civil war and established a military government under an American naval commander.

Wilson feared in 1915 that Germany might annex Denmark and its Caribbean possession, the Danish West Indies or Virgin Islands. After extended negotiations, the

United States purchased the islands from Denmark by treaty on August 4, 1916, for $25 million and took possession of them on March 31, 1917.

In 1913, Wilson refused to recognize the government of Mexican military dictator Victoriano Huerta, and offered unsuccessfully to mediate between Huerta and his Constitutionalist opponent, Venustiano Carranza. When the Huerta government arrested several American seamen in Tampico in April 1914, American forces occupied the port of Veracruz, an action condemned by both Mexican political factions. In July 1914, Huerta abdicated his power to Carranza, who was soon opposed by his former general Francisco "Pancho" Villa (1878–1923). Seeking American intervention as a means of undermining Carranza, Villa shot 16 Americans on a train in northern Mexico in January 1916 and burned the border town of Columbus, New Mexico, in March 1916, killing 19 people. Carranza reluctantly consented to Wilson's request that the United States be allowed to pursue and capture Villa in Mexico, but did not expect the force of about 6,000 army troops under the command of General John J. Pershing which crossed the Rio Grande on March 18. The force advanced more than 300 miles into Mexico, failed to capture Villa, and became, in effect, an army of occupation. The Carranza government demanded an American withdrawal, and several clashes with Mexican troops occurred. War threatened, but in January 1917 Wilson removed the American forces.

John Barrett, head of the Pan-American Union (formerly Blaine's International Bureau of American Republics), called for multilateral mediation to bring about a solution to Mexico's internal problems and remove the United States from Mexico. Although Wilson initially refused, Argentina, Brazil, and Chile did mediate among the Mexican factions and Wilson withdrew American troops. Barrett hoped to replace the unilateral Monroe Doctrine with a multilateral Pan-American policy to promote collective responses and mediation to difficult hemispheric problems. Wilson, however, refused to share power with Latin America.

THE ROAD TO WAR IN EUROPE

When World War I broke out in Europe, Wilson issued a proclamation of American neutrality on August 4, 1914. The value of American trade with the Central Powers fell from $169 million in 1914 to almost nothing in 1916, but trade with the Allies rose from $825 million to $3.2 billion during the same period. In addition, the British and French had borrowed about $3.25 billion from American sources by 1917. The United States had become a major supplier of Allied munitions, food, and raw materials.

The sinking of the British liner *Lusitania* off the coast of Ireland on May 7, 1915, with the loss of 1,198 lives, including 128 Americans, brought strong protests from Wilson. Secretary of State Bryan, who believed Americans should stay off belligerent ships, resigned rather than insist on questionable neutral rights and was replaced by Robert Lansing. Following the sinking of another liner, the *Arabic*, on August 19, the Germans gave the "*Arabic* pledge" to stop attacks on unarmed passenger vessels.

The House-Grey Memorandum: Early in 1915, Wilson sent his friend and adviser Colonel Edward M. House on an unsuccessful visit to the capitals of the belligerent nations on both sides to offer American mediation in the war. Late in the year, House returned to London to propose that Wilson call a peace conference; if Germany refused to attend or was uncooperative at the conference, the United States could enter the war on the Allied side. An agreement to that effect, called the House-Grey memorandum, was signed by the British foreign secretary, Sir Edward Grey, on February 22, 1916.

On December 12, 1916, the Germans, confident of their strong position, proposed a peace conference, but were evasive and stated that they did not want Wilson at the conference. In an address to Congress on January 22, 1917, Wilson made his last offer to serve as a neutral mediator. He proposed a "peace without victory," based not on a "balance of power" but on a "community of power."

Germany announced on January 31, 1917, that it would sink all ships, belligerent or neutral, without warning in a large war zone off the coasts of the Allied nations in the eastern Atlantic and the Mediterranean. The Germans realized that the United States might declare war, but they believed that, after cutting the flow of supplies to the Allies, they could win the war before the Americans could send any sizable force to Europe. Wilson broke diplomatic relations with Germany on February 3. During February and March several American merchant ships were sunk by submarines.

The British intercepted a secret message from the German foreign secretary, Arthur Zimmerman, to the German minister in Mexico, and turned it over to the United States on February 24, 1917. The Germans proposed that, in the event of a war between the United States and Germany, Mexico attack the United States. After the war, the "lost territories" of Texas, New Mexico, and Arizona would be returned to Mexico. In addition, Japan would be invited to join the alliance against the United States. When the telegram was released to the press on March 1, many Americans became convinced that war with Germany was necessary.

A declaration of war against Germany was passed by the Senate on April 4 by a vote of 82 to 6, and by the House on April 6 by a vote of 373 to 50. It was signed by Wilson on April 6.

Wilson believed that the Zimmerman telegram showed that the Germans were not trustworthy and would eventually go to war against the United States. He also felt that armed neutrality could not adequately protect American shipping. The democratic government established in Russia after the revolution in March 1917 also proved more acceptable as an ally than the tsarist government. Finally, he was convinced that the United States could hasten the end of the war and ensure a major role for itself in designing a lasting peace.

World War I: The Military Campaign

The American force of about 14,500, which had arrived in France by September 1917, was assigned a quiet section of the line near Verdun. As numbers increased, the American role became more significant. When the Germans mounted a major drive toward Paris in the spring of 1918, the Americans experienced their first important engagements. In June, they prevented the Germans from crossing the Marne at Chateau-Thierry, and cleared the area of Belleau Woods. In July, eight American divisions aided French troops in attacking the German line between Reims and Soissons. The American First Army, with over half a million men under Pershing's immediate command, was assembled in August 1918, and began a major offensive at St. Mihiel on the southern part of the front on September 12. Following the successful operation, Pershing began a drive against the German defenses between Verdun and Sedan, an action called the Meuse-Argonne offensive. He reached Sedan on November 7. During the same period the English in the north and the French along the central front also broke through the German lines. The fighting ended with the armistice on November 11, 1918.

Mobilizing the Home Front

A number of volunteer organizations sprang up around the country to search for draft dodgers, enforce the sale of bonds, and report any opinion or conversation considered suspicious. Perhaps the largest such organization was the American Protective League with about 250,000 members, which claimed the approval of the Justice Department. Such groups publicly humiliated people accused of not buying war bonds, and perse-cuted, beat, and sometimes killed people of German descent. As a result of the activities of the CPI and the vigilante groups, German language instruction and German music were banned in many areas, German measles became "liberty measles," pretzels were prohibited in some cities, and so on. The anti-German and antisubversive war hysteria in the United States far exceeded similar public moods in Britain and France during the war.

The Espionage Act of 1917 provided for fines and imprisonment for persons who made false statements which aided the enemy, incited rebellion in the military, or ob-structed recruitment or the draft. Printed matter advocating treason or insurrection could be excluded from the mails. The Sedition Act of May 1918 forbade any criticism of the government, flag, or uniform, even if there were not detrimental consequences, and expanded the mail exclusion. The laws sounded reasonable, but they were applied in ways that trampled on civil liberties. Eugene V. Debs, the perennial Socialist candidate for president, was given a 10–year prison sentence for a speech at his party's convention in which he was critical of American policy in entering the war and warned of the dangers of militarism. Movie producer Robert Goldstein released the movie *The Spirit of '76* about the Revolutionary War. It naturally showed the British fighting the Americans. Goldstein was fined $10,000 and sentenced to 10 years in prison because the film de-picted the British, who were now fighting on the same side as the United States, in an unfavorable light. The Espionage Act was upheld by the Supreme Court in the case of *Shenk v. United States* in 1919. The opinion, written by Justice Oliver Wendell Holmes, Jr. (1841–1935), stated that Congress could limit free speech when the words represented a "clear and present danger," and that a person cannot, in effect, scream "fire" in a crowded theater. The Sedition Act was similarly upheld in *Abrams v. United States* a few months later. Ultimately 2,168 persons were prosecuted under the laws, and 1,055 were convicted, of whom only 10 were charged with actual sabotage.

WARTIME SOCIAL TRENDS

Large numbers of women, mostly white, were hired by factories and other enter-prises in jobs never before open to them. They were often resented and ridiculed by male workers. When the war ended, almost all returned to traditional "women's jobs" or to homemaking. Returning veterans replaced them in the labor market. Women continued to campaign for women's suffrage. In 1917, six states, including New York, Ohio, Indiana, and Michigan, gave the vote to women. Wilson changed his position in 1918 to advocate women's suffrage as a war measure. In January 1918, the House of Representatives adopted a suffrage amendment to the constitution which was defeated later in the year by southern forces in the Senate. The way was paved for the victory of the suffragists after the war.

The labor shortage opened industrial jobs to Mexican-Americans and to African-Americans. W.E.B. DuBois, among the most prominent African-American leader of the time, supported the war effort in the hope that the war would make the world safe for democracy and bring a better life for African-Americans in the United States. About half a million rural southern African Americans migrated to cities, mainly in the North and Midwest, to obtain employment in war and other industries, especially in steel and meatpacking. In 1917, there were race riots in 26 cities in the North and South, with the worst in East St. Louis, Illinois.

In December 1917, a constitutional amendment to prohibit the manufacture and sale of alcoholic beverages in the United States was passed by Congress and submitted to the states for ratification. While alcohol consumption was being attacked, cigarette consumption climbed from 26 billion in 1916 to 48 billion in 1918.

PEACEMAKING AND DOMESTIC PROBLEMS (1918–1920)

From the time of the American entry into the war, Wilson had maintained that the war would make the world safe for democracy. He insisted that there should be peace without victory, meaning that the victors would not be vindictive toward the losers, so that a fair and stable international situation in the postwar world would ensure lasting peace. In an address to Congress on January 8, 1918, he presented his specific peace plan in the form of the Fourteen Points. The first five points called for open rather than secret peace treaties, freedom of the seas, free trade, arms reduction, and a fair adjustment of colonial claims. The next eight points were concerned with the national aspirations of various European peoples and the adjustment of boundaries, as, for example, in the creation of an independent Poland. The fourteenth point, which he considered the most important and had espoused as early as 1916, called for a "general association of nations" to preserve the peace. The plan was disdained by the Allied leadership, but it had great appeal for many people on both sides of the conflict in Europe and America.

Wilson decided that he would lead the American delegation to the peace conference which opened in Paris on January 12, 1919. In doing so he became the first president to leave the country during his term of office. The other members of the delegation were Secretary of State Robert Lansing, General Tasker Bliss, Colonel Edward M. House, and attorney Henry White. Wilson made a serious mistake in not appointing any leading Republicans to the commission and in not consulting the Republican leadership in the Senate about the negotiations. In the negotiations, which continued until May 1919, Wilson found it necessary to make many compromises in forging the text of the treaty.

Following a protest by 39 senators in February 1919, Wilson obtained some changes in the League of Nations structure to exempt the Monroe Doctrine and domestic matters from League jurisdiction. Then, on July 26, 1919, he presented the treaty with the League within it to the Senate for ratification. Almost all of the 47 Democrats supported Wilson and the treaty, but the 49 Republicans were divided. About a dozen were "irreconcilables" who thought that the United States should not be a member of the League under any circumstances. The remainder included 25 "strong" and 12 "mild" reservationists who would accept the treaty with some changes. The main objection centered on Article X of the League Covenant, where the reservationists wanted it understood that the United States would not go to war to defend a League member without the approval of Congress. The leader of the reservationists was Henry Cabot Lodge of Massachusetts, the chairman of the Foreign Relations Committee. More senators than the two-thirds necessary for ratification favored the treaty either as written or with reservations.

On September 3, 1919, Wilson set out on a national speaking tour to appeal to the people to support the treaty and the League and to influence their senators. He collapsed after a speech in Pueblo, Colorado, on September 25, and returned to Washington, where he suffered a severe stroke on October 2 which paralyzed his left side. He was seriously ill for several months, and never fully recovered. In a letter to the Senate Democrats on November 18, Wilson urged them to oppose the treaty with the Lodge reservations. In votes the next day, the treaty failed to get a two-thirds majority either with or without the reservations.

Many people, including British and French leaders, urged Wilson to compromise with Lodge on reservations, including the issue of Article X. Wilson, instead, wrote an open letter to Democrats on January 8, 1920, urging them to make the election of a

Democratic president in 1920 a "great and solemn referendum" on the treaty as written. Such partisanship only exacerbated the situation. Many historians think that Wilson's ill health impaired his judgment, and that he would have worked out a compromise had he not had the stroke. The Senate took up the treaty again in February 1920, and on March 19 it was again defeated both with and without the reservations. The United States officially ended the war with Germany by a resolution of Congress signed on July 2, 1921, and a separate peace treaty was ratified on July 25. The United States did not join the League.

Prohibition: In January 1919, the Eighteenth Amendment to the Constitution prohibiting the manufacture, sale, transportation, or importation of intoxicating liquors was ratified by the states, and it became effective in January 1920. The Nineteenth Amendment, providing for women's suffrage, which had been defeated in the Senate in 1918, was approved by Congress in 1919. It was ratified by the states in time for the election of 1920.

Labor Strife: The great increase in prices prompted 2,655 strikes in 1919, involving about four million workers, or 20 percent of the labor force. Unions were encouraged by the gains they had made during the war and thought they had the support of public opinion. However, the Communist revolution in Russia in 1917 soon inspired a fear of violence and revolution by workers. While most of the strikes in early 1919 were successful, the tide of opinion gradually shifted against the workers.

Specter of Communism: Americans feared the spread of the Russian Communist revolution to the United States, and many interpreted the widespread strikes of 1919 as Communist-inspired and the beginning of the revolution. Bombs sent through the mail to prominent government and business leaders in April 1919 seemed to confirm their fears, although the origin of the bombs has never been determined. The membership of the two Communist parties founded in the United States in 1919 was less than 100,000, but many Americans were sure that many workers, all foreign-born persons, radicals, and members of the International Workers of the World (known as "Wobblies"), a radical union in the western states, were Communists. The anti-German hysteria of the war years was transformed into the anti-Communist and antiforeign hysteria of 1919 and 1920, and continued in various forms through the 1920s.

Anarchists Deported: Attorney General A. Mitchell Palmer, who aspired to the 1920 presidential nomination, was one of the targets of the anonymous bombers in the spring of 1919. In August 1919, he named J. Edgar Hoover (1895–1972) to head a new Intelligence Division in the Justice Department to collect information about radicals. In November 1919, Palmer's agents arrested almost 700 persons, mostly anarchists, and deported 43 of them as undesirable aliens. On January 2, 1920, Justice Department agents, local police, and vigilantes in 33 cities arrested about 4,000 people accused of being Communists. Many people caught in the sweep were neither Communists nor aliens. Eventually 556 were shown to be Communists and aliens, and were deported. Palmer then announced that huge Communist riots were planned for major cities on May Day (May 1, 1920). Police and troops were alerted, but the day passed with no radical activity. Palmer was discredited and the Red Scare subsided.

Race Riots: White hostility based on competition for lower-paid jobs and black encroachment into neighborhoods led to race riots in 25 cities, with hundreds killed or wounded and millions of dollars in property damage. The Chicago riot in July was the worst, lasting 13 days and leaving 38 dead, 520 wounded, and 1,000 families homeless. Fear of returning African-American veterans in the South led to an increase of lynchings from 34 in 1917 to 60 in 1918 and 70 in 1919. Some of the victims were veterans still in uniform.

17. THE ROARING TWENTIES AND ECONOMIC COLLAPSE (1920–1929)

The Republican Convention: Senator Warren G. Harding (1865–1923) of Ohio was nominated as a dark-horse candidate, and Governor Calvin Coolidge (1872–1933) of Massachusetts was chosen as the vice presidential nominee. The platform opposed the League and promised low taxes, high tariffs, immigration restriction, and aid to farmers.

The Democratic Convention: Governor James Cox was nominated on the 44th ballot, and Franklin D. Roosevelt (1882–1945), an assistant secretary of the Navy and distant cousin of Theodore, was selected as his running mate. The platform endorsed the League, but left the door open for reservations.

THE 1920s: ECONOMIC ADVANCES AND SOCIAL TENSIONS

The United States experienced a severe recession from mid-1920 until the end of 1921. Europe returned to normal and reduced its purchases in America, and domestic demand for goods not available in wartime was filled. Prices fell, and unemployment exceeded 12 percent in 1921.

The principal driving force of the economy of the 1920s was the automobile. There were 8,131,522 motor vehicles registered in the United States in 1920, and 26,704,825 in 1929. By 1925, the price of a Ford Model T had been reduced to $290, less than three months pay for an average worker. Ford plants produced 9,000 Model Ts per day. Automobile manufacturing stimulated supporting industries such as steel, rubber, and glass, as well as gasoline refining and highway construction. During the 1920s, the United States became a nation of paved roads. The Federal Highway Act of 1916 started the federal highway system and gave matching funds to the states for construction. One estimate stated that the automobile industry directly or indirectly employed 3.7 million people in 1929.

Unlike earlier boom periods, which had involved large expenditures for capital investments such as railroads and factories, the prosperity of the 1920s depended heavily on the sale of consumer products. Purchases of "big ticket" items such as automobiles, refrigerators, and furniture were made possible by installment or time payment credit. The idea was not new, but the availability of consumer credit expanded tremendously during the 1920s. Consumer interest and demand was spurred by the great increase in professional advertising, which used newspapers, magazines, radio, billboards, and other media.

There was a trend toward corporate consolidation during the 1920s. In most fields, an oligopoly of two to four firms dominated. This was exemplified by the automobile industry, where Ford, General Motors, and Chrysler produced 83 percent of American vehicles in 1929. Government regulatory agencies such as the Federal Trade Commission and the Interstate Commerce Commission were passive and generally controlled by persons from the business world. The public generally accepted the situation and viewed businessmen with respect. Illustrating the attitudes of the time, *The Man Nobody Knows*, a book by advertising executive Bruce Barton published in 1925, became a best-seller. It described Jesus as the founder of modern business and his apostles as an exemplary business management team.

There was also a trend toward bank consolidation. Because corporations were raising much of their money through the sale of stocks and bonds, the demand for business loans declined. Commercial banks then put more of their funds into real estate loans, loans to brokers against stocks and bonds, and the purchase of stocks and bonds themselves. By doing so they made themselves vulnerable to economic disaster when the depression began in late 1929. Even during the prosperous 1920s, 5,714 banks failed, most of them in rural areas or in Florida. Banks in operation in 1929 numbered 25,568.

By 1920, for the first time, a majority of Americans (51 percent) lived in an urban area with a population of 2,500 or more. A new phenomenon of the 1920s was the tremendous growth of suburbs and satellite cities, which grew more rapidly than the central cities. Streetcars, commuter railroads, and automobiles contributed to the process, as well as the easy availability of financing for home construction. The suburbs had once been the domain of the wealthy, but the technology of the 1920s opened them to working-class families.

Changing Mores

Traditional American moral standards regarding premarital sex and marital fidelity were widely questioned for the first time during the 1920s. There was a popular misunderstanding by people who had not read his works that Sigmund Freud had advocated sexual promiscuity. Movies, novels, and magazine stories were more sexually explicit. The "flaming youth" of the Jazz Age emphasized sexual promiscuity and drinking, as well as new forms of dancing considered erotic by the older generation. The automobile, by giving people mobility and privacy, was generally considered to have contributed to sexual license. Journalists wrote about "flappers," young women who were independent, assertive, and promiscuous. Birth control, though illegal, was promoted by Margaret Sanger (1883–1966) and others and was widely accepted. But compared with the period from 1960 to the present, it was a relatively conservative time.

Many feminists believed that the passage of the Nineteenth Amendment in 1920 providing women's suffrage would solve all problems for women. When it became apparent that women did not vote as a block, political leaders gave little additional attention to the special concerns of women. The sexual revolution brought some emancipation. Women adopted less bulky clothing, and could smoke and socialize with men in public more freely than before. Divorce laws were liberalized in many states at the insistence of women. Domestic service was the largest job category. Most other women workers were in traditional female occupations such as secretarial and clerical work, retail sales, teaching, and nursing. Rates of pay were below those for men. Most women still pursued the traditional role of housewife and mother, and society accepted that as the norm.

The migration of southern rural African-Americans to the cities continued, with about 1.5 million moving during the 1920s. By 1930, about 20 percent of American blacks lived in the North, with the largest concentrations in New York, Chicago, and Philadelphia. While they were generally better off economically in the cities than they had been as tenant farmers, they generally held low-paying jobs and were confined to segregated areas of the cities. The Harlem section of New York City, with an African-American population of 73,000 in 1920 and 165,000 in 1930, was the largest African-American urban community. It became the center for African-American writers, musicians, and intellectuals. African-Americans throughout the country developed jazz and blues. W.E.B. DuBois, the editor of *The Crisis*, continued to call for integration and to attack segregation despite his disappointment with the lack of progress after World War I. The National Association for the Advancement of Colored People was a more conservative but active voice for civil rights, and the National Urban League concentrated on employment and economic advancement.

A native of Jamaica, Marcus Garvey (1887–1940) founded the Universal Negro

Improvement Association there in 1914. He moved to New York in 1916. Garvey advocated African-American racial pride and separatism rather than integration, and called for a return of African-Americans to Africa. Some of his ideas soon alienated the older African-American organizations. He developed a large following, especially among southern African-Americans. He urged his followers to buy only from African-Americans, and founded a chain of businesses, including grocery stores, restaurants, and laundries. In 1921, he proclaimed himself the provisional president of an African empire, and sold stock in the Black Star Steamship Line which would take migrants to Africa. The line went bankrupt in 1923, and Garvey was convicted and imprisoned for mail fraud in the sale of the line's stock and then deported. His legacy was an emphasis on African-American pride and self-respect.

Many writers of the 1920s were disgusted with the hypocrisy and materialism of contemporary American society. Often called the "Lost Generation," many of them, such as novelists Ernest Hemingway (1899–1961) and F. Scott Fitzgerald (1896–1940) and poets Ezra Pound (1885–1972) and T. S. Eliot (1888–1965) moved to Europe. Typical authors and works include Ernest Hemingway's *The Sun Also Rises* (1926) and *A Farewell to Arms* (1929); Sinclair Lewis's (1885–1951) *Babbitt* (1922), *Arrowsmith* (1925), and *Elmer Gantry* (1927); F. Scott Fitzgerald's *The Great Gatsby* (1925) and *Tender Is the Night* (1929); John Dos Passos's (1896–1970) *Three Soldiers* (1921); and Thomas Wolfe's (1900–1938) *Look Homeward, Angel* (1929). H. L. Mencken (1880–1956), a journalist who began publication of the *American Mercury* magazine in 1922, ceaselessly attacked the "booboisie," as he called middle-class America, but his literary talent did not match that of the leaders of the period.

Social Conflicts: The Rise of Nativism

Many white Protestant families saw their traditional values gravely threatened. The traditionalists were largely residents of rural areas and small towns, and the clash of farm values with the values of an industrial society of urban workers was evident. The traditionalist backlash against modern urban industrial society expressed itself primarily through intolerance.

KKK Founded: On Thanksgiving Day in 1915, the Knights of the Ku Klux Klan, modeled on the organization of the same name in the 1860s and 1870s, was founded near Atlanta by William J. Simmons. Its purpose was to intimidate African-Americans, who were experiencing an apparent rise in status during World War I. The Klan remained small until 1920, when two advertising experts, Edward Y. Clark and Elizabeth Tyler, were hired by the leadership. Clark and Tyler used modern advertising to recruit members. By 1923, the Klan had about five million members throughout the nation. The largest concentrations of members were in the South, the Southwest, the Midwest, California, and Oregon. The use of white hoods, masks, and robes, and the secret ritual and jargon seemed to appeal mostly to lower middle-class men.

The "Red" Scare: There had been calls for immigration restriction since the late nineteenth century. Labor leaders believed that immigrants depressed wages and impeded unionization. Some progressives believed that they created social problems. In June 1917, Congress, over Wilson's veto, had imposed a literacy test for immigrants and excluded many Asian nationalists. During World War I and the Red Scare, almost all immigrants were considered radicals and Communists. With bad economic conditions in postwar Europe, over 1.3 million came to the United States between 1919 and 1921. As in the period before the war, they were mostly from south and east Europe and mostly Catholics and Jews, the groups most despised by nativist Americans. In 1921, Congress passed the

Emergency Quota Act, which limited immigration by nation to three percent of the number of foreign-born persons from that nation in the United States in 1910. In practice, the law admitted about as many as wanted to come from such nations as Britain, Ireland, and Germany, while severely restricting Italians, Greeks, Poles, and east European Jews. It became effective in 1922 and reduced the number of immigrants annually to about 40 percent of the 1921 total. Congress then passed the National Origins Act of 1924, which set the quotas at two percent of the number of foreign-born persons of that nationality in the United States in 1890, excluded all Asians, and imposed an annual maximum of 164,000.

Immigration from Western Hemisphere nations was not limited. The law further reduced the number of south and east Europeans, and cut the annual immigration rate to 20 percent of the 1921 figure. In 1927, the annual maximum was reduced to 150,000.

Fundamentalist Protestants, under the leadership of William Jennings Bryan, began a campaign in 1921 to prohibit the teaching of evolution in the schools, and thus protect belief in the literal biblical account of creation. The idea was especially well received in the South. In 1925, the Tennessee legislature passed a law that forbade any teacher in the state's schools or colleges to teach evolution. The American Civil Liberties Union found a young high school biology teacher, John Thomas Scopes, who was willing to bring about a test case by breaking the law. Scopes was tried in Dayton, Tennessee, in July 1925. Bryan came to assist the prosecution, and Chicago trial lawyer Clarence Darrow (1857–1938) defended Scopes. The trial attracted national attention through newspaper and radio coverage. The judge refused to allow expert testimony, so the trial was a strictly duel of words between Darrow and Bryan. As was expected, Scopes was convicted and fined $100. Bryan died of exhaustion a few days after the trial. Both sides claimed a moral victory. The antievolution crusaders secured enactment of a statute in Mississippi in 1926, which was followed by statutes in several other states.

Sacco and Vanzetti: On April 15, 1920, two unidentified gunmen robbed a shoe factory and killed two men in South Braintree, Massachusetts. Nicola Sacco and Bartolomeo Vanzetti, Italian immigrants and admitted anarchists, were tried for the murders. Judge Webster Thayer clearly favored the prosecution, which based its case on the political radicalism of the defendants. After Sacco and Vanzettiwere convicted and sentenced to death in July 1921, there was much protest in the United States and in Europe that they had not received a fair trial. After six years of delays, they were executed on August 23, 1927. A half-century later, on July 19, 1977, Sacco and Vanzetti would be vindicated by Governor Michael Dukakis.

GOVERNMENT AND POLITICS IN THE 1920s: THE HARDING ADMINISTRATION

Warren G. Harding was a handsome and amiable man of limited intellectual and organizational abilities. He had spent much of his life as the publisher of a newspaper in the small city of Marion, Ohio. He recognized his limitations, but hoped to be a much-loved president. He showed compassion by pardoning socialist Eugene V. Debs for his conviction under the Espionage Act and by inviting him to dinner at the White House. He also persuaded U.S. Steel to give workers the eight-hour work day. A convivial man, he liked to drink and play poker with his friends, and kept the White House stocked with bootleg liquor despite prohibition. He was accused of keeping a mistress named Nan Britton. His economic philosophy was conservative.

Harding appointed some outstanding persons to his cabinet, including Secretary of State Charles Evans Hughes, a former Supreme Court justice and presidential candidate;

Secretary of the Treasury Andrew Mellon (1855–1937), a Pittsburgh aluminum and banking magnate and reportedly the richest man in America; and Secretary of Commerce Herbert Hoover, a dynamic multimillionaire mine owner famous for his wartime relief efforts. Less impressive was his appointment of his cronies Albert B. Fall as secretary of the interior and Harry M. Daugherty as attorney general. Other cronies, some of whom were dishonest, were appointed to other government posts.

Harding apparently was honest, but several of his friends whom he appointed to office became involved in major financial scandals. Most of the information about the scandals did not become public knowledge until after Harding's death.

Teapot Dome: The Teapot Dome Scandal began when Secretary of the Interior Albert B. Fall in 1921 secured the transfer of several naval oil reserves to his jurisdiction. In 1922, he secretly leased reserves at Teapot Dome in Wyoming to Harry F. Sinclair of Monmouth Oil and at Elk Hills in California to Edward Doheny of Pan-American Petroleum. A Senate investigation later revealed that Sinclair had given Fall $305,000 in cash and bonds and a herd of cattle, while Doheny had given him a $100,000 unsecured loan. Sinclair and Doheny were acquitted in 1927 of charges of defrauding the government, but in 1929, Fall was convicted, fined, and imprisoned for bribery.

Vice President Calvin Coolidge became president. He had a reputation for honesty, although he did not remove Daugherty from the cabinet until March 1924.

The Election of 1924 (Republicans): Calvin Coolidge was nominated, and Charles G. Dawes (1865–1951) was his running mate. The platform endorsed business development, low taxes, and rigid economy in government. The party stood on its record of economic growth and prosperity since 1922.

The Election of 1924 (Progressives): Robert M. LaFollette, after failing in a bid for the Republican nomination, formed a new Progressive party, with support from Midwest farm groups, socialists, and the American Federation of Labor. The platform attacked monopolies, and called for the nationalization of railroads, the direct election of the president, and other reforms.

The '24 Vote: Coolidge received 15,725,016 votes and 382 electoral votes, more than his two opponents combined. Davis received 8,385,586 votes and 136 electoral votes, while LaFollette had 4,822,856 votes and 13 electoral votes from his home state of Wisconsin.

The Coolidge Adminstration

Coolidge was a dour and taciturn man. Born in Vermont, his adult life and political career were spent in Massachusetts. "The business of the United States is business," he proclaimed, and "the man who builds a factory builds a temple." His philosophy of life was stated in the remark that "four-fifths of all our troubles in this world would disappear if only we would sit down and keep still." Liberal political commentator Walter Lippmann wrote that "Mr. Coolidge's genius for inactivity is developed to a very high point." He intentionally provided no presidential leadership.

The Election of 1928 (Republicans): Coolidge did not seek another term, and the convention quickly nominated Herbert Hoover, the secretary of commerce, for president, and Charles Curtis (1860–1936) as his running mate. The platform endorsed the policies of the Harding and Coolidge administrations.

The Election of 1928 (Democrats): Governor Alfred E. Smith (1873–1944) of New York, a Catholic and an antiprohibitionist, controlled most of the nonsouthern delegations. Southerners supported his nomination with the understanding that the platform would not advocate repeal of prohibition. Senator Joseph T. Robinson of Arkansas, a Protestant and a prohibitionist, was the vice-presidential candidate. The platform differed little from the Republican, except in advocating lower tariffs.

Stock Market Crashes

Herbert Hoover, an Iowa farm boy and an orphan, graduated from Stanford University with a degree in mining engineering. He became a multimillionaire from mining and other investments around the world. After serving as the director of the Food Administration under Wilson, he became secretary of commerce under Harding and Coolidge. He believed that cooperation between business and government would enable the United States to abolish poverty through continued economic growth.

Stock prices increased throughout the decade. The boom in prices and volume of sales was especially active after 1925, and was intensive during 1928–29. The Dow Jones Industrial Average for the year 1924 was 120; for the month of September 1929 it was 381; and for the year 1932 it dropped to 41. Stocks were selling for more than 16 times their earnings in 1929, well above the rule of thumb of that time of 10 times their earnings.

Careful investors, realizing that stocks were overpriced, began to sell to take their profits. During October 1929, prices declined as more stock was sold. On "Black Thursday," October 24, 1929, almost 13 million shares were traded, a large number for that time, and prices fell precipitously. Investment banks tried to boost the market by buying, but on October 29, "Black Tuesday," the market fell about 40 points, with 16.5 million shares traded.

18. THE GREAT DEPRESSION AND THE NEW DEAL (1929–1941)

REASONS FOR THE DEPRESSION

A stock-market crash does not mean that a depression must follow. A similar crash in October 1987 did not lead to depression. In 1929, a complex interaction of many factors caused the decline of the economy.

Many people had bought stock on a margin of 10 percent, meaning that they had borrowed 90 percent of the purchase through a broker's loan and put up the stock as collateral. Broker's loans totaled $8.5 billion in 1929, compared with $3.5 billion in 1926. When the price of a stock fell more than 10 percent, the lender sold the stock for whatever it would bring and thus further depressed prices. The forced sales brought great losses to the banks and businesses that had financed the broker's loans, as well as to the investors.

There were already signs of recession before the market crash in 1929. Because the gathering and processing of statistics was not as advanced then as now, some factors were not so obvious to people at the time. The farm economy, which involved almost 25 percent of the population, had been depressed throughout the decade. Coal, railroads, and New England textiles had not been prosperous. After 1927, new construction declined and auto sales began to sag. Many workers had been laid off before the crash of 1929.

During the early months of the depression, most people thought it was just an adjustment in the business cycle which would soon be over. As time went on, the worst depression in American history set in, reaching its bottom point in early 1932. The gross national product fell from $104.6 billion in 1929 to $56.1 billion in 1933. Unemployment reached about 13 million in 1933, or about 25 percent of the labor force, excluding farmers. Industrial production dropped about 51 percent. The banking system suffered; 5,761 banks, more than 22 percent of the total, failed by the end of 1932.

HOOVER'S DEPRESSION POLICIES

The Agricultural Marketing Act: Passed in June 1929, before the market crash, this law, proposed by the president, created the Federal Farm Board. It had a revolving fund of $500 million to lend agricultural cooperatives to buy commodities, such as wheat and cotton, and hold them for higher prices. Until 1931, it did keep agricultural prices above the world level. Then world prices plummeted, the board's funds ran out, and there was no period of higher prices in which the cooperatives could sell their stored commodities.

The Hawley-Smoot Tariff: This law, passed in June 1930, raised duties on both agricultural and manufactured imports. It did nothing of significance to improve the economy, and historians argue over whether it contributed to the spread of the international depression.

The Reconstruction Finance Corporation: Chartered by Congress in 1932, the RFC had an appropriation of $500 million, and authority to borrow $1.5 billion for loans to railroads, banks, and other financial institutions. It prevented the failure of basic firms, on which many other elements of the economy depended, but was criticized by some as relief for the rich.

The Federal Home Loan Bank Act: This law, passed in July 1932, created home-loan banks, with a capital of $125 million, to make loans to building and loan associations, savings banks, and insurance companies to help them avoid foreclosures on homes.

The Bonus Army: The Bonus Expeditionary Force, which took its name from the American Expeditionary Force of World War I, was a group of about 14,000 unemployed veterans who went to Washington in the summer of 1932 to lobby Congress for immediate payment of the bonus that had been approved in 1926 for payment in 1945. At Hoover's insistence, the Senate did not pass the bonus bill, and about half of the BEF accepted a congressional offer of transportation home. The remaining five or six thousand, many with wives and children, continued to live in shanties along the Anacostia River and to lobby for their cause. After two veterans were killed in a clash with the police, Hoover, calling them insurrectionists and Communists, ordered the army to remove them. On July 28, 1932, General Douglas MacArthur, the army chief of staff, assisted by majors Dwight D. Eisenhower (1890–1969) and George S. Patton (1885–1945), personally commanded the removal operation. With machine guns, tanks, cavalry, infantry with fixed bayonets, and tear gas, MacArthur drove the veterans from Washington and burned their camp.

THE FIRST NEW DEAL

The heir of wealthy family and fifth cousin of Theodore Roosevelt, Franklin Delano Roosevelt was born in 1882 on the family estate at Hyde Park, New York. He graduated from Harvard and Columbia Law School, married his distant cousin, Anna Eleanor Roosevelt (1884–1962) in 1905, and practiced law in New York City. He entered state politics, then served as assistant secretary of the Navy under Wilson, and was the Democratic vice-presidential candidate in 1920. In 1921, he suffered an attack of polio which left him paralyzed for several years and on crutches or in a wheelchair for the rest of his life. In 1928, he was elected governor of New York, succeeding Al Smith. He was reelected in 1930. As governor, his depression programs for the unemployed, public works, aid to farmers, and conservation attracted national attention.

Roosevelt did not have a developed plan of action when he became president. He intended to experiment and to find what worked. As a result, many programs overlapped or contradicted others and were changed or dropped if they did not work.

In February 1933, before Roosevelt took office, Congress passed the Twenty-first Amendment to repeal prohibition, and sent it to the states. In March, the new Congress legalized light beer. The amendment was ratified by the states and took effect in December 1933.

In February 1933, as the inauguration approached, a severe banking crisis developed. Banks could not collect their loans or meet the demands of their depositors for withdrawals and runs occurred on many banks. Eventually banks in 38 states were closed by the state governments, and the remainder were open for only limited operations. An additional 5,190 banks failed in 1933, bringing the depression total to 10,951.

When Roosevelt was inaugurated on March 4, 1933, the American economic system seemed to be on the verge of collapse. Roosevelt assured the nation that "the only thing we have to fear is fear itself," called for a special session of Congress to convene on March 9, and asked for "broad executive powers to wage war against the emergency." Two days later, he closed all banks and forbade the export of gold or the redemption of currency in gold.

Legislation of the New Deal

The special session of Congress, from March 9 to June 16, 1933, passed a great body of legislation which has left a lasting mark on the nation. The period has been referred to ever since as the "Hundred Days." Historians have divided Roosevelt's legislation into the First New Deal (1933–1935) and a new wave of programs beginning in 1935 called the Second New Deal.

The Emergency Banking Relief Act was passed on March 9, the first day of the special session. The law provided additional funds for banks from the RFC and the Federal Reserve, allowed the Treasury to open sound banks after 10 days and to merge or liquidate unsound ones, and forbade the hoarding or export of gold. Roosevelt, on March 12, assured the public of the soundness of the banks in the first of many "fireside chats," or radio addresses. People believed him, and most banks were soon open with more deposits than withdrawals.

The Banking Act of 1933, or the Glass-Steagall Act, established the Federal Deposit Insurance Corporation (FDIC) to insure individual deposits in commercial banks, and separated commercial banking from the more speculative activity of investment banking.

The Truth-in-Securities Act required that full information about stocks and bonds be provided by brokers and others to potential purchasers.

The Home Owners Loan Corporation (HOLC) had authority to borrow money to refinance home mortgages and thus prevent foreclosures. Eventually it lent more than three billion dollars to more than one million home owners.

Gold was taken out of circulation following the president's order of March 6, and the nation went off the gold standard. Eventually, on January 31, 1934, the value of the dollar was set at $35 per ounce of gold, 59 percent of its former value. The object of the devaluation was to raise prices and help American exports.

The Securities and Exchange Commission was created in 1934 to supervise stock exchanges and to punish fraud in securities trading.

The Federal Housing Administration (FHA) was created by Congress in 1934 to insure long-term, low-interest mortgages for home construction and repair.

These programs, intended to provide temporary relief for people in need, were to be disbanded when the economy improved.

The Federal Emergency Relief Act appropriated $500 million for aid to the poor to be distributed by state and local governments. It also established the Federal Emergency Relief Administration under Harry Hopkins (1890–1946).

The Civilian Conservation Corps enrolled 250,000 young men aged 18 to 24 from families on relief to go to camps where they worked on flood control, soil conservation, and forest projects under the direction of the War Department. A small monthly payment was made to the family of each member. By the end of the decade, 2.75 million young men had served in the corps.

The Public Works Administration, under Secretary of the Interior Harold Ickes, had $3.3 billion to distribute to state and local governments for building projects such as schools, highways, and hospitals. The object was to "prime the pump" of the economy by creating construction jobs. Additional money was appropriated later.

In November 1933, Roosevelt established the Civil Works Administration to hire four million unemployed workers. The temporary and makeshift nature of the jobs, such as sweeping streets, brought much criticism, and the experiment was terminated in April 1934.

The Agricultural Adjustment Act of 1933 created the Agricultural Adjustment Administration (AAA), headed by George Peek. It sought to return farm prices to parity with those of the 1909 to 1914 period. Farmers agreed to reduce production of principal farm commodities and were paid a subsidy in return. The money came from a tax on the processing of the commodities. Farm prices increased, but tenants and sharecroppers were hurt when owners took land out of cultivation. The law was repealed in January 1936 on the grounds that the processing tax was not constitutional.

The Federal Farm Loan Act consolidated all farm credit programs into the Farm Credit Administration to make low-interest loans for farm mortgages and other agricultural purposes.

The Commodity Credit Corporation was established in October 1933 by the AAA to make loans to corn and cotton farmers against their crops so that they could hold them for higher prices.

The Frazier-Lemke Farm Bankruptcy Act of 1934 allowed farmers to defer foreclosure on their land while they obtained new financing, and helped them to recover property already lost through easy financing.

The National Industrial Recovery Act, passed on June 16, 1933, the last day of the Hundred Days, was viewed as the cornerstone of the recovery program. It sought to stabilize the economy by preventing extreme competition, labor-management conflicts, and overproduction. A board composed of industrial and labor leaders in each industry or business drew up a code for that industry which set minimum prices, minimum wages, maximum work hours, production limits, and quotas. The antitrust laws were temporarily suspended.

The Tennessee Valley Authority, a public corporation under a three-member board, was proposed by Roosevelt as the first major experiment in regional public planning. Starting from the nucleus of the government's Muscle Shoals property on the Tennessee River, the TVA built 20 dams in an area of 40,000 square miles to stop flooding and soil erosion, improve navigation, and generate hydroelectric power. It also manufactured nitrates for fertilizer, conducted demonstration projects for farmers, engaged in reforestation, and attempted to rehabilitate the whole area. It was fought unsuccessfully in the courts by private power companies. Roosevelt believed that it would serve as a yardstick to measure the true cost of providing electric power.

The economy improved but did not recover. The GNP, money supply, salaries, wages, and farm income rose. Unemployment dropped from about 25 percent of nonfarm workers in 1933 to about 20.1 percent, or 10.6 million, in 1935. But it was a long way from the 3.2 percent of predepression 1929, and suffering as a result of unemployment was still a major problem.

THE SECOND NEW DEAL: OPPOSITION FROM THE RIGHT AND LEFT

The Share Our Wealth Society was founded in 1934 by Senator Huey "The King-fish" Long (1893–1935) of Louisiana. Long was a populist demagogue who was elected governor of Louisiana in 1928, established a practical dictatorship over the state, and moved to the United States Senate in 1930. He supported Roosevelt in 1932, but then broke with him, calling him a tool of Wall Street for not doing more to combat the depression. Long called for the confiscation of all fortunes over five million dollars and a tax of one hundred percent on annual incomes over one million. With the money, the government would provide subsidies so that every family would have a "homestead" of house, car, and furnishings, a minimum annual income of $2,000, and free college education for those who wanted it. His slogan was "Every Man a King." Long talked of running for president in 1936, and published a book entitled *My First Days in the White House*. His society had more than five million members when he was assassinated on the steps of the Louisiana Capitol on September 8, 1935. The Reverend Gerald L. K. Smith appointed himself Long's successor as head of the society, but he lacked Long's ability.

The Second New Deal Begins

With millions of Democratic voters under the sway of Townsend, Long, and Coughlin, with the destruction of the NRA by the Supreme Court imminent, and with the election of 1936 approaching, Roosevelt began to push through a series of new programs in the spring of 1935. Much of the legislation was passed during the summer of 1935, a period sometimes called the Second Hundred Days.

The Works Progress Administration (WPA) was started in May 1935, following the passage of the Emergency Relief Appropriations Act of April 1935. Headed by Harry Hopkins, the WPA employed people from the relief rolls for 30 hours of work a week at pay double the relief payment but less than private employment.

The National Youth Administration (NYA) was established as part of the WPA in June 1935, to provide part-time jobs for high school and college students to enable them to stay in school, and to help young adults not in school to find jobs.

The Rural Electrification Administration (REA) was created in May 1935, to provide loans and WPA labor to electric cooperatives so they could build lines into rural areas not served by private companies.

The Social Security Act was passed in August 1935. It established a retirement plan for persons over age 65, which was to be funded by a tax on wages paid equally by employee and employer. The first benefits, ranging from $10 to $85 per month, were paid in 1942. Another provision of the act had the effect of forcing the states to initiate unemployment insurance programs.

The Banking Act of 1935 created a strong central Board of Governors of the Federal Reserve system with broad powers over the operations of the regional banks.

The Election of 1936: Roosevelt had put together a coalition of followers who made the Democratic party the majority party in the nation for the first time since the Civil War. While retaining the Democratic base in the South and among white ethnics in the big cities, Roosevelt also received strong support from midwestern farmers. Two groups that made a dramatic shift into the Democratic ranks were union workers and African Americans. Unions took an active political role for the first time since 1924, providing both campaign funds and votes. African Americans had traditionally been Republican since emancipation, but by 1936 about three-fourths of the African American voters, who lived mainly in the northern cities, had shifted into the Democratic party.

The Last Years of the New Deal

Frustrated by a conservative Supreme Court which had overturned much of his New Deal legislation, Roosevelt, after receiving his overwhelming mandate in the election of 1936, decided to curb the power of the court. In doing so, he overestimated his own political power. In February 1937, he proposed to Congress the Judicial Reorganization Bill, which would allow the president to name a new federal judge for each judge who did not retire by the age of $70^1/_2$. The appointments would be limited to a maximum of 50, with no more than six added to the Supreme Court. At the time, six justices were over the proposed age limit. The president was astonished by the wave of opposition from Democrats and Republicans alike, but he uncharacteristically refused to compromise. In doing so, he not only lost the bill but control of the Democratic Congress, which he had dominated since 1933. Nonetheless, the Court changed its position, as Chief Justice Charles Evans Hughes and Justice Owen Roberts began to vote with the more liberal members. The National Labor Relations Act was upheld in March 1937, and the Social Security Act in April. In June, a conservative justice retired, and Roosevelt had the opportunity to make an appointment.

Most economic indicators rose sharply between 1935 and 1937. The gross national product had recovered to the 1930 level, and unemployment, if WPA workers were considered employed, had fallen to 9.2 percent. During the same period, there were huge federal deficits. Roosevelt decided that the recovery was sufficient to warrant a reduction in relief programs and a move toward a balanced budget. The budget for fiscal year 1938 was reduced from $8.5 billion to $6.8 billion, with the WPA experiencing the largest cut. During the winter of 1937–1938, the economy slipped rapidly and unemployment rose to 12.5 percent. In April 1938, Roosevelt requested and received from Congress an emergency appropriation of about $3 billion for the WPA, as well as increases for public works and other programs. In July 1938, the economy began to recover, and it regained the 1937 levels in 1939.

SOCIAL DIMENSIONS OF THE NEW DEAL ERA

Unemployment for African-Americans was much higher than for the general population, and before 1933 they were often excluded from state and local relief efforts. African-Americans did benefit from many New Deal relief programs, but about 40 percent of African-American workers were sharecroppers or tenants who suffered from the provisions of the first Agricultural Adjustment Act. Roosevelt seems to have given little thought to the special problems of African-Americans, and he was afraid to endorse legislation such as an anti-lynching bill for fear of alienating the southern wing of the Democratic party. Eleanor Roosevelt and Harold Ickes strongly supported civil rights, and a "Black Cabinet" of advisors was assembled in the Interior Department. More African-Americans were appointed to government positions by Roosevelt than ever before, but the number was still small. When government military contracts began to flow in 1941, A. Philip Randolph (1889–1979), the president of the Brotherhood of Sleeping Car Porters, proposed a march on Washington to demand equal access to defense jobs. To forestall such an action, Roosevelt issued an executive order on June 25, 1941, establishing the Fair Employment Practices Committee to ensure consideration for minorities in defense employment.

John Collier, the commissioner of the Bureau of Indian Affairs, persuaded Congress to repeal the Dawes Act of 1887 by passing the Indian Reorganization Act of 1934. The law restored tribal ownership of lands, recognized tribal constitutions and government, and provided loans to tribes for economic development. Collier also secured the creation of the Indian Emergency Conservation Program, a Native American CCC for projects on the reservations. In addition, he helped Native Americans secure entry into the WPA, NYA, and other programs.

Labor Unions

Labor unions lost members and influence during the 1920s and early 1930s. The National Industrial Recovery Act gave them new hope when it guaranteed the right to unionize, and during 1933 about 1.5 million new members joined unions. But enforcement of the industrial codes by the NRA was ineffective, and labor leaders began to call it the "National Run Around." As a result, in 1934, there were many strikes, sometimes violent ones.

The passage of the National Labor Relations or Wagner Act in 1935 resulted in a massive growth of union membership, but at the expense of bitter conflict within the labor movement. The American Federation of Labor was made up primarily of craft unions. Some leaders, especially John L. Lewis, the dynamic president of the United Mine Workers, wanted to unionize the mass-production industries, such as automobiles and rubber, with industrial unions. In November 1935, Lewis and others established the Committee for Industrial Organization to unionize basic industries, presumably within the AFL. President William Green of the AFL ordered the CIO to disband in January 1936. When the rebels refused, they were expelled by the AFL executive council in March 1937. The insurgents then reorganized the CIO as the independent Congress of Industrial Organizations.

During its organizational period, the CIO sought to initiate several industrial unions, particularly in the steel, auto, rubber, and radio industries. In late 1936 and early 1937, it used a tactic called the sit-down strike, with the strikers occupying the workplace to prevent any production. There were 477 sit-down strikes involving about 400,000 workers. The largest was in the General Motors plant in Flint, Michigan, where the union sought recognition by the automaker. In February 1937, General Motors recognized the United Auto Workers as the bargaining agent for its 400,000 workers. By the end of 1941, the CIO had about 5 million members, the AFL about 4.6 million, and other unions about one million. Union members constituted about 11.5 percent of the work force in 1933 and 28.2 percent in 1941.

NEW DEAL DIPLOMACY AND THE ROAD TO WAR

Roosevelt and Secretary of State Cordell Hull continued the policies of their predecessors by endeavoring to improve relations with Latin American nations, and formalized their position by calling it the Good Neighbor Policy.

At the Montevideo Conference of American Nations in December of 1933, the United States renounced the right of intervention in the internal affairs of Latin American countries. In 1936, in the Buenos Aires Convention, the United States agreed to submit all American disputes to arbitration. The marines were removed from Haiti, Nicaragua, and the Dominican Republic by 1934. The Haitian protectorate treaty was allowed to expire in 1936, the right of intervention in Panama was ended by treaty in 1936, and the receivership of the finances of the Dominican Republic ended in 1941.

The United States did not intervene in the Cuban revolution in the spring of 1933, but it did back a coup by Fulgencio Batista to overthrow the liberal regime of Ramon Grau San Martin in 1934.

UNITED STATES NEUTRALITY LEGISLATION

Belief that the United States should stay out of foreign wars and problems began in the 1920s and grew in the 1930s. Examinations of World War I profiteering and revisionist history that asserted Germany had not been responsible for World War I and that the United States had been misled were also influential during the 1930s. A Gallup poll in April 1937 showed that almost two-thirds of those responding thought that American entry into World War I had been a mistake. Leading isolationists included Congressman Hamilton Fish (1888–1946) of New York, Senator William Borah (1865–1940) of Idaho, and Senator George Norris (1861–1944) of Nebraska, all Republicans. Pacifist movements, such as the Fellowship of Christian Reconciliation, were influential among college and high school students and the clergy.

The Johnson Act of 1934: This law prohibited any nation in default on World War I payments from selling securities to any American citizen or corporation.

The Neutrality Acts of 1935: On outbreak of war between foreign nations, all exports of American arms and munitions to them would be embargoed for six months. In addition, American ships were prohibited from carrying arms to any belligerent, and the president was to warn American citizens not to travel on belligerent ships.

The Neutrality Acts of 1936: The laws gave the president authority to determine when a state of war existed, and prohibited any loans or credits to belligerents.

The Neutrality Acts of 1937: The laws gave the president authority to determine if a civil war was a threat to world peace and if it was covered by the Neutrality Acts. It also prohibited all arms sales to belligerents, and allowed the cash-and-carry sale of nonmilitary goods to belligerents.

THREATS TO WORLD ORDER

The United States looked on as Japan invaded Manchuria, Italy invaded Ethiopia, and Germany occupied the Rhineland.

In a speech in Chicago in October 1937, Roosevelt proposed that the democracies unite to quarantine aggressor nations, but when public opinion did not pick up the idea, he did not press the issue.

THE AMERICAN RESPONSE TO THE WAR IN EUROPE

Even before the outbreak of World War II, Roosevelt began a preparedness program to improve American defenses. Congress greatly increased defense appropriations. In August 1939, Roosevelt created the War Resources Board to develop a plan for industrial mobilization in the event of war. The next month, he established the Office of Emergency Management in the White House to centralize mobilization activities.

The Neutrality Act of 1939: Roosevelt officially proclaimed the neutrality of the United States on September 5, 1939. He then called Congress into special session on September 21 and urged it to allow the cash-and-carry sale of arms. Despite opposition from isolationists, the Democratic Congress, in a vote that followed party lines, passed a new Neutrality Act in November. It allowed the cash-and-carry sale of arms and short-term loans to belligerents, but forbade American ships to trade with belligerents or Americans to travel on belligerent ships. The new law was helpful to the Allies because they controlled the Atlantic.

Almost all Americans recognized Germany as a threat. They divided on whether to aid Britain or to concentrate on the defense of America. The Committee to Defend America by Aiding the Allies was formed in May 1940, and the America First Committee, which opposed involvement, was incorporated in September 1940.

In April 1940, Roosevelt declared that Greenland, a possession of conquered Denmark, was covered by the Monroe Doctrine, and he supplied military assistance to set up a coastal patrol there.

In May 1940, Roosevelt appointed a Council of National Defense, chaired by William S. Knudson (1879–1948), the president of General Motors, to direct defense production and to build 50,000 planes. The Office of Production Management was created to allocate scarce materials, and the Office of Price Administration was established to prevent inflation and protect consumers. In June, Roosevelt made Republicans Henry L. Stimson (1867–1950) and Frank Kellogg (1856–1937) secretaries of war and navy, respectively, partly as an attempt to secure bipartisan support.

Congress approved the nation's first peacetime draft, the Selective Service and Training Act, in September 1940. Men 21 to 35 were registered, and many were called for one year of military training.

Roosevelt determined that to aid Britain in every way possible was the best way to avoid war with Germany. In September 1940, he signed an agreement to give Britain 50 American destroyers in return for a 99-year lease on air and naval bases in British territories in Newfoundland, Bermuda, and the Caribbean.

The Election of 1940 (Republicans): Passing over their isolationist front-runners, Senator Robert A. Taft (1889–1953) of Ohio and New York attorney Thomas E. Dewey (1902–1971), the Republicans nominated Wendell L. Willkie (1892–1944) of Indiana, a dark-horse candidate. Willkie, a liberal Republican who had been a Democrat most of his life, was the head of an electric utility holding company which had fought against the TVA. The platform supported a strong defense program, but severely criticized New Deal domestic policies.

The Election of 1940 (Democrats): Roosevelt was nominated for a third term, breaking a tradition which had existed since George Washington. Only with difficulty did Roosevelt's managers persuade the delegates to accept his choice of vice president, Secretary of Agriculture Henry A. Wallace, to succeed Garner. The platform endorsed the foreign and domestic policies of the administration. Roosevelt told the public, "Your boys are not going to be sent to any foreign wars."

The Vote: Roosevelt won by a much narrower margin than in 1936, with 27,243,466 votes, 54.7 percent, and 449 electoral votes. Willkie received 22,304,755 votes and 82 electoral votes. Socialist Norman Thomas had 100,264 votes, and Communist Earl Browder (1891–1973) received 48,579.

AMERICAN INVOLVEMENT WITH THE EUROPEAN WAR

The Lend-Lease Act: This let the United States provide supplies to Britain in exchange for goods and services after the war. It was signed on March 11, 1941. In effect, the law changed the United States from a neutral to a nonbelligerent on the Allied side.

In April 1941, Roosevelt started the American Neutrality Patrol. The American navy would search out but not attack German submarines in the western half of the Atlantic and warn British vessels of their location. Also in April, U.S. forces occupied Greenland, and in May, the president declared a state of unlimited national emergency.

American marines occupied Iceland, a Danish possession, in July 1941 to protect it from seizure by Germany. The American navy began to convoy American and Icelandic ships between the United States and Iceland.

On August 9, 1941 Roosevelt and Winston Churchill issued the Atlantic Charter.

Germany invaded Russia in June 1941, and in November the United States extended lend-lease assistance to the Russians.

The American destroyer *Greer* was attacked by a German submarine near Iceland on September 4, 1941. Roosevelt ordered the American military forces to shoot on sight any German or Italian vessel in the patrol zone. An undeclared naval war had begun. The American destroyer *Kearny* was attacked by a submarine on October 16, and the destroyer *Reuben James* was sunk on October 30, with 115 lives lost. In November, Congress authorized the arming of merchant ships.

THE ROAD TO PEARL HARBOR

To halt Japanese expansion in Asia, the Vichy government granted the Japanese government the right to build military bases and station troops in French Indochina. In late July, the United States placed an embargo on the export of aviation gasoline, lubricants, and scrap iron and steel to Japan, and granted an additional loan to China. In December, the embargo was extended to include iron ore and pig iron, some chemicals, machine tools, and other products.

Negotiations to end the impasse between the United States and Japan were conducted in Washington between Secretary Hull and Japanese Ambassador Kichisaburo Nomura. Hull demanded that Japan withdraw from Indochina and China, promise not to attack any other area in the western Pacific, and withdraw from its pact with Italy and Germany in return for the reopening of American trade. The Japanese offered to withdraw from Indochina when the Chinese war was satisfactorily settled, to promise no further expansion, and to agree to ignore any obligation under the Tripartite Pact to go to war if the United States entered a defensive war with Germany. Hull refused to compromise.

In October 1941, a new military cabinet headed by General Hideki Tojo took control of Japan. The Japanese secretly decided to make a final effort to negotiate, and to go to war if no solution was found by November 25. A new round of talks followed in Washington, but neither side would make a substantive change in its position, and on November 26, Hull repeated the American demand that the Japanese remove all their forces from China and Indochina immediately. The Japanese gave final approval on December 1 for an attack on the United States.

The Japanese planned a major offensive to take the Dutch East Indies, Malaya, and the Philippines in order to obtain the oil, metals, and other raw materials they needed. At the same time, they would attack Pearl Harbor in Hawaii to destroy the American Pacific fleet to keep it from interfering with their plans.

The United States had broken the Japanese diplomatic codes and knew that trouble was imminent. Between December 1 and December 6, 1941, it became clear to administration leaders that Japanese task forces were being ordered into battle. American commanders in the Pacific were warned of possible aggressive action there, but not forcefully. Apparently most American leaders thought that Japan would attack the Dutch East Indies and Malaya, but would avoid American territory so as not to provoke action by the

United States. Some argue that Roosevelt wanted to let the Japanese attack so that the American people would be squarely behind the war.

At 7:55 a.m. on Sunday, December 7, 1941, the first wave of Japanese carrier-based planes attacked the American fleet in Pearl Harbor. A second wave followed at 8:50 a.m. American defensive action was almost nil, but by the second wave a few anti-aircraft batteries were operating and a few army planes from another base in Hawaii engaged the enemy. The United States suffered the loss of two battleships, which were sunk, six more damaged and out of action, three cruisers and three destroyers sunk or damaged, and a number of lesser vessels destroyed or damaged. All of the 150 aircraft at Pearl Harbor were destroyed on the ground. Worst of all, 2,323 American servicemen were killed and about 1,100 wounded. The Japanese lost 29 planes, five midget submarines, and one fleet submarine.

In what could be construed as one of the luckier breaks in modern military history, the U.S. fleet of aircraft carriers based at Pearl Harbor happened to be out on maneuvers at the time of the Japanese strike. The carriers would soon play a significant role in the Pacific theater, as the United States entered World War II.

19. WORLD WAR II AND THE POSTWAR ERA (1941–1960)

THE U.S. DECLARES WAR

On December 8, 1941, Roosevelt told a joint session of Congress that the day before had been a "date that would live in infamy." Congress declared war on Japan, with one dissenting vote. On December 11, Germany and Italy declared war on the United States. Great Britain and the United States then established the Combined Chiefs of Staff, headquartered in Washington, to direct Anglo-American military operations.

On January 1, 1942, representatives of 26 nations met in Washington, D.C., and signed the Declaration of the United Nations, pledging themselves to the principles of the Atlantic Charter and promising not to make a separate peace with their common enemies.

THE HOME FRONT

War Production Board: The WPD was established in 1942 by President Franklin D. Roosevelt for the purpose of regulating the use of raw materials.

Wage and Price Controls: In April 1942, the General Maximum Price Regulation Act froze prices and extended rationing. In April 1943, prices, wages, and salaries were frozen.

Revenue Act of 1942: The Revenue Act of 1942 extended the income tax to the majority of the population. Payroll deduction for the income tax began in 1944.

Social Changes: Rural areas lost population as people went to work in factories. Population in coastal areas rose rapidly, as defense contracting and other wartime activities were concentrated there. African-Americans moved from the rural South to northern and western cities, finding employment opportunities in factories. This migration led to racial tensions, often resulting in rioting—most notably in the June 1943 racial riot in Detroit.

Smith-Connolly Act: Passed in 1943, the Smith-Connolly Antistrike Act authorized government seizure of a plant or mine idled by a strike if the war effort was impeded. It expired in 1947.

Korematsu v. United States: In 1944, the Supreme Court upheld President

Roosevelt's 1942 order that Issei (Japanese-Americans who had emigrated from Japan) and Nisei (native-born Japanese-Americans) be relocated to concentration camps. The camps were closed in March 1946.

Smith v. Allwright: In 1944, the Supreme Court struck down the Texas primary elections, which were restricted to whites, for violating the fifteenth Amendment.

Presidential Election of 1944: President Franklin D. Roosevelt, together with new vice-presidential candidate Harry S. Truman (1884–1972) of Missouri, defeated his Republican opponent, Governor Thomas E. Dewey of New York.

Roosevelt died on April 12, 1945, at Warm Springs, Georgia. Harry S. Truman became president.

THE NORTH AFRICAN AND EUROPEAN THEATERS

Nearly 400 ships were lost in American waters of the Atlantic to German submarines between January and June 1942.

The United States joined in the bombing of the European continent in July 1942. Bombing increased during 1943 and 1944 and lasted to the end of the war.

The Allied army under Dwight D. Eisenhower attacked French North Africa in November 1942. The Vichy French forces surrendered.

In the Battle of Kassarine Pass, North Africa, February 1943, the Allied army met General Erwin Rommel's Africa Korps. Although the battle is variously interpreted as a standoff or a defeat for the United States, Rommel's forces were soon trapped by the British moving in from Egypt. In May 1943, Rommel's Africa Korps surrendered.

Allied armies under George C. Patton (1885–1945) invaded Sicily from Africa in July 1943, and gained control by mid-August. Moving from Sicily, the Allied armies invaded the Italian mainland in September. Benito Mussolini had already fallen from power, and his successor, Marshal Pietro Badoglio, surrendered. The Germans, however, put up a stiff resistance, with the result that Rome did not fall until June 1944. With the death of Mussolini and the surrender of Marshal Badoglio, Italy became occupied by Nazi Germany.

In March 1944, the Soviet Union began pushing into Eastern Europe.

On "D-Day," June 6, 1944, Allied armies under Dwight D. Eisenhower, now commander in chief of the Allied Expeditionary Forces, began an invasion of Normandy, France. Allied armies under General Omar Bradley (1893–1981) took the transportation hub of St. Lo, France, in July.

Allied armies liberated Paris in August. By mid-September, they had arrived at the Rhine, on the edge of Germany.

Beginning December 16, 1944, at the Battle of the Bulge, the Germans counterattacked, driving the Allies back about 50 miles into Belgium. By January, the Allies were once more advancing toward Germany. The Allies crossed the Rhine in March 1945. In the last week of April, Eisenhower's forces met the Soviet army at the Elbe. On May 7, 1945, Germany surrendered.

THE PACIFIC THEATER

By the end of December 1941, Guam, Wake Island, the Gilbert Islands, and Hong Kong had fallen to the Japanese. In January 1942, Raboul, New Britain, fell, followed in February by Singapore and Java, and in March by Rangoon, Burma.

The U.S. air raids on Tokyo in April 1942 were militarily inconsequential, but they raised Allied morale.

U.S. forces surrendered at Corregidor, Philippines, on May 6, 1942.

In the Battle of the Coral Sea, May 7–8, 1942 (northeast of Australia, south of New Guinea and the Solomon Islands), planes from the American carriers *Lexington* and *Yorktown* forced Japanese troop transports to turn back from attacking Port Moresby. The battle stopped the Japanese advance on Australia.

At the Battle of Midway, June 4–7, 1942, American air power destroyed four Japanese carriers and about 300 planes. The United States lost the carrier *Yorktown* and one destroyer. The battle proved to be the turning point in the Pacific.

A series of land, sea, and air battles took place around Guadalcanal in the Solomon Islands from August 1942 to February 1943, stopping the Japanese.

The Allied strategy of island hopping, begun in 1943, sought to neutralize Japanese strongholds with air and sea power and then move on. General Douglas MacArthur commanded the land forces moving from New Guinea toward the Philippines, while Admiral Chester W. Nimitz directed the naval attack on important Japanese islands in the central Pacific.

U.S. forces advanced into the Gilberts (November 1943), the Marshalls (January 1944), and the Marianas (June 1944).

In the Battle of the Philippine Sea, June 19–20, 1944, the Japanese lost three carriers, two submarines, and more than 300 planes, while the Americans lost 17 planes. After the American capture of the Marianas, General Tojo resigned as premier of Japan.

The Battle of Leyte Gulf, October 25, 1944, involved three major engagements which resulted in Japan's loss of most of its remaining naval power. It also brought the first use of the Japanese kamikaze or suicide attacks by Japanese pilots who crashed into American carriers.

Forces under General Douglas MacArthur (1880–1964) liberated Manila in March 1945.

Between April and June 1945, in the battle for Okinawa, nearly 50,000 American casualties resulted from the fierce fighting, but the battle virtually destroyed Japan's remaining defenses.

THE ATOMIC BOMB

The Manhattan Engineering District was established by the army engineers in August 1942 for the purpose of developing an atomic bomb (it eventually became known as the Manhattan Project). J. Robert Oppenheimer directed the design and construction of a transportable atomic bomb at Los Alamos, New Mexico.

On December 2, 1942, Enrico Fermi (1901–1954) and his colleagues at the University of Chicago produced the first atomic chain reaction.

On July 16, 1945, the first atomic bomb was exploded at Alamogordo, New Mexico.

The *Enola Gay* dropped an atomic bomb on Hiroshima, Japan, on August 6, 1945, killing about 78,000 persons and injuring 100,000 more. On August 9, a second bomb was dropped on Nagasaki, Japan.

On August 8, 1945, the Soviet Union entered the war against Japan.

Japan surrendered on August 14, 1945. The formal surrender was signed on September 2.

DIPLOMACY

Casablanca Conference: On January 14–25, 1943, Franklin D. Roosevelt and Winston Churchill, prime minister of Great Britain, declared a policy of unconditional surrender for "all enemies."

Moscow Conference: In October 1943, Secretary of State Cordell Hull obtained Soviet agreement to enter the war against Japan after Germany was defeated, and to participate in a world organization after the war was over.

Declaration of Cairo: Issued on December 1, 1943, after Roosevelt met with General Chiang Kai-shek in Cairo from November 22 to 26, the Declaration of Cairo called for Japan's unconditional surrender and stated that all Chinese territories occupied by Japan would be returned to China and that Korea would be free and independent.

Teheran Conference: The first "Big Three" conference met at Casablanca in January 1943. They later met at Teheran, Yalta, and Potsdam.

The Emergence of the Cold War and Containment

In a speech in Fulton, Missouri, in 1946, Winston Churchill stated that an "Iron Curtain" had spread across Europe, separating the democratic from the authoritarian Communist states.

In 1946, career diplomat and Soviet expert George F. Kennan warned that the Soviet Union had no intention of living peacefully with the United States. The next year, in July 1947, he wrote an anonymous article for *Foreign Affairs* in which he called for a counterforce to Soviet pressures, for the purpose of "containing" communism.

Truman Doctrine: In February 1947, Great Britain notified the United States that it could no longer aid the Greek government in its war against Communist insurgents. The next month President Harry S. Truman asked Congress for $400 million in military and economic aid for Greece and Turkey. In what became known as the "Truman Doctrine," he argued that the United States must support free peoples who were resisting Communist domination.

Marshall Plan: Secretary of State George C. Marshall (1880–1959) proposed in June 1947 that the United States provide economic aid to help rebuild Europe. Meeting in July, representatives of the European nations agreed on a recovery program jointly financed by the United States and the European countries. The following March, Congress passed the European Recovery Program, popularly known as the Marshall Plan, which provided more than $12 billion in aid.

After the United States, France, and Great Britain announced plans to create a West German Republic out of their German zones, the Soviet Union in June 1948 blocked surface access to Berlin. The United States then instituted an airlift to transport supplies to the city until the Soviets lifted their blockade in May 1949.

NATO

In April 1949, the North Atlantic Treaty Organization was signed by the United States, Great Britain, France, Italy, Belgium, the Netherlands, Luxembourg, Denmark, Norway, Portugal, Iceland, and Canada. The signatories pledged that an attack against one would be considered an attack against all. Greece and Turkey joined the alliance in 1952, and West Germany in 1954. The Soviets formed the Warsaw Treaty Organization in 1955 to counteract NATO.

NATO was strengthened by the Korean War.

INTERNATIONAL COOPERATION

Representatives from Europe and the United States, at a conference held July 1–22, 1944, signed agreements for an international bank and a world monetary fund to stabilize international currencies and rebuild the economies of war-torn nations.

At Yalta in February 1945, Roosevelt, Churchill, and Stalin called for a conference on world organization to meet in April 1945 in the United States.

From April to June 1945, representatives from 50 countries met in San Francisco to establish the United Nations. The U.N. charter created a General Assembly composed of all member nations which would act as the ultimate policy-making body. A Security Council, made up of 11 members, including the United States, Great Britain, France, the Soviet Union, and China as permanent members and six additional nations elected by the General Assembly for two-year terms, would be responsible for settling disputes among U.N. member nations.

Containment in Asia

General Douglas MacArthur headed a four-power Allied Control Council which governed Japan, allowing it to develop economically and politically.

Between 1945 and 1948, the United States gave more than $2 billion in aid to the Nationalist Chinese under Chiang Kai-shek, and sent George C. Marshall to settle the conflict between Chiang's Nationalists and Mao Tse-tung's Communists. In 1949, however, Mao defeated Chiang and forced the Nationalists to flee to Formosa (Taiwan). Mao established the People's Republic of China on the mainland.

KOREAN WAR

On June 25, 1950, North Korea invaded South Korea. President Truman committed U.S. forces commanded by General MacArthur, but under United Nations auspices. By October, the U.N. forces (mostly American) had driven north of the 38th parallel, which divided North and South Korea. Chinese troops attacked MacArthur's forces on November 26, pushing them south of the 38th parallel, but by spring 1951, the U.N. forces had recovered their offensive. MacArthur called for a naval blockade of China and bombing north of the Yalu River, criticizing the president for fighting a limited war. In April 1951, Truman removed MacArthur from command.

Armistice talks began with North Korea in the summer of 1951. In June 1953, an armistice was signed, leaving Korea divided along virtually the same boundary that had existed prior to the war.

EISENHOWER-DULLES FOREIGN POLICY

Dwight D. Eisenhower, elected president in 1952, chose John Foster Dulles (1888–1959) as secretary of state. Dulles talked of a more aggressive foreign policy, calling for "massive retaliation" and "liberation" rather than containment. He wished to emphasize nuclear deterrents rather than conventional armed forces. Dulles served as secretary of state until ill health forced him to resign in April 1959. Christian A. Herter (1895–1961) took his place.

In 1954, the French asked the United States to commit air forces to rescue French forces at Dien Bien Phu, Vietnam, where they were being besieged by the nationalist forces led by Ho Chi Minh. Eisenhower refused. In May 1954, Dien Bien Phu surrendered.

France, Great Britain, the Soviet Union, and China signed the Geneva Accords in July 1954, dividing Vietnam along the 17th parallel. The North would be under Ho Chi Minh and the South under Emperor Bao Dai. Elections were scheduled for 1956 to unify the country, but Ngo Dinh Diem overthrew Bao Dai and prevented the elections from taking place. The United States supplied economic aid to South Vietnam.

Dulles attempted to establish a Southeast Asia Treaty Organization parallel to NATO, but was able to obtain only the Philippine Republic, Thailand, and Pakistan as signatories in September 1954.

President Eisenhower announced in January 1957 that the United States was prepared to use armed force in the Middle East against Communist aggression. Under this doctrine, U.S. marines entered Beirut, Lebanon, in July 1958 to promote political stability during a change of governments. The marines left in October.

The United States supported the overthrow of President Jacobo Arbenz Guzman of Guatemala in 1954 because he began accepting arms from the Soviet Union.

Vice President Nixon had to call off an eight-nation goodwill tour of Latin America after meeting hostile mobs in Venezuela and Peru in 1958.

In January 1959, Fidel Castro overthrew Fulgencio Batista, dictator of Cuba. Castro soon began criticizing the United States and moved closer to the Soviet Union, signing a trade agreement with the Soviets in February 1960. The United States prohibited the importation of Cuban sugar in October 1960, and broke off diplomatic relations in January 1961.

THE POLITICS OF AFFLUENCE: DEMOBILIZATION AND DOMESTIC POLICY

Harry S. Truman, formerly a senator from Missouri and vice president of the United States, became president on April 12, 1945. In September 1945, he proposed a liberal legislative program, including expansion of unemployment insurance, extension of the Employment Service, a higher minimum wage, a permanent Fair Employment Practices Commission, slum clearance, low-rent housing, regional TVA-type programs, and a public-works program, but was unable to put it through Congress.

Congress created the Atomic Energy Commission in 1946, establishing civilian control over nuclear development and giving the president sole authority over the use of atomic weapons in warfare.

Taft-Hartley Act (1947): The Republicans, who had gained control of Congress in 1946, sought to control the power of the unions through the Taft-Hartley Act. This act made the "closed-shop" illegal; labor unions could no longer force employers to hire only union members. The act did allow the "union-shop," in which newly-hired employees were required to join the union. It also established an 80–day cooling-off period for strikers in key industries, ended the practice of employers collecting dues for unions, forbade such actions as secondary boycotts, jurisdictional strikes, featherbedding, and contributing to political campaigns, and required an anti-Communist oath from union officials. The act slowed down efforts to unionize the South, and by 1954, 15 states had passed "right to work" laws, forbidding the "union-shop."

In 1946, Truman appointed the President's Committee on Civil Rights, which one year later produced its report *To Secure These Rights*. The report called for the elimination of all segregation. In 1948, the president banned racial discrimination in federal government hiring practices and ordered desegregation of the armed forces.

The Presidential Succession Act of 1947 placed the Speaker of the House and the president pro tempore of the Senate ahead of the secretary of state and after the vice president in the line of succession. The twenty-second Amendment to the Constitution, ratified in 1951, limited the president to two terms.

Election of 1948: Truman was the Democratic nominee, but the Democrats were split by the States' Rights Democratic party (Dixiecrats) which nominated Governor Strom Thurmond of South Carolina, and the Progressive party, which nominated former

Vice President Henry Wallace. The Republicans nominated Governor Thomas E. Dewey of New York. After traveling widely, and attacking the "do-nothing Congress," Truman won a surprise victory.

THE FAIR DEAL

Truman sought to enlarge and extend the New Deal, including extending Social Security to more people, rural electrification, and farm housing. He also introduced bills dealing with civil rights, national health insurance, federal aid to education, and repeal of the Taft-Hartley Act. A coalition of Republicans and Southern Democrats prevented little more than the maintenance of existing programs.

ANTICOMMUNISM

In 1950, Julius and Ethel Rosenberg and Harry Gold were charged with giving atomic secrets to the Soviet Union. The Rosenbergs were convicted and executed in 1953.

On February 9, 1950, Senator Joseph R. McCarthy (1908–1957) of Wisconsin declared that he had a list of known Communists who were working in the State Department. He later expanded his attacks to diplomats and scholars and contributed to the electoral defeat of two senators. After making charges against the army, he was censured and discredited by the Senate in 1954. He died in 1957.

EISENHOWER'S DYNAMIC CONSERVATISM

The Republicans nominated Dwight D. Eisenhower, most recently NATO commander, for the presidency and Richard M. Nixon, senator from California, for the vice presidency. The Democrats nominated Governor Adlai E. Stevenson (1900–1965) of Illinois for president. Eisenhower won by a landslide; for the first time since Reconstruction, the Republicans won some southern states.

Eisenhower sought to balance the budget and lower taxes but did not attempt to roll back existing social and economic legislation. Eisenhower first described his policy as "dynamic conservatism," and then as "progressive moderation." The administration abolished the Reconstruction Finance Corporation, ended wage and price controls, and reduced farm price supports. It cut the budget and in 1954 lowered tax rates for corporations and individuals with high incomes; an economic slump, however, made balancing the budget difficult.

Social Security was extended in 1954 and 1956 to an additional 10 million people, including professionals, domestic and clerical workers, farm workers, and members of the armed services. In 1959, benefits were increased 7 percent. In 1955, the minimum wage was raised from 75 cents to $1.00 an hour.

The Rural Electrification Administration announced in 1960 that 97 percent of American farms had electricity. In 1954, the government began financing the export of farm surpluses in exchange for foreign currencies, and later provided surpluses free to needy nations and to the poor in exchange for governmentally issued food stamps.

In 1954, Eisenhower obtained congressional approval for joint Canadian–U.S. construction of the St. Lawrence Seaway, which was intended to give oceangoing vessels access to the Great Lakes. In 1956, Congress authorized construction of the Interstate Highway System, with the federal government supplying 90 percent of the cost and the states 10 percent.

The launching of the Soviet space satellite *Sputnik* on October 4, 1957, created fear that America was falling behind technologically. Although the United States launched

Explorer I on January 31, 1958, the concern continued. In 1958, Congress established the National Aeronautics and Space Administration (NASA) to coordinate research and development, and passed the National Defense Education Act to provide grants and loans for education.

On January 3, 1959, Alaska became the 49th state, and on August 21, 1959, Hawaii became the 50th.

CIVIL RIGHTS

Eisenhower completed the formal integration of the armed forces, desegregated public services in Washington, D.C., naval yards, and veterans' hospitals, and appointed a Civil Rights Commission.

Brown v. Board of Education of Topeka: In this 1954 case, NAACP lawyer Thurgood Marshall challenged the doctrine of "separate but equal" (*Plessy v. Ferguson*, 1896). The Court declared that separate educational facilities were inherently unequal. In 1955, the Court ordered states to integrate "with all deliberate speed."

Although at first the South reacted cautiously, by 1955 there were calls for "massive resistance." White Citizens Councils emerged to spearhead the resistance. State legislatures used a number of tactics to get around *Brown*. By the end of 1956, desegregation of the schools had advanced very little.

Although he did not personally support the Supreme Court decision, Eisenhower sent 10,000 National Guardsmen and 1,000 paratroopers to Little Rock, Arkansas, to control mobs and enable African-Americans to enroll at Central High in September 1957. A small force of soldiers was stationed at the school throughout the year.

On December 11, 1955, in Montgomery, Alabama, Rosa Parks, a black woman, refused to give up her seat on a city bus to a white and was arrested. Under the leadership of Martin Luther King (1929–1968), an African-American pastor, African-Americans of Montgomery organized a bus boycott that lasted for a year, until in December 1956, the Supreme Court refused to review a lower court ruling that stated that separate but equal was no longer legal.

Eisenhower proposed the Civil Rights Act of 1957, which established a permanent Civil Rights Commission and a Civil Rights Division of the Justice Department empowered to prevent interference with the right to vote. The Civil Rights Act of 1960 gave the federal courts power to register African-American voters.

In 1959, state and federal courts nullified Virginia laws that prevented state funds from going to integrated schools. This proved to be the beginning of the end for "massive resistance."

In February 1960, four African-American students who had been denied service staged a sit-in at a segregated Woolworth lunch counter in Greensboro, North Carolina. This action inspired sit-ins elsewhere in the South and led to the formation of the Student Nonviolent Coordinating Committee (SNCC). The SNCC's chief aims included ending segregation in public accommodations and protecting blacks' voting rights.

The Election of 1960: Vice President Richard M. Nixon won the Republican presidential nomination, and the Democrats nominated Senator John F. Kennedy (1917–1963) for the presidency, with Lyndon B. Johnson (1908–1973), majority leader of the Senate, as his running mate.

Kennedy's Catholicism was a major issue until, on September 12, Kennedy told a gathering of Protestant ministers that he accepted separation of church and state and that he wouldn't allow Catholic leaders would not tell him how to act as president.

A series of televised debates between Kennedy and Nixon helped create a positive image for Kennedy and may have been a turning point in the election.

Kennedy won the election by slightly more than 100,000 popular votes and 94 electoral votes, based on majorities in New England, the Middle Atlantic, and the South.

20. THE NEW FRONTIER, VIETNAM, AND SOCIAL UPHEAVAL (1960–1972)

KENNEDY'S "NEW FRONTIER" AND THE LIBERAL REVIVAL

Kennedy was unable to get much of his program through Congress because of an alliance of Republicans and southern Democrats. He proposed plans for federal aid to education, urban renewal, medical care for the aged, reductions in personal and corporate income taxes, and the creation of a Department of Urban Affairs. None of these proposals passed.

Kennedy did gain congressional approval for raising the minimum wage from $1.00 to $1.25 an hour and extending it to 3 million more workers.

The 1961 Housing Act provided nearly $5 billion over four years for the preservation of open urban spaces, development of mass transit, and the construction of middle-class housing.

CIVIL RIGHTS

In May 1961, blacks and whites, sponsored by the Congress on Racial Equality, boarded buses in Washington, D.C., and traveled across the South to New Orleans to test federal enforcement of regulations prohibiting discrimination. They met violence in Alabama but continued to New Orleans. Others came into the South to test the segregation laws.

The Justice Department, under Attorney General Robert F. Kennedy (1925–1968), began to push for civil rights, including desegregation of interstate transportation in the South, integration of schools, and supervision of elections.

In the fall of 1962, President Kennedy called the Mississippi National Guard to federal duty to enable an African American, James Meredith, to enroll at the University of Mississippi.

Kennedy presented a comprehensive civil rights bill to Congress in 1963. It banned racial discrimination in public accommodations, gave the attorney general power to bring suits on behalf of individuals for school integration, and withheld federal funds from state-administered programs that practiced discrimination. With the bill held up in Congress, 200,000 people marched, demonstrating on its behalf on August 28, 1963, in Washington, D.C. Martin Luther King gave his "I Have a Dream" speech.

THE COLD WAR CONTINUES

Under Eisenhower, the Central Intelligence Agency had begun training some 2,000 men for an invasion of Cuba to overthrow Fidel Castro, the left-leaning revolutionary who had taken power in 1959. On April 19, 1961, this force invaded at the Bay of Pigs, but was pinned down and forced to surrender. Some 1,200 men were captured.

After a confrontation between Kennedy and Khrushchev in Berlin, Kennedy called up reserve and National Guard units and asked for an increase in defense funds. In

August 1961, Khrushchev responded by closing the border between East and West Berlin and ordering the erection of the Berlin Wall.

The Soviet Union began the testing of nuclear weapons in September 1961. Kennedy then authorized resumption of underground testing by the United States.

On October 14, 1962, a U-2 reconnaissance plane brought photographic evidence that missile sites were being built in Cuba. Kennedy, on October 22, announced a blockade of Cuba and called on Khrushchev to dismantle the missile bases and remove all weapons capable of attacking the United States from Cuba. Six days later, Khrushchev backed down, withdrew the missiles, and Kennedy lifted the blockade. The United States promised not to invade Cuba, and removed missiles from bases in Turkey, claiming they had planned to do so anyway.

Afterwards, a "hot line" telephone connection was established between the White House and the Kremlin to effect quick communication in threatening situations.

In July 1963, a treaty banning the atmospheric testing of nuclear weapons was signed by all the major powers except France and China.

In 1961, Kennedy announced the Alliance for Progress, which would provide $20 million in aid to Latin America.

JOHNSON AND THE GREAT SOCIETY

On November 22, 1963, Kennedy was assassinated by Lee Harvey Oswald in Dallas, Texas. Jack Ruby, a nightclub owner, killed Oswald two days later. Conspiracy theories emerged. Chief Justice Earl Warren led an investigation of the murder and concluded that Oswald had acted alone, but suspicions of a conspiracy have continued.

Succeeding Kennedy, Johnson had extensive experience in both the House and Senate, and as a Texan, was the first southerner to serve as president since Woodrow Wilson. He pushed hard for Kennedy's programs, which were languishing in Congress.

A tax cut of more than $10 billion passed Congress in 1964, and an economic boom resulted.

The 1964 Civil Rights Act outlawed racial discrimination by employers and unions, created the Equal Employment Opportunity Commission to enforce the law, and eliminated the remaining restrictions on black voting.

Michael Harrington's *The Other America* (1962) showed that 20 to 25 percent of American families were living below the governmentally defined poverty line. This poverty was created by increased numbers of old and young, job displacement produced by advancing technology, and regions bypassed by economic development. The Economic Opportunity Act of 1964 sought to address these problems by establishing a Job Corps, community action programs, educational programs, work-study programs, job training, loans for small businesses and farmers, and Volunteers in Service to America (VISTA), a "domestic peace corps." The Office of Economic Opportunity administered many of these programs.

Election of 1964: Lyndon Johnson was nominated for president by the Democrats, with Senator Hubert H. Humphrey of Minnesota for vice president. The Republicans nominated Senator Barry Goldwater, a conservative from Arizona. Johnson won more than 61 percent of the popular vote and could now launch his own "Great Society" program.

The Medicare Act of 1965 combined hospital insurance for retired people with a voluntary plan to cover physician's bills. Medicaid provided grants to states to help the poor below retirement age.

EMERGENCE OF BLACK POWER

In 1965, Martin Luther King announced a voter registration drive. With help from the federal courts, he dramatized his effort by leading a march from Selma to Montgomery, Alabama, between March 21 and 25. The Voting Rights Act of 1965 authorized the attorney general to appoint officials to register voters.

Seventy percent of African-Americans lived in city ghettos. It did not appear that the tactics used in the South would help them. Frustration built up. In August 1965, Watts, an area of Los Angeles, erupted in a riot. More than 15,000 National Guardsmen were brought in; 34 people were killed, 850 wounded, and 3,100 arrested. Property damage reached nearly $200 million. In 1966, New York and Chicago experienced riots, and the following year there were riots in Newark and Detroit. The Kerner Commission, appointed to investigate the riots, concluded that they were directed at a social system that prevented African-Americans from getting good jobs and crowded them into ghettos.

Stokely Carmichael, was by 1964 unwilling to work with white civil-rights activists. In 1966, he called for the civil rights movements to be "black-staffed, black-controlled, and black-financed." Later, he moved on to the Black Panthers, self-styled urban revolutionaries based in Oakland, California. Other leaders such as H. Rap Brown also called for Black Power.

On April 4, 1968, Martin Luther King was assassinated in Memphis. Riots in more than 100 cities followed. James Earl Ray, an escaped convict, pleaded guilty to the murder—he later sought to retract his plea—and was sentenced to 99 years.

THE NEW LEFT

Students at the University of California at Berkeley staged sit-ins in 1964 to protest the prohibition of political canvassing on campus. Led by Mario Savio, the movement changed from emphasizing student rights to criticizing the bureaucracy of American society. In December, police broke up a sit-in; protests spread to other campuses.

Student protests began focusing on the Vietnam War. In the spring of 1967, 500,000 gathered in Central Park in New York City to protest the war, many burning their draft cards. SDS (Students for a Democratic Society) became more militant and willing to use violence. It turned to Lenin for its ideology.

More than 200 large campus demonstrations took place in the spring, culminating in the occupation of buildings at Columbia University to protest the university's involvement in military research and its perceived poor relations with minority groups. Police wielding clubs eventually broke up the demonstration. In August, thousands gathered in Chicago to protest the war during the Democratic convention. Although police violence against the demonstrators aroused anger, the antiwar movement began to split between those favoring violence and those opposing it.

Beginning in 1968, SDS began breaking up into rival factions. After the more radical factions began using bombs, Tom Hayden left the group. By the early 1970s, the New Left had lost political influence, having abandoned its original commitment to democracy and nonviolence.

WOMEN'S LIBERATION

In *The Feminine Mystique* (1963), Betty Friedan argued that middle-class society stifled women and did not allow them to use their individual talents. She attacked the cult of domesticity.

Friedan and other feminists founded the National Organization for Women (NOW) in 1966, calling for equal employment opportunities and equal pay.

VIETNAM

After the French defeat in 1954, the United States sent military advisors to South Vietnam to aid the government of Ngo Dinh Diem. The pro-Communist Vietcong forces gradually grew in strength, partly because Diem failed to follow through on promised reforms. They received support from North Vietnam, the Soviet Union, and China. The U.S. government supported a successful military coup against Diem in the fall of 1963.

In August 1964—after claiming that North Vietnamese gunboats had fired on American destroyers in the Gulf of Tonkin—Lyndon Johnson pushed the Gulf of Tonkin resolution through Congress, authorizing him to use military force in Vietnam. After a February 1965 attack by the Vietcong on Pleiku, Johnson ordered operation "Rolling Thunder," the first sustained bombing of North Vietnam. Johnson then sent combat troops to South Vietnam; under the leadership of General William C. Westmoreland, they conducted search and destroy operations. The number of troops increased to 184,000 in 1965, 385,000 in 1966, 485,000 in 1967, and 538,000 in 1968.

"Hawks" defended the president's policy and, drawing on containment theory, said that the nation had the responsibility to resist aggression. Secretary of State Dean Rusk became a major spokesman for the domino theory, which justified government policy by analogy with England's and France's failure to stop Hitler prior to 1939. If Vietnam should fall, it was said, all Southeast Asia would eventually go. The administration stressed its willingness to negotiate the withdrawal of all "foreign" forces from the war.

Opposition began quickly, with "teach-ins" at the University of Michigan in 1965 and a 1966 congressional investigation led by Senator J. William Fulbright. Antiwar demonstrations were gaining large crowds by 1967. "Doves" argued that the war was a civil war in which the United States should not meddle. "Doves" said that the South Vietnamese regimes were not democratic, and opposed large-scale aerial bombings, use of chemical weapons, and the killing of civilians. "Doves" rejected the domino theory, pointing to the growing losses of American life (over 40,000 by 1970) and the economic cost of the war.

On January 31, 1968, the first day of the Vietnamese New Year (Tet), the Vietcong attacked numerous cities and towns, American bases, and even Saigon. Although they suffered large losses, the Vietcong won a psychological victory, as American opinion began turning against the war.

Setting the Stage for a Nixon Victory

The Election of 1968: In November 1967, Senator Eugene McCarthy of Minnesota announced his candidacy for the 1968 Democratic presidential nomination, running on the issue of opposition to the war.

In February, McCarthy won 42 percent of the Democratic vote in the New Hampshire primary, compared with Johnson's 48 percent. Robert F. Kennedy then announced his candidacy for the Democratic presidential nomination.

Lyndon Johnson withdrew his candidacy on March 31, 1968, and Vice President Hubert H. Humphrey took his place as a candidate for the Democratic nomination.

Robert Kennedy is Assassinated: After winning the California primary over McCarthy, Robert Kennedy was assassinated by Sirhan Sirhan, a young Palestinian. This event assured Humphrey's nomination.

Nixon Nominated: The Republicans nominated Richard M. Nixon, who chose Spiro T. Agnew, governor of Maryland, as his running mate in order to appeal to southern voters. Governor George C. Wallace of Alabama, a longtime segregationist, ran for the presidency under the banner of the American Independent party, appealing to fears generated by protestors and big government.

Johnson suspended air attacks on North Vietnam shortly before the election. Nonetheless Nixon, who emphasized stability and order, defeated Humphrey by a margin of 1 percent. Wallace's 13.5 percent was the best showing by a third-party candidate since 1924.

THE NIXON CONSERVATIVE REACTION

The Nixon administration sought to block renewal of the Voting Rights Act and delay implementation of court-ordered school desegregation in Mississippi. After the Supreme Court ordered busing of students in 1971 to achieve school desegregation, the administration proposed an antibusing bill, which was blocked in Congress.

In 1969, Nixon appointed Warren E. Burger, a conservative, as chief justice, but ran into opposition with the nomination of southerners Clement F. Haynesworth, Jr., and G. Harrold Carswell. After these nominations were defeated, he nominated Harry A. Blackmun, who received Senate approval. He later appointed Lewis F. Powell, Jr., and William Rehnquist as associate justices. Although more conservative than the Warren court, the Burger court did declare the death penalty, as used at the time, unconstitutional in 1972, and struck down state antiabortion legislation in 1973.

VIETNAMIZATION

Nixon proposed that all non-South Vietnamese troops be withdrawn in phases, and that an internationally supervised election be held in South Vietnam. The North Vietnamese rejected this plan.

The president then turned to "Vietnamization," the effort to build up South Vietnamese forces while withdrawing American troops. In 1969, Nixon reduced American troop strength by 60,000, but at the same time ordered the bombing of Cambodia, a neutral country.

In April 1970, Nixon announced that Vietnamization was succeeding and that another 150,000 American troops would be out of Vietnam by the end of the year. A few days later, he sent troops into Cambodia to clear out Vietcong sanctuaries and resumed bombing of North Vietnam.

Protests against escalation of the war were especially strong on college campuses. During a May 1970 demonstration at Kent State University in Ohio, the National Guard opened fire on protestors, killing four students. Soon after, two black students were killed by a Mississippi state policeman at Jackson State University. Several hundred colleges were soon closed down by student strikes, as moderates joined the radicals. Congress repealed the Gulf of Tonkin Resolution.

The publication in 1971 of classified Defense Department documents, called "The Pentagon Papers," revealed that the government had misled the Congress and the American people regarding its intentions in Vietnam during the mid-1960s.

Nixon drew American forces back from Cambodia but increased bombing. In March 1972, after stepped-up aggression from the North, Nixon ordered the mining of Haiphong and other northern ports.

In the summer of 1972, negotiations between the United States and North Vietnam began in Paris. A draft agreement was developed by October which included a cease-fire, return of American prisoners of war, and withdrawal of U.S. forces from Vietnam. A few days before the 1972 presidential election, Henry Kissinger, the president's national security advisor, announced that "peace was at hand."

Nixon resumed bombing of North Vietnam in December 1972, claiming that the North Vietnamese were not bargaining in good faith. In January 1973, the opponents reached a settlement in which the North Vietnamese retained control over large areas of the South and agreed to release American prisoners of war within 60 days. After the prisoners were released, the United States would withdraw its remaining troops. Nearly 60,000 Americans had been killed and 300,000 more wounded and the war had cost Americans $109 billion. On March 29, 1973, the last American combat troops left South Vietnam.

FOREIGN POLICY

Initiatives with China and the U.S.S.R.: With his national security advisor, Henry Kissinger, Nixon took some bold diplomatic initiatives. Kissinger traveled to China and the Soviet Union for secret sessions to plan summit meetings with the Communists. In February 1972, Nixon and Kissinger went to China to meet with Mao Tse-tung and his associates. The United States agreed to support China's admission to the United Nations and to pursue economic and cultural exchanges.

Nixon and Kissinger called their policy *détente*, a French term meaning a relaxation in the tensions between two governments. The agreements were significant in part because they were made before the United States withdrew from Vietnam.

A NIXON LANDSLIDE

The Election of 1972: The Democrats nominated Senator George McGovern of South Dakota for president and Senator Thomas Eagleton for vice president. After the press revealed that Eagleton had previously been treated for psychological problems, McGovern eventually eased him off the ticket; Sargent Shriver took Eagleton's place. This severely stalled the campaign, and McGovern was further hampered by a party divided over the war and social policies, as well as his own perceived radicalism.

Alabama Governor George Wallace, running as the American Independent party candidate, aborted his campaign after being shot, on May 15, 1972, and left paralyzed below the waist. Arthur C. Bremer, 21, was sentenced to 63 years for shooting Wallace and three bystanders at a Maryland shopping mall.

Richard M. Nixon and Spiro T. Agnew, who had been renominated by the Republicans, won a landslide victory, receiving 521 electoral votes to McGovern's 17.

21. WATERGATE, CARTER, AND THE NEW CONSERVATISM (1972–1997)

WATERGATE

What became known as the Watergate crisis began during the 1972 presidential campaign. Early on the morning of June 17, James McCord, a security officer for the Committee to Reelect the President (CREEP), and four other men broke into Democratic headquarters at the Watergate apartment complex in Washington, D.C., and were caught while going through files and installing electronic eavesdropping devices. On June 22, Nixon announced that the administration was in no way involved in the burglary attempt.

In March 1974, a grand jury indicted Haldeman, Ehrlichman, former Attorney

General John Mitchell, and four other White House aides and named Nixon an unindicted coconspirator.

In April, Nixon released edited transcripts of the White House tapes, the contents of which led to further calls for his resignation. Jaworski subpoenaed 64 additional tapes, which Nixon refused to turn over, and the case went to the Supreme Court.

Meanwhile, the House Judiciary Committee televised its debate over impeachment, adopting three articles of impeachment. It charged the president with obstructing justice, misusing presidential power, and failing to obey the committee's subpoenas.

Before the House began to debate impeachment, the Supreme Court ordered the president to release the subpoenaed tapes to the special prosecutor. On August 5, Nixon, under pressure from his advisors, released the tape of June 23, 1972, to the public. This tape, recorded less than a week after the break-in, revealed that Nixon had used the CIA to keep the FBI from investigating the case. Nixon announced his resignation on August 8, 1974, to take effect at noon the following day. Gerald Ford then became president.

THE FORD PRESIDENCY

Gerald Ford was in many respects the opposite of Nixon. Although a partisan Republican, he was well liked and free from any hint of scandal. Ford almost immediately encountered controversy when in September 1974 he offered to pardon Nixon. Nixon accepted the offer, although he admitted no wrongdoing and had not yet been charged with a crime.

VIETNAM

As North Vietnamese forces pushed back the South Vietnamese, Ford asked Congress to provide more arms for the South. Congress rejected the request, and in April 1975 Saigon fell to the North Vietnamese.

CARTER'S MODERATE LIBERALISM

Ronald Reagan, a former movie actor and governor of California, opposed Ford for the Republican presidential nomination, but Ford won by a slim margin. The Democrats nominated James Earl Carter, formerly governor of Georgia, who ran on the basis of his integrity and lack of Washington connections. Carter narrowly defeated Ford in the election.

Carter sought to conduct the presidency on democratic and moral principles. His administration gained a reputation for proposing complex programs to Congress and then not continuing to support them through the legislative process.

Carter offered amnesty to Americans who had fled the draft and gone to other countries during the Vietnam War. He established the Departments of Energy and Education and placed the civil service on a merit basis. He created a "superfund" for cleanup of chemical waste dumps, established controls over strip mining, and protected 100 million acres of Alaskan wilderness from development.

CARTER'S FOREIGN POLICY

Human Rights Emphasized: Carter sought to base foreign policy on human rights, but was criticized for inconsistency and lack of attention to American interests.

Panama Canal Treaty: Carter negotiated a controversial treaty with Panama, affirmed by the Senate in 1978, that provided for the transfer of ownership of the canal to Panama in 1999 and guaranteed its neutrality.

China Recognized: Carter ended official recognition of Taiwan and in 1979 recognized the People's Republic of China. Conservatives called the decision a "sell-out."

SALT Ratified: In 1979, the administration signed the Strategic Arms Limitation Treaty (SALT II) with the Soviet Union. The treaty set a ceiling of 2,250 bombers and missiles for each side, and established limits on warheads and new weapons systems. It never passed the Senate.

Camp David Accords: In 1978, Carter negotiated the Camp David Accords between Israel and Egypt. Bringing Anwar Sadat, president of Egypt, and Menachem Begin, prime minister of Israel, to the presidential retreat in Camp David, Maryland, for two weeks in September 1978, Carter sought to end the state of war that existed between the two countries. Israel promised to return occupied land in the Sinai to Egypt in exchange for Egyptian recognition, a process completed in 1982. An agreement to negotiate the Palestinian refugee problem proved ineffective. Nonetheless, Camp David stood as a major foreign policy achievement.

THE IRANIAN CRISIS

In 1978, a revolution forced the shah of Iran to flee the country, replacing him with a religious leader, Ayatollah Ruhollah Khomeini. Because the United States had supported the shah with arms and money, the revolutionaries were strongly anti-American, calling the United States the "Great Satan."

After Carter allowed the exiled shah to come to the United States for medical treatment in October 1979, some 400 Iranians broke into the American embassy in Teheran on November 4, taking the occupants captive. They demanded that the shah be returned to Iran for trial and that his wealth be confiscated and given to Iran. Carter rejected these demands; instead, he froze Iranian assets in the United States and established a trade embargo against Iran. He also appealed to the United Nations and the World Court. The Iranians eventually freed the African American and women hostages, but retained 52 others.

In April 1980, Carter ordered a marine rescue attempt, but it collapsed after several helicopters broke down and another crashed, killing eight men. Secretary of State Cyrus Vance resigned in protest before the raid began, and Carter was widely criticized for the attempted raid. The failure of the hostage rescue attempt, on the eve of Carter's bid for re-election, severely damaged his credibility as a capable president.

The Election of 1980: Reagan won by a large electoral majority, and the Republicans gained control of the Senate and increased their representation in the House.

After extensive negotiations with Iran, in which Algeria acted as an intermediary, Carter released Iranian assets and the hostages were freed on January 20, 1981, 444 days after being taken captive and on the day of Reagan's inauguration.

THE REAGAN PRESIDENCY: ATTACKING BIG GOVERNMENT

An ideological though pragmatic conservative, Ronald Reagan acted quickly and forcefully to change the direction of government policy. He placed priority on cutting taxes. His approach was based on "supply-side" economics, the idea that if government left more money in the hands of the people, they would invest rather then spend the excess on consumer goods. The results would be greater production, more jobs, and greater prosperity, and thus more income for the government despite lower tax rates.

Reagan asked for a 30 percent tax cut, and despite fears of inflation on the part of Congress, in August 1983 obtained a 25 percent cut, spread over three years. The percentage was the same for everyone; hence high-income people received greater savings than middle- and low-income individuals. To encourage investment, capital gains, gift, and inheritance taxes were reduced and business taxes liberalized. Anyone with earned income was also allowed to invest up to $2,000 a year in an individual retirement account (IRA), deferring all taxes on both the principle and its earnings until retirement.

Congress passed the Budget Reconciliation Act in 1981, cutting $39 billion from domestic programs, including education, food stamps, public housing, and the National Endowments for the Arts and Humanities. While cutting domestic programs, Reagan increased the defense budget by $12 billion.

By December 1982, the economy was experiencing recession because of the Federal Reserve's "tight money" policy, with over 10 percent unemployment. From a deficit of $59 billion in 1980, the federal budget was running $195 billion in the red by 1983. The rate of inflation, however, helped by lower demand for goods and services and an oversupply of oil as non-OPEC countries increased production, fell from a high of 12 percent in 1979 to 4 percent in 1984. The Federal Reserve Board then began to lower interest rates, which, together with lower inflation and more spendable income because of lower taxes, resulted in more business activity. Unemployment fell to less than 8 percent.

Because of rising deficits, Reagan and Congress increased taxes in various ways. The 1982 Tax Equity and Fiscal Responsibility Act reversed some concessions made to business in 1981. Social Security benefits became taxable income in 1983. In 1984, the Deficit Reduction Act increased taxes by another $50 billion. But the deficit continued to increase.

John W. Hinckley shot Reagan in the chest on March 30, 1981. The president was wounded but made a swift recovery. Reagan's popularity increased, possibly helping his legislative program.

Reagan ended ongoing antitrust suits against International Business Machines and American Telephone and Telegraph, thereby going a significant distance toward delivering on his promise to reduce government interference with business.

Asserting American Power

Reagan took a hard line against the Soviet Union, calling it an "evil empire." He placed new cruise missiles in Europe, despite considerable opposition from Europeans.

In Nicaragua, Reagan encouraged the opposition (*contras*) to the leftist Sandinista government with arms, tactical support, and intelligence, and supplied aid to the government of El Salvador in its struggles against left-wing rebels. In October 1983, the president also sent American troops into the Caribbean island of Grenada to overthrow a newly established Cuban-backed regime.

The Election of 1984: Walter Mondale, a former senator from Minnesota and vice president under Carter, won the Democratic nomination over Senator Gary Hart and Jesse Jackson, an African-American civil-rights leader. Mondale chose Geraldine Ferraro, a congresswoman from New York, as his running mate. Mondale criticized Reagan for his budget deficits, high unemployment and interest rates, and reduction of spending on social services. However, Reagan was elected to a second term in a landslide.

Second-Term Foreign Concerns

Reagan challenged Muammar al-Qadhafi, the anti-American leader of Libya, by sending Sixth Fleet ships within the Gulf of Sidra, which Qadhafi claimed. When Libyan gunboats challenged the American ships, American planes destroyed the gunboats and bombed installations on the Libyan shoreline. Soon after, a West German night club popular among American servicemen was bombed, killing a soldier and a civilian. Reagan, believing the bombing had been ordered directly by Qadhafi, launched an air strike from Great Britain against Libyan bases in April 1986.

After Mikhail S. Gorbachev became the premier of the Soviet Union in March 1985 and took a more flexible approach toward both domestic and foreign affairs, Reagan softened his anti-Soviet stance. Nonetheless, although the Soviets said that they would honor the unratified SALT II agreement, Reagan argued that they had not adhered to the pact and sought to expand and modernize the American defense system.

Reagan concentrated on obtaining funding for the development of a computer-controlled strategic defense initiative system (SDI), popularly called "Star Wars" after the widely seen movie, that would destroy enemy missiles from outer space. Congress balked, skeptical about the technological possibilities and fearing enormous costs.

SDI also appeared to prevent Reagan and Gorbachev from reaching an agreement on arms limitations at summit talks in 1985 and 1986. Finally, in December 1987, they signed an agreement eliminating medium-range missiles from Europe.

The Iran-Contra Scandal

Near the end of 1986, a scandal arose involving William Casey, head of the CIA, Lieutenant Colonel Oliver North of the National Security Council, Admiral John Poindexter, national security advisor, and Robert McFarlane, former national security advisor. In 1985 and 1986, they had sold arms to the Iranians in hopes of encouraging them to use their influence in getting American hostages in Lebanon released. The profits from these sales were then diverted to the Nicaraguan *contras* in an attempt to get around congressional restrictions on funding the *contras*. The president was forced to appoint a special prosecutor, and Congress held hearings on the affair in May 1987.

Second-Term Domestic Affairs

The Economy: The Tax Reform Act of 1986 lowered tax rates, changing the highest rate on personal income from 50 percent to 28 percent and on corporate taxes from 46 percent to 34 percent. At the same time, it removed many tax shelters and tax credits. The law did away with the concept of progressive taxation, the requirement that the percentage of income taxed increased as income increased. Instead, over a two-year period it established two rates, 15 percent on incomes below $17,850 for individuals and $29,750 for families and 28 percent on incomes above these amounts. The tax system would no longer be used as an instrument of social policy.

The federal deficit reached $179 billion in 1985. At about the same time, the United States experienced trade deficits of more than $100 billion annually, partly because management and engineering skills had fallen behind Japan and Germany, and partly because the United States provided an open market to foreign businesses. In the mid-1980s, the United States became a debtor nation for the first time since World War I. Consumer debt also rose from $300 billion in 1980 to $500 billion in 1986.

Black Monday: On October 19, 1987, the Dow-Jones stock-market average dropped more than 500 points. Between August 25 and October 20, the market lost over a trillion dollars in paper value. Fearing a recession, Congress in November 1987 reduced 1988 taxes by $30 billion.

NASA: The explosion of the shuttle *Challenger* soon after take off on January 28, 1986 damaged NASA's credibility and reinforced doubts about the complex technology required for the SDI program.

Supreme Court Appointments: Reagan reshaped the Court in 1986, replacing Chief

Justice Warren C. Burger with Associate Justice William H. Rehnquist, probably the most conservative member of the Court. Although failing in his nomination of Robert Bork for associate justice, Reagan did appoint other conservatives to the Court: Sandra Day O'Connor, Antonin Scalia, and Anthony Kennedy.

The Election of 1988: After a sex scandal eliminated Senator Gary Hart from the race for the Democratic presidential nomination, Governor Michael Dukakis of Massachusetts emerged as the victor over his major challenger, Jesse Jackson. He chose Senator Lloyd Bentsen of Texas as his vice-presidential running mate. Vice President George Bush, after a slow start in the primaries, won the Republican nomination. He chose Senator Dan Quayle of Indiana as his running mate. Bush easily defeated Dukakis, winning 40 states and 426 electoral votes, while Dukakis won only 10 states and 112 electoral votes. Nonetheless, the Republicans were unable to make any inroads in Congress.

BUSH ABANDONS REAGANOMICS

Soon after George Bush took office as president on January 20, 1989, the budget deficit for 1990 was estimated at $143 billion. With deficit estimates continuing to grow, Bush held a "budget summit" with Congressional leaders in May 1990, and his administration continued talks throughout the summer. In September the administration and Congress agreed to increase taxes on gasoline, tobacco, and alcohol, establish an excise tax on luxury items, and raise Medicare taxes. Cuts were also to be made in Medicare and other domestic programs. The 1991 deficit was now estimated to be over $290 billion. The following month Congress approved the plan, hoping to cut a cumulative amount of $500 billion from the deficit over the next five years. In a straight party vote, Republicans voting against and Democrats voting in favor, Congress in December transferred the power to decide whether new tax and spending proposals violated the deficit cutting agreement from the White House Office of Management and Budget to the Congressional Budget Office.

The Commission on Base Realignment and Closure proposed in December 1989 that 54 military bases be closed. In June 1990 Secretary of Defense Richard Cheney sent to Congress a five-year plan to cut military spending by 10 percent and the armed forces by 25 percent. The following April, Cheney recommended the closing of 43 domestic military bases plus many more abroad.

In May 1989, Bush vetoed an increase in the minimum wage from $3.35 to $4.55 an hour. But the following November, Bush signed an increase to $4.25 an hour, to become effective in 1991.

With the savings and loan industry in financial trouble in February 1989, largely because of bad real estate loans, Bush proposed to close or sell 350 institutions, to be paid for by the sale of government bonds. In July he signed a bill that created the Resolution Trust Corporation to oversee the closure and merging of savings and loans, and which provided $166 billion over 10 years to cover the bad debts. Estimates of the total costs of the debacle were over $300 billion.

The Gross National Product slowed from 4.4 percent in 1988 to 2.9 percent in 1989. Unemployment gradually began to increase, reaching 6.8 percent in March 1991, a three year high. Every sector of the economy, except for medical services, and all geographical areas experienced the slowdown. The "Big Three" automakers posted record losses, while Pan American and Eastern Airlines entered bankruptcy proceedings. In September 1991 the Federal Reserve lowered the interest rate.

Other Domestic Issues Under Bush

Exxon Valdez: After the oil tanker Exxon *Valdez* spilled more than 240,000 barrels of oil into Alaska's Prince William Sound in March 1989, the federal government ordered Exxon Corporation to develop a clean-up plan, which it carried out until the weather prevented the company from continuing in September. *Valdez* captain, Joseph Hazelwood, was found guilty of negligence the following year. Exxon Corporation, the State of Alaska, and the U.S. Justice Department reached a settlement in October 1991 requiring Exxon to pay $1.025 billion in fines and restitution through 2001.

Congressional Ethics Violations: After the House Ethics Committee released a report charging that Speaker of the House Jim Wright had violated rules regulating acceptance of gifts and outside income, Wright resigned in May 1989. A short time later, the Democratic Whip, Tony Coelho, resigned because of alleged improper use of campaign funds.

Flag Burning: In May 1989 the Supreme Court ruled that the Constitution protected protesters who burned the United States flag. Bush denounced the decision and supported an amendment barring desecration of the flag. The amendment failed to pass Congress.

HUD Scandal: In July 1989 Secretary of Housing and Urban Development Jack Kemp revealed that the department had lost more than $2 billion under his predecessor, Samuel Pierce. A special prosecutor was named in February 1990 to investigate the case and the House held hearings on HUD during the next two months.

Medicare: In July 1988 the Medicare Catastrophic Coverage Act had placed a cap on fees Medicare patients paid to physicians and hospitals. After many senior citizens, particularly those represented by the American Association of Retired Persons (AARP), objected to the surtax that funded the program, Congress repealed the Act in November 1989.

Pollution: The Clean Air Act, passed in October 1990 and updating the 1970 law, mandated that the level of emissions was to be reduced 50 percent by the year 2000. Cleaner gasolines were to be developed, cities were to reduce ozone, and nitrogen oxide emissions were to be cut by one-third.

Civil Rights: The Americans with Disabilities Act, passed in July 1990, barred discrimination against people with physical or mental disabilities. In October 1990 Bush vetoed the Civil Rights Act on the grounds that it established quotas, but a year later he accepted a slightly revised version that, among other things, required that employers in discrimination suits prove that their hiring practices are not discriminatory.

Supreme Court Appointments: Bush continued to reshape the Supreme Court in a conservative direction when, upon the retirement of Justice William J. Brennan, he successfully nominated Judge David Souter of the U.S. Court of Appeals in 1989. Two years later, Bush nominated a conservative African-American judge, Clarence Thomas, also of the U.S. Court of Appeals, upon the retirement of Justice Thurgood Marshall. Thomas's nomination stirred up opposition from the NAACP and other liberal groups which supported affirmative action and abortion rights. Dramatic charges of sexual harassment against Thomas from Anita Hill, a University of Oklahoma law professor, were revealed only days before the nomination was to go to the Senate, and provoked a reopening of Judiciary Committee hearings which were nationally televised. Nonetheless, Thomas narrowly won confirmation in October 1991.

BUSH'S ACTIVIST FOREIGN POLICY

Panama: Since coming to office, the Bush administration had been concerned with Panamanian dictator Manuel Noriega because he allegedly served as an important link in the drug traffic between South America and the United States. After economic sanctions, diplomatic efforts, and an October 1989 coup failed to oust Noriega, Bush ordered 12,000 troops into Panama on December 20. The Americans installed a new government headed by Guillermo Endara, who had earlier apparently won a presidential election which was promptly nullified by Noriega. On January 3, 1990, Noriega surrendered to the Americans and was taken to the United States to stand trial on drug trafficking charges; he was convicted and jailed for assisting the Medellín drug cartel. Twenty-three United States soldiers and three American civilians were killed in the operation. The Panamanians lost nearly 300 soldiers and more than 500 civilians.

Nicaragua: After years of civil war, Nicaragua held a presidential election in February 1990. Because of an economy largely destroyed by civil war and large financial debt to the United States, Violetta Barrios de Chamorro of the National Opposition Union defeated Daniel Ortega of the Sandinistas, thereby fulfilling a long-standing American objective. The United States lifted its economic sanctions in March and put together an economic aid package for Nicaragua. In September 1991, the Bush administration forgave Nicaragua most of its debt to the United States.

China: After the death in April 1989 of reformer Hu Yaobang, formerly general secretary and chairman of the Chinese Communist party, students began pro-democracy marches in Beijing. By the middle of May, more than one million people were gathering on Beijing's Tiananmen Square, and other protestors elsewhere in China, calling for political reform. Martial law was imposed and in early June the army fired on the demonstrators. Estimates of the death toll in the wake of the nationwide crackdown on demonstrators ranged between 500 and 7,000. In July 1989, United States National Security Advisor Brent Scowcroft and Deputy Secretary of State Lawrence Eagleburger secretly met with Chinese leaders. When they again met the Chinese in December and revealed their earlier meeting, the Bush administration faced a storm of criticism for its policy of "constructive engagement" from opponents arguing that sanctions should be imposed. While establishing sanctions in 1991 on Chinese high-technology satellite-part exports, Bush continued to support renewal of Most Favored Nation trading status.

Africa: To rescue American citizens threatened by civil war, Bush sent 230 marines into Liberia in August 1990, evacuating 125 people. South Africa in 1990 freed Nelson Mandela, the most famous leader of the African National Congress, after 28 years of imprisonment. South Africa then began moving away from apartheid, and in 1991 Bush lifted economic sanctions imposed five years earlier. Mandela and his wife, Winnie, toured the U.S. in June 1990 to a tumultuous welcome, particularly from African-Americans. During their visit, they also addressed Congress.

COLLAPSE OF EAST EUROPEAN COMMUNISM

In August 1989 Hungary opened its borders with Austria. The following October, the Communists reorganized their party, calling it the Socialist party. Hungary then proclaimed itself a "Free Republic."

With thousands of East Germans passing through Hungary to Austria, after the opening of the borders in August 1989, Erich Honecker stepped down as head of state in October. On November 1, the government opened the border with Czechoslovakia and eight days later the Berlin Wall fell. On December 6, a non-Communist became head of state, followed on December 11 by large demonstrations demanding German reunification. Reunification took place in October 1990.

After anti-government demonstrations were forcibly broken up in Czechoslovakia in October 1989, changes took place in the Communist leadership the following month.

Then, on December 8, the Communists agreed to relinquish power and Parliament elected Václav Havel, a playwright and anti-Communist leader, to the presidency on December 29.

When anti-government demonstrations in Romania were met by force in early December, portions of the military began joining the opposition which captured dictator Nicolae Ceausescu and his wife, Elena, killing them on December 25, 1989. In May 1990 the National Salvation Front, made up of many former Communists, won the parliamentary elections.

In January 1990 the Bulgarian national assembly repealed the dominant role of the Communist party. A multi-party coalition government was formed the following December.

Albania opened its border with Greece and legalized religious worship in January 1990, and in July ousted hardliners from the government.

Amid the collapse of Communism in Eastern Europe, Bush met with Mikhail Gorbachev in Malta from December 1 through December 3, 1989; the two leaders appeared to agree that the Cold War was over. On May 30 and 31, 1990, Bush and Gorbachev met in Washington to discuss the possible reunification of Germany, and signed a trade treaty between the United States and the Soviet Union. The meeting of the two leaders in Helsinki on September 9 addressed strategies for the developing Persian Gulf crisis. At the meeting of the "Group of 7" nations (Canada, France, Germany, Italy, Japan, United Kingdom, and the United States) in July 1991, Gorbachev requested economic aid from the West. A short time later, on July 30 and 31, Bush met Gorbachev in Moscow where they signed the START treaty, which cut U.S. and Soviet nuclear arsenals by 30 percent, and pushed for Middle Eastern talks.

PERSIAN GULF CRISIS

Saddam Hussein of Iraq charged that Kuwait had conspired with the United States to keep oil prices low and began massing troops at the Iraq-Kuwait border.

On August 2, Iraq invaded Kuwait, an act that Bush denounced as "naked aggression." One day later 100,000 Iraqi soldiers were poised south of Kuwait City near the Saudi Arabian border. The United States quickly banned most trade with Iraq, froze Iraq's and Kuwait's assets in the United States, and sent aircraft carriers to the Persian Gulf. After the United Nations Security Council condemned the invasion, on August 6 Bush ordered the deployment of air, sea, and land forces to Saudi Arabia, dubbing the operation "Desert Shield." At the end of August there were 100,000 American soldiers in Saudi Arabia.

Bush encouraged Egypt to support American policy by forgiving Egypt its debt to the United States and obtaining pledges of financial support from Saudi Arabia, Kuwait, and Japan, among other nations, to help pay for the operation. On October 29, the Security Council warned Hussein that further actions might be taken if he did not withdraw from Kuwait. In November Bush ordered that U.S. forces be increased to more than 400,000. On November 29, the United Nations set January 15, 1991, as the deadline for Iraqi withdrawal from Kuwait.

On January 9, Iraq's foreign-minister, Tariq Aziz, rejected a letter written by Bush to Hussein. Three days later, after an extensive debate, Congress authorized the use of force in the Gulf. On January 17, an international force including the United States, Great Britain, France, Italy, Saudi Arabia, and Kuwait launched an air and missile attack on Iraq and occupied Kuwait. The U.S. called the effort "Operation Desert Storm." Under the overall command of Army General H. Norman Schwarzkopf, the military effort emphasized high-technology weapons, including F-15 E fighter-bombers, F-117 A stealth fighters, Tomahawk cruise missiles, and Patriot anti-missile missiles. Beginning on January 17, Iraq fired SCUD missiles into Israel in an effort to draw that country into the war and splinter the U.S.-Arabian coalition. On January 22 and 23, Hussein's forces set Kuwaiti oil fields on fire and spilled oil into the Gulf.

On February 23, the allied ground assault began. Four days later Bush announced that Kuwait was liberated and ordered offensive operations to cease. The United Nations established the terms for the cease-fire: Iraqi annexation of Kuwait to be rescinded, Iraq to accept liability for damages and return Kuwaiti property, Iraq to end all military actions and identify mines and booby traps, and Iraq to release captives.

On April 3, the Security Council approved a resolution to establish a permanent cease-fire; Iraq accepted U.N. terms on April 6. The next day the United States began airlifting food to Kurdish refugees on the Iraq-Turkey border who were fleeing the Kurdish rebellion against Hussein, a rebellion that was seemingly encouraged by Bush, who nonetheless refused to become militarily involved. The United States estimated that 100,000 Iraqis had been killed during the war while the Americans had lost about 115 lives.

On February 6, 1991, the United States had set out its postwar goals for the Middle East. These included regional arms control and security arrangements, international aid for reconstruction of Iraq and Kuwait, and resolution of the Israeli-Palestinian conflict. Immediately after cessation of the conflict, Secretary of State James Baker toured the Middle East attempting to promote a conference to address the problems of the region. After several more negotiating sessions, Saudi Arabia, Syria, Jordan, and Lebanon had accepted the United States proposal for an Arab-Israeli peace conference by the middle of July; Israel conditionally accepted in early August. Despite continuing conflict with Iraq, including United Nations inspections of its nuclear capabilities, and new Israeli settlements in disputed territory—which kept the conference agreement tenuous—the nations met in Madrid, Spain, at the end of October. Bilateral talks in early November between Israel and the Arabs concentrated on procedural issues.

BREAKUP OF THE SOVIET UNION

Following the collapse of Communism in Eastern Europe, the Baltic republic of Lithuania, which had been taken over by the Soviet Union in 1939 through an agreement with Adolph Hitler, declared its independence from the Soviet Union on March 11, 1990.

Two days later, on March 13, the Soviet Union removed the Communist monopoly of political power, allowing non-Communists to run for office. The process of liberalization went haltingly forward in the Soviet Union. Perhaps the most significant event was the election of Boris Yeltsin, who had left the Communist party, as president of the Russian republic on June 12, 1991.

On August 19, Soviet hard-liners attempted a coup to oust Gorbachev, but a combination of their inability to control communication with the outside world, a failure to quickly establish military control, and the resistance of Yeltsin, members of the military, and people in the streets of cities such as Moscow and Leningrad, ended the coup on August 21, returning Gorbachev to power.

In the aftermath of the coup, much of the Communist structure came crashing down, including the prohibition of the Communist party in Russia. The remaining Baltic republics of Latvia and Estonia declared their independence, which was recognized by the United States several days after other nations had done so. Most of the other Soviet republics then followed suit in declaring their independence. The Bush administration wanted some form of central authority to remain in the Soviet Union; hence, it did not seriously consider recognizing the independence of any republics except the Baltics.

Bush also resisted offering economic aid to the Soviet Union until it presented a radical economic reform plan to move toward a free market. However, humanitarian aid such as food was pledged in order to preserve stability during the winter.

In September 1991, George Bush announced unilateral removal and destruction of ground-based tactical nuclear weapons in Europe and Asia, removal of nuclear-armed Tomahawk cruise missiles from surface ships and submarines, immediate destruction of intercontinental ballistic missiles covered by START, and an end to the 24-hour alert for strategic bombers that the U.S. had maintained for decades. Gorbachev responded the next month by announcing the immediate deactivation of intercontinental ballistic missiles covered by START, removal of all short-range missiles from Soviet ships, submarines, and aircraft, and destruction of all ground-based tactical nuclear weapons. He also said that the Soviet Union would reduce its forces by 700,000 troops, and he placed all long-range nuclear missiles under a single command. Gorbachev's hold on the presidency progressively weakened in the final months of 1991, with the reforms he had put in place taking on a life of their own. The dissolution of the U.S.S.R. led to his resignation in December, making way for Boris Yeltsin, who had headed popular resistance.

THE DEMOCRATS RECLAIM THE WHITE HOUSE

William Jefferson Clinton, governor of Arkansas, overcame several rivals to win the Democratic presidential nomination in 1992 and with his running mate, Senator Albert Gore of Tennessee, went on to win the White House. During the campaign, Clinton and independent candidate H. Ross Perot, a wealthy Texas businessman, emphasized jobs and the economy, while attacking the mounting federal debt. The incumbent, Bush, stressed traditional values and his foreign policy accomplishments. In the 1992 election, Clinton won 43 percent of the popular vote and 370 electoral votes, defeating Bush and Perot. Perot took 19 percent of the popular vote, but was unable to garner any electoral votes.

Clinton came to be dogged by a number of controversies, ranging from alleged ill-gotten gains in a complex Arkansas land deal that came to be known as the Whitewater Affair to charges of sexual misconduct, brought by a former Arkansas state employee, that dated to an incident she said had occurred when Clinton was governor.

On the legislative front, Clinton was strongly rebuffed in an attempt during his first term to reform the nation's healthcare system. In the 1994 mid-term elections, in what Clinton himself considered a repudiation of his administration, the Republicans took both houses of Congress from the Democrats and voted in Newt Gingrich of Georgia as Speaker of the House. Gingrich had helped craft the Republican congressional campaign strategy to dramatically shrink the federal government and give more power to the states.

Clinton, however, was not without his successes, both on the legislative and diplomatic fronts. He signed a bill establishing a five-day waiting period for handgun purchases, and he signed a Crime Bill emphasizing community policing. He signed the Family Leave Bill, which required large companies to provide up to 12 weeks' unpaid leave to workers for family and medical emergencies. He also championed welfare reform (a central theme of his campaign), but made it clear that the legislation he signed into law in August 1996 radically overhauling FDR's welfare system disturbed him on two counts—its exclusion of legal immigrants from getting most federal benefits and its deep cut in federal outlays for food stamps; Clinton said these flaws could be repaired with further legislation. In foreign affairs, Clinton, with debated North American Free Trade Agreement, which, as of January 1994, lifted most trade barriers with Mexico and Canada. Clinton sought to ease tensions between Israelis and Palestinians, and he helped bring together Itzhak Rabin, prime minister of Israel, and Yasir Arafat, chairman of the Palestine Liberation Organization, for a summit at the White House. Ultimately, the two Middle East leaders signed an accord in 1994 establishing Palestinian self-rule in the Gaza Strip and Jericho. In October 1994 Israel and Jordan signed a treaty to begin the process of establishing full diplomatic relations. Rabin was assassinated a year later by a radical, right-wing Israeli. The Clinton administration also played a central role in hammering out a peace agreement in 1995 in war-torn former Yugoslavia—where armed conflict had broken out in 1991 between Serbs, Croats, Bosnian Muslims, and other factions and groups.

Clinton recaptured the Democratic nomination without a serious challenge, while longtime GOP Senator Robert Dole of Kansas, the Senate majority leader, had to overcome several opponents, but orchestrated a harmonious nominating convention with running mate Jack Kemp, a former New York congressman and Cabinet member. In November 1996, with most voters citing a healthy economy and the lack of an enticing alternative in Dole or the Reform Party's Perot, Clinton received 49 percent of the vote, becoming the first Democrat to be re-elected since FDR, in 1936. The GOP retained control of both houses of Congress.

Clinton, intent on mirroring the diversity of America in his Cabinet appointments, chose Hispanics Henry Cisneros (Housing and Urban Development) and Federico Peña (Transportation and, later, Energy) African Americans Ron Brown (Commerce) and Mike Espy (Agriculture), and women, including the nation's first woman attorney general, Janet Reno, and Madeleine Albright, the first woman secretary of state in U.S. history (Albright succeeded Warren Christopher, who served through Clinton's first term). Brown and 34 others on a trade mission died when his Air Force plane crashed in Croatia in April 1996. Cisneros and Espy both resigned under ethics clouds.

LATE 20TH CENTURY SOCIAL AND CULTURAL DEVELOPMENTS

AIDS: In 1981 scientists announced the discovery of Acquired Immune Deficiency Syndrome (AIDS), which was especially prevalent among homosexual males and intravenous drug users. Widespread fear resulted, including an upsurge in homophobia. The Centers for Disease Control and the National Cancer Institute, among others, pursued research on the disease. The Food and Drug Administration responded to calls for fast-tracking evaluation of drugs by approving the drug AZT in February 1991. With the revelation that a Florida dentist had infected three patients, there were calls for mandatory testing of healthcare workers. Supporters of testing argued before a House hearing in September 1991 that testing should be regarded as a public health, rather than a civil rights, issue. In early 1998, the Centers for Disease Control estimated that between 400,000 and 650,000 Americans were HIV-positive, meaning that they had the virus that causes AIDS. Public health officials expressed concern about the difficulties in tracking the spread of AIDS, as the HIV infection was being reported to health agencies only when patients developed symptoms, which could be years after infection. New drug therapies, meanwhile, were preventing AIDS symptoms from ever appearing, creating the specter of growing numbers of people going unseen by public-health agencies as they spread the virus. These developments came against the backdrop of a marked change in the demographic makeup of the epidemic's victims—from mostly white homosexual males to African Americans, Hispanics, and women, particularly those who are poor, intravenous drug users, or the sex partners of drug users.

Families: More than half the married women in the United States continued to hold jobs outside the home. Nearly one out of every two marriages was ending in divorce, and there was an increase in the number of unmarried couples living together, which contributed to a growing number of illegitimate births. So-called family values became a major theme in presidential politics, powered in part by the publication of leading conservative William J. Bennett's best-selling anthology *The Book of Virtues: A Treasury of Great Moral Stories*. Bennett had served as Bush's secretary of education and, later, as director of the Office of National Drug Control Policy, which the press shortened to "drug tsar."

Terrorism Hits Home: While terrorist attacks continued to be a grim reality overseas through the 1980s and early 1990s—with Americans frequently targeted—such incidents had come to be perceived as something the United States wouldn't have to face on its own soil—until February 26, 1993, when a terrorist bomb ripped through the underground parking garage of the World Trade Center in New York City, killing six people and injuring more than 1,000. The blast shattered America's "myth of invulnerability," wrote foreign policy analyst Jeffrey D. Simon in his book *The Terrorist Trap*. Convicted and sentenced to 240 years each were four Islamic militants. On April 19, 1995, in the deadliest act of domestic terrorism in U.S. history, the Oklahoma City federal building was bombed: 168 people were killed and 500 injured. Timothy James McVeigh, a gun enthusiast involved in the American militia movement who had often expressed hatred toward the U.S. federal government and was particularly aggrieved over the government's assault exactly two years earlier on a self-proclaimed prophet's compound in Waco, Texas, was convicted and sentenced to death in June 1997. A second defendant, Terry Nichols, was convicted of conspiracy.

Murder Trial a National Spectacle: In Los Angeles, former pro-football star, broadcaster, and actor O.J. Simpson was tried for the brutal murder in June 1994 of his ex-wife, Nicole Brown Simpson, and her friend Ronald Goldman. The nationally televised trial became a running spectacle for months, with the lengthy, tortuous courtroom proceedings transfixing the nation. Simpson was found not guilty, but would later, in a civil trial, be found responsible for the slaying of Goldman and for committing battery against Nicole. The civil judgment awarded the plaintiffs, Ronald's parents and Nicole's estate, $33.5 million in damages. (The Browns refrained from bringing a wrongful-death suit to spare the young Simpson children the agony of having to testify.)

Crime and Politics: George Bush had won the presidency in 1988 on a strong anti-crime message, crystallized in a controversial TV spot that demonized Willie Horton, an African-American inmate in the Massachusetts jail system who was released while then-presidential candidate Michael Dukakis was the Democratic governor. Bill Clinton co-opted the traditional Republican crime issue by pushing through legislation for more community policing, an approach that, together with aggressive central management, was credited for the plummeting crime rate in New York City, for example.

U.S. Prisoner Count Grows: Between 1987 and 1997, the period spanning the Bush administration and Clinton's first term, the number of Americans in prison doubled, soaring from 800,000 to 1.6 million.

Drug Abuse Continues: Drug abuse continued to be widespread, with cocaine becoming more readily available, particularly in a cheaper, stronger form called "crack."

Labor: Labor union strength continued to ebb in the 1990s (though some observers pointed to the success of the 1997 Teamsters strike against United Parcel Service, the giant shipper, as a sign that labor was rebounding), with the U.S. Department of Labor's Bureau of Labor Statistics reporting that union membership as a percent of wage and salary employment dropped to 14.5 percent in 1996, down from 14.9 percent in 1995. In 1983, union members made up 20.1 percent of the work force. Unions continued to be responsible for higher wages for their members: organized workers reported median weekly earnings of $615, as against a median of $462 for non-union workers, according to the bureau.

Abortion and the High Court: In a July 1989 decision, *Webster v. Reproductive Health Services*, the U.S. Supreme Court upheld a Missouri law prohibiting public employees from performing abortions, unless the mother's life is threatened. With this decision came a shift in focus on the abortion issue from the courts to the state legislatures. Pro-life (anti-abortion rights) forces moved in several states to restrict the availability of abortions, but their results were mixed. Florida rejected abortion restrictions in October 1989, the governor of Louisiana vetoed similar legislation nine months later, and in early 1991 Maryland adopted a liberal abortion law. In contrast, Utah and Pennsylvania enacted strict curbs on abortion during the same period. At the national level, Bush in October 1989 vetoed funding for Medicaid abortions. The conflict between pro-choice (pro-abortion) and pro-life forces gained national attention through such events as a pro-life demonstration held in Washington in April 1990, and blockage of access to abortion clinics by Operation Rescue, a militant anti-abortion group, in the summer of 1991. Abortion clinics around the country continued to be the targets of protests and violence through the mid-'90s.

Gap Between Rich and Poor Widens: Kevin Phillips's *The Politics of Rich and Poor* (1990) argued that 40 million Americans in the bottom fifth of the population experienced a 1 percent decline in income between 1973 and 1979 and a 10 percent decline between 1979 and 1987. Meanwhile, the top fifth saw a rise of 7 percent and 16 percent during the same periods. The number of single-parent families living below the poverty line (annual income of $11,611 for a family of four) rose by 46 percent between 1979 and 1987. Nearly one-quarter of American children under age six were counted among the poor, said Phillips.

Censorship: The conservative leaning of the electorate in recent years revealed its cultural dimension in a controversy that erupted over the National Endowment for the Arts in September 1989. Criticism of photographer Robert Mapplethorpe's homoerotic and masochistic pictures, among other artworks which had been funded by the Endowment, led Senator Jesse Helms of North Carolina to propose that grants for "obscene or indecent" projects, or those derogatory of religion, be cut off. Although the proposal ultimately failed, it raised questions of the government's role as a sponsor of art in an increasingly pluralistic society. The Mapplethorpe photographs also became an issue the following summer when Cincinnati's Contemporary Art Center was indicted on charges of obscenity when it exhibited the artist's work. A jury later struck down the charges. Meanwhile, in March 1990, the Recording Industry Association of America, in a move advocated by, among others, Tipper Gore, wife of Democratic Senator Al Gore of Tennessee (the man who would be elected vice-president in 1992), agreed to place new uniform warning labels on recordings that contained potentially offensive language.

Crisis in Education: The National Commission on Excellence in Education, appointed in 1981, argued in "A Nation at Risk" that a "rising tide of mediocrity" characterized the nation's schools. In the wake of the report, many states instituted reforms, including higher teacher salaries, competency tests for teachers, and an increase in required subjects for high school graduation. In September 1989 Bush met with the nation's governors in Charlottesville, Virginia, to work on a plan to improve the schools. The governors issued a call for the establishment of national performance goals to be measured by achievement tests. In February 1990 the National Governors' Association adopted specific performance goals, stating that achievement tests should be administered in grades four, eight, and twelve. As the new millenium approached, however, signs began to emerge that the tide might be turning: a major global comparison found in June 1997 that America's 9- and 10-year-olds were among the world's best in science and also scored well above average in math.

Literary Trends: The 1980s and 1990s saw the emergence of writers who concentrated on marginal or regional aspects of national life. William Kennedy wrote a series of novels about Albany, New York, most notably *Ironweed* (1983). The small-town West attracted attention from Larry McMurtry, whose *Lonesome Dove* (1985) used myth to explore the history of the region. The immigrant experience gave rise to Amy Tan's *The Joy-Luck Club* (1989) and Oscar Hijuelos's *The Mambo Kings Play Songs of Love* (1990). Tom Wolfe satirized greed, and class and racial tensions in New York City in *The Bonfire of the Vanities* (1987). Toni Morrison's *Beloved* (1987) dramatized the African-American slavery experience.

HISTORY AND SOCIAL SCIENCES

court-packing plan" called for

w justices if present justices offer the age of 70 did

ry removal of all Supreme Court justices over the

ory removal of all Supreme Court justices who
slation.

justices if present justices over the age of 70 did

the U.S. flag and in order to hasten the downfall
rta, President Woodrow Wilson

shing to take U.S. troops across the border into

U.S. diplomatic recognition of Huerta's regime.

xico City by U.S. troops.

the Mexican port city of Vera Cruz.

oodrow Wilson's Fourteen Points EXCEPT

    (C)   freedom of the seas.

    (D)   a restoration of the balance of power.

4.   Which of the following was among the objectives of Booker T. Washington?

    (A)   To keep up a constant agitation of questions of racial equality

    (B)   To encourage blacks to be more militant in demanding their rights

    (C)   To encourage blacks to work hard, acquire property, and prove they were worthy of their rights

    (D)   To urge blacks not to accept separate but equal facilities

5.   The term "Seward's Folly" referred to Secretary of State William Seward's

    (A)   advocacy of a lenient policy toward the defeated Southern states.

(B) break with the majority radical faction of the Republican party in order to back President Andrew Johnson.

(C) belief that the Civil War could be avoided and the Union restored by provoking a war with Britain and France.

(D) negotiation of the purchase of Alaska from Russia.

6. In response to southern intransigence in the face of President Andrew Johnson's mild reconstruction plan, Congress did all of the following EXCEPT

(A) exclude Southern representatives and senators from participating in Congress.

(B) pass the Civil Rights Act of 1866.

(C) order the arrest and imprisonment of former Confederate leaders.

(D) approve and send on to the states the Fourteenth Amendment.

7. When President Andrew Johnson removed Secretary of War Edwin M. Stanton without the approval of the Senate, contrary to the terms of the recently passed Tenure of Office Act, he

(A) was impeached and removed from office.

(B) came within one vote of being impeached.

(C) was impeached and came within one vote of being removed from office.

(D) was impeached, refused to resign, and his term ended before a vote could be taken on his removal from office.

8. In speaking of "scalawags," white Southerners of the Reconstruction era made reference to

(A) former slaves who had risen to high positions within the Reconstruction governments of the Southern states.

(B) Northerners who had come south to take high positions within the Reconstruction governments of the Southern states.

(C) the U.S. Army generals who served as military governors in the South.

(D) Southerners who supported or participated in the Reconstruction regimes.

9. The first individual who served as Prime Minister of Great Britain was

(A) William Pitt   (C) Lord Palmerston

(B) William Gladstone   (D) Robert Walpole

10. Friederich Nietzsche advanced his philosophy in such works as

(A) *Thus Spake Zarathustra* and *The Will to Power*.

(B) *The Golden Bouth* and *The Wild Duck*.

(C)   *The Return of the Native* and *Jude the Obscure*

(D)   *Civilization and Its Discontents* and *The Riddle of the Universe.*

HISTORY AND SOCIAL SCIENCES

ANSWERS TO PRACTICE QUESTIONS

1. **(A)**   6. **(C)**

2. **(D)**   7. **(C)**

3. **(D)**   8. **(D)**

4. **(C)**   9. **(D)**

5. **(D)**   10. **(A)**

MSAT

Multiple Subjects Assessment for Teachers

CHAPTER 5

Science Review

Chapter 5

Science Review

The Science portion of the MSAT accounts for 18 percent of the overall exam. It is primarily concerned with the ability to understand and apply scientific concepts, demonstrated through the formulation of hypotheses, the testing of these hypotheses through experimentation, and the ability to evaluate the resulting data. This depends on the core knowledge of scientific information provided in the review that follows. The MSAT Science test is divided into three sections:

Life Science (33–34 percent)
- Cellular biology
- Biology of organisms
- Ecology
- Evolution

Geoscience (33–34 percent)
- Astronomy
- Geology
- Meteorology
- Oceanography

Physical Science (33–34 percent)
- Matter / reactions and interactions
- Macromechanics
- Energy
- Modern physics

These three sections, equally distributed in the MSAT Science test, form the core of what an elementary school teacher should know about scientific concepts and their applications. Each topic is covered in the following review, and careful study should guarantee success on this portion of the MSAT. Scientific concepts are often interrelated, so equal attention should be paid to every section. Answering the practice questions that follow the review will give you a good idea of which areas present the greatest challenge to you.

STRATEGIES FOR SCIENCE SECTIONS

- Carefully read the passage, graph, chart, figure, and/or other information on which the questions are based. Then read the first question.

- Make sure you clearly understand what the question is asking. Misinterpreting a question will cost you time and points. Scan the passage, graph, chart, or figure again to make sure the answer is accurately based upon this given information.

- If a word is unfamiliar to you, try to figure out its meaning from the context in which it is used.

- When a question asks you to apply an unfamiliar idea or principle, try to apply it to a familiar situation first. Next, apply the principle, in the same manner, to the given question. This often aids in the understanding of the problem.

- Often, when an answer choice repeats information from a passage, it is a trick. Be sure to read all of the choices before making a hasty decision.

- Although the answer you choose may seem logical and correct, make sure it is supported by the given information.

PART I: BIOLOGY

Themes and General Vocabulary

Biology is an independent set of explanatory concepts. Thus, we describe biology as the study of living organisms/things.

A hypothesis is very tentative and is something to be proven; it is only tentatively held and must be checked out fully and possibly proven. A hypothesis is an educated guess.

There are many fields of study in the biological sciences. A few examples are:

- zoology, the study of animal life;

- botany, the study of plant life;

- ecology, the study of the relationship of living things to their environment;

- embryology, the study of the formation and development of organisms in their earliest stages of life;

- anatomy, the study of structures of the body;

- physiology, the study of the functions of the body;

- genetics, the study of heredity;

- cytology, the study of the cell;

- histology, the study of tissues; and

- bacteriology, the study of bacteria and/or one-celled plant life.

The Cell

The cell is the basic structure of all living things. This is the foundation of cell theory. Some cells are total living organisms while other cells are the basic units of structure of complex living things. Most cells can reproduce to form new cells which are almost identical to the original cell. Sex cells reproduce by meiosis while somatic cells (autosomes or body cells) reproduce by mitosis.

Cells are of two types: prokaryotic or eukaryotic. Prokaryotes are cells that do not have a nuclear membrane or membrane-bound organelles. Bacteria and blue-green bacteria are examples of prokaryotes. Eukaryote refers to most cells making up all other living organisms.

A generalized cell will contain:

1. a cell membrane which is a double layer of lipids that surrounds the cell, thus acting as a "gatekeeper," controlling what moves into and out of the cell.

2. a nucleus which is separated from the cytoplasm by a thickened membrane that is more selective than the cell membrane.

3. cytoplasm, the gel-like material that surrounds and protects by cushioning the organelles. It also contains all the chemicals for that particular cell to carry out its living activities.

Depending upon the kind of cell and the function of the cell, any cell can contain any number of the following organelles:

1. **Mitochondria:** the powerhouse of the cell. It is the site where energy is obtained from food consumed and made available for the cell's use.

2. **Chloroplast:** the site of photosynthesis.

3. **Plastids:** store chlorophyll for use by the chloroplasts.

4. **Lysosomes:** carry out digestive functions and store digestive enzymes as needed by the cell.

5. **Smooth endoplasmic reticulum:** does not have ribosomes attached and is the transportation system of the cell.

6. **Rough endoplasmic reticulum:** has ribosomes attached and also carries out cell transportation, but mainly of necessary protein materials needed by the cell.

7. **Golgi apparatus:** manufacture, synthesize, store, and distribute hormones, enzymes, and other protein materials needed by the individual cell or by the organism.

8. **Peroxisomes:** manufacture, store and secrete oxidation enzymes needed by the cell.

9. **Vacuoles:** fluid-filled sacs which usually contain water, proteins, pigments, organic acids, or metabolic wastes. Some are active in cell metabolism, while others act as storage containers.

10. **Basal bodies:** short, cylindrical microtubules which play a role in cell movement by directing the formation of cilia and flagella.

11. **Cell wall:** a non-living, inflexible, outer component of plant cells which supports and protects the cell. The main component is often cellulose.

12. **Centrioles:** small cylindrical bodies which lie just outside the nucleus in animal cells in a specialized area of cytoplasm. They play a role in cell division and in cell motility.

13. **Nucleolus:** a dark-staining organelle within the nucleus which contains RNA, proteins, and some DNA. It plays a role in the synthesis of ribosomal RNA.

14. **Chromosomes:** threadlike structures composed mainly of DNA which is arranged in genes. This is the hereditary information of the cell.

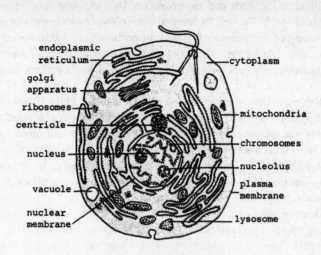

endoplasmic reticulum

golgi apparatus

ribosomes

centriole

nucleus

vacuole

nuclear membrane

cytoplasm

mitochondria

chromosomes

nucleolus

plasma membrane

lysosome

Typical animal cell

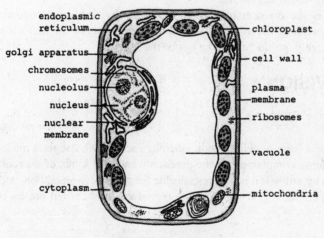

endoplasmic reticulum

golgi apparatus

chromosomes

nucleolus

nucleus

nuclear membrane

cytoplasm

chloroplast

cell wall

plasma membrane

ribosomes

vacuole

mitochondria

Typical plant cell

Cells maintain a balance or working equilibrium that is optimum for their needs. This balance, obtained by this internal control, is called homeostasis. This accounts for all movement into and out of the cell. Though the cell can adjust to a wide range of environmental needs and amounts, there is a limit to how much and how often it can adjust.

To understand homeostasis, one must understand how molecules move by osmosis and diffusion. When molecular movement has met needed concentrations of materials on either side of the cell membrane, the state of equilibrium exists. It is in this state that the cell operates most efficiently.

Materials move into and out of the cell either by active transport, passive transport, endocytosis, phagocytosis, or exocytosis. The exact method used depends on the type, function, and environment of the cell. A cell exists in a constantly changing environment and has constantly changing needs which must be met in order to stay alive and function. All transport occurs over a semipermeable membrane. Turgor pressure is necessary for the cell to adjust to its needs and environment. This pressure determines the amount of water maintained inside the cell to counterbalance the environment outside the cell. It is by the maintaining of this pressure that all transportation needed in the cell is determined.

Proteins are used by the cell or organism to provide energy, general maintenance, growth, and reproduction functions. All living material needs carbon, nitrogen, hydrogen, and oxygen to survive. Also, these elements are essential for the construction of organic molecules that constitute what it means to be "living." Only protein will supply the necessary nitrogen for life within a cell or organism. Protein degradation is the process by which proteins are broken down into the smallest units, called amino acids. Then, the amino acids are reconstructed into peptide chains (by the process of protein synthesis) that can be used by cell organelles or other materials as needed by the cell. This process of combining amino acids to produce peptide chains to reconstruct proteins is called protein synthesis.

Reproduction is a process that is necessary for life to continue. Reproduction is the process the organism or cell utilizes to create an offspring like itself. Reproduction can be asexual or sexual. Asexual reproduction occurs when one split produces a carbon-copy of the cell itself. Asexual processes are called fission, budding, fragmentation, regeneration, conjugation, or sporulation. The asexual methods of reproduction are used by one-cell organisms or lower life organisms.

Mitosis is the division of a body cell. The division or reproduction is for the purpose of maintaining life as a productive and efficient organism. Meiosis is the division of sex cells, namely, production of the egg or the sperm.

CELL DIVISION

Mitosis

Mitosis is a form of cell division whereby each of two daughter nuclei receives the same chromosome complement as the parent nucleus. All kinds of asexual reproduction are carried out by mitosis; it is also responsible for growth, regeneration, and cell replacement in multicellular organisms. Asexual reproduction is carried out by mitosis in eukaryotic cells.

Interphase

Interphase is no longer called the resting phase because a great deal of activity occurs during this phase. In the cytoplasm, oxidation and synthesis reactions take place. In the nucleus, DNA replicates itself and forms messenger RNA, transfer RNA and ribosomal RNA.

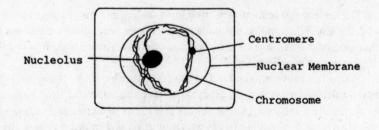

Interphase

Prophase

Chromatids shorten and thicken during this stage of mitosis. The nucleoli disappear and the nuclear membrane breaks down and disappears as well. Spindle fibers begin to form. In an animal cell, there is also division of the centrosome and centrioles.

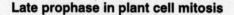

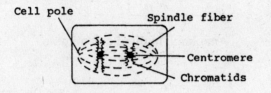

Late prophase in plant cell mitosis

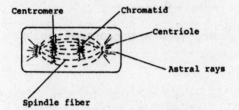

Prophase in animal cell mitosis

Metaphase

During this phase, each chromosome moves to the equator, or middle of the spindle. The paired chromosomes attach to the spindle at the centromere.

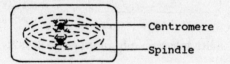

Metaphase in plant cell mitosis

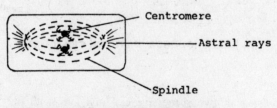

Metaphase in animal cell mitosis

Anaphase

Anaphase is characterized by the separation of sister chromatids into a single-stranded chromosome. The chromosomes migrate to opposite poles of the cell.

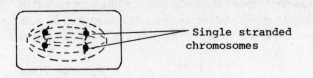

Anaphase in plant cell mitosis

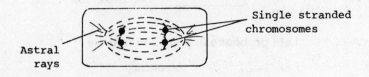

Anaphase in animal cell mitosis

Telophase

During telophase, the chromosomes begin to uncoil and the nucleoli as well as the nuclear membrane reappear. In plant cells, a cell plate appears at the equator which divides the parent cell into two daughter cells. In animal cells, an invagination of the plasma membrane divides the parent cell.

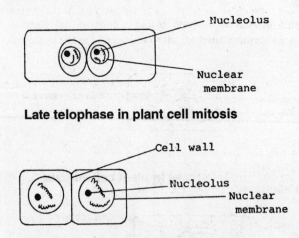

Late telophase in plant cell mitosis

Late telophase in animal cell mitosis

Meiosis

Meiosis consists of two successive cell divisions with only one duplication of chromosomes. This results in daughter cells with a haploid number of chromosomes or one-half of the chromosome number in the original cell. This process occurs during the formation of gametes and in spore formation in plants.

Spermatogenesis

This process results in sperm cell formation with four immature sperm cells with a haploid number of chromosomes.

Oogenesis

This process results in egg cell formation with only one immature egg cell with a haploid number of chromosomes, which becomes mature and larger as yolk forms within the cell.

First Meiotic Division

Interphase I

Chromosome duplication begins to occur during this phase.

Prophase I

During this phase, the chromosomes shorten and thicken and synapsis occurs with pairing of homologous chromosomes. Crossing-over between non-sister chromatids will also occur. The centrioles will migrate to opposite poles and the nucleolus and nuclear membrane begin to dissolve.

Metaphase I

The tetrads, composed of two doubled homologous chromosomes, migrate to the equatorial plane during Metaphase I.

Anaphase I

During this stage, the paired homologous chromosomes separate and move to opposite poles of the cell. Thus, the number of chromosomes types in each resultant cell is reduced to the haploid number.

Telophase I

Cytoplasmic division occurs during telophase I. The formation of two new nuclei with half the chromosomes of the original cell occurs.

Second Meiotic Division

Prophase II

The centrioles that had migrated to each pole of the parental cell, now incorporated in each haploid daughter cell, divide, and a new spindle forms in each cell. The chromosomes move to the equator.

Metaphase II

The chromosomes are lined up at the equator of the new spindle, which is at right angles to the old spindle.

Anaphase II

The centromeres divide and the daughter chromatids, now chromosomes, separate and move to opposite poles.

Telophase II

Cytoplasmic division occurs. The chromosomes gradually return to the dispersed form and a nuclear membrane forms.

Nucleic Acid Biochemistry

A living organism could be called a chemical factory. More chemical activity is carried on inside the cell or inside the living organism than any other place. Chemical bonds are broken, constructed and reconstructed in a continuous operation. Chemical reactions occur simultaneously throughout the organism so that life will be an ongoing process. Carbohydrates, starches, lipids, proteins, water, and nucleic acids are the chemicals (organic molecules) and compounds that are basic to all life.

DNA was discovered in 1869. It was not until the development of the electron microscope in the mid-1940s, however, that scientists gained a true realization of the functioning of DNA.

DNA (deoxyribonucleic acid) is the basic chemical of life. It is a giant molecule made of four different nitrogenous bases (adenine, guanine, cytosine, thymine), phosphate groups, and 5-carbon sugars that collectively are called a nucleotide. It is a self-duplicating molecule that is in a double helix (spiral staircase appearance). It is found inside the nucleus of the cell. It contains the directions, or "blueprints," for the making of all the proteins that a cell needs. Proteins play a major role in cell metabolism and are the basic building blocks of a cell. DNA is the controller of heredity and all life activities of the cell. Its function is linked to the functioning of a companion chemical called RNA (ribonucleic acid).

Ribonucleic acid differs from DNA in that uracil replaces thymine as a nitrogenous base. The sugar used by DNA has one less oxygen present. Also, RNA is a single-stranded, straight chain. The genetic information in DNA is carried out of the nucleus by what is called messenger RNA (mRNA). This mRNA contains the genetic message which is used to accomplish protein synthesis in the cytoplasm of the cell by transfer RNA (tRNA) using ribosomes which are composed of ribosomal RNA (rRNA) and proteins.

The DNA acts as an interpreter or decoder for the many chemical messages that are carried through the cell as a part of the life activities. The DNA cannot leave the nucleus and, therefore, must have a messenger and translator working directly with it. In addition, the tRNA picks up and delivers necessary amino acids to complete the needed activity. This process enables the cell to carry out digestion, oxidation, assimilation, synthesis, and other necessary cell activities.

The basic functions of life comprising total cell metabolism are:

1. **Ingestion:** taking in of food.

2. **Digestion:** breaking down of food by enzymes to simpler, soluble forms.

3. **Secretion:** formation of useful substances.

4. **Absorption:** diffusion of dissolved material through cell membranes.

5. **Respiration:** release of energy by oxidation of food.

6. **Excretion:** getting rid of wastes of the cells.

The Chemical Composition of DNA:

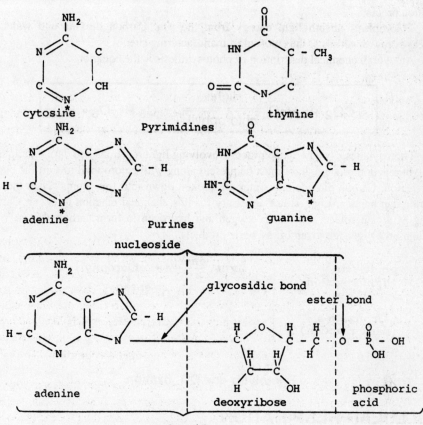

Structural formulas of purines (adenine and guanine), pyrimidines (thymine and cytosine), and a nucleotide

7. **Transportation:** circulation of materials throughout the organism.

8. **Assimilation:** formation of more protoplasm, resulting in growth and repair.

9. **Regulation:** maintaining stability of organism's chemical makeup under constantly changing internal and external environment (homeostasis).

10. **Synthesis:** building up of complex molecules from simple compounds.

11. **Reproduction:** production of more living individuals.

12. **Irritability:** response to stimuli.

13. **Movement:** the ability to change position. In some rare cases, as in plants, movement is coupled with irritability.

14. **Bioluminescence:** production of internal light within some organisms.

PHOTOSYNTHESIS

Photosynthesis is a process that occurs within all plant cells which supply all of the carbohydrates used by both plants and animals. Not only are essential organic compounds formed, but needed water and oxygen are given off as by-products in this autotrophic nutrition process.

Chloroplasts absorb light energy from the sun. Carbon dioxide and water are present as raw materials at the chloroplast manufacturing site.

An overall chemical description of photosynthesis is the equation:

$$6\,CO_2 + 6\,H_2O \underset{\text{chlorophyll}}{\overset{\text{light}}{\rightleftharpoons}} C_6H_{12}O_6 + 6\,O_2$$

Photosynthesis is a two-step process involving light reactions and dark reactions. In the light reaction process, light must be present along with chlorophyll to start the chemical reaction. Carbon dioxide and water are broken down into free atoms. Then the dark reaction can happen. Light is not necessary for this chemical reaction to occur. Carbon, acting as a centerpiece, joins with oxygen and hydrogen to form carbohydrates. Water and unused oxygen are given off as waste products.

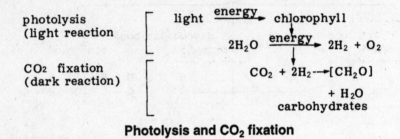

photolysis (light reaction)

$$\text{light} \xrightarrow{\text{energy}} \text{chlorophyll}$$

$$2H_2O \xrightarrow{\text{energy}} 2H_2 + O_2$$

CO₂ fixation (dark reaction)

$$CO_2 + 2H_2 \dashrightarrow [CH_2O]$$
$$+ H_2O$$
$$\text{carbohydrates}$$

Photolysis and CO$_2$ fixation

CELLULAR RESPIRATION

Cellular respiration is the process by which the cell or organism gets energy for all of its activities. It is through this respiration process that chemical energy is released. This process occurs in the mitochondria through a series of steps.

Step 1
  ATP ⟩
  ADP ⟩
Glucose (6 carbons)

Step 2
Glucose Phosphate (6 carbons)

Sugar Phosphate (6 carbons)
  ATP ⟩
  ADP ⟩

Step 3
Sugar Diphosphate (6 carbons)

2 PGAL (3 carbons each)

Step 4
  4 ADP ⟩   2NAD
  4 ATP ⟩   2 NADH₂
2 Molecules of pyruvic acid (3 carbons each)

The steps are summarized as follows:

Step 1 — Activation of glucose

Step 2 — Formation of sugar diphosphate

Step 3 — Formation of oxidation of PGAL, phosphoglyceraldehyde

Step 4 — Formation of pyruvic acid ($C_3H_4O_3$). Net gain of two ATP molecules

Cellular respiration can be either aerobic or anaerobic. In aerobic respiration, release of energy from organic compounds occurs in the presence of oxygen. The oxidation, or process of breaking down and releasing energy, is stimulated by enzymes and acids present in and around the mitochondria. In anaerobic respiration, there is no oxygen present and it must occur by a fermentation process. Lactic acid is produced as a by-product of this process. Lactic acid in muscles results in muscle fatigue and soreness.

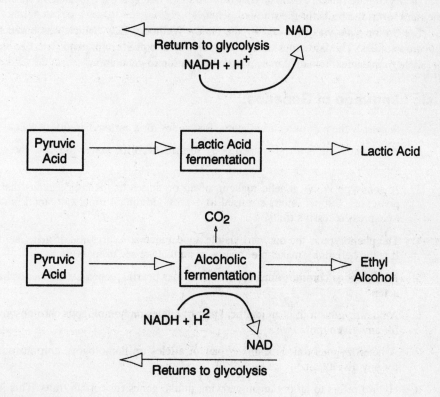

GENETICS

Everyone is aware of how offspring will resemble their parents. Yet, the offspring may have traits that are not present in either parent. In 1857, Gregor Mendel developed his laws of genetics after seven years of studying the garden green pea. Mendel's laws of genetics are:

1. **Law of Dominance:** Every organism receives a trait from the mother and a trait from the father. One trait may have dominance over the other and mask the recessive trait to keep it from showing in the offspring. Dominant traits are often the darker, heavier, or larger of the two traits.

2. **Law of Segregation:** The genes carried in the same place on homologous chromosomes will separate when gametes form. Then when the egg and sperm cell unite to form a new individual, the equal contribution of each parent is assured.

3. **Law of Independent Assortment:** The genes for one characteristic (alleles) are inherited independently of the genes for another characteristic (a second pair of alleles) except when gene linkage occurs (two genes are located on the same chromosome). Genes on separate chromosomes are inherited independently.

In 1900, Walter Sutton began further studies based on Mendel's studies. Sutton compared the behavior of the chromosomes to the principles of inheritance. He confirmed all that Gregor Mendel had formulated. Sutton learned that the "factors" Mendel referred to were units located in the chromosomes. Sutton named these factors "genes." The chromosomal theory of inheritance, established by Sutton, states that genes are located on chromosomes and forms the basis for the study of genetics.

The Sutton Law was followed by the Hardy-Weinberg Law, which was based on population studies. The law states that in a population at equilibrium, genotypic frequencies (allele frequencies) remain constant from generation to generation.

Basic Language of Genetics:

1. A gene is the part of a chromosome that codes for a certain hereditary trait.

2. A chromosome is a rod-shaped body formed from the genes found in the cell nucleus.

3. A genotype is the genetic makeup of an organism or the set of genes that it possesses. Capital letters are used to express dominant traits and small letters to express recessive traits.

4. The phenotype is the outward visible appearance or expression of gene action. It is the hereditary makeup of an organism that we see or measure.

5. Homologous chromosomes are chromosomes bearing genes for the same characters.

6. A homozygous trait is an identical pair of alleles on homologous chromosomes for any given trait.

7. A heterozygous trait is a mixed pair of alleles on homologous chromosomes for any given trait.

8. Hybrid refers to an organism carrying unlike genes for certain traits. This is a preferred trait when breeding for the "best of both" traits.

9. Mutation is a sudden appearance of a new trait or variation which is inherited.

10. Lethal means deadly. This trait will cause death of the organism.

Each gene has a particular location on a chromosome (allele). Genes carried on the X chromosome are called sex-linked genes. Males carrying a recessive allele on their single X chromosome express a recessive phenotype. Females must carry recessive alleles on both X chromosomes to express a recessive phenotype.

Mutations can affect either chromosomes or individual genes. Chromosomal aberrations like mutations occur in reproductive cells and may be passed on to the offspring.

Nondisjunction of the chromosomes results in gametes that have too few or too many chromosomes. In polyploidy, organisms have an extra set of chromosomes. In the disease called trisomy 21, or Down's Syndrome, a person has an extra twenty-first chromosome. Gene mutations occur due to a change in the DNA sequence for that particular gene at that particular time. A mutated gene does not give correct directions for protein synthesis and normally harms the organism. There are a few mutations that have proven to be beneficial, however.

The Punnett Square is a method used to predict the probable outcome of a particular genetic cross. This testcross will help determine information about an organism or potential organism. Study the basic cross worked out below.

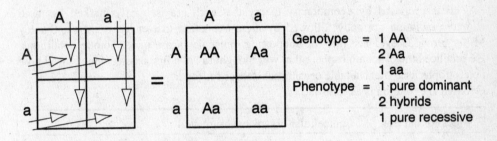

Genotype = 1 AA
2 Aa
1 aa

Phenotype = 1 pure dominant
2 hybrids
1 pure recessive

BREAKING THE CODE OF LIFE

More is being learned about the code of life that is locked into the DNA of every cell. Every living organism has its own unique pattern of DNA that accounts for the individualism in each organism. Prior to mitosis or meiois occurring within the cell, that is the reason for organisms to grow, develop, and reproduce, so replication of the DNA must occur. In this process, DNA unspirals, unzips, and separates, and new strands of DNA are constructed from nucleotides present in the nucleus. Then the process of cell division may occur. This occurrence is what holds the code of life. Although this may be the key to answering questions about cancer and other life-threatening diseases that affect certain organisms, much research still needs to be done.

EVOLUTION OF ORGANISMS

Several theories have been formulated on how life evolves. One such theory was advanced by Jean Lamarck in 1809, when he proposed that an organism evolves in response to its environment by acquiring a trait which would adapt them to live in its changing environment. For instance, if a giraffe's neck was too short, he posited, the constant stretching during its lifetime would lead to offspring that would have longer necks.

In 1859, Darwin formulated his theory in his book *The Origin of Species*. The book supported the theory of evolution but gave a completely different twist to the evolution idea. After studying many plants and animals, Darwin concluded that no two organisms are exactly alike, but instead differ in size, shape, color, etc., and that these traits are inherited from the parents to the offspring and not acquired. Individuals who inherit adaptive traits have a greater chance for survival. Thus, Darwin called his theory natural selection.

Evidence that supports evolutionary theories includes adaptations to the environment, homologous organs, vestigial organs, similarity of embryonic development, similarity of nucleic acids, and similar protein structure. With the groundwork laid by Lamarck and Darwin, modern evolutionists include speciation, adaptive radiation, convergent evolution, divergent evolution, and population genetics as phenomena that support evolutionary theory.

Over time, there have been marked changes in atmospheric content, climate, and environment. If a species did not have the necessary adaptive traits to change with the external changes, the species became extinct.

Fossils are evidence of living things that existed long ago. The most common fossils are found in sedimentary rock that can be dated by using radioactive isotopes to measure the amount of carbon in the remains. This amount determines a close approximation to the exact age of the fossil remains.

It is proposed by evolutionary theory that each era is briefly marked by rapid adaptive radiation normally followed by mass extinction that ended each era. Stanley Miller provided evidence that life-supporting molecules arose under abiotic conditions. He produced the exact atmosphere that was thought to have first existed and showed how heterotrophs used the available organic substances for food.

Geological evolution is as follows:

Precambrian Era	unicellular organisms originated
Paleozoic Era	multicellular animals and fern-like plants originated
Mesozoic Era	birds, mammals, reptiles, and flowering plants originated
Cenozoic Era	radiation of birds, mammals, reptiles, and flowering plants occurred

CLASSIFICATION

Classification is a method of organizing information based on similarities. Aristotle was the first scientist to attempt to classify living things by grouping them into two major groups—plants or animals. Then they were divided into three major sub-groups as to their habitat—land, water, or air. Since Aristotle's first attempt at classification, man has used various systems of classifying living things in an effort to identify them. With so many languages and word meanings, a standard language had to be developed so that the use of common names in each language could be avoided. Thus, scientists began to use the genus and species names, with the intention of creating a consistent international language. This classification system is called binomial nomenclature.

The levels of classification from largest to smallest are kingdom, phylum class, order, family, genus, and species. All living organisms are classified into one of five kingdoms to start the identifying procedure. Then the organism will be studied, compared to specific requirements, and placed in an appropriate level until a species is finally established. The biological name would be the genus and species.

A classification key can be used as an aid to identify organisms. It uses an organism's general characteristics and special features to find its appropriate placement. (Study the following mini-key.)

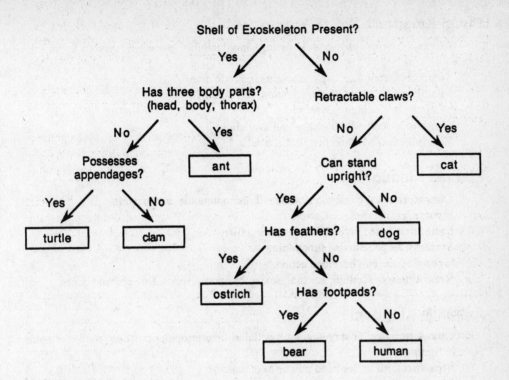

Often, as seen throughout time, organisms change in order to survive. Natural selection causes all species to adapt to changing environmental conditions. This change is called adaptation. The organisms change to adapt to their new environments and through time they evolve into entirely different organisms. This is called speciation.

Monera Kingdom

Bacteria and blue-green bacteria

Characteristics: prokaryotes, microscopic, lives as a single cell or in colonies in water, autotrophic, few heterotrophic

Structures: flagella, capsules

Functions: food getting, respiration, reproduction

Systems: none

Growth: cell membrane and availability of food set growth limit

Reproduction Method: binary fission

Protista Kingdom

Animal-like organism, distinguished by method of locomotion

Characteristics: eukaryotes, mainly microscopic, single-celled or multicellular; some autotrophic and many heterotrophic

Structures: cilia, flagella, cell organelles membrane bound, photosynthetic

Functions: organelles function as organ systems

Systems: none

Growth: cell membrane and availability of food set growth limit

Reproduction Method: asexual or sexual

Fungi Kingdom

Characteristics: eukaryotes, mainly multicellular, parasitic, symbiotic, mycor-rhizae

Structures: root-like, caps, filaments, reproductive
Functions: digestive-like, respiration, reproductive
Systems: beginning to develop
Growth: based on food source and availability
Reproduction Method: asexual, sexual

Plantae Kingdom

Characteristics: eukaryotes, multicellular, nonmotile, autotrophic
Structures: cellulose cell walls
Functions: based on cell and tissue chemistry
Systems: all present and functioning
Growth: based on hormone action
Reproduction Method: asexual, sexual by spores, seeds, flowers, and cones

Animalia Kingdom

Characteristics: eukaryotes, multicellular, heterotrophic, most are motile at some point in lifetime
Structures: all present and unique to organism
Functions: based on nutrition, cell and tissue chemistry, and individual demands
Systems: all present and functioning
Growth: based on hormone action and nutrition
Reproduction Method: asexual, sexual

HUMAN SYSTEMS BIOLOGY

Digestive System

The digestive system is responsible for both mechanical and chemical digestion that break down food into molecules so they can move into the cell and be used for the living process. The mouth, teeth, and tongue begin the mechanical digestion by breaking down the food through the chewing process. The addition of saliva begins the chemical digestion process. The enzyme amylase breaks down carbohydrates and starts the break-down of starches. Food moves from the mouth to the stomach by way of the esophagus. In the stomach, other digestive enzymes and hydrochloric acid begin the breakdown of proteins. The stomach churns and mixes the food. Food, now in a liquid-like state, moves from the stomach into the small intestine, where it is absorbed through the villa into the bloodstream where it is delivered and assimilated by the cells of the body. Waste materials and unused food are carried back to the large intestine where they mix with roughage and water. The undigested materials are excreted from the body.

Circulatory System

The circulatory system is composed of the heart, arteries, veins, red blood cells, white blood cells, antibodies, thrombin, water, and plasma. A four-chambered heart, controlled by the pacemaker, rhythmically controls the pumping action by alternating contractions of the atria and ventricles. Blood circulates through the body in two loops—

arteries carrying oxygenated blood away from the heart to all parts of the body, and veins returning deoxygenated blood to the heart and lungs to be reoxygenated. An auxiliary portion is the lymphatic system, which drains excess tissue fluids back into the circulatory system along with white blood cells that destroy harmful microorganisms.

Skeletal System

The skeleton is the basic framework of the human body and is made of connective tissue—bones and cartilage. Bone is living tissue with vitamins, collagen, and minerals to give it strength and hardness. The process by which the bones harden is called ossification. Bones are joined by cartilage at joints. Joints are classified as to the amount of movement they allow: stationary (skull), hinge (elbow), or ball and socket (hip).

Muscular System

The three human muscle types are skeletal, cardiac, and smooth. All muscle tissue exerts force when it contracts; therefore, muscles are responsible for all movement of the body, voluntary or involuntary. Energy for all movement is derived from an ample supply of mitochondria in the muscle cell. ATP, a high level energy carrier, is produced by the mitochondria for use by other cells and tissue parts during movement or exercise. Muscles are paired to accomplish full movement. Each contracting muscle will be paired with an antagonistic muscle, and tendons attach paired muscle groups to bones to complete the movement action. The skeletal muscles make up this grouping of muscles and are mainly voluntary.

Cardiac muscle is found only in the heart. The heart is the strongest muscle of the body. It is responsible for keeping the blood flowing through the circulatory system at a given pressure. The cardiac muscle is an involuntary muscle.

Smooth muscles are found in the linings of the body such as the digestive system and internal organs. They are generally involuntary muscles.

Nervous System

The basic unit of the nervous system is the neuron (nerve cell). Its structure allows electrochemical signals to travel across synapses to activate muscles, glands, or organ tissue. The nervous system is divided into two parts: the central nervous system, which includes the brain and spinal cord; and the peripheral nervous system, which is a vast network of nerves that totally connects all parts of the body. Receptors located in sense organs and in the skin send information along the sensory neurons to the spinal cord and then to the brain where the information is chemically interpreted, causing a motor response.

Respiratory System

Respiration involves actions started by nerves stimulating muscles and bones to mechanically enlarge the respiratory cavity of the body. The breathing rate is controlled by nerves originating in the brain based on carbon dioxide content. The human nasal passages are adapted to clean, moisten, and warm the air before it enters the lungs by way of the trachea and bronchi. The lungs are made up of many tiny air sacs called alveoli that are found at the end of the bronchiole in clusters. The exchange of gases between the lungs and circulatory system occurs in the alveoli.

Excretory System

The excretory system is made up of the kidney, bladder, connecting tubes, and capillaries joined to the kidney. Urine is collected by structures in the kidney called nephrons. From the nephrons, the liquid wastes are collected and stored in the bladder. Urine leaves the body through the urethra.

Endocrine System

The endocrine system produces hormones which travel by way of the bloodstream to specific target cells. The manner in which the hormone acts on the target cells depends on whether it is a protein or steroid. Each will cause a feedback, which is one way to regulate hormones secreted into the body. Homeostasis depends on the actions of the nervous and endocrine systems. Organs, like the kidney, function based on endocrine stimulation.

Integumentary System

The integumentary covering of the body is called the skin. Skin consists of two layers, the epidermis and the dermis. Skin protects the body, rids the body of mineral salts and wastes, regulates body temperature, and picks up environmental signals. The skin is the bonding or holding agent that keeps the body intact and functioning. Also part of the integumentary system are the hair and nails.

Immunity and Diseases

Important Lymphatic Organs

A defense against pathogens

Adenoids and Tonsils—Organs that filter out antigens (substances, such as viruses, which stimulate antibody synthesis) that enter the body via the upper-respiratory and gastrointestinal tracts.

Thymus—Produces cells that eventually become what are called peripheral T cells, which possess surface receptors for antigens.

Bone Marrow—Produces blood-forming stem cells.

Spleen—Has three functions:

1. Can mount an immune response to antigens in the blood stream.

2. Scavenges old red blood cells.

3. Serves as reserve site for making blood-forming stem cells.

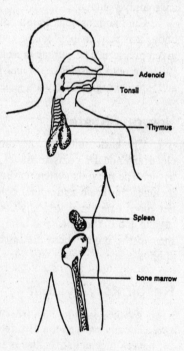

Disorders of the Immune System

Lupus—Humans develop immune reactions to their own nucleic acids.

Allergies—Humans become hypersensitive to environmental substances, called allergens.

AIDS (Acquired Immune Deficiency Syndrome)—

1. Humans have reduced numbers of helper T cells.

2. Humans may not be able to form antibodies against diseases like pneumonia.

ECOLOGY

Ecology can be defined as the study of interactions between groups of organisms and their environment. Groups are referred to as populations. Ecology is the basis of all life and all support systems of life. It is made up of chains—the food chain, carbon/oxygen chain, energy chain, and water chain. It is through the linking of the chains that life continues. Each organism has a specific habitat in an ecosystem carrying out a specific role (niche).

Ecology and behavior are closely linked. It is because of learned and innate behaviors that organisms are equipped to meet the ever-changing environmental demands and the interactions with other living organisms.

Life on earth exists in a thin layer known as the biosphere. The land, air, and water that make up the biosphere each have their own areas where life exists. The land, or terrestrial, biomes are determined mainly by climate. Water, or aquatic, biomes are classified as freshwater or marine, depending upon the amount of salt (salinity) in the water. Marine life occurs in various zones depending on depth, temperature, and light intensity. Freshwater abiotic factors are depth, turbidity, temperature, and light intensity. Estuaries are mixtures of salt and fresh water. They are more protected than the ocean, but more nutrient-rich than rivers and support a wide variety of species.

The size of a population at a given time is determined by its growth rate. Growth rate is determined by the factors of birth rate, immigration, death rate, and emigration. Other factors like natural disasters, availability of food, and disease also independently affect population. Environmental resistance to increased population often depends on population density. Crowding of organisms can reduce nutrients, spread disease, and interfere with reproduction. Competition for an environment's limited resources occurs between members of a population (intraspecific competition) and between different species in an area (interspecific competition). Competition also limits population size.

Humans are unique in their ability to modify the carrying capacity of their environment to be favorable for population growth. Most scientists agree that it is only a matter of time before humans will be unable to increase the earth's carrying capacity any further. At that time, the birth rate must decrease and the death rate must increase to balance population growth.

Natural resources are necessary for human survival and the making of necessary products. The natural resources are water, soil, air, wildlife, and forests. Problems that are now being faced are related to erosion, soil depletion, species extinction, deforestation, desertification, and water shortages. Efforts to reverse these problems and their environmental damages are found in the planned programs of reforestation, captive breeding, biological harvesting, or planned farming through efficient plowing and planting procedures.

Pollution is damaging both the ecosystems and living organisms. Air, water, soil, and food resources are being affected by pollution. Pollutants include automobile exhaust, fertilizers, pesticides, industrial wastes, radioactive wastes, and most of all, household wastes. The growing population and modern conveniences greatly contribute to this insurmountable problem. Government regulations, community efforts, and changes in the habits of industries and individuals are necessary to solve pollution problems.

PART II: CHEMISTRY

INTRODUCTION TO CHEMISTRY

Chemistry is one of the oldest branches of science. The study of chemistry can be traced back as far as the Babylonian Period. The field of chemistry seeks to transform one molecule into another to tailor or refine such chemicals as plastics, drugs, food technology, fuels, and dyes. Out of these raw materials, countless products required to meet our needs of daily living can be manufactured. Chemistry is defined as the study of the composition and behavior of elements in combination with each other.

Chemistry began to grow as knowledge spread about the atomic theory proposed by Thomas Dalton about 1807. He advocated that all matter is composed of small indivisible particles which he named "atoms" and described as little round balls. He believed these particles could combine with one another in many forms to produce all possible substances. It was remarkable how close his theory was to being correct considering the lack of experimental techniques available at that time. He was correct in stating that atoms join together to form complex substances. Dalton was incorrect in his assumption that all atoms are alike.

A great growth was experienced in the field of chemistry after the discovery of the group-forming pattern by D. L. Mendeleev in 1896. With the newly acquired information, a listing of all of the known chemical elements was placed on a chart in the order of their increasing atomic weights and number of energy levels. This charted information was the first periodic table.

As information in the field of chemistry grew, studies branched into the areas of organic chemistry and inorganic chemistry. Organic chemistry deals with the carbon compounds while inorganic chemistry deals with all the other elements and compounds.

The field of chemistry has vastly expanded based on the study of the atomic structure of elements and their behavior. Atomic structure is related to the properties and arrangement of elements in the periodic chart. The elements are classified into groups, periods, and families. It is from these groupings that matter is classified and its behavior is studied based on the ability of an element to combine or react with other elements. The study of the behavior of matter is based on properties of the elements and their ability to combine through the transfer and sharing of electrons to form compounds and other matter. This is commonly referred to as the process of bonding.

Every element has its own letter symbol. With these letter symbols and atomic numbers used together correctly, one can construct a formula. The formulas can be combined to show the composition of compounds, reactions between elements, chemical equilibrium, and oxidation and reaction rates. This is accomplished by the process of balancing equations.

It is necessary that everyone understand the basics of chemistry since our lives revolve around this subject. Also, how far we can progress is based on our ability to understand chemical concepts and apply them to our everyday life.

STRUCTURE OF MATTER

Matter is anything that occupies space and has mass. Matter resists changes in motion. It takes force to accelerate matter. There are four states of matter—solid, liquid, gas, and a fourth state called the plasma state. This state only exists at extremely high temperatures, such as those found on the sun. Plasma consists of high-energy, electrically charged particles. Plasma is created when a fluorescent lamp is turned on. Most of the matter in the universe is in the plasma state.

The structure of matter depends on the number and types of atoms that combine or react to form the matter. Matter is measured by the force with which gravity pulls on the mass toward the center of the earth. Matter can also be measured by its capacity for doing work, or the energy that it contains. This energy can be either activation, potential, or kinetic energy. Activation energy is that energy necessary to start a reaction. Potential energy is stored energy, while kinetic energy is the energy that matter possesses due to motion.

It can be shown experimentally that potential energy can be transformed into kinetic energy without any energy loss. This is an illustration of the Law of Conservation of Matter or Energy, which states that under ordinary conditions, matter or energy can neither be created nor destroyed but can be converted from one form to another.

One method of classifying matter is to find out if it is a substance or a mixture of substances. If a substance is composed of only one kind of atom, it is an element. If the substance is composed of two or more kinds of atoms, the matter can be a mixture or a compound, depending on how the atoms are joined and react to each other under normal conditions.

Mixtures do not follow the law of definite proportions, which means that the two substances can be mixed in almost any proportion. Thus, the properties of a mixture vary with composition. If the substances in a mixture are spread out evenly, it is considered to be a homogeneous mixture. If the substances in a mixture are not spread out evenly, it is considered to be a heterogeneous mixture. Vinegar is a homogeneous mixture as the substances are spread out evenly throughout. A homogeneous mixture can be called a solution. Other solutions include seawater, soft drinks, tea, or milk.

A suspension is a heterogeneous mixture in which the particles are large enough to be seen by a microscope or the eye. These particles are affected by gravity and may settle out of the mixture. The particles can be temporarily suspended again by shaking. The mixing of water and pepper is an example of a suspension. Stirring up the bottom of a river will produce a suspension. With time, the action of gravity on the sand and soil will cause the particles to settle back to the bottom of the river.

If particles of a mixture are larger than those found in a solution, yet smaller than particles found in a suspension, the mixture is referred to as a colloid. Colloidal particles appear to be evenly distributed and they will not settle out. The small size of the particles causes gravity to have less of an effect. Thus, there is less possibility of settling out caused by gravity.

All matter can be identified as having either physical or chemical properties. A physical property is a characteristic of matter that can be observed without changing the makeup of the substance. Boiling points and freezing points are examples of physical properties. Other physical properties are color, odor, hardness, density, and the ability to conduct heat or electricity. Physical properties can be used to separate mixtures. A mixture of iron and sand can be separated by a magnet. Iron is magnetic. Sand is not, and thus they can be separated with ease.

A physical change occurs when matter changes in size, shape, color, or state. A physical change does not change the chemical composition of a substance. When a glass breaks, the size and shape of the glass change, but the chemical makeup remains the same no matter in how many pieces the glass might exist.

A chemical property is a characteristic that determines how a substance reacts to form other substances. Chemical properties are determined by chemical changes. When a chemical change occurs, the substance will seldom, if ever, return to its original state. For example, iron will rust in the presence of water and oxygen. Rusting is an example of the chemical property known as corrosion. Corrosion occurs when metals are destroyed as they combine chemically with other substances.

In a chemical change, a substance is changed to a new substance which has different properties. Chemical changes may release thermal energy, light, or electricity. Some chemical changes need energy. All changes, chemical and physical, involve an energy change of some kind. Many compounds are formed from elements by chemical changes. In the same respect, many compounds are broken down by a chemical change.

When wood burns, heat is given off and a small amount of ashes is left. The substance of the wood has changed. Wood is made of carbon, hydrogen, and oxygen. When wood burns, the elements unite with atmospheric oxygen resulting in the formation of carbon dioxide and water. Also, carbon is the element of the ash substance that remains. This is a chemical change as energy is used to bring about the change and heat (an energy form) is given off; other compounds have been formed and the elements can never return to the state of wood (unless they again become integrated into the growth of a tree).

EQUATIONS SHOWING STRUCTURE OF MATTER

Matter can be identified not only by name, but also by the way an element fits together with other elements to form matter. It is important for one to know if the proposed combination actually exists. For example, no chemist has ever been able to prepare hydrogen nitrate. Additionally, in making combinations, one must have a positive and a negative component. Generally speaking, metals are positive components, while nonmetals are negative components (with the exception of ammonia and radicals). When elements combine in varying proportions, prefixes are used for the naming of the compound and for formula writing. Mono- means one, bi- or di- mean two, tri- means three, tetra- means four, pent- means five, and so on. Common suffixes and meanings are -ide (for naming monatomic anions), -ous (for the ion with the lower charge), and -ic (for the ion with the higher charge).

PERIODICITY OF ELEMENTS

The latter half of the 19th century brought about the updating of the Periodic Law: the properties of the elements are periodic functions of their atomic numbers. Atomic numbers represent the number of protons and also the number of electrons in a neutral atom. The electron structures of the atoms provide information showing the properties of the elements. Vertical columns represent the chemical families while horizontal columns represent the period or row. Proceeding across a row, the ability to hold electrons decreases. For example, lithium is the most metallic, while fluorine is the least metallic.

Some atoms tend to join with other atoms, while others will show no tendency to join with like atoms or like elements. The results of this tendency or attraction of the atoms involved in joining is called a chemical bond. When atoms combine to form new molecules, there is a shifting or transfer of valence electrons found in the outer shell of each atom. This usually results in the completing of outer shells by each atom. A more stable compound or form is achieved by the gaining, losing, or sharing of pairs of electrons. In forming chemical bonds, there is a release of energy or an absorption of energy. The bonds can be ionic, covalent, or metallic.

The kinetic model explains the forces between molecules and the energy they possess in three basic assumptions:

1. All matter is composed of extremely small particles.

2. The particles making up all matter are in constant motion.

3. When these particles collide with each other or with the walls of the container, there is no loss of energy.

BEHAVIOR OF MATTER

The behavior and classification of matter is dependent upon the electron attraction and interaction of electrons forming the matter. When atoms react with one another, it is the electrons that are involved in bonding, whether it be ionic or covalent.

All reactions need to receive a certain amount of energy before they can start. The amount of energy needed or received to start the chemical reaction is called activation energy. Some reactions require so little energy that it can be absorbed from the surroundings. This is called a spontaneous reaction which takes place with so little energy that it seems as if no energy was needed. A reaction that gives off energy is called an exothermic reaction. A reaction that absorbs energy is called an endothermic reaction. Combustion is a decomposition reaction. A catalyst can be added to a chemical reaction to control the reaction rate.

Acids

Acid properties are:

1. Water solutions of acids conduct electricity.

2. Acids will react actively with metals.

3. Acids will change blue litmus to pink.

4. Acids will react with bases resulting in both a loss of water and leaving a salt (neutralization).

5. Weak acid solutions taste sour.

6. Acids react with carbonates to release carbon dioxide.

Bases

Base properties are:

1. Bases are conductors of electricity in strong solutions.

2. Bases change red litmus paper to blue.

3. Bases react with acids to neutralize each other and to form a salt and water.

4. Bases react with fats to form a class of compounds called soaps.

5. Bases feel slippery and strong solutions are caustic to the skin.

Salts

A salt is an ionic compound containing positive ions other than hydrogen and a negative ion other than hydroxide ions. It is usually formed by neutralization when certain acids and bases are combined and form water and salt as the products.

Formula

A formula is a sort of road map, or a detailed description, of how something is organized or produced. A formula will not reveal the hidden structures of substances. In some reactions, no product is formed at completion, or reactants and products may react both ways. The reaction is said to have reached equilibrium when the rate of the forward reaction is equal to the rate of the reverse reaction. Factors that affect chemical equilibrium are changing concentration, temperature, and pressure.

Electro-Chemistry

Reactions that do not occur spontaneously can be forced by an external supply of energy. This is called an electrolytic reaction. Many chemicals and useful products are produced in this manner. Electroplating, electrolysis of water or salts, and the cathode functioning of a battery all are examples of electro-chemistry.

Simple electrochemical cells, in which electrons produced by the oxidation of zinc atoms are transferred through an external circuit into a copper solution, are called galvanic cells or voltaic cells. All electrochemical cells have the same general components: an oxidation half-cell, a reduction half-cell, and a means of separation so that the electrons produced by the oxidation reaction can be supplied through an external circuit into the reduction reaction. The voltage of the cell is the net voltage or potential voltage of two half-cell reactions. Lead storage cells contain a series of lead grids separated by an insulating material. The grids are alternately filled with spongy lead and lead dioxide that compose what are called dry cells. As long as the grids remain intact, the cell will deliver about two volts of electric current.

SOLUTIONS

Forces of attraction between particles produce a solution. One must mix a solute and a solvent to produce a solution. The particles making up each have certain forces of attraction that produce bonds. The bonds produced by these forces of attraction will determine the solubility of the solute. Temperature also affects the solubility of a solution. If the solution is made of gases, the solubility will be affected by pressure. Pressure does not affect the solubility of solids and liquids. If no more solute can be dissolved in the solvent, the solution is said to be saturated. In an unsaturated solution, more solute can be added to the solvent, while in a supersaturated solution, the solution is holding more dissolved solute than normal at that given temperature.

Matter exists as a substance or a mixture. If a substance is made of only one kind of atom, it is an element. If it is made of two or more kinds of atoms in a definite grouping, it is a compound. A compound always occurs in a definite composition based on the Law of Definite Composition, which states, "A compound is composed of two or more elements chemically combined in a definite ratio by weight." Compounds always have a fixed composition and will be classified as ionic or covalent depending on the type of bonding that occurs when the atoms are combined. The ability to combine is dependent upon the valence of the atom or element. An ionic compound contains ionic bonds—a force of attraction between oppositely charged ions. A covalent compound is a compound that is composed of covalent bonds—a bond in which the electrons are shared between atoms. When a compound is formed, the elements or atoms making up the compound lose their properties and take on the properties of the compound formed.

It is important to remember that the gain of electrons is reduction, and the loss of electrons is oxidation. The oxidation number of a bonded atom is the number of electrons gained, lost, or shared in a chemical reaction. The metal elements that lose electrons easily and become positive ions are placed high in the electromotive series.

The metal elements that lose electrons with greater difficulty are placed lower on the periodic chart. The energy required to remove electrons from metallic atoms can be assigned numeral values called electrode potentials. Binary compounds are named by changing the name of the element that has the negative oxidation number to end in -ide.

The rate of the reaction is defined as the quantity of product formed in some stated interval or the rate at which the reaction will take place. The rate of the chemical reaction can be defined in terms of the change in concentration of any species in the reaction with respect to time. The rate of the reaction can be determined by measuring how fast the product is formed after the reactants are mixed, or how many moles are formed per second. Also, increase in temperature will increase frequency of molecular collision and increase rate of reaction. Activation energy is necessary to produce enough energy to break or weaken bonds before new bonds can be formed. Some reactions produce energy in the formation of new compounds or the products have more energy than the reactants (exothermic reactions) while other reactants need a greater amount of energy than the activation energy (endothermic reactions). The study of reaction rate factors is called chemical kinetics.

PART III: EARTH SCIENCE

ASPECTS OF EARTH SCIENCE

An understanding of the beginnings of the solar system and the Earth's development within it is essential to environmental survival. This understanding is filled with curiosity, and may be the price of environmental survival. A lack of curiosity and understanding may signal the environment's demise.

Hipparchus, in 150 B.C.E., determined the distance of the moon from the Earth, based on his calculations on the Earth's diameter. The Greeks added to the study of astronomy by determining that an eclipse was caused by the Earth passing between the sun and the moon, and, that the sun was at the center of the solar system. These and other basic studies concerning the sun, moon, planets, galaxies, and solar system have led to questions like, Does the universe go on forever? Where does it all end? Is space infinite? It is because of such challenging questions that astronomy has developed into an exact science.

Theories

The theory developed by Sir Isaac Newton is in direct opposition to the theory developed by Albert Einstein. Newton stated that a planet moves around the sun because of the gravitational force exerted by the sun. This theory holds true if one is studying the velocities of small objects compared to light. Einstein's theory of relativity states that the planet chooses the shortest possible path throughout the four-dimensional world which is defined by the presence of the sun. According to this theory, if you were to leave home and walk in a straight line, you would eventually return home. Both of these theories sprang from human minds and have been used to create many of our scientific explanations (theories). New theories will show weaknesses and limitations to each theory.

Most scientists tend to believe the theory that the solar system probably developed as a nebula (cloud of gas and dust) that once swirled around the sun and slowly flattened out. Sections of the cloud began to spin like eddies in a stream, collecting gases and dust and causing the sections to grow and form planets. They slowly developed into spinning planets that now travel around the sun.

The generally accepted theory of the origin of the universe, known as the Big Bang Theory, describes the universe as the product of an explosion of a singularity—a point in space with infinite mass, but without surface area. According to this theory all matter in the universe was at one time contained within this singularity, compressed to infinite density. The explosion of this singularity some 10 to 20 billion years ago, both created and filled the space now occupied by our universe. All particles contained in this singularity sped away from the point of explosion. This expansion continues today, with galaxies moving away from one another at great speed.

In the early 1700s, Abraham Werner presented his theory that one large ocean once covered the Earth. The chemicals in the water slowly settled to the bottom of the water where they formed granite and other forms of rock layers. The Earth was completely formed with the settling of the water and no other changes occurred. All life, according to Werner, began with the settling of the water and the formation of the Earth.

The Hutton Theory of 1785 claimed that the Earth was gradually changing and would continue to change in the same ways. According to Hutton, these changes could be used to explain the past. He died before he could get other scientists to accept his ideas, yet after his death and publication of his ideas, they became a leading guide for the geological thinkers.

Some maintain that the Creation Theory rooted in the narrative of the first chapters of Genesis is the true story of the creation of the universe. Various attempts have been made to work out the date of the creation on the basis of the data given in the Bible and the date of creation has been set at 3760 B.C.E. This creation theory is but one of the many religion-based theories, as all religions take as their foundation some version of the idea that the creation of the universe was the action of an omnipotent being.

Battle lines have been drawn. One theorist will research and develop a possible strategy for solving the age-old question, only for another theorist to come along and find a flaw in that research and then develop a new theory. Thus new theories are constantly developed. Each theory developed is viewed in a manner to gain an understanding of the information presented pertaining to the Earth's formation for the purpose of survival and prosperity of the universe.

Solar System

The solar system includes the sun, nine planets and their moons, asteroids, meteoroids, comets, interplanetary dust, and interplanetary plasma that is circular in shape. The sun is the center of the solar system, with a mass 750 times greater than that of all of the planets combined. The planets rotate around the sun, with Mercury being the closest to and Pluto being the farthest from the sun. The terrestrial (earth-like) planets—Mercury, Venus, Mars, and the Earth—are composed chiefly of iron and rock. These planets are smallest in comparison to the four largest planets, Jupiter, Saturn, Uranus, and Neptune, which are called the Major planets. They are composed chiefly of hydrogen, helium, ammonia, and methane. Pluto is believed to be less than one-fifth the size of Earth, which makes it smaller than our moon.

Asteroids or planetoids are small, irregularly-shaped objects orbiting between Jupiter and Mars. Meteoroids are chunks of iron resulting from collisions between asteroids. Comets are round heads consisting of dust particles mixed with frozen water, frozen methane, and frozen ammonia, and a tail made of dust and gases escaping from the head.

Meteors and Meteorites

A meteor is a metallic or stony mass belonging to the solar system that is hurtled into the Earth's atmosphere. The meteor cannot be seen until it enters the atmosphere, at which time the friction with the air makes it glow and shine for only a few seconds as it falls to the Earth. Thus, it is called a falling, or shooting, star.

Meteorites seldom do damage, yet they have devastating potentiality. Meteorites are pieces of extraterrestrial matter that are studied to determine the origins of the universe and the solar system. Meteorites make up only a tiny fraction of the matter falling into the Earth's atmosphere from space. They sometimes explode into fragments with a noise that can be heard for many miles when they strike the surface of the Earth.

Stars

When you look at the sky, you see only a tiny part of the universe consisting mainly of stars, clouds of dust, and the solar system. Astronomers study the brightness and color of the stars. Brightness indicates the mass of the stars, while the color indicates the temperature of the star's surface. The distance is difficult to determine as most stars are so far away. Stars have been studied as early as 3000 B.C.E.; yet, they still remain a mystery.

Stars and star groupings (constellations) are used as compasses at night, as a navigational aid, as a basis for astrology, for study, and for viewing at the planetarium. What appears as movement of the stars and the nearly 80 constellations is actually the spinning and placement of the Earth. Seasonally and yearly, the constellations that can be seen will differ, causing the sky to appear to move west during the year.

Galaxies

Galaxies are groups or systems of stars located millions to billions of light-years from Earth. Sometimes called stellar universes, galaxies include billions of stars, and are classified as to their appearance. Irregular systems have no special form or symmetry. The spiral system resembles a large pinwheel with arms extending from the dense central core. Elliptical systems appear round without the spiral arms.

Our solar system is in the Milky Way Galaxy. The Milky Way is a spiral galaxy and is held together by gravity. It slowly rotates, with its spiral arms turning once in about 200 million years. The Milky Way contains clouds of gas, dust, and millions or billions of star clusters which form their own distinct patterns. Bands of stars making-up the spiral arms of our galaxy can be seen in the night sky. The Andromeda Nebula Galaxy, first studied in 1612, resembles the Milky Way. It is the nearest galaxy that northern hemisphere observers can see.

In the past few decades, radio astronomy has played a great role in studying celestial objects. In 1959, the first quasar was discovered. It was noticed that some sources of celestial radio waves appeared to be point-like—"quasi-stellar"—instead of looking like radio waves emitted by galaxies. These "quasi-stellar radio sources," or quasars, as they are known, give off radio waves and light at a rate over 100,000 billion times as fast as the sun. Quasars appear to be far smaller than ordinary galaxies, and are believed by some astronomers to be the core of violently exploding galaxies. Quasars appear to be among the most distant objects in the universe. Today, astronomers have identified over 1,000 quasars.

PHYSICS AND CHEMISTRY OF THE EARTH

Physical Properties

The Earth has three motions: it spins like a top, moves in the spinning motion around the sun, and all the while moves through the Milky Way with the rest of the solar system. The Earth spins around on its axis, an imaginary line that connects the North and South poles at either end of the planet Earth. The spinning motion makes the sun seem to move from east to west and causes the occurrence of day and night. While it is spinning the Earth follows a path around the sun. This is called the orbit. The Earth has only one moon. The sun's gravity acts on both the Earth and the moon, causing the moon to travel in an oval-like orbit around the Earth. Because of this movement, we have the seasons of spring, summer, fall, and winter. The seasons are a result of the tilting of the Earth on its axis, as well as the movement and position of the Earth in relation to the sun.

Chemical Composition

The Earth's surface is about 70% water, with most of the water being oceans. The deepest oceanic ridge has been measured at 11,022 meters. The land surface makes up the remaining 30% and extends an average of 850 meters above the division of land and water. The highest peak is Mount Everest in Asia, at 8,848 meters above sea level. Oceans, lakes, rivers, and all other bodies of water and ice make up a part of the Earth called the hydrosphere. Land bodies surrounded by water make up the continents. Together, land and water surfaces that support life are called the biosphere.

The chemical composition of the Earth is 46.6% oxygen, 27.72% silicon, 8.13% aluminum, 5.0% iron, 3.60% calcium, 2.83% sodium, 2.59% potassium, 2.09% magnesium, 0.44% titanium, and all other elements total 1.0%. A geologist is a person who studies the Earth and its contents. It is through the work of geologists that the chemical composition of the Earth has been established.

Rocks

The hard, solid part of the Earth's surface is called rock. Rock may be exposed from its soil cover when highways are cut through hillsides or mountain regions. River channels or shorelines frequently cut through rock beds. Some mountain chains expose rock beds when weathering exposes the rock base. Rocks are useful in many ways as granite (igneous), marble (metamorphic), or limestone (sedimentary) can be used in buildings, dams, highways, or the making of cement. Metals like aluminum, iron, lead, and tin are removed from rock that is called ore.

Minerals

Minerals are the most common form of solid material found in the Earth's crust. Even soil contains bits of minerals that have broken away from its rock source. Minerals are dug from the Earth and are used to make a variety of products. To be considered a mineral, the element must be found in nature and never have been a part of any living organism. Atoms making up the element or substance must be arranged in regular patterns to form crystals.

Ores

Ores are mineral deposits high enough in an element content that it would be economically feasible to be mined and sold for a profit. Ore deposits are located from geological knowledge about crustal movements and ore formations along with sophisticated instruments and a lot of luck. Once the ore has been located, the mining process is based on the most economical method to remove the highest amount of the mineral from the rock with the least amount of environmental damage. Processes include leaching or separating the mineral from the rock by heat, brine solutions, evaporation of seawater, or chemically removing the metal from the ore.

Earth's Magnetism

Imaginary lines curve from the North pole to the South pole, making up the Earth's magnetic field. The Earth acts as though its center is a large magnet. These imaginary lines aid the compass needle to determine directions based on the Earth's natural magnetic field. Scientists are not sure what produces the enormous currents that are deep within the Earth and responsible for the Earth's magnetic fields.

EVOLUTION AND CRUSTAL PROCESS

Changing of the Earth

The moon's gravitational pull produces tides both in the ocean and in the Earth's solid crust. Throughout time, slow evolutionary changes have taken place and continue to take place. As shorelines are inched away in one location, mud and silt build up in other areas, adding to the land surface. With all these changes occurring slowly over long periods of time, little difference can be recorded as to variations in land or water surfaces of the Earth.

Continental Drifts

The continental shelves are zones of relatively shallow portions of the continent extending out under the oceans. The continental shelves or edges are a part of the continent they adjoin and the edge of the shelf is the true boundary of the continent. The continental shelf is not a small area. In some areas, they may contain the same area as the size of the Soviet Union under the waters of the ocean. The shelves were formed eighteen to twenty thousand years ago due to the melting of the glaciers, along with time, wave-cutting terraces, erosion and sedimentation all part of the formation explanation. At the edge of the shelf, the continental slope leads downward to the deep ocean. At the bottom of the slope, an area of deposition called the continental rise may form a gentler slope. Other features included in the continental margin are trenches, ridges, and submarine canyons. A reef is a rocky or coral elevation dangerous to the surface navigation which may or may not be covered by water. A rocky reef is always detached from shore; a coral reef may or may not be connected to the shoreline.

Nature's Recycling

Nature's method of recycling is evident through many processes. Some processes are the water cycle, carbon cycle, oxygen cycle, and energy cycle as demonstrated by prey and predators. These concepts are explained through the following drawings.

SURFACE PROCESSES

Atmosphere

Air, an odorless and colorless gas, surrounds the Earth and extends approximately 1,000 miles above the surface of the Earth. This is called the atmosphere. It is made up of 78% nitrogen and 21% oxygen; the remaining 1% consists mainly of argon, water vapor, dust particles, and other gases. Cloud formations float in the lowest portion of the atmosphere, called the troposphere. Weather occurrences are formed in the troposphere. It is also the more dense portion of the atmosphere, followed by the stratosphere, mesosphere and exosphere.

The ionosphere is a belt of radiation surrounding the Earth. Outside the atmosphere, in what used to be considered "empty" space, man's satellites in 1958 disclosed the existence of magnetism. The aurora borealis or "northern dawn/lights" is a beautiful display of moving, colored streamers or folds of light. Its counterpart in the Antarctic is the aurora australis, or "southern dawn/lights," both connected to the Earth's magnetic field or lines of force. During magnetic storms, aurora borealis can be seen as far south as Boston and New York.

Water

The most important source of sediment is Earth and rock material carried to the sea by rivers and streams; the same materials may also have been transported by glaciers and winds. Other sources are volcanic ash and lava, shells and skeletons of organisms, chemical precipitates formed in seawater, and particles from outer space.

Water is a most unusual substance because it exists on the surface of the Earth in its three physical states: ice, water, and water vapor. There are other substances that might exist in a solid and liquid or gaseous state at temperatures normally found at the Earth's surface, but there are fewer substances which occur in all three states.

Water is odorless, tasteless, and colorless. It is the only substance known to exist in a natural state as a solid, liquid, or gas on the surface of the Earth. It is a universal solvent. Water does not corrode, rust, burn, or separate into its components easily. It is chemically indestructible. It can corrode almost any metal and erode the most solid rock. A unique property of water is that it expands and floats on water when frozen or in the solid state. Water has a freezing point of 0°C and a boiling point of 100°C. Water has the capacity for absorbing great quantities of heat with relatively little increase in temperature. When distilled, water is a poor conductor of electricity but when salt is added, it is a good conductor of electricity.

Sunlight is the source of energy for temperature change, evaporation, and currents for water movement through the atmosphere. Sunlight controls the rate of photosynthesis for all marine plants, which are directly or indirectly the source of food for all marine animals. Migration, breeding, and other behaviors of marine animals are affected by light.

Water, as the ocean or sea, is blue because of the molecular scattering of the sunlight. Blue light, being of short wavelength, is scattered more effectively than light of longer wave lengths. Variations in color may be caused by particles suspended in the

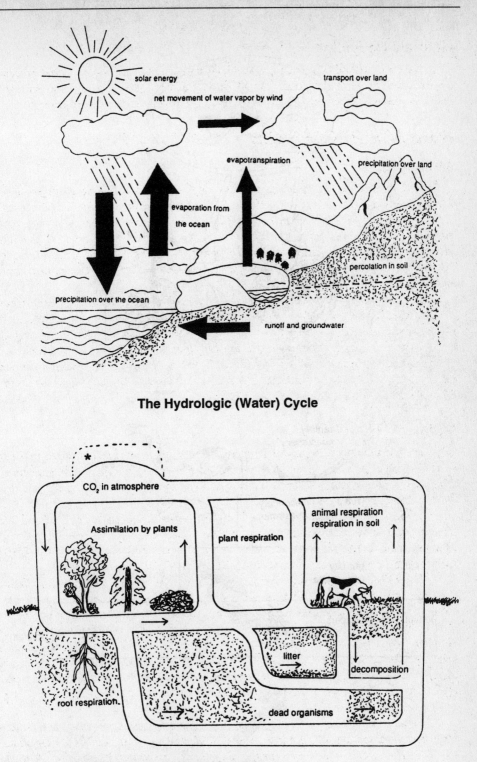

The Hydrologic (Water) Cycle

* A seasonal change in atmospheric CO_2 levels is caused by variations in the distribution of vegetation on the earth.

Carbon Cycle

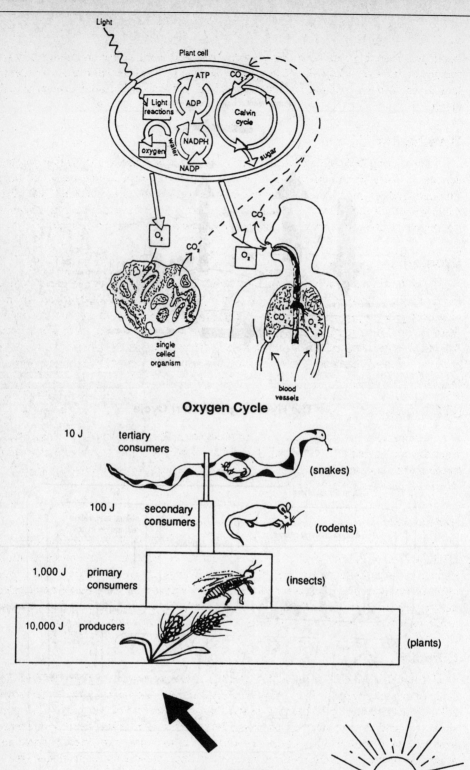

Light

Plant cell

ATP

CO₂

Light reactions

ADP

Calvin cycle

oxygen

water

NADPH

NADP

sugar

O₂

CO₂

O₂

CO₂

single celled organism

CO₂

O₂

blood vessels

Oxygen Cycle

10 J   tertiary consumers   (snakes)

100 J   secondary consumers   (rodents)

1,000 J   primary consumers   (insects)

10,000 J   producers   (plants)

1,000,000 J of sunlight

10% of the energy in one level is transferred to the next higher level. Most energy (~90%) is lost as heat.

Energy Cycle

water, water depth, cloud cover, temperature, and other variable factors. Heavy concentrations of dissolved materials cause a yellowish hue, while algae will cause the water to look green. Heavy populations of plant and animal materials will cause the water to look brown.

Weathering

Weathering is the natural wearing away of rock or soil due to chemical or physical actions on these Earth surfaces. This occurs very slowly over a long period of time. Through chemical weathering, rocks break down as oxygen, carbon dioxide, and water vapor react with rock until it is finally changed into soil. Physical weathering occurs in dry regions by the wind action constantly wearing away the surface of the rock.

Erosion

The first concept of erosion was that natural weathering that we call erosion led to the formation of mountains and mountain chains. The main causes of erosion are air and/or water movement across rock or soil, changes in the temperature, or any combination of these factors. Chemical erosion can occur as carbon dioxide and water vapor are removed from dead organic matter. These are all natural forms of erosion. Man can cause erosion with poor crop-planting procedures, lack of crop rotation, and the cutting of trees without planning or replacement.

Temperature

Temperature is controlled by the position of the Earth on its axis and its distance from the sun at rotation. At the equator, the air would be warmest and always pushing upward while cold air would be flowing in to be warmed. The constant changing of air will cause changes in the temperature.

Pressure

Air pressure also plays an important role in the movement of air and the changing of air temperatures and weather changes. Next to the equator, a low pressure cell is formed because the air is warmer, lighter, and moving upward. The low pressure is a result of the molecules of air being further apart. The colder air has closer air molecules; thus, a high pressure cell is formed. Extreme weather conditions, such as flooding, may result when both low cells and high cells occupy the same air space.

Climate

Climate is the usual weather that occurs in a general area over a period of time. The study of climate is called climatology. When referring to climate, one takes into consideration air temperature, wind speed, sunshine, humidity, amount of precipitation, air pressure, and general geographic conditions. Climate has a direct effect upon living organisms and the type(s) of life that can exist in the region being considered. Climate also affects our method of transportation, outdoor activities, choices for employment, type of clothing, type of housing, and food naturally available or that can be grown.

Alternate Energy Forms

About 90% of today's energy is supplied from fossil fuels as crude oil, natural gas, and coal. These materials are a result of nature providing such supplies for man's use. Thus, these are considered our nonrenewable resources as they cannot be replaced after they have been used. With conservation and suitable alternate energy sources, our natural resources will last longer and these fossil fuels can be usable for many more years. Alternate energy sources include methanol, ethanol, wood and wood wastes, garbage and plant material, corn, other grains, solar energy, photovoltaic cells, hydroelectricity, nuclear power, wind energy (windmills), tidal energy, geothermal energy (geysers), and fusion using nuclear waste materials.

EARTH'S HAZARDS AND RESOURCES

Earthquakes

Earthquakes are vibrations due to the movements within and beneath the Earth's crust. They occur as a result of faulting or other structural processes happening as a result of a strain on the rocks at the edge of the crust. A long series of quakes with none being greater than the others is called an Earth swarm and occurs near volcanic regions. Imperial Valley, California, is known for having Earth swarms. Earth tremors are vibrations of low intensity and can be felt only by those located directly over the affected area.

Earthquake intensity is measured on a scale from 0 to 9, where each number represents an energy release ten times that of the previous number. This energy release is measured by the "Richter Scale" as it was introduced by Charles F. Richter in 1935. Richter was an American seismologist. About 80% of earthquake energy is released in the areas bordering the vast Pacific Ocean, with 15% released in an east-west band across the Mediterranean. The remaining 5% occur sporadically throughout the remaining parts of the world bordering large bodies of water.

Volcanoes

Volcanoes are a natural phenomenon whose most deleterious effects are generally confined to a small area. About 500 volcanoes are known to have been active, with two-thirds of them in the Pacific Ocean area. Modern research into volcanoes and their role in forming much of the Earth's crust began with the French geologist Jean Etienne Guettard in the mid-eighteenth century.

Volcanoes discharge a large amount of carbon dioxide into the air; the weathering of rocks utilizes carbon dioxide. This presents a pair of mechanisms for possible long-term climatic changes. A period of greater than normal volcanic action might initiate a warming of the Earth. The mountains built by the volcanic ash might expose large areas of new and unweathered rock to the air, which will lower the carbon dioxide levels, thus reducing the atmospheric temperature.

Oceans

It is estimated the world's oceans extend over 328 million cubic miles, with the greatest depth being 36,198 feet off the coast of Guam. The deepest of all oceans is the Pacific Ocean, averaging 14,048 feet, and the most shallow is the Baltic Sea at 180.4 feet deep. Sedimentary rock at the bottom of the oceans has been dated at 3 billion years old with the water dated at 4 billion years old.

The oceans supply man with a means of transportation, habitat for aquatic life that is used for food, a source of minerals, and a means of weather control. Also, the ocean offers various sources of energy for consumption and use in the future. Currently, oil and gas are being derived from the ocean as sources of energy. Much research is now being conducted as to the feasibility of waves or water of the ocean being used to produce power. Also, the ocean is being used to simulate islands of lush plant growth to increase the photosynthesis process as a possible way to reduce the depletion of the ozone layer.

Hot Springs

Hot springs are naturally occurring bodies of water that are warmer than their surrounding air. Hot springs (thermal springs) occur in regions of faulted or folded rock due to volcanic action. The water that comes from underground where the rocks are hot will produce hot water that rises to the Earth's surface in the form of a spring. Not all hot springs are a direct result of volcanoes; some are produced by geysers.

Migration

Migration is the movement of people or animals from one area to another area. Migration occurs because of seasonal changes, wars, famines, floods, volcanic eruptions, weather, and other natural disasters for the purpose of survival. Migration practices began with prehistoric man. Little is known about the pattern of movement or why migrations took place. It is believed the first migrations were to escape the spread of the great glaciers and ice sheets. The most common application of migration is that of birds and other animals moving to survive winters or for the purpose of reproduction as illustrated by the salmon moving into the colder waters.

Flooding

Flooding is the natural occurrence of an extremely large amount of water flowing into a given area faster than it can leave the area. As a result, the stream, lake, or river will overflow its natural level. Estuary zones and sand dunes are natural flood control devices. Man-made devices include dams and sandbagging to control flood waters. The control of flood waters is important to the survival of coastal habitats for wading marsh birds, birds of prey, migratory birds, water fowl, and other aquatic life, as well as man.

Water-Based Formations

The commonly seen waves on the surface of water are caused principally by wind. When a breeze blows over calm water, it forms small ripples or capillary waves. As the wind speed increases, larger, more visible gravity waves are formed. When the wind reaches high speeds, whitecaps are formed. However, submarine earthquakes, volcanic eruptions, and tides also cause waves. Waves will always break parallel to the shoreline.

The tide is the continuous cycle of alternating rise and fall of the sea level observed along the coastlines and bodies of water connected to the sea. On most coastlines, the cycle occurs about every 12 hours. Along the Gulf coastline, a tidal cycle can occur about every 24–25 hours. The rise and fall of sea level observed along coastlines is produced by waves of extreme length; high water is the crest of the wave; low water is the trough. Tides can be predicted once observations have been mathematically related to the positions of Earth, moon, and sun. Tides are caused by the gravitational interaction between the sun, moon, and Earth. The moon exercises the greatest influence on our tide; although its mass is much less than the sun's, it is closer to the Earth and its tide-producing effect is more than twice as great.

The maximum height reached by a rising tide is called high water. This is due solely to the periodic tidal force, but at times, the meteorological effects of severe storms or strong winds may be superimposed on the normal tide to produce high water.

Low water is the minimum height reached by a falling tide. Usually this is due solely to the influence of a periodic tidal force, but sometimes the influence of severe storms or strong winds may be superimposed on the normal tide to produce low water.

Tides are classified as semidiurnal, diurnal, and mixed. Areas having semidiurnal tides have two high waters and two low waters each day; this is the most common type. Diurnal tides consist of one high water and one low water each day. Tides are classified as mixed when they are diurnal on some days and semidiurnal on others.

Hurricanes occur when the atmospheric conditions, tail movements, winds, and pressure change severely. Hurricanes begin with winds moving in a circular motion over bodies of water, picking up both speed and rainy weather conditions. When a hurricane approaches a coastline, the sea level will go 20 feet above normal tide level. The months of June through November are considered hurricane season. August, September, and October normally have more hurricanes documented than any other months with September having the greatest number of hurricanes. May and December, on rare occasions, have logged hurricanes. Hurricanes can cause both property damage and personal damage when they move from the water to land surfaces with a tornado resulting from its wind force as it moves further inland.

A typhoon is a severe storm over the oceans that is made of rain, wind, and water and will affect tidal movements of shorelines of islands near their occurrences.

Currents are water movements in horizontal or vertical flow occurring at differing depths of the water. Currents stabilize the climate of adjacent land areas, preventing extremes of temperatures. Currents are also influenced/affected by the moon and its position relative to the equator.

Density differences may produce both horizontal and vertical movement of water, causing modifications to the wind-driven surface currents. Water tends to flow from an area of low density to an area of high density. Water may tend to become of greater density as the temperature decreases.

Fog is a hydrometer which consists of a visible collection of minute water droplets suspended in the atmosphere near the Earth's surface. It will interfere with the ability to see at a distance over the area that it covers. It is caused by atmospheric humidity and a warm temperature layer being transported over a cold body of water or land surface.

Economics of Earth's Resources

Conservation is the protection and wise management of Earth's resources or natural resources, for the benefit of not only man, but all living things. Without wise practices of conservation and concern for the quality of the environment, all natural resources necessary for life, such as air, animals, energy, minerals, plants, soil, water, and other elemental forms would be damaged, wasted, or destroyed. With greater conservation enforcement, the cost of living will be lower for everyone and more ideal surroundings will be present. The Earth not only has limited resources, but the demands are greater as populations increase, which means there must be a wiser use of Earth's resources if they are to last as long as man or if man is to survive. The cost of man's poor resource management can be life itself.

PART IV: PHYSICS

BASIC CONCEPTS OF PHYSICS

Physics is the study of matter, energy, and the relationships between the two phenomenal areas of study. Relationships between matter and energy have existed as long as the universe has existed, though man has not totally understood all relationships. Every time you lift a baby, push a wheelbarrow, or physically work out, you are demonstrating or applying the principles of physics. Basic principles or concepts of physics may be divided into eight general areas: mechanics (motion and force), energy, magnetism, sound, light, heat, waves, and electricity.

A scientific law is usually constructed after a limited number of experiments or observations have been tried. It summarizes the order that is believed to exist within certain prescribed conditions and can only occasionally be modified or extended to fit new situations. A scientific law is a statement that (1) fits new facts, (2) uses inductive and deductive reasoning, and (3) successfully predicts what is found in nature.

Law of Acceleration

The amount of acceleration is directly proportional to the acting force and inversely proportional to mass:

$F = ma.$

Drop a rock and it falls to the ground. The rock starts its fall from a resting position and gains speed as it falls. This gain in speed indicates the acceleration of the rock as it falls. Gravity (acting force) causes the rock to fall downward once it moves from its resting position. Remember, acceleration is equal to the change in speed divided by the time interval.

Archimedes' Law of Buoyancy or Archimedes' Principle

The relationship between buoyancy and displaced liquid was discovered in ancient times by the Greek philosopher Archimedes in the third century B.C.E. It states that "an immersed object is pushed up by a force equal to the weight of the fluid it displaces." When an object is suspended in water, the pressures on opposite sides cancel each other. The pressure increases with depth, and the upward force on the bottom of the object will be greater than the downward forces on the top. Thus, an object is lighter in water than in air. This relationship, called Archimedes' Principle, is found to be true of both liquids and gases.

Bernoulli's Law

"A moving stream of gas or liquid appears to exert less sideways pressure than if it were at rest." Bernoulli studied the relationship of fluid speed and pressure, and wondered how the fluid got the energy for extra speed. He discovered that the pressure in a fluid decreases as the speed of the fluid increases. This principle is a consequence of the conservation of energy and supports the concept of steady flow. If the flow speed is too great, then it becomes turbulent and follows changing, curling paths known as eddies. Also, this same principle application accounts for the flight of birds and aircraft abilities.

Boyle's Law

If the temperature of a gas remains constant,

$V = 1/P$

where P and V are the pressure and volume, respectively. When the density of the gas increases in a given space, the pressure is increased. The density of the gas also can be doubled by simply compressing the air to half its volume. This law is applied when one inflates a tire, balloon, or any other such object.

Charles' Law

"The volume of gas increases as its temperature increases if the pressure stays the same." Charles' measurements suggested that the volume of a gas would become zero at a temperature of –273°C. Thus, this temperature is called absolute zero. This law applies only to gases. Scientists have found all gases become liquids or solids before they are cooled to the temperature of –273°C. Charles' Law is used to explain the kinetic theory as four factors are needed to describe a gas—the mass, the volume, the pressure, and the temperature. Charles' Law explains the increase in volume within tires after traveling long distances or traveling on hot days.

Hooke's Law

The amount of stretch or compression, x, is directly proportional to the applied force F:

$(x = F)$.

This law is used to explain the property of elasticity. Elasticity is the ability of a body to change shapes when a force is applied and then return to its original shape when that force is removed. Steel is an example of an elastic material. It can be stretched and it can be compressed. Because of its strength and elastic properties, it is used to make springs for construction girders. Also, spring construction and functioning is based on Hooke's Law.

Newton's Laws

Sir Isaac Newton's laws describe how forces change the motion of an object and are stated in the Three Laws of Motion.

The First Law (Law of Inertia) states that every body remains in a state of rest or uniform motion unless acted upon by forces from the outside.

The Second Law (Law of Constant Acceleration) states that the acceleration of an object increases as the amount of net force applied from outside the object increases. The formula of this law is

Force = mass × acceleration

Force = mass × meter divided by seconds squared (m/s^2) = $\dfrac{\text{kg} \cdot \text{m}}{\text{s}^2}$.

Therefore, applying the formula to determine one newton is the force needed to give a mass of one kilogram an acceleration of one meter per second squared, or:

Force (1 newton) = mass 1 (kg) × acceleration (1 m/s^2) 1 N = 1 kg × 1 m/s^2

Newton's Third Law (Law of Conservation of Momentum) states that forces always come in pairs: to every action there is an equal and opposite reaction. When one object exerts a force on a second object, the second object exerts a force that would be equal to and opposite the force of the first object. Mass is a measure of the amount of inertia of a body. The product of mass and velocity is the amount of momentum an object possesses. A quantity that is not changed is said to be conserved. In a collision the total momentum of the colliding bodies is not changed. This is the Law of Conservation of Momentum or Newton's Third Law. Momentum is conserved provided there are no outside forces acting on a set of objects.

Law of Conservation of Energy

Energy cannot be created or destroyed; it changes forms but does not cease to exist. This law explains how energy can change from one form to another. As energy can never be created or destroyed, the total energy of the universe remains the same.

Law of Conservation of Mechanical Energy

In the absence of friction, energy stored in a machine remains constant and work done by the machine is equal to the work done on it. The energy of an object enables it to do work. Mechanical energy is due to the position of something (potential energy) or the movement of something (kinetic energy). Mechanical energy is produced by a machine that is a device for multiplying forces or changing the directions of forces.

Law of Gravitation

Any two bodies in the universe attract each other with a force that is directly proportional to their masses and inversely proportional to the square of their distance apart:

$$F = Gm_1m_2/d^2.$$

Forces are always applied at several different places under normal circumstances, not just at one point. This force on objects found on the Earth is what we call gravity.

Lenz's Law

The direction of an induced current is always such that its magnetic field opposes the operation that causes it. This law is the basis for the design of a generator and its ability to function by converting mechanical energy into electrical energy. A changing magnetic field induces an electric field. A generator uses the electromagnetic induction to convert mechanical energy into electrical energy.

Ohm's Law

The current in a wire is proportional to the potential difference between the ends of the wire:

V (voltage) = I (current) × R (resistance)

Ohm's Law determines the strength of the current that flows into the circuit and the basis for the concept of electrical current. Any path along which electrons can flow is a circuit. A complete circuit is needed to maintain a continuous electron flow.

Law of Reflection

The angle of the incidence equals the angle of reflection. This law explains how a wave changes its direction or how it is reflected back. When light is reflected from a flat surface or plane such as a mirror, the incoming light ray (incident ray) and the reflected ray of light (reflected ray) are measured with respect to a line perpendicular to the flat surface. When a light ray strikes a flat surface, the angle of incidence always equals the angle of reflection. Sunlight is an example showing this law.

Law of Refraction

Light rays passing through a transparent substance are bent, or refracted; the thicker the substance is, the farther apart its actual and apparent locations will be. The law also states that the incident ray and the refracted ray both lie on one plane.

A theory applies to a broad range of phenomena and is applied to a small aspect of nature. A theory attempts to explain the "how's" and "why's" of science. It is in the establishing and testing of theories that discoveries are made. The primary purpose of a theory is to enable us to see a natural phenomenon as a part of a simple, unified whole as it:

1. correlates many facts in a single concept or reasonable assumption;

2. suggests or accommodates new ideas;

3. stimulates research;

4. is useful in solving long-range problems; and

5. makes predictions.

Albert Einstein developed the Theory of Relativity, which is often referred to as Einstein's Theory. The relativity theory is based on mathematical formulas and calculations dealing with gravitation, mass, motion, space, and time. Basic principles of this theory are:

1. Motion in a straight line will have constant velocity. All other motion is judged from this frame of reference.

2. The speed of light in empty space will always have the same value regardless of the motion of the source or the motion of the observer.

Before a hypothesis can be scientific, it must conform to the scientific rule of being testable. Then, one must test by following the scientific method:

1. recognize the problem;

2. formulate your hypothesis;

3. complete related research;

4. perform test-to-test prediction;

5. collect data while performing the test;

6. summarize research and test results in an orderly manner; and

7. draw conclusions.

MATTER, MASS, AND DENSITY

Matter is found in everything. Everything is made of atoms. All matter, living or nonliving, is a combination of elements (atoms). Matter is anything that has mass and occupies space. Matter can exist in four states dependent upon its Brownian Motion: (1) solid, (2) liquid, (3) gas, or (4) plasma, which makes up the greatest quantity of matter.

Mass is the quantity of matter in a body that exhibits a response to any effort (energy or movement) made to start it, stop it, or change in any way its state of motion. Mass is measured by the amount of inertia an object has. The greater the mass, the greater the force necessary to change its state of motion. Mass is often confused with weight. Weight is a specific numerical measurement or unit, while mass is anything that takes up space and has weight.

Density is the measure of compactness of a material. It being as light as a feather or heavy as a rock is dependent upon its density. Density is not mass nor is it volume. Density cannot be equated to size in all cases; rather, it is the compactness of the mass per unit of volume. Both the mass of the atoms making up the substance or material and the spacing between the atoms determine the density of materials or state of materials.

Motion

Motion is all around us. Our bodies, no matter how still we think we are, are in a constant state of motion. Motion is easy to see but almost impossible to describe or define. Therefore, when speaking of motion, one must address it as relative to an object rate.

Velocity

Velocity is the speed in a given direction. Speed and velocity can be used interchangeably if the description is asking for how fast a movement occurs in a certain direction. Velocity can be described as constant or changing. A constant velocity requires that both the speed stay the same and direction not be changed or altered. Motion at constant velocity is motion in a straight line at a constant speed. A body may be moving at a constant speed along a curved path or the speed may vary along a constant path. The latter is referred to as changing velocity.

Acceleration

Acceleration is a rate that applies to a decreasing speed (deceleration) as well as an increasing speed (acceleration). Acceleration applies to a change in direction as well as the change in speed. Pressing the gas pedal of a car will accelerate the speed of the car; pressing the brakes will retard the speed, or decelerate the car. Like velocity, acceleration is directional.

Momentum

Momentum is the mass of an object multiplied by its velocity

momentum = mass $\times$ velocity – $m = m \times v$.

If the momentum of an object changes, either the mass or the velocity or both change. Thus, acceleration occurs.

Gravity causes a rock to fall downward once it has been dropped. This action on movement is referred to as gravitational motion. If there were no gravitational action, the motion would be called free fall. The time that it takes an object to fall from the beginning of the fall to the point of rest is called elapsed time. The concept of gravity effects was first credited to Isaac Newton after he was hit on the head with an apple that fell from a tree he was sitting beneath.

Speed

Speed is a measure of how fast something is moving or the rate at which a distance is being covered. Speed is calculated as the distance covered divided by the unit of time. Speed is the rate of change of the position of an object. The average speed describes the motion of objects even if they are not moving at a constant speed. This average speed can be calculated by the total distance traveled divided by the total time taken for travel.

Inertia

Inertia is the resistance an object has to a change in its state of motion. Inertia can be measured by its mass depending upon the amount and type of matter in it. The idea of inertia while in motion is called momentum in reference to moving objects.

FORCE

Force is the push or pull one body exerts on another body. "For every action, there is an equal and opposite reaction" is another way of describing force. Force is the product of acceleration. The combination of all the forces that act on an object is called the net force. When a body is at rest, a force is at work. The fact that the body is at rest rather than accelerating shows another force at work. Force is necessary to maintain balance and reach net force zero. For a book to be at rest on a table, the sum of the forces acting upon the book must equal zero.

The process of determining the components of a vector is called resolution. A person pushes a lawn mower. This in turn applies force against the ground causing the lawn mower to roll forward. In this example, the vector is a combination of two components. Any vector can be represented by a pair of components that are at right angles to each other.

Friction is the name given to the force that acts between materials that are moving past each other. Friction is a result that arises from irregularities in the surfaces of sliding objects. If no friction was present, a moving object would need no force whatever for its motion to continue. Even for a surface that appears to be smooth, there are microscopic irregularities causing friction to occur.

Parallel

When the forces on two opposite sides are equal, this is said to be a parallel force. Thus, this produces, considering all forces are equal, an action-reaction situation.

ENERGY

Energy is the ability of an object to cause change; energy is the ability to do work. Energy is produced when forces are at work. Objects in motion cause change. The greater the speed, the greater the change that occurs. If you experience an energy surge, then you can work more or move faster. Objects as well as people can have energy. Energy can exist in various forms and can change from one form to another form. This energy and its changes can be measured. The unit of measurement of energy is called a joule.

Energy exists in three states: potential, kinetic, and activation energies. An object possessing energy because of its motion has kinetic energy. The energy that an object has as the result of its position or condition is called potential energy. The energy necessary to transfer or convert potential energy into kinetic energy is called activation energy.

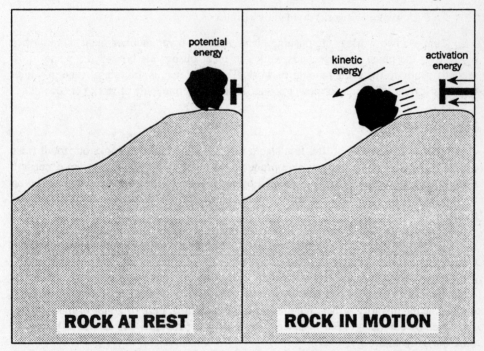

potential energy

kinetic energy

activation energy

ROCK AT REST

ROCK IN MOTION

Study the diagram to see that a rock at rest is considered to be potential energy. If a force is used to set that rock in motion, that force would be the activation energy. The rock rolling down the hill until it reaches a point of rest (potential energy) is considered kinetic energy.

Other forms of energy are a result of conditions or combinations of the states of energy. When kinetic and potential energy of lifting, bending, and stretching are grouped together, they are called mechanical energy. If one considers the total energy of the particles that make up an object or body, this is thermal energy. A raised weight possesses potential energy called gravitational potential energy. When it is released, it will return to its former level. This is the principle applied to the functioning of a spring or stretching an object.

Work is the transfer of energy as the result of motion. Most people think of work as an amount of effort exerted. However, if you attempted to move a boulder without any success, you expended energy but no work was accomplished. Work is a derived unit; it may be expressed as any force unit times any distance unit. The only thing that matters in calculating work is the distance moved in the direction of the force.

A machine is any device by which energy can be transferred from one place to another or one form to another. Think back to the diagram of the rock rolling down the hill. This is an example of a machine. Often, when we think of a machine or using a machine, some outside agent—a motor, a battery, your muscles—does the work on the machine. The machine then delivers work to something on which it acts.

The principle of conservation of mechanical energy deals with the functioning of a machine. This principle dictates how two kinds of work are related. "In the absence of other forces that dissipate energy, the total mechanical energy of a system remains constant." So long as any energy that is stored within a machine remains constant, and in the absence of friction, the work done by the machine is exactly equal to the work done on it.

Power is the rate of doing work per unit of time. This is calculated by:

P (power) = W (work) divided by t (time).

Suppose two workers are pushing identical boxes up an inclined plane. One pushes his box up the plane in 20 seconds while the other pushes his box up the plane in 40 seconds. Both do the same amount of work. The difference is the rate of time in which the work is done. The unit for power is watt. One watt is one joule of work per second.

HEAT

Heat is a necessity of life. It is also a very valuable tool that cooks our food, frees metals from ores, and creates usable products (to mention a few of its uses). Heat is a form of energy and that energy is created by the motion of the molecules making up an object. Heat is the transfer of energy from an object of high temperature to one of lower temperature.

Heat has several properties: it is a conductor, it can be measured, it can be transferred or radiated, and can travel by convection. Nearly all materials will either expand or contract when heat is added or taken away. When the amount of heat within an object or around an object varies, that object will vary. There is an exact point at which the variation will occur. We call this the specific heat. The specific heat of any substance is defined as the quantity of heat required to raise the temperature of a unit of mass of that substance by one degree. For instance, a gram of water requires one calorie of energy to raise the temperature 1°C.

Heat is commonly measured in calories or kilocalories, although scientifically the SI or joule is preferred. SI is the abbreviation of Le Système International d'Unites (French), which is the international system of measurement. The term applied here would be the degree. The degree is a measure of temperature. Temperature is a measure of the average kinetic energy of the particles in a body. The degree might be stated in terms of Fahrenheit (F), Kelvin (K), or Celsius (C).

Celsius is based on the freezing temperature of a body or substance being 0 degrees. To remove all possible internal heat within a body or substance, one must reduce the temperature to −273° C. This point is considered to be 0 on the Kelvin scale and is called absolute zero. The Fahrenheit scale measures the freezing point at 32°F. To convert from the Fahrenheit scale to the Celsius scale use the formula:

$$°C = {}^5/_9 (°F - 32) \quad \text{or} \quad °C = (°F - 32) \div 1.8$$

unless the temperature is below zero on either scale. In that case, you must place a minus sign in front of its number in the equation.

Heat and work are similar when discussing the transfer of energy. Heat is transferred by convection, conduction, or radiation. As work is accomplished, heat is transferred. One way that heat passes from one object to another is by conduction. Not all objects will conduct heat at the same rate; therefore, they are considered poor heat conductors. A very poor conductor of heat is called an insulator.

Most gases and liquids are poor conductors. They can transfer heat by convection, the mass movement of the heated gas or liquid. This is accomplished by spurring, or sporadic movement of molecules in the mass that pass heat when they bump together. Another method of heat transfer is called radiation. Unlike conduction and convection, radiation does not require direct contact between bodies or masses. Almost all of the energy that comes to Earth is by radiation from the sun. The amount of heat that a body can radiate depends not only on its temperature but on the nature of its surface. Dark, rough surfaces tend to send out more heat than smooth, light-colored surfaces.

WAVES

A British physicist, Edward Victor Appleton, received a Nobel Prize in 1947 for his work dealing with waves. His discoveries led to defining an important region of the atmosphere called the "ionosphere." It was established that there were definite layers that would reflect and absorb various radio waves, and thus, the Appleton layers were established. These layers reflect and absorb only the long radio waves used in ordinary radio broadcasts. The shorter waves, used for television broadcasting, pass through, and that is why televisions have a limited range and must use satellite relay stations. The ionosphere is the strongest at the end of the day, after the day-long effect of the sun's radiation, and weakens by dawn because many ions and electrons have recombined. Storms on the sun, intensifying the streams of particles and high-energy radiation sent to the Earth, cause the ionized layers to strengthen and thicken. The regions above the ionosphere also flare up into aurora displays.

A wave is a wiggle in space and time that can extend from one place to another. Light and sound are both forms of energy that move through space as waves. If this wiggle only occurs in time, it is called a vibration. A wave is measured in wavelengths. The high points are called the crests, the low points the troughs, and the distance from the midpoint to the crest is the amplitude. How frequently a vibration occurs is described by its frequency. The time necessary for the wave to complete one cycle is called a period.

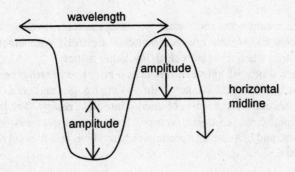

LIGHT

The only thing that we can really see is light. Most objects are made visible by the light they reflect from such light sources. Scientists agree that light has a dual nature—part particle and the other part wave. The particles may be measured as photons. The waves are measured by the distance the light travels in one year. This is called a light year. Light is defined as the only visible portion of the electromagnetic spectrum. Light is produced by vibrating electrically charged atoms that have the ability to absorb energy and emit it as light. The transfer of energy by electromagnetic waves is called radiation.

Properties

The properties of light are reflection, refraction, diffraction, and interference. The amount of the property being demonstrated depends on the amount of light, angle of the light ray, object composition and density. Material that allows all the light to pass through is called transparent. Material that blocks the light is called opaque.

Quantum is an elemental unit that describes the smallest amount of anything. One quantum of light energy is called a photon. In the micro-world, one quantum of anything is an atom. The Quantum Theory is the study of the behavior of the basic elemental form of anything. This can be adapted to all branches of science to explain behavior of matter.

Reflection occurs when a wave bounces off an object. Waves that strike the object are called incident waves, while waves that bounce off are called reflected waves. The angle between the reflected wave and the normal is called the angle of reflection. When the waves are reflected from a surface, the angle of incidence always equals the angle of reflection.

Refraction is the bending of waves toward the direction of slower wave velocity. When wavelengths become shorter, the frequency does not change. Thus, the material will determine the amount of light that is refracted.

Diffraction

The bending of light around the edge of the object blocking its path is called diffraction. The effects of diffraction occur when waves pass either through an opening or around an object that blocks their path.

Light travels in waves that are transverse. This is called polarization. Other waves are longitudinal as they travel. Polarized light waves are waves that travel on one plane. Light vibrating parallel to a molecule is absorbed. The light vibrating at right angles to the rows passes through. This concept is used in the sunglass industry—sunglass lenses are designed to reduce glare.

Illumination is the process of making an object bright by increasing the amount of light per unit of area of a surface.

X-rays are electromagnetic waves with the shortest wavelength and the highest amount of energy. Electrically charged particles are filled with kinetic energy that is changed to radiation when these rays crash into other matter.

Lasers are a source of light that produces a bright and narrow beam of light of one color length and is coherent. Coherent light has the troughs and crests of the light lined up together. Lasers convert one form of energy into light energy. The laser is very bright but extremely inefficient as a light source. They are used extensively by surveyors, welders, surgeons, and by code interpreters for barcoding, as a method of ringing up sales at the supermarket.

SOUND

Sound travels about 4.5 times faster in seawater than in air. Its speed is affected by temperature, salinity, and pressure; an increase in any of these results in an increase in the speed of sound.

Sound energy does not travel in straight lines in the ocean because of density differences in water. It is refracted, or bent, by variations in sound speed of the water, scattered by suspended material or marine organisms, reflected and scattered by the surface and bottom, and attenuated by the water through which it travels.

Ambient noise refers to any noise or sound produced by the environment or living creatures or organisms.

There are many varieties of sounds that are produced to be captured by the ear and interpreted by the brain. The brain easily distinguishes one sound from another, yet sound is only a longitudinal wave, a rhythmic disturbance of the air that carries energy. Sound waves are compression waves produced by vibrating matter. Ultrasound is used extensively in medical treatment. One way is through picturing a fetus in the womb without any danger to the fetus or the mother.

When any frequency of forced vibrations on an object matches the natural frequency of the object, the measure of the sound increases. The use of tuning forks adjusted to the same frequency and spaced a meter apart is the most common way to demonstrate resonance.

ELECTRICITY

An electrical charge resting on an object is called static electricity. If this static electricity is placed in motion, it becomes an electrical current. It is the electrical current that we use in most electrical appliances. This same static electricity can be produced by rubbing a hard rubber rod or sealing wax with a piece of fur or flannel. Also, the same result can be accomplished by rubbing a glass rod with a piece of silk.

Electricity can be carried by matter that is a conductor. Sometimes this is accomplished by a spark, which is a static discharge, or a transfer of static electricity. Materials that are poor conductors, such as wood, plastic, rubber, or glass, are used as insulators or grounds which allow an object to lose its charge in a given direction.

A flow of electrons or charged particles through a conductor is called an electric current. This is demonstrated by use of an electroscope.

Electrical circuits function very efficiently within homes. Most circuits are either alternating current (AC) or direct current (DC). Electricity can be supplied to a water heater to heat water, or through wiring and a bulb to produce artificial light. The energy is carried by means of electrical current from a power plant. One common electrical circuit is the series circuit. A path is formed by electric conductors in the form of wire to carry the current. The series circuit has only one path for the current so the current will be the same through every part.

Another circuit is the parallel circuit, in which there are two or more separate branches for the current to flow. This is the type of circuit used in string lights for a Christmas tree such that when one light goes out, the rest of the lights will stay on. Also, this type of wiring pattern is used for the outlets in our homes. It is not necessary for all the outlets to be in use at all times for electricity to be available at the flip of a switch.

One electronic device that is commonly used is the battery. A battery acts like a pump forcing electrons through a conductor. There are two types of batteries: wet cell battery and dry cell battery. A wet cell battery contains two different metals in a solution containing an electrode. The car battery is an example of the wet cell battery. The dry cell battery contains a carbon rod set in the middle of a zinc holder. A moist paste sets up a chemical reaction that causes electrons to be released.

MAGNETISM

Magnetism is the ability to attract iron and certain other metals that have a molecular structure similar to iron. Magnetism is related to electricity in that it travels in currents. Magnets exert a force on another magnet just like an electrical charge. They can attract or repel each other without touching because of their electrical charges. The strength of their interaction depends on the distance of separation of the two magnets.

Magnetism was explained by Albert Einstein in 1905 in his theory of special relativity when he showed that a magnetic field is a by-product of the electric field. Charges in motion have associated with them both an electric and a magnetic field. A magnetic field is produced by the motion of the electric charge.

A voltmeter is a calibrated device used to measure the electric potential. This electrical current produces a magnetic field. The same principal construction is used in the making of an electric motor. The principal difference is that the current is made to change direction every time the coil makes a half revolution.

Speakers used in car radios, home stereos, and loudspeaker systems belong in the grouping of electromagnets. A speaker consists of a coil of thin wire that goes between the poles of a magnet. The coil is attached to a cone-shaped piece of stiff paper that converts the electrical current into sound.

SCIENCE

PRACTICE QUESTIONS

1. Which cellular component is responsible for the regulation of exchanges of substances between a cell and its environment?

    (A) The endoplasmic reticulum

    (B) The cell nucleus

    (C) The cytoplasm

    (D) The cell membrane

2. Genetic information that needs to move out of the nucleus can not leave by way of the DNA. Therefore, it is carried out by the

    (A) tRNA.   (C) tDNA.

    (B) mDNA.   (D) mRNA.

3. A nucleotide consists of

    (A) a sugar, a protein, and uracil.

    (B) a sugar, a phosphate group, and a nitrogenous base.

    (C) a starch, a nitrogenous base, and a sugar.

    (D) a protein, a starch, and a sugar.

4. Matter is group-based on its ability to

    (A) react with itself in the presence of other elements.

    (B) be studied.

    (C) react and combine with other elements.

    (D) change.

5. For a chemical equilibrium involving gaseous reactants and products, an increase in pressure

    (A) always displaces the equilibrium in the direction in which the number of molecules decrease.

    (B) displaces the equilibrium to form more of the reactants.

    (C) displaces the equilibrium to form more of the products.

    (D) has no effect on the equilibrium.

6. "Planets move around the sun because of the gravitational force exerted by the sun" is part of which scientist's theory?

   (A) Aristotle   (C) Einstein

   (B) Newton   (D) Hipparchus

7. The sun has a mass of 750 times greater than

   (A) all terrestrial planets.

   (B) the four largest planets.

   (C) the Earth, moon, and sun combined.

   (D) all planets combined.

8. Charles' Law can be used to explain

   (A) why car tires are slightly larger after a long trip on a hot day.

   (B) how a liquid-filled thermometer works.

   (C) why a bottle of water cracks when it freezes.

   (D) how large amounts of gas are stored in small containers.

9. Most of the matter of the universe is in which state?

   (A) Liquid   (C) Gas

   (B) Solid   (D) Plasma

10. Cellular respiration occurs in the

   (A) golgi apparatus   (C) mitochondria

   (B) nucleus   (D) lungs

SCIENCE

ANSWERS TO PRACTICE QUESTIONS

1.	**(D)**	6.	**(B**
2.	**(D)**	7.	**(D)**
3.	**(B)**	8.	**(A)**
4.	**(A)**	9.	**(D)**
5.	**(A)**	10.	**(C)**

MSAT

Multiple Subjects Assessment for Teachers

CHAPTER 6

Visual and Performing Arts Review

Chapter 6

Visual and Performing Arts Review

The Visual and Performing Arts section of the MSAT focuses on the four major disciplines of the arts: visual arts, dance, music, and drama. This section accounts for 10 percent of the overall exam—14 of the 134 multiple-choice questions, and 2 of the Content Area Exercises. While this is not a large portion of the test, it does cover a wide variety of material with which you should be familiar. The Visual and Performing Arts portion of the test has three elements:

Aesthetic Perception / Creative Expression (40 percent)
- Basic art elements, vocabulary, and principles

Cultural Heritage (40 percent)
- Relationships of artwork to one another, and to their historical and geographical context
- Differentiation among various styles, movements and schools

Aesthetic Valuing
- Development of aesthetic criteria
- Interpretation of a work's meaning

The following review addresses each of these points directly in both historical and comparitive contexts. The test questions may require you to blend knowledge of more than one of the artistic disciplines, however they usually are more concerned with a general understanding of aesthetic principles than names and dates of specific artists, works of art, etc.

AESTHETIC PERCEPTION AND CREATIVE EXPRESSION

The visual and performing arts have served to express humanity's basic spiritual beliefs and the need to organize its environment from prehistoric times to the present. Seventeen thousand years ago, before cities and settled villages, paleolithic people at Lascaux (modern France)—and at Altimira (modern Spain) about 2,000 years later—

Venus of Willendorf
c. 25,000–20,000 BC Stone Museum of Natural History, Vienna

produced realistic animal paintings on cave walls in an attempt to capture the essences of the creatures they hunted and encountered. The urge to create art existed even earlier in the paleolithic period, and numerous small female figures (now called Venuses) and carved weapons dating from perhaps as early as 30,000 B.C. have been discovered in Europe. Megalithic structures, such as Stonehenge in England, and monuments of ancient civilizations, such as the Egyptian pyramids, were precisely calculated architectural forms that answered sophisticated needs of astronomical calculation, paid homage to the mysteries and power of the sun and stars, and attempted to master the passage to the afterlife. Tribal people throughout history have used dance and music to control their environment, communicate with animals, and comprehend the unseen world, as well as to merely celebrate, and have produced masks, weavings, textiles, pottery, and jewelry of harmonious form and color and complex abstract patterns.

Beginning with the first great civilized society, the Sumerians in Mesopotamia more than 5,000 years ago, the peoples of the world have continued on a consistent path in the area of fine, applied, and performing arts. Visual fine art has come to mean a self-conscious creation of aesthetically sophisticated works, usually by one individual, in an attempt to further knowledge, expand style and technology, and create beauty. Applied art is practical and often evolves directly from the needs, culture, and tastes of a community; crafts and decorative art, utilitarian or commercial objects in which quality of technique is primary, are examples. Increasingly, the lines between fine art and craft have become blurred, so that it is no longer necessary to arbitrarily enthrone a work of art merely because it is, for example, a painting rather than a piece of pottery or jewelry. In the performing arts, folk dance and music are a natural outgrowth of a community's recreational, entertainment, celebratory, and ritualistic needs. The great masterpieces of ballet, opera, and classical music each represent the conscious manipulation of form and idea in a new way to create an individualistic work, usually for the purposes of an audience's edification and amusement.

All of the arts on all levels may be judged as either successful or not, as good or mediocre, and have a beauty and legitimacy that operates on an aesthetic level and arises from its culture.

The visual and performing arts basically encompass the categories of sculpture, architecture, painting and graphics, music, dance, and theater. Each of these has its own rules and requirements and aesthetic appeal, its own distinct way of satisfying a basic human means of expression.

Sculpture is concerned with molding shapes in three-dimensional forms. Sculptures may be cast—molten metals poured into molds to create cast-bronze figures—and such works would include ancient Greek statues of warriors, equestrian monuments of the Italian Renaissance, Auguste Rodin's *Thinker*, and Frederic Bartholdi's enormous Statue of Liberty. They may also be carved—from wood, stone, or marble—shaped from clay, or in the twentieth century, welded together from metal pieces.

Painting is a two-dimensional means of re-creating reality or arranging abstract forms in color on a flat surface. Surfaces have traditionally been walls, wooden panels, canvas, paper and parchment, even decorative objects such as vases. The color is usually applied with a brush, using pigments mixed with media such as linseed oil or water. Types of painting include watercolor, oil, tempera, and acrylic; for frescoes, pigments are applied directly over wet plaster to seal in the art on a wall or ceiling. Other two-dimensional art, in color or black and white, are **drawing**—with graphite (pencil), ink applied by pen or brush, and chalk or crayons—and **printmaking.** In etching, woodcuts, lithographs, and the many variations on these methods, multiple copies of a drawing are made by creating either a raised or recessed surface (metal, wood, or stone) that takes ink and pressing paper against the surface.

Architecture is the conscious organization of space and form to provide a structure for living, working, worshipping, or for other residential or civic needs. Great architecture has always been intimately connected with new technologies and building materials, as well as with the immediate cultural needs of a community, city, or nation. Gothic cathedrals, for example, soar to the heavens with massive vertical elements to reflect the religious devotion of medieval Europe. The simple shapes and unadorned facades of many twentieth-century buildings reveal a fascination with the era's ease of using such materials as glass, steel, and concrete and a rejection of what was considered the overly decorated architecture of the previous century.

Dance is an art form based on physical movement and expression—by humans singly, or in couples or groups. Folk and tribal dancing are often related to communal celebration or religious ritual. Dance created to entertain an audience by one person may be choreographed and worked out in strict steps and gestures, such as in ballet or musical theater.

Music is the arrangement of sounds for voice and musical instruments, and, like dance, requires training and repetitive practice. For most of history, music has been an outgrowth of a community's or an ethnic group's need to celebrate, and has often been linked to story-telling or poetry. Traditional instruments have been indigenous variations on drums, horns, pipes (such as flutes), and hollow boxes fitted with vibrating strings (such as lyres or lutes). In Europe, a system of musical notation developed during the Middle Ages, and the use of notation (written symbolic indications of pitch and duration of tones) is a convenient way to distinguish "art" (or classical, or complexly composed) music from folk and ethnic music. Since the seventeenth century, orchestral instruments of the West have multiplied to include pianos, saxophones, clarinets, cellos, and in our own era, electronic synthesizers.

Theater is the performance, for the sake of an audience's education or entertainment, of a story, usually of drama, comedy, or some combination thereof. The West's tradition of theater originated chiefly with the ancient Greeks—the tragedies of Aeschylus and Sophocles, the comedies of Aristophanes—and many feel reached its high point in the late sixteenth and early seventeenth centuries in England with the plays of William Shakespeare, who is revered throughout the world for his mastery of the form. Theater requires vocal declamation, acting, costumes, sometimes masks, usually a scenic backdrop or constructed set, and poetic expression. Music is often an integral part of the performance as well. Theater may be said to encompass all the art forms, since a theatrical production of ballet, opera, or musical drama/comedy can include all the disciplines, employing set decoration, costuming, dance, song, and instrumental music.

CULTURAL HERITAGE

Artistic expression in dance, theater, music, and the visual arts has undergone many stylistic changes in the passing centuries of the world's civilizations. It can be affected by the era's spirit, by evolving economic and social changes, and by religion. The form the art takes, and the way it fits into the lives of a people, depends on its geographical source and the ethnic group from which it originates. For example, one form of dance in Europe by the seventeenth century evolved into the sophisticated high-art form of ballet, which is both entertaining and cerebral. In India, four types of dance are considered classical, but these have very different forms and purposes than European ballet. Even within a society, the representations and needs of an art form change with the cultural forces of an age. While the religious-symbolic paintings, sculptures, and manuscript illuminations of the Middle Ages saw no need to relate human beings realistically to each other in size, or place them in a natural-looking environment or realistic space, the Renaissance artists, seeing humans as the center of the universe and seeking rational knowledge, depicted a world of visual beauty, of perfectly observed persons in perfectly proportioned environments.

In theater, twentieth-century drama may emphasize psychological portraits of individuals and realistic dialogue. But the ancient Greeks sought to portray—using masks and chorus (a group of dancer-singers) commentary on the main action—great themes of fate, honor, and pride. In the tradition of Japanese Noh plays, which originated in the fifteenth century and derive from Zen Buddhism, five plays separated by three comic interludes are marked by stylized acting, masks, mime, and folk dance.

In music, the system of tonal scales and preferences are often unique to a culture: for example, the Chinese prefer the pentatonic scale of five notes, while the West has primarily used a scale of seven notes (eight with the repeated first note for an octave). Indian musical pieces are often built upon *ragas* (meaning "mood" or "color"), which are melodic patterns of five to seven tones. Indian compositions feature repetitive patterns and use scales whose octaves have 22 intervals, or steps.

Architecture is related to the most basic needs of a society and the technology and materials available to a culture or in a geographic location. Because the ancient Egyptians needed grandeur in their funerary monuments and they were able to master the complicated calculations to perfectly cut and arrange huge stones, the magnificent pyramids were created. Architecture is the measure of the prevailing philosophy of an age. The Renaissance architects, for example, sought to express their rediscovery of ancient humanism and search for knowledge, as well as their new-found joy in earthly life and beauty, through the application of perfect proportions, the use of classical engineering techniques, and by perfecting of the art of constructing domes.

HISTORICAL SURVEY

Visual Arts

Paleolithic people in Europe painted animal pictures on the cave walls at Lascaux and Altimira about 15,000-13,000 B.C. Some examples of even older art, dating from 30,000 to 20,000 B.C., are the various "Venuses"—small stylized stone carvings of women as symbols of fertility, found in modern France, Italy, and Austria. The artists of the ancient civilizations of Sumer, Babylon, and Assyria were skilled in carving even the hardest rocks, such as granite and basalt, into narratives of battles and historical records. Egyptian statues, like their architectural monuments the pyramids, were often of colossal size, to further exalt the power of the society's leaders and gods. The art of ancient Greece has its roots in the Minoan civilization on the island of Crete, which flourished about 2500-1400 B.C.: the palace at Knossos is known for characteristic wall paintings revealing a people enamored of games, leisure, and the beauty of the sea. The mainland Greeks of the classical period, about a thousand years later, were fascinated by physical beauty. Their Olympian gods were fashioned in the human image, and a universe of perfection, guided by a master plan, was re-created in their idealized and gracefully proportioned sculptures, architecture, and paintings. In the Hellenistic period, these various objects came to be appreciated as art, for their beauty alone.

The culture of Rome excelled in engineering and building, whose purpose it was to efficiently organize a vast empire and provide an aesthetic environment for private and public use. The Romans built temples, roads, bath complexes, civic buildings, palaces, and aqueducts. One of the greatest of their artistic and engineering accomplishments was the massive-domed temple of all the gods, the Pantheon, which is today one of the most perfectly preserved of all classical-period buildings.

The early Christian period era borrowed the basilica form of Roman architecture for its churches, particularly evident in churches in the town of Ravenna in northeast Italy. The seventh-century church of San Vitale echoes the mosaic mastery of the eastern Roman, or Byzantine, empire in Constantinople (which flourished as a center of civilization for a thousand years after the decline of Rome). Its grandiose apse mosaic depicts Emperor Justinian and Empress Theodora.

The Romanesque style of art and architecture was preeminent from about 800 to 1200. By then many local styles, including the decorative arts of the Byzantines, the Near East, and the German and Celtic tribes, were contributing to European culture. Common features of Romanesque churches are round arches, vaulted ceilings, and heavy walls that are profusely decorated—primarily with symbolic figures of Christianity, the realism of which for its creators had became less and less important and was, instead, subordinate to the message.

View from the Apse of San Vitale, Ravenna, Italy 526 B.C.–47 A.D.

Gothic art flourished in Europe for the next 300 years. The cathedrals in this style are some of the purest expressions of an age. They combine a continued search for engineering and structural improvement with stylistic features that convey a relentless verticality, a reach toward heaven, and the unbridled adoration of God. Soaring and airy, these cathedrals were constructed using such elements as flying buttresses and pointed arches and vaults, and were decorated by a profusion of sculptures and stained-glass windows that were, for the worshippers, visual encyclopedias of Christian teachings and stories.

The Italian Renaissance's roots are found as early as the 1300s, when the painter Giotto began to compose his figures into groups and depict expressive human gestures. During the fifteenth century, art, architecture, literature, and music were invigorated. Renaissance artists developed new forms and revived classical styles and values, with the belief in the importance of human experience on Earth. Great sculptors approached true human characterization and realism. Lorenzo Ghiberti created the bronze doors of the Florence Baptistry (early fifteenth century) and Donatello produced *Gattamelata*, the first equestrian statue since the Roman era.

Architecture, in the hands of Filippo Brunelleschi and Leon Battista Alberti, revived the Greek elements and took a scientific, ordered approach, one similarly expressed in painting, with the emphasis on the calculated composition of figures in space known as perspective. The Renaissance artists sought to produce works of perfect beauty and engaged in a constant search for knowledge, most often portraying religious subjects and wealthy patrons. The stylistic innovations of such fifteenth-century painters as Masaccio, Paolo Uccello, Fra Angelico, Piero della Francesca, Andrea Mantegna, and Sandro Botticelli were built upon in the High Renaissance of the next century.

Art became more emotional and dramatic, color and movement were heightened, compositions were more vigorous, and there were increased references to classical iconography and the pleasures of an idyllic golden age. These aspects can be seen in Michelangelo's magnificent Sistine Chapel frescoes and his powerful sculptures of *David* and *Moses,* Leonardo's *Mona Lisa,* Raphael's *School of Athens* fresco, and the increasingly dramatic and colorful works of the Venetian and northern Italian masters Titian, Correggio, Giorgione, and Bellini. The northern European Renaissance also emphasized a renewed interest in the visible world, and works by Albrecht Dürer, Lucas Cranach, Matthias Grunewald, and Albrecht Altdorfer reveal an emphasis on the symbolism of minutely observed details and accurate realism based on observation of reality rather than prescribed rules.

Presaged by the works of the Venetian artist Tintoretto (the radiating *Last Supper*) and El Greco in Spain (*View of Toledo; The Immaculate Conception*), the baroque period of the seventeenth century produced artists who added heightened drama to the forms of Renaissance art. Caravaggio (*The Calling of Saint Matthew; The Conversion of Saint Paul*) and the sculptor Gianlorenzo Bernini (*Saint Teresa in Ecstasy*) in Italy; the Flemish masters Peter Paul Rubens (*Marie de Medici Lands at Marseilles)* and Jacob Jordaens portrayed figures in constant motion, draperies of agitated angles, and effects of lighting and shadow that amplified emotional impact and mystery.

In this spirit followed such painters of court life and middle-class portraiture as Velazquez, Rembrandt, Anthony Van Dyck, and Frans Hals. Rembrandt used expressive brushwork and mysterious light contrasts to enliven genre painting and portraiture, particularly of groups. Rembrandt's influence has remained potent, since his art appears to impart universal truths, and sections of his compositions glow with a mysterious inner light often unrelated to realistic effects (*The Night Watch,* many self-portraits).

The art of the early eighteenth century is often called rococo. Painters like Jean-Antoine Watteau (*Embarkation for Cythera*), Giambattista Tiepolo (frescoes of the Wurzberg Residenz), Francois Boucher, and Jean-Honore Fragonard, often for decorative wall and ceiling schemes, turned the agitated drama of the baroque into light, pastel-toned, swirling compositions that seem placed in an idyllic land of a golden age. In the seventeenth and eighteenth centuries, European artists also responded to middle-class life and everyday objects and created genre paintings (Jan Vermeer, Adriaen van Ostade, Jean-Baptiste Chardin). Jean-Baptiste Greuze in France and William Hogarth in England endowed their everyday subjects with a wealth of narrative detail that aimed to impart a specific moral message.

Such narrative art combined in the nineteenth century with romantic literature— Goethe, Byron, Shelley, Scott, Wordsworth, and others—and political events to produce works with a political point of view or a story to tell, in a variety of styles. Jacques-Louis David used a severe classical sculptural style (neoclassical) in his paintings to revive classical art and ennoble images of the French Revolution and Napoleon's empire (*The Death of Marat; The Oath of the Horatii; Napoleon in His Study*). Neoclassical sculpture

The Death of Marat
Jacques Louis David, 1793. Royal Museums of Fine Arts, Brussels.

revived the aloof severity and perfection of form of ancient art (Jean-Antoine Houdon, Antonio Canova, Bertel Thorvaldsen, Horatio Greenough)—a style also reflected in Thomas Jefferson's architectural designs for his Monticello home and the University of Virginia.

The Spanish painter Francisco de Goya commented powerfully on political events in his painting *May 3, 1808*. In France, Eugene Delacroix (*The Death of Sardanapalus; Liberty Leading the People*) and Theodore Gericault (*The Raft of the Medusa*) imbued subjects from literature, the Bible, exotic lands, and current events with dramatic and heroic intensity. The grandeur and transcendence of nature, the emotional reaction to inner dreams and metaphysical truths of romanticism are seen in the work of such mystical artists as England's William Blake, Henry Fuselli, and John Martin, and America's Thomas Cole. Caspar David Friedrich in Germany and the English Pre-Raphaelites (William Holman Hunt, John Everett Millais, Dante Gabriel Rossetti, Ford Madox Brown, Arthur Hughes, and others) endowed their keenly observed, minutely detailed works with a romantic spirit of poetic yearning and literary references, and accurately re-created the natural world in brilliantly colored landscapes.

In the first half of the nineteenth century, landscape painting in England reached a zenith with the works with Constable and Turner. Turner's awe-inspiring landscapes form a bridge between the spirit of romanticism and the expressionistic brushwork and realism of the Barbizon School in France, whose chief painters were Charles Daubigny and Jean-Baptiste-Camille Corot. Beginning with Barbizon, the French painters of the nineteenth century concentrated more and more on the reporterlike depiction of everyday life and the natural environment in a free, painterly (gesture and brushwork) style.

The realist pioneers were Gustave Courbet (*The Stone Breakers; A Burial at Ormans*), Jean-Francois Millet (*The Sower; The Angelus*), and Honore Daumier (*The Third-Class Carriage*). Renowned as a political caricaturist, Daumier's chief medium was the lithograph and paved the way for the stylistic and subject innovations of the Impressionists. Traditional means of composing a picture, academic methods of figure modeling, of color relations, and accurate and exact rendering of people and objects, were rejected in favor of an art that emphasized quickly observed and sketched moments from life, the relation of shapes and forms and colors, the effects of light, and the act of painting itself.

Beginning with Edouard Manet (*Le Dejeuner sur l'Herbe; Olympia*) in the 1860s, French artists continually blurred the boundaries of realism and abstraction, and the landscapes and everyday-life paintings of such Impressionist artists as Claude Monet, Camille Pissarro, Auguste Renoir, Alfred Sisley, and Edgar Degas gave way to the more experimental arrangements of form and color of the great Postimpressionists—Paul Gauguin, Vincent Van Gogh, Georges Seurat, and Toulouse-Lautrec. Auguste Rodin produced powerful sculptures with the freedom of Impressionist style.

Greatly influenced by Japanese art and particularly the flattened space, distinctive shapes, and strong colors of Japanese woodblock prints, artists from Manet and Degas to the American Impressionist Mary Cassatt, from Toulouse-Lautrec to the Nabis (Edouard Vuillard, Pierre Bonnard, and Maurice Denis) used paintings, pastels, and lithography to further break down the boundaries between representational art and abstraction. The new freer form of art, centered around the personality of the artist and celebrating personal style and the manipulation of form and color, in the late nineteenth and early twentieth century evolved in a number of directions.

Some artists turned inward to explore mystical, symbolic, and psychological truths: Symbolists, Expressionists, and exponents of art nouveau, such as Odilon Redon, Jan Toorop, Edvard Munch (*The Scream*), James Ensor (*The Entry of Christ into Brussels*), Gustav Klimt (*The Kiss*), Ernst Kirchner, Max Pechstein. Others pursued formal innovations, among them Paul Cezanne, Henri Matisse, Pablo Picasso, Georges Braque, and Juan Gris. Picasso's Cubism (*Les Demoiselles d'Avignon*) seemed the most direct call for the total destruction of realistic depiction; his use of African and Oceanic tribal art, and his emphasis on taking objects apart and reassembling them—thus showing a subject's multiplicity of aspects and dissolving time and space—led to similar experiments by Fernand Leger, Marcel Duchamp, the sculptors Alexander Archipenko and Jacques Lipchitz, and the Italian Futurist Umberto Boccioni (*Unique Forms of Continuity in Space*).

Pure abstraction, with little or no relation to the outside world, was approached in the more emotional, expressionistic, and color-oriented paintings of Wassily Kandinsky, Roger Delauney, and Paul Klee. More cerebral arrangements of abstract geometrical shapes and colors were the mark of Kasimir Malevich, Piet Mondrian, and the Bauhaus School of Design in Germany, whose stripped-down, simplified, and usually geometrically-oriented aesthetic influenced architecture, industrial and commercial design, sculpture and the graphic arts for half a century.

In architecture can be seen the most obvious results of this new tradition, from the simplified, sleek structures of Le Corbusier and Walter Gropius to the boxlike glass

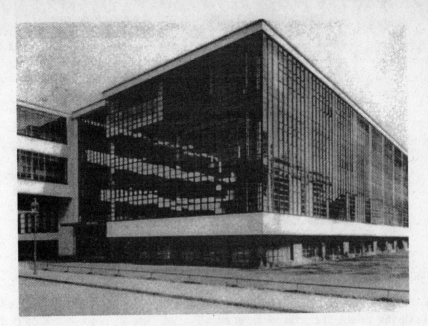

Shop Block, The Bauhaus.
Walter Gropius. 1925–26, Dessau, Germany

skyscrapers of Philip Johnson. The pioneering giant of twentieth-century architecture was Frank Lloyd Wright, whose rejection of eclectic decorative styles of the previous century's architecture and use of new engineering techniques paralleled the Bauhaus aesthetic. From the early 1900s, Wright's buildings (the Robie House, Fallingwater, and Tokyo's Imperial Hotel) exhibited a personal and bold originality, based on a philosophy of "organic architecture," a belief that the form of a structure should be dictated by its natural surroundings, purpose, and building materials.

Inspired by the psychoanalytic writings of Sigmund Freud and Carl Jung, the subconscious and the metaphysical became another important element in art, especially in the work of the Surrealist artists Salvador Dali (*The Persistence of Memory*), Giorgio de Chirico, Max Ernst, Rene Magritte, Joan Miro, and Yves Tanguy. Important sculptors who manipulated abstract shapes and were influenced by tribal arts in the twentieth century include Constantin Brancusi, Henry Moore, Hans Arp, and Alberto Giacometti; Alexander Calder created floating assemblies called mobiles, and Louise Nevelson made constructions and wall sculptures from scraps of everyday objects.

Obsession with self and with abstraction also led to the major American art movement after World War II, known as Abstract Expressionism. The chief proponents of this style were Clifford Still, Jackson Pollock, Willem de Kooning, and Robert Motherwell. Other Americans took this movement into the area of color-field painting, a cooler, more reserved formalism of simple shapes and experimental color relationships. Artists in this movement include Mark Rothko, Barnett Newman, Joseph Albers, and Ad Reinhardt.

Other important trends in American art in the twentieth century were reflective of a democratic and consumer society. The muralists and social realists between the wars created art that was physically interesting and whose subjects were accessible to the average person. John Sloan, George Bellows, Edward Hopper, Thomas Hart Benton, Grant Wood, and John Stuart Curry were among those who celebrated the American

Three Flags
Jasper Johns, 1958. Collection of Mr. and Mrs. Burton Tremaine, Meriden, CT.

scene in paintings, and frequently in murals for public buildings and through widely available fine prints. The great Mexican muralists, who usually concentrated on political themes—Diego Rivera, Jose Clemente Orozco, and David Siqueiros—brought their work to the public both in Mexico and in the United States. The icons of American popular culture found their way, in the movement known as Pop Art, into canvases by Andy Warhol, Robert Indiana, Larry Rivers, Jasper Johns, Roy Lichtenstein, and Robert Rauschenberg.

Music

In the ancient world, Egyptian, Sumerian, and Hebrew cultures used song and such instruments as lyres, harps, drums, flutes, cymbals, and trumpets. The ancient Greeks accompanied the recitation of poetry with the stringed lyre, and Athenian drama was accompanied by the *aulos* or double-piped oboe (an instrument used in the worship of Dionysus), and choral songs were heard between recited passages.

In the early Christian era, plainsong, or unaccompanied religious chant, was codified and arranged, with early forms of music notation, by Pope Gregory the Great (late sixth century). This is the origin of Gregorian chant. By the twelfth and thirteenth centuries, the important form of polyphony, upon which the distinctive art music of the West is based, enabled supportive melodies to be added to the main chant. The basic form of music notation, representing pitch through the use of a staff, was invented by the Italian Benedictine monk Guido d'Arezzo. Throughout the later Middle Ages both religious and secular polyphonic music was composed, and melodies and rhythms became more diversified: new musical forms included the ballade, the rondeau, and the virelai of the troubadours. The first polyphonic setting of the Catholic mass was composed by Guillaume de Machaut in the fourteenth century.

During the Renaissance, the spirit of humanism and rationalism pervaded polyphonic music, technical problems of composition were eagerly resolved, and music began to be seen as a mark of culture. More and more emphasis was placed upon secular music and dance and instrumental music ensembles, as well as on increasingly complex combinations of voices and instruments. Major composers were Giovanni da Palestrina, Josquin des Pres, Orlando di Lasso, William Byrd, and Giovanni Gabrieli.

Baroque music of the seventeenth and early eighteenth centuries employed a greater complexity of contrapuntal, or multimelodic, form, and the beginnings of harmony, the use of colorful instrumental ensembles, and great drama and emotion. The new dramatic forms became popular entertainment, particularly the operas of Claudio Monteverdi (*The Coronation of Poppea*). Other innovative forms included the oratorio, the cantata, the sonata, the suite, the concerto, and the fugue. The great works of baroque music were composed by Dietrich Buxtehude, Johann Pachelbel, Alessandro Scarlatti, Antonio Vivaldi (*The Four Seasons*), Henry Purcell, Jean Phillipe Rameau, George Frederic Handel (*The Messiah; Israel in Egypt*) and Johann Sebastian Bach (Brandenberg concertos; *Saint Matthew Passion*).

The greatest composers of the classical period of the latter half of the eighteenth century, marked by clarity of form, logical thematic development, and strict adherence to sonata form, were Franz Joseph Haydn and Wolfgang Amadeus Mozart. Mozart's structurally exquisite works approach perfection of form while adding to music inventive melodic diversity. Mozart wrote 41 symphonies, as well as such innovative operas as *The Marriage of Figaro* and *The Magic Flute.* The German composer Ludwig van Beethoven (Fifth and Ninth symphonies, *Moonlight* and *Pathetique* sonatas) ushered in the romantic school of symphonic music. His symphonies and piano sonatas, concertos, and string quartets explode with dramatic passion, expressive melodies and harmonies, and complex thematic development.

Much of the romantic music that followed was less formal and more expressive, often associated with grandiose concepts and literary themes, and increasingly more colorful instrumentally. Art songs, piano concertos and sonatas, and symphonic poems (which seek to paint a musical picture or tell a story) became important forms for romantic composers. These included Fredric Chopin (mainly piano music, some of which he called nocturnes), Hector Berlioz (*Symphonie Fantastique; Les Troyans*), Franz Liszt (*Mephisto Waltz,* piano concertos), Richard Strauss (*Also Sprach Zarathustra, Don Juan,* the operas *Salome* and *Elektra*), and Felix Mendelssohn (four symphonies, incidental music to *A Midsummer Night's Dream*). Other important symphonic composers of the nineteenth century were Robert Schumann, Johannes Brahams, Peter Ilich Tchaikovsky, and Gustav Mahler.

Throughout the century, musical development continued in the direction of a greater richness of harmony, a more varied use of musical instruments and orchestral color, and a greater use of chromaticism (the freedom to use tones not related to the key of the composition).

Other important influences in nineteenth-century music include the use of ethnic influences or folk melodies and music of a nationalistic vein, as well as of popular song—often linked to composers who were outstanding melodists and harmonic innovators—pieces such as this were written by Giacomo Rossini (*The Barber of Seville; William Tell*), Georges Bizet (*Carmen*), Giuseppe Verdi (*Aida; La Traviata*), Giacomo Puccini (*La Boheme; Tosca*), and the American Louis Moreau Gottschalk (*A Night in the Tropics; The Banjo*), and the Russians—Mikhail Glinka (*A Life for the Tsar*), Alexander Borodin (*Prince Igor, In the Steppes of Central Asia*), Modest Mussorgsky (*Boris Gudonov, A Night on Bald Mountain*), and Nicholas Rimsky-Korsakov (*Russian Easter Overture, Sherherazade*).

One of the great innovators in opera, Richard Wagner, sought to create a new form of music drama, using continuous music and relentless, swirling harmonies to underlie massive spectacle and recitative, or sung dialogue. Mussorgky and Wagner's idiomatic and chromatic harmonies greatly influenced the French "impressionist" composers, Claude

Debussy (*La Mer; Prelude to the Afternoon of a Faun; Children's Corner Suite*) and Maurice Ravel (*Rhapsodie Espagnole; Mother Goose Suite; Tombeau de Couperin*), who for the most part eschewed the traditional larger forms and wrote emotional, dramatic, and colorful tone pictures and sonatas, using oriental tonalities and free rhapsodic forms.

The concert music of the twentieth century increasingly endeavored to enlarge the boundaries of rhythm, form, and harmony, seemingly parallel to the direction in the visual arts away from traditional structure and melodic-harmonic connections with listeners and toward more personal or intellectual experiments in abstraction. Thus, Igor Stravinsky may be seen as the musical equivalent of Picasso; the composer who, during the years before World War I, broke apart rhythms and introduced radical harmonies in works like *The Rite of Spring* and *Petrushka,* which set the stage for further trends away from traditional ideas of tonality and harmony. Francis Poulenc (*Les Biches*) and Stravinsky himself sought to use the new rhythms and harmonies in more structurally clear, and less orchestrally dense, neoclassical pieces. The Austrian composers Arnold Schoenberg, Anton von Webern, and Alban Berg employed a new, 12-tone system, which was a highly intellectualized method of composing music without a fixed key and by establishing an arbitrary "tone row."

Ethnic and popular influences continued to exert an important pull in the creation of twentieth-century music. Folk music was a major element in the works of the English composers Ralph Vaughan Williams and Gustav Holst, of the Hungarian composers Bela Bartok and Zoltan Kodaly, and often in the music of Stravinsky and the Soviet Union's Sergei Prokofiev and Aram Khachaturian. Ragtime, blues, jazz, and other popular folk, dance, and commercial music provided material for some of the most innovative and exciting work in twentieth-century music: Stravinsky's *Ragtime for Eleven Instruments* and *A Soldier's Tale;* Ravel's *Les Enfants et Les Sortileges* and Piano Concerto in G; Darius Milhaud's *La Creation du Monde* and *Le Boeuf sur le Toit*; Kurt Weill's *Threepenny Opera;* Erik Satie's *Parade;* George Gershwin's *Rhapsody in Blue* and *Porgy and Bess;* and many pieces by Poulenc, Paul Hindemith, Leonard Bernstein, and Bohuslav Martinu. Composers after World War II continued to employ the intellectual methods of Schoenberg and to experiment with tape-recorded sound (Edgard Varese) and conceptual music based on indeterminacy or chance (John Cage). Since the 1970s, American music has seen a return to romanticism, reflected in the renewed interest in the music of Samuel Barber and David Diamond and in the lush scores of David Del Tredici (*Final Alice*). The minimalists, whose work is built upon gradual shifts of consistently repeated melodies and harmonies, include Philip Glass (*Einstein on the Beach*) and John Adams (*Nixon in China*).

DANCE, THEATER, OPERA, POPULAR MUSICAL THEATER, AND ETHNIC/FOLK TRADITIONS

Tribal people believe that through imitative dance they can gain knowledge of the mysterious powers of nature and influence the unseen world. Most dancing of this kind is communal. Dances of the ancient civilizations were often reserved for priests and religious rituals. But even the pharaohs of ancient Egypt enjoyed dancing as spectacle, and the ancient Greeks held dancing in high esteem, establishing many different styles for different purposes: the *gymnopedia,* for example, was a vigorous dance for athletic young men, and the *dithyramb* was a processional dance employing poetry and narrative, from which Greek drama arose. Romans enjoyed dancing as entertainment and pioneered the use of pantomime.

During the Middle Ages, the common folk enjoyed dancing, much of it related to fertility or seasonal rituals such as Maypole and wedding dances. The frenzied dance of death was the popular response to the spread of the plague in Europe, and dances in parades and pageants were also popular. Secular dance with more formalized steps and forms became important among the upper classes after the Renaissance period. Stylized and formalized dances included the pavanne, the galliard, the sarabande, the gigue, the minuet, the gavotte, and the chaconne.

Among Western and non-Western cultures alike the folk traditions of the performing arts often link the disciplines of dance, theater, and music. Ethnic dance with the longest and most sophisticated tradition is the classical dance of India, of which there are four main schools. Kathakali is the most theatrical of the Indian dances: actor-dancers perform stories based on mythological tales, and extensive use is made of costumes, masks, drums, makeup, and shouts.

Bharata Natyam, of southern India, is the oldest form, whose principles were described in Hindu scriptures 2,000 years ago. It requires extensive body movements, complex rhythms for the feet, and complex facial movements and hand gestures. Kathek is the Moslem-influenced dance of northern India, which values virtuosity and emotional expression. Manipuri dancing is strictly religious, and one of the annual village dance festivals is a ballet of the creation of the world. Indian dance has exerted great influence over the court and temple dances of Indonesia, Thailand, Japan, and other Asian countries.

Dance is primarily linked with theatrical entertainments in China (the opera) and Japan. Japanese Kabuki theater employs masks, singing, and dancing in a highly stylized manner, and the Noh plays of Japan are dance-dramas with stylized scenery and acting. In Indonesia, the Javanese *gamalen,* an orchestra of tuned percussion instruments consisting of up to 80 pieces, is played softly to accompany song and gentle dancing, and powerfully for heroic dances. Native American tribal dances are essentially ritualistic (such as the ghost dance of the Paiutes), but the hoop and eagle dances of the western Indian peoples are theatrical and intricate.

Folk dancing for pure recreation is also an important tradition, and in the West among the most significant dances are the Scottish Highland fling, the Italian tarantella, the American Virginia reel and square dances, and the Argentine tango. Popular American social dancing, usually requiring two persons, in the twentieth century has adopted many Latin American dances, including the rhumba, mambo, and tango, and is related to both popular songs and jazz-band arrangements—first spread through sales of sheet music, then records, and often derived from musical theater and films.

The importance of social dancing and the continual interest in new popular dance steps was essentially begun by the American dance team of Irene and Vernon Castle in the period during and after World War I. Popular dances have included the Charleston, the jitterbug, the fox trot, the twist and, increasingly after the 1950s, other youth-oriented dances related to rock music.

Self-consciously created dance, as a form of theater and as ballet, has been used alone or as part of a larger production. Ballet has origins in both the ancient Roman pantomime and the Italian *commedia dell'arte.* France led the way in establishing the essentials of the classical ballet, beginning with the founding of the Royal Academy of Dancing in Paris in 1661. France created a theatrical tradition of opera ballets, and dance rules and steps were strictly formalized.

Into the nineteenth century it was nearly impossible for an acceptable opera not to include a ballet section. In Italy the ballet was affiliated with the opera company at La

Scala in Milan, and in Russia academies of ballet in Moscow and St. Petersburg won worldwide fame. By the end of the nineteenth century significant ballets were being composed by Tchaikovsky (*Swan Lake; The Nutcracker*). It was another Russian, Sergei Diaghilev, who made ballet one of the most important independent art forms of the twentieth century. Diaghilev, who was essentially a producer, brought together such great choreographers and dancers as Michael Fokine, Leonide Massine, and Vasilav Nijinsky with composers such as Stravinsky, Prokofiev, Debussy, Poulenc, and Satie. One of Diaghilev's greatest Ballet Russe choreographers, George Balanchine, became the most important American choreographer, director of the New York City Ballet, after World War II. The traditional elements of ballet were enlarged by the use of more abstract patterns, nontraditional steps and forms, greater individual expression, less virtuosic display, greater athleticism, and more incorporation of folk/popular-dance elements. Pioneering choreographers in the first half of the twentieth century include Isadora Duncan, Ruth St. Denis, Ted Shawn, Martha Graham, Agnes De Mille, and Jerome Robbins.

Agnes De Mille and Jerome Robbins were the leading figures of ballet-dance as used in American musical theater. Their folk- and jazz-inflected dances added significantly to the ballet idiom and revolutionized the American musical—De Mille with Rodgers and Hammerstein's *Oklahoma* and Robbins with Leonard Bernstein's *West Side Story*.

Music and theater have always been linked, and the traditions of opera, operetta, and musical comedy/drama in Europe and America have produced enduring theatrical masterpieces: the operas of Rossini, Verdi, Puccini, Bizet, Wagner, Weill, and Gershwin; the operettas of Gilbert and Sullivan (*The Pirates of Penzance; The Mikado; Patience*), Johann Strauss, Jr. (*Die Fledermaus*), Jacques Offenbach (*Tales of Hoffmann*), and Franz Lehar (*The Merry Widow*); and the musical comedies (a term loosely applied; musical theater is more accurate) of Jerome Kern (*Show Boat*), Richard Rodgers (*Carousel; Oklahoma; The King and I*), George Gershwin (*Strike Up the Band; Of Thee I Sing*), Leonard Bernstein (*On the Town; West Side Story*), and Stephen Sondheim (*Follies; Sweeney Todd*).

Drama and comedy have sought without music to portray humanity's deepest passions and most universal concerns, and simply to amuse or entertain. Medieval drama was primarily religious, with the stylized mystery and miracle plays often presented in cathedrals and monasteries. Most theatrical performances in Europe until the sixteenth century took place in booths or courtyards or an outside open area. The great plays of Shakespeare and his contemporaries were presented in theaters, but these were merely stages set against the side of a building with spectators gathered around the stage on three sides in the yard or in galleries, with no provisions for scenery. Over the next hundred years, theaters were gradually enclosed and a separated stage, demarcated by a proscenium opening, hosted theatricals with elaborate scenery and even indoor lighting. Molière in the seventeenth century and Beaumarchais in the eighteenth wrote comedies of manners and farces; the latter's *Barber of Seville* and *Marriage of Figaro* were adapted for operas by Rossini and Mozart, respectively.

Similar plays, with somewhat more realism and characters reflecting the interests and values of the middle class, were written in the nineteenth century by Oscar Wilde (*The Importance of Being Earnest; Lady Windemere's Fan*), George Bernard Shaw (*Pygmalion*), and Anton Chekov (*The Cherry Orchard*). Drama became more psychological and sought to reveal truths about real people and their inner and interpersonal conflicts with the dramas of August Strindberg (*Miss Julie*) and Henrik Ibsen (*A Doll's House*). Great American twentieth-century playwrights include Eugene O'Neill (*Long*

Day's Journey into Night; The Iceman Cometh), Tennessee Williams (*The Glass Menagerie; A Streetcar Named Desire*), and Arthur Miller (*Death of a Salesman; The Crucible*).

AESTHETIC VALUING

In addition to understanding the history of the visual and performing arts, it is important to be able to confront a work and judge its aesthetic merits—regardless of whether we specifically recognize it from memory. Questions one may ask are: A) What is the purpose of the work? Religious? Entertainment? Philosophical? Emotional? Didactic? Pure form? Social or political commentary? B) To what culture does it belong, and to what geographical region and time period—and how does it reflect these? C) Is its origin and/or function popular or commercial? Does it derive organically from the needs or celebratory functions of a community, or is it a self-conscious artistic creation of one individual? D) What style is it in? For example: Is this music baroque, classical, or romantic? Is it influenced by ethnic or popular music? Often after answering such questions, one may even be able to determine the specific artist—by putting all the clues together as in a detective story.

In looking at a work of visual art, in order to judge its quality—whether it is or isn't good art—we need to assess: A) whether it succeeds in its purpose; B) if the artist has spoken with a unique voice—regardless of style—or could this artwork just as easily be the work of someone else? C) if the style is appropriate to the expressed purpose of the work; D) if the work is memorable and distinctive; E) if the artist has used all the technical elements available to the particular discipline with accomplished skill.

Although such basic questions as these can be applied in evaluating all good art, it is important to remember that beyond these kinds of questions there are other criteria that apply only to certain art forms, for certain purposes, in certain cultures. For example, it is inappropriate to look for the use of perspective of the Western-realist tradition in Japanese or Chinese art. In music, the improvisitory style and variation forms of American jazz, and other musical vocabulary unique to the jazz (as played by such musician/composers as Duke Ellington and King Oliver) allows its quality to be judged on equal but different terms than a symphony by Beethoven. In Islamic art, the beauties of manuscripts and textiles and architectural decoration are normally limited to exquisite patterns, beautiful script for texts, and stylized naturalistic forms for ornamentation; in the religious tradition, the realistic representation of human figures is purposely avoided.

The intensity of the Hindu religious feeling in India, the workings of the universe, the endless cycles of rebirth, the goal of the ultimate blissful union with the divine, especially the intense experience of erotic love—all are embodied in Kandarya Mahaveda and other temples at Khajuraho. The profusion of sculptures rising up the temple walls at Khajuraho occupy the senses and mind in ways similar to the religious instruction afforded by the profusion of sculptural and stained-glass stories and images of the European Gothic cathedrals, such as Rheims, Chartres, and Naumberg.

In opera, the masterful works by Puccini and Weill succeed on very different levels, and were created using different styles and for different purposes. While Puccini's *La Boheme, Tosca, Madama Butterfly,* and *La Fanciulla del West* are affecting melodramas of the highest order, with ravishing music serving drama and emotion in a perfect union, Kurt Weill's and Bertolt Brecht's *Threepenny Opera* and *The Rise and Fall of the City of Mahagonny* excoriate the excesses of modern societies built on greed and bloated bourgeois values—by using oblique satire and austerely constructed music that incorporates jazz rhythms and harmonies and popular-music-type melodies. Similarly, style and purpose are served brilliantly by the naturalism and accurate depiction of observed nature in the works of such masters as Rembrandt, Gainsborough, Van Dyck, Courbet, and Renoir.

Just as successful and affecting is the personal, mystical vision of William Blake appropriately expressed in his watercolors and hand-colored prints of symbolic, contorted figures. And just as aesthetically brilliant are the agitated woodcuts and paintings depicting the psychological introspection and emotional turmoil of expressionist artists such as Edvard Munch, Oskar Kokoschka, Egon Schiele, and Max Beckman.

VISUAL AND PERFORMING ARTS

PRACTICE QUESTIONS

1. The graphic art of the early nineteenth century poet-artist William Blake is a product of

   (A) neoclassical style

   (B) Pre-Raphaelitism.

   (C) political events following the French Revolution.

   (D) a mystical, personal, metaphysical vision.

2. The plays of Shakespeare were performed

   (A) on a stage in an open area.

   (B) in fields.

   (C) in a large amphitheater.

   (D) in the courts of English nobility.

3. The operas of Puccini were written in a style called verismo, or realism. *La boheme,* for example, takes place

   (A) in China.

   (B) in Bohemia.

   (C) among the starving artists in Paris.

   (D) among cowboys in the American West.

4. Intaglio, relief, and planographic all describe what kind of art technique?

   (A) Printmaking

   (B) Sculpture

   (C) Carved monument inscriptions

   (D) Frescoes

5. Albrecht Dürer's Renaissance paintings in Germany differed from those of the Italian Renaissance in that they

   (A) depicted only common people.

   (B) observed nature more closely.

   (C) were not religious.

   (D) never depicted animals.

VISUAL AND PERFORMING ARTS

ANSWERS TO PRACTICE QUESTIONS

   1. **(D)**
   2. **(A)**
   3. **(C)**
   4. **(A)**
   5. **(B)**

MSAT
Multiple Subjects Assessment for Teachers

CHAPTER 7

Human Development
Review

Chapter 7

Human Development Review

The Human Development portion of the MSAT is unlike the others in that it seeks to assess your understanding of the developmental needs of your students rather than the subject matter that you will be responsible to teach. Seven percent of the overall exam is devoted to this area, comprising 8 of the 120 multiple-choice questions, and 2 of the Content Area Exercises. Questions cover the following subject areas:

Implications and Applications of Theory (20 percent)
- Behavioral, cognitive, and psychosocial development

Implications and Applications of Research (30 percent)
- Family, personality, and moral development
- Achievement factors
- Aggression
- Play
- Intellectual development
- Affects of pre- and post-natal substance abuse

Major Developmental Perspectives (15 percent)
- Continuity vs. discontinuity
- Nature vs. nurture
- Adult-directed vs. child-centered learning

Gathering and Using Information (10 percent)
- Formal and informal methods
- Ethical issues

Human Diversity (25 percent)
- Questions posed within the above areas, but pertaining to diverse populations

The review that follows provides information on each of these topics as they apply to the beginning teacher. All questions are posed in a pedagogical context, and the review should augment the developmental knowledge attained in your education and psychology courses.

In order for teachers to successfully teach students of all ages and in all disciplines, it is necessary that teachers understand learners. Benjamin Bloom (1976) has suggested that students' cognitive entry skills and intelligence (or IQ) account for about 50 percent of what students achieve academically; 25 percent can be attributed to the quality of instruction students receive; 25 percent can be attributed to affective characteristics of the students. Those affective characteristics include such things as the learner's personality, self-concept, locus of control, attitudes, level of anxiety, and study habits. Therefore, although it is important that teachers acquire and utilize effective teaching techniques and provide quality instruction to students, it can be argued that it is even more important in terms of educational outcomes that teachers understand cognitive and affective factors which influence student performance.

The traditional view of education saw the learner as a *tabula rasa*, a blank slate, upon which the teacher wrote knowledge. In this model, the student was assumed to be an empty vessel; he or she came into the classroom knowing nothing. It was the teacher's responsibility, as the expert, to impart knowledge or to fill the empty vessel.

Today, cognitive psychologists have corrected this faulty notion. Educators now recognize that students bring to the classroom an array of personal characteristics and experiences upon which they base their present knowledge. Those characteristics and experiences may or may not be congruent to the teacher's background; nonetheless, they constitute a knowledge base for the learner. Therefore, the teacher's role is to activate the learner's prior knowledge and help the student connect new information with what is known already. Thus, in today's educational model, the student is seen as an active learner who brings much to the classroom.

The effective teacher, then, must go beyond assuming the role of a "sage on the stage." The effective teacher must be more than just an expert who has mastered a discipline or body of knowledge. The effective teacher must be a facilitator of learning; an effective teacher empowers students to learn for and by themselves. The effective teacher, in other words, is a "guide by the side" of students, assisting them in the process of learning and enhancing that process for students.

The importance of teachers' having a basic understanding of the principles of human development in its many dimensions: physically, mentally, emotionally, and socially cannot be overstated. It is also important that teachers appreciate a dynamic and interactive view of human development. This approach to understanding human development is one which recognizes that human beings do not develop in a vacuum. People exist in an environment which, friendly or unfriendly, supportive or nonsupportive, evokes and provokes reactions from individuals; moreover, it is not a one-way street with the environment doing all the driving. People also act in certain ways to shape and form their environment. There is a constant interaction or interplay between people and their environments. Thus, effective teachers must be sensitive to and knowledgeable of both personal characteristics of students and characteristics of their environment.

STUDENT DEVELOPMENT AND MATURATION

A teacher does not have to be an expert in anatomy and physiology to see the physical changes that accompany students' growth and maturity. The preschool child has trouble grasping pencils or crayons in a manner to facilitate handwriting; however, even most two-year olds can grasp crayons sufficiently to make marks on papers and, thus, enjoy the creative excitement of art.

Physiological changes play a significant role in the development of children as they increase their control of bodily movements and functions and refine their motor skills. Their ability to engage in simple to complex classroom and playground activities increases as they develop. Classroom and playground activities must be adjusted and adapted in order to be developmentally appropriate for the skill levels of the children.

As students enter junior high or begin their secondary education, they again experience important physiological changes with the onset of puberty. With puberty comes changes in primary sexual characteristics and the emergence of secondary sexual characteristics. In addition to bodily characteristics, there is a change in bodily feelings, and there is an increase in sex drive.

Girls, on average, reach maturational milestones before boys. Physical changes may cause embarrassment to both females and males when they draw unwelcome attention; moreover, these changes almost always create some discomfort as adolescents find the body they were familiar and comfortable with to be quite different, sometimes seemingly overnight.

David Elkind has noted two developmental characteristics of adolescence which share a relationship to the physiological changes accompanying maturation. These two characteristics are the *imaginary audience* and the *personal fable*. First, adolescents, preoccupied with their own physiological changes, often assume that others are equally intrigued by these changes in appearance and behavior; they may feel that others are staring at them, watching their every move, scrutinizing their behavior for one misstep or their appearance for any flaws. If everyone is watching, then it's imperative to be, to act, and to look just right. In today's culture, that means wearing the right clothes and having all the right brand names and status symbols. Because of adolescents' sensitivity to attention (especially the wrong kind of attention, that is, not fitting in, not being "right"), it is especially important that teachers of this age group be aware of the *imaginary audience* phenomenon and be sensitive to social interactions in the classroom. It, indeed, is important that teachers not contribute to creating unwanted attention or to stigmatizing or stereotyping students.

Personal fable refers to the belief that "My life is different from everyone else's; therefore, no one can understand how I feel or what I think. No one has ever felt or thought what I feel and think." This out-of-focus view tends to support both a feeling of isolation (which may be precipitated by the changing sensations from a body that is undergoing biological changes) and a willingness to engage in risky behaviors (thinking that only others have car accidents when they drive dangerously—"It won't happen to me"—or, only other girls get pregnant when they have unprotected sexual relations—"It won't happen to me.").

In sum, these two characteristics of adolescence are examples of how physical changes accompany and, perhaps even evoke, emotional and cognitive changes as individuals grow and mature. Both phenomena of *imaginary audience* and *personal fable* have emotional features (fear of rejection, fear of isolation, fear of difference, shame, guilt from increased sexual feelings, frustration, and so forth) and both describe a feature of adolescent cognitive ability: the ability to think about one's self as an object of one's own and of other's thought. The developmental epistemologist Jean Piaget explained that this way of thinking represents the cognitive stage of formal operations.

Cognition is a term commonly used to refer to all the processes whereby knowledge is acquired; the term can be used to cover very basic perceptual processes, such as smell, touch, sound, and so forth, to very advanced operations, such as analysis, synthesis, and critical thinking.

THEORIES OF COGNITIVE DEVELOPMENT

Until his death in 1980, Jean Piaget was a predominant figure in the field of cognitive psychology. It is safe to postulate that perhaps no other single individual has had greater influence on educational practices than Piaget. Basically, his theory of cognitive development is based on the notion that cognitive abilities (or one's ability to think) are developed as individuals mature physiologically, and they have opportunities to interact with their environment. Piaget described these interactions as the *equilibration* of *accommodation* and *assimilation* cycles or processes. In other words, when individuals (who, according to Piaget, are innately endowed with certain cognitive predispositions and capabilities) encounter a new or novel stimulus, they are brought into a state of *disequilibrium.*

That is a way of saying that they are thrown off balance; they do not know or understand that which is new or unfamiliar. However, through the complementary processes of *accommodation* (or adjusting prior knowledge gained through former experiences and interactions) and *assimilation* (fitting together the new information with what has been previously known or understood), individuals come to know or understand that which is new. Once again, individuals are returned to a state of *equilibrium* where they remain until the next encounter with an unfamiliar something. For Piaget, this is how learners learn.

Piaget also predicted that certain behaviors and ways of thinking characterize individuals at different ages. For this reason, his theory is considered a *stage* theory. *Stage* theories share the common tenet that certain characteristics will occur in predictable sequences and at certain times in the life of the individual.

According to Piaget, there are four stages of cognitive development, beginning with the *sensorimotor* stage describing individuals from birth to around the age of two. The second stage, *preoperational* (describing cognitive behavior between the ages of two and seven), is characterized by egocentrism, rigidity of thought, semilogical reasoning, and limited social cognition; some cognitive psychologists have observed that this stage seems to describe how individuals think more in terms of what they can't do than what they can do. This stage describes the way that children in preschool and kindergarten go about problem-solving; also, many children in the primary grades may be at this stage in their cognitive development.

The next two stages, however, may be most important for elementary and secondary school teachers since they describe cognitive development during the times that most students are in school. The third stage, *concrete operations,* is the beginning of operational thinking and describes the thinking of children between the ages of 7 and 11. Learners at this age begin to decenter. They are able to take into consideration viewpoints other than their own. They can perform transformations, meaning that they can understand reversibility, inversion, reciprocity, and conservation. They can group items into categories. They can make inferences about reality and engage in inductive reasoning; they increase their quantitative skills, and they can manipulate symbols if they are given concrete examples with which to work. This stage of cognitive development is the threshold to higher-level learning for students.

Finally, *formal operations* is the last stage of cognitive development and opens wide the door for higher-ordered, critical thinking. This stage describes the way of thinking for learners between the ages of 11 and 15, and for Piaget, constitutes the ultimate stage of cognitive development (thus also describing adult thinking). Learners at this stage of cognitive development can engage in logical, abstract, and hypothetical thought;

they can use the scientific method, meaning they can formulate hypotheses, isolate influences, and identify cause-and effect-relationships. They can plan and anticipate verbal cues. They can engage in both deductive and inductive reasoning, and they can operate on verbal statements exclusive of concrete experiences or examples. These cognitive abilities characterize the highest levels of thought.

Another theoretical approach to understanding human development is offered by Erik Erikson, another important stage theorist, who described pyschosocial development. For each of eight stages, he identified a developmental task explained in terms of two polarities. For the purposes of this discussion, only those stages describing school-age individuals will be included.

According to Erikson, preschoolers and primary-school aged children must be able to function in the outside world independently of parents; when children are able to do this, they achieve a sense of *initiative*; when children are not able to move away from total parental attachment and control, they experience a sense of *guilt*. Thus, this stage of psychosocial development is the stage of initiative versus guilt. The child's first venture away from home and into the world of school has considerable significance when viewed in light of this theory; it is imperative that teachers assist students in their first experiences on their own, away from parental control.

Erikson's next stage of development is one involving a tension between *industry* and *inferiority*. For example, if the child who enters school (thus achieving initiative) acquires the skills (including academic skills such as reading, writing, and computation, as well as social skills in playing with others, communicating with others, forming friendships, and so forth) which enable her or him to be successful in school, then the child achieves a sense of industry; failure to achieve these skills leads to a sense of inferiority.

IDENTITY ACHIEVEMENT AND DIFFUSION

Around the time students enter junior high, they begin the developmental task of achieving *identity*. According to Erikson, the struggle to achieve identity is one of the most important developmental tasks and one which creates serious psychosocial problems for adolescents. For example, even the individual who has successfully achieved all the important developmental milestones (such as initiative and industry) now finds him- or herself in a state of flux: Everything (body, feelings, thoughts) is changing. The adolescent starts to question, "Who am I?" Erikson believed that if adolescents find out what they believe in, what their goals, ideas, and values are, then they attain identity achievement; failure to discover these things leads to identity diffusion.

By the time many students reach high school, they are entering a stage of young adulthood, for Erikson, a psychosocial stage characterized by the polarities of *intimacy* and *isolation*. Individuals at this stage of development begin to think about forming lasting friendships, even marital unions. Erikson would argue that many psychosocial problems experienced by young adults have their origin in the individual's failure to achieve identity during the preceding stage; the young man or woman who does not know who he or she really is cannot achieve true intimacy.

For the classroom teacher, knowledge of psychosocial stages of human development can result in greater effectiveness. For example, the effective teacher realizes the importance of helping students to achieve skills necessary to accomplish crucial developmental tasks. According to Erikson's theory, teachers of elementary school-aged learners would do well to focus on teaching academic and social skills, helping students to gain proficiency in skills that will enable learners to be productive members of society. On the other hand, secondary school teachers would do well to keep in mind, as they engage students in higher-ordered thinking activities appropriate to their stage of cognitive development, that students have pressing psychological and social needs in their struggle to achieve identity and to attain intimacy.

By understanding key principles of human development in its multiple dimensions, effective teachers provide students with both age-appropriate and developmentally-appropriate instruction. This, in sum, is the best instruction. It is instruction that addresses all the needs of students, their physical, emotional, and social needs, as well as their cognitive (or intellectual) needs.

The preceding discussion on human development emphasized primarily the characteristics of learners or what may be considered internal factors. Internal factors, beyond the general characteristics that humans share as they grow and mature, also include factors such as students' personality characteristics, their self-concept and sense of self-esteem, their self-discipline and self-control, their ability to cope with stress, and their general outlook on life.

External factors are those things outside the student personally but which impact on the student. They include the home environment and family relationships, peer relationships, community situations, and the school environment. In other words, external factors constitute the context in which the student lives and learns.

MASLOW'S HIERARCHY OF NEEDS

Abraham Maslow's hierarchy of human needs is a model applicable to many diverse fields, including education, business and industry, health and medical professions, and more. Maslow identified different levels of individuals' needs in a hierarchical sequence, meaning that lower level needs must be satisfied before individuals could ascend to higher levels of achievement. He identified the fulfillment of basic physiological needs as fundamental to individuals' sense of well-being and their ability to engage in any meaningful activity. Simply stated, students' physiological needs (to have hunger and thirst satisfied, to have sleep needs met, to be adequately warm, and so forth) must be met before students can perform school tasks. Today's schools provide students with breakfast and lunch when needed, and great effort and expense is often directed towards heating and cooling school buildings.

Maslow's second level of need concerned safety. Again, students must feel safe from harm and danger before they are ready to learn. Today, schools often are equipped with metal detectors to increase students' sense of safety. In some schools, guards and security officers patrol the halls.

The third level of need, according to Maslow's theory, is the need for affiliation or the need to belong and to be accepted by others. Although this need may, at first glance, seem less related to the student's environment, it does, indeed, refer to the student's social environment. Students need the opportunity to develop social relationships and to establish friendships among their peers. In essence, Maslow, through his theory, determined that environmental factors are important in education.

Another significant principle of human development arises from a long debate between those experts who believed that innate characteristics (those the individual is born with) play the most important role in determining who the individual will become and what he or she will do versus those who believed that environmental characteristics are most important. This argument is referred to in the literature as the *nature* versus *nurture* debate.

NATURE AND NURTURE

After experts on both sides of the argument stated their positions, the conclusion seemed to be that both *nature* (the internal variables) and *nurture* (the environment) play equally important roles in determining the outcome of individuals' growth and maturation. Again, it is important to remember the interaction of the individual with her or his environment, recalling that this view is the *dynamic* view of human development.

Before proceeding, teachers would do well to understand that perception plays an important role for learners to the extent that perception creates our individual reality. The world as we know it is a result of our selective perception. We cannot attend to all events and variables in our environment. We select certain events and variables to notice, to attend to, and these phenomena which we observe form our perceptions; thus, we create our own reality. External and internal phenomena grab our attention and shape reality for each of us.

Thus, it is one thing for teachers to be aware of and sensitive to the students' environment; it is, however, impossible for teachers to see, feel, and understand the individual's environment in exactly the same way that it is seen, felt, and understood by the student.

Carol Tavris, a social psychologist and author of the book, *Anger the Misunderstood Emotion*, notes that emotion plays a significant role in students' perceptions. For example, guilt is an emotion aroused by thoughts such as, "I should study or my parents will kill (be disappointed in) me." This is easily contrasted with the emotion of fear generated by the thought, "I should study or I will be a failure in life." Furthermore, guilt and fear can be compared to the emotion of anger which is prompted by thoughts such as, "Why should I study when my teacher is out to get me?" Today's student often sees the teacher as an enemy, not as an authority figure or a friend. Tavris has identified anger as a primary emotion experienced by many students today and one which plays a significant role in shaping their academic perceptions which, in turn, forms their reality of classroom experiences.

Explaining further, Tavris observes that unfulfilled expectations lead to anger. For example, if a student is led to believe (by teachers, school administrators, their peers, or by parents and siblings) that attending class is somehow irrelevant to academic achievement, then the student who is frequently absent still has the expectation of being successful. The student's perception is that absenteeism is compatible with academic achievement. If, because of absenteeism, the student fails to master essential elements of the curriculum and does not succeed, then the student will feel anger, the appropriate and anticipated emotion.

Anger, however, can be diffused by addressing perceptions, correcting false impressions, and establishing appropriate and realistic expectations. To illustrate, if all those significant individuals to the student emphasize the importance of class attendance, then students acquire the correct perception (in this case) that attendance is important for academic achievement and that absenteeism leads to academic failure.

For the sake of illustration only, let's consider what might happen if the teacher stresses attendance and the parents do not. In this case, the best route for the teacher to take is to show empathy for the student's dilemma. The teacher can acknowledge how difficult it is for the student to attend class when the parents are not supporting attendance, but the teacher also must seek to empower the student to make choices and to take responsibility for her or his own behavior.

In the situation described here, the student undergoes stress because of conflicting messages, and stress is faced by students and faculty alike. In fact, in the above example, the teacher is stressed too in that the teacher faces the conflict between supporting the parents of the student and supporting that which is in the best educational interests of the student.

Stress is the product of any change; both negative and positive changes produce stress. Environmental, physiological, and psychological factors cause stress. For example, environmental factors such as noise, air pollution, and crowding (among others) create stress; physiological factors such as sickness and physical injuries create stress; and, finally, psychological factors such as self-deprecating thoughts and negative self-image cause stress. In addition to the normal stressors that everyone experiences, some students are living in dysfunctional families; some students are dealing with substance abuse and addictions; some are experiencing sexual abuse. There are numerous sources of stress in the lives of students.

Since life is a stressful process, it is important that students and faculty learn acceptable ways to cope with stress. The first step in coping with stress is to recognize the role that stress plays in our lives. A teacher might lead a class through a brainstorming activity to help the students become aware of the various sources of stress affecting them. Next, the teacher could identify positive ways of coping with stress such as the importance of positive self-talk, physical exercise, proper nutrition, adequate sleep, balanced activities, time-management techniques, good study habits, and relaxation exercises.

Students who are stressed often become angry rather easily; however, students are not just angry. They experience a wide range of emotions, and may be sad, depressed, frustrated, afraid, and, on the positive side, happy and surprised. Effective teachers realize that students' emotions, as explained in this section and the preceding section on human development, play a significant role in students' classroom performance and achievement. Thus, effective teachers seek to create a classroom environment supportive of students' emotional needs. They have appropriate empathy and compassion for the emotional conflicts facing students, yet their concern is tempered by a realistic awareness of the importance of students attaining crucial academic and social skills that will grant them some control over their environment as they become increasingly independent and, eventually, must be prepared to be productive citizens.

Effective teachers recognize the effects of students' perceptions on the learning process and the effects of many environmental factors; as a result, they plan instruction to enhance students' self-esteem and to promote realistic expectations. It is important that teachers be able to differentiate positive and negative environmental factors, maximizing the positive variables and minimizing the negative ones. The teacher has the primary responsibility of creating a classroom environment that recognizes the different environmental factors affecting each student and that encourages each learner to excel, to achieve her or his personal best. Effective teachers work hard at creating learning environments in which all students are ready to learn—where students feel safe, accepted, competent, and productive.

Effective teachers also realize that students bring to the classroom a variety of characteristics, both personal and social, that create within the classroom a microcosm reflective of American society at large. Indeed, America has long held to the notion of being a "melting pot" whereby members of various racial, ethnic, religious, and national origin groups have contributed to the wealth of our culture.

Ethnocentrism is a sociological term used to describe the natural tendency of viewing one's own cultural or familial way of doing things as the right, correct, or best way. Because ethnocentrism is a natural tendency, all people are likely to engage in ethnocentric thinking and behaviors at times.

Some social critics have pointed out that ethnocentrism has played a notable role in American education. They assert that educational institutions often have been guilty of assuming a Eurocentric viewpoint, that is, solely recognizing the contributions of European writers, artists, scientists, philosophers, and so forth, at the expense of those from other cultures. These critics have also noted that the contributions of men often are disproportionately recognized over like achievements of women (Sadker & Sadker, 1994).

In fact, David and Myra Sadker (1994) have found that teachers, both male and female, at all grade levels, are more likely to call on male than female students, are more likely to give positive reinforcement to males' correct responses than to those of females, and to provide coaching or instructional help to males when their responses are incorrect than to females. Their research has led them to conclude that teachers are usually unaware of gender bias in their teaching, but that such bias is pervasive in American schools. Their research also has persuaded them that bias can be eliminated once teachers become sensitive to its debilitating effects on students.

The point made here is that ethnocentrism, in any form, can be damaging because it is exclusive rather than inclusive. Eurocentric and other ethnocentric perspectives are equally limited in that they narrowly focus attention on one set of ideas at the neglect of others. Therefore, effective teachers will wisely expend a degree of effort in avoiding ethnocentric thinking and behaviors. Effective teachers will attempt to include all students in all classroom activities. The race, ethnicity, religion, national origin, and gender of learners will be viewed as strengths which enable students to learn with and from each other.

Historically speaking, educational experiments have demonstrated the importance of teachers' avoiding bias and ethnocentric thinking. The *Hawthorne effect,* or the phenomenon whereby what teachers expected became reality, was demonstrated when teachers were told that some students in their classes were extremely intelligent whereas others were extremely slow or mentally retarded. In fact, all students had normal range intelligence. Nonetheless, at the end of the experiment, students who had been identified to the teachers as being extremely intelligent all had made significant academic progress and were not only at the top of their class, but also performing at the top on national achievement tests. Those students who had been identified as retarded had made no progress at all; in fact, they had lost previously-made gains. Thus, it was demonstrated that teachers' expectations for students often become self-fulfilling prophecies.

Because multiculturalism and/or cultural diversity can be a controversial issue with many sides to consider, a reasonable approach to diversity for the classroom teacher is to distinguish between cultural diversity and learning diversity and *to focus on diversity in learning*. This approach transcends cultural boundaries and recognizes that all people have distinct learning preferences and tendencies. Furthermore, this approach acknowledges that all preferences and tendencies are equally valid and that each style of learning has strengths. The teacher who understands learning styles can validate all students in the class.

ENVIRONMENTAL FACTORS

Many factors play a role in determining a student's learning style. Among those most often cited in the research literature on learning style are environmental, emotional, sociological, physiological, and psychological factors (Dunn & Dunn, 1993). Although there are several different models for understanding learning differences and many good instruments for assessing learning styles, the Dunn and Dunn (1993) model is one widely used in public schools with versions suitable for students in elementary and secondary classrooms. It will serve as the basis for the following discussion.

Environmental factors include students' reactions to such stimuli as sound, light, temperature, and room design. Do students prefer to study and learn with or without sound, with bright or soft lights, in warm or cool rooms, with standard classroom furniture or alternative seating? Classroom teachers observe that some students are easily distracted by any noise and require absolute quiet when studying or working on assignments. On the other hand, some students seem to learn best when they can listen to music. Some researchers have found evidence that students who prefer sound learn best when classical or instrumental music is played in the background.

Light is another environmental factor with students' preferences for light appearing to be basically inherited. Family members often exhibit the same preference. Some students prefer bright, direct illumination while others prefer dim, indirect lighting.

Temperature and design are two other environmental factors affecting learning style. Some students will prefer warmer temperatures whereas others will prefer cooler temperatures. Finally, some students will prefer to sit in straight-backed chairs at desks while others may prefer to sit on soft, comfy chairs or to sit or recline on the floor.

Although traditional classrooms are structured to provide quiet, brightly illuminated study and work areas with straight-backed chairs and desks, classroom teachers will observe that this environment meets the needs of only some of the learners in the class. An effective teacher will take into consideration the learning styles of all students and experiment with different room designs, study centers, and creating different environments in the classroom. Although classroom temperature may seem to be beyond the control of the teacher, students can be advised to dress in layers so that they can remove outer garments when they are too warm and put on more layers when they are too cool.

EMOTIONAL FACTORS

According to Rita and Kenneth Dunn, emotional factors include motivation, persistence, responsibility, and structure. To explain, some students are motivated intrinsically: they undertake and complete tasks because they see the value in doing so. Other students are motivated extrinsically: They undertake and complete tasks because they desire to please others or to earn good marks. In regard to persistence, some students, when they undertake assignments, become totally and completely engaged in their work; they seem to lose track of time and can work for long periods without interruption or without feeling fatigued. Other students seem to work in short spurts of energy, needing to take frequent breaks.

When it comes to responsibility, some students are nonconforming, always doing the unexpected (and sometimes unwanted), whereas other students are conforming, always following the rules. Structure refers to whether or not students need detailed and precise instructions. Some students have lots of questions about how assignments should be done, and they desire detailed, step-by-step instructions on each phase of the assignment. Other students, however, seem to work from general concepts and are usually eager to begin assignments, often beginning their work before the directions have been given.

Sociological factors include whether or not students are social learners—preferring to work in pairs or in groups—or whether they are independent learners—preferring to work alone. Another sociological factor is whether or not students work best under the close guidance and supervision of an authority figure, be it teacher or parent, or whether they work best with a minimum of adult guidance and are best left primarily on their own to do their work.

Physiological factors include students' preferences for food or drink while they study, what time of day they learn best, their mobility needs, and their perceptual strengths. Briefly, some students may need to eat or drink in order to effectively and efficiently learn. Rita Dunn says that to make sure that students do not abuse this privilege, she allows them to eat only carrot or celery sticks (cooked so that the snacks will not crunch when eaten by students) and to drink water. This way, she is certain that only students who really need intake when they are learning will take advantage of this concession.

Some students may learn best early in the morning, some later in the morning, some in early afternoon, and some later in the afternoon. Researchers have found that merely manipulating the time of day that certain students take tests can significantly affect their test performance.

Mobility needs refer to the fact that some students need to move around when they study, whereas other students can sit still for longer periods of time. Although all of these factors are important, and a growing body of literature tends to support the idea that these factors play a significant role in increasing students' performance and in increasing teachers' effectiveness with students, perhaps one of the most important elements in understanding learning style is to identify students' perceptual strengths. Perceptual strengths refer to students' learning modalities, such as whether they are visual, auditory, tactile, or kinesthetic learners. Basically, these perceptual modalities refer to whether students learn best by seeing, hearing, or doing.

Some students can be given a book or handout to read and then perform a task well based on what they have read. These students tend to have visual (iconic or semantic) perceptual strength. Other students are visual learners, too, but they tend to learn best from images. These are the students who seem to recall every event, even minor details, from films, videos, or classroom demonstrations.

Although evidence indicates that less than 15 percent of the school-age population is auditory (Dunn, 1993), much of the classroom instruction takes the form of teachers telling students information. Most students do not learn auditorially. Therefore, these students must be taught how to listen and learn from oral instructions and lecture.

Teachers who rely on telling students the information that is important would do well to remember that females are more likely to learn auditorially than males. Teachers should also keep in mind that whether or not students benefit from lectures is likely to depend on several other elements as well as whether or not the students are auditory learners, such as whether or not the students like the teacher, whether or not they think the information being presented is important, or whether or not they think that listening to the teacher will help them to achieve their goals (Baxter-Magolda, 1992).

On the other hand, there are students who do not seem to benefit much from lectures, textbook assignments, or visual aids. These students' perceptual strengths are tactile and kinesthetic. They learn from movement and motion, from being able to touch, handle, and manipulate objects. Often these students may have been identified as having learning disabilities. Sometimes they have been relegated to shop or cooking classes or have found their success in athletics, music, or art. Interestingly, many of the "hands on" skills that often identify a student for a career as an auto mechanic are also important skills for mechanical engineers and surgeons.

LEARNING STYLES

The obvious benefit of knowing whether or not students are auditory, visual, tactile, or kinesthetic learners is not simply to cater to the learners' preferences or strengths. The significance is that once strengths are identified, then teachers can teach students to use those strengths in situations which are not easy or natural. For example, students who are not auditory learners (but tactile and kinesthetic) must learn responsibility for their own learning; they must learn to become involved in lecture classes. Becoming involved means that they learn to take copious notes, participate in class discussions, ask questions, and answer questions posed by the teacher.

Visual learners must sit where they can see what's going on in class, where they can see the teacher and the board. They need opportunities to draw pictures, to diagram, to take good notes, to create mind maps, and to use flashcards. They must be taught how to visualize the abstract concepts they are being taught, and they need opportunities to practice all these techniques.

For visual learners who learn best by reading, teachers can provide adequate opportunities to read in class. Students need to learn specific note-taking methods, and reading and comprehension strategies. They also can be taught to use supplemental readings, to use the library effectively, and to use workbooks.

Auditory learners need to learn attention-directing activities. They can learn to use audio cassettes as learning aids. They can learn to ask questions in class and to participate in class discussions. They must be taught how to summarize and paraphrase—especially how to state in their own words the concepts they are trying to master. They may need the teacher to repeat or to restate ideas. Students must learn to pay close attention to verbal cues such as voice tone and inflection. Reciting what they have heard (or read) is an important strategy for auditory learners as is finding someone to whom they can explain ideas they have acquired. It may be helpful for auditory learners to work on some assignments with students who are visual learners (Nolting, 1993).

Tactile, kinesthetic learners may benefit from study groups, discussion groups, role-playing situations, lab settings, computer activities, learning games, and using flashcards and other manipulatives. They must get involved in class by asking questions and participating in discussions. They learn best when they can convert what they are learning into real-life, concrete experiences; for example, they may learn fractions by cutting a pizza into slices. Often, they need to work math problems immediately after being shown examples to check their understanding. They often need to move around while they are studying, reviewing ideas while exercising, or doing chores. Many times, they do their best work when they are using tools such as computers, calculators, or even their fingers.

When classroom teachers assess students' learning styles and then begin to teach to empower students to learn more effectively and perform tasks with greater proficiency, the result is that students also learn a tremendous lesson about diversity. They learn that not everyone learns in the same way, but that everyone can achieve. The products of learning can meet the same high standards although the processes for learning may be different for different students.

This is a rich lesson for students and faculty alike. It tells students that it is okay to be different; in fact, everyone is different. It tells students that it is okay to be the way they are. Apart from their race, ethnicity, religious beliefs, national origin, or gender, they are special, and they are good. They can learn. This may be one of the most important lessons that students ever learn and one that all teachers can be proud and eager to teach.

It is one thing for teachers to have command of their subject matter. It is a given that English teachers will be able to write well, that math teachers will be able to compute and calculate, that science teachers will know and understand science, and so forth. However, it is something else—and something at least as important—that teachers know how to teach.

When teachers understand learners, that is, when teachers understand developmental processes common to all learners, and how environmental features and learning styles, varied and diverse, affect learning, then teachers are better able to design and deliver effective instruction. Although there may be some intuitive aspects to teaching (and it seems that some people were born to teach), teaching skills can be acquired through processes of introspection, observation, direct instruction, self-evaluation, and experimentation.

How teachers teach should be directly related to how learners learn. Theories of cognitive development describe how learners learn new information and acquire new skills. There are many theories of cognitive development, two of which will be included in this review; they are (a) the Piagetian (or Neo-Piagetian) theory, and (b) information processing theory.

Piagetian theory (including Neo-Piagetian theory), describes learning in discrete and predictable stages. Therefore, teachers who understand this theory can provide students with developmentally-appropriate instruction. This theory also describes learners moving from simpler ways of thinking to more complex ways of problem-solving and thinking. For teachers, there are many important implications of this theoretical perspective. For example, teachers must create enriched environments that present learners with multiple opportunities to encounter new and unfamiliar stimuli—be they objects or ideas. Teachers must also provide learners with opportunities to engage in extended dialogue with adults; according to Piaget's theory, conversational interactions with adults are a key component in cognitive development, especially the acquisition of formal operations (or higher-ordered thinking skills). Moreover, it is important that adults (and teachers in particular) model desired behaviors; teachers must reveal their own complex ways of thinking and solving problems to students.

On the other hand, information processing theories of human development take a different approach to describing and understanding how learners learn. Based on a computer metaphor and borrowing computer imagery to describe how people learn, information processing theories begin by determining the processing demands of a particular cognitive challenge (or problem to solve) necessitating a detailed task-analysis of how the human mind changes external objects or events into a useful form according to certain, precisely-specified rules or strategies, similar to the way a computer programmer programs a computer to perform a function. Thus, information processing theories focus on the process, how the learner arrives at a response or answer.

A brief analysis of one information processing theory will serve to illustrate this point. Sternberg's (1985) triarchic theory of intelligence is a theory taking into account three features of learning. Those three features are (a) the mechanics or components of intelligence (including both higher-ordered thinking processes, such as planning, decision making and problem solving, and lower-ordered processes, such as making inferences, mapping, selectively encoding information, retaining information in memory, transferring new information in memory, and so forth); (b) the learner's experiences; and (c) the learner's context (including the adaptation to and the shaping and selecting of environments).

According to Sternberg, learners' use of the mechanics of intelligence is influenced by learners' experiences. To illustrate, some cognitive processes (such as those required in reading) become automatized as a result of continued exposure to and practice of those skills. Learners who come from homes where parents read and where there are lots of different reading materials tend to be more proficient readers; certainly, learners who read a lot become more proficient readers. Those learners who are exposed to reading activities and who have ample opportunities to practice reading have greater skill and expertise in reading; and in a cyclical manner, students who have skills in reading like to read. Conversely, those who lack reading skills don't like to read. Students who don't like to read, don't read; thus, their reading skills, lacking practice, fail to improve.

An information processing approach acknowledges that not only are individuals influenced by their environments and adapt to those environments, individuals also are active in shaping their own environments. In other words, a child who wants to read but who has no books at home may ask parents to buy books, or may go to the library to read, or check out books to read at home.

Information processing theory is of interest to educators because of its insistence on the idea that intelligent performance can be facilitated through instruction and direct training. In sum, intelligent thinking can be taught. Sternberg has urged teachers to identify the mental processes that academic tasks require and to teach learners those processes; he challenges teachers to teach learners what processes to use, when and how to use them, and how to combine them into strategies for solving problems and accomplishing assignments.

Teachers who wish to follow Sternberg's advice might choose to begin teaching by identifying *instructional objectives*, that is, what should students be able to do as a result of instruction. Second, teachers would analyze the objectives in terms of identifying the *instructional outcomes*, those being the tasks or assignments that students can perform as a result of achieving the instructional objectives. Third, teachers would analyze instructional outcomes in terms of the *cognitive skills* or mental processes required to perform those tasks or assignments. After following these three steps and identifying instructional objectives, instructional outcomes, and cognitive skills involved, the teacher is ready to conduct a *preassessment* (or pretest) to determine what students already know.

Instruction is then based on the results of the preassessment with teachers focusing on teaching directly the cognitive skills needed in order for students to perform the task(s). Following instruction, teachers would conduct a *post-assessment* (or post-test) to evaluate the results of instruction. Further instruction would be based on the results of the post-assessment, that is, whether or not students had achieved expected outcomes and whether or not teachers had achieved instructional objectives.

Regardless of which theoretical perspective is adopted by teachers, and, at times, teachers may find themselves taking a rather eclectic approach and borrowing elements from several theoretical bases, it is helpful for teachers to consider if they are structuring their classrooms to satisfy learners' needs or merely their own needs as teachers. Furthermore, if the teachers' goal is to increase teaching effectiveness by facilitating learners' knowledge and skill acquisition, then teachers will engage continuously in a process of self-examination and self-evaluation.

METACOGNITION

Self-examination and self-evaluation are both types of *metacognitive* thinking. *Metacognition* is a term used to describe what, how, and why people know what they know when they know it. In short, it is thinking about thinking and knowing about knowing. Cognitive psychologists describe metacognition as a characteristic of higher-ordered, mature, and sophisticated thinking. Generally speaking, as learners achieve higher levels of cognitive skills, they also increase their metacognitive skills. Therefore, not only should teachers engage in metacognitive thinking, they should model that thinking for their students, and encourage their students to develop metacognitive skills.

Metacognition can be understood in terms of (a) metacognitive knowledge and (b) metacognitive control (Flavell, 1987). Basically, metacognitive knowledge is what learners need to know and metacognitive control is what learners need to do. Metacognitive control, therefore, is in the hands of the learner. Teachers cannot control learners' behavior although they can encourage and admonish. The best that teachers can do is help learners expand their metacognitive awareness and knowledge.

Awareness can be increased by talking about metacognition. Flavell has explained that there are three kinds of metacognitive knowledge, those three kinds being (a) person knowledge, (b) task knowledge, and (c) strategy knowledge.

Person knowledge falls into one of three categories: (a) intraindividual knowledge, (b) interindividual knowledge, and (c) universal knowledge. First, intraindividual knowledge is what the learner knows or understands about him- or herself. Therefore, it is important that learners have opportunities to learn about themselves, about their interests, abilities, propensities, and so forth. For this reason (among others), it is important that learners have opportunities to learn about their own learning style and their perceptual strengths. It is also helpful for them to have opportunities to examine their personalities, values, and goals.

Furthermore, in a model that recognizes the dynamic nature of instruction, that is, one which recognizes that the learner also knows certain things and can contribute to the classroom, the teacher realizes that she or he is a learner, too. Teachers, then, can benefit from examining their own learning style, perceptual strengths, personalities, values, and goals. Moreover, it can be extremely beneficial for teachers to consider their own instructional style.

INSTRUCTIONAL STYLE ASSESSMENT

One instrument that assesses instructional style, the Instructional Style Inventory (Canfield & Canfield, 1988), identifies instructional styles in four general categories (although there also can be combinations of different styles). The four categories are *social, independent, applied,* and *conceptual.* Briefly stated, the social style is one which describes the teacher who values classroom interactions, who stresses teamwork and group work; the independent style describes the teacher who emphasizes working alone and is likely to rely on self-paced, individualized, and programmed instruction; the applied style is one which stresses real-world experiences and avoids lecture and preparatory reading, but focuses on practicums and site visits, and so forth; finally, the conceptual style is one describing the teacher who is language-oriented and likes highly organized materials and tends to depend on lectures and readings.

Returning to the discussion on metacognitive knowledge, the second kind of person knowledge is interindividual knowledge, how learners are alike and how they are different. Again, this is another reason why the recognition of diversity brought about by studying learning styles can inform learners and improve their cognitive performance. As they learn about their own learning style, learners also observe that their classmates have some similarities and some differences when it comes to the various elements or factors in determining learning style. Interindividual knowledge is increased as students realize that there are many different ways to learn.

Finally, the third kind of personal knowledge is universal knowledge, the knowledge that there are degrees of understanding. Examples are the realization that short-term memory is fallible and has limited capacity, that people can make mistakes, that it is easier to remember things if they are written down, that memory work requires repetition, and so forth. To examine students' understanding of universal knowledge, teachers might ask students to identify what they know about learning, for example, by asking students to write down on notecards what they know about how people learn things or by brainstorming the question in class.

The second broad category of metacognitive knowledge, according to Flavell, is task knowledge. Task knowledge includes several different variables, such as whether information is interesting or boring, or if it is new or familiar, or if it is easy or difficult. Task knowledge enables learners to plan appropriately for undertaking tasks (for example, if something is hard to learn, then it may take more time, more concentration, and more effort) and tells them how to go about accomplishing the task (for example, if the task requires memory, then a memory strategy is needed).

Specific tasks relevant to academic disciplines can be identified by classroom teachers; however, there are academic tasks that are generally applicable to all content-areas. These academic tasks include what are broadly referred to as study skills, but which are foundational skills for all learning. They include such tasks as time management, directing attention, processing information, finding main ideas, studying, and taking tests, among others (Weinstein, Schulte, & Palmer, 1988).

Flavell's final category of metacognitive knowledge is strategy knowledge which takes into account how learners can best accomplish particular tasks and how they can be reasonably certain that they have reached their cognitive goals. Strategy knowledge also equips learners to monitor their cognitive activities and to gain confidence in their abilities. To illustrate, if the task is to find main ideas, then learners need strategies for finding main ideas. Strategies for this task include learning (a) to preview or survey reading assignments (reading headings, words in bold print; looking at illustrations and graphic aids); (b) to ask questions (What is this about?, Who is this about?, When did it happen?, Where did it happen?, How did it happen?, Why did it happen?); and (c) to read the first and last sentences in each paragraph (knowing that the first and last sentences in paragraphs are most likely to be topic sentences).

STUDY STRATEGIES

If the task is to study, then learners need specific strategies for studying. These strategies can include, among others, (a) outlining, mapping, or summarizing text (from books or notes); (b) marking text (using margins for notetaking and summarizing); (c) participating in group review sessions; (d) comparing notes with a friend, tutor, or teacher; (e) getting extra help (from a tutor, teacher, or parent); and, (f) going to the library (to get additional information from alternative sources). Of course, strategies such as outlining can be further delineated into specific steps for various kinds of outlines.

Obviously, there is an interaction between person, task, and strategy knowledge. For example, if the task is studying, then a visual learner who learns well by reading (individual characteristic) might choose to go to the library to find an alternative source of information (strategy characteristic); in this example, there is a three-way interaction involving task, individual, and strategy.

Although teachers willingly expend considerable energy teaching students about tasks, they often erroneously assume that students will automatically or tacitly acquire learning strategies. However, the fact is that many students do not acquire these strategies and that even those who may learn some strategies would benefit from direct instruction in the use of specific learning strategies. The research literature indicates that the use of think-aloud protocols, spontaneous private speech, skimming, rereading, context clues, error-detection, grouping skills, examination/evaluation skills (distinguishing between con-

ceptual versus superficial features, or between major themes and minor details and between decoding and comprehension, between verbatim recall and recall for gist) can
significantly enhance learners' performance.

Teachers who incorporate an understanding of the role played by metacognition
(especially in teaching middle-school and older students) into their instruction will find
that they are preparing their students well for a lifetime of learning. Flavell (1979)
explained that metacognition is necessary for the oral communication of information, oral
persuasion, oral comprehension, reading comprehension, writing, language acquisition,
attention, memory, problem-solving, social cognition, self-control, and self-instruction. It
is hard to imagine a task that one might do that wouldn't require metacognition.

A recent critique of education in America includes the observation that the movement to teach basic academic skills in America's schools may have resulted in more
students performing well on tests of basic skills; however, thinking skills, not just basic
skills, are needed in the real world of jobs, families, and citizenship. To better prepare
students for the real world, teachers need to focus on the *process* of learning, teaching
students *how to think and learn*. Teaching metacognitive awareness and fostering the
development of metacognitive knowledge are steps in the right direction.

Students often say that they like teachers who can motivate students when, in fact,
teachers are not responsible for students' motivation. Motivation is a student's responsibility; motivation comes from within the student. However, effective teachers will help
students develop self-discipline, self-control, and self-motivation. These skills of self-
management can be taught, yet they require a great deal of effort and practice in order for
students to gain true proficiency.

When students say that they like or want teachers who motivate them, they are
probably referring to some characteristics that teachers possess which are attractive and
interesting to learners. So, while it is true that teachers are not responsible for students'
motivation, it is also true that teachers can influence motivation, that teachers can promote and/or inhibit motivation in the classroom by their attitudes and their actions.

One researcher has offered three principles to guide teachers that will lead to
greater effectiveness in the classroom (Baxter-Magolda, 1992). Interestingly, each of
these principles leads to empowering students and, thus, are motivational in nature.

The first principle is to *validate students as knowers*. This principle is based on the
idea of the active learner who brings much to the classroom (the dynamic view of human
development). How can teachers validate students? Baxter-Magolda suggests that teachers display a caring attitude towards students. This means that it's appropriate for teachers to take an interest in students, to learn about their likes and dislikes, their interests and
hobbies, both in school and outside school. This also means that it's okay for teachers to
show enthusiasm and excitement for their classes, not only the subject-matter they teach,
but the students they teach as well. It also means, as Carol Tavris (1994) noted, that it's
good for teachers to show empathy for students' emotional needs.

Baxter-Magolda also recommends that teachers question authority by example and
let students know that they, as teachers, can also be questioned. This means that teachers
model critical thinking skills in the classroom. Teachers can question authority when they
examine and evaluate readings—whether from textbooks or other sources. Teachers can
question authorities when they teach propaganda techniques, exposing advertising claims
and gimmicks. Teachers can question authority when they discuss the media and how so-
called news sources shape and form public opinion. There are numerous opportunities for
teachers in dealing with current affairs and public opinion to question authority and
inculcate in their students critical thinking and higher-ordered reasoning skills.

Also, when teachers allow students to question them, teachers are acknowledging that everyone is a learner. Everyone should participate in a lifelong process of continuous learning. It is no shame or disgrace for the teacher to admit that sometimes he or she doesn't know the answer to every question. This gives the teacher the opportunity to show students how adults think, how they have a level of awareness (metacognition) when they don't know something, and about how they go about finding answers to their questions. Teachers who admit that they don't have all the answers thus have the opportunity to show students how answers can be found and/or to reveal to students that there are no easy answers to some of life's most difficult questions.

Third, to validate students as knowers, teachers can value students' opinions, ideas, and comments. Teachers' affirmations include smiles and nods of approval, positive comments (such as, "That's a good answer."), and encouraging cues (such as, "That may seem like a reasonable answer, but can you think of a better answer?" or "Can you explain what you mean by that answer?"). Validating students as knowers also means supporting students' voices, that is, giving them ample opportunities to express their own ideas, to share their opinions, to make their own contributions to the classroom. These opportunities can include times of oral discussion as well as written assignments.

JOINTLY CONSTRUCTED MEANING

Another principle in Baxter-Magolda's guidelines for teaching effectiveness is for teachers and students to recognize that learning is *a process of jointly-constructing meaning*. To explain, Baxter-Magolda says that it is important for teachers to dialogue with students (also an important concept in Piagetian theory) and that teachers emphasize mutual learning. Also in agreement with Piagetian principles, Baxter-Magolda recommends that teachers reveal their own thinking processes as they approach subjects and as they analyze and understand new subjects and as they solve problems and reach decisions. She further advises that teachers share leadership and promote collegial learning (group work), acknowledging that individual achievement is not the sole purpose or focus for learning. By allowing students to collaborate, they also will learn significant lessons directly applicable to work situations where most accomplishments are the result of team efforts, not the sole efforts of individuals.

Baxter-Magolda's final principle for teachers is to *situate learning in the students' own experiences*. She suggests that this be done by letting students know that they are wanted in class, by using inclusive language (avoiding ethnic and cultural bias and stereotyping, instead using gender-neutral and inclusive language), and focusing on activities. Activities are important for motivation because they give learners things to do, to become actively involved in, arousing their attention and interest, and giving them an outlet for their physical and mental energy. Activities can have an additional positive benefit in that they can serve to connect students to each other, especially when students are given opportunities to participate in collaborative learning (the way things happen in the "real world") and to work in groups. Finally, in situating learning in students' own experiences, it is important to consider the use of personal stories in class, as appropriate (that is, without violating anyone's right to privacy and confidentiality). Moreover, teachers can share personal stories which allow them to connect with students in a deeper and more personal way.

The child psychologist, Harvard professor, and author of numerous scholarly and popular books, Robert Coles, recently wrote of his experiences teaching in a Boston inner-city high school. He told of his disillusionment and his struggle to claim students' respect and attention so that he could teach them. Finally, there was a classroom confrontation, followed by a self-revelation (that being to show his students what he was like as a person). He shared some of his thoughts and feelings about loneliness. He told about his own boyhood experiences of visiting museums with his mother and what she taught him about art. In the end, he, too, had a revelation; he concluded that when teachers share what we have learned about ourselves with our students, we often can transcend the barriers of class and race. A teacher can change a "me" and a "them" (the students) into an "us." Building camaraderie this way then becomes an optimal starting point for teaching and learning (Coles, 1993). Dr. Coles' experience was that telling his story to the class was a step towards helping his students claim some motivation of their own.

When students assume responsibility for their own motivation, they are learning a lesson of personal empowerment. Unfortunately, although personal empowerment is probably one of the most important lessons anyone ever learns, it is a lesson infrequently taught in classrooms across the country.

Empowerment has at least four components, one of which is self-esteem. A good definition of self-esteem is that it is my opinion of me, your opinion of you. It is what we think and believe to be true about ourselves, not what we think about others and not what they think about us. Self-esteem appears to be a combination of self-efficacy and self-respect as seen against a background of self-knowledge.

Self-efficacy, simply stated, is one's confidence in one's own ability to cope with life's challenges. Self-efficacy refers to having a sense of control over life or, better, over one's responses to life. Experts say that ideas about self-efficacy get established by the time children reach the age of four. Because of this early establishment of either a feeling of control or no control, classroom teachers may find that even primary grade students believe that they have no control over their life, that it makes no difference what they do or how they act. Therefore, it is all the more important that teachers attempt to help all students achieve coping skills and a sense of self-efficacy.

Control, in this definition of self-efficacy, can be examined in regard to external or internal motivators. For example, external motivators include such things as luck and the roles played by others in influencing outcomes. Internal motivators are variables within the individual. To explain, if a student does well on a test and is asked, "How did you do so well on that test?," a student who relies on external motivators might reply, "Well, I just got lucky," or "The teacher likes me." If the student failed the test and is asked why, the student dependent on external motivators might answer, "Well, it wasn't my lucky day," or "The teacher doesn't like me," or "My friends caused me to goof off and not pay attention so I didn't know the answers on the test." A student who relies on internal motivators and who does well on a test may explain, "I am smart and always do well on tests," or "I studied hard and that's why I did well." On the other hand, even the student who relies on internal motivators can do poorly on tests and then may explain, "I'm dumb and that's why I don't do well," or "I didn't think the test was important and I didn't try very hard." Even though students have similar experiences, in regard to issues of control, what is important is how students explain their experiences. If students have external motivators, they are likely to either dismiss their performance (success or failure) as matters of luck or to credit or blame the influence of others. If students have internal motivators, then they are likely to attribute their performance to either their intelligence and skills (ability) or their effort.

Students who have external motivators need help understanding how their behavior contributes to and influences outcomes in school. Students need clarification as to how grades are determined and precise information about how their work is evaluated. Students who have internal motivators but low self-esteem (such as thinking, "I'm dumb") need help identifying their strengths and assets (something that can be accomplished when students are given information about learning styles). Self-efficacy can be enhanced.

Another factor in empowerment is self-respect. Self-respect is believing that one deserves happiness, achievement, and love. Self-respect is treating one's self as least as nicely as one treats other people. Many students are not aware of their internal voices (which are established at an early age). Internal voices are constantly sending messages, either positive or negative. Psychologists say that most of us have either a generally positive outlook on life, and our inner voice sends generally positive messages ("You're okay," "People like you," "Things will be all right," and so forth) or a generally negative outlook on life, and an inner voice sending negative messages ("You're not okay," "You're too fat, skinny, ugly, stupid," and so forth).

Many students need to become aware of their inner voice and how it can be setting them up for failure. They need to learn that they can tell their inner voice to stop sending negative messages, and that they can reprogram their inner voice to be kinder, gentler, and to send positive messages. However, it does require effort, practice, and time to reprogram the inner voice.

Two tools which can help students in the reprogramming process are affirmations and visualizations (Ellis, 1991). Affirmations are statements describing what students want. Affirmations must be personal, positive, and written in the present tense. What makes affirmations effective are details. For example, instead of saying, "I am stupid," students can be encouraged to say, "I am capable. I do well in school because I am organized, I study daily, I get all my work completed on time, and I take my school work seriously." Affirmations must be repeated until they can be said with total conviction.

Visualizations are images students can create whereby they see themselves the way they want to be. For example, if a student wants to improve his or her typing skills, then the student evaluates what it would look like, sound like, and feel like to be a better typist. Once the student identifies the image, then the student has to rehearse that image in her or his mind, including as many details and sensations as possible. Both visualization and affirmation can restructure attitudes and behaviors. They can be tools for students to use to increase their motivation.

Finally, the fourth component of empowerment is self-knowledge. Self-knowledge refers to an individual's strengths and weaknesses, assets and liabilities; self-knowledge comes about as a result of a realistic self-appraisal (and can be achieved by an examination of learning styles). Achieving self-knowledge also requires that students have opportunities to explore their goals and values.

Students who know what their goals and values are can more easily see how education will enable them to achieve those goals and values. Conversely, students cannot be motivated when they do not have goals and values, or when they do not know what their goals and values are. In other words, without self-knowledge, motivation is impossible. Therefore, teachers who follow Baxter-Magolda's guidelines for effective instruction and who teach their students about personal empowerment are teachers who realize the importance of motivation and who set the stage for students to claim responsibility for their own successes and failures. Such teachers help students to become motivated to make changes and to accomplish more.

HUMAN DEVELOPMENT

PRACTICE QUESTIONS

1. Rueben Stein is a middle-school teacher who wants to teach his class about the classification system in the animal kingdom. He decides to introduce this unit to his class by having the students engage in general classification activities. He brings to class a paper bag filled with 30 household items. He dumps the contents of the bag onto a table and then asks the students, in groups of three or four, to put like items into piles and then to justify or explain why they placed certain items into a particular pile.

    By assigning this task to his students, Mr. Stein is providing his students with a developmentally-appropriate task because

    (A) middle-school students like to work in groups.

    (B) the items in the bag are household items with which most students will be familiar.

    (C) the assignment gives students the opportunity to practice their skills at categorizing.

    (D) the assignment will give students a task to perform while the teacher finishes grading papers.

2. Maria Smith is a high school English teacher who is concerned about a student who is failing her junior English class. The student has not turned in any outside assignments, and Ms. Smith has noticed a definite decline in the quality of work the student completes in class. Ms. Smith also has observed that the student has great difficulty staying awake in class and that she seems irritable and distracted most of the time.

    In her efforts to help the student, Ms. Smith decides to ask the student

    (A) if she has been having family problems.

    (B) if she realizes that the quality of her classwork is suffering and if she knows of any reasons for the decline.

    (C) to work on better time-management skills.

    (D) to start coming in early or to stay after class to receive extra help with her work.

3. Elva Rodriguez teaches fourth grade. She has structured her class so that students can spend thirty minutes daily, after lunch, in sustained, silent reading activities with books and reading materials of their own choosing.

    In order to maximize this reading opportunity and to recognize differences among learners, Ms. Rodriguez

(A) allows some students to sit quietly at their desks while others are allowed to move to a reading area where they sit on floor cushions or recline on floor mats.

(B) makes sure that all students have selected appropriate reading materials.

(C) plays classical music on a tape player to enhance student learning.

(D) dims the lights in the classroom in order to increase students' reading comprehension.

4. Karla Dixon is a second-grade teacher who has selected a book to read to her class after lunch. She shows the students the picture on the cover of the book and reads the title of the book to them. She then asks, "What do you think this book is about?"

By asking this question, Ms. Dixon is

(A) learning which students are interested in reading strategies.

(B) trying to keep the students awake since she knows they usually get sleepy after lunch.

(C) encouraging students to make a prediction, a precursor of hypothetical thinking.

(D) finding out which students are good readers.

5. Ben Douglas is a high school history teacher. His class is studying the Korean Conflict when a student brings up a question about the morality of the war in Vietnam. This is not a subject that Mr. Douglas is prepared to teach at the time.

In response to the student's question, Mr. Douglas

(A) tells the student that the day's topic is the Korean Conflict and suggests that the student bring up the question later on in the term.

(B) invites the class to respond to the student's question.

(C) gives the student a cursory response, eliminating the need for any further discussion.

(D) disciplines the student for not paying attention to the topic under discussion.

HUMAN DEVELOPMENT

ANSWERS TO PRACTICE QUESTIONS

1. **(C)**
2. **(B)**
3. **(A)**
4. **(C)**
5. **(B)**

REFERENCES

Baxter-Magolda, M. B. (1992). *Knowing and reasoning in college: Gender-related patterns in students' intellectual development.* San Francisco: Jossey Bass.

Bloom, B. (1976). *Human characteristics and school learning.* New York: McGraw-Hill.

Canfield, A. A. & Canfield, J. S. (1988). Instructional styles inventory. Los Angeles: Western Psychological Services.

Coles, R. (1993). Point of view: When earnest volunteers are solely tested. *Chronicle of Higher Education*, May 5, A52.

Dunn, R. (1993). Presentation on the Productivity Environmental Preferences Scale (PEPS) at Learning Styles Institute, Lubbock, Texas, June 5-9. (Sponsored by Education Service Center, Region XVII.)

Dunn, R., & Dunn, K. (1993). Presentation on Using Learning Styles Information to Enhance Teaching Effectiveness at Learning Styles Institute, Lubbock, Texas, June 5-9. (Sponsored by Education Service Center, Region XVII.)

Elkind, D. (1967). Egocentrism in adolescence. *Child Development*, 38, 1025-34.

Ellis, D. (1991). *Becoming a master student.* Rapid City, SD: College Survival.

Erikson, E. (1963). *Childhood and society.* New York: Horton.

Flavell, J. H. (1979). Metacognition and cognitive monitoring: A new area of cognitive-developmental inquiry. *American Psychologist*, 34, 906-911.

Flavell, J. H. (1987). Speculations about the nature and development of metacognition. In R. H. Kluwe & F. E. Weinert (Eds.), *Metacognition, motivation, and learning* (pp. 21-30). Hillsdale, NJ: Erlbaum.

Maslow, A. (1968). *Toward a psychology of being.* New York: Van Nostrand Reinhold.

Nolting, P. (1993). Presentation on Meeting Learners' Special Needs at West Texas Regional TASP Workshop, Lubbock, Texas, August 7. (Sponsored by Texas Tech University.)

Piaget, J. (1950). *The psychology of intelligence.* London: Routledge and Kegan Paul.

Sadker, M., & Sadker, D. (1994). *Failing at fairness: How America's schools cheat girls.* New York: Charles Scribner's Sons.

Sternberg, R. J. (1985). *Beyond IQ: A triarchic theory of human intelligence.* Cambridge: Cambridge University Press.

Tavris, C. (1994). Presentation on Coping with Student Conflict Inside and Outside the Classroom at Texas Junior College Teachers Conference, San Antonio, February 25.

Weinstein, C. E., Schulte, A.C., & Palmer, D. R. (1988). The learning and study strategies inventory. Clearwater, FL: H & H Publishing.

MSAT

Multiple Subjects Assessment for Teachers

CHAPTER 8

Physical Education Review

Chapter 8

Physical Education Review

The Physical Education section of the MSAT accounts for 7 percent, or 8 questions, in the Content Knowledge exam, and 2 items in the Content Area Exercises. The Physical Education review addresses the specific knowledge needed in the physical, biological, and social sciences to teach physical education. There are three main elements to the test and the review.

Movement Concepts (50 percent)
- Fundamental locomotor and nonlocomotor movements
- Fitness
- Movement forms

Physical and Biological Foundations (40 percent)
- Growth and Development
- Motor learning
- Anatomy
- Exercise physiology
- Kinesiology

Social Science Foundations (10 percent)
- Social and psychological aspects of physical education

More specifically, the review covers knowledge necessary to a physical education instructor, such as diet and nutrition, and specific games and tasks that teach specific skills.

One of the primary reasons for the teaching of physical education is to instill a willingness to exercise. To that end it is important to understand the benefits in participating in a lifelong program of exercise and physical fitness.

Fortunately it is not difficult to find justification for exercising and maintaining a consistently high level of fitness. The benefits of a consistent program of diet and exercise are many. Improved cardiac output, improved maximum oxygen intake, and improvement of the blood's ability to carry oxygen are just a few of these benefits. Exercise also lowers the risk of heart disease by strengthening the heart muscle, lowering pulse and blood pressure, and lowering the concentration of fat in both the body and the blood. It can also improve appearance, increase range of motion, and lessen the risk of back problems associated with weak bones and osteoperosis.

PRINCIPLES OF PHYSICAL FITNESS

Physical fitness is the ability of the entire body to work together efficiently—to be able to do the most amount of work with the least amount of effort. Physical fitness is composed of four basic components: strength and power, endurance, agility, and speed and flexibility. Training is required to develop consistent physical fitness, and training is comprised of several principles. To begin, a warm-up is essential. An effective warm-up will increase body temperature and blood flow, as well as guard against strains and tears to muscles, tendons, and ligaments. A good warm-up consists of stretching exercises, calisthenics, walking and slow jogging.

While exercising, a student must be aware of his or her body's adaptations to the demands imposed by training. Some of these adaptations are improved heart function and circulation, improved respiratory function, and improved muscular strength and endurance. All of these adaptations lead to improved vigor and vitality. In order to affect these adaptations, the students must exert themselves to a far greater degree than their normal daily activities. This exertion is referred to as overload. Despite what this term suggests, it does not imply that trainers should work beyond healthy limits, however it does imply that they must push themselves in order to see results. The rate of improvement and adaptation is directly related to the frequency, intensity and duration of training.

In addition to regular training, you must gear your students' training toward those adaptations which are important to them. This is know as specificity. Performance improves when the training is specific to the activity being performed. That is to say, certain activities will have more effect on cardiovascular health than overall muscle tone and appearance, and vice versa. Therefore, you should always try to maintain a balance in your exercise.

The body thrives on activity and therefore, the axiom "use it or lose it" certainly holds true. Lack of activity can cause many problems, including flabby muscles, a weak heart, poor circulation, shortness of breath, obesity, and a degenerative weakening of the skeletal system. It is important to note, however, that when many people begin a program of exercise, they expect to see results immediately. More often than not, this is not the case. Individual response to exercise varies greatly from person to person. This can be affected by heredity, age, general physical fitness, rest and sleep habits, an individual's motivation, their environmental influences, and any handicap, disease or injury that may impede the body's adaptation to training. The sum of all these factors is an individual's potential for maximizing his or her own physical fitness. Unfortunately, very few people live up to this full potential.

Finally, a good program of exercise always ends with a cooling off period. Very much like the warm-up, and just as essential, the same low impact exercises used during a warm up may be used to cool off after a period of intense exertion. Without cooling off, blood will pool and slow the removal of waste products. With this basic introduction in mind, let's look at some more specific forms of exercise, and the positive effects they have on the body.

AEROBIC EXERCISE

Aerobic Exercise involves both muscle contraction and movement of the body. Aerobic exercise requires large amounts of oxygen and when done regularly will condition the cardiovascular system. Some aerobic exercises are especially suited to developing aerobic training benefits, with a minimum of skill and time involved. Examples of good aerobic activities are walking, running, swimming, rope skipping, and bicycling. These activities are especially good in the development of fitness because all of them can be done alone and with a minimum of special equipment. In order to be considered true aerobic conditioning, an activity must require a great deal of oxygen, it must be continuous and rhythmic, it must exercise major muscle groups, burn fat as an energy source, and it must last for at least twenty minutes at an individual's target heart rate. You may determine your target heart rate by subtracting 80% of your age from 220.

Interval training is also a good way to develop fitness. This type of exercise involves several different aerobic activities performed at intervals to comprise one exercise session. If a student learns about interval training he or she will be better able to create his or her own fitness program. All the above mentioned activities provide examples of methods of interval training.

LOW IMPACT AEROBICS

For some people, low impact aerobics may have some advantages over traditional, or high impact aerobics. Because low impact aerobic exercise is easier to perform, it is an option for all ages and levels of fitness. It is easier to monitor your heart rate, there is less warm up and cool down required. Because one foot is on the ground at all times, there is less chance of injury. In all other respects, such as duration and frequency, low impact aerobic exercise is identical to high impact.

ANATOMY AND PHYSIOLOGY

Anatomy describes the structure, position and size of various organs. Because our bones adapt to fill a specific need, exercise is of great benefit to the skeletal system. Bones which anchor strong muscles thicken to withstand the stress. Weight bearing bones can develop heavy mineral deposits while supporting the body. Because joints help provide flexibility and ease of movement, it is important to know how each joint moves. Types of joints are ball and socket, (shoulder and hip) hinge, (knee) pivot (head of the spine), gliding (carpal and tarsal bones) angular (wrist and ankle joints) partially moveable (vertebrae) and immovable (bones of the adult cranium).

Muscles are the active movers in the body. In order to properly teach any physical education activity the functions and physiology of the muscles must be understood. Since muscles move by shortening or contracting, proper form should be taught so the student can get the most out of an activity. It is also important to know the location of each muscle. This knowledge will help in teaching proper form while doing all physical education activities. Understanding the concept of antagonistic muscles, along with the related information concerning flexors and extensors, is also vital to the physical educator. Imagine trying to teach the proper form of throwing a ball if you do not understand the mechanics involved. Knowledge of anatomy and physiology is also necessary to teach proper techniques used in calisthenics as well as all physical activities. Some physical education class standbys are frequently done improperly or done when the exercise itself can cause harm. Examples of these are squat thrusts, straight leg sit-ups, straight leg toe touches, straight leg push-ups for girls and double leg lifts.

SPORTS AND GAMES

Individual, dual and team sports all have a prominent place in a successful physical education curriculum. Since one of the attributes of a quality physical education program is carry over value, it is easy to justify the inclusion of these activities in a curriculum. That is not to say that "rolling out the ball" is enough to create learning situations through the use of sports and games. Learning the rules and keeping score supplies a framework for goals and learning how to deal with both victory and defeat. Examples of some sports and games that are useful to achieve the aforementioned goals are as follows:

Team Sports

Volleyball —6 players, two out of three games. Winner scores 15 points with a margin of two.

Basketball —5 players. Most points at the end of the game wins.

Softball —9 or 10 players. Most runs at the end of seven innings wins.

Field Hockey —11 players. Most goals wins.

Soccer —11 players. Most goals wins.

Flag Football —9 or 11 players (can be modified to fit ability and size of the class). Six points for a touchdown, one or two for a point after, and two for a safety.

Dual Sports

Tennis—Either doubles or singles. Four points–fifteen, thirty, forty, and game. Tie at forty–deuce. Winner must win by a margin of two. Remember, love means nothing in tennis.

Badminton—Either doubles or singes. Winner in doubles 15 points, singles 21 by a margin of two.

Table Tennis—Either doubles or singles. 21 points by a margin of two.

Shuffleboard—Either singles or doubles. 50, 75, or 100 points. Determined by participants before the game begins.

Individual Sports

Swimming—Very good for cardiovascular conditioning and can be done almost anywhere there is water.

Track and field—Scoring varies with event.

Bowling—Scoring is unique and good math skills are encouraged.

Weight training—No scoring involved but the benefits are many. Muscles are toned and strengthened through the use of weight training. Either weight machines or free weights can be used. It is important for students to learn the proper techniques and principles of weight training so they can reap the benefits while avoiding injury. When weight training, participants must consider the concept of muscular balance– this is equal strength in opposing muscle groups. All opposing groups (antagonistic muscles) i.e., triceps and biceps, hamstrings and quadriceps need to be equal or body parts may become improperly aligned. The responsibility of the physical educator is to teach accurate information about the human body as well as teach ways to prevent injury and achieve efficiency in movement. Understanding that abdominal strength is important to lower back strength can help students create an exercise program to help avoid back injuries.

Gymnastics—Includes tumbling. Excellent activity for developing coordination and grace. Also requires strength which is developed by the activities done. This training can begin at a very early age with tumbling activities and progress to gymnastics.

Golf—A fantastic carry over activity that can be taught on campus, at the golf course or both. Requires coordination, concentration and depth perception.

Rhythmics—Includes ball gymnastics and other activities that may require music. Rhythmics can be taught in early elementary physical education, enabling students to develop music appreciation as well as spatial awareness.

Dance—Can be either individually or with a partner. Dance is especially good at developing spatial awareness and the ability to follow instructions. Dance instruction should begin in elementary school. Basic steps are walk and/or skip and are suitable to teach to first and second graders. Skip, slide, and run and/or skip are suitable for second and third graders, and the more difficult step-hop can be taught to grades three through six. The ability to dance can also aid in the development of social skills and teamwork. Dance also provides an excellent framework for multicultural education. Many dances are indigenous to certain cultures and students can learn about different races and cultures while learning dances. Having the class walk through the dances without the music and then adding the music is effective. The instructor must be careful not to teach too many steps before the dance is tried with the music. Most students enjoy dance in spite of themselves.

Adaptive Physical Education

Public Law 94-142 provides the legal definition for the term "handicapped children." It includes children who have been evaluated as being mentally impaired, deaf, speech impaired, visually handicapped, seriously emotionally disturbed, orthopedically impaired, multi-handicapped, having learning disabilities or having other health impairments (anemia, arthritis, etc.). P.L. 94-142 states that these children need special education and services. The challenge in teaching physical education to handicapped children is tailoring activities to fit each child. For example blind or partially sighted students can participate in weightlifting, dance, and some gymnastic and tumbling activities. These students can also participate in some other activities with modifications. A beeper ball can be used for softball; a beeper can be used for archery. If a beeper is not available for archery the teacher can put the student in position and assist in aiming. Many games and activities can be modified for the handicapped. Sometimes all it takes is a little ingenuity to change activities so handicapped people can enjoy participating.

There are many students who are only temporarily disabled who will benefit from adaptive physical education. Examples of temporary disabilities are pregnancy, broken bones, and recovery from surgery and disease. It is very important when teaching the handicapped and temporarily handicapped not to have a very large class. The optimum class size for handicapped students would be less than ten with fifteen being the absolute maximum.

HEALTH AND DIET

Along with exercise, a knowledge of and participation in a healthy life style is vital to good health and longevity. What constitutes good nutrition, the role of vitamins, elimination of risk factors and strategies to control weight are all part of a healthy lifestyle.

Good Nutrition

Complex carbohydrates should comprise at least half of the diet. This is important because these nutrients are the primary and most efficient source of energy. Examples of complex carbohydrates are: vegetables, fruits, high-fiber breads and cereals. Fiber in the diet is very important because it promotes digestion, reduces constipation and has been shown to help reduce the risk of colon cancer. Another benefit of complex carbohydrates is that they are high in water content which is vital to the functioning of the entire body.

Proteins should comprise about one fifth of the diet. Protein is a food which builds and repairs the body. Sources of protein are beans, peas, lentils, peanuts and other pod plants. Another source is red meat, which unfortunately contains great deal of saturated fat.

There are two categories of fat; unsaturated, which is found in vegetables, and saturated which comes from animals or vegetables. Cocoa butter, palm oil and coconut oil are saturated fats that come from vegetables. Unsaturated vegetable fats are preferable to saturated fats because they appear to offset the rise in blood pressure that accompanies too much saturated fat. These fats may also lower cholesterol and help with weight loss. Whole milk products contain saturated fat but the calcium found in them is vital to health. For this reason, most fat limiting diets suggest the use of skim milk and low fat cheese.

Research indicates a link between high fat diets and many types of cancer. Diets high in saturated fats are also dangerous because fats cause the body to produce to much low-density lipoprotein in the system. Cholesterol, a substance only found in animals, is of two different kinds, LDL (Low Density Lipoproteins) and HDL (High Density Lipoproteins). Some cholesterol is essential in order for the body to function properly. It is vital to the brain and an important component of the creation of certain hormones. The body produces cholesterol in the liver. Excess cholesterol found in the blood of so many people usually comes from cholesterol in their diet rather than from internal production. LDL cholesterol encourages the build up of plaque in the arteries. HDLs do just the opposite. LDL cholesterol can be controlled through proper diet, and HDL cholesterol levels can be raised by exercise. Triglycerides are another form of fat found in the blood which are important to monitor because high triglycerides seem to be inversely proportional to HDLs.

Vitamins

Vitamins are essential to good health. One must be careful, however, not to take too much of certain vitamins. Fat soluble, A, D, E, and K vitamins will be stored in the body and in excessive amounts will cause some dangerous side effects. Water soluble vitamins, all the rest, are generally excreted through the urinary system and the skin when taken to excess. A brief synopsis of the vitamins and minerals needed by the body follows:

Vitamin A: Needed for normal vision and prevention of night blindness, healthy skin, resistance to disease and tissue growth and repair. Found in spinach, carrots, broccoli and other dark green or yellow orange fruits and vegetables; also found in liver and plums.

Vitamin D: Promotes absorption of calcium and phosphorous, normal growth of healthy bones, teeth, and nails. Formed by the action of the sun on the skin. Also found in halibut liver oil, herring, cod liver oil, mackerel, salmon, and tuna, and is added to many milk products.

Vitamin E: Protects cell membranes, seems to improve elasticity in blood vessels, also may prevent formation of blood clots and protect red blood cells from damage by oxidation. Found in wheat germ oil, sunflower seeds, raw wheat germ, almonds, pecans, peanut oil, and cod liver oil.

Thiamin / B1: Functioning of nerves, muscle growth and fertility. Also production of energy, appetite and digestion. Found in pork, legumes, nuts, enriched and fortified whole grains, and liver.

Riboflavin / B2: Aids in the production of red blood cells, good vision, healthy skin and mouth tissue, and production of energy. Found in lean meat, dairy products, liver, eggs, enriched and fortified whole grains, and green leafy vegetables.

Niacin / B3: Promotes energy production, appetite, digestive and nervous system, healthy skin and tongue.

Pyridoxine / B6: Red blood cell formation and growth. Found in liver, beans, pork, fish, legumes, enriched and fortified whole grains and green leafy vegetables.

Vitamin B12: Healthy nerve tissue, energy production, utilization of folic acid, and aids in the formation of healthy red blood cells. Found in dairy products, liver, meat, poultry, fish and eggs.

Vitamin C: Promotes healing and growth, resists infection, increases iron absorption, aids in bone and tooth formation/repair. Found in citrus fruits, cantaloupe, potatoes, strawberries, tomatoes and green vegetables.

Minerals

Sodium: Normal water balance inside and outside cells. Blood pressure regulation and electrolyte and chemical balance. Found in salt, processed foods, bread and bakery products.

Potassium: Volume and balance of body fluids. Prevents muscle weakness and cramping, important for normal heart rhythm and electrolyte balance in the blood. Found in citrus fruits, leafy green vegetables, potatoes and tomatoes.

Zinc: Taste, appetite, healthy skin, and wound healing. Found in lean meat, liver, milk, fish, poultry, whole grain cereals, and shellfish.

Iron: Red blood cell formation, oxygen transport to the cells, prevents nutritional anemia. Found in liver, lean meats, dried beans, peas, eggs, dark green leafy vegetables, and whole grain cereals.

Calcium: Strong bones, teeth, nails, muscle tone, prevents osteoporosis, prevents muscle cramping. Helps the nerves function and the heart beat. Found in milk, yogurt, and other dairy products, and dark leafy vegetables.

Phosphorous: Regulates blood chemistry and internal processes, strong bones and teeth. Found in meat, fish, poultry, and dairy products.

Magnesium: Energy production, normal heart rhythm, nerve/muscle function, and prevents muscle cramps. Found in dried beans, nuts, whole grains, bananas and leafy green vegetables.

Elimination of Risk Factors

Another aspect of physical education concerns awareness and avoidance of the risks that are present in our everyday lives. Some risk factors include being overweight, smoking, use of drugs, unprotected sex, and stress. Education is the key to minimizing the presence of these risk factors. Unfortunately, because of the presence of peer pressure and lack of parental control the effect of education is sometimes not enough.

Weight-Control Strategies

Statistics show that Americans get fatter every year. Even though countless books and magazine articles are written on the subject of weight control, often the only place a student gets reliable information about diet is in a classroom. For example, it is an unfortunate reality that fat people do not live as long, on average, as thin ones. Being overweight has been isolated as a risk factor in various cancers, heart disease, gall bladder problems, and kidney disease. Chronic diseases such as diabetes and high blood pressure are also aggravated, or caused by, being overweight.

Conversely, a great many problems are presented by being underweight. Our society often places too much value on losing weight, especially on women. Ideal weight, as well as a good body-fat ratio, is the goal when losing weight. A study done at the Cooper clinic shows a correlation between body fat and high cholesterol. Exercise is the key to a good body-fat ratio. Exercise helps to keep the ratio down thus improving cholesterol levels, and helps in preventing heart disease.

In order to lose weight, calories burned must exceed calories going in. No matter what kind of diet is tried, this principle applies. There is no easy way to maintain a healthy weight. Here again, the key is exercise. If calorie intake is restricted too much, the body goes into its starvation mode and operates by burning fewer calories. Just a 250-calorie drop a day combined with a 250-calorie burn will result in a loss of one pound a week. Crash diets, which bring about rapid weight loss, are not only unhealthy but also are not very effective. Slower weight loss is more lasting. Aerobic exercise is the key to successful weight loss. Exercise speeds up metabolism and causes the body to burn calories. Timing of exercise will improve the benefits. Exercise before meals speeds up metabolism and has been shown to suppress appetite. Losing and maintaining weight is not easy. Through education, people will be better able to realize that losing weight is hard work and is a constant battle.

FIRST AID

First aid is the immediate, temporary care of an injured or ill person. Occasionally during physical education classes, injuries and illnesses can occur. For this reason a basic knowledge of first aid is important for physical education teachers.

Fractures—Any break in a bone is a fracture. Fractures can be *simple*—a break in the bone, *comminuted* or shattered—many breaks, or many breaks in the bone, or *compound*—a break in the bone and the skin. First aid: immobilize, use ice to control swelling, seek medical aid. In the case of a compound fracture it is important to stop bleeding.

Shock—Traumatic shock is a severe compression of circulation caused by injury or illness. Symptoms include, cool clammy skin and rapid weak pulse. First aid: minimize heat loss and elevate the legs without disturbing the rest of the body. Seek medical help.

Sprain—An injury to a joint caused by the joint being moved too far or away from its range of motion. Both ligaments and tendons can be injured. Ligaments join bone to bone and tendons join muscle to bone. First Aid: R.I.C.E.—rest, immobilization, compression, and elevation.

Strain—A muscle injury caused by overwork. First aid: use ice to lessen swelling, some heat after can be beneficial. Opinion on the value of heat varies.

Dislocation—A joint injury in which bone ends are moved out of place at the joints and ligaments holding them are severely stretched and torn. First Aid: immobilize and seek medical help. Some people advocate "popping" the dislocation back into place but this can be risky for both the injured person and person giving the first aid (liability).

Heat Exhaustion—Symptoms include, cold clammy skin, nausea, dizziness and paleness. First Aid: not as severe as heat stroke but must be treated by increase in water intake, replacing salt, and getting out of the heat.

Heat Stroke—High fever, dry skin, and may be unconscious. First Aid: attempt to cool off gradually, get them into the shade, seek medical attention immediately.

CPR—Cardio Pulmonary Resuscitation. First aid technique used to provide artificial circulation and respiration. Remember- A=airway, B=breathing, C=circulation. Check the airway to make sure it is open, check breathing, and circulation.

Heart Attack—Symptoms may include any or all of the following: shortness of breath, pain in the left arm, pain in the chest, nausea, and sweating. First aid: elevate the head and chest, give CPR if indicated, seek medical assistance.

Seizures—Generally caused by epilepsy. First aid: clear the area so victim is not injured during the seizure, do not place anything in the mouth, seek medical help after the seizure if necessary.

MOVEMENT EDUCATION

Movement education is the process by which a child is helped to develop competency in movement. It has been defined as learning to move and moving to learn. Movement competency requires the student to manage his or her body. This body management is necessary to develop both basic and specialized activities. Basic skills are needed by the child for broad areas of activity which are related to daily living and child's play. Specialized skills are required to perform sports and have very clear techniques. Basic skills must be mastered before the child can develop specialized ones. The child controls his or her movement during nonlocomotor (stationary) activities, in movements across the floor or field, through space, and when suspended on apparatus. To obtain good body management skills is to acquire, expand, and to integrate elements of motor control. This is done through wide experiences in movement, based on a creative and exploratory approach. It is important that children not only to manage the body with ease of movement but also realize that good posture and body mechanics are important parts of their movement patterns.

Perceptual motor competency is another consideration in body management. Perceptual motor concepts which are relevant to physical education include those which give attention to balance, coordination, lateral movement, directional movement, awareness of space, and knowledge of one's own body. Basic skills can be divided into three categories, locomotor, nonlocomotor and manipulative skills. A movement pattern might include skills from each category.

Locomotor Skills

Locomotor skills are moving the body from place to place: walking, running, skipping, leaping, galloping, and sliding. Skills which move the body upward such as jumping or hopping are also locomotor skills.

Nonlocomotor Skills

Nonlocomotor skills are done in place or with very little movement from place to place. Examples of nonlocomotor skills are: bending and stretching, pushing and pulling, raising and lowering, twisting and turning, shaking and bouncing.

Manipulative Skills

Manipulative skills are skills used when the child handles a play object. Most manipulative skills involve using the hands and the feet, but other parts of the body may be used as well. Hand-eye and foot-eye coordination are improved with manipulative objects. Throwing, batting, kicking and catching are important skills to be developed using balls and beanbags. Starting a child at a low level of challenge and progressing to a more difficult activity is an effective method for teaching manipulative activities. Most activities begin with individual practice and later move to partner activities. Partners should be of similar ability. When teaching throwing and catching, the teacher should emphasize skill performance, principles of opposition, weight transfer, eye focus, and follow-through. Some attention should be given to targets when throwing because students need to be able to catch and throw to different levels.

Specialized Skills

Specialized skills are related to various sports and other physical education activities such as dance, tumbling, gymnastics and specific games. To teach a specialized skill the instructor must present and use explanation, demonstration, and drill. Demonstration can be done by other students provided the teacher monitors the demonstration and gives cues for proper form. Drills are excellent to teach specific skills but can become tedious unless they are done in a creative manner. Using game simulations to practice skills is an effective method to maintain interest during a practice session.

Teachers must also remember to use feedback when teaching a skill or activity. Positive feedback is much more conducive to skill learning than negative feedback. Feedback means correcting with suggestions to improve. If a student continually hits the ball into the net while playing tennis he or she is aware that something is not right. The teacher should indicate what the problem is and tell the student how to succeed in getting the ball over the net.

Movement education enables the child to make choices of activity and the method they wish to employ. Teachers can structure learning situations so the child can be challenged to develop his or her own means of movement. The child becomes the center of learning and is encouraged to be creative in carrying out the movement experience. In this method of teaching the child is encouraged to be creative and progress according to his/her abilities. The teacher is not the center of learning, but suggests and stimulates the learning environment. Student centered learning works especially well when there is a wide disparity of motor abilities. If the teacher sets standards that are too high for the less talented students they may become discouraged and not try to perform.

Basic movement education attempts to develop the children's awareness not only of what they are doing but how they are doing it. Each child is encouraged to succeed in his or her own way according to his or her own capacity. If children succeed at developing basic skills in elementary school they will have a much better chance at acquiring the specialized skills required for all sports activities.

PSYCHOLOGICAL AND SOCIAL ASPECTS OF PHYSICAL EDUCATION

Physical education is a very important part of a student's elementary school education. It is not only an opportunity to "blow off steam," but it is also an arena of social interaction. One psychological aspect of physical education is the enhancement of self esteem. Often students who have limited success in other classes can "shine" in physical education. This does not happen automatically, it is up to the teacher to create situations that enable students to gain self esteem. Teachers must also be careful not to damage self esteem. An example of a potentially damaging situation occurs during the exercise of choosing members of a team. Teachers should not have the captains chosen and then choose the teams in front of the whole class. Nothing is more demeaning than to be the last person chosen. A better method is for the teacher to select the captains (this is also a very good way to separate the superstars-have the six best athletes be the captains). The captains then go to the sidelines and pick the teams from a class list. The teacher can then post or read the team lists after mixing up the order chosen so no one knows who were the first and last picked.

Gender Equity

It is important to choose both girls and boys as captains so the girls do not feel left out. Lack of gender equity can contribute to serious self esteem problems for girls. Frequently girls are ignored in co-ed classes even when they have good skills. If students have been in co-ed classes for a long period of time, gender equity seems to be less of a problem, but it still exists. Teachers can, through example, foster an atmosphere of fairness. A teacher's attention to students has been proven to affect self-esteem and self-confidence.

Another method to enhance self-esteem is to use students, whenever possible, to demonstrate skills. When students are used to demonstrate, classmates will realize that they too may possess that skill. As they demonstrate, students can give cues and suggestions to improve performance. Most students enjoy being involved in demonstrations, so the instructor should be careful to use as many students as possible. The teacher must not abdicate his or her authority, but rather provide direction and examples of proper form when teaching skills.

Social Interaction

Being a member of a team provides many opportunities for social interaction. The team concept emulates life situations. Team members can practice leadership and followership skills. Students can learn to win and lose gracefully when playing any sport. Another concept teamwork teaches is that everyone makes his or her own contributions to the team.

Physical education will also provide many opportunities to develop social skills. Both same-sex classes and co-ed classes provide many opportunities for social interaction. Getting along with others is a valuable skill that can be promoted by physical education. If teachers create an atmosphere of equal treatment to all students it will be easier for all to coexist. Teachers who have "pets" and exclude others in the class because of gender or behavior spoil the atmosphere of the class. If students don't feel that they are worthy of the teacher's attention, their self-esteem will suffer. The physical education class can provide tremendous benefits to students, but it takes a skilled teacher to create situations to provide those benefits.

PHYSICAL EDUCATION

PRACTICE QUESTIONS

1. Which of the following is not a principle of training?

   (A) overload

   (B) adaptation

   (C) calorie burn

   (D) specificity

2. The ability of the entire body to work together efficiently is called

   (A) kinesiology

   (B) physical fitness

   (C) potential

   (D) physiology

3. Abdominal strength will enable which of the following areas to also be strong?

   (A) the hamstrings

   (B) trapezius

   (C) the chest muscles

   (D) the back

4. Dance instruction should begin in elementary school with which steps?

   (A) step-hop

   (B) gallop

   (C) walk and/or skip

   (D) skip and slide

5. The active movers of the body are

   (A) bones

   (B) ligaments

   (C) tendons

   (D) muscles

PHYSICAL EDUCATION

ANSWERS TO PRACTICE QUESTIONS

1. **(C)**
2. **(B)**
3. **(D)**
4. **(C)**
5. **(D)**

MSAT

Multiple Subjects Assessment for Teachers

PRACTICE
MSAT I

Content Knowledge I

TIME: 2 Hours
          134 Questions

> **DIRECTIONS:** Each of the questions or incomplete statements below is followed by four suggested answers or completions. Select the one that is best in each case.

Section I: Literature and Language Studies

QUESTIONS 1–6 are based on the following excerpt from a longer poem. Read the poem carefully before choosing your answers.

> One speaks the glory of the British Queen,
> And one describes a charming Indian screen;
> A third interprets motions, looks, and eyes;
> At every word a reputation dies.
> Snuff, or the fan, supply each pause of chat,
> With singing, laughing, ogling, and all that.
> Meanwhile, declining from the noon of day,
> The sun obliquely shoots his burning ray;
> The hungry judges soon the sentence sign,
> And wretches hang that jurymen may dine;

From "The Rape of the Lock" (Canto 3 lines 13–22) by Alexander Pope

1.   The last two lines suggest that this society

   (A) takes pride in its justice system.

   (B) speedily administers justice for humanitarian reasons.

   (C) sentences the wrong people to death.

   (D) sentences people for the wrong reasons.

2.   Lines 1–6 suggest that this society

   I.   indulges in gossip that slanders the Queen.

   II. engages in serious discussions about affairs of state.

III. engages in gossip that ruins reputations.

(A) I and III. (C) II only.

(B) III only. (D) I, II, and III.

3. The juxtaposition in lines 1 and 2 suggest that the people

(A) talk of trivia.

(B) revere the monarchy and Indian screens equally.

(C) are Imperialists.

(D) are Royalists.

4. The word "obliquely" (line 8) in this context could mean or function as all of the following EXCEPT

(A) perpendicularly.

(B) at a steep angle.

(C) a pun on hidden meanings.

(D) a pun on stealth.

5. The rhyming couplets reflect that the poet is

(A) poking gentle fun at the society.

(B) lampooning the society.

(C) savagely satirizing the society.

(D) amusingly parodying Homer.

6. The change in voice from the first half of the excerpt into the second is best described as one from

(A) light to dark.

(B) amused to critical.

(C) light-hearted to sarcastic.

(D) amused to sadness.

QUESTIONS 7–14 are based on the following passage. Read the passage carefully before choosing your answers.

"What is he, then?"

"Why, I'll tell you what he is," said Mr. Jonas, apart to the young ladies, "he's precious old, for one thing; and I an't best pleased with him for that, for I think my father must have caught it of him. He's a strange old chap, for another," he added in a louder voice, "and don't understand any one hardly, but him!" He pointed to his honoured parent with the carving-fork, in order that they might know whom he meant.

"How very strange!" cried the sisters.

"Why, you see," said Mr. Jonas, "he's been addling his old brains with figures and book-keeping all his life; and twenty years ago or so he went and took a fever. All the time he was out of his head (which was three weeks) he never left off casting up; and he got to so many million at last that I don't believe he's ever been quite right since. We don't do much business now though, and he an't a bad clerk."

"A very good one," said Anthony.

"Well! He an't a dear one at all events," observed Jonas; "and he earns his salt, which is enough for our look-out. I was telling you that he hardly understands any one except my father; he always understands him, though, and wakes up quite wonderful. He's been used to his ways so long, you see! Why, I've seen him play whist, with my father for a partner; and a good rubber too; when he had no more notion what sort of people he was playing against, than you have."

From *Martin Chuzzlewit* by Charles Dickens.

7. From this passage it can be inferred that Mr. Jonas is all of the following EXCEPT

   (A) irritated that the old clerk understands hardly anyone except the father.

   (B) unconcerned about hurting the old clerk's feelings.

   (C) worried that the old clerk might make a serious error.

   (D) intent upon impressing the sisters.

8. If the old clerk is not "quite right" in the head, then why is he kept on as an employee?

   (A) Mr. Jonas will not go against his father's wishes.

   (B) Mr. Jonas does not want to offend the ladies.

   (C) Mr. Jonas reveres people of the older generation.

   (D) Mr. Jonas is somewhat afraid of the "strange old chap."

9. As used in the passage, the word "precious" means

   (A) very. (C) beloved.

   (B) of high value. (D) very overrefined in behavior.

10. What has made the old clerk not "quite right" in the head?

    (A) going a bit deaf in his old age.

    (B) working with numbers and bookkeeping all his life.

    (C) working sums and figures in his fever.

    (D) having to put up with Mr. Jonas' abuse.

11. The sentence "He an't a dear one at all events." can best be interpreted to mean which of the following?

    (A) Mr. Jonas does not like the old clerk.

    (B) The customers of the business do not like the old clerk.

    (C) Sometimes the clerk creates serious problems.

    (D) His wages do not cost the company very much money.

12. All of the following are things Mr. Jonas dislikes about the clerk EXCEPT that he is

    (A) old.

    (B) a bit strange.

    (C) a good whist player.

    (D) not always aware of who is around him.

13. What is the meaning of "he got to so many million at last"?

    (A) He irritated countless customers.

    (B) He had trouble keeping up with the high figures.

    (C) He became quite advanced in years.

    (D) He thought the three weeks was a million days.

14. A reasonable description of the old man is that he

    (A) knows what he is doing when it is something he has been accustomed to doing.

    (B) only pretends to be deaf and addled in order to irritate Mr. Jonas.

    (C) can do only the simplest of tasks, although he would like to be able to do more.

    (D) can do anything he wants to do, but only chooses to do what pleases him.

15. Which of the following, according to current linguistic theories, is the best definition of the meaning of a word?

    (A) Its general, dictionary definition.

    (B) Its use in a particular situation.

    (C) Its referent (the object to which it refers).

    (D) Its thought or corresponding idea in the mind.

16. Saussure's major breakthrough in linguistics was his insistence that

    (A) there is an inherent, one-to-one correspondence between a word and its referent.

    (B) the meaning of a word is subject to change over the course of time.

    (C) there are different words for the same referent in different languages.

    (D) the connection between a word and its referent is an arbitrary convention.

17. Which of the following best describes the acquisition of language by children?

    (A) A logical process by which a child learns to express his or her thoughts.

    (B) A series of imitative stages occurring in a necessary succession, where each advance is built on the previous one.

    (C) A series of imitative stages occurring in a rough, overlapping sequence, including possible regressions.

    (D) A random developmental sequence indivisible into stages.

18. Adults acquire new words and expressions primarily through

    (A) casual explanation from peers.

    (B) formal instruction in school.

    (C) exposure to their use.

    (D) use of a dictionary or thesaurus.

19. The intention of an utterance is

    (A) private, available only to the speaker of the utterance.

    (B) public, measurable by various outward criteria.

    (C) unknowable to either the speaker or the listener of the utterance.

    (D) translatable into the "deep structure" of the utterance.

20. The best way to judge whether or not an intention has been fulfilled is by

    (A) observing the actions which follow from the utterance.

    (B) consulting the speaker of the utterance for confirmation.

    (C) asking the listener of the utterance if he or she understood the intention.

    (D) consulting the rules of standard American English.

21. Which of the following statements, based on information in the Literature and Language Studies Review, is true?

    (A) Good language skills are important to every occupation or field of endeavor.

    (B) Good language skills must be emphasized in the humanities, but tend to over-complicate scientific or mathematical writing.

    (C) Good language skills are helpful but non-essential to practical, non-academic professions.

    (D) Good language skills demonstrate social grooming and manners, but most of us can "get by" without them.

22. Which of the following best describes "standard American English"?

    (A) A set of rules drawn from the underlying logic of spoken English.

    (B) The rules by which Americans actually speak.

    (C) An arbitrary set of rules and conventions imposed upon spoken English.

    (D) The correct method for learning and speaking English.

QUESTIONS 23–27 refer to the following passage.

The house of fiction has in short not one window, but a million—a number of possible windows not to be reckoned, rather; every one of which has been pierced, or is still pierceable, in its vast front, by the need of the individual vision and by the pressure of the individual will. These apertures, of dissimilar shape and size, hang so, all together, over the human scene that we might have expected of them a greater sameness of report than we find. They are but windows at the best, mere holes in a dead wall, disconnected, perched aloft; they are not hinged doors opening straight upon life. But they have this mark of their own that at each of them stands a figure with a pair of eyes, or at least with a field-glass, which forms, again and again, for observation, a unique instrument, insuring to the person making use of it an impression distinct from every other. He and his neighbours are watching the same show, but one seeing more where the other sees less, one seeing black where the other sees white, one seeing big where the other sees small, one seeing coarse where the other sees fine. And so on, and so on; there is fortunately no saying on what, for the particular pair of eyes, the window may <u>not</u> open; "fortunately" by reason, precisely, of this incalculability of range. The spreading field, the human scene, is the "choice of subject"; the pierced aperture, either broad or balconied or slitlike and low-browed, is the "literary form"; but they are, singly or together, as nothing without the posted presence of the watcher—without, in other words, the consciousness of the artist. Tell me what the artist is, and I will tell you of what he has *been* conscious. Thereby I shall express to you at once his boundless freedom and his "moral" reference.

23. The phrase "they are not hinged doors opening straight upon life" (line 8) implies that

    (A) fiction does not directly mirror life.

    (B) works of fiction are windows not doors.

    (C) fiction presents twisted versions of life.

    (D) fictional works are not easily created.

24. What is the antecedent of "they" in line 6?

    (A) Windows (line 7).

    (B) Apertures (line 4).

    (C) Holes (line 7).

    (D) Need (line 3) and pressure (line 4).

25. The shifts in point of view from "we" (lines 5–6) to "he" (line 12) to "I" (line 22) has which of the following effects?

    (A) The shifts indicate the speaker's distinguishing himself/herself from the critics who inhabit the house of fiction.

    (B) The shifts symbolize the speaker's alienation from the genre.

    (C) The movement from group to individual parallels the movement from the group "house of fiction" (line 1) to individual "figure with a pair of eyes" (line 9).

    (D) The movements separate the readers from the authors.

26. Which of these phrases contains an example of antithesis?

    (A) "These apertures, of dissimilar shape and size, hang so, all together, over the human scene" (lines 4–5).

(B) "They are but windows at the best, mere holes in a dead wall, disconnected, perched aloft; they are not hinged doors" (lines 6–8).

(C) "...at each of them stands a figure with a pair of eyes, or at least with a field-glass" (lines 9–10).

(D) "...one seeing more where the other sees less, one seeing black where the other sees white, one seeing big where the other sees small, one seeing coarse where the other sees fine" (lines 12–15).

27. Which of the following does the speaker consider to be the most important element in the "house of fiction"?

(A) The "figure with a pair of eyes" (line 9).

(B) The "apertures" (line 4).

(C) The "hinged doors" (line 8).

(D) The "human scene" (line 5).

Section II: Mathematics

28. Simplify the following expression: $6 + 2(x - 4)$

    (A) $4x - 16$ (C) $2x - 2$

    (B) $2x - 14$ (D) $-24x$

29. If six cans of beans cost $1.50, what is the price of eight cans of beans?

    (A) $.90   (C) $1.60

    (B) $1.00   (D) $2.00

30. Bonnie's average score on three tests is 71. Her first two test scores are 64 and 87. What is her score on test three?

    (A) 62   (C) 74

    (B) 71   (D) 151

31. In the figure below, what is the perimeter of square $ABCD$ if diagonal $AC = 8$?

    (A) 32

    (B) 64

    (C) $4\sqrt{2}$

    (D) $16\sqrt{2}$

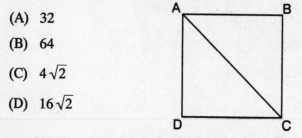

32. If $2x^2 + 5x - 3 = 0$ and $x > 0$, then what is the value of x?

    (A) $-\dfrac{1}{2}$ (C) 1

    (B) $\dfrac{1}{2}$ (D) $\dfrac{3}{2}$

33. A jar contains 20 balls. These balls are labeled 1 through 20. What is the probability that a ball chosen from the jar has a number on it which is divisible by 4?

    (A) $\dfrac{1}{20}$ (C) $\dfrac{1}{4}$

    (B) $\dfrac{1}{5}$ (D) 4

34. According to the chart below, in what year were the total sales of Brand X televisions the greatest?

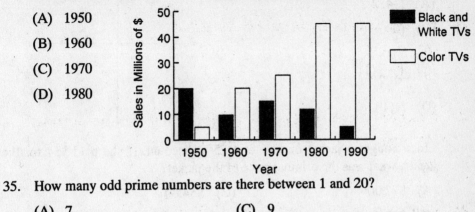

Sales of Brand X Televisions

(A) 1950

(B) 1960

(C) 1970

(D) 1980

35. How many odd prime numbers are there between 1 and 20?

(A) 7   (C) 9

(B) 8   (D) 10

36. Two concentric circles are shown in the figure below. The smaller circle has radius $OA = 4$ and the larger circle has radius $OB = 6$. Find the area of the shaded region.

(A) 4π

(B) 16π

(C) 20π

(D) 36π

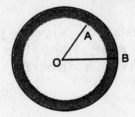

37. Solve the following inequality for x: $8 - 2x \le 10$

(A) $x \le 1$ (C) $x \le -1$

(B) $x \ge -9$ (D) $x \ge -1$

38. In the figure shown below $l_1 \parallel l_2$, $\triangle RTS$ is an isosceles triangle, and the measure of $\angle T = 80°$. Find the measure of $\angle OPR$.

(A) 50°

(B) 80°

(C) 130°

(D) 105°

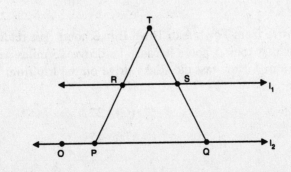

39. What is the midpoint of $\overline{MN}$ in the figure below?

    (A) (−4, 2)

    (B) (0, 0)

    (C) $\left(-\frac{3}{2}, 1\right)$

    (D) (1, 0)

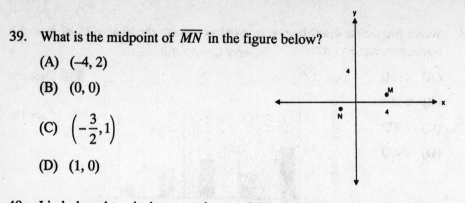

40. Linda bought a jacket on sale at a 25% discount. If she paid $54 for the jacket, what was the original price of the jacket?

    (A) $72.00   (C) $54.00

    (B) $67.50   (D) $40.50

41. In the number 72104.58, what is the place value of the 2?

    (A) Thousands   (C) Ten-thousands

    (B) Millions   (D) Tenths

42. Mrs. Wall has $300,000. She wishes to give each of her six children an equal amount of her money. Which of the following methods will result in the amount that each child is to receive?

    (A) 6 x 300,000   (C) 300,000 ÷ 6

    (B) 6 + 300,000   (D) 6 − 300,000

43. Bob wants to bake some cupcakes. His recipe uses $2^2/_3$ cups of flour to produce 36 cupcakes. How many cups of flour should Bob use to bake 12 cupcakes?

    (A) $\frac{1}{3}$ (C) 1

    (B) $\frac{8}{9}$ (D) $1\frac{2}{9}$

44. Ricky drove from Town A to Town B in 3 hours. His return trip from Town B to Town A took 5 hours because he drove 15 miles per hour slower on the return trip. How fast did Ricky drive on the trip from Town A to Town B?

    (A) 25.5   (C) 37.5

    (B) 32   (D) 45

45. Which of the following inequalities represents the shaded region in the figure below?

    (A) $x \geq 2$

    (B) $x \leq 2$

    (C) $y \geq 2$

    (D) $y \leq 2$

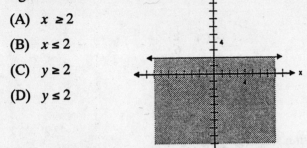

46. Round the following number to the nearest hundredths place: 287.416

    (A) 300   (C) 287.42

    (B) 290   (D) 287.41

47. If $a = b^3$ and $a = {}^1/_8$, what is the value of b?

    (A) $\dfrac{1}{512}$ (C) $\dfrac{3}{8}$

    (B) $\dfrac{1}{8}$ (D) $\dfrac{1}{2}$

48. In a barn there were cows and people. If we counted 30 heads and 104 legs in the barn, how many cows and how many people were in the barn?

    (A) 10 cows and 20 people.

    (B) 16 cows and 14 people.

    (C) 18 cows and 16 people.

    (D) 22 cows and 8 people.

49. If two lines, l_1 and l_2, which lie in the same plane, are both perpendicular to a third line, l_3, in the same plane as the first two, what do you definitely know about l_1 and l_2?

    (A) l_1 and l_2 are perpendicular.

    (B) l_1 and l_2 are parallel.

    (C) l_1 and l_2 intersect.

    (D) l_1 and l_2 are skew.

50. What is $\frac{1}{2} + \frac{1}{3}$?

(A) $\frac{1}{5}$ (C) $\frac{1}{6}$

(B) $\frac{2}{5}$ (D) $\frac{5}{6}$

51. Which of the following sets is graphed below?

(A) $\{x \mid x \geq -1\}$

(B) $\{x \mid x > -1\}$

(C) $\{x \mid x \leq -1\}$

(D) $\{x \mid x < -1\}$

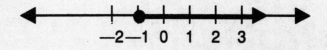

52. According to the graph below, during how many months was supply greater than demand?

(A) 0   (C) 2

(B) 1   (D) 3

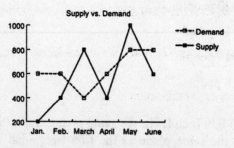

53. What is the greatest common divisor of 120 and 252?

(A) 2   (C) 6

(B) 3   (D) 12

54. How many negative integers are between −9 and 5?

(A) 13   (C) 9

(B) 10   (D) 8

Section III: History and Social Sciences

55. Which observation about California's unique geography is false?

    (A) Its isolation kept it free from European settlement, even after centuries of European settlement on the Pacific coast.

    (B) Its large population and industrial centers are located in arid and semi-arid environments.

    (C) It's semi-tropical, Mediterranean climate has been a perpetual source of attraction since people first entered the region.

    (D) Its long, navigable rivers facilitated the movement of produce to the state's multiple ports.

56. The demise of the California missions can ultimately be traced to

    (A) Mexican independence.

    (B) low productivity and the inability of the missions to sustain themselves.

    (C) imperial policies which recalled the Franciscans back to Spain.

    (D) the desires of missionaries to seek out "virgin" territories elsewhere.

57. What made Los Angeles especially attractive to many immigrants from 1890–1910 was

    (A) the city's large, natural harbor capable of facilitating an international trade.

    (B) the city's bountiful and dependable water supply from the Los Angeles river.

    (C) the city's booming wheat industry.

    (D) None of the above.

58. The Haymarket Incident involved

    (A) a riot between striking workers and police.

    (B) a scandal involving corruption within the Grant administration.

    (C) allegations of corruption on the part of Republican presidential candidate James G. Blaine.

    (D) a disastrous fire that pointed out the hazardous working conditions in some factories.

59. In its decision in the case of *Dred Scott v. Sanford*, the Supreme Court held that

    (A) separate facilities for different races were inherently unequal and there-fore unconstitutional.

    (B) no black slave could be a citizen of the United States.

    (C) separate but equal facilities for different races were constitutional.

    (D) Affirmative Action programs were acceptable only when it could be proven that specific previous cases of discrimination had occurred within the institution or business in question.

60. In coining the phrase "Manifest Destiny," journalist John L. O'Sullivan meant that

    (A) the struggle for racial equality was the ultimate goal of America's existence.

    (B) America was certain to become an independent country sooner or later.

    (C) it was the destiny of America to overspread the continent.

    (D) America must eventually become either all slave or all free.

61. All of the following were causes of the Mexican War EXCEPT

    (A) American desire for California.

    (B) Mexican failure to pay debts and damages owed to the U.S.

    (C) U.S. annexation of the formerly Mexican-held Republic of Texas.

    (D) Mexican desire to annex Louisiana.

62. In order to deal with the crisis in banking at the time of his inauguration, Franklin Roosevelt

    (A) drastically curtailed government spending and cut taxes.

    (B) declared a four-day "banking holiday" and prohibited the export of money.

    (C) urged Congress to pass legislation banning fractional reserve banking and holding bank trustees responsible for all deposits.

    (D) announced a multi-billion dollar federal bailout package.

63. The greatest significance of the Supreme Court's decision in *Marbury v. Madison* was that it

    (A) claimed for the first time that the Supreme Court could issue directives to the president.

    (B) claimed that the Supreme Court alone was empowered to say what the Constitution meant.

    (C) claimed for the first time that the Supreme Court could declare an act of Congress to be unconstitutional.

    (D) was openly defied by President Thomas Jefferson.

64. The term "Trail of Tears" refers to

    (A) the Mormon migration from Nauvoo, Illinois, to what is now Utah.

    (B) the forced migration of the Cherokee tribe from the southern Appalachians to what is now Oklahoma.

    (C) the westward migration along the Oregon Trail.

    (D) the migration into Kentucky along the Wilderness Road.

65. Which of the following was passed into law during the presidency of Woodrow Wilson?

    (A) The Pure Food and Drug Act.

    (B) A progressive income tax.

    (C) A high protective tariff.

    (D) A national old-age pension.

66. The Bay of Pigs incident involved

    (A) the presence of Soviet nuclear missiles in Cuba.

    (B) a U.S. sponsored attempt to overthrow Castro.

    (C) a confrontation between U.S. and Soviet troops in Europe.

    (D) a clash between a U.S. Navy destroyer and North Vietnamese patrol boats.

67. During the late 17th century Austria confronted several decades of almost continuous warfare on two fronts against

    (A) Italy and Prussia.

    (B) England and Russia.

(C) France and the Ottoman Empire.

(D) Prussia and the Ottoman Empire.

68. The characteristics of fascism include all of the following EXCEPT

(A) totalitarianism.

(B) democracy.

(C) romanticism.

(D) militarism.

69. The industrial economy of the 19th century was based upon all of the following EXCEPT

(A) the availability of raw materials.

(B) an equitable distribution of profits among those involved in production.

(C) the availability of capital.

(D) a distribution system to market finished products.

70. Oscar Wilde's *The Picture of Dorian Gray* and Thomas Mann's *Death in Venice*

(A) are examples of the romantic literature which dominated the literary scene at the turn of the 20th century.

(B) embodied a new symbolist direction in literature which addressed themes which were ignored previously.

(C) emphasized a new sense of realism in literature.

(D) were representative of a literary movement known as expressionism.

71. The response of the Catholic Church to the Reformation was delayed because

(A) the Papacy feared the remnants of the Conciliar Movement within the church itself.

(B) Rome wanted to coordinate its policy with secular Catholic leaders.

(C) church leaders thought that the opposition would self-destruct.

(D) the situation did not appear to be that serious from the Roman perspective.

72. The Russian Revolution of 1905

(A) led Nicholas II to issue the October Manifesto, and from the Duma.

(B) was immediately suppressed by Nicholas II.

(C) led to the issuing of the October Manifesto which introduced democratic government to Russia.

(D) was the primary cause for the defeat of Russia in the Russo-Japanese War.

73. Among the non-French intellectuals who participated in the Enlightenment were all of the following EXCEPT

(A) Edward Gibbon.

(C) Benjamin Franklin.

(B) David Hume.

(D) Leopold von Ranke.

74. The chart provided below indicates that

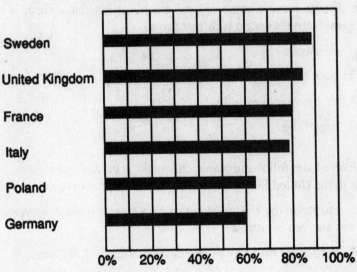

Number of Persons Employed in 1932 as a Percentage of 1929

(A) nations with large populations were better able to respond to the impact of the Depression than nations with smaller populations.

(B) advanced industrial societies had lower rates of unemployment during this period.

(C) the post-war economies in Central and Eastern Europe were fragile and subject to rapid deterioration during an economic collapse.

(D) Sweden and the United Kingdom had the strongest economic systems in the world.

75. In 1910 the most powerful state in Europe was

   (A) France.   (C) Russia.

   (B) Germany.   (D) Great Britain.

76. Which of the following is used to effect the release of a person from improper imprisonment?

   (A) A writ of mandamus.

   (B) A writ of habeas corpus.

   (C) The Fourth Amendment requirement that police have probable cause in order to obtain a search warrant.

   (D) The Supreme Court's decision in *Roe vs. Wade*.

77. When a member of the House of Representatives helps a citizen from his or her district receive some federal aid to which that citizen is entitled, the Representative's action is referred to as

   (A) casework.

   (B) pork barrel legislation.

   (C) lobbying.

   (D) logrolling.

78. Which of the following statements most accurately compares political parties in the United States with those in other Western democracies?

   (A) Parties in the United States exert a greater influence over which candidates run for office.

   (B) Parties are much more centralized in the United States.

   (C) There are usually more political parties in other Western democracies.

   (D) Party members in the national legislature are much freer to vote against the party line in other Western democracies.

Section IV: Science

QUESTIONS 79–83 refer to the following passage.

Scientific investigation involves two areas: pure science and applied science. Pure science is basic research, or the attempt to answer questions simply for the sake of knowledge itself. Applied science uses the knowledge gained from pure science to solve practical problems. Consider the following example: A biologist wants to know how insects attract mates. After much research, observation, and experimentation she discovers a substance called a pheromone is produced by the female insect and released into the air as an invisible gas, much like perfume. Pheromones are chemicals that are given off by organisms and affect or influence the behavior or the development of an individual organism. Pheromones are also known as "sex attractants" and are specific according to the type of organism. She found that pheromones produced by some organisms can be detected miles away by male organisms of the same species. This allows the male to find the female much faster than by looking or listening for the female insect. Pheromones are so powerful that the insect attracted pays no attention to anything other than trying to reach the female so that mating can begin.

79. The biologist that did the research on pheromones was engaged in

    (A) basic research.

    (B) applied research.

    (C) government research.

    (D) library research.

80. Pheromones

    (A) are used only in insects.

    (B) are used by all animals.

    (C) are found in many organisms.

    (D) can be seen.

81. If another biologist placed a cockroach pheromone on a cork and then placed the cork in a dish containing a solution poisonous to cockroaches, what would probably be the result?

    (A) No cockroaches would be affected.

    (B) Over a period of time, the dish would gradually be filled with dead cockroaches that crawled through the poison in an attempt to mate with the cork.

(C) Moths would be attracted to the pheromone-impregnated cork.

(D) Cockroaches would surround the dish but not cross the poison.

82. If a biologist used pheromones to attract male cockroaches to a cork containing a contact poison in hopes of ridding his home of cockroaches, what would this be an example of?

(A) Pure science.

(C) Applied science.

(B) Basic research.

(D) Government research.

83. Pheromones are sexual attractants of insects. This has been a great discovery in itself. If scientists took this information and used it to make a trap where the insects would die, this would be an example of

(A) entomology.

(C) applied science.

(B) botany.

(D) pure science.

QUESTIONS 84–86 refer to the following table.

ERA	PERIOD	EVENTS	BEGAN MILLIONS OF YEARS AGO
CENOZOIC	Quaternary	Humans. Four major glacial advances.	2
	Tertiary	Increase in mammals. Appearance of primates. Mountains appear in Europe and Asia.	65
MESOZOIC	Cretaceous	Dinosaurs disappear. Increase in flowering plants and reptiles.	140
	Jurassic	Birds. Mammals. Dominance of dinosaurs. Mountain building in western North America.	195
	Triassic	Beginning of dinosaurs and primitive mammals.	230
PALEOZOIC	Permian	Reptiles spread and develop. Evaporate deposits. Glaciation in Southern Hemisphere.	280
	Carboniferous	Abundant amphibians. Reptiles appear.	345
	Devonian	Fishes. First amphibians. First abundant forests on land.	395
	Silurian	First land plants. Mountain building in Europe.	435
	Ordovician	First fishes and vertebrates.	500
	Cambrian	Marine invertebrates.	600
PRECAMBRIAN TIME		Five times longer than all geologic time following.	

84. Which of the following statements is true?

    (A) Earth's history is divided into time blocks, determined by geologic events only.

    (B) Earth's history is divided into equal divisions of time.

    (C) Earth's history is divided into time blocks of differing amounts of time.

    (D) Each period of Earth's history is divided into time blocks called eras.

85. Which sequence of life is correct?

    (A) Invertebrates, Fish, Reptiles, Mammals.

    (B) Fish, Invertebrates, Mammals, Birds.

    (C) Plants, Invertebrates, Forests, Fish.

    (D) Invertebrates, Mammals, Birds, Plants.

86. According to the table, what period would have marked the appearance of the first relatives of the common alligator?

    (A) Silurian.   (C) Tertiary.

    (B) Triassic.   (D) Carboniferous.

QUESTIONS 87–90 refer to the following information.
Relative Masses and Average Separations
Moon, Earth, and Sun

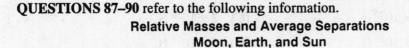

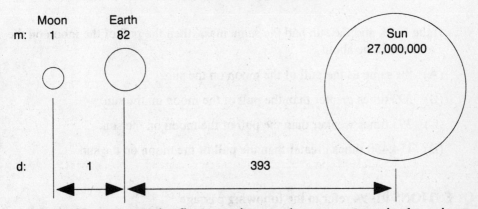

Isaac Newton was the first to point out that every mass in the universe attracts every other mass. This statement is known as the Law of Universal Gravitation. This attraction between bodies is proportional to the mass of each and is inversely proportional to the square of the distance between their centers. Also, by Newton's Third Law of Motion, this attraction must be the same on each pair of masses but in an opposite direction. For example, it is known that the Earth pulls on the moon with an average force of 2×10^{20} N and the moon pulls on the Earth with an average force of 2×10^{20} N.

87. Newton's Universal Law of Gravitation implies that

   (A) the attraction between the moon and the sun is the same as that between the moon and the Earth.

   (B) the attraction between the Earth and the sun is the same as that between the moon and the Earth.

   (C) the pull of the sun on the Earth is the same as the pull of the Earth on the sun.

   (D) the pull of the sun on the moon must be 3×10^{19} N.

88. The pull of the sun on the Earth is

   (A) about 82 times stronger than the pull of the sun on the moon.

   (B) about 82 times weaker than the pull of the sun on the moon.

   (C) about 393 times stronger than the pull of the sun on the moon.

   (D) about 393 times weaker than the pull of the sun on the moon.

89. If the distance between the moon and the Earth was doubled, then the gravitational pull of the Earth on the moon would be

   (A) 8×10^{20} N.   (C) 2×10^{20} N.

   (B) 4×10^{20} N.   (D) 5×10^{19} N.

90. If the Earth and the sun had the same mass, then the pull of the moon on the Earth would be about

   (A) the same as the pull of the moon on the sun.

   (B) 393 times greater than the pull of the moon on the sun.

   (C) 393 times weaker than the pull of the moon on the sun.

   (D) 154,450 times greater than the pull of the moon on the sun.

QUESTIONS 91–94 refer to the following passage.

When an Earthquake occurs, some of the energy released travels through the ground as waves. Two general types of waves are generated. One type, called the P wave, is a compression wave that alternately compresses and stretches the rock layers as it travels. A second type is a Shear wave, called the S wave, which moves the rocks in an up and down manner.

A graph can be made of the travel times of these waves:

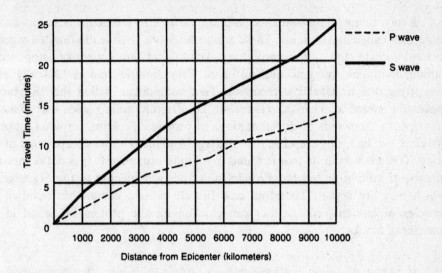

Distance from Epicenter (kilometers)

91. The main reason that a Time-Travel graph can be used to determine distance to an Earthquake's point of occurrence is that

   (A) S waves move up and down.

   (B) P waves are compressional.

   (C) P waves travel faster than S waves.

   (D) S waves travel faster than P waves.

92. Approximately how many minutes does it take a P wave to travel 8000 km?

   (A) 6 minutes.   (C) 3 minutes.

   (B) 12 minutes.   (D) 15 minutes.

93. An Earthquake occurs at noon, and the recording station receives the S wave at 12:05 P.M. How far away is the Earthquake?

   (A) 1000 km.   (C) 3000 km.

   (B) 2000 km.   (D) 4000 km.

94. How far away is an Earthquake if the difference in arrival time between the P and S waves is 7 minutes?

   (A) 1000 km.   (C) 4000 km.

   (B) 3000 km.   (D) 7000 km.

QUESTIONS 95–98 are based on the following passage.

Every living thing contains proteins. A protein molecule is composed of molecules called amino acids. These amino acids are chemically bonded together to form a chain (the protein molecule). Amino acids are generally composed of carbon, hydrogen, oxygen, and nitrogen. Every amino acid is basically alike except for one molecular component. That component, called the "R" factor, makes the amino acid unique. There are 20 different amino acids that make up hundreds of thousands of different kinds of proteins. Proteins are what make up our skin, our hair, our muscles, our cartilage, and many other components of our body. There is very little that is found in a living organism that is not composed, in part, of protein molecules. Protein molecules are specific to the organism of which they are a part. Therefore cow muscle protein cannot be found in the muscles of humans, and neither can chicken muscle protein be found in the muscles of hawks.

95. If a chain of amino acids makes up a protein molecule, then one protein can be different from another protein by

 (A) only the length of the protein molecule.

 (B) the length of protein molecule, and the order and type of amino acids in the protein molecule.

 (C) only the type of amino acids found in the protein molecule.

 (D) only the number of chemical bonds found in the protein molecule.

96. How many different kinds of "R" factors are there?

 (A) 20   (C) 100

 (B) 50   (D) 1000

97. Proteins are

 (A) chains of amino acids.

 (B) chains of fat molecules.

 (C) rings of carbon.

 (D) loops of cellulose molecules.

98. Which of the following is not made of protein?

 (A) Hair.   (C) Rock.

 (B) Fingernails.   (D) Skin.

QUESTIONS 99–102 refer to the following paragraph.

Cells contain chromosomes. The number of chromosomes in a cell varies. In sexually reproducing organisms, the cells usually have two sets of chromosomes. Cells like these are said to be "diploid." In organisms that reproduce asexually, the cells are usually "haploid," or having one set of chromosomes. Cells reproduce themselves by means of a process called mitosis. Some organisms can reproduce themselves by budding, or breaking, when there is no sexual reproduction. Sexually reproducing organisms undergo a process whereby they produce haploid cells from diploid cells. These haploid cells are called sperms or eggs. When a sperm and an egg are united, they fuse to form a single cell called a zygote. The zygote of a human has 46 chromosomes. A zygote is a diploid cell and will undergo mitosis to produce a mature organism.

99. There are 46 chromosomes found in the cheek cell of a human male. If this cell were to undergo mitosis, how many chromosomes would be found in each resulting daughter cell?

   (A) 2   (C) 24

   (B) 10   (D) 46

100. Humans have 46 chromosomes in their body cells. How many chromosomes are found in the zygote?

   (A) 2   (C) 23

   (B) 10   (D) 46

101. If mitosis were not to occur in both a male and a female human and their sperm and egg were to unite to form a zygote, how many chromosomes would the zygote have?

   (A) 2   (C) 46

   (B) 23   (D) 92

102. Which of the following relates to a zygote?

   (A) A single organism composed of two cells.

   (B) Haploid.

   (C) Undergoes meiosis to produce four sperm.

   (D) Diploid.

Section V: Visual and Performing Arts

103. The great ziggurat at Ur was produced by a Mesopotamian civilization known as the

    (A) Egyptians.   (C) Assyrians.

    (B) Sumerians.   (D) Babylonians.

104. Flying buttresses, pointed arches, and stained glass windows are characteristic of which historic style of architecture?

    (A) Romanesque.   (C) Renaissance.

    (B) Byzantine.   (D) Gothic.

105. Jackson Pollock's *Lucifer* of 1947 is an example of what post World War II artistic movement?

    (A) Fauvism.   (C) Cubism.

    (B) Futurism.   (D) Abstract Expressionism.

106. Caravaggio's *The Conversion of St. Paul* (below) exhibits all of the following characteristics EXCEPT

    (A) a contrast of deep shadows and bright highlights.

    (B) a sense of drama.

(C) a preference for soft contours and loose brushwork.

(D) a strongly foreshortened figure.

107. A printmaking process that involves the use of a limestone block is

(A) lithography.   (C) etching.

(B) engraving.   (D) woodcutting.

108. One of the leaders in the USA of art education reform, the author of *Educating Artistic Vision*, is

(A) Ralph Nader.   (C) Bill Honig

(B) Mortimer Adler.   (D) Elliot Eisner.

109. In art education circles, the acronym DBAE stands for

(A) Design Basics for Aesthetic Education.

(B) Design By Advanced Education.

(C) Discipline-Based Art Education.

(D) Developing Brainpower through Arts Education.

110. Which of the following is a complimentary color pair?

(A) Blue and green.

(B) Yellow and red.

(C) Red and green.

(D) Purple and red.

QUESTIONS 111–112 are based on the following works of art.

(A)*Venus of Willendorf*, Naturhistorisches Museum, Vienna.

(B) Alexander Archipenko, *Woman Combing Her Hair*, Museum of Modern Art, New York.

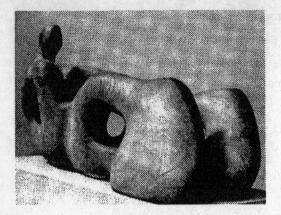

(C) Henry Moore, *Reclining Figure*,
Detroit Instititute of Art.

(D) Henri Matisse, *Back I*,
Tate Gallery, London.

(A) *Venus of Willendorf,* Naturhistorisches Museum, Vienna.

(B) Alexander Archipenko, *Woman Combing Her Hair,* Museum of Modern Art, New York.

(C) Henry Moore, *Reclining Figure,* Detroit Institute of Art.

(D) Henri Matisse, *Back I,* Tate Gallery, London.

111. Which of the above figures seems to best embody the compositional principles of Cubism?

112. Which of the above may have served as a Paleolithic fertility idol?

113. The previous illustration is of a Buddhist burial mound located in India. Completed in the first century A.D., structures like this one are among the most important ancient architectural monuments of southern Asia. They are called

    (A) pagodas.   (C) mastabas.

    (B) stupas.   (D) mandorlas.

114. "Form Follows Function" is an expression coined by

    (A) Frank Lloyd Wright.   (C) Le Corbusier.

    (B) Louis Sullivan.   (D) Mies van der Rohe.

115. The painting below, entitled *Nude Descending a Staircase #2* was painted by

    (A) Marcel Duchamp.

    (B) Pablo Picasso.

    (C) Georges Braque.

    (D) Piet Mondrian.

116. In a perspective drawing, the lines that appear to be perpendicular to the picture plane and which intersect at the vanishing point are called

(A) epigones.

(C) hatchings.

(B) orthogonals.

(D) imagines.

Section VI: Human Development

QUESTIONS 117–119 refer to the following passage.

Miss Sharp's fourth-grade class is studying a unit entitled "Discoveries" in social studies and science. Miss Sharp has prepared four learning centers for the class. In Learning Center #1 students use information from their science and social studies textbooks to prepare a time line of discoveries that occurred between 1800 and 1990. In Learning Center #2 students use a variety of resource materials to research one particular discovery or discoverer they have selected from a prepared list. Each student then records what they learned about this discovery or discoverer on an individual chart that will later be shared with the whole class. In Learning Center #3 students add small amounts of five different substances to jars of water and record the results over a period of five minutes. In Learning Center #4 students write a description of the need for a new discovery to solve a problem or answer a question. Then students suggest several possible areas of research that may contribute to this new discovery.

117. Miss Sharp introduces the learning centers by explaining the purpose of each center and giving directions for each activity. Next she divides the class of 22 into four groups and assigns each group to a different center. After 20 minutes, some students are completely finished with one center and want to move on, but other students have only just begun working. What would be the best solution to this situation?

   (A) Each learning center should be revised so that the activities will require approximately the same amount of time to complete.

   (B) Students who finish one center early should be given additional work to complete before moving to the next center.

   (C) Students should be permitted to move from center to center as they complete each activity so long as no more than six students are working at each center.

   (D) Students should be permitted to work through the activities in each center as quickly as possible so that the class can move on to the next unit.

118. Which of the following would be the most appropriate concluding activity for the Discoveries Unit?

   (A) Students should have a class party celebrating the birthday of Marie Curie, Jonas Salk, and Thomas Edison.

   (B) Each student should be required to prepare a verbal report detailing what they learned about an important medical discovery.

(C) Each student should take a multiple-choice test containing questions related to each learning center.

(D) Each student should design a concluding activity, or select one from a prepared list, that reflects what they learned about a discovery they studied.

119. In selecting resource materials for Learning Center #2, Miss Sharp carefully chooses materials that present information about a variety of discoveries made by both men and women from several different countries. Her purpose in making these selections is most probably to ensure that materials

(A) are challenging but written at the appropriate reading level.

(B) demonstrate the diversity of individuals who have made discoveries.

(C) contain information about discoveries included in the textbook.

(D) will be of interest to the majority of the students.

QUESTIONS 120–121 refer to the following passage.

The fourth-grade students in Mrs. Alvarez's class are studying Native Americans. Mrs. Alvarez wants to strengthen her student's ability to work independently. She also wants to provide opportunities for the students to use a variety of print and media resources during this unit of study. Mrs. Alvarez plans to begin the unit by leading the class in a brainstorming session to formulate questions to guide their research about Native Americans.

120. Which of the following criteria should guide Mrs. Alvarez as she leads the brainstorming session?

(A) The questions should emphasize the factual content presented in the available print materials.

(B) The questions should emphasize higher order thinking skills, such as comparison, analysis, and evaluation.

(C) The questions should reflect the interest of the students.

(D) The questions should include all of the fourth-grade objectives for this unit.

121. Mrs. Alvarez has collected a variety of print and media resources for the students to use in their research. Which of the following will probably be the best way to motivate students to research the questions they have prepared?

(A) The teacher should assign two to three questions to each student so that all the questions are covered.

(B) The teacher should allow individual students to select the questions they would like to research.

(C) The teacher should select three key questions and assign them to all the students.

(D) The teacher should assign one topic to each student, then provide the students with additional information.

QUESTIONS 122–125 refer to the following passage.

Mrs. Gettler teaches 26 third graders in a large inner city school. About one-third of her students participate in the ESL program at the school. Mrs. Gettler suspects that some of the students parents are unable to read or write in English. Four of the students receive services from the learning resource teacher. At the beginning of the year, none of the students read above 2.0 grade level, and some of the students did not know all the letters of the alphabet.

122. Which of the following describes the instructional strategy that is most likely to improve the reading levels of Mrs. Gettler's students?

(A) An intensive phonics program that includes drill and practice work on basic sight words.

(B) An emergent literacy program emphasizing pattern books and journal writing using invented spelling.

(C) An instructional program that closely follows the third-grade basal reader.

(D) All the students should participate in the school's ESL program and receive services from the learning resource center.

123. Mrs. Gettler is selecting books for the classroom library. In addition to student interest, which of the following would be the most important considerations?

(A) The books should have a reading level that matches the students' independent reading ability.

(B) The books should only have a reading level that is challenging to the students.

(C) The books should include separate word lists for student practice.

(D) A classroom library is not appropriate for students at such a low reading level.

124. Which of the following individual and small group learning centers is suitable for Mrs. Gettler's class?

   I.   A post office center where students can write letters to friends and family.

   II.   A restaurant center where students read menus, write food orders, and pay the bill with play money.

   III. A weather center where students record current conditions, including temperature, cloud cover and wind direction, and prepare graphs of weather patterns.

   IV. A science center where students record the results of experiments with combining liquids such as bleach, vinegar, cooking oil, food coloring, and rubbing alcohol.

(A) I only.

(B) I and II.

(C) I, II, and III.

(D) II, III, and IV.

125. Mrs. Gettler realizes that an individual's preferred learning style contributes to that individual's success as a student. Mrs. Gettler wants to accommodate as many of her student's individual learning styles as possible. Which of the following best describes the way to identify the student's learning styles?

(A) Mrs. Gettler should record her observations of individual student's behaviors over a period of several weeks.

(B) Each of the students should be tested by the school psychologist.

(C) Mrs. Gettler should administer a group screening test for identifying learning styles.

(D) Mrs. Gettler should review the permanent file of each student and compare the individual's previous test scores with classroom performance.

Section VII: Physical Education

126. The handicapping conditions represented by Public Law 94–142 includes children defined as

    I.   Mentally retarded

    II. Hard of hearing

    III. Learning disabled

    (A) I and II.   (C) III only.

    (B) I only.   (D) I, II, and III.

127. Most children with a history of epileptic seizures

    (A) can take part in physical education programs with non-epileptics.

    (B) may participate in limited activities, depending on the type of seizure experienced.

    (C) may experience minor motor seizures during physical activity.

    (D) will have an abnormal increase in heart rate and blood pressure during physical activity.

128. Activities that develop gross motor-visual skills almost always involve the use of a

    (A) ball.   (C) trampoline.

    (B) balance beam.   (D) exercise mat.

129. A volleyball game scores for

    (A) 12 points, and the serving team must win by 1 point.

    (B) 11 points, and the serving team must win by 1 point.

    (C) 15 points, and the serving team must win by 2 points.

    (D) 14 points, and the serving team must win by 2 points.

130. Exercise systems commonly used to develop muscular strength include

    I.   Weight training

    II. Interval training

    III. Isometric training

    IV. Isokinetic training

(A) I, II, and III.   (C) I and II.

(B) I, III, an IV.   (D) III and IV.

131. During prolonged exercise in the heat, fluid balance is reestablished by

(A) consuming salt tablets.   (C) drinking water.

(B) taking vitamins.   (D) taking mineral supplements.

132. Most of the calories in an athlete's diet should be derived from

I. Fats

II. Carbohydrates

III. Proteins

(A) I and II.   (C) II only.

(B) I only.   (D) III only.

133. Of the following, which test does NOT measure muscular strength and endurance in children?

(A) Pull ups.   (C) Grip strength test.

(B) Flexed arm hang.   (D) Sit and reach test.

134. Dance steps most appropriate for younger children (grades 1–2) are

(A) walk and/or skip.   (C) skip and slide.

(B) run and/or skip.   (D) skip and step-hop.

Content Area Exercises I

DIRECTIONS: Respond to each of the items below in a brief, well constructed essay.

I. Literature and Language Studies

1. In the selection below, Joseph Conrad is describing a trip up the Congo River, and the psychological and physical effects this trip has on the narrator. Read the passage carefully and using specific references to the text, describe how Conrad illustrates these effects. You may focus on either diction, syntax, or sentence structure.

There were moments when one's past came back to one, as it will sometimes when you have not a moment to spare to yourself; but it came in the shape of an unrestful and noisy dream, remembered with wonder amongst the overwhelming realities of this strange world of plants, and water, and silence. And this stillness of live did not in the least resemble a peace. It was the stillness of an implacable force brooding over an inscrutable intention. It looked at you with a vengeful aspect. I got used to it afterwards; I did not see it any more; I had no time. I had to keep guessing at the channel; I had to discern, mostly by inspiration, the signs of hidden banks; I watched for sunken stones; I was learning to clap my teeth smartly before my heart flew out, when I shaved by a fluke some infernal sly old snag that would have ripped the life out of the tin-pot steamboat and drowned all the pilgrims; I had to keep a lookout for the signs of dead wood we could cut up in the night for next day's steaming. When you have to attend to things of that sort, to the mere incidents of the surface, the reality—the reality, I tell you— fades. The inner truth is hidden—luckily, luckily. But I felt it all the same; I felt often its mysterious stillness watching me at my monkey tricks....

From *Heart of Darkness* by Joseph Conrad.

2. Discuss one major difference between the methods used to convey a social message in a novel and the methods used to convey a similar message in a persuasive essay.

3. "Setting" is a term that describes the locale and historical period in which the action of a narrative work takes place. Setting can be used to help describe meaning, create atmosphere, establish thematic devices and so on. Some works depend very heavily on their setting, and for some it is a secondary factor. Choose one of the works listed below, or another of comparable quality, and discuss the importance of setting to the work.

The Scarlet Letter	*Catch-22*
The Jungle	*Portrait of the Artist as a Young Man*
Sister Carrie	*Moll Flanders*
David Copperfield	*Moby-Dick*
The Grapes of Wrath	*The Glass Menagerie*
1984	*The Tempest*

4. Discuss one effect of the standardization of grammar.

II. Mathematics

5. The following figure is a graph of the unemployment rate for Town A from June through December. Explain why this graph is misleading.

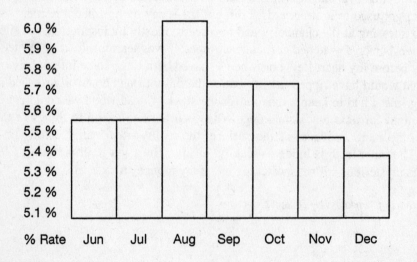

6. The following is a list of yearly salaries for Company A:

> $20,000
>
> $20,000
>
> $25,000
>
> $32,000
>
> $33,000
>
> $90,000
>
> $95,000

The median salary for Company A is $32,000.

The mean salary for Company A is $45,000.

Why is the median salary, rather than the mean salary, a better indication of the average salary of this company.

7. A child's kite is on top of a straight pine tree. A ladder is placed against the tree and touches the kite. The ladder forms a 45 degree angle with the flat ground. The base of the tree is 4 feet away from the ladder.

With only this information, how can you determine the height of the tree?

8. Given that the figure below is a unit circle, prove that the sec α = d.

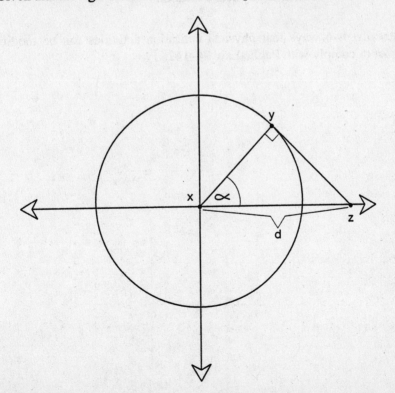

III. Visual and Performing Arts

9. It has been said that a society's values and needs can be seen in its architecture. Briefly support or refute this statement.

10. Briefly describe ways in which theater can be said to encompass all the artistic disciplines.

IV. Human Development

11. Briefly describe two different styles of learning, and ways in which a teacher must adapt to these styles.

12. Briefly describe the last two stages of Piaget's theory of cognitive development, and include why they are important to elementary educators.

V. Physical Education

13. Briefly describe two ways in which teachers can enhance students' self-esteem in the context of physical education.

14. Describe two ways that physical education activities can be modified in order to comply with Public Law 94–142.

Content Area Exercises II

DIRECTIONS: Respond to each of the items below in a brief, well constructed essay.

I. History and Social Sciences

1. Briefly describe the wave of fear and subsequent events that culminated in the famous Sacco and Vanzetti trial of 1921. Include the major facts of the trial.

2. Give a definition of and relation between the following:

   a) Jim Crow laws.

   b) *Plessy vs. Ferguson*

3. Describe the events surrounding, and the significance of, the entrance of the People's Republic of China into North Korea on November 26, 1950.

4. Name at least one of the three major heroes of Italian unification and describe briefly how they created a united Italy.

II. Science

5. A small population of a particular species of snake thought to be extinct was found on an isolated island near Florida. Discuss the genetic disadvantages of this small population.

6. Propose the advantages and disadvantages of using hydrogen gas as a major energy source.

7. Some scientists believe that life on Earth began due to the environmental conditions found at that time:

>   atmospheric gases: water vapor, hydrogen, methane, ammonia

>   weather conditions: lightning and rain.

How could an experiment in the lab test this hypothesis?

8. Listed below are groups of two surfaces and the associated friction value (known as the coefficient of friction). Explain friction and the meaning of the value.

Steel on steel	.47
Copper on steel	.36
Waxed wood on snow	.10
Rubber on wet concrete	.70
Steel on ice	.06

Content Knowledge I

ANSWER KEY

1.	(D)	35.	(A)	69.	(B)	103.	(B)
2.	(B)	36.	(C)	70.	(B)	104.	(D)
3.	(B)	37.	(D)	71.	(A)	105.	(D)
4.	(A)	38.	(C)	72.	(A)	106.	(C)
5.	(A)	39.	(D)	73.	(D)	107.	(A)
6.	(D)	40.	(A)	74.	(C)	108.	(D)
7.	(C)	41.	(A)	75.	(B)	109.	(C)
8.	(A)	42.	(C)	76.	(B)	110.	(C)
9.	(A)	43.	(B)	77.	(A)	111.	(B)
10.	(C)	44.	(C)	78.	(C)	112.	(A)
11.	(D)	45.	(D)	79.	(A)	113.	(B)
12.	(C)	46.	(C)	80.	(C)	114.	(B)
13.	(B)	47.	(D)	81.	(B)	115.	(A)
14.	(A)	48.	(D)	82.	(C)	116.	(B)
15.	(B)	49.	(B)	83.	(C)	117.	(C)
16.	(D)	50.	(D)	84.	(C)	118.	(D)
17.	(C)	51.	(A)	85.	(A)	119.	(B)
18.	(C)	52.	(C)	86.	(D)	120.	(C)
19.	(B)	53.	(D)	87.	(C)	121.	(B)
20.	(A)	54.	(D)	88.	(A)	122.	(B)
21.	(A)	55.	(D)	89.	(D)	123.	(A)
22.	(C)	56.	(A)	90.	(D)	124.	(C)
23.	(A)	57.	(D)	91.	(C)	125.	(A)
24.	(B)	58.	(A)	92.	(B)	126.	(D)
25.	(C)	59.	(B)	93.	(A)	127.	(A)
26.	(D)	60.	(C)	94.	(C)	128.	(A)
27.	(A)	61.	(D)	95.	(B)	129.	(C)
28.	(C)	62.	(B)	96.	(A)	130.	(B)
29.	(D)	63.	(C)	97.	(A)	131.	(C)
30.	(A)	64.	(B)	98.	(C)	132.	(C)
31.	(D)	65.	(B)	99.	(D)	133.	(D)
32.	(B)	66.	(B)	100.	(D)	134.	(A)
33.	(C)	67.	(C)	101.	(D)		
34.	(D)	68.	(B)	102.	(D)		

DETAILED EXPLANATIONS
OF ANSWERS

1. **(D)** The prisoners are speedily sentenced because the judges and the jurymen are hungry and want to go home for supper as the day ends — the prisoners may be guilty, but the wrong reasons determine their sentences (D). No doubt the people do believe in the system, but the sarcasm of the piece suggests that this society uses the system for personal selfish benefits — certainly not a humanitarian society.

2. **(B)** The society depicted is shallow and trivial, engaging in chatty conversations that everyone takes seriously. Serious as the discussions may be, they possibly involve extramarital affairs rather than affairs of state (C, D) — such gossip ruins reputations (B). The gossiping involves the Queen but it is not revealed that she is slandered (which would involve maliciousness), which, if you hadn't already done so, eliminates (D) along with (A).

3. **(B)** The question wants you to analyze the clash or conflict of two very different concepts in conversation: the glory of the Queen in one breath and a fire screen (or room divider) in another. The juxtaposition is not so much to suggest trivia or seriousness (the Queen's glory is serious but the furniture is not), but that this society holds both in equal reverence (B). No real evidence is given that the people are Royalists or Imperialists.

4. **(A)** There is a clever use of the language in this one adverb. It stands for the angle of the sun as it declines at a steep angle but also for the hidden meanings behind the word as it refers to this society: the deceit, the amorality. It certainly does not mean that the sun is at a perpendicular angle (A).

5. **(A)** You need to know the meanings of words like doggerel: crude irregular couplets of a burlesque nature, and lampoon: sharp, often virulent attack on a person or society. Neither of these definitions fits these highly stylized couplets, which are gentle — certainly not savage — in their satire and criticism (A). There is a parody of Homer in the poem which is a mock epic, but not in the couplets employed.

6. **(D)** The move is light to dark in the physical movement of the day but not specifically in the voice. On analysis you will find the "coming down" of mood from amusement at the chat of the day — the trivia — to a sadness of the effect of the hunger of the court officials, a hunger that sends men to the gallows. The answer is (D).

7.   **(C)**   Evidence in the passage indicates the old clerk is still a good records keeper. Mr. Jonas observes that he "an't a bad clerk," to which Anthony adds, "A very good one." Mr. Jonas is obviously unconcerned about hurting the old clerk's feelings (B) as he says terribly rude things in front of his father and the old clerk. Mr. Jonas says the clerk is "old" and he is not "pleased with him for that." Mr. Jonas' irritation with the old man shows through when he points out the clerk's inability (A) to hear no one but Mr. Jonas' father. Perhaps Mr. Jonas is trying to impress the young ladies (D) as he addresses them "apart."

8.   **(A)**   Mr. Jonas' father is described in the passage as "honored parent." This wording might be taken ironically, and perhaps is humorous given the way he speaks in front of his parent, but Mr. Jonas goes on to say how the two old men are used to each other. As it would probably upset Mr. Jonas' father to do without his longtime companion, (A) is the logical conclusion. Choice (C) is a possible option, but "revere" is too strong a word given the tone Mr. Jonas uses. Mr. Jonas is more concerned with impressing than offending the young ladies (B), and there is no evidence to support (D).

9.   **(A)**   Although "precious" can be defined in any of the ways listed as possible answers, only "very old" can be considered the best meaning for "precious old" because the rest of the passage details the old clerk's eccentricities brought on by the passing of time. Choices (B) and (C) may apply to the way Mr. Jonas' father feels about the clerk, but they do not fit *Mr. Jonas'* feelings. Nowhere in the passage is (D) discussed.

10.   **(C)**   When the old clerk took a fever "twenty years ago or so," he was delirious for three weeks. The entire time he had fever, he "never left off" running figures in his head, and the figures eventually became so high that his brain became addled. Choice (B) may have contributed to the clerk's problem, but it is not the immediate cause. Choice (A) is incorrect as the fever happened many years before he grew deaf. Choice (D) may have contributed, but there is no evidence in the passage to indicate it.

11.   **(D)**   During the conversation between Mr. Jonas and Anthony about the clerk's worth as a worker, Mr. Jonas comments, "He an't a dear one" and then explains how he "earns his salt." The idiom "earns his salt" means he "earns his wages," so "dear" can be taken to mean "expensive" in this context: the old clerk does not have to be paid much but he earns his pay. Although (A) may be true, it is not the meaning in this context. There is no evidence to support (B) or (C).

12.   **(C)**   The clerk's being a good whist player seems to strike a bit of admiration in Mr. Jonas because the old man can play well even when he "had no more notion what sort of people he was playing against, than you have." Even though he seems to be amazed at the old clerk's whist game, Mr. Jonas seems irritated

the old man is unaware of anyone else but the "honored parent" (D). Mr. Jonas speaks disparagingly of the clerk's age (A), and strangeness (B).

13. **(B)** During his fever, the old clerk added numbers for three weeks. The numbers mounted steadily into "so many million at last." Choice (D) is a possibility, but evidence in the passage does not indicate this probability. The fever happened before (C) became a factor. Choice (A) has no evidence to support it.

14. **(A)** The old clerk seems sharp enough dealing with accustomed things — clerking, whist, responding to Mr. Jonas' father — but he has difficulties with responding to new people and situations. There is no evidence (B) is correct: The passage references a problem he has with *understanding* what is being said, not hearing it. Keeping books and playing whist are not "the simplest of tasks" (C). What the old clerk "would like" (C) to do or is pleased (D) to do is not a consideration in this passage. It seems as if the old man's mind is permanently afflicted; Mr. Jonas says of him after the fever, "I don't believe he's ever been quite right since."

15. **(B)** According to current linguistic theories, use is the criterion by which the meaning of a word may be measured. The meaning of any particular word or utterance is context-bound, changing from situation to situation and dependent on the specific circumstances of that situation. Meaning thus conceived is a public event, which people can observe and assess; choice (B) is correct. A general, dictionary definition of a word is inadequate to explain the meaning of a word, because it only applies to one particular type of situation. Even if a dictionary offers several possible meanings for a word, it doesn't provide any method by which to select from these possibilities to assess the meaning of a word in a particular situation; choice (A) is incorrect. Words are sometimes used to refer to objects, but this is by no means the only way in which they are used, thus (C) is not the best choice. Thoughts or ideas "in the mind" are not visible and we could never be sure that what occurs in the speaker's mind when he or she utters a word is the same as what occurs in the listener's mind; choice (D) is not correct.

16. **(D)** Saussure was one of the first linguists to propose that there was no particular or logical connection between a word and what it refers to. While the connection between a word and its referent is arbitrary, it is nonetheless held in place by conventional practice; words are thus not used at random by each speaker of a language but rather according to the ways previous speakers have used them; choice (D) is correct. Choices (B) and (C), while both correct statements in and of themselves, were not discoveries of Saussure's, but rather generally-available empirical information which he used in order to arrive at his conclusion. Neither (B) nor (C) is the best answer. The notion that a word has an inherent, one-to-one correspondence with its referent, choice (A), is the prior linguistic theory against which Saussure made his claim of arbitrariness. Choice (A) is incorrect.

17. **(C)** According to the studies of Maurice Merleau-Ponty, there are a number of generally discernible stages in childhood language development. While warning against the danger of insisting too heavily on artificial divisions, Merleau-Ponty nonetheless recognized several particular stages in the child's acquisition of language, based on increasingly sophisticated operations of imitation. He also allowed for the possibility of temporary regression in these stages, in addition to that of precocious advancement where the child suddenly manifests a linguistic capacity previously absorbed but hitherto undisplayed. Choice (C) is the correct answer. The conception of the acquisition of language as a child's learning to express his or her thoughts is an incoherent notion, because it necessarily presupposes a prior language in which the child is having such thoughts; choice (A) is therefore incorrect. As Merleau-Ponty's study indicates, the child's acquisition of language is able to be divided roughly into successive stages, avoiding either extreme of a strict series of stages each logically dependent on the previous one, or of a chaotic, undefinable development. Both extremes, choice (B) and choice (D), are not correct.

18. **(C)** Merleau-Ponty, as we have seen in the article above, denies that there is a radical distinction between the way children learn language and the way adults continue to expand their linguistic repertoire. As children learn language by being surrounded by it, so too do adults acquire new verbal possibilities primarily by dint of their exposure to them. Choice (C) is therefore correct. It is only rarely that adults find it necessary to interrupt a conversational sequence for explanation of a specific unfamiliar term or phrase; hence (A) is not the best answer. Similarly, even in technical or academic situations, the meaning of a new term or expression is generally established by the use a given writer or speaker is making of it; thus (B) is not the correct choice. The use of a dictionary or thesaurus, choice (D), is generally not an effective means of learning language, as such reference books cannot tell you how the new linguistic item in question is used in its various, particular applications. Choice (D) is not correct.

19. **(B)** Like meaning, the intention of an utterance is "on the surface," manifested within the particular situation and measurable by outward criteria pertinent to the situation. Choice (B) is thus correct. Intention is not a private act occurring in the mind of a speaker; if one couldn't express one's intentions verbally to another person, one wouldn't be able to articulate them to oneself. Therefore choice (B) is correct. For the same reason, choice (A) cannot be correct. If intentions were unknowable, it would make no sense to speak of intentions at all; hence choice (C) is incorrect. Finally, the notion that intention is public and "on the surface" contradicts previous linguistic theories of "deep structure," which maintained that one must translate a given sentence into another set of words in order for its intention to be clear. The problem with such a notion is that there is nothing to guarantee the adequacy of the translation and thus we are involved in an infinite regress. If the intention of an utterance cannot be made clear by the

utterance itself, it is unlikely another set of words would possess such clarity. Choice (D) is therefore incorrect.

20. **(A)** Because intention is a public event, measurable by outward criteria, the best way to judge whether or not a given intention has been fulfilled is to observe the actions that follow from it. Choice (A) is therefore correct. Both choices (B) and (C) attempt to remove intention from what is publicly observable and to locate it in the mind, either of the speaker or the listener. Neither (B) nor (C) can be the correct choice. Consulting the rules of standard American English, choice (D) would similarly focus our attention away from the situation itself to an abstract concept of language. But because an intention is manifested in the given situation of the utterance, it would be impossible to consider in the abstract, by a set of rules not bound to any particular set of circumstances. Choice (D) is thus incorrect.

21. **(A)** Because we are, for all intents and purposes, constantly immersed in language, it follows that good linguistic skills are vital no matter what particular situation is at hand; choice (A) is thus correct (see review, p. 45). It is incorrect to assume that, because one is dealing with scientific phenomena or numerical equations, one is not involved with language. Results from scientific investigations are understood and explained in language, and mathematical relationships constitute a language in and of themselves. (B) cannot be the correct choice. Even in non-academic occupations, linguistic skills are important; one is frequently called upon to read and/or generate text in the course of working as well as to communicate with co-workers. Choice (C) is incorrect. Good language skills are not to be simply equated with manners and polite conversation; rather, such skills indicate one's capacity to understand and use a variety of different types of language to different purposes. Choice (D) is simply mistaken.

22. **(C)** "Standard American English" is an arbitrary regularization and formalization of a particular set of rules for English usage; such rules are useful for particular purposes, such as the teaching of English to speakers of foreign languages. Choice (C) is correct. Because the permutations of English in this country are so various and inconsistent, there cannot be said to be a single underlying logic to American English; hence, choice (A) is false. The multitude of English languages spoken in this country also rules out choice (B), for there is no single way Americans "actually" speak. Finally, while "standard American English" may be used to assist in the teaching of English, its limitations in actual speaking situations are many, and it is best viewed as the beginning, not the end, of training in the English language. (D) is thus not the best choice.

23. **(A)** A door that would open "straight upon life" would directly reveal life: fictional works are not such doors and do not strictly imitate life (A). (A) is a better answer than (B) because (B) interprets the phrase literally, not as the metaphor it is. (C) is incorrect because it relies upon a misinterpretation of

"not...opening straight." There are no contextual references to the making of fiction (D).

24. **(B)** "Apertures" (openings) precedes "they" and is synonymous with its predicate "windows" (B). (A) and (C) are incorrect because they follow "they" and are its predicates. "Need" and "pressure" (D) describe the formation of the windows, not the windows themselves.

25. **(C)** The shift in point of view from "we" to "he" to "I" mimics the description of fiction that moves from building/genre housing all authors to each watcher at a window with an individual perspective (C). (A) is incorrect because the "house of fiction" contains authors, not their critics. The speaker neither affirms nor denies that he/she is a writer of fiction, making (B) incorrect. The use of "we" draws readers in and allies them with, rather than alienating them from, the speaker's perspective (D).

26. **(D)** (D), with its parallel pairs of contrasting words, exemplifies antithesis. There are no such contrasts in the other four choices. Shape and size (A), windows and doors (B), eyes and field-glass (C), are not opposites.

27. **(A)** The speaker states that human scene/choice of subject and window/literary form are nothing without the "consciousness of the artist" (line 21). (B) and (D) are consequently incorrect. Hinged doors (C) are dismissed because they do not have the same function as the windows.

28. **(C)** When simplifying algebraic expressions, always work from left to right. First perform all multiplications and divisions; then, once this is done, start again from the left and do all additions and subtractions.

SUGGESTION: It can be helpful to translate the algebraic statement to English. For example, $6 + 2(x - 4)$ is "six plus two *times* the quantity x minus 4." The word *times* indicates multiplication, so we must first perform $2(x - 4)$ by using the *distributive property* $a(b - c) = ab - ac$:

$$6 + 2(x - 4) = 6 + 2 \times x - 2 \times 4 = 6 + 2x - 8.$$

Then we perform the subtraction to combine the terms 6 and 8:

$$6 + 2x - 8 = 2x + (6 - 8) = 2x - 2.$$

Note that we did not combine the $2x$ term with the other terms. This is because they are not *like terms*. Like terms are terms which have the same variables (with the same exponents). Since the terms 6 and 8 have no variable x, they are not like terms with $2x$.

29. **(D)** Let x be the cost of one can of beans. Then $6x$ is the cost of six cans

of beans. So $6x = \$1.50$. Dividing both sides of the equation by 6, we get $x = \$.25$ and, hence, since $8x$ is the cost of eight cans of beans, we have $8x = 8 \times \$.25 = \$2.00$.

30. **(A)** Let t_1, t_2, t_3 represent Bonnie's scores on tests one, two, and three, respectively. Then the equation representing Bonnie's average score is

$$\frac{t_1 + t_2 + t_3}{3} = 71.$$

We know that $t_1 = 64$ and $t_2 = 87$. Substitute this information into the equation above:

$$\frac{64 + 87 + t_3}{3} = 71.$$

Combining 64 and 87 and then multiplying both sides of the equation by 3 gives us

$$3 \times \frac{151 + t_3}{3} = 3 \times 71 \text{ or } 151 + t_3 = 213.$$

Now subtract 151 from both sides of the equation so that

$$t_3 = 213 - 151 = 62.$$

31. **(D)** Let s be the length of each side of square $ABCD$. Since triangle ADC is a right triangle, we can use the Pythagorean Theorem to solve for s. We have $AD^2 + DC^2 = AC^2$ or $s^2 + s^2 = 8^2$. Simplifying the equation, we get: $2s^2 = 64$. Now divide both sides of the equation by two:

$$s^2 = 32 \text{ so } s = \sqrt{32} = \sqrt{16} \times \sqrt{2} = 4\sqrt{2}.$$

Therefore, the perimeter of square $ABCD$ is

$$P = 4s = 4 \times 4\sqrt{2} = 16\sqrt{2}.$$

32. **(B)** To solve the equation $2x^2 + 5x - 3 = 0$, we can factor the left side of the equation to get $(2x - 1)(x + 3) = 0$. Then use the following rule (this rule is sometimes called the Zero Product Property): If $a \times b = 0$ then either $a = 0$ or $b = 0$. Applying this to our problem gives us

$$2x - 1 = 0 \text{ or } x + 3 = 0.$$

Solve these two equations:

$$2x - 1 = 0 \rightarrow 2x = 1 \rightarrow \frac{1}{2} \text{ or } x + 3 = 0 \rightarrow x = -3.$$

But $x > 0$, so $x = \dfrac{1}{2}$.

33. **(C)** Note that the numbers 4, 8, 12, 16, and 20 are the only numbers from 1 through 20 that are divisible by 4. The probability that a ball chosen from the jar has a number on it which is divisible by 4 is given by

$$\dfrac{\text{total quantity of balls whose numbers are divisible by four}}{\text{total number of possible outcomes}} = \dfrac{5}{20} = \dfrac{1}{4}$$

34. **(D)** First find the total sales for each year by reading the graph for the sales of (i) black and white televisions and (ii) color televisions. Then combine these numbers:

1950	$20,000,000 + $5,000,000	= $25,000,000
1960	$10,000,000 + $20,000,000	= $30,000,000
1970	$15,000,000 + $25,000,000	= $40,000,000
1980	$10,000,000 + $45,000,000	= $55,000,000
1990	$5,000,000 + $45,000,000	= $50,000,000

The greatest total sales occurred in 1980.

35. **(A)** A prime number is an integer which is greater than one and which has no integer divisors other than 1 and itself. So, the prime numbers between 1 and 20 (not including 1 and 20) are: 2, 3, 5, 7, 11, 13, 17, 19. But 2 is not an odd number, so the odd primes between 1 and 20 are: 3, 5, 7, 11, 13, 17, 19. Hence, there are seven odd primes between 1 and 20.

36. **(C)** The area of the shaded region is equal to the area of the large circle (which has $\overline{OB}$ as a radius), minus the area of the smaller circle (which has $\overline{OA}$ as a radius). Since the area of a circle with radius r is $A = \pi r^2$, the area of the shaded region is:

$$\pi\,(OB)^2 - \pi\,(OA)^2 = 36\pi - 16\pi = 20\pi.$$

37. **(D)** To solve this inequality, we shall use the following rules:

(i)   If $a \le b$ and c is any number then $a + c \le b + c$.

(ii)   If $a \le b$ and $c < 0$ then $ca \ge cb$.

The goal in solving inequalities, as in solving equalities, is to change the inequality so that the variable is isolated (i.e., by itself on one side). So, in the equation $8 - 2x \le 10$, we want the term $-2x$ by itself. To achieve this, use rule (i) above and add –8 to both sides obtaining $8 - 2x + (-8) \le 10 + (-8)$ or $-2x \le 2$. Now we use rule (ii) and multiply both sides of the inequality by $-^1/_2$ as follows:

$$-\frac{1}{2} \times 2x \ge -\frac{1}{2} \times 2 \text{ or } x \ge -1.$$

38. **(C)** Since $\angle OPQ$ is a straight angle, $m\angle OPQ = 180°$. But

$m\angle OPQ = m\angle OPR + \angle RPQ$, so

$m\angle OPR + m\angle RPQ = 180°$ or $m\angle OPR = 180° - m\angle RPQ$.

Thus, we need to find $m\angle RPQ$. Now, $l_1 \parallel l_2$, therefore, $mRPQ = m\angle TRS$ since $\angle RPQ$ and $\angle TRS$ are corresponding angles. Recall that corresponding angles are two angles which lie on the same side of the transversal (i.e., a line intersecting other lines, in this case line TP is a transversal since it intersects both line l_1 and l_2), are not adjacent, and one is interior ($\angle RPQ$ in this problem) while the other is exterior ($\angle TRS$). Also, we know that the sum of the measures of the interior angles of a triangle is 180° and

$m\angle T = 80°$, so $m\angle TRS + m\angle RST = 180° - m\angle T = 100°$.

But $m\angle TRS = m\angle RST$ since $\triangle RST$ is isosceles. Thus, $m\angle TRS = 50°$. Thus,

$m\angle RPQ = 50°$ and $m\angle OPR = 180° - m\angle RPQ = 180° - 50° = 130°$.

39. **(D)** The midpoint of a segment with endpoints (x_1, y_1) and (x_2, y_2) is

$$\left(\frac{x_1 + x_2}{2}, \frac{y_1 + y_2}{2}\right).$$

Our endpoints are $M = (4,1)$ and $N = (-2, -1)$, so the midpoint of $\overline{MN}$ is

$$\left(\frac{4 + (-2)}{2}, \frac{1 + (-1)}{2}\right) = (1, 0).$$

40. **(A)** Let p be the original price of the jacket. Linda received a 25% discount so she paid 75% of the original price. Thus, 75% of p equals 54. Writing this in an equation, we get:

$$0.75p = 54 \text{ or } \frac{3}{4}p = 54.$$

To solve this equation, multiply both sides of the equation by the reciprocal of $^3/_4$ which is $^4/_3$. This will isolate the variable p.

$$\frac{4}{3}\left(\frac{3}{4}p\right) = \left(\frac{4}{3}\right)54 \text{ or } p = \frac{216}{3} = 72.$$

41. **(A)** 72104.58 is read "seventy-**two thousand**, one hundred four and fifty-eight hundredths."

42. **(C)** Another way to phrase the second sentence is: She wants to divide her money equally among her six children. Therefore, each child is to receive $300{,}000 \div 6$.

43. **(B)** Bob wants to bake 12 cupcakes. The recipe is for 36 cupcakes. Therefore, Bob wants to make $^{12}/_{36}$ or $^{1}/_{3}$ of the usual amount of cupcakes. Thus, Bob should use $^{1}/_{3}$ of the recipe's flour or

$$\left(\frac{1}{3}\right)\left(\frac{8}{3}\right) = \frac{8}{9}.$$

Note we used $^{8}/_{3}$ since

$$2\frac{2}{3} = \frac{8}{3}.$$

44. **(C)** Let s_1 and s_2 be Ricky's speed (rate) on the trip from A to B and the return trip from B to A, respectively. Then, since he drove 15 miles per hour slower on the return trip, $s_2 = s_1 - 15$. Recall that rate times time equals distance. So the distance from A to B is $(s_1) 3 = 3s_1$ and the distance from B to A is $(s_2)5 = 5s_2 = 5(s_1 - 15) = 5s_1 - 75$. But the distance from Town A to Town B is the same as the distance from Town B to Town A so we have the following equation:

$$3s_1 = 5s_1 - 75.$$

To solve this equation, first add 75 to both sides of the equation:

$$3s_1 + 75 = 5s_1 - 75 + 75 \text{ or } 3s_1 + 75 = 5s_1.$$

Now isolate the variable, subtract $3s_1$ from both sides:

$$3s_1 + 75 - 3s_1 = 5s_1 - 3s_1 \text{ or } 75 = 2s_1.$$

To finish the problem, divide both sides of the equation by 2:

$$s_1 = \frac{75}{2} = 37.5$$

Thus, Ricky drove 37.5 miles per hour on his trip from Town A to Town B.

45. **(D)** The shaded region consists of all the points on the horizontal line passing through the point (0, 2) and those below the line. All of these points have $y =$ coordinate less than or equal to 2: Thus, our answer is $y \leq 2$.

46. **(C)** The 1 is in the hundredths place. If the number to the immediate

right of the 1 (i.e., the number in the thousandths place) is greater than or equal to 5 we increase 1 to 2, otherwise do not change the 1. Then we leave off all the numbers to the right of the 1. In our problem a 6 is in the thousandths place so we change the 1 to a 2 to get 287.42 as our answer.

47. **(D)** If $a = b^3$ and $a = \frac{1}{8}$, then substituting into the first equation we have:

$$\frac{1}{8} = b^3 \text{ or } \left(\frac{1}{2}\right)^3 = b^3 \text{ so } b = \frac{1}{2}.$$

48. **(D)** Let x be the number of people in the barn. Then, since each person and cow has only one head, the number of cows must be $30 - x$. Since people have two legs, the number of human legs totals $2x$. Similarly, since the number of legs each cow has is 4, the total number of cow legs in the barn is $4(30 - x)$. Thus, we have this equation:

$$2x + 4(30 - x) = 104.$$

To solve this equation, use the distributive property:

$$a(b - c) = ab - ac.$$

We get:

$$4(30 - x) = (4 \times 30) - (4 \times x) = 120 - 4x.$$

Our equation reduces to:

$$2x + 120 - 4x = 104 \text{ or } 120 - 2x = 104.$$

Now subtract 120 from both sides or the equation to get $-2x = 104 - 120 = -16$. Dividing both sides of the equation by -2: $x = 8$. Therefore, there were 8 people and $30 - 8 = 22$ cows in the barn.

49. **(B)** If two lines l_1 and l_2 which lie in the same plane, are both perpendicular to a third line, l_3, l_1 and l_2 are parallel.

50. **(D)** First of all the least common multiple (LCM) of 2 and 3 is $2 \times 3 = 6$, so let's rewrite the expression so that both fractions have 6 as a common denominator:

$$\frac{1}{2} + \frac{1}{3} = \frac{3}{3} \times \frac{1}{2} + \frac{2}{2} \times \frac{1}{3} = \frac{3}{6} + \frac{2}{6} = \frac{5}{6}.$$

51. **(A)** Note that there is a solid dot on -1 which means to include -1 in the set. The numbers to the right of -1 are shaded; this means to include these numbers also. Hence, this is the graph of all numbers greater than or equal to

$-1 (\{x \mid x \geq -1\})$.

52. (C) According to the graph, the supply was greater than the demand in March and May only.

53. (D) The greatest common divisor (GCD) is the greatest integer which divides both 120 and 252. To find the GCD, factor both numbers and look for common factors.

$$120 = 2^3 \times 3 \times 5 \text{ and } 2^2 = 2^2 \times 3^2 \times 7,$$

so the GCD $= 2^2 \times 3 = 12$.

54. (D) The list of all the negative integers between -9 and 5 is:

$$-8, -7, -6, -5, -4, -3, -2, -1.$$

55. (D) The answer is (D). While California has a number of rivers for white-water rafting, none of them are used for commerce. Therefore, (A), (B), and (C) are incorrect.

56. (A) The answer is (A). Mexican liberals who controlled the new government demanded the secularization of the missions. The missions were highly productive (B), (D), and the Franciscans had no intention of abandoning them. Moreover, by "pacifying" the natives, missionaries were an integral part of Spanish imperial policy (C) and supported by the crown.

57. (D) The answer is (D). Los Angeles had no natural harbor (A), no dependable water supply (B), and no industry. Wheat was extracted in Northern California (C). Los Angeles's growth sprung from the efforts of boosters and land speculators, who shrewdly used their great wealth, as well as municipal and federal subsidies, to build the necessary infrastructure in advance of demand.

58. (A) The Haymarket Incident involved the throwing of a bomb at Chicago police and a subsequent riot involving police and striking workers. There were plenty of scandals within the Grant administration (B), but this was not one of them. Allegations of corruption on the part of Republican presidential candidate James G. Blaine (C) were contained in the Mulligan Letters. The disastrous fire that pointed out the hazardous working conditions in some factories (D) was New York's Triangle Factory fire.

59. (B) In the 1857 case *Dred Scot v. Sanford* the Supreme Court held that no black slave could be a citizen of the United States. It was in the 1954 case *Brown v. Topeka Board of Education* that the court held separate facilities for the races to be unconstitutional (A). The reverse (C) was the court's holding in the 1896 case *Plessy v. Ferguson*. Affirmative Action was limited (D) in the 1970s and '80s.

60. **(C)** O'Sullivan spoke of America's "manifest destiny to overspread the continent." The idea that America must eventually become either all slave or all free (D) was expressed by Lincoln in his "House Divided" speech and was called by William H. Seward the "Irresponsible Conflict." Racial equality (A) was still not a popular idea when O'Sullivan wrote in the first half of the nineteenth century. By that time, of course, America was already an independent country (B).

61. **(D)** Mexico did expect to win the war, invade the U.S., and dictate a peace in Washington, but whatever desire, if any, the Mexicans may have had for the state of Louisiana was not a factor in the coming of the war. The U.S. did, however, desire to annex California (A) and did annex Texas (C); Mexico did refuse to pay its debts (B) and did claim Texas (C).

62. **(B)** Roosevelt declared a banking holiday, closing all banks to prevent anxious depositors from demanding their money and causing the banks to default. Curtailing government spending and taxes (A) was the last thing Roosevelt wanted to do and would probably have had little effect on the immediate banking crisis at the time of Roosevelt's inauguration. Banning fractional reserve banking (C) would at least have addressed the root problem but was as extreme in another direction and was not suggested by anyone in government at that time. A multi-billion dollar federal bailout (D) has been the federal government's response to the savings and loan crisis of the late 1980s and early 1990s.

63. **(C)** *Marbury v. Madison* asserted for the first time the Supreme Court's right to declare an act of Congress unconstitutional. It did not, however, go so far as to claim that the Supreme Court alone was empowered to say what the Constitution meant (B). In the decision of this case, Chief Justice John Marshall wisely avoided issuing a directive (A) that President Thomas Jefferson would have defied (D) had it been issued.

64. **(B)** The term "Trail of Tears" is used to describe the relocation of the Cherokee tribe from the southern Appalachians to what is now Oklahoma. The migration of Mormons from Nauvoo, Illinois, to the Great Salt Lake in Utah (A), the westward movements along the Oregon Trail (C), and, much earlier, the Wilderness Road (D), all took place and could at times be as unpleasant as the Cherokees' trek. They were, however, voluntary and therefore did not earn such sad titles as the "Trail of Tears."

65. **(B)** The income tax became law under Wilson. The Pure Food and Drug

Act (A) was passed under Taft. The old-age pension (D) had to wait for Franklin Roosevelt. High protective tariffs (C) have existed at a number of time throughout U.S. history. The Underwood Tariff passed under Wilson represented a lowering of tariff rates.

66. **(B)** The Bay of Pigs incident involved a U.S.-sponsored attempt by free Cubans to overthrow Communist dictator Fidel Castro. The presence of Soviet nuclear missiles in Cuba was at issue in the Cuban Missile Crisis. The clash between a U.S. Navy destroyer and North Vietnamese patrol boats (D) was the Tonkin Gulf incident and related to the Vietnam War.

67. **(C)** The correct answer is (C) France and the Ottoman Empire. Austria was attacked twice during the period from 1660 to 1685 by the Ottoman Turks and was confronted during the same time by wars with France. (A) is incorrect because Italy did not exist as a nation-state, and Austria and Prussia were allies. (B) is incorrect because England was allied with Austria and Russia was undergoing political crises which were not stabilized until Peter the Great seized power and reformed the government. (D) is incorrect because of Austria's alliance with Prussia.

68. **(B)** Democracy is the correct response because it is the antithesis of the authoritarianism of fascism. Indeed, the totalitarian, romantic, militaristic, and nationalistic characteristics were, in large part, a reaction against the perceived inadequacies of democracy.

69. **(B)** The industrial economy of the 19th century was not based upon an equitable distribution of profits among all those who were involved in production. Marxists and other critics of capitalism condemned the creed of capitalists and the abhorrent conditions of the industrial proletariat. Raw materials, a constant labor supply, capital, and an expanding marketplace were critical elements in the development of the industrial economy.

70. **(B)** Oscar Wilde's *The Picture of Dorian Gray* and Thomas Mann's *Death in Venice* embodied a new symbolists' direction in literature which addressed themes which were ignored previously; these themes include fantasies relating to the perpetual "youth" in exchange for the soul, and homosexuality. These works and others of this vintage could not be (A) construed as examples of romantic literature in the literary tradition of romanticism nor can they be categorized as examples of the (C) new sense of realism in literature or examples (D) of any expressionist literary movement. Both of these works were applauded by intellectuals at the time of their publication.

71. **(A)** The response of the Catholic Church to the Reformation was delayed because the Papacy feared the remnants of the Conciliar Movement within the

church itself. The Conciliar Movement, which was clearly evident at the Council of Constance (1414) and later at the Councils of Basel and Florence, was a tradition in the Roman Catholic Church which asserted that authority within the church resided in the assembly of bishops; it was a challenge to the concept of Petrine Supremacy and the authority of the Papacy. Rome (B) had little interest in coordinating its policy with secular leaders, although the early support of Charles V and Henry VIII was well received. By the 1530s most intelligent Church leaders did not (C) think that Protestantism would self-destruct or that (D) the situation was not a serious crisis.

72. **(A)** The Russian Revolution of 1905 led Nicholas II to issue the October Manifesto which called for an advisory assembly (the Duma) to be formed. It was not suppressed by Nicholas II (B). The October Manifesto was not (C) democratic in nature; the Revolution of 1905 occurred after Russian forces were being defeated in the Russo-Japanese war. The death in the war was a factor which stimulated the revolution.

73. **(D)** Leopold van Ranke, the 19th century German historian was not a contributor to the Enlightenment. Edward Gibbon (*The Decline and Fall of the Roman Empire*), David Hume (*History of England* and many works in philosophy), and Adam Smith (*Wealth of Nations*) were English contributors. Benjamin Franklin, American, was a multi-faceted genius of the Enlightenment.

74. **(C)** The chart indicates that the post-war economics in Central and Eastern Europe were fragile and subject to rapid deterioration during an economic collapse.

75. **(B)** In 1910 the most powerful state in Europe was Germany. While Great Britain (D) and France (A) had significant power—especially, Great Britain in its overseas holdings—Germany had the most powerful industrial economy and the most effective military organization in Europe, and Russia (C) were developing economies and military powers at this time.

76. **(B)** A writ of habeas corpus is a court order which directs an official who is detaining someone to produce the person before the court so that the legality of the detention may be determined. The primary function of the writ is to effect the release of someone who has been imprisoned without due process of law. For example, if the police detained a suspect for an unreasonable time without officially charging the person with a crime, the person could seek relief from a court in the form of a writ of habeas corpus. (A) is incorrect because a writ of mandamus is a court order commanding an official to perform a legal duty of his or her office. It is not used to prevent persons from being improperly imprisoned. The Fourth Amendment requirement that police have probable cause in order to obtain a search warrant regulates police procedure. It is not itself a mechanism for

affecting release of a person for improper imprisonment, so (C) is incorrect. Answer (D) is incorrect since the decision in *Roe v. Wade* dealt with a woman's right to have an abortion. It had nothing to do with improper imprisonment.

77. **(A)**   (A) is the best answer since the term "casework" is used by political scientists to describe the activities of congressmen on behalf of individual constituents. These activities might include helping an elderly person secure social security benefits, or helping a veteran obtain medical services. Most casework is actually done by congressional staff, and may take as much as a third of the staff's time. Congressmen supply this type of assistance for the good public relations it provides. Answer (B) fails because pork barrel legislation is rarely if ever intended to help individual citizens. Pork barrel legislation authorizes federal spending for special projects, such as airports, roads, or dams, in the home state or district of a congressman. It is meant to help the entire district or state. Also, there is no legal entitlement on the part of a citizen to a pork barrel project, such as there is with social security benefits. (C) is not the answer because lobbying is an activity directed toward congressmen, not one done by congressmen. A lobbyist attempts to get congressmen to support legislation that will benefit the group which the lobbyist represents. Logrolling, (D), is incorrect, because it does not refer to congressional service for constituents. It refers instead to the congressional practice of trading votes on different bills. Congressman A will vote for Congressman B's pork barrel project and in return B will vote for A's pork barrel project.

78. **(C)**   The three largest countries of Western Europe—the United Kingdom, France, and the Federal Republic of Germany—have either a multi-party system or a two-plus party system. A multi-party system is one in which three or more major parties compete for seats in the national legislature, while a two-plus party system has two large parties and one or more small parties. The United Kingdom has a two-plus party system. There are two large parties, the Conservatives and Labour. The Liberals are a smaller third party and there are even smaller regional parties in Scotland, Northern Ireland, and Wales. France has a multi-party system. The Socialists, Neo-Gaullists, and Republicans are major parties, while the Communists and the National Front are small parties with few seats in parliament. The Federal Republic of Germany has a two-plus party system. The major parties are the Christian Democratic Union and the Social Democratic Party. At the fringes of public life are the Greens and the Neo-Nazis. The United States, by contrast, has only two parties which successfully compete on a national basis from one election to the next. These are, of course, the Democrats and the Republicans. Answer (A) is incorrect. In Western European countries, party leaders determine which persons will run for office under the party banner. In the United States, on the other hand, candidates for office are selected by the voters in primary elections. Sometimes in the United States a candidate whom the party leadership detests wins the primary, and thus the right

to run for office under the party banner. In most Western European countries, political parties are much more centralized than in the United States; therefore, (B) is false. Answer (D) is false. Because parties are centralized in Western Europe, and because party leaders select candidates for national office, a party member in the national legislature seldom votes against the party. If one did, party leaders would remove his or her name from the ballot in future elections.

79. **(A)**   Answer choice (A), "basic research," is the correct answer since the biologist was interested in gaining the knowledge simply for the sake of curiosity or knowledge itself. "Applied research" (B) cannot be the correct answer since it involves using knowledge that has been gained from basic research or pure research and used to solve a problem. "Government research" (C) cannot be the correct answer since it may be either basic research or applied research, and in the paragraph there is no mention of who is funding the research. "Library research" (D) cannot be the correct answer even though in scientific research there is work done in the library; the paragraph deals with the major theme of a biologist doing "basic research."

80. **(C)**   Answer choice (C), "are found in many organisms," is the correct answer since there are organisms other than insects that produce chemical sexual attractants. "Are used only in insects" (A) cannot be the correct answer since there are other animals that produce chemical sexual attractants. "Are used by all animals" (B) cannot be the correct answer since there are some animals, especially the "lower" such as sponges and coelenterates, that have not been found to produce sexual attractants. "Can be seen" (D) cannot be the correct answer since the pheromones are invisible.

81. **(C)**   Answer choice (C), "over a period of time, the dish would gradually be filled with dead cockroaches that crawled through the poison in an attempt to mate with the cork," is the correct answer since they would attempt to crawl to the cork thinking that it is a female. "No cockroaches would be affected" (A) cannot be the correct answer since the pheromone would definitely affect the insect. "Moths would be attracted to the pheromone impregnated cork" (C) cannot be the correct answer since the biologist in the question was not using a moth pheromone and pheromones are specific. "Cockroaches would surround the dish but not cross the poison" (D) cannot be the correct answer since the cockroach would not notice what it is crawling through.

82. **(C)**   Answer choice (C), "Applied science," would be the correct answer since the biologist is solving a problem by applying the information gained from the basic research or pure science. "Pure science" (A) cannot be the correct answer since the biologist is not experimenting out of curiosity or for only the sake of knowledge. "Basic research" (B) cannot be the correct answer since it is the same thing as "pure science." "Government research" (D) cannot be the

correct answer since "government" would imply who is sponsoring the research, and not whether it is pure science/basic research or applied science/research.

83. **(C)** Answer choice (C), "applied science" would be the correct answer since the scientists are using information gained from basic research/pure science to solve a problem. "Entomology" (A) cannot be the correct answer since it is the study of insects. "Botany" (B) cannot be the correct answer since it is the study of plants. "Pure science" (D) cannot be the correct answer since the scientists are not trying to gain knowledge simply for the sake of knowledge itself.

84. **(C)** Examination of the fourth column reveals that there is no pattern to the divisions of time, therefore (C) is the correct answer. (A) is incorrect because the events listed are biological in nature rather than geological. (B) is incorrect, as the time blocks are of differing amounts. (D) is wrong because the eras are divided into periods and not the reverse.

85. **(A)** The sequence of life listed is correct, so answer choice (A) should be chosen. (B) is incorrect because invertebrates evolved before fish. (C) is incorrect because the first fish appeared much earlier than the first forests. Plants were present before birds, so (D) is wrong.

86. **(D)** The common alligator is a reptile. Answer choice (D) is correct because the Carboniferous Period saw the emergence of the first reptiles. Answer choices (A), (B), and (C) are incorrect, because they represent the emergence periods of organisms other than reptiles.

87. **(C)** By Newton's Third Law of Motion, the gravitational pull of a first body on a second must be equal and opposite to the pull of the second back on the first, no matter what the mass of each body is or what the motion of each body is. Therefore, I pull back on the Earth with the same force the Earth pulls on me, but in the opposite direction. But, because my mass is so small, I accelerate downward a great deal (9.8 m/s^2) while the mass of the Earth is so large that it accelerates minutely.

88. **(A)** The gravitational pull between two masses is proportional to the product of their masses. Hence, doubling the two masses would increase the pull by 4 times. Since the Earth is 82 times more massive than the moon, the pull between the sun and Earth must be 82 times greater than the pull between the Earth and moon if their separations were the same. Actually, the smaller distance between the Earth and moon makes the pull between the sun and Earth only 175 times the pull between the Earth and moon.

89. **(D)** The gravitational pull between any two masses is inversely proportional to the square of the distance between them. The pull between the moon and

Earth was given as 2×10^{20} N. If their separation was increased by two, then the force between them would have to decrease by four. A force of 2×10^{20} N divided by four is 5×10^{19} N.

90. **(D)** Since each answer given involves the pull between the moon and sun, the key factor is the relative distances between the bodies. The distance between the sun and moon is on the average 393 times greater than the distance between the moon and Earth. Remembering that the pull is inversely proportional to the square of the distance, the pull between the moon and Earth must be 393^2 or 154,450 times the pull between the sun and moon.

91. **(C)** (C) is correct, because of the difference between the P and S waves, the P wave travels faster. It can be seen on the graph that the P wave covers a greater distance in less time. (A) and (B) are incorrect as they are descriptions of the waves rather than an explanation. (D) is incorrect as an examination of the graph reveals the S wave to be slower.

92. **(B)** (B) is correct, locate the position labeled 8000 km and look up until you reach the P wave line and read across to the time. (A) is incorrect, it would be 3000 km. (C) is incorrect, it would be 1000 km. (D) is incorrect, it would be > 10,000 km.

93. **(A)** (A) is correct, you must locate the place on the graph where the S wave has traveled 5 minutes and read down to find the distance. (B) is incorrect; it would be 7 minutes. (C) is incorrect; it would be 10 minutes. (D) is incorrect; it would be 13 minutes.

94. **(C)** (C) is correct. You must locate on the graph the place where the space between the P and S wave lines is 7 minutes; then look down and read the distance scale. (A) is incorrect; it would be 2 minutes. (B) is incorrect; it would be 4 minutes. (D) is incorrect; it would be 9 minutes.

95. **(B)** Answer choice (B), "the length of the protein molecule, and the order and type of amino acids in the protein molecule" is the correct answer since proteins can be of different lengths; they can contain different types of amino acids; the amino acids can be in different orders in the protein. "Only the length of the protein molecule" (A) cannot be the correct answer since proteins can also differ by the order of their amino acids and /or by the types of amino acids they contain. "Only the type of amino acids in the protein molecule" (C) cannot be the correct answer since proteins can also differ in length and/or by the order of their amino acids. "Only the number of chemical bonds found in the protein molecule" (D) cannot be the correct answer since it is not mentioned as being one of the factors by which proteins can be different.

96. **(A)**   Answer choice (A), 20, is the correct choice since there are 20 differ-ent types of "R" factor which produce 20 different types of amino acids. As their only 20 different types of amino acids producing an equal number of types of "R" factor, it is not possible for (B), (C), or (D) to be correct.

97. **(A)**   Answer choice (A), "chains of amino acids" is the correct choice since amino acids are bonded together to form a chain. "Chains of fat molecules" (B) cannot be the correct answer since fat molecules are not part of a protein chain, and they are not mentioned in the paragraph. "Rings of carbon" (C) cannot be the correct answer since carbon rings form structures other than protein, and proteins which are composed of amino acids have no carbon rings. "Loops of cellulose molecules" (D) cannot be the correct answer since proteins are com-posed of amino acid chains.

98. **(C)**   Answer choice (C), "rock" is the correct choice since rock is not composed of amino acids. "Hair" (A) cannot be the correct answer since hair is composed of protein. "Fingernails" (B) cannot be the correct answer since they are composed of protein. "Skin" (D) cannot be the correct answer since its major components are protein.

99. **(D)**   Answer choice (D), "46" is the correct answer since a cell undergo-ing mitosis will first double its chromosome number and then divide and during that division the chromosomes will be evenly and correctly divided between the two daughter cells. "2" (A) cannot be the correct answer since the information in the question states that a cell starts out with 46 chromosomes. "10" (B) cannot be the correct answer since this number is still too small to make up even one set of chromosomes, much less two. "24" (C) cannot be the correct answer since hu-mans are sexually reproducing organisms and in a body cell there are two sets of chromosomes; therefore, 24 would be more than a single set but less than two sets.

100. **(D)**   Answer choice (D), "46," is the correct answer since the zygote of a human is a cell derived from a sperm containing 23 chromosomes and an egg containing 23 chromosomes. "2" (A) cannot be the correct answer since it repre-sents too few chromosomes for either a haploid sex cell or a diploid body cell. "10" (B) cannot be the correct answer since it also represents too few chromo-somes for either a haploid sex cell or a diploid body cell. "23" (C) cannot be the correct answer since it represents the number of chromosomes in a sperm or an egg.

101. **(D)**   Answer choice (D), "92" is the correct answer since the egg and sperm, in this case, would have the diploid number of chromosomes (46), and if they were to unite, then the number of chromosomes would be doubled. "2" (A)

cannot be the correct answer since this number represents too few chromosomes for even a human sex cell. "23" (B) cannot be the correct answer since this is the haploid chromosome number of a normal human sex cell. "46" (C) cannot be the correct answer since this is the diploid chromosome number of a normal zygote.

102. **(D)**   Answer choice (D), "diploid" is the correct answer since a zygote is a diploid cell formed from the union of two haploid sex cells. "A single organism composed of two cells" (A) cannot be the correct answer since a zygote is not composed of two cells, it is composed of one cell. "Haploid" (B) cannot be the correct answer since a zygote is formed from the union of two haploid sex cells and is a diploid cell. "Undergoes meiosis to produce four sperm" (C) cannot be the correct answer since zygotes do not undergo meiosis.

103. **(B)**   The ziggurat at Ur is the finest extant example of Sumerian architecture; actually, it is the best preserved ancient temple tower in all of Mesopotamia (present-day Iraq). To be specific, the ziggurat at Ur was built about 2100 B.C. by a group known as the Neo-Sumerians, the last civilization to embrace the customs and language of the earlier Sumerians (active from about 3000 to 2350 B.C.). The Egyptians neither lived in Mesopotamia nor built ziggurats, although their pyramids (which served as royal tombs not temple platforms) are sometimes confused with ziggurats. The Assyrians and Babylonians lived in Mesopotamia, but these civilizations had nothing to do with the great ziggurat at Ur, built centuries before the Assyrians and Babylonians came along.

104. **(D)**   Flying buttresses, pointed arches and stained glass windows appear together only on Gothic style buildings, most of which were built between 1150 and 1500. Buildings of the Romanesque period (c. 1050-1150) usually employ wall buttresses and rounded arches; only a few employ pointed arches. The flying buttress was a device invented specifically to support the high vaults of Gothic churches. Byzantine buildings, like the famous Hagia Sophia in Istanbul, are characterized by domes and rounded arches, among other things. The same is true for Renaissance architecture.

105. **(D)**   Pollock's *Lucifer* is a monument of Abstract Expressionism, one of the most influential artistic movements of the 20th century. Pollock's work is characterized by drips and splotches of paint arranged in rhythmic patterns on large canvases. Pablo Picasso is the best known practitioner of Cubism, an early 20th century style characterized by fractured, though straight, lines, and, at least at times, recognizable subject matter. Henri Matisse was the leader of the Fauvists, a group of French artists active in the early 20th century and known for their use of intensely bright colors.

106. **(C)**   St. Paul (or Saul as he was known at this point) has just been knocked from his horse and blinded by the light of God. Caravaggio renders the scene with a dark background strongly broken by a beam of light coming from above. It is a dramatic scene, a climactic moment in the life of the apostle. The figure of Paul has been foreshortened such that his head is closer to the viewer than the rest of his body. The artist has filled the composition almost completely; there is very little unoccupied, or "negative," space. He has also used clear, precise contour lines and detailed brushwork.

107. **(A)**   In conventional lithography a limestone block, obtained preferably from quarries in Bavaria, is used as the support for the crayon marks, acids, and inks needed for a lithograph. The support for woodcuts is wood. Metal plates, usually of zinc or copper, serve for engravings and etchings.

108. **(D)**   Elliot Eisner became one of the leaders in art education with his book *Educating Artistic Vision* (1972). This was followed by other seminal books like *The Arts, Human Development and Education* (1976). Ralph Nader is a consumer advocate and author of *Unsafe at Any Speed*. Mortimer Adler is a nationally recognized philosopher, author and educator, author of *The Paideia Program*, and advocate of learning through the great books. Bill Honig is an educational administrator for the state of California, noted for his reform of grade school textbooks and for his own book *Last Chance for Our Children: How You Can Help Save Our Schools*.

109. **(C)**   Discipline-Based Art Education is an approach to the teaching of art that integrates art history, art criticism, aesthetics, and art production. Teachers versed in DBAE have their students do much more than traditional arts and crafts; they also encourage the reading, writing, and critical analysis of art.

110. **(C)**   Red, yellow, and blue are the primary colors. Their respective complements are green, purple, and orange.

111. **(B)**   Produced in 1915 at the height of the movement known as Cubism, Archipenko's *Woman Combing Her Hair* is composed of the facet-like planes and displaced body parts typical of Cubist art.

112. **(A)**   One of best known artifacts of the Paleolithic or Old Stone Age era, the so-called *Venus of Willendorf*, was made around 20,000 B.C. The statue's emphasis on genitalia and breasts suggests its purpose had something to do with human reproduction.

113. **(B)** "Stupas" is the correct response. Pagodas are towers, usually with curved-up roofs, that are built as temples or memorials in the Far East (A). Mastabas are tombs built by Egyptians during the Old Kingdom (C). A mandorla is an almond-shaped halo surrounding medieval images of Christ (D).

114. **(B)** Louis Sullivan, an architect best known for his late 19th century skyscrapers, promoted the idea that a building's form should follow its function. His slogan "form follows function" became one of the Great Truths for modern architects of the 20th century, among them Gropius and Mies van der Rohe.

115. **(A)** Exhibited in 1913 at the famous Armory Show in New York City, Duchamp's *Nude Descending a Staircase* became one of the most vilified (and celebrated) paintings of the 20th century. For many Americans this painting represented everything that was perverse about modern European painting. Stylistically, Duchamp's work relies on the slightly earlier Cubist compositions of Picasso and Braque. However, unlike the static figures of Picasso and Braque, Duchamp's nude is captured in the process of moving.

116. **(B)** Developed in Italy in the 15th century, one-point linear perspective uses a mathematical system based on orthogonals, where all lines appear to recede perpendicular to the picture plane, converging at a single vanishing point on the horizon. Imagines are wax ancestor portraits favored by the ancient Romans (D). Hatching is a drawing and printmaking technique in which fine lines are placed close together to achieve an effect of shading (C). Epigones are members of any generation that is less distinguished than the one before, e.g., the artists who followed Giotto (A).

117. **(C)** The correct response is (C). This response recognizes that children learn at different rates and suggests a structured method to limit the number of children per center. It is impossible for all students to work at the same rate (A). Children who finish early should not be given extra work merely to keep them busy (B). Speed is not the primary goal of this activity (D).

118. **(D)** The correct response is (D). A concluding activity should encourage students to summarize what they have learned and share this information with other students. A class party celebrating scientists is a valuable experience but does not allow students to share what they have learned (A). A topic for cumulative reviews should not be limited to only medical discoveries when the unit's topic was much broader (B). A test is considered an evaluation technique and should not be confused with a concluding activity (C).

119. **(B)** The correct response is (B). Materials should represent a wide range of topics and people, thereby fostering an appreciation for diversity in the students. An appropriate reading level (A), related information (C), and a majority of interest (D) are all important, but cannot be called the main reason for selecting a book.

120. **(C)**   The correct response is (C). The use of instructional strategies that make learning relevant to individual student interests is a powerful motivating force that facilitates learning and independent thinking. (A) and (B) are both important factors to consider during a brainstorming session of this type, but both of these factors should influence the teacher only after the student interests have been included. (D) indicates a misunderstanding of the situation described. The students are setting the objectives for the unit as they brainstorm questions.

121. **(B)**   The correct response is (B). Choice is an important element in motivating students to learn. (A) is contradictory with the stated purpose of the activity. The students proposed the questions, so covering all the questions should not be a problem. (C) is incorrect because the students have chosen what they consider to be key questions; the teacher should select different or additional key questions. (D) is a possibility, but only if there is a specific reason why all the students should not research all the questions.

122. **(B)**   The correct response is (B). The best way to teach children to read, regardless of grade level, is to use a program of emergent literacy which includes pattern books and journal writing with invented spelling. (A) is incorrect because although an intensive phonics program that includes drill and practice seat work on basic sight words may be effective with some students, it is not the most effective way to teach all students to read. (D) is incorrect because an ESL program is intended to provide assistance to only those students who are learning English as a second language. Additionally, the learning resource teacher should provide assistance to only those students who have been identified as having a learning disability that qualifies them to receive services.

123. **(A)**   The correct response is (A). By selecting books for the classroom library that match students' independent reading abilities, the teacher is recognizing that students must improve their reading ability by beginning at their own level and progressing to more difficult materials. (B) is incorrect because books that are so difficult that they are challenging will most likely be frustrating to many students. (C) is incorrect because the presence or absence of separate word lists should not be a determining factor in selecting books for a classroom library. (D) is incorrect because all children need access to a classroom library regardless of their reading abilities.

124. **(C)**   The correct response is (C). A post office center, restaurant center, and a weather center all encourage a variety of reading and writing activities which is what these students need most. (A) and (B) are incorrect because they are incomplete. (D) is incorrect because the science center is included and combining the chemicals in that center poses an obvious danger to young children.

125. **(A)**   The correct response is (A). One of the most reliable ways to identify individual learning styles is to observe the students over a period of time and make

informal notes about their work habits and the choices they make within the classroom. (B) is incorrect because although a school psychologist could provide information about each student's learning style, the teacher can identify this information on his or her own. (C) is incorrect because although administering a group screening test will identify learning styles, such a test may be difficult to obtain, and the teacher could gain the same knowledge through simple observation. (D) is incorrect because each student's permanent file may or may not contain this information, and an individual student's learning style may have changed over the years and there is no guarantee that this change will be noted in the permanent record.

126. **(D)**   Public Law 94-142 provides a legal definition for the term "handicapped children." It includes children who have been evaluated as being mentally retarded, hearing impaired, deaf, speech impaired, visually handicapped, seriously emotionally disturbed, orthopedically impaired, having other health impairments (e.g., anemia, arthritis, etc.), deaf-blind, multi-handicapped, or with specific learning disabilities. P.L. 94–142 states that these children need special education and services.

127. **(A)**   Epilepsy refers to different kinds of seizures. Most epileptic children can participate in regular physical education classes, regardless of the type of seizure previously experienced (B). Seizures are caused by an electrochemical imbalance in the brain. A minor motor seizure (C) causes localized contractions of muscles on one side or in one part of the body. Sweating and rapid heart rate (D) are characteristic of an autonomic seizure.

128. **(A)**   Gross visual-motor skills involve movement of the body's large muscles as visual information is processed. A ball is always used to perfect these skills. In some cases a bat or racquet will also aid in developing these skills.

129. **(C)**   A volleyball game ends with 15 points, as long as the serving team has won by 2 points. One point is scored by the serving team if the receiving team cannot return the ball that was propelled across the net within the boundaries.

130. **(B)**   Interval training (A), (C), is associated with the development of cardiovascular endurance and performance of aerobic activities (e.g., swimming, running, and cycling). Weight training involves a progressive increase in workload to develop muscular strength. With isometric exercise, the muscle does not change its length as a person exerts force against a resistance. In this case the force is static. However, with isokinetic exercise, the resistance pushes back with force equal to the one that the person exerts.

131. **(C)**   Fluid is always reestablished by drinking water. A common practice is to drink before, during and after an event. It is not necessary to take salt tablets (A) since normal salting of food is adequate to replenish the salt lost with sweat.

Sugared drinks and juice (E) draw water to the gastrointestinal tract and cause cramps. Vitamin (B) and mineral supplements (D) will not replenish water.

132. **(C)**   Roughly 60% of the calories consumed should be derived from carbohydrates. These should mostly include complex carbohydrates that come from foods such as bread and pasta.

133. **(D)**   The grip strength test (C), pull ups (for boys) (A), and flexed arm hang (for girls) (B), are all tests to measure muscular strength and endurance. The sit and reach test measures flexibility.

134. **(A)**   The skills required to master a certain dance will determine the suggested grade level for that dance. The simplest steps used are "walk and/or skip" and are therefore appropriate for grades 1–2. The steps "run and/or skip" (B), and "skip and slide" (C), are more difficult, and therefore suggested for grades 2–3. Even more difficult is the "step-hop" (D), and it is incorporated in dances appropriate for grades 3–6.

Content Area Exercises
Scoring Guide

3 • The examinee demonstrates a comprehensive understanding of the material presented.

• The examinee has responded effectively to every part of the question.

• The examinee has provided well supported explanations.

• The examinee has demonstrated a strong knowledge of the subject matter, including relevant theories, concepts, and procedures.

2 • The examinee demonstrates a basic understanding of the material presented.

• The examinee has responded effectively to most parts of the question.

• The examinee has provided explanations.

• The examinee has demonstrated an adequate knowledge of the subject matter, including relevant theories, concepts, and procedures.

1 • The examinee demonstrates some misunderstanding of the material presented.

• The examinee fails to respond effectively to every part of the question.

• The examinee has provided only weak explanations.

• The examinee has demonstrated insufficient knowledge of the subject matter, including relevant theories, concepts, and procedures.

0 • The examinee has either not responded, responded off-topic, has responded completely incorrectly, or simply rephrased the question.

CONTENT AREA EXERCISES I

I. Literature and Language Studies

1.   Response that received a score of 3:
Conrad's sentence structure is perhaps the most prominent device used to give his reader a vivid description of the psychological and physical stress that his narrator is experiencing. In the latter portion of the passage, Conrad uses a number of sentences linked by semicolons to give the reader the feeling of the slow, rhythmic passage up the river. Repetition of the narrator's "I" makes the narrative very personal, allowing the reader to place him or herself into the action, making the descriptions very realistic. In the same section, Conrad specifically outlines the variety of tedious tasks that the narrator must carry out, creating a tension that underlies the futility and paranoia of the last sentence.

Response that received a score of 1:
Conrad's choice of words illustrates that the narrator is very worried about the trip that he is making. He spends most of the passage just describing what the narrator is doing, and how bored and scared he must be. In the last line of the passage, the narrator describes himself as a monkey, meaning that he feels like he is no longer human in this situation. Overall, Conrad has provided a vivid description of what it must be like to be sailing up the Congo River.

2.   Response that received a score of 3:
The expansive scope of a novel allows the author to convey a message through the actions of his or her characters. A novelist has the ability to place his or her characters in any situation they choose, and allow them to react in a way that demonstrates his or her point of view. The author can use his characters' actions as an example to the reader. For example, in Nathaniel Hawthorne's *The Scarlet Letter*, Hesther Prynne is established as the scapegoat for a society's social ills, and her grace in handling the situation is an example to his readers. In addition, her character makes the rest of the society stand out as judgmental and reactionary.
In a persuasive essay, the author is not bound to develop characters and move a plotline along. An essayist may present his or her argument in any context they wish, and the quality of the essay will be judged primarily by the quality of the argument. Generally, however, an essay is designed to be read in one sitting. Therefore, the essayist must pack everything they want to say in a small space. While the novelist has nuance on his or her side, the essayist may more freely express his or her opinions in their own context, rather than having to place them in a "believable" environment.

Response that received a score of 1:

A novelist is telling a story, and a social message may or may not be a part of that story. If the novelist wants to convey a message, they can just pick a character and have that character express their point of view. They just have to make sure that if they agree with that character, he doesn't end up dead in the end.

A persuasive essay doesn't use characters. The essayist just says whatever he wants to say, and the reader can agree with it or not. He or she just lays out their argument, and let's the reader be the judge, but the novelist tries to make you think a certain way.

3.   Response that received a score of 3:

Moby-Dick, by Herman Melville is set on a whaling ship called The Pequod. This setting is crucial to understanding the motivations of the characters. The bond that grows between Ishmael, the narrator, and his fellow travelers is a direct result of the fact that they are, for all practical purposes, trapped on the ship together. They must work together, eat together and sleep together for the three years which the voyage is supposed to last. They are dependent on each other for their livelihood and their happiness. Any story about whaling must, by necessity take place on a ship, however it would be difficult to imagine the tensions and bonds that develop between characters to exist anywhere other than the micro-cosmic world of The Pequod.

Another aspect of the setting that affects the reader is the fact that now, in the late twentieth century, the once noble occupation of whaling has become severely discredited. For this reason, the novel offers a perspective on a different time, when commerce was more important than the destruction of endangered species.

Response that received a score of 1:

In The Jungle, by Upton Sinclair, setting is not very important. It's the story of the hardships faced by an immigrant family, and could happen anywhere and anytime a family picks up and moves from one place to another. The particulars of the plot make up the context of the story, but for the most part, you could move it anywhere and it would stay the same. The main character, Jergis is just like anybody else. He's a guy trying to make a living in an unfair world. I could probably write the same story about my grandfather when he moved to this country.

4.   Response that received a score of 3:

While the standardization of grammar has made it easier to test entire groups of students on the basis of specific criteria, this may have dramatic effects on the self-esteem of these students. If we think of grammar as a rigid set of rules that one must follow, we deny the fact that language is generative, and changes with use. The idea of standardized grammar insists that in order to be understood, an individual must conform to a strict set of rules. This would suggest, for example, that someone who used an "ungrammatical expression, such as "ain't" would not be understood. Obviously this is not true. In another way, standardization of grammar can stigmatize students from a variety of ethnic backgrounds. For example, speakers of Black English are following another set of grammar rules and speech patterns, and are often scolded during their education. This can deal a severe blow to the self-esteem of these students, as well as suggest to them that their teachers feel that there is something wrong with their cultural heritage.

Response that received a score of 1:
Standardized grammar is an outdated idea. You can't tell people how to talk, because the language they use is their own. Anyone who would think that a person was not intelligent just because they didn't follow some hundred year old rule is simply wrong. Of course, you have to follow some rules, like where to put the verb in a sentence, or where to put a conjunction, but overall, if somebody can be understood, that should be good enough. People have been talking long before grammar was standardized, and they did just fine. Standardized grammar just has the function of making people feel bad for how they express themselves, and people should never be discouraged from expressing themselves.

II. Mathematics

5. Response that received a score of 3:
This graph is misleading because it is an example of a truncated graph. By looking at only the graph, it appears that the unemployment rate doubled from June to August, then dropped significantly from August through December. However, the unemployment rate only changed by a few percentage points throughout the period. If the graph was not truncated it would better reflect the minor fluctuation of the unemployment rate during this period.

Response that received a score of 1:
This graph is misleading because it appears to be skewed. The unemployment rate left of the graph does not appear to be correlated to the graph.

6. Response that received a score of 3:
The median salary is a more appropriate method of determining the measure of central tendency in this example because of the small sample size and the sensitivity of a few large values to skew the average ($90,000 and $95,000). The mean value is influenced too much by the two high salaries and is not a good representation of average salary of this company.

Response that received a score of 1:
Because of the small sample size, the mean would not be a good method of

calculating this company's average salary. By taking the mean value, this company's average salary appears higher than it is. Therefore, the median salary is a more appropriate indication of this company's average salary.

7. **Response that received a score of 3:**
    Given the information above, it can be assumed that the ladder, tree, and ground form a right triangle. Therefore, it the tangent of 45 degrees is multiplied by 4 (the distance from the tree to the ladder), the height of the tree can be calculated.

Response that received a score of 1:
    Since the ladder forms a 45 degree angle with the ground, the tree's height has to equal the distance from the tee to the ladder.

8. **Response that received a score of 3:**
    Since the figure is a unit circle, we know that the distance from X to Y is equal to 1. The secant of an angle is the inverse cosine of the angle. In this example, it would be $d/1$, or d.

Response that received a score of 1:
    There is not enough information to complete this problem, unless a unit circle indicates that the distance from X to Y is equal to 1. If this is true than secant equals d because $1/d$ equals the cosine.

III. Visual and Performing Arts

9. **Response that receive a score of 3:**
    Architecture has always been a reflection of the values and needs of a given culture. For an example of this, one need only go into any city in any country and look for the tallest building. During times when religion was the dominant cultural influence, cathedrals climbed toward heaven. In our own modern society, office buildings concerned with commerce and consumerism dominate our cityscapes. Architecture also tells us a great deal about our fears. Buildings in California are considered great architecture if they are earthquake-proof, and government buildings are considered great architecture if they are invulnerable to attack.

Response that received a score of 1:
    Architecture is important because people's homes reflect their values. Someone who lives in a nice house with bars on the windows will probably have very different values from someone whose house is not really protected. Also, big housing developments where poor people are stacked up floor after floor on top of one another shows how society doesn't care about them.

10. Response that received a score of 3:

Theater can be said to encompass all the artistic disciplines because in many cases, music, dance, and visual art work in concert to create the overall mood. For example, song and dance have long been a staple of many theatrical productions, from opera to Broadway musicals, and set dressing and costume design are carried out by visual artists. When all these things function together, they create a comprehensive artistic experience.

Response that received a score of 1:

When I saw *Cats*, by Andrew Lloyd Weber, it was clear that a true artist created this show. Many people don't think of him as an artist because he's modern, but I disagree. I think that it doesn't matter what time period your from, if you can make people happy like that, your an artist. He wrote the music and the dialogue, and it was such an original idea!

IV. Human Development

11. Response that received a score of 3:

Educators now realize that individual students often learn best in ways that are very different from one another. For example, some students are visually oriented, and some others are more geared toward auditory education. Visual learners are those students that learn best by reading. Teachers can encourage these students to pursue supplemental reading, or they can teach them how to read more effectively. Teachers can encourage these students to underline in their texts when they read, or to write margin notes. Auditory learners learn best by listening. They can use audio cassettes as supplementary learning materials, and should be encouraged to participate in class discussions, and should be taught to take effective notes based on what they hear in class.

Response that received a score of 1:

Two styles of learning are motivated and unmotivated. Motivated students don't require as much attention from teachers and can basically be left on their own to pursue their studies. Unmotivated students will not work on they're own, and teachers must constantly keep after them to make sure that they are working. Motivated students should be rewarded by allowing them to study on their own, reading materials that they chose themselves. Teachers should make sure that unmotivated students do not waste their time on things like comic books, but rather read only school oriented material.

12. Response that received a score of 3:

The last two stages in Piaget's theory of cognitive development are concrete operations and formal operations. The concrete operations stage occurs between the ages of 7 and 11. This stage is extremely important to educators because this is the time when students become able to take into consideration opinions other than their own. In this stage, the student can begin to learn that there are many opinions that surround a single issue. The final stage is formal operations. This is very important because this is the beginning of what we would call adult thinking, and generally occurs between the ages of 11 and 15. This is the stage when students become able to engage in logical, hypothetical thought. They can make educated guesses about a situation, and identify cause and effect relationships.

Response that received a score of 1:

The final stages in Piaget's theory of cognitive development are preoperational and concrete operations. The preoperational stage in when students are convinced that their opinion is the only one with any validity. Students at this age (2-7) are very rigid in their thinking, and what thinking they do is very low level. This age is very frustrating for educators.

The concrete operations stage is the time when students begin to think like adults. They have the capacity for logic and understanding, although they don't always use it. This is when students really begin to learn, and that is why it is very important to educators.

V. Physical Education

13. Response that received a score of 3:

One of the best ways a physical education teacher can enhance their students' self-esteem is to ask individual students to demonstrate skills to be learned. Many students who are not successful in the academic arena find that they can achieve in their physical education classes. Most students enjoy this type of demonstration, and are made to feel successful by modeling the proper execution of an activity.

Another way to enhance student's self-esteem is to be absolutely sure that gender equity is practiced in their physical education classes. Too often, girls are ignored in phys ed. Girls should be chosen as "captains" as often as their male counterparts, and should be encouraged to live up to their full physical potential.

Response that received a score of 1:

One way to enhance self-esteem in physical education classes is to accentuate the achievements of the best athletes. Often these students don't do well in their other classes, so they should be chosen as captains every time, and should always be used to demonstrate whatever they are good at, like hitting or running.

Another way is to take make the captains pick teams, because this will enhance the self-esteem of the first student's picked, and for the last students picked, physical education is probably not a priority for them anyway.

14. **Response that received a score of 3:**
    Public Law 94-142 outlines the legal definition of "handicapped children." Too often these students are left out of physical education classes because not enough effort is made on the part of the teacher to adapt to their needs. One step that can be taken is to modify the program for them, gearing it toward activities that are not impacted by their disability. For example, a blind student can be encouraged to try weight training. Another method of tailoring phys ed classes to handicapped students is to limit class size. The optimum class size for handicapped students is ten students, with the absolute maximum being fifteen.

Response that received a score of 1:
    One way to adapt physical education classes to handicapped students would be to reduce the physical demands placed on them. For example, if the rest of the class is playing basketball, a handicapped student could write a paper on the game. Another way is to modify activities to suit the student's needs. For example, a beeper ball can be used for a blind student to play softball.

CONTENT AREA EXERCISES II

I. History and Social Sciences

1.   Response that received a score of 3:
The Red Scare led to the Sacco and Vanzetti trial. During the last months of World War I, Americans became very fearful of immigrants and foreigners, as they were suspected of being anarchists or communists. The labor strikes of 1919, which occurred when the International Workers of the World and other unions went on strike in many cities, caused much of the panic. Also, causing fear was the fact that bombs were being sent through the mail to prominent citizens, and there was much violence in the streets. The Palmer raids, led by U.S. attorney general Palmer, heightened tensions. During the raids, government agents, without warrants, broke into suspected IWW members' homes and meeting places and arrested thousands. Then in 1921, Sacco and Vanzetti, two Italian immigrant anarchists, were then accused of murder. Although there was no evidence that they were guilty, they were executed. After the trial, immigrant restriction became a hotly debated topic among Americans.

Response that received a score of 1:
The trial occurred when Americans were afraid of immigrants. Sacco and Vanzetti were Italians who were accused of murder. It was wrong to accuse them because they had done nothing wrong, but were only immigrants.

2.   Response that received a score of 3:
The Supreme Court case *Plessy vs. Ferguson*, of 1896, established that "separate but equal" status for blacks was constitutions. After Reconstruction failed, white Southerners kept blacks separate from whites by establishing Jim Crow laws, which were legal because the *Plessy* case made them so. Jim Crow laws were passed by individual cities and created separate public facilities for blacks and whites, such as restrooms, drinking fountains, hospitals, schools, and other facilities. The facilities for blacks were separate, but not equal, in fact, they were famously inferior to the whites' facilities.

Response that received a score of 1:
Jim Crow laws were passed in the South. These laws made black people use separate drinking fountains and bathrooms, and made them sit in separate areas in theatres and restaurants.

3.   Response that received a score of 3:
The U.S. was fighting the Korean War when this event occurred. Communist North Korea had attacked non-Communist South Korea, and the U.S. had

joined in South Korea's effort to ward off the North Koreans. Led by Genreal MacArthur, the American troops crossed over into North Korean territory. The Chinese warned the Americans to back off, but MacArthur instead moved his troops to the Chinese border. When the Chinese troops entered the war in November, 1950, they moved the U.S. troops back to the 38th parallel and greatly embarrassed MacArthur, who asked the U.S. government for permission to use nuclear weapons against the Chinese. This request was denied, a stalemate then occurred, and it was decided through talks that Communist North Korea and non-Communist South Korea would remain separated by the 38th parallel.

Response that received a score of 1:
The Korean war was lost when the Chinese crossed over their border and entered North Korea. They had a lot of troops and the U.S. troops could not fight them off. It was terrible for the U.S. when the Chinese entered North Korea.

4.   Response that received a score of 3:
Count Cavour was one of the architects of the Risorgimento. Cavour made an agreement with France that if Cavour started a war with Austria, to make her leave Central and Southern Italy, then France would support Cavour in return for small tracts of land. Although Napolean backed out of the agreement after war had begun, the war with Austria sparked uprisings in many Italian territories, and these new governments became part of greater Italy. Garibaldi also wanted a united Italy. Garibaldi led in the liberation of the Land of the Two Sicilies from the Bourbon ruler. Instead of then ruling this land himself, he offered it to the cause for a united Italy, and it then became part of a greater Italy.

Response that received a score of 1:
Italy had not been one country, but several principalities. Mazzini helped to unite Italy. He led troops into Southern Italy and, after winning the territory, declared it part of greater Italy.

II. Science

5.   Response that received a score of 3:
This small population of snakes would be susceptible to genetics defects. This is because the small breeding population's genetic makeup would be limited by lack of variation in the gene pool. Therefore, genetic defects would be more easily passed to the next generations. Additionally, once the population grows and mutations exist, the gene pool would become more dynamic and less susceptible to genetic defects.

Response that received a score of 1:
Genetic defects would be found more readily in this population because of

the small sample size of the population. These defects would be passed on from generation to generation developing this type of snake into a weak species.

6. Response that received a score of 3:

The major disadvantage of using hydrogen as an energy source is that it is highly explosive and potentially dangerous. However, as technology advances, it may be possible to overcome this obstacle. There are several qualities that make hydrogen an excellent alternative energy source. Hydrogen, although very explosive, releases more energy than any fossil fuel when burned. Hydrogen is also environmentally safe; when hydrogen burns it forms only oxygen and water vapor. Additionally, hydrogen can be obtained by separating a water molecule into its component atoms, oxygen and hydrogen. Thus, hydrogen is a potentially endless source of energy.

Response that received a score of 1:

Hydrogen is very volatile which is its major disadvantage. Currently there is not method to contain hydrogen safely. Also, hydrogen is difficult to find in the atmosphere which would make it a very costly alternative fuel source. The only advantage to hydrogen is that it can be liquified at cold temperatures allowing for easy and low cost transportation.

7. Response that received a score of 3:

The experiment would have to simulate the conditions found on Earth at that time. In a closed container (to eliminate possible contamination), the atmospheric gases could be mixed. At the mixing point of the gases, an electrode could cause a spark to represent lightning. Once this occurs, the gases could be cooled to cause condensation of the gases. This would simulate rain. This process could be repeated several times to ensure that organic compounds would have an opportunity to form. After the experiment was complete, the resulting solution would be checked for organic compounds.

Response that received a score of 1:

The gases could be placed in a jar and heated by a flame. The flame would represent the lightning. Next, the gaseous solution would be placed in a cooler to cause condensation. The new solution could now be examined for organic compounds.

8. Response that received a score of 3:

Using the data in this chart, friction can be explained as the resulting force of the surfaces of two objects interacting with each other. The data in the chart suggests that the objects' density effects the friction value. It seems that the two dense objects (steel on steel) have a high friction value and the two objects varying in density (steel on ice) have a low friction value. However, this does not account for the friction value associated with rubber and wet concrete which suggests that other factors may effect friction.

Response that received a score of 1:

Friction is defined as the force of two or more objects on each other. The data in the chart explains this theory. The objects in the chart interact with each other which results in a force (friction value). The values differ from surface to surface due to the chemical composition of each object.

MSAT

Multiple Subjects Assessment for Teachers

PRACTICE
MSAT II

Content Knowledge II

TIME: 2 Hours
        134 Questions

DIRECTIONS: Each of the questions or incomplete statements below is followed by four suggested answers or completions. Select the one that is best in each case.

Section I: Literature and Language Studies

QUESTIONS 1–2 are based on the following poem. Read the poem carefully before choosing your answers.

> Now thou art dead, no eye shall ever see,
> For shape and service, spaniel like to thee.
> This shall my love do, give thy sad death one
> Tear, that deserves of me a million.

1.   The above poem is an example of a(n)

   (A)   allegory.   (C)   ballad.

   (B)   elegy.   (D)   kenning.

2.   Lines 3-4 contain an example of

   (A)   enjambment.   (C)   onomatopoeia.

   (B)   personification.   (D)   Homeric simile.

QUESTIONS 3–4 are based on the following poem.

> Study is like the heaven's glorious sun,
> That will not be deep-searched with saucy looks.
> Small have continual plodders won
> Save base authority from others' books.
> These earthly godfathers of heaven's lights,
> That give a name to every fixed star

Have no more profit of their shining nights
Than those who walk and wot* not what they are.
(*know)

3. The speaker of these lines is most likely a

(A) student.

(C) clergyman.

(B) professor.

(D) thief.

4. The lines "Small have continual plodders won / Save base authority from others' books" mean

(A) only one's opinions are important—not facts found in books.

(B) study is long and tedious, but ultimately rewarding.

(C) knowledge and authority are eventually given to those who pursue them.

(D) all that is gained by study are the simple and worthless opinions of others.

QUESTION 5 is based on the following passage.

There was a time when I went every day into a church, since a girl I was in love with knelt there in prayer for half an hour in the evening and I was able to look at her in peace.

Once when she had not come and I was reluctantly eyeing the other supplicants I noticed a young fellow who had thrown his whole lean length along the floor. Every now and then he clutched his head as hard as he could and sighing loudly beat it in his upturned palms on the stone flags.

5. By using the term "supplicants," the author implies that

(A) everyone in the church is there to celebrate a mass.

(B) everyone in the church is devout.

(C) everyone in the church is guilty of something.

(D) everyone in the church is a hypocrite.

QUESTIONS 6–7 are based on the following poem.

WHEN BRITAIN REALLY RULED THE WAVES
When Britain really ruled the waves
   (In good Queen Bess's time)—
The House of Peers made no pretense
To intellectual eminence,
   Or scholarship sublime;
Yet Britain won her proudest bays*
In good Queen Bess's glorious days!
When Wellington thrashed Bonaparte,
   As every child can tell,
The House of Peers, throughout the war,
Did nothing in particular,
   And did it very well:
Yet Britain set the world ablaze
In good King George's glorious days!
And while the House of Peers withholds
   Its legislative hand,
And noble statesman do not itch
To interfere with matters which
   They do not understand,
As bright will shine Great Britain's rays
As in good King George's glorious days!
(*honors)

6.   In this poem, the ruling body of Britain is described as

   (A) a very successful legislative institution.

   (B) a body which makes wise decisions.

   (C) a body which is supported by the British.

   (D) a group of disinterested and unintelligent noblemen.

7.   The tone of this poem can be described as

   (A) lauding.   (C) satiric.

   (B) parodic.   (D) satisfied.

QUESTIONS 8–9 are based on the following passage.

It was the best of times, it was the worst of times, it was the age of wisdom, it was the age of foolishness, it was the epoch of belief, it was the epoch of incredulity, it was the season of Light, it was the season of Darkness, it was the spring of hope, it was the winter of despair, we had everything before us, we had nothing before us, we were all going direct to Heaven, we were all going direct the other way—in short, the period was so far like the present period, that some of its noisiest authorities insisted on its being received, for good or for evil, in the superlative degree of comparison only.

There were a king with a large jaw, and a queen with a plain face, on the throne of England; there were a king with a large jaw, and a queen with a fair face, on the throne of France. In both countries it was clearer than crystal to the lords of the State preserves of loaves and fishes, that things in general were settled for ever.

8. The vast comparisons in the above passage indicate that the speaker is describing

(A) a placid historical time period.

(B) a time of extreme political upheaval.

(C) a public event.

(D) a time when anything was possible.

9. The last sentence of the passage

(A) mocks the self-assuredness of the governments of England and France.

(B) comments on the horrible poverty of the two nations.

(C) most likely foreshadows an upcoming famine or drought.

(D) attacks the two governments for neglecting the poor, hungry masses.

QUESTIONS 10–12 are based on the following passages.

(A) Once upon a time and a very good time it was there was a moocow coming down along the road and this moocow that was coming down along the met a nicens little boy named baby tuckoo...

(B) And thus have these naked Nantucketers, these sea hermits, issuing from their ant-hill in the sea, overrun and conquered the watery world like so many Alexanders...

(C) A large rose tree stood near the entrance of the garden: the roses growing on it were white, but there were three gardeners at it, busily painting them red. Alice thought this a very curious thing, and she went nearer to watch them, and, just as she came up to them, she heard one of them say "Look out now, Five!"

(D) Emma was not required, by any subsequent discovery to retract her ill opinion of Mrs. Elton. Her observation had been pretty correct. Such as Mrs. Elton appeared to her on the second interview, such she appeared whenever they met again—self-important, presuming, familiar, ignorant, and ill-bred. She had a little beauty and a little accomplishment, but so little judgement that she thought herself coming with superior knowledge of the world, to enliven and improve a country neighborhood...

10. Which passage makes use of allusion?

11. Which passage employs a thematic device to imitate the speech of a character?

12. Which passage is most likely taken from a 19th century novel of manners?

QUESTIONS 13–15 are based on the following passages.

(A) My life closed twice before its close;
It yet remains to see
If immortality unveil
A third event to me,

(B) Hark, hark!
Bow-wow,
The watch-dogs bark!
Bow-wow.
Hark, hark! I hear
The strain of strutting chanticleer
Cry, "Cock-a-doodle-doo!"

(C) A narrow fellow in the grass
Occasionally rides;
You may have met him. Did you not,
His notice sudden is:
The grass divides as with a comb,
A spotted shaft is seen,
And then it closes at your feet
And open further on.

(D) Gather ye rosebuds while ye may,

Old Time is still a-flying;
And this same flower that smiles today
Tomorrow will be dying.

13. Which passage espouses the philosophy of *carpe diem*?

14. Which passage employs the technique of onomatopoeia?

15. Which passage employs the technique of alliteration?

16. It pleased God that I was still spared, and very hearty and sound in health, but very impatient of being pent up within doors without air, as I had been for fourteen days or thereabouts, and I could not restrain myself, but I would go to carry a letter for my brother to the post-house.

    The above is most likely an excerpt from which of the following?

    (A) Poem.   (C) Journal.

    (B) Play.   (D) Myth.

17. As he walked through the office, Raskolnikov noticed that many people were looking at him. Among them he saw the two porters from *the* house whom he had invited that night to the police-station. They stood there watching. But he was no sooner on the stairs than he heard the voice of Porfiry Petrovitch behind him. Turning around, he saw the latter running after him, out of breath.

    The above paragraph is most probably an excerpt from which of the following?

    (A) British spy novel.

    (B) 19th century Russian novel.

    (C) A modern romance.

    (D) An existentialist short story.

18. Which of the following lines is an example of iambic pentameter?

    (A) The an/gry spot / doth glow /on Cae/sar's brow, /

    (B) Here goes / the try / I've al/ways known/

$$\overset{\cup\ \ \cup\ \ /}{} \quad \overset{\cup\ \ //}{} \quad \overset{\cup\ \ /}{}$$

(C) She loves the / way I hold / her hand/

(D) Although I / knew the road / led home/

QUESTIONS 19–20 refer to the following passage.

>Oh God, do you hear it, this persecution,
>These my sufferings from this hateful
>Woman, this monster, murderess of children?
>Still what I can do that I will do:
>I will lament and cry upon heaven,
>Calling the gods to bear me witness
>How you have killed my boys to prevent me from
>Touching their bodies or giving them burial.
>I wish I never begot them to see them
>Afterward slaughtered by you.

19. These lines are spoken by

    (A) the murderer.   (C) one of the gods.

    (B) the father of dead children   (D) a bystander.

20. It can be inferred from this passage that

    (A) the woman had a right to kill her children.

    (B) the man deserved to lose his children.

    (C) the rites and ceremonies of burial are extremely important.

    (D) the gods decreed the death of the children.

QUESTIONS 21–23 are based on the following passage.

It is very seldom that mere ordinary people like John and myself secure ancestral halls for the summer.

A colonial mansion, a hereditary estate, I would say a haunted house and reach the height of romantic felicity—but that would be asking too much of fate!

Still I will proudly declare that there is something queer about it.

Else, why should it be let so cheaply? And why have stood so long untenanted?

John laughs at me, of course, but one expects that.

John is practical in the extreme. He has no patience with faith, an intense horror of superstition, and he scoffs openly at any talk of things not to be felt and seen and put down in figures.

John is a physician, and *perhaps* (I would not say it to a living soul, of course, but this is dead paper and a great relief to my mind)—*perhaps* that is one reason I do not get well faster.

You see, he does not believe I am sick! And what can one do?

If a physician of high standing, and one's own husband, assures friends and relatives that there is really nothing the matter with one but temporary nervous depression—a slight hysterical tendency—what is one to do?

My brother is also a physician, and also of high standing, and he says the same thing.

So I take phosphates or phosphites—whichever it is—and tonics, and air and exercise, and journeys, and am absolutely forbidden to "work" until I am well again.

Personally, I disagree with their ideas.

21. John is characterized by the speaker as

(A) arrogant.   (C) cunning.

(B) trustworthy.   (D) condescending.

22. The speaker views writing as

(A) annoying.   (C) laborious.

(B) therapeutic.   (D) painful.

23. We can infer from the passage that the speaker

(A) is insane.

(B) is of no solid mental health.

(C) feels limited by her husband.

(D) strongly dislikes her husband.

QUESTION 24 refers to the following passage.

It was Phaethon who drove them to Fiesole that memorable day, a youth all irresponsibility and fire, recklessly urging his master's horses up the stony hill. Mr. Beebe recognized him at once. Neither the Ages of Faith not the Age of Doubt had touched him; he was on the way, saying that she was his sister— Persephone, tall and slender and pale, returning with the Spring to her mother's cottage, and still shading her eyes from the unaccustomed light. To her Mr. Eager objected, saying that here was the thin edge of the wedge, and one must guard against imposition. But the ladies interceded, and when it had been made clear that it was a very great favour, the goddess was allowed to mount beside the god.

24. Which of the following helps characterize Phaethon and Persephone as a "god" and "goddess?"

 I. Their names. III. Her eyes.

 II. His occupation. IV. Her build.

 (A) I only. (C) I, II, and III.

 (B) I and II. (D) II, III, and IV.

25. According to Merleau-Ponty, what defines language?

 (A) Its referent.

 (B) The speaker's intention.

 (C) The value of its use.

 (D) The definition of the words used.

26. Ludwig Wittgenstein would be LEAST likely to agree with which of the following statements:

 (A) Meaning is "on the surface."

 (B) Meaning refers to some "deep structure" of language.

 (C) Language allows for multiple, even conflicting usage.

 (D) Meaning is derived from the way people use language.

27. Sassure was one of the first linguists to assert that

 (A) the association between a word and its meaning is arbitrary.

 (B) meaning is use.

 (C) language is a monolithic structure.

 (D) language acquisition falls into rigid, successive stages.

Section II: Mathematics

28. If 406.725 is rounded off to the nearest tenth, the result is

    (A) 406.3   (C) 406.7

    (B) 406.5   (D) 406.8

29. The mean IQ score for 1,500 students is 100, with a standard deviation of 15. Assuming normal curve distribution, how many students have an IQ between 85 and 115? Refer to the figure shown below.

    (A) 510

    (B) 750

    (C) 1,020

    (D) 1,275

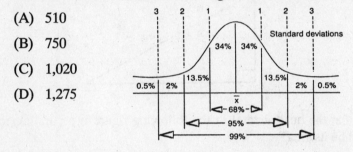

30. Twice the sum of 10 and a number is 28. Find the number.

    (A) 4   (C) 12

    (B) 8   (D) 14

31. You can buy a telephone for $24. If you are charged $3 per month for renting a telephone from the telephone company, how long will it take you to recover the cost of the phone if you buy one.

    (A) 6 months   (C) 8 months

    (B) 7 months   (D) 9 months

32. Two college roommates spent $2,000 for their total monthly expenses. A circle graph below indicates a record of their expenses.

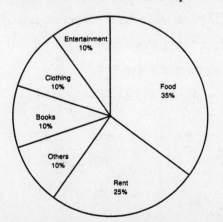

Based on the above information, which of the following statements is accurate?

(A) The roommates spent $700 on food alone.

(B) The roommates spent $550 on rent alone.

(C) The roommates spent $300 on entertainment alone.

(D) The roommates spent $300 on clothing alone.

33. What would be the measure of the third angle in the following triangle?

(A) 45°

(B) 50°

(C) 60°

(D) 70°

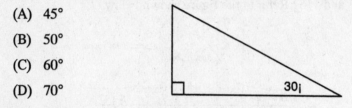

34. Assuming that the quadrilateral in the following figure is a parallelogram, what would be its area?

(A) 32 cm

(B) 40 cm

(C) 40 cm²

(D) 64 cm²

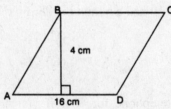

35. Which of the following is *not* a proper subset of {1, 2, 3, 4}?

(A) {1, 2}   (C) {1, 2, 4}

(B) {1, 2, 5}   (D) {1, 3, 4}

36. Which of the following statements includes a cardinal number?

(A) There are 15 volumes in the set of periodicals.

(B) I received my 14th volume recently.

(C) The students meet at Room 304.

(D) My phone number is 213-617-8442.

37. Find the next three terms in this sequence: 1, 4, 9, 16,...

(A) 19, 24, 31   (C) 21, 28, 36

(B) 20, 25, 31   (D) 25, 36, 49

38. Assume that one pig eats 4 pounds of food each week. There are 52 weeks in a year. How much food do 10 pigs eat in a week?

    (A) 40 lbs.   (C) 208 lbs.

    (B) 520 lbs.   (D) 20 lbs.

39. Suppose that a pair of pants and a shirt cost $65 and the pants cost $25 more than the shirt. What did they each cost?

    (A) The pants cost $35 and the shirt costs $30.

    (B) The pants cost $40 and the shirt costs $25.

    (C) The pants cost $43 and the shirt costs $22.

    (D) The pants cost $45 and the shirt costs $20.

40. There are five members in a basketball team. Supposing every member shakes hands with each of the other members of the team before the game starts, how many handshakes will there be in all?

    (A) 6   (C) 9

    (B) 8   (D) 10

41. Which figure can be obtained from figure Y by translation?

    (A) a

    (B) b

    (C) c

    (D) d

42. Tom bought a piece of land selling for $20,000. If he had to pay 20% of the price as a down payment, how much was the down payment?

    (A) $2,500   (C) $4,000

    (B) $3,000   (D) $4,500

43. A certain company produces two types of lawnmowers. Type A is self-propelled while type B is not. The company can produce a maximum of 18 mowers per week. It can make a profit of $15 on mower A and a profit of $20 on mower B. The company wants to make at least 2 mowers of type A but not more than 5. They also plan to make at least 2 mowers of type B. Let x be the number of type A produced, and let y be the number of type B produced.

From the previous page, which of the following is *not* one of the listed constraints?

(A) $x \le 2$ (C) $x + y \le 18$

(B) $x \le 5$ (D) $y < 5$

44. Mr. Smith died and left an estate to be divided among his wife, two children, and a foundation of his choosing in the ratio of 8:6:6:1. How much did his wife receive if the estate was valued at $300,000?

(A) $114,285.71   (C) $85,714.29

(B) $120,421.91   (D) $14,285.71

45. There were 19 hamburgers for 9 people on a picnic. How many whole hamburgers were there for each person if they were divided equally?

(A) 1   (C) 3

(B) 2   (D) 4

46. George has four ways to get from his house to the park. He has seven ways to get from the park to the school. How many ways can George get from his house to school by way of the park?

(A) 4   (C) 28

(B) 7   (D) 3

47. If it takes 1 minute per cut, how long will it take to cut a 15-foot long timber into 15 equal pieces?

(A) 5   (C) 14

(B) 10   (D) 20

48. Ed has 6 new shirts and 4 new pairs of pants. How many combinations of new shirts and pants does he have?

(A) 10   (C) 18

(B) 14   (D) 24

49. Ralph kept track of his work time in gardening. Refer to the broken-line graph below:

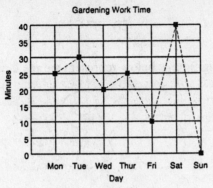

Gardening Work Time

How many minutes did he average per day?

(A) 10 min.

(B) 20 min.

(C) 21.43 min.

(D) 23.05 min.

50. Mary had been selling printed shirts in her neighborhood. She made this pictograph to show how much money she made each week.

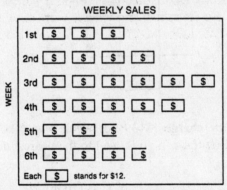

WEEKLY SALES

How many weeks were sales more than $55?

(A) 1 week.

(B) 2 weeks.

(C) 3 weeks.

(D) 4 weeks.

51. In a biology class at International University, the grades on the final examination were as follows:

91	81	65	81
50	70	81	93
36	90	43	87
96	81	75	81

Find the mode.

(A) 36   (C) 81

(B) 70   (D) 87

52. Which of the following figures below represent simple closed curves?

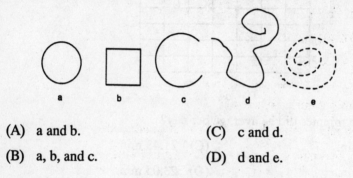

a   b   c   d   e

(A) a and b.   (C) c and d.

(B) a, b, and c.   (D) d and e.

53. How many lines of symmetry, if any, does the following figure have?

(A) 1
(B) 2
(C) 3
(D) 4

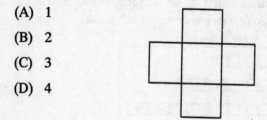

54. A car rental agency charges $139 per week plus $0.08 per mile for an average size car. How far can you travel to the nearest mile on a maximum budget of $350?

(A) 2,637 mi.   (C) 2,110 mi.

(B) 2,640 mi.   (D) 1,737 mi.

Section III: History and Social Sciences

55. The nomadic warriors who would later become the lords of feudal Japan arrived in the:

   (A) Kofun Era.

   (B) Heian Era.

   (C) Sengoku Era.

   (D) Warring States Era.

56. *Bakfu*, literally translated, means:

   (A) Shogunate.   (C) Landed estate.

   (B) Tent government.   (D) Feudal lord.

57. All of the following were unifiers of feudal Japan EXCEPT:

   (A) Oda Nobunaga.

   (B) Toyotomi Hideyoshi.

   (C) Tokugawa Ieyasu.

   (D) Minamoto no Yorimoto.

58. The conversion of Asoka to which of the following religions facilitated its passage into Indian society:

   (A) Taoism.   (C) Buddhism.

   (B) Hinduism.   (D) Jainism.

59. Which of the following Meso-American civilizations first established the concept of zero?

   (A) Toltec.   (C) Aztec.

   (B) Maya.   (D) Inca.

60. Which of the following is NOT one of the five pillars of the Islamic faith?

   (A) Confession of faith.

   (B) Payment of alms.

   (C) Fasting from sunrise to sunset during Ramadhan.

   (D) The jihad.

61. Which of the following Sub-Saharan peoples created life-sized figures of humans and animals in terra cotta?

    (A) The Nok.   (C) The Ghana.

    (B) The Songhai.   (D) The Bantu.

62. Which of the following Pre-Columbian American cultures were sun worshippers?

    (A) Aztec.   (C) Inca.

    (B) Andean.   (D) Hohokam.

63. All of the following were New Deal reforms EXCEPT

    (A) the National Industrial Recovery Act.

    (B) the Tennessee Valley Authority.

    (C) the Reconstruction Finance Corporation.

    (D) the Agricultural Adjustment Act.

64. Which of the following were characteristics of the U.S. economy during the 1980s?

    I.   Declining foreign investment

    II.   Declining unemployment rates

    III. Declining stock prices

    IV.   Declining inflation

    V.   Declining imbalance between imports and exports.

    (A) I and V.   (C) II, III, and V.

    (B) II and IV.   (D) I, III, IV, and V.

65. Which of the following was most crucial in bringing about U.S. participation in the First World War?

    (A) British propaganda.

    (B) German violation of Belgian neutrality.

    (C) German use of submarines against merchant and passenger ships.

    (D) German atrocities against French and Belgian civilians in the occupied areas of those countries.

66. All of the following helped shape the development of colonial American agriculture EXCEPT

    (A) availability of land.

    (B) abundance of capital.

    (C) limitations of climate and land.

    (D) shortage of labor.

67. The Credit Mobilier Scandal involved

    (A) a dummy construction company used by railroad magnates to defraud the government.

    (B) a tax-collection contract sold in exchange for a kickback to Republican campaign coffers.

    (C) a conspiracy to defraud the government of large amounts of money from the excise tax on whiskey.

    (D) an attempt by Congress to raise its own pay retroactively.

68. The LEAST important issue during the era of "Jacksonian Democracy" was

    (A) the removal of Indians from southeastern states.

    (B) federal financing of internal improvements.

    (C) the right of states to nullify federal laws.

    (D) the growing trend toward industrialization.

69. Spanish explorers Hernan de Soto and Francisco Vasquez de Coronado sought

    (A) an all-water route to the Orient.

    (B) rich Indian civilizations to plunder.

    (C) a route to East Asia.

    (D) sources of raw materials for Spain.

70. Which of the following was NOT one of the purposes of the Lewis and Clark expedition?

    (A) Establishing friendly relations with the western Indians.

    (B) Gaining geographic knowledge about the western part of North America.

    (C) Discovering sources of gold.

    (D) Gaining scientific knowledge about the flora and fauna of western North America.

71. The Black Death of the 14th century resulted in the

    (A) decline of the movement toward nation-states in Western Europe.

    (B) rise of modern medicine.

    (C) enhancement of the value of labor.

    (D) flight of millions of Europeans overseas.

72. The major responsibility of the Federal Reserve Board is to

    (A) implement monetary policy.

    (B) control government spending.

    (C) regulate commodity prices.

    (D) help the president run the executive branch.

73. Which of the following best describes the relationship between educational background and participation in politics?

    (A) The more schooling one has, the more likely one is to vote.

    (B) The less schooling one has, the more likely one is to run for public office.

    (C) There is no relationship between educational background and participation in politics.

    (D) People with a high school education are more likely to vote than either those who did not finish high school or those with a college degree.

74. The 1985 Gramm-Rudman Act

    (A) outlawed the use of federal funds for abortions.

    (B) established a mechanism for balancing the federal budget.

    (C) prohibited the use of any federal funds for aiding the Contras in Nicaragua.

    (D) changed the tax code to eliminate loopholes for the wealthy.

75. Which of the following best defines the term "judicial restraint?"

    (A) A decision by judges to limit the number of cases they decide per year.

    (B) Refusal by judges to lobby Congress for funds.

    (C) A practice by which judges remove themselves from cases in which they have a personal interest.

    (D) The tendency of judges to interpret the Constitution in light of the original intent of its framers

76. Which of the following statement about the Equal Rights Amendment is false?

   (A) It passed both houses of Congress, but was never ratified by three-fourths of the states.

   (B) Congress extended the time limit for ratification of the amendment.

   (C) Some states that ratified the amendment later tried to rescind their ratification.

   (D) The amendment was intended to restore certain rights to blacks and Hispanics that had been restricted by a series of Supreme Court decisions.

77. During the past three decades, all of the following changes have occurred in political behavior and public opinion in the United States EXCEPT

   (A) the declining importance of political ideology as a factor influencing presidential nominations to the Supreme Court.

   (B) an increase in support for Republican presidential candidates in the South.

   (C) an increase in the influence of the conservative wing on the Republican Party.

   (D) a drop in voter turnout for congressional and presidential elections.

78. The Constitution places legislative power in Congress and Executive power in the President. This is an example of

   (A) separation of power.   (C) constitutional interpretation.

   (B) checks and balances.   (D) fundamental rights.

Section IV: Science

QUESTIONS 79–82 refer to the following passage.

Skin is the flexible outer covering on the bodies of vertebrate animals. The thickness varies on different body areas. Human skin is composed of an outer layer called the epidermis and an inner layer called the dermis. The epidermis has several layers. Near the outside is the stratum corneum. Under it is the layer of Malpighi which quickly grows to replace the cells of the stratum corneum which wear away. Human skin protects the body from injury, helps get rid of waste products, regulates water, and regulates temperature.

79. What area of the skin is most likely the thinnest?

    (A) The soles of the feet.
    (B) The palms of the hand.
    (C) Skin covering the eyeballs.
    (D) The back.

80. What is the order of the layers of skin from the outside of the body proceeding inward?

    (A) stratum corneum, layer of Malpighi, dermis.
    (B) stratum corneum, layer of Malpighi, epidermis.
    (C) dermis, layer of Malpighi, stratum corneum.
    (D) dermis, stratum corneum, layer of Malpighi.

81. How does the body regulate temperature or water through the skin?

    (A) Respiration.
    (B) Transpiration.
    (C) Perspiration.
    (D) Sensation.

82. Since the stratum corneum is constantly wearing away, structures such as blood vessels, nerve endings, and sweat glands must be found in

    (A) the layer of Malpighi.
    (B) the stratum corneum.
    (C) the epidermis.
    (D) the dermis.

QUESTIONS 83–85 refer to the following passage.

The discoveries of Galileo Galilei (1564–1642) and Isaac Newton (1642–1727) precipitated the scientific revolution of the 17th century. Stressing the use of detailed measurements during experimentation enabled them to frame several universal laws of nature and to overthrow many of Aristotle's (384–322 B.C.E.) erroneous ideas about motion which were based on sheer reasoning alone. One of these universal laws is now known as the "Law of Inertia" or Newton's First Law of Motion. According to this law, objects in motion tend to stay in motion and objects at rest tend to stay at rest unless acted upon by external force. The more mass (inertia) an object has, the more resistance it offers to changes in its state of motion.

83. According to the Law of Inertia, which of the following would offer the greatest resistance to a change in its motion?

   (A) A pellet of lead shot.   (C) A large watermelon.

   (B) A golf ball.   (D) A feather.

84. When astronauts sleep aboard the Space Shuttle, they strap themselves to a wall or bunk. In the event thruster rockets were fired, resulting in a change in Shuttle velocity, any unstrapped, sleeping astronauts could be injured by slamming into a Shuttle wall. The sleeping astronauts need to be strapped down because

   (A) their bodies have inertia.

   (B) gravity is not strong enough to keep them touching their beds.

   (C) their body functions need to be constantly monitored.

   (D) astronauts cannot sleep while floating free in space.

85. In Einstein's famous equation, $E = mc^2$, which of the following is most closely associated with a body's inertia?

   (A) The energy $= E$.

   (B) The mass $= m$.

   (C) The speed of light $= c$.

   (D) The speed of light squared $= c^2$.

QUESTIONS 86–89 refer to the following graph.

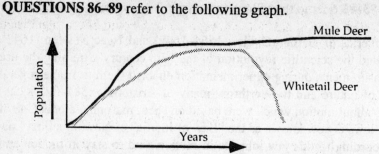

In the graph above, the dark black line represents the growth in a ranch's population of mule deer. The shaded line represents the growth of a population of whitetail deer in the same area. In both cases, sufficient food is supplied, and no other outside influences or diseases affect either populations.

86. According to the graph, two species with the same living requirements cannot live long together in the same environment. Competition will eliminate one of the two.

    (A) This conclusion is supported by the data.

    (B) This conclusion is not supported by the data.

    (C) This conclusion includes the effect of hunting and is supported by the data.

    (D) This conclusion includes the effect caused by a drought and is supported by the data.

87. If one comes to the conclusion that the idea of survival of the fittest is supported by this graph, then

    (A) the conclusion is supported by the data.

    (B) the conclusion is refuted by the data.

    (C) the conclusion is refuted because only one kind of deer survived.

    (D) the conclusion is refuted because the two kinds of deer do not compete with each other, and the data supports this.

88. If one comes to the conclusion that the mule deer are better adapted to the environment than the whitetail deer, then

    (A) the conclusion is supported by the data.

    (B) the conclusion is refuted by the data.

    (C) the conclusion is neither supported nor refuted by the data.

    (D) the data gives plenty of information concerning the mule deer's adaptability, which supports the conclusion.

89. One could come to the conclusion that for a period of time the mule deer and the whitetail deer did not compete, so one could see a significant growth in the whitetail population. In this case

    (A) the conclusion is supported by the data.

    (B) the conclusion is refuted by the data.

    (C) the conclusion is neither supported or refuted by the data.

    (D) the data gives plenty of information concerning the mule deer's adaptability, which supports the conclusion.

QUESTIONS 90–91 refer to the following diagram.

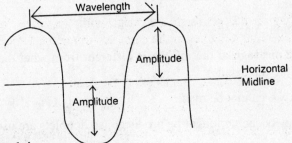

90. The wavelength is

    (A) the distance between any two peaks.

    (B) the distance between two adjacent peaks.

    (C) the distance between the height of a wave and the low point of a wave.

    (D) the rate of motion of the peak.

91. A wave does not carry along the medium through which it travels. Thus, it follows that

    (A) molecules of water in the ocean are pushed to shore by waves.

    (B) the ocean's water molecules are thoroughly mixed each day be waves.

    (C) debris in the ocean is washed ashore by waves.

    (D) individual water molecules do not travel toward shore, but wave peaks do.

QUESTIONS 92–95 refer to the following passage.

Protein synthesis is very important in living things. All cells contain protein and the making of protein is controlled by DNA (deoxyribonucleic acid), which is a major constituent of the chromosomes. DNA molecules contain information in the form of 64 chemical "code words." This information is also known as the "genetic code." Since DNA is only found in the nucleus of cells, the information that is needed for protein synthesis must be carried to the portion of the cell involved with protein synthesis, the endoplasmic reticulum (ER) and the ribosomes. This is done by a molecule called messenger ribonucleic acid (mRNA), which is made by DNA. Once the mRNA is in the ER, the ribosomes begin to "read" the instructions on the mRNA. As the instructions are read, transfer ribonucleic acid (tRNA) brings to the ribosomes, from the cytoplasm, the proper amino acids. The ribosomes then bond these amino acids together in the proper order until a long chain of amino acids (the protein) is formed.

92. Imagine that a cosmic ray obliterates a "code word" in a single DNA molecule. What happens when the DNA molecule is read so that mRNA can be built?

(A) Nothing happens.

(B) The message of the mRNA is different from what the DNA code was before the event.

(C) mRNA cannot be made.

(D) Triplets can no longer be produced, so doublets are used.

93. DNA nucleotides are found in what part of the cell?

(A) The lysosomes.

(B) The endoplasmic reticulum.

(C) The cytoplasmic matrix.

(D) The nucleus.

94. DNA strands that are coiled around and interwoven with protein molecules form

(A) RNA.   (C) nucleotides.

(B) chromosomes.   (D) genes.

95. If the "code words" for a DNA molecule were changed around, or reversed, what would happen to the resulting protein?

(A) The resulting protein would be changed in some way, either in length, number, or arrangement of amino acids.

(B) The resulting protein would definitely be smaller.

(C) The resulting protein would definitely be larger.

(D) The resulting protein would be wrapped around the DNA.

QUESTIONS 96–98 refer to the following passage.

For five years Charles Darwin traveled around the world aboard the H.M.S. Beagle. During that time he observed many things, especially the plants and animals of South America and the Galapagos Islands. Later, he published his famous book, *On The Origin of Species*, which made sense of what he saw. His theory may be summarized by the following four observations: (1) individuals vary genetically; (2) generally, organisms will produce more offspring than the environment can support; (3) even though there are large numbers of offspring, the population remains fairly constant; and (4) the environment all over the planet is in a constant state of change. From these four observations Darwin concluded that: (1) in every population there is competition for available resources, (2) those organisms that have favorable genetic variation will be able to live and reproduce, and (3) those genetic variations that allowed the parents to survive will be handed down to offspring through generations and will accumulate in the population until the whole population will have these favorable genes. In this way, Darwin could see how things change or evolve.

96. It is a well-known fact that clams release millions of eggs and sperm. If 50% of all eggs were fertilized, would this be consistent with Darwin's conclusions?

    (A) Yes, because favorable variations occur.

    (B) Yes, because there are more offspring produced than the environment could support, and only some of the clams would survive.

    (C) Yes, because the environment is constantly changing.

    (D) No, because individual sperm and egg are different genetically.

97. It is estimated that a single fern can produce upwards of 50 million spores in a single year. It is easy to realize that all of the spores do not grow into a mature adult fern, because if they did, whole continents would be covered with ferns. What did Darwin observe that would explain this?

    (A) Organisms produce more offspring than the environment can support, so a population will remain constant because there are not enough resources for all offspring.

    (B) The environment is slowly changing all over the world, which prevents all of the offspring from maturing.

    (C) Genetic variation is allowing the ferns to keep the same level of population.

    (D) Genetic variation, which allows for survival, will increase.

98. Which person would be helped by having a better understanding of Darwin's observations and conclusions in order to have a more productive business?

(A) Cattle rancher.

(C) Engineer.

(B) Oil worker.

(D) Refinery Chemist.

QUESTIONS 99–100 refer to the following passage.

Most substances are denser during the solid phase than during the liquid phase. Water is an exception to this rule. Additionally, water has a very high boiling point compared to other hydrides of nonmetals. Water has several other unusual properties that are related to the structure and composition of the water molecules.

99. Which of the following statements is NOT a true statement about water?

(A) Ice cubes float because solid water is less dense than liquid water.

(B) Water exists as both a liquid and a solid at normal Earth temperatures.

(C) Hydrogen bonding is especially weak in water.

(D) The bonds between the oxygen and the hydrogens of water are covalent.

100. The unusually high boiling and melting points of water result from

(A) a great amount of intermolecular attraction in water.

(B) low surface tension.

(C) low amount of hydrogen bonding between water molecules.

(D) the low heat capacity of water.

QUESTIONS 101–102 refer to the following passage.

The average home use of electricity in the United States as compared to a developing country like Brazil is shown in the table below. The amount of electrical energy used is given in kilowatt-hours (KWH) per household per year. (October 1990, *Scientific American*, p. 113)

Use	United States	Brazil
Lighting	1000	350
Cooking	635	15
Water Heating	1540	380
Air-Conditioning	1180	45
Refrigeration	1810	470
Other	1180	200

101. Which of the statements below is the best conclusion based on the data provided?

   (A) The total electrical consumption by the average U.S. household is about twice that of the typical Brazilian home wired for electricity.

   (B) Because it is warmer in Brazil, the percentage of electricity used in air-conditioning is greater than that used in the United States.

   (C) Both countries have a somewhat similar pattern of electricity consumption.

   (D) United States households use more electricity for water heating than lighting, while Brazilian households use more electricity for lighting than water heating.

102. How much more electrical energy per household does the United States consume than developing Brazil?

   (A) 3 times

   (B) 4 times

   (C) 5 times

   (D) 6 times

Section V: Visual and Performing Arts

Georges Pompidou National Center of Art and Culture, Paris

103. Which of the following seems most true of the building pictured above?

(A) It relies on broad areas of unbroken surfaces.

(B) It uses industrial forms and materials to suggest a living organism.

(C) It is conceived and designed on a human scale.

(D) It owes a debt to the Classical past.

Chartres Cathedral, France

104. Which of the following best describes the sculpture on the building pictured above?

    (A) It tells a detailed story with a definite sequence.

    (B) It dominates the facade of the building.

    (C) It draws heavily on Classical mythology.

    (D) It is contained by the architectural forms of the doorways.

105.

106.

Kiyotada, *Dancing Kabuki Actor*, c. 1725
Metropolitan Museum of Art, New York

Antonio Pollaiuolo, *Hercules and Antaus*, c. 1475. Museo Nazionale, Florence

105. In the example pictured above, the folds of the garment serve to

    (A) create a dynamic surface pattern which dominates the composition.

    (B) counteract the vigorous motion of the figure.

    (C) establish a sense of three-dimensional space.

    (D) help tell the story behind the figure's movements.

106. The sculpture pictured above suggests which of the following?

    (A) The rolling motion of a wheel.

    (B) The balanced action of a lever.

    (C) The twisting spiral of a screw.

    (D) The flowing motion of liquid.

107. In the example shown above, which of the following contributes most to the effect of a photographic snapshot?

    (A) The inclusion of the horse and dog.

    (B) The middle-class character of the subjects.

    (C) The perspective grid behind the figures.

    (D) The off-center composition and the random cropping of figures.

Abbey church of St. Michael, Hildesheim, West Germany

108. The building pictured above depends for its effect on:

    (A) the interplay of diagonal and vertical lines.

    (B) the broad expanse of window glass.

    (C) a subtle arrangement of curving, rhythmic forms.

    (D) the bold massing of simple cubic forms.

Temple of Hera at Psestum, Italy

109. Which of the following is fundamental to the design of the building pictured above?

(A) A combination of intersecting diagonal lines.

(B) A simple repetition of vertical and horizontal forms.

(C) A continuous expanse of unbroken wall surface.

(D) A combination of columns and arches.

QUESTIONS 110–112 refer to the following pictures

(A) National Gallery, Washington, D.C.

(B) Metropolitan Museum of Art, New York

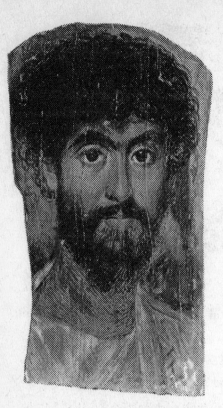

(C) Albright-Knox Art Gallery,
Buffalo

(D) Sammlung Thyssen-Bornemisza,
Lugano, Italy

110. Which of the examples pictured above makes the most direct contact with the viewer?

111. In which example does the pose and expression of the sitter convey artistic disdain?

112. Which example breaks down the forms of the subject and merges them with the background?

Wu Chen, *Bamboo*, National Palace Museum, Taipai, Taiwan

113. Which of the following seems most true of the example pictured above?

   (A) The artist attempted a realistic depiction of three-dimensional space.

   (B) The picture probably illustrates an episode in a narrative.

   (C) The execution was slow, painstaking, and deliberate.

   (D) Both the script and the leaves share a quality of quick, fluid calligraphy.

(A)

(B) JeanBaptiste Camille Corot, *The Harbor of La Rochelle,* 1851.

(C) John Sloan, *The Lafayette,* 1927.

(D) Andrew Wyeth, *Christina's World*, 1948. Museum of Modern Art, New York.

114. In which example does the landscape act as a backdrop for a carefully composed figure group?

115. In which example does the location of the horizon line emphasize the figure's isolation?

116. The costume key pictured above would be most appropriate for which of the following plays?

(A) Ibsen's *A Doll's House.*   (C) Shaw's *Pygmalion.*

(B) Shakespeare's *Twelfth Night.* (D) Aristophane's *The Birds.*

Section VI: Human Development

Mr. Drake is a first-grade teacher who is using the whole language method while teaching about animals.

117. Before reading a story to the students, Mr. Drake tells the students what he is expecting to learn from reading the story. What is his reason for doing this?

   (A) The students should know why the instructor chose this text over any other.

   (B) It is important for teachers to share personal ideas with their students in order to foster an environment of confidence and understanding.

   (C) Mr. Drake wants to verify that all students are on-task before he begins the story.

   (D) Mr. Drake is modeling a vital pre-reading skill in order to teach it to the young readers.

118. Mr. Drake has a heterogeneously grouped reading class. He has the students in groups of two—one skilled reader and one remedial reader—reading selected stories to one another. The students read the story and question each other until they feel that they both understand the story. By planning the lesson this way, Mr. Drake has

   (A) set a goal for his students.

   (B) condensed the number of observations necessary, thereby creating more time for class instruction.

   (C) made it possible for another teacher to utilize the limited materials.

   (D) utilized the student's strength and weaknesses to maximize time, materials, and the learning environment.

119. Before reading a story about a veterinary hospital, Mr. Drake constructs a semantic map of related words and terms using the students' input. What is his main intention for doing this?

   (A) To demonstrate a meaningful relationship between the concepts of the story and the prior knowledge of the students.

   (B) To serve as a visual means of learning.

   (C) To determine the level of understanding the students will have at the conclusion of the topic being covered.

   (D) To model proper writing using whole words.

Mr. Dobson teaches fifth-grade mathematics at Valverde Elementary. He encourages students to work in groups of two or three as they begin homework assignments so they can answer questions for each other. Mr. Dobson notices immediately that some of his students chose to work alone even though they had been asked to work in groups. He also notices that some students are easily distracted even though the other members of their group are working on the assignment as directed.

120. Which of the following is the most likely explanation for the students' behavior?

   (A) Fifth-grade students are not physically or mentally capable of working in small groups; small groups are more suitable for older students.

   (B) Fifth-grade students vary greatly in their physical development and maturity; this variance influences students' interests and attitudes.

   (C) Fifth-grade students lack the ability for internal control, and therefore learn best in structured settings. It is usually best to seat fifth graders in single rows.

   (D) Mr. Dobson needs to be more specific in his expectations for student behavior.

121. Mr. Dobson wants to encourage all of his students to participate in discussions related to the use of math in the real world. Five students in one class are very shy and introverted. Which of the following would most likely be the best way to encourage these students to participate in the discussion?

   (A) Mr. Dobson should call on these students by name at least once each day and give participation grades.

   (B) Mr. Dobson should not be concerned about these students because they will become less shy and introverted as they mature during the year.

   (C) Mr. Dobson should divide the class into small groups for discussion so these students will not be overwhelmed by speaking in front of the whole class.

   (D) Mr. Dobson should speak with these students individually and encourage them to participate more in class discussions.

122. In the same class, Mr. Dobson has two students who are overly talkative. These two students volunteer to answer every question. Which of the following is the best way to deal with these students?

   (A) Mr. Dobson should call on the overly talkative students only once during each class.

(B) Mr. Dobson should ask these students to be the observers in small group discussions, and take notes about participation and topics discussed.

(C) Mr. Dobson should place these students in a group by themselves so they can discuss all they want and not disturb the other students.

(D) Mr. Dobson should recognize that overly talkative students need lots of attention and should be called on to participate throughout the class period.

123. Mr. Dobson wants to use a variety of grouping strategies during the year. Sometimes he groups students with others of similar ability; sometimes he groups students with varying ability. Sometimes he permits students to choose their own groupings. Sometimes he suggests that students work with a particular partner; sometimes he assigns a partner. Sometimes he allows students to elect to work individually. This flexibility in grouping strategies indicates that Mr. Dobson recognizes that

(A) fifth graders like surprises and unpredictable teacher behavior.

(B) grouping patterns affect students' perceptions of self-esteem and competence.

(C) frequent changes in the classroom keep students alert and interested.

(D) it is not fair to place the worst students in the same group consistently.

Genevieve Thompson is a first-year teacher who has accepted a position as a first-grade teacher. In college, Genevieve's elementary teaching field was science. She is eager to begin working with her first graders so that in addition to teaching them literacy skills, she can teach them to enjoy science and mathematics.

124. Of all of her students who do not have documented handicaps, which of her students are likely to be poor readers?

(A) Those whose parents seldom read aloud to them.

(B) Those whose parents place them in daycare for more than three hours per day.

(C) Those whose parents allow them to watch more than two hours of television daily.

(D) Those who are being raised by a grandparent.

125. One advantage of using interactive videodisk technology is that students have the opportunity to actually observe demonstrations of how such phenomena as sound waves work. Teaching students by allowing them to see the natural phenomenon of sound waves taking place instead of merely offering complex theoretical descriptions of sound waves is most important for students at what stage of development?

(A) Piaget's sensorimotor stage.

(B) Piaget's concrete operational stage.

(C) Piaget's formal operational stage.

(D) Piaget's interpersonal concordance stage.

Section VII: Physical Education

126. Which of the following conditions would cause a child to be classified as handicapped according to P.L. 94–142?

    (A) Pregnancy.   (C) Obesity.

    (B) Deafness.   (D) Acne.

127. Which of the following vitamins is not fat soluble?

    (A) Vitamin D   (C) Vitamin E

    (B) Vitamin C   (D) Vitamin K

128. The primary and most efficient energy source of the body comes from

    (A) proteins.   (C) complex carbohydrates.

    (B) fats.   (D) simple sugars.

129. The body produces cholesterol in the

    (A) liver.   (C) stomach.

    (B) pancreas.   (D) pituitary gland.

130. A break in the bone with a corresponding break in the skin is called a

    (A) comminuted fracture.   (C) compound fracture.

    (B) simple fracture.   (D) complex fracture.

131. In order to achieve lasting weight loss, people should

    (A) enter a commercial diet program.

    (B) combine permanent dietary changes with exercise.

    (C) cut calories to below 100 per day.

    (D) exercise for two hours a day.

132. Which of the following is a locomotive skill?

    (A) Bouncing.   (C) Throwing.

    (B) Catching.   (D) Leaping.

133. Exercises that cause actual contraction of the muscle fibers are called

    (A) isotonic   (C) static.

    (B) isometric.   (D) aerobic.

134. Which is NOT a principle of aerobic conditioning?

    (A) Requires oxygen.

    (B) Continuous and rhythmic.

    (C) Burns protein for energy.

    (D) Uses major muscle groups.

Content Area Exercises I

TIME: 2 Hours
14 Questions

DIRECTIONS: Respond to each of the items below in a brief, well constructed essay.

I. Literature and Language Studies

1. Ludwig Wittgenstein wrote: "The limits of my language are the limits of my world," meaning that it is impossible to really know anything in the absence of language to describe it. Please support or refute this statement.

2. Compare the ways in which adults acquire language to the ways in which children acquire language.

3. Chose one of the poetic forms below and describe how its structure enhances its meaning.

    free verse   elegy   limerick

    villanelle   sistina   haiku

    blank verse   epigram

4. Briefly define and compare romanticism, realism, and naturalism.

II. Mathematics

5. If you square an integer and subtract 1, the result equals the product of that integer plus 1 and that integer minus 1. Why?

6. Given that:

   x and a are real numbers

   n is a natural number

   Show that $x^n = a$ is not always true.

7. Why does the product of two irrational numbers not have to be another irrational number?

8. A builder measures the angles A, B, C of the new house's roof. How does he know that sides 1, 2, and 3 are equivalent? (Refer to the following figure.)

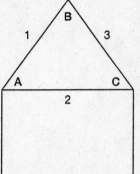

III. Visual and Performing Arts

9. Briefly describe two methods of aesthetic evaluation. You may illustrate your methods with examples from any artistic discipline.

10. Most art historians agree that people began to create art in the paleolithic period, about thirty thousand years ago, carving small female fertility symbols, now called Venuses. What about this prehistoric art connects it with the art of today?

IV. Human Development

11. Choose any one of Maslow's hierarchy of human needs and briefly describe how it is relevant to elementary educators.

12. Briefly define ethnocentrism, and its relevance to elementary education.

V. Physical Education

13. Briefly describe two ways in which organized sports and games can help a student in academic areas.

14. Elimination of everyday risk factors is an important part of physical education. Briefly describe two of these risk factors, and how phys ed can be used to help reduce them.

Content Area Exercises II

TIME: 1 Hour
8 Questions

DIRECTIONS: Respond to each of the items below in a brief, well constructed essay.

I. History and Social Sciences

1. Fascism is a word that is widely used but difficult to define. List at least 2 major tenets of Italian fascism.

2. "A shadow has fallen upon the scenes so lately lighted by the Allied victory...From Stettin in the Baltic to Triste in the Adriatic, an iron curtain has descended across the Continent." Describe the significance of the above quote. Include who made the speech, what the speech is commonly called, and describe what differing ideologies it addresses.

3. Describe the major events of the Russian Revolution of 1917. Include the names of both the leader that was murdered and the leader that eventually took his place.

4. In *The Souls of Black Folk,* W.E.B. Du Bois offers his opinion of black education. Briefly describe his views.

II. Science

5. Explain the phenomena depicted in the illustration below:

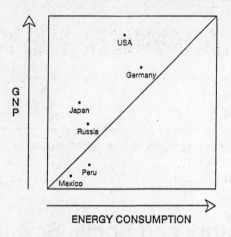

6. Explain why the composition of the Earth's atmosphere at an altitude of 750 km is He, H, and O (He is atomic helium, H is atomic hydrogen, O is atomic oxygen) instead of heavier molecules such as O_2 and N_2.

7. Using the material provided below, explain how a solar distillation machine could be built to desalinate seawater.

   glass sheet   container for water   shovel

8. Most national airports have a wind shear detection system composed of a network of ground based anemometers. Using the configuration below, explain how wind shear could be detected.

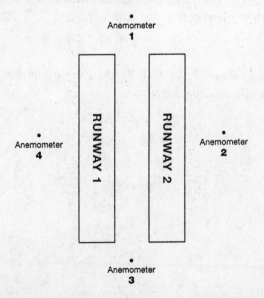

Content Knowledge II

ANSWER KEY

1.	(B)	35.	(B)	69.	(B)	103.	(B)
2.	(A)	36.	(A)	70.	(C)	104.	(D)
3.	(A)	37.	(D)	71.	(C)	105.	(A)
4.	(D)	38.	(A)	72.	(A)	106.	(B)
5.	(C)	39.	(D)	73.	(A)	107.	(D)
6.	(D)	40.	(D)	74.	(B)	108.	(D)
7.	(C)	41.	(C)	75.	(D)	109.	(B)
8.	(D)	42.	(C)	76.	(D)	110.	(C)
9.	(A)	43.	(D)	77.	(A)	111.	(B)
10.	(B)	44.	(A)	78.	(A)	112.	(A)
11.	(A)	45.	(B)	79.	(C)	113.	(D)
12.	(D)	46.	(C)	80.	(A)	114.	(A)
13.	(D)	47.	(C)	81.	(C)	115.	(D)
14.	(B)	48.	(D)	82.	(D)	116.	(B)
15.	(C)	49.	(C)	83.	(C)	117.	(D)
16.	(C)	50.	(B)	84.	(A)	118.	(D)
17.	(B)	51.	(C)	85.	(B)	119.	(A)
18.	(A)	52.	(A)	86.	(A)	120.	(B)
19.	(B)	53.	(D)	87.	(A)	121.	(C)
20.	(C)	54.	(A)	88.	(C)	122.	(B)
21.	(D)	55.	(A)	89.	(A)	123.	(B)
22.	(B)	56.	(B)	90.	(B)	124.	(A)
23.	(C)	57.	(D)	91.	(D)	125.	(B)
24.	(B)	58.	(C)	92.	(B)	126.	(B)
25.	(C)	59.	(B)	93.	(D)	127.	(B)
26.	(B)	60.	(D)	94.	(B)	128.	(C)
27.	(A)	61.	(A)	95.	(A)	129.	(A)
28.	(C)	62.	(C)	96.	(B)	130.	(C)
29.	(C)	63.	(C)	97.	(A)	131.	(B)
30.	(A)	64.	(B)	98.	(A)	132.	(D)
31.	(C)	65.	(C)	99.	(C)	133.	(A)
32.	(A)	66.	(B)	100.	(A)	134.	(C)
33.	(C)	67.	(A)	101.	(C)		
34.	(D)	68.	(D)	102.	(C)		

DETAILED EXPLANATIONS
OF ANSWERS

1.   **(B)**   An elegy is a serious poem lamenting the death of an individual or group of individuals. Passage (B) is Robert Herrick's "Upon His Spaniel Tracy," an elegy which mourns the death of his favorite dog. Thus, passage (B) is the correct answer.

2.   **(A)**   Enjambment occurs when a line of poetry "runs on" to the next line, causing a slight pause in mid-sentence or thought. Line three reads, "This shall my love do, give thy sad death one." The reader is left wondering, "One what?" It is not until line four that the poet explains that he will give one "Tear." Thus, choice (A) is the correct answer.

3.   **(A)**   The speaker of these lines is Berowne, a reluctant student in Shakespeare's *Love's Labor's Lost*. You can discern that the lines are spoken by a student because they are a reaction *against* study and those who pursue it ("Small have continual plodders won...") It would be highly unusual for a professor to say such things, and the other three choices are, of course, possible, but not within the limited context of the passage.

4.   **(D)**   Restated, the lines mean, "Little (small) have those who constantly (continually) plod through their studies gained (won), except (save) for some common, throwaway knowledge (base authority) from others' books." Choice (D) comes closest to this, and is thus the correct answer.

5.   **(C)**   A supplicant is one who seeks forgiveness in a religious sense. Therefore, by labeling the parishioners as such, the author is implying that they are all guilty of various crimes against their religion, and have come to the church seeking forgiveness.

6.   **(D)**   This poem, written by William S. Gilbert in 1882, is a satiric look at the ineffectuality of the British Parliament and its inability (in the poet's opinion) to do anything worthwhile. Phrases such as "The House of Peers made no pretense / To intellectual eminence" and "The House of Peers, throughout the war, / Did nothing in particular, / And did it very well" show the author's disdain for the noble men who inherited their Parliament seats and had no real interest in the political goings-on of England. The fact that, as the poet mentions, Britain becomes an empire in spite of the House of Peers adds to the satiric yet humorous tone of the poem.

7.   **(C)**   The satire in the poem is evident in the author's depiction of the success of Britain in spite of the ineffectual "House of Peers," and the satire is given a prophetic nature as the author wonders if the same success will continue, as if the Parliament will always be useless. The poem certainly does not laud (praise) the Parliament (A), and the poet is not satisfied (D), with the House's past performances. The poem is not a parody (B).

8.   **(D)**   The passage, which opens Charles Dickens's *A Tale of Two Cities*, contains numerous and vast comparisons. By making these comparisons and descriptions of the time period ("we had everything before us, we had nothing before us, we were all going direct to Heaven, we were all going direct the other way," etc.), Dickens is illustrating how during this period (just before the French Revolution) anything was possible: "wisdom", "foolishness", "Light", or "Darkness". This "anything is possible" tone also foreshadows the French Revolution, which the Aristocracy never expected. Dickens will, later in the novel, describe extreme political upheaval, but does not here, so (B) is wrong. (A) is wrong because "placid" implies settled and calm; if "anything is possible," then the times are exact opposite. There is no mention of a public event or the attitudes of people at war, so (C) is incorrect.

9.   **(A)**   The Bible tells of how Christ was able to feed hundreds of hungry people with only 7 loaves of bread and fish until all were satiated. By jokingly suggesting that the two governments contain the positions "lords of the state preserves of loaves and fishes," Dickens mocks their self-assuredness and unflinching certainty that the "preserves" will never be depleted and that "things in general [are] settled for ever." The phrase "clearer than crystal" helps, through it sarcasm, to give this attack more sting. All of the other choices are not alluded to or discussed in the passage, and are thus incorrect.

10.   **(B)**   This passage from Melville's *Moby Dick* contains an allusion in the phrase, "like so many Alexanders." Melville is illustrating the strength and power of whalers ("naked Nantucketers") by alluding and comparing them to Alexander the Great, the famous conqueror who died in 323 B.C.

11.   **(A)**   This passage, which opens James Joyce's *A Portrait of the Artist as a Young Man* is written in "baby talk" ("moocow," "nicens," "baby tuckoo") to convey to readers the age, speech and mental set of the narrator.

12.   **(D)**   Nineteenth century novels of manners employed such themes as the importance (or unimportance) of "good breeding," the elation (and suffocation) caused by society, and the interaction of individuals within the confines of a closed country community (to name just a few). This passage, taken from Jane Austen's *Emma*, mentions "opinions" of other characters, the importance of "beauty" and "accomplishment" (note how Emma sees them as almost saving graces for Mrs. Elton), and the "improvement" of a "country neighborhood."

13. **(D)**   The theme of *carpe diem*, Latin for "seize the day," urges people to enjoy their present pleasures and lives, because the future is so uncertain. Passage (D), taken from Robert Herrick's, "To the Virgins to Make Much of Time," urges its readers to act now ("Gather ye...while ye may") because time will never stop and all things must come to an end ("...Tomorrow will be dying").

14. **(B)**   Onomatopoeia refers to the formation of words imitating the sound of the object or action expressed, such as "Buzz," "clang," "boom," and "meow." Passage (B) contains two examples of onomatopoeia: "Bow-wow" to imitate the barking of a dog, and "Cock-a-doodle-doo" to imitate the sound of the rooster.

15. **(C)**   Alliteration refers to the repetition of consonant sounds at the beginning of successive (or nearly successive) words in a line (or lines) of poetry. Passage (C) contains the line, "A spotted shaft is seen, which alliterates the "s" sound for poetic effect. Thus, choice (C) is correct.

16. **(C)**   You are asked to decide the literary form of the quote. Since it seems to have no poetic form, the first choice is easily negated. Although a long speech in a play could be similar to this, there is no dialogue, which would normally indicate a play (B). A journal, or diary, is written in first person, as the excerpt is. Also, it puts forth everyday events and feelings, the purpose we normally associate with a journal. A myth (D) is a traditional story, usually connected with the religion of people, and attempts to account for something in nature. This quote gives no indication of mythological allusions. The correct answer is (C).

17. **(B)**   This question asks you to judge, from the paragraph given, the type of literature from which the excerpt was taken. The only choice for which any support is given is choice (B), because the names given are Russian. The other choices can be ruled out, because there is not anything in the paragraph to support them as choices. We see no evidence of British terminology or dialect (A), nor are there specific elements of a modern romance (C). Likewise, there is not enough information to determine whether or not this is a short story with existential qualities (D). Therefore, you must choose the answer you *can* support, which is choice (B).

18. **(A)**   Choice (A) is the only correct scanned line. It contains five iambic feet and is an example of iambic pentameter. The other examples have incorrectly marked accents and feet.

19. **(B)**   This passage comes from the Greek play *Medea*, by Euripides. Medea, a woman who is being cast aside so her husband, Jason, can marry a princess, kills their two sons in retaliation. This passage shows Jason lamenting over the boys' deaths and invoking the gods to punish his ex-wife.

20. **(C)**   In the passage Jason mourns that Medea killed the boys "to prevent

me/Touching their bodies or giving them burial." In Greek society, the dead were honored by elaborate burial rites and ceremonies. To be buried without ceremony was considered to be dishonorable to the dead, especially when they were related to great warriors, such as Jason.

21. **(D)** John is portrayed by the speaker as condescending. The speaker tells us that she thinks that there is something queer about the house and that "John laughs at me, of course, but one expects that." The speaker expects her husband to laugh at her, which indicates that that is his usual reaction to her ideas. Also, the speaker reports that John does not believe that she is sick, and dismisses her illness as "temporary nervous tension" and "a slight hysterical tendency," he believes he knows more about her than she does herself. Choice (D) is the correct answer.

22. **(B)** The speaker says of her story that she "would not say it to living soul, of course, but this is dead paper and a great relief to my mind." Writing is, for her, an outlet, a way for her to address her problems. Choice (B) is the correct answer.

23. **(C)** The speaker feels limited by her husband. She tells us that she thinks the reason she does not get well faster is because John does not believe that she is sick. To cure her depression and "hysteria" he perscribes, in addition to tonics and exercize, a prohibition on her writing. She disagrees with him, as her writing serves as an outlet and is "a great relief to (her) mind."

24. **(B)** Phaethon was (in classical myth) the son of Helios, the Sun, who at one time undertook to drive his father's chariot. Persephone was (in classical myth) queen of the underworld and the reviving crops. Thus, their names (I) as well as Phaethon's occupation (II) characterize them as "gods"; choice (B) is correct.

25. **(C)** According to Merleau-Ponty, language is defined by the value of its use. The referent / meaning connection (A), was studied by Sassure. The speaker's intention (B) is important, but must be clear to the audience for language to function. Definition (D), Merleau-Ponty would say, is often a group of definitions, and therefore not precise enough.

26. **(B)** Wittgenstein applied a common-sense approach to language in this case, asserting that "Meaning is use." Therefore, he would agree with every statement but (B), that there is an implicit "deep structure" to which language refers.

27. **(A)** Sassure was one of the first linguists to assert that the connection between a word and it's referent is arbitrary. Ludwig Wittgenstein was the first to assert that meaning is use (B), and this theory was the beginning of the end for the idea that language is a monolithic structure (C). Merleau-Ponty studied language acqusition, and warned against the idea that it falls into rigid, successive stages (D).

28. **(C)** 7 is in the tenth's place. Since the next digit (2) is below 5, drop this digit and retain the 7. The answer, therefore, is 406.7.

29. **(C)** The mean IQ score of 100 is given. One standard deviation above the mean is 34% of the cases, with an IQ score up to 115. One standard deviation below the mean is another 34% of the cases, with an IQ score ranging to 85. So, a total of 68% of the students have an IQ between 85 and 115. Therefore, $1,500 \times .68 = 1,020$.

30. **(A)**

$$(10 + x)2 = 28$$
$$20 + 2x = 28$$
$$2x = 28 - 20$$
$$2x = 8$$
$$x = \frac{8}{2}$$
$$x = 4$$

31. **(C)** Let x = length of time (# of months) to recover cost.

$$3x = 24$$
$$x = \frac{24}{3}$$
$$x = 8 \text{ mos.}$$

32. **(A)** $2,000 \times .35 = $700. The rest have wrong computations.

33. **(C)** With one right angle (90°) and a given 30° angle, the missing angle, therefore, is a 60° angle. ($90° + 30° = 120°$; $180° - 120° = 60°$.)

34. **(D)** The area of a parallelogram is base ×height. Therefore, $A = bh = (16\text{cm}) \times 4 \text{ cm}) = 64 \text{ cm}^2$.

35. **(B)** Only B has an element (which is 5) not present in the given set of {1,2,3,4}.

36. **(A)** 15 is used as a cardinal number. The rest are either ordinal (B) or nominal (C,D) numbers.

37. **(D)** The sequence 1, 4, 9, 16 is the sum of serialized odd numbers.

1.	1	5.	$1 + 3 + 5 + 7 + 9 = 25$
2.	$1 + 3 = 4$	6.	$1 + 3 + 5 + 7 + 9 + 11 = 36$
3.	$1 + 3 + 5 = 9$	7.	$1 + 3 + 5 + 7 + 9 + 11 + 13 = 49$
4.	$1 + 3 + 5 + 7 = 16$		

38. **(A)** Here one must use only needed information. Do not be distracted by superfluous data. Simple multiplication will do. If one pig eats four pounds of food per week, how much will 10 pigs eat in one week? $10 \times 4 = 40$ pounds. The problem intentionally contains superfluous data (52 weeks), which should not distract the reader from its easy solution. Ratio and proportion will also work here

$$\frac{1}{10} = \frac{4}{x},$$

$x = 40$ pounds/week.

39. **(D)** Let the variable S stand for the cost of the shirt. Then the cost of the pair of pants is $S + 25$ and

$$S + (S + 25) = 65$$
$$2S = 65 - 25$$
$$2S = 40$$
$$S = 20$$

$20 (cost of shirt)

$20 + $25 = $45 (cost of pants)

40. **(D)** The possible handshakes are illustrated by listing all the possible pairs of letters, thus

AB   AC   AD   AE

BC   BD   BE

CD   CE

DE

(a total of 10 handshakes)

41. **(C)** Only C involves a change by only translation.

547

42. **(C)** Let

D = down payment

D = $20,000 × .20

D = $4,000

43. **(D)** All but D are constraints. The constraint for *y* is to at least make 2 mowers.

44. **(A)** The ratio 8:6:6:1 implies that for each $8 the wife received, each child received $6 and the foundation $1. The estate is divided into 8 + 6 + 6 + 1, or 21 equal shares. The wife received $8/21$ of $300,000 or $114, 285.71, each child received $6/21$ of $300,000, or $85,714.29, and the foundation received $1/21$ of $300,000 or $14,285.71. As a check, $114,285.71 + $85,714.29 + $85,714.29 + $14,285.71 = $300,000.

45. **(B)** Simple division. $19/9$ = 2 whole hamburgers with one left over.

46. **(C)** Simple multiplication. 7 × 4 = 28.

47. **(C)** For a 15 ft. log, it will take 14 cuts to make 15 equal pieces. Therefore, 14 minutes for 14 cuts.

48. **(D)** Simple multiplication. 6 × 4 = 24.

49. **(C)** Find the sum of the seven days. Thus:

M = 25;

T = 30;

W = 20;

Th = 25;

F = 10;

Sat = 40;

Sun = 0,

or a total of 150 minutes. Find the average by dividing 150 by 7 = 21.43 minutes.

50. **(B)** If each $ stands for $12, only weeks 3 and 4 had a sale of $72 and $60, respectively. The rest are below $55.

51. **(C)** Mode is the most frequent score. 81 appeared five times and is therefore the mode.

52. **(A)** By definition, a simple curve is a curve that can be traced in such a way that no point is traced more than once with the exception that the tracing may stop where it started. A closed curve is a curve that can be traced so that the starting and stopping points are the same. Therefore, A and B are simple closed curves. The rest are not.

53. **(D)** A line of symmetry for a figure is a line in which you can stand a mirror, so that the image you see in the mirror is just like the part of the figure that the mirror is hiding. In this case there are four lines.

54. **(A)**

m = number of miles you can travel

$0.08 m$ = amount spent for m miles travelled at 8 cents per mile,

rental fee + mileage charge = total amount spent

$$\$139 + \$0.08 \, m = \$350$$

Solution: $139 - 139 + 0.08 \, m = 350 - 139$

$$0.08 \, m = 211$$

$$\frac{0.08m}{0.08} = \frac{211}{0.08}$$

$$m = 2{,}637.5$$

$$m = 2{,}637$$

Therefore, you can travel 2,637 miles (if you go 2,638 miles you have travelled too far).

55. **(A)** The nomadic warriors who would later become the lords of feudal Japan arrived in the Kofun Era. The Heian Era (B) marked their rise to power, and the Sengoku Era (C), also called the Warring States Era (D) marked the beginning of the decline of their power due to political fragmentation.

56. **(B)** Literally translated, *bakfu* means tent government. Shogunate (A) refers to the customary translation of the term. A landed estate (C) was known as a *shoen*, and a local feudal lord was called a *daimyo*.

57. **(D)** (A), (B), and (C) were all unifiers of Japan, while Minamoto no Yorimoto was the founder of the first, or Kamakura Shogunate.

58. **(C)**   Asoka converted to Buddhism in the third century B.C.E., facilitating its acceptance by Indian society. Taoism (A), and Jainism (D) flourished in China rather than the Indian subcontinent. Hinduism (B) was the prominent religion in India before as well as after the conversion of Asoka.

59. **(B)**   The Maya were the first of these civilizations to develop the concept of zero. While each of the other civilizations achieved a great deal artistically, mathematically, and culturally, the Maya were the first to develop this esoteric concept.

60. **(D)**   The jihad, or holy war, is a concept central to the Islamic faith; however, it is not one of the five pillars. In addition to (A), (B), and (C), Muslims are expected to make a pilgrimage to Mecca once in their lifetime, completing the five pillars of faith.

61. **(A)**   The Nok created life-sized terra cotta figures. The Songhai (B) were originally part of the Mali Empire, and were known for gaining their independence in the early 1400s. The Ghana (C) were noted for their building of impressive stone structures, but their society mysteriously disappeared after an invasion by the Mali in the thirteenth century. The Bantu (D) society was loosely organized throughout Sub-Saharan Africa, and their walled city, Great Zimbabwe was a prominent trading center.

62. **(C)**   The Incas were a sun worshipping people, and believed themselves to be the viceregent of the sun god on Earth. The Aztec (A) were a polytheistic culture, and practiced routine human sacrifice for the appeasment of their chief diety. The term Andean (B) refers to the Andes Mountains of South America, where several cultures flourished. The Hohokam (D) were mound builders that lived in what is now the southwestern United States.

63. **(C)**   The Reconstruction Finance Corporation was not part of the New Deal but was created in 1932, during the presidency of Herbert Hoover, as an attempt to reexpand credit by extending loans to distressed businesses. This was part of Hoover's response to the Depression. The National Industrial Recovery Act (A) (1933), the Tennessee Valley Authority (B) (1933), and the Agricultural Adjustment Act (D) (1933), were all part of Roosevelt's New Deal program.

64. **(B)**   The economy of the 1980s was generally characterized by declining inflation (IV) and falling unemployment rates (II). On the other hand, stock prices (III) generally increased, despite a sharp drop in October 1987, while the imbalance between imports and exports (V), the so-called "trade deficit," and the level of foreign investment in the U.S. economy (D) remained high.

65. **(C)**   The German use of submarines against merchant and passenger ships was the most crucial factor in bringing the United States into the First World

War. German violation of Belgian neutrality (B) helped bring Britain into the war, and British propaganda (A), which did play a role in securing U.S. involvement, made much of German atrocities in Belgium (D). However, torpedoing unarmed ships without giving warning and making provision for the safety of passengers and crew—which a submarine was incapable of doing in 1917—was seen as akin to piracy.

66. **(B)**   Though the land was abundant (A), capital (B) and labor (D) were scarce in early America. Limitations of climate and land (C) prevented New England from developing the staple-crop agriculture in demand in Europe.

67. **(A)**   Credit Mobilier was the name of the dummy construction company set up by officials of Union Pacific in order to embezzle millions of dollars the government was paying to subsidize the construction of a transcontinental railroad. The contract for the collection of $427,000 in unpaid taxes, for a 50% commission that later found its way into Republican campaign coffers (B), was the centerpiece of a scandal known as the Sanborn Contract Fraud. The Whiskey Ring Fraud was the name given to the conspiracy of distillers and treasury officials to defraud the government of large amounts of money from the excise tax on whiskey (C), and Congress's attempt to raise its own pay retroactively (D) was christened the Salary Grab Act. The exposure of all of these sordid affairs during the presidency of U. S. Grant helped give his administration a reputation for corruption.

68. **(D)**   While farms were disappearing and industry was growing during the era of Jacksonian Democracy, industrialization would not become an issue until after the Civil War. Federal financing of internal improvements (B), states' rights (C), and the removal of southeastern Indians to reservations (A) all were, with other issues such as the Second Bank of the United States, important issues during this era.

69. **(B)**   De Soto and Coronado hoped to repeat the success of Hernando Cortes, who had sacked the rich Aztec Empire of Mexico. For Coronado, the hope first focused on the mythical "Seven Cities of Cibola" and then on the equally fictional "Gran Quivira." Both Spaniards were disappointed but did play important roles in exploring the hitherto unknown interior of North America and in establishing Spain's claims to the southern portions of the continent.

70. **(C)**   In sending out the Lewis and Clark expedition, President Thomas Jefferson was not concerned with the possibility that they might discover gold (they did not). He did desire that they establish friendly relations with the western Indians (A), gain both geographic (B) and scientific (D) knowledge about western North America.

71. **(C)** The devastation of the Black Death enhanced the value of labor during the 14th century because of the enormous depletion of the labor pool. The plague did not have any meaningful impact on the development of nation-states (A), nor was a flight of millions of Europeans overseas (D) associated with this event. (B) is incorrect because modern medicine did not develop for centuries.

72. **(A)** The Federal Reserve Board is a government agency consisting of seven members appointed for 14-year terms by the president, with the consent of the Senate. This board is at the head of the Federal Reserve System, which is comprised of member banks across the country. The primary function of the Federal Reserve Board is to implement monetary policy. The Federal Reserve Board has three methods of implementing monetary policy. First, it can change the reserve requirement, which is the amount of cash that member banks must keep on deposit in a regional Federal Reserve Bank. An increase in the requirement reduces the amount of cash a bank has on hand to loan. Second, the board can change the discount rate, which is the interest rate that member banks must pay to borrow money from a Federal Reserve Bank. A higher rate discourages a member bank from borrowing and lending more money. Third, the board can buy and sell government securities. To increase the money supply the board sells securities. To decrease the money supply the board buys securities. Answer (B) is the most plausible alternative to (A), but fails because controlling government spending is a function of Congress and the president. Answer (C) is incorrect because the Federal Reserve Board has nothing to do with regulating commodity prices. Answer (D) is incorrect because the Board does not help the president run the executive branch.

73. **(A)** There is a direct correlation between voter turnout and educational level. Those with four years or more of college are more likely to vote than those with one to three years of college. Those with one to three years of college are more likely to vote than are high school graduates. High school graduates are, in turn, more likely to vote than are those with less than a high school education. The answer is (A), the more schooling one has, the more likely one is to vote. Voting is only one form of political participation. Other forms are running for office, working in political campaigns, and contributing to campaigns. While it is difficult to find statistics which show the correlation between educational status and running for office, we do know that most people who are completely inactive (that is, do not participate in politics in any way) typically have little education and low incomes and are relatively young. Therefore, it is safe to conclude that the less education one has, (B), the *less* likely one is to run for office; so (B) is not the answer. Answer (C) is clearly wrong, since many studies have shown a direct correlation between advanced educational status and political participation by voting. Answer (D) is wrong, as is clear from the graph. Those with a high school education are *not* more likely to vote than are those with a college degree.

74. **(B)** In 1985, Congress passed the Gramm-Rudman Act with the intent to balance the federal budget by 1992. The law created a plan whereby the budget deficit for each year from 1986 through 1991 could not exceed a specified, declining amount. Therefore, the correct response is (B). (A) is incorrect because the Hyde Amendment of 1976 outlawed the use of federal funds for abortions, except where the life of the mother is at stake. (C) is incorrect because the Boland Amendments outlawed the use of federal funds to aid the Nicaraguan Contras. (D) is incorrect because the Gramm-Rudman Act did not change the tax code.

75. **(D)** There are two schools of thought on the proper method of constitutional interpretation by the judiciary. One is called "judicial activism." Advocates of this school believe that the intentions of those who wrote the Constitution should not be authoritative for the decision of controversial matters in the present. They say that judges should be free to adapt the Constitution to changing political and social circumstances. The other school is called "judicial restraint." Advocates of this school stress that the Constitution was a great contract by which the American people created a government. This contract laid the ground rules for the operation of the government, and it provided a formal process of amendment for changing those ground rules. In order to understand the ground rules, say advocates of restraint, one must determine the original intentions of those who wrote and ratified the Constitution. For unelected judges to assume to themselves the power to change the Constitution, according to this school, is for the judges to usurp a power that was not given them by the Constitution or the people. Therefore, the correct answer is (D). Answer (A) is incorrect because there is no general process by which judges limit the number of cases they hear in a year. Justices on the Supreme Court do have a lot of control over which cases they hear, through a process called certiorari. When litigants appeal to the Court to have their cases heard, the justices vote on the merits of the cases. If four justices vote to hear a particular case, they issue a "writ of certiorari" to the lower court, ordering all documents relevant to the case to be sent up to the Supreme Court. Answer (B) is incorrect because judges do not lobby funds from Congress. Answer (C) is incorrect because when judges remove themselves from a case they are said to recuse themselves.

76. **(D)** The question asks which statement is false. The correct answer is (D) since the purpose of the equal rights amendment was to protect and enlarge the rights of women, not of blacks and Hispanics. The operative clause read "Equality of rights under the law shall not be denied or disparaged by the United States or any State on account of sex." (A) is not a false statement because both houses of Congress passed the amendment in 1972, and sent it to the states for ratification. The necessary three-fourths of the state legislatures never ratified the amendment, so it died in 1982. (B) is not a false statement because Congress did extend the time limit for ratification. The original time limit expired in 1979, but before

that date arrived Congress extended the time limit to 1982. (C) is not a false statement because Nebraska and Tennessee, which had ratified the amendment, tried to rescind their ratification.

77. **(A)** Presidents Reagan and Bush emphasized political ideology as a factor in choosing their nominees to the Supreme Court. The single most important issue has been a potential candidate's stand on *Roe vs. Wade*, 1973. In that case, the Supreme Court held that the right to privacy included a woman's right to choose an abortion, at least in the first trimester of pregnancy. Roe is perhaps the most controversial decision of the Court in the last 30 years. Republican presidents have tried to nominate Justices who would vote to overrun Roe, while Democratic senators have done their best to thwart those nominations. (B) is incorrect because there has, in fact, been an increase in support for Republican presidential candidates in the South in the last 30 years. From the end of the Reconstruction until the 1950s, the Democratic candidate for president could count on solid support from the states of the old Confederacy. However, that began to change in the 1960s. In six elections since 1964, the Democratic candidate for president has won a majority of southern states only once, in 1976, when Georgia's Jimmy Carter did so. The Democratic candidate has not won Virginia and has won Mississippi, Alabama, Florida, South Carolina, and North Carolina only once each, since 1964. (C) is incorrect because the conservative wing of the Republican Party has increased in influence in the past 30 years. After a bitter battle at the 1964 Republican National Convention, conservative Republicans managed to nominate Barry Goldwater as the party's candidate for president. This was the beginning of the takeover of the party by its conservative wing. In 1968, the party nominated Richard Nixon, a strongly anti-communist conservative. In 1980 and 1984, the party nominated Ronald Reagan, long a conservative influence within the party. The conservative wing of the party has also managed to dominate the party's platform at most of the last seven party conventions. (D) is incorrect because voter turnout has decreased in the last 30 years. In 1960, about 62% of the voting age population voted in the presidential election. In 1988, less than 50% did.

78. **(A)** The distribution of governmental powers between the branches is known as "separation of powers." A related concept, "checks and balances" (B) most frequently refers to situations where power is "shared," and is therefore "checked" by the power of another branch. Federalism (A) refers to the distribution of power between levels of government (state, national), while constitutional interpretation (C) could refer to any aspect of the constitution, not just the distribution of power. The notion of fundamental rights would refer to such basic liberties as freedom of the press.

79. **(C)** Skin covering the eyeballs is generally the thinnest skin on the body. The soles of the feet (A) and the palms of the hand (B) are often involved in laborious activities, and the skin is thick in this area. The back (D) also has thick skin. Thus, (C) is the correct answer.

80. **(A)**   The epidermis is made of two layers: the layer of Malpighi and the stratum corneum. The stratum corneum is the outer layer, and the layer of Malpighi is directly under it. Under these two layers of the epidermis is the dermis.

81. **(C)**   The body regulates water and heat through perspiration. Transpiration describes a process not involving humans. Thus, (B) is not correct. Respiration (A) is breathing in humans and will cause some water loss. However, the question asks for how the body regulates substances through the skin. (D), sensation, is the ability to process or perceive. The skin does have nerve endings that can sense, but this does not involve temperature or water regulation.

82. **(D)**   The nerve endings, blood vessels, and sweat glands are found in the dermis. They are not in the layer of Malpighi, since this layer's main function is to grow to replace the stratum corneum that quickly wears away. Thus, (A) is wrong. It would not be beneficial to have these important structures in a layer that wears away; thus, they are not found in the stratum corneum. (B) must be wrong. Since the layer of Malpighi and the stratum corneum are the two layers of the epidermis, (C) must be wrong. (D) must be correct.

83. **(C)**   The property of an object which determines the object's resistance to motion is its mass. A large watermelon (C) has a far greater mass than the pellet of lead shot, golf ball, or feather. The mass of an object never changes. It is equal to an object's weight divided by the acceleration due to gravity "g" at its current position in space.

84. **(A)**   The sleeping astronauts would continue their motion in a straight line if the Shuttle suddenly changed velocity due to the firing of its thrusters. If the Shuttle slowed down, the astronauts would move forward relative to the walls. This is all due to the fact that the astronauts have mass, or inertia. Gravity is so weak that it is negligible on the astronauts. They can be monitored by battery driven devices which allow them to move around, and they can certainly sleep without being strapped. Bodies do not need a reaction force to sleep.

85. **(B)**   Inertia is measured by mass, m, which is choice (B). Choice (A) does contain mass but also involves other complicating factors like the speed of light, c, which invalidate the choice. There are two ways to measure mass: gravitationally through an object's weight, and inertially through an object's resistance to motion. Both measures, gravitational mass and inertial mass, have always been found to be the same for a given object.

86. **(A)**   Answer choice (A), "this conclusion is supported by the data," is the correct answer since the gray line representing the whitetail deer population drops over a period of time, and the mule deer (black line) stays the same or shows an increase in population. "This conclusion is not supported by the data" (B) cannot be the correct answer since one can determine that there are fewer

whitetail deer over a period of time. "This conclusion includes the effect of hunting and is supported by the data" (C) cannot be the correct answer since it is stated in the paragraph that hunting was not allowed. "This conclusion includes the effect caused by drought and is supported by the data" (D) cannot be the correct answer since no drought was mentioned in the data.

87. **(A)** Answer choice (A), "the conclusion is supported by the data," is the correct answer since the mule deer survived and the whitetail deer did not survive. "The conclusion is refuted by the data" (B) cannot be the correct answer since the fittest, in this case, were the mule deer. "The conclusion is refuted because only one survived" (C) cannot be the correct answer since there is no data indicating that any of the whitetail deer survived. "The conclusion is refuted because both deer do not compete with each other and the data supports this" (D) cannot be the correct answer since both animals had the same food and opportunities.

88. **(C)** Answer choice (C), "the conclusion is neither supported nor refuted by the data," is the correct answer since there is no data concerning any special adaptations to the environment. "The conclusion is supported by the data" (A) cannot be the correct answer since there is no data concerning any special adaptations to the environment. "The conclusion is refuted by the data" (B) cannot be the correct answer since environmental adaptations are not addressed by the graph. "The data gives plenty of information concerning the mule deers' adaptability, which supports the conclusion" (D) cannot be the correct answer since there are no data about adaptability.

89. **(A)** Answer choice (A), "the conclusion is supported by the data," is the correct answer since the graph shows an early increase in both populations of deer. "The conclusion is refuted by the data" (B) cannot be the correct answer since the graph shows an early increase in both populations of deer. "The conclusion is neither supported nor refuted by the data" (C) cannot be the correct answer since the conclusion is supported by the early increase in both populations of deer. "The data gives plenty of information concerning the mule deer's adaptability, which supports the conclusion" (D) cannot be the correct answer since adaptability is not a part of the graph.

90. **(B)** is correct since, as the diagram shows, the distance between the two adjacent peaks is labelled as the wavelength. If the peaks are not adjacent, more than one wavelength will be measured, as in (A). (C) is wrong because the distance described is twice the wave amplitude, not wavelength. (D) is describing velocity, not wavelength.

91. **(D)** is correct. The water molecules, which is the medium, is not carried, but the wave peaks do move toward shore. (A) states the opposite of what is mentioned in the question. (B) is wrong because although the ocean is somewhat

mixed each day, this mixing is due to currents and turbulence, not by waves. (C) is wrong because debris washes ashore by currents and turbulence, not by waves.

92.   **(B)**   Answer choice (B), "the message of the mRNA is different from what the DNA code was before the event," is the correct choice. Since the DNA contains the information for the mRNA, the mRNA made after the event will be different because the DNA will be changed. "Nothing happens" (A) cannot be the correct answer since the removal of a "code word" is at least considered a point mutation, and the resulting mRNA will be changed. "mRNA cannot be made" (C) cannot be the correct answer since many of the DNA "code words" would have to be destroyed before this would happen. "Triplets can no longer be produced, so doublets are used" (D) cannot be the correct answer since "code words" are always "read" by three (triplets).

93.   **(D)**   Answer choice (D), the nucleus, is the correct answer since the nucleus contains the chromosomes, which are composed of DNA nucleotides and some protein. The lysosomes (A) cannot be the correct answer since lysosomes contain digestive enzymes. The endoplasmic reticulum (B) cannot be the correct answer since it is a series of membranes found in the cytoplasm and it serves as a site of protein synthesis. "They are found floating in the cytoplasmic matrix" (C) cannot be the correct answer since DNA nucleotides are not found outside the nucleus.

94.   **(B)**   Answer choice (B), chromosomes, is the correct answer since DNA and its associated proteins form these rodlike or threadlike structures. RNA (A) cannot be the correct answer since RNA does not interweave itself with proteins to form chromosomes. Nucleotides (C) cannot be the correct answer since DNA strands are composed of nucleotides. Genes (D) cannot be the correct answer since genes are composed of DNA and make up chromosomes.

95.   **(A)**   Answer choice (A), "the resulting protein would be changed in some way, either in length, number or type of arrangement of amino acids" would be the correct answer since all proteins are made of amino acids, which are bonded together sequentially as dictated by the mRNA which was made by the DNA. "The resulting protein would definitely be smaller" (B) cannot be the correct answer since only the order of the amino acids would be changed. "The resulting protein would definitely be larger" (C) cannot be the correct answer since only the order of the amino acids would be changed. "The resulting protein would be wrapped around the DNA" (D) cannot be the correct answer since DNA does not enter into the actual construction of the protein molecule.

96.   **(B)**   Answer choice (B), "yes, because there are more offspring produced than the environment could support, and only some of the clams would survive" would be the correct answer since it is consistent with the second of Darwin's observations and the first of his conclusions. "Yes, because favorable variations occur" (A) cannot be the correct answer since the question has nothing to do with

the variation. "Yes, because the environment is constantly changing" (C) cannot be the correct answer since even though the environment is constantly changing, the change is not fast enough to affect the single release of clam's sex cells. "No, because individual sperm and egg are different" (D) cannot be the correct answer since this is not consistent with any of Darwin's observations nor with any of his conclusions.

97. **(A)** Answer choice (A), "organisms produce more offspring than the environment can support so a population will remain constant since there are not enough resources for all offspring," is the correct answer since it is consistent with Darwin's observations and conclusions. "The environment is slowly changing all over the world which prevents all of the offsprings from maturing." (B) cannot be the correct answer since the environment does not change that quickly. "Genetic variation is allowing the ferns to keep the same level of population" (C) cannot be the correct answer since genetic variation has nothing to do with the leveling of the population of ferns. "Genetic variation that allows for survival will accumulate" (D) cannot be the correct answer since the survival characteristics, which can accumulate, do not do so quickly enough for this to occur in a single year.

98. **(A)** Answer choice (A), "cattle rancher," is the correct answer since cattle ranchers are always trying to have the best-bred cattle. "Oilman" (B) cannot be the correct answer since this person would be more interested in the finding and refining of oil. "Engineer" (C) cannot be the correct answer since engineers function in constructing things. "Refinery chemist" (D) cannot be the correct answer since a refinery chemist's main function is to develop new products or to maintain the quality control of the products produced at the refinery.

99. **(C)** is the answer. Hydrogen bonding is especially strong in water, not weak. (A), (B), (D) are all true statements about water.

100. **(A)** is correct. Intermolecular attraction, namely, hydrogen bonding, leads to the high boiling and melting point. (B) is wrong because water has high surface tension. (C) is wrong because there is a great deal of hydrogen bonding between water molecules. (D) is wrong because water has a high heat capacity.

101. **(C)** Choice (A) is unacceptable because in each area of use, the U.S. household utilizes far more than twice the electrical energy of the Brazilian household. Choice (B) is incorrect because the percent used in air-conditioning is greater in the U.S. than in Brazil. Choice (D) is incorrect since in Brazil more electrical energy is used for water heating than for lighting.

102. **(C)** Both columns of electrical energy in KWH must be totaled. The U.S. household consumes 7345 KWH while the Brazilian household consumes 1460

KWH per year. This is a ratio of 5 to 1. It is interesting to note that the Third World developing countries mimic the United States in their usage of technology.

103. **(B)**   The building pictured in the example—the contemporary "Beaubourg" art museum and cultural center in Paris—dispenses entirely with the ideas and philosophies of the classical past and with the styles and forms of traditional architecture. It is conceived instead on a huge industrial scale and, rather than projecting an atmosphere of quiet balance and poetic calm, it seeks to involve itself and its visitors in the dynamic life and culture of the modern city. Therefore, rather than concealing its structural and mechanical components behind a finished, exterior wall, the Beaubourg intentionally exposes its "anatomy", using pipes, ducts, tubes, and funnels of a modern industrial plant to reveal both its structure and its functions to the people in attendance. The visitor's ability to perceive the building's processes at work creates the sense that both building and people are part of a huge living organism.

104. **(D)**   The jamb statues on the Early Gothic cathedral at Chartres, France (c. A.D. 1145–1170) draw their subject matter and thematic content not from classical mythology but from Christian ideology and belief. The figure groupings in the three main portals illustrate scenes from the Life and Passion of Christ, such as His birth, the Presentation in the Temple, and, in the center, the Second Coming. However, these scenes are not specifically arranged in a continuous narrative sequence and do not "tell a story". The sculpture itself, though it covers much of the building's facade, cannot be said to dominate, since it is strictly controlled and contained within the space allotted to it. The static, motionless figures conform closely to their architectural framework and are therefore subordinate to the structural forms of the doorways.

105. **(A)**   In the eighteenth century Japanese woodblock print pictured in the example, the artist used the folds of the garment and its bold design to create an animated surface pattern of diagonal lines and shapes. These diagonals, far from minimizing the motion of the dancer, emphasize his athletic leaps and turns, although they give no specific information about the story behind his dance. Further, the drapery folds do not cling to the dancer's body and define the three-dimensional forms of his anatomy, as they would in a Western tradition, but, rather, obscure his body almost completely, reassert the picture surface, and deny any sense of actual, three-dimensional space.

106. **(B)**   The Renaissance sculptor who created the small figure group shown in the example was intent on conveying the physical stresses and strains of two wrestlers in violent conflict. To express the ferocity of the fight he has exaggerated the tautness of the muscles and the rigid tension of the bodies; to illustrate the climactic moment at which one fighter lifts the other from the ground to break his back, he has shown the brief instant during which the raised figure is balanced against his opponent's stomach. In the viewpoint shown, there is no

suggestion of either the rolling motion of a wheel or the flowing of liquid, and there is apparently none of the spiral torsion of a screw. The figures do seem to interlock somewhat like a set of gears, but the simple machine they most resemble is the lever, with the fulcrum located at the balance point between the two men's abdomens.

107. **(D)** Edgar Degas (1834–1917), the French Impressionist artist who painted the picture shown in the example, was strongly influenced by the ability of the camera to capture a subject in a fleeting moment and in a spontaneous, seemingly unposed manner. In *Viscount Lepic and His Daughters*, 1873, the artist has constructed an off-center composition in which the main subject moves to the right and seems about to exit the picture. Both the viscount and his two young daughters are abruptly cut off at or near the waist, the dog is half-hidden behind one of the children, and the man standing to the left barely enters the picture. This random cropping of objects is reminiscent of a photographic snapshot. Further, the focal center of the picture is located in the empty plaza behind the figures. The painting therefore owes little either to Greek sculpture, which usually represented the full human figure in idealized form, or to Renaissance perspective, which carefully balanced its figures within an illusionistic space. It also shows no apparent debt to the numerous styles of children's book illustration or to the severe abstractions of much primitive art.

108. **(D)** The example shows the church of St. Michael's at Hildesheim, Germany (c. A.D. 1001–1003). It is typical of Early Romanesque architecture in its dependence on thick blank walls with little or no ornamental decoration, and in its massing of simple cubic and cylindrical forms. The effect of this building is less that of a structural framework supporting walls, roofs, and windows, than of a combination of building blocks which have been sectioned and than glued together. Except for the arched shape of the windows, with their tiny glassed areas, the building completely avoids curving forms, while the only diagonals are those of the roof lines, which are functionally necessary but not fundamental to the building's cubic character. Finally, a spectator's ground-level point of view might make this building seem larger and more dramatic, but it, too, is not essential to the architects' conception.

109. **(B)** The Greek Doric temple pictured in the example illustrates a type of architecture known as post-and lintel (or *trabeated*) construction, in which long horizontal beams rest atop a series of vertical supports. In the Greek temple, the cylindrical columns act as supports for the large marble "beam" (or the *architrave*), which, in turn, supports the roof. The Doric temple thus achieves an appearance of Classical balance and perfection through the calculated repetition of a minimum variety of forms. The temple avoids unbroken wall surfaces, instead playing off the solids and voids of the columns and the spaces between, while the only diagonals are those of the triangular front gable (the *pediment*).

The building is completely devoid of arches, which were known to the Greeks but were rarely used and gained prominence only in Roman architecture.

110. **(C)** One of the examples shown, choices (D) is a profile portrait, in which the sitter does not turn her gaze out of the picture space, thus eliminating any possibility of eye contact with the viewer. Two other examples, choices (A) and (B), show the subjects in nearly full face, but the sitter in choice (A) glances introspectively down to his left, while the subject in choice (B) looks toward us but, with aristocratic remove, keeps his own gaze just out of the line of our view. Only choice (C) presents a subject in full face who looks directly at the viewer with his large, warm eyes. This sarcophagus portrait from Roman Egypt, c. A.D. 160, intent on expressing the warmth and humanity of the deceased subject, not only effected full eye contact with the viewer, but also portrayed the subject's eyes as abnormally large and deep.

111. **(B)** Neither the clothing, the sitters, the expressions, nor the styles of choices (A) and (C) convey in any specific way that the subjects are aristocrats. Only choices (B) and (D) show subjects who are clearly wealthy, well-born, and well-bred. Choice (D), however, is a profile portrait which is so formalized as to be neutral and devoid of expression. Choice (B), by contrast, presents a subject whose rich clothing, haughty posture, elegantly cocked wrists, and, especially, distant expression mark him as a wealthy young man whose circumstances make him superior to most.

112. **(A)** The two Renaissance portraits, choices (B) and (D), show the forms and features of their subjects as clearly-defined, well-modelled, and set within a basically naturalistic space. The portrait in choice (C), too, though painted in a sketchier style, models the forms of the face in a lucid, convincing, realistic manner in order to project the sitter's personality. Only choice (A) begins to abstract the figure and undermine the conventional sense of form in the search for new pictorial styles. Only in choice (A), the *Boy in a Red Vest* by the French painter Paul Cézanne, is the specific subject less important that the way the artist treats it. Here, the painter breaks the outlines of the figure and disintegrates its forms, linking them with the background space in a new kind of picture and construction.

113. **(D)** In the Chinese ink painting shown in the example, the artist exploited the fluid, calligraphic character of the ink-and-brush technique. In rendering the graceful bamboo leaves, he did not attempt to suggest illusionistic three-dimensional space, as a Western artist might, but let his forms lie firmly on the two-dimensional picture plane. Further, he restricted his range of tones to a dense black and one grey, and, even though written script is included in the picture, this isolated image of the bamboo plant does not relate an episode in a story. Instead, the artist has drawn upon years of technical training and practice to create a

picture in which both the script and the plant forms act as kind of spontaneous, rhythmic "writing."

114. **(A)** Of the four answer choices, only (A) and (B) can be said to show groups of figures in a landscape; choice (D) shows one or two isolated figures in a landscape setting, and choice (C) contains no landscape elements at all. Choice (B), however, though it presents a number of figures within a topographic view, carefully avoids formally composed and arranged groups and seeks instead to achieve an effect of direct, unposed observation. Only choice (A) uses a composed group as its focal point: the line of schoolboys, seemingly engaged in a moment of spontaneous play, has been painstakingly arranged to lead the viewer's eye from the darker forms at the right to the white-shirted boy at the center. The entire group is set in a broad meadow against a distant, level horizon line which lends balance and stability to the whole composition.

115. **(D)** Only choices (A), (B), and (D) include visible horizon lines: in choice (A) the horizon is integrated with the figure group, and in choice (B) the figures, though small and insignificant within the broad landscape space, are busy in normal workaday activities and do not seem especially isolated. Choice (D), however, Andrew Wyeth's *Christina's World*, 1948, places a solitary figure in a broad, empty landscape space bounded by a high, distant horizon. The helpless isolation of the stricken woman in the field is emphasized by the distance which separates her from her home high on the horizon.

116. **(B)** This question asks you to look at a set of costumes for a play and to match the costumes with the appropriate play. The costumes are definitely from the Elizabethan era, and even if you do not know the other authors and titles listed, you should be able to match a Shakespearean play with these Elizabethan costumes. The correct answer is (B).

117. **(D)** The correct response is (D). Comprehension is shown when the reader questions his or her intent for reading. For example, one may be reading a story to find out what terrible things may befall the main character. The rationale for choosing a book may be an interesting bit of information (A), but it is not a major topic of discussion with the students. Sharing personal information (B) creates a certain bond, but this is not directly relevant to the question. It is also important that all students are on-task before the beginning of a lesson (C), but this is a smaller part of the skill modeled in response (D).

118. **(D)** The correct response is (D). By having a mixed level pair read together, the remedial student receives instruction and the skilled student receives reinforcement. It uses alternative teaching resources, the students themselves, to enhance the learning environment. A certain goal, comprehension, has been set (A), but this is not the most likely outcome. The teacher will need to observe less groups (B), but it is unlikely that this will change the time needed to work with

all groups as long as quality is to be maintained. Although reading in pairs, each student should have a book, and it would be impractical to permit another teacher to utilize the books while one teacher is using them.

119. **(A)**   The correct response is (A). By mapping out previous knowledge, information already known can be transferred to support new information. Although words on the board are visual (B), this is not the underlying motive. Semantic mapping done at the beginning of a story tests how much prior knowledge the students have about the topic at the outset (C). This does model proper use of words (D), but this is not the main intent of the exercise.

120. **(B)**   The correct response is (B). The variance in fifth graders' physical size and development has a direct influence on their interests and attitudes, including their willingness to work with others and a possible preference for working alone. Working in small groups enhances student achievement. It is a learned skill that must be practiced. (A) is incorrect because fifth graders do have the physical and mental maturity to work in small groups. (C) is incorrect because not all fifth-grade students lack the ability for internal control. (D) is incorrect because although Mr. Dobson might need to be more specific in his directions to the students, this is not the main reason for the behavior.

121. **(C)**   The correct response is (C). Students who are naturally shy are usually more willing to participate in small groups than in discussions involving the entire class. Answer (A) is incorrect because calling on each student once per day will not necessarily assist shy students to participate in class discussions even if participation grades are assigned. (B) is incorrect because although students may become less shy as the year progresses, the teacher still has a responsibility to encourage students to participate. Choice (D) is incorrect because although speaking to each student individually may help some students participate, it is likely more students will participate if the procedure outlined in choice (A) is implemented.

122. **(B)**   The correct response is (B). Student's who are overly talkative are usually flattered to be asked to take a leadership role. Asking these students to take notes also assigns them a task that allows other students to voice their opinions uninterrupted. Choice (A) is incorrect because calling on these students only once during the class period will most likely frustrate them and create problems. Answer (C) is incorrect because placing overly talkative students in a group by themselves does not teach them to listen to other student's opinions. (D) is incorrect because although overly talkative students usually need attention, they must be helped to recognize that other student's also have opinions, even though they may not be assertive in voicing them.

123. **(B)**   The correct response is (B). Grouping patterns affect a student's perceptions of self-esteem and competence. Maintaining the same groups through-

out the year encourages students in the average group to view themselves as average, students in the above-average group to view themselves as above average. Choice (A) is incorrect because most students do not like unpredictable teacher behavior. Response (C) is incorrect because changes in the classroom often create an atmosphere of mistrust and uneasiness, and do not cause students to be more alert. Answer (D) is incorrect because although the explanation is correct, it is incomplete when compared to (B).

124. **(A)** The correct response is (A). The most important predictor variable of reading success is whether or not a child's parents immerse her in print (read to her) before she starts school. An enriched daycare environment can be beneficial to a child's development (B), especially if shared reading and story activities are stressed. While research suggests that excessive television watching by young students may have deleterious effects, the amount of time spent watching television is not the important predictor of reading success that being read to by a parent is (C). Being raised by a grandparent is not a predictor of poor reading ability (D).

125. **(B)** The correct response is (B). Children operating at the concrete operating stage greatly benefit from direct observation. Infants operate at the sensorimotor stage; observing a demonstration of how sound waves work would be of no use to infants (A). While students operating at the formal operational level would greatly benefit from direct observation of sound waves in addition to complex theoretical descriptions, the direct observation is absolutely essential to the understanding of the concrete thinker (C). There is no Piagetial interpersonal concordance stage. Interpersonal concordance is a stage of moral development described by Lawrence Kohlberg.

126. **(B)** Deafness is the only one that would cause a child to be classified as handicapped. Pregnancy (A) is not a permanent condition, and obesity (C) and acne (D) are not debilitating enough to be considered handicaps.

127. **(B)** Vitamin C is water soluble—the remaing choices are fat soluble.

128. **(C)** Complex carbohydrates are the most efficient energy source for the body. While other choices provide some energy, they are not nearly as efficient as complex carbohydrates.

129. **(A)** Cholesterol is produced naturally in the liver. The pancreas (B) produces insulin and digestive enzymes, the stomach (C) is the organ of digestion, and the pituitary gland (D) produces a variety of hormones.

130. **(C)** A broken bone with a corresponding break in the skin is called a compound fracture. A comminuted bone (A) has been shattered. A simple frac-

ture (B) does not break the skin. A complex fracture (D) concerns a bone with more than one break.

131. **(B)**   Permanent dietary changes and exercise are the only way to produce lasting weight loss. Commercial diets (A) do not always include a program of exercise, but rather concentrate on diet. Radically reducing calorie intake (C) will cause the body to go into starvation mode and slow down digestion to conserve energy. Two hours of daily exercise is not very practical and without controlling calorie intake, it would be ineffective.

132. **(D)**   Leaping is the only locomotive skill listed. Bouncing (A), catching (B), and throwing (C), are manipulative movements.

133. **(A)**   Isotonic exercises cause the muscles to contract. Isometric (B) exercises do not affect a change in muscle length. Static (C) is not a type of exercise, and an exercise does not have to change muscle length to be considered aerobic (D).

134. **(C)**   (A), (B), and (D) are principles of aerobic conditioning. (C) is not.

Content Area Exercises
Scoring Guide

---

3 • The examinee demonstrates a comprehensive understanding of the material presented.

   • The examinee has responded effectively to every part of the question.

   • The examinee has provided well supported explanations.

   • The examinee has demonstrated a strong knowledge of the subject matter, including relevant theories, concepts, and procedures.

---

2 • The examinee demonstrates a basic understanding of the material presented.

   • The examinee has responded effectively to most parts of the question.

   • The examinee has provided explanations.

   • The examinee has demonstrated an adequate knowledge of the subject matter, including relevant theories, concepts, and procedures.

---

1 • The examinee demonstrates some misunderstanding of the material presented.

   • The examinee fails to respond effectively to every part of the question.

   • The examinee has provided only weak explanations.

   • The examinee has demonstrated insufficient knowledge of the subject matter, including relevant theories, concepts, and procedures.

---

0 • The examinee has either not responded, responded off-topic, has responded completely incorrectly, or simply rephrased the question.

CONTENT AREA EXERCISES I

I. Literature and Language Studies

1. Response that received as score of 3:

With all due respect to Mr. Wittgenstein, his statement is purely theoretical and has little to do with the way people actually think. No one is a stranger to having some feeling, some emotion, some sensation that they are simply unable to describe. All the poets, painters, and sculptors throughout the ages have been unable to adequately describe the feeling of being in love. If someone has never experienced it, it is impossible to convey. By Mr. Wittgenstein's argument then, love is beyond the limits of his world. As much as language can accomplish, it is no substitute for experience.

Response that received a score of 1:

I agree with that statement because you can really only think in the context of the language you have. If you don't have words for things, and you can't describe them to somebody else, then how can you prove to your audience that this thing really exists. For example, if someone doesn't know nothing about sports, and you try to explain it to them, if they don't have the vocabulary for things like a touchdown, or a home run, how can you make them understand? In order to understand something, you have to understand its language.

2. Response that received a score of 3:

Adults acquire language in very much the same way that children do. Both adults and children learn new words by observing the context in which they are used. Children are bombarded with language even before they are born, and began to observe and imitate what they hear. As they get older, they begin to develop the skills that we recognize as facility with language. They become able to relate words and objects to one another, they become able to refer to objects in their absence, etc. Once these skills are developed, language acquisition occurs by relating new information to old information, by observing the use of new language, and people retain this ability throughout their lives. Adults learn new language through exposure to new fields that often have a language of their own, such as philosophy or new technology.

Response that received a score of 1:

Children are born with an incredible ability to acquire language very quickly. As a person ages, this ability decreases, until eventually, it becomes very difficult, even impossible to learn new things. Examples of this can be found in how hard it is for adults to do simple tasks that children find so easy, like programming a VCR, or opening a child-proof bottle. Adults lose their ability to learn with age, and that includes learning new words.

3. Response that received a score of 3:

A villanelle is one of the most restrictive modes of closed form poetry. A well written villanelle is so structured that the form becomes part of the context of the meaning. A great deal of restraint or control is obvious in this form, and depending upon the meaning, this can either underscore it, or give it an ironic twist. For example, a poem about the necessity for morality, law, and order in a disordered society would be emphasized by this form, showing the beauty that order has the potential to create. A poem about the glory of anarchy would be ironic in this highly ordered form, and might be better suited for free verse.

Response that receive a score of 1:

An elegy is a sad poem, often written about the death of some important person. Elegys are usually very long, and this enhances its meaning. As you read it, you get sadder and sadder, as the poem emphasizes the good things about a person's life. By the end, the person that the elegy is written for becomes very present in your mind, and you miss them even more. An elegy is the saddest kind of poem.

4. Response that received a score of 3:

Romanticism is the idea that the world is a perfect place, or if not perfect, at least perfectible by human reason reason and emotion. Realism is a view of the world based primarily upon empirical observation, stating that the world contains both good and evil, more or less in balance. Naturalism states that the world is fundamentally imperfect, and that quite often evil triumphs over good. The naturalist does not always see the balance that the realist proclaims, and rarely if ever sees the perfect state of existence that the romantic sees as an attainable goal.

Response that received a score of 1:

The romantic person believes that love can conquer all. He is very idealistic and unrealistic. The realist is very cinical, and believes that the world is full of just as much evil as good, if not more. The naturalist is somewhere in between, believing that the world is always in some kind of natural balance.

II. Mathematics

5. Response that received a score of 3:

The is true is because of polynomial factors. It can be shown in the equation:

$$n^2 - 1 = (n+1)(n-1)$$

$n+1$ and $n-1$ are factor of the polynomial n^2-1. The factors of every polynomial equal that polynomial if multiplied together.

Response that received a score of 1:
When multiplied together, the product of $(n+1)$ and $(n-1)$ equals $n^2 - 1$. This is due to polynomials and factoring.

6. **Response that received a score of 3:**
First, I will prove that $x^n = a$ is sometimes true. If $x>0$ and $n>0$ than $x^n = a$ is true. However, if $x/2$ is a natural number and $a<0$, then $x^n = a$ is false.

Response that received a score of 1:
If x is an even number and $a<0$, then $x^n = a$ is false.

7. **Response that received score of 3:**
The product of two irrational numbers is not limited to the set of irrational numbers. A irrational number is a nonterminating, nonrepeating decimal number. The product of two irrational numbers can be a rational number. The best way to illustrate this is by an example,

$$\sqrt{2} \times \sqrt{2} = 2$$

Therefore, the product of 2 irrational numbers can be a rational number.

Response that received a score of 1:
The product of two irrational numbers can be a rational number. This is because products of any real number are not limited to the set of irrational numbers.

8. **Response that received a score of 3:**
The builder measured each angle to be 60 degrees. Since the roof forms an isosceles triangle, he knows that each side of the roof must be equivalent.

Response that received a score of 1:
There is not enough information to answer this question. The builder could only know if the sides are equal if angles A, B, and C are 60 degrees.

III. Visual and Performing Arts

9. **Response that received a score of 3:**
There are several questions that one may ask in order to make an aesthetic judgement on a work of art. First, one may inquire as to the purpose of a piece of art, and then decide whether or not that purpose has been achieved. For example,

Picasso's *Guernica* is supposed to demonstrate the horror of war, and the terrified expressions of the figures clearly illustrate this.

Another means of aesthetic evaluation is concerned with the voice of the artist. Is is unique, or could this easily be the work of another artist? The cubist influence is very clear in this painting, so Picasso's voice certainly comes through.

Response that received a score of 1:

When you look at a piece of art, the most important question you can ask is whether or not it has accomplished what it set out to do. For example, a horror movie, if it scares you, it has succeeded in its purpose. Now you may say that this isn't art, but it has succeeded in its purpose. Another way to tell if something is good art is to see how well the artist used what was available to him. For example, if an artist paints a picture, has he used the entire canvas, or are parts of it blank? Or have they used many colors, or is the painting mostly in one or two colors?

10.   Sample response that received a score of 3:

Paleolithic art reflects the same impulses that are alive in the art world today. The conscious manipulation of materials based upon some aesthetic criteria is the one constant in the art world. The motivations for this creativity might be different, but the art is the same. Perhaps they were trying to manipulate and influence the world around them. Perhaps these Venuses had some religious significance, or maybe they were just pretty to look at, but in any case, the result is the same. Art is created when people take one thing, like a rock, or some paint, and transform it into something completely different based upon their own unique creativity.

Sample response that received a score of 1:

This art is the same as the art of today because it has no practical use. Paleolithic peoples were the first to create objects that they didn't really need, just liked to have around. Just like today, art might be nice to look at, but it doesn't do anything. Upon until the paleolithic times, people only made things that they actually needed, like weapons or axes. In paleolithic times, people actually started being creative instead of just making things that they needed to stay alive.

IV. Human Development

11.   Response that receive a score of 3:

The second level of need in Maslowe's hierarchy concerns an individual's need to feel safe. With violence in our schools becoming an increasing problem, a student's need to feel safe is more important than ever. Maslowe's hierarchy states that until these basic needs are met, it is impossible for a student to engage in real, productive learning. Many schools have taken steps to make students feel safer such as the installation of metal detectors. There is an argument to be made, however, that metal detectors make students feel less safe, both as a reminder of the presence of weapons in the school, and also the feeling that the school's administration is an oppressive omnipresent authority figure.

Response that received a score of 1:
The first level of Maslow's hierarchy has to do with the very basic needs of life. The need not to be hungry or thirsty, and to be warm enough in winter and cool enough in summer. I know that my elementary school did not satisfy any of these needs. It was always either too hot or too cold, and the food was so bad that students often went hungry rather than eat it. Then they were surprised when we didn't do well on tests. If teachers hope that their students will perform well in school, they should press the administration to get better food, as well as better heaters and air conditioners.

12. **Response that a score of 3:**
Ethnocentrism in education refers to the unequal attention applied to a given ethnic background at the expense of all other ethnic backgrounds. Ethnocentrim is most frequently discussed in the context of Eurocentrism, the view that holds the accomplishments of European civilization as being more important than all others. It also revolves around judging all other cultures on the basis of European ideals such as imperialism or superiority in warfare. The only solution to the problem of Eurocentrism is the equal treatment of all cultures in the classroom, and the acknowledgment that the dominant culture is only one in a world of many.

Response that received a score of 1:
Ethnocentrism is a politically correct term that suggests that students should be taught about all cultures, not just the one that they are a part of. It stresses the fact that students should know about cultures other than Europe or the United States, like China or Africa. Ethnocentrism means that all cultures are valued equally in the classroom, and no one culture is said to be any more important than any other.

V. Physical Education

13. **Response that received a score of 3:**
The skills involved in sports and games can carry over to academics in many ways. For example, a game that has a somewhat complicated scoring process, such as bowling, can be used to practice math skills. In addition, the discipline involved in weight training, for example, can carry over into academic areas.

Response that received a score of 1:

Sports can teach leadership skills and teach students how to work as part of a team. Another way that sports help in academic skills is comes from the very technical aspects of sports. Students can be encouraged to memorize statistics like batting averages to improve study skills.

14. Responses that received a score of 3:

Students face threats to their health and well being every day, and one of the best ways that phys ed can combat their effects is to instill the value of a healthy life. For example, students that are encouraged to gain self-esteem through their physical fitness will be less likely to compromise that fitness by smoking or using drugs.

Another method is to make use of the more relaxed environment present in many physical education classes for a frank discussion about safer sex practices—what they are and why they are important.

Response that received a score of 1:

Phys ed can be used to reduce risks by educating students about what the risks are and how to avoid them. For example, a student who smokes can be asked to perform several aerobic exercises and when they can't do anymore, a student who doesn't smoke can be asked to do the same thing. When the non-smoking student performs better, the other student can see the risk of smoking first hand. Another way physical education can be used is to teach stress relieving activities like yoga.

CONTENT AREA EXERCISE II

I. History and Social Sciences

(handwritten: #1 priority · State · Ruler)

1. Response that received a score of 3:

Italian fascism was based on the belief that the future of the state and Mussolini were the most important factors in an Italian's life. Mussolini also extolled the necessity of Italy expanding and conquering, or the necessity of war, as a means to make Italy more powerful. Propaganda was a major tenet of Italian fascism, as it constantly portrayed enemies of fascism in grotesque ways and reminded Italian people of their duties as Italians to their state and leader. The phrase, "Believe! Obey! Fight!" shows the connection between fascism's warlike state and propaganda. The fascists also believed that Italy had to be a homogenous society, people who did not fit in were in danger of losing their lives.

(handwritten margin: propaganda, grotesque, depicting propaganda of enemies)

Response that received a score of 1:

(handwritten: homogenous or PEITH!)

Italian fascists believed that Jews, foreigners, mentally handicapped, and other "outcasts" were dangerous to Italian society. Mussolini, Italian fascists' leader, also believed that Italy had to attack other countries in order to enhance Italy's status in the world.

2. Response that received a score of 3:

(handwritten: indicative of Cold War)

Winston Churchill made the Iron Curtain speech soon after the Second World War. In this speech Churchill clearly defined the Cold War. In the speech, given at a college in the United States, Churchill defines the two sides of the Cold War. On one side, the Soviet communists lie, and all of the territory that Churchill believes they control, including Eastern Europe. On the other side lies the Western democracies, including the Americans that believe in capitalism, democracy, and all of the other countries that believe in the same ideology.

(handwritten margin: 2 sides, evil / angel, USSR / US., comm unism / Democracy, liars ↓ honest)

Response that received a score of 1:

The speech is called the "Iron Curtain speech". It tells of the world being divided between the communists and the non-communist.

3. Response that received a score of 3:

(handwritten: Romanovs lead for 300 yrs. ↓)

During World War I, when Tsar Nicholas II was leader of Russia, economic conditions in the country became very severe. Many strikes and street demonstrations occurred, and these became a revolution. The Romanov dynasty, after 300 years of rule, came to an end. A Provisional Government ruled the country while two groups, the anti-communists (the Whites) and the communists (the Reds or Bolsheviks), fought over control of the country. In 1918 a Bolshevik group killed the Tsar and his family. By 1920, with the help of the peasant class, Lenin and the Communist party took control over the country.

(handwritten: Russian revolution)

(handwritten: REDS = BOLSHEVIKS = COMMUNISTS vs WHITES = NON COMMUNISTS (ANTI))

Response that received a score of 1:

The communists started a revolution in Russia. After a lot of fighting, the Tsar was murdered and Lenin became ruler of Russia.

4.   **Response that received a score of 3:** *educational opportunities* *FOUGHT FOR*

W.E.B. Du Bois, from the 1890's, until long after the First World war, *because* argued against industrial education for all blacks, and instead, argued that some *TRAP* black students should attend a liberal arts college. Most "Progressives" were *FOR* arguing for industrial education only, including the famous black leader Booker *BLACK* T. Washington. One of the major tenets of Du Bois's argument is that not all black students are capable of undertaking a liberal arts education, just like not all whites are capable of undertaking one. In order for black industrial schools like Tuskegee to exist, black teachers are needed, in order for the black community to be self-sufficient. Black industrial schools need black teachers that are well educated, and this, for Du Bois, means a liberal arts education. Du Bois calls this elite group of educated blacks the "talented tenth". → *LiBeRal aRTS eDuCATeD*

Response that received a score of 1:

Du Bois, in his book, advocates the "talented tenth". This tenth of the black population would be very well educated, and most people were against this. Most people from this period did not think that blacks should be educated.

II. Science

5.   **Response that received a score of 3:**

This diagram illustrates how a nation's Gross National Product (GNP) correlates to its energy consumption. I would hypothesize that these two characteristics are dependent on each other. Thus, the GNP will increase in parallel to the energy consumption. Hence, one could assume that a nation with a high energy consumption would also have a high GNP. The converse of this statement is also true; a nation with a low energy consumption would have a low GNP. One possible explanation of this phenomena is that industry needs energy to produce goods. This explains why the more industry produces (GNP) the higher the energy consumption would be.

Response that received a score of 1:

This diagram represents the capitalistic tendency of democratic nations. The nations with high Gross National Products consume higher energy because of the increased wealth in those nations.

6.   **Response that received a score of 3:**

I will hypothesize that these atoms (He, H, and O) are found at this altitude instead of molecules found closer to the surface because of the atmospheric density. Heavier elements descend to the surface and lighter elements ascend to the upper atmosphere.

Response that received a score of 1:
    In the atmosphere the barometric pressure is too low to support heavier elements and molecules. Therefore, only lighter substances can be found.

7.   **Response that received a score of 3:**
    A hole could be dug in the ground. The hole would then have to be filled with the seawater. Next, the glass sheet would be placed from the edge of the hole to water's surface, forming an angle. The container would be placed in the small gap between the water and the glass sheet. When solar energy heated the apparatus, the seawater would evaporate, leaving salt and other particles behind. The water would then condense of the angled glass. The droplets would accumulate on the glass until gravity pulled the droplets toward the container. The pure water would now accumulate in the container.

Response that received a score of 1:
    A hole could be dug in the sand. The container could be used to carry seawater to the hole. Once the hole had a substantial amount of seawater in it, the glass sheet would cover the hole. Once the sun heated the glass, the seawater would evaporate. It is unknown how the evaporated water could be condensed and used as pure water.

8.   **Response that received a score of 3:**
    Wind speed and direction is measured at each anemometer. These readings are constantly compared with one another. If one anemometer gives a reading that is inconsistent with the others, it would be reasonable to assume that there is a wind shear in that area.

Response that received a score of 1:
    An anemometer is used to measure wind speed and direction. If the anemometer show very high wind speed blowing in varying directions, then there might be a wind shear.

MSAT

Multiple Subjects Assessment for Teachers

ANSWER
SHEETS

MSAT – Test 1 Answer Sheet

1. Ⓐ Ⓑ Ⓒ Ⓓ
2. Ⓐ Ⓑ Ⓒ Ⓓ
3. Ⓐ Ⓑ Ⓒ Ⓓ
4. Ⓐ Ⓑ Ⓒ Ⓓ
5. Ⓐ Ⓑ Ⓒ Ⓓ
6. Ⓐ Ⓑ Ⓒ Ⓓ
7. Ⓐ Ⓑ Ⓒ Ⓓ
8. Ⓐ Ⓑ Ⓒ Ⓓ
9. Ⓐ Ⓑ Ⓒ Ⓓ
10. Ⓐ Ⓑ Ⓒ Ⓓ
11. Ⓐ Ⓑ Ⓒ Ⓓ
12. Ⓐ Ⓑ Ⓒ Ⓓ
13. Ⓐ Ⓑ Ⓒ Ⓓ
14. Ⓐ Ⓑ Ⓒ Ⓓ
15. Ⓐ Ⓑ Ⓒ Ⓓ
16. Ⓐ Ⓑ Ⓒ Ⓓ
17. Ⓐ Ⓑ Ⓒ Ⓓ
18. Ⓐ Ⓑ Ⓒ Ⓓ
19. Ⓐ Ⓑ Ⓒ Ⓓ
20. Ⓐ Ⓑ Ⓒ Ⓓ
21. Ⓐ Ⓑ Ⓒ Ⓓ
22. Ⓐ Ⓑ Ⓒ Ⓓ
23. Ⓐ Ⓑ Ⓒ Ⓓ
24. Ⓐ Ⓑ Ⓒ Ⓓ
25. Ⓐ Ⓑ Ⓒ Ⓓ
26. Ⓐ Ⓑ Ⓒ Ⓓ
27. Ⓐ Ⓑ Ⓒ Ⓓ
28. Ⓐ Ⓑ Ⓒ Ⓓ
29. Ⓐ Ⓑ Ⓒ Ⓓ
30. Ⓐ Ⓑ Ⓒ Ⓓ
31. Ⓐ Ⓑ Ⓒ Ⓓ
32. Ⓐ Ⓑ Ⓒ Ⓓ
33. Ⓐ Ⓑ Ⓒ Ⓓ
34. Ⓐ Ⓑ Ⓒ Ⓓ

35. Ⓐ Ⓑ Ⓒ Ⓓ
36. Ⓐ Ⓑ Ⓒ Ⓓ
37. Ⓐ Ⓑ Ⓒ Ⓓ
38. Ⓐ Ⓑ Ⓒ Ⓓ
39. Ⓐ Ⓑ Ⓒ Ⓓ
40. Ⓐ Ⓑ Ⓒ Ⓓ
41. Ⓐ Ⓑ Ⓒ Ⓓ
42. Ⓐ Ⓑ Ⓒ Ⓓ
43. Ⓐ Ⓑ Ⓒ Ⓓ
44. Ⓐ Ⓑ Ⓒ Ⓓ
45. Ⓐ Ⓑ Ⓒ Ⓓ
46. Ⓐ Ⓑ Ⓒ Ⓓ
47. Ⓐ Ⓑ Ⓒ Ⓓ
48. Ⓐ Ⓑ Ⓒ Ⓓ
49. Ⓐ Ⓑ Ⓒ Ⓓ
50. Ⓐ Ⓑ Ⓒ Ⓓ
51. Ⓐ Ⓑ Ⓒ Ⓓ
52. Ⓐ Ⓑ Ⓒ Ⓓ
53. Ⓐ Ⓑ Ⓒ Ⓓ
54. Ⓐ Ⓑ Ⓒ Ⓓ
55. Ⓐ Ⓑ Ⓒ Ⓓ
56. Ⓐ Ⓑ Ⓒ Ⓓ
57. Ⓐ Ⓑ Ⓒ Ⓓ
58. Ⓐ Ⓑ Ⓒ Ⓓ
59. Ⓐ Ⓑ Ⓒ Ⓓ
60. Ⓐ Ⓑ Ⓒ Ⓓ
61. Ⓐ Ⓑ Ⓒ Ⓓ
62. Ⓐ Ⓑ Ⓒ Ⓓ
63. Ⓐ Ⓑ Ⓒ Ⓓ
64. Ⓐ Ⓑ Ⓒ Ⓓ
65. Ⓐ Ⓑ Ⓒ Ⓓ
66. Ⓐ Ⓑ Ⓒ Ⓓ
67. Ⓐ Ⓑ Ⓒ Ⓓ
68. Ⓐ Ⓑ Ⓒ Ⓓ

69. Ⓐ Ⓑ Ⓒ Ⓓ
70. Ⓐ Ⓑ Ⓒ Ⓓ
71. Ⓐ Ⓑ Ⓒ Ⓓ
72. Ⓐ Ⓑ Ⓒ Ⓓ
73. Ⓐ Ⓑ Ⓒ Ⓓ
74. Ⓐ Ⓑ Ⓒ Ⓓ
75. Ⓐ Ⓑ Ⓒ Ⓓ
76. Ⓐ Ⓑ Ⓒ Ⓓ
77. Ⓐ Ⓑ Ⓒ Ⓓ
78. Ⓐ Ⓑ Ⓒ Ⓓ
79. Ⓐ Ⓑ Ⓒ Ⓓ
80. Ⓐ Ⓑ Ⓒ Ⓓ
81. Ⓐ Ⓑ Ⓒ Ⓓ
82. Ⓐ Ⓑ Ⓒ Ⓓ
83. Ⓐ Ⓑ Ⓒ Ⓓ
84. Ⓐ Ⓑ Ⓒ Ⓓ
85. Ⓐ Ⓑ Ⓒ Ⓓ
86. Ⓐ Ⓑ Ⓒ Ⓓ
87. Ⓐ Ⓑ Ⓒ Ⓓ
88. Ⓐ Ⓑ Ⓒ Ⓓ
89. Ⓐ Ⓑ Ⓒ Ⓓ
90. Ⓐ Ⓑ Ⓒ Ⓓ
91. Ⓐ Ⓑ Ⓒ Ⓓ
92. Ⓐ Ⓑ Ⓒ Ⓓ
93. Ⓐ Ⓑ Ⓒ Ⓓ
94. Ⓐ Ⓑ Ⓒ Ⓓ
95. Ⓐ Ⓑ Ⓒ Ⓓ
96. Ⓐ Ⓑ Ⓒ Ⓓ
97. Ⓐ Ⓑ Ⓒ Ⓓ
98. Ⓐ Ⓑ Ⓒ Ⓓ
99. Ⓐ Ⓑ Ⓒ Ⓓ
100. Ⓐ Ⓑ Ⓒ Ⓓ
101. Ⓐ Ⓑ Ⓒ Ⓓ
102. Ⓐ Ⓑ Ⓒ Ⓓ

103. Ⓐ Ⓑ Ⓒ Ⓓ
104. Ⓐ Ⓑ Ⓒ Ⓓ
105. Ⓐ Ⓑ Ⓒ Ⓓ
106. Ⓐ Ⓑ Ⓒ Ⓓ
107. Ⓐ Ⓑ Ⓒ Ⓓ
108. Ⓐ Ⓑ Ⓒ Ⓓ
109. Ⓐ Ⓑ Ⓒ Ⓓ
110. Ⓐ Ⓑ Ⓒ Ⓓ
111. Ⓐ Ⓑ Ⓒ Ⓓ
112. Ⓐ Ⓑ Ⓒ Ⓓ
113. Ⓐ Ⓑ Ⓒ Ⓓ
114. Ⓐ Ⓑ Ⓒ Ⓓ
115. Ⓐ Ⓑ Ⓒ Ⓓ
116. Ⓐ Ⓑ Ⓒ Ⓓ
117. Ⓐ Ⓑ Ⓒ Ⓓ
118. Ⓐ Ⓑ Ⓒ Ⓓ
119. Ⓐ Ⓑ Ⓒ Ⓓ
120. Ⓐ Ⓑ Ⓒ Ⓓ
121. Ⓐ Ⓑ Ⓒ Ⓓ
122. Ⓐ Ⓑ Ⓒ Ⓓ
123. Ⓐ Ⓑ Ⓒ Ⓓ
124. Ⓐ Ⓑ Ⓒ Ⓓ
125. Ⓐ Ⓑ Ⓒ Ⓓ
126. Ⓐ Ⓑ Ⓒ Ⓓ
127. Ⓐ Ⓑ Ⓒ Ⓓ
128. Ⓐ Ⓑ Ⓒ Ⓓ
129. Ⓐ Ⓑ Ⓒ Ⓓ
130. Ⓐ Ⓑ Ⓒ Ⓓ
131. Ⓐ Ⓑ Ⓒ Ⓓ
132. Ⓐ Ⓑ Ⓒ Ⓓ
133. Ⓐ Ⓑ Ⓒ Ⓓ
134. Ⓐ Ⓑ Ⓒ Ⓓ

MSAT – Test 2 Answer Sheet

1. Ⓐ Ⓑ Ⓒ Ⓓ	35. Ⓐ Ⓑ Ⓒ Ⓓ	69. Ⓐ Ⓑ Ⓒ Ⓓ	103. Ⓐ Ⓑ Ⓒ Ⓓ
2. Ⓐ Ⓑ Ⓒ Ⓓ	36. Ⓐ Ⓑ Ⓒ Ⓓ	70. Ⓐ Ⓑ Ⓒ Ⓓ	104. Ⓐ Ⓑ Ⓒ Ⓓ
3. Ⓐ Ⓑ Ⓒ Ⓓ	37. Ⓐ Ⓑ Ⓒ Ⓓ	71. Ⓐ Ⓑ Ⓒ Ⓓ	105. Ⓐ Ⓑ Ⓒ Ⓓ
4. Ⓐ Ⓑ Ⓒ Ⓓ	38. Ⓐ Ⓑ Ⓒ Ⓓ	72. Ⓐ Ⓑ Ⓒ Ⓓ	106. Ⓐ Ⓑ Ⓒ Ⓓ
5. Ⓐ Ⓑ Ⓒ Ⓓ	39. Ⓐ Ⓑ Ⓒ Ⓓ	73. Ⓐ Ⓑ Ⓒ Ⓓ	107. Ⓐ Ⓑ Ⓒ Ⓓ
6. Ⓐ Ⓑ Ⓒ Ⓓ	40. Ⓐ Ⓑ Ⓒ Ⓓ	74. Ⓐ Ⓑ Ⓒ Ⓓ	108. Ⓐ Ⓑ Ⓒ Ⓓ
7. Ⓐ Ⓑ Ⓒ Ⓓ	41. Ⓐ Ⓑ Ⓒ Ⓓ	75. Ⓐ Ⓑ Ⓒ Ⓓ	109. Ⓐ Ⓑ Ⓒ Ⓓ
8. Ⓐ Ⓑ Ⓒ Ⓓ	42. Ⓐ Ⓑ Ⓒ Ⓓ	76. Ⓐ Ⓑ Ⓒ Ⓓ	110. Ⓐ Ⓑ Ⓒ Ⓓ
9. Ⓐ Ⓑ Ⓒ Ⓓ	43. Ⓐ Ⓑ Ⓒ Ⓓ	77. Ⓐ Ⓑ Ⓒ Ⓓ	111. Ⓐ Ⓑ Ⓒ Ⓓ
10. Ⓐ Ⓑ Ⓒ Ⓓ	44. Ⓐ Ⓑ Ⓒ Ⓓ	78. Ⓐ Ⓑ Ⓒ Ⓓ	112. Ⓐ Ⓑ Ⓒ Ⓓ
11. Ⓐ Ⓑ Ⓒ Ⓓ	45. Ⓐ Ⓑ Ⓒ Ⓓ	79. Ⓐ Ⓑ Ⓒ Ⓓ	113. Ⓐ Ⓑ Ⓒ Ⓓ
12. Ⓐ Ⓑ Ⓒ Ⓓ	46. Ⓐ Ⓑ Ⓒ Ⓓ	80. Ⓐ Ⓑ Ⓒ Ⓓ	114. Ⓐ Ⓑ Ⓒ Ⓓ
13. Ⓐ Ⓑ Ⓒ Ⓓ	47. Ⓐ Ⓑ Ⓒ Ⓓ	81. Ⓐ Ⓑ Ⓒ Ⓓ	115. Ⓐ Ⓑ Ⓒ Ⓓ
14. Ⓐ Ⓑ Ⓒ Ⓓ	48. Ⓐ Ⓑ Ⓒ Ⓓ	82. Ⓐ Ⓑ Ⓒ Ⓓ	116. Ⓐ Ⓑ Ⓒ Ⓓ
15. Ⓐ Ⓑ Ⓒ Ⓓ	49. Ⓐ Ⓑ Ⓒ Ⓓ	83. Ⓐ Ⓑ Ⓒ Ⓓ	117. Ⓐ Ⓑ Ⓒ Ⓓ
16. Ⓐ Ⓑ Ⓒ Ⓓ	50. Ⓐ Ⓑ Ⓒ Ⓓ	84. Ⓐ Ⓑ Ⓒ Ⓓ	118. Ⓐ Ⓑ Ⓒ Ⓓ
17. Ⓐ Ⓑ Ⓒ Ⓓ	51. Ⓐ Ⓑ Ⓒ Ⓓ	85. Ⓐ Ⓑ Ⓒ Ⓓ	119. Ⓐ Ⓑ Ⓒ Ⓓ
18. Ⓐ Ⓑ Ⓒ Ⓓ	52. Ⓐ Ⓑ Ⓒ Ⓓ	86. Ⓐ Ⓑ Ⓒ Ⓓ	120. Ⓐ Ⓑ Ⓒ Ⓓ
19. Ⓐ Ⓑ Ⓒ Ⓓ	53. Ⓐ Ⓑ Ⓒ Ⓓ	87. Ⓐ Ⓑ Ⓒ Ⓓ	121. Ⓐ Ⓑ Ⓒ Ⓓ
20. Ⓐ Ⓑ Ⓒ Ⓓ	54. Ⓐ Ⓑ Ⓒ Ⓓ	88. Ⓐ Ⓑ Ⓒ Ⓓ	122. Ⓐ Ⓑ Ⓒ Ⓓ
21. Ⓐ Ⓑ Ⓒ Ⓓ	55. Ⓐ Ⓑ Ⓒ Ⓓ	89. Ⓐ Ⓑ Ⓒ Ⓓ	123. Ⓐ Ⓑ Ⓒ Ⓓ
22. Ⓐ Ⓑ Ⓒ Ⓓ	56. Ⓐ Ⓑ Ⓒ Ⓓ	90. Ⓐ Ⓑ Ⓒ Ⓓ	124. Ⓐ Ⓑ Ⓒ Ⓓ
23. Ⓐ Ⓑ Ⓒ Ⓓ	57. Ⓐ Ⓑ Ⓒ Ⓓ	91. Ⓐ Ⓑ Ⓒ Ⓓ	125. Ⓐ Ⓑ Ⓒ Ⓓ
24. Ⓐ Ⓑ Ⓒ Ⓓ	58. Ⓐ Ⓑ Ⓒ Ⓓ	92. Ⓐ Ⓑ Ⓒ Ⓓ	126. Ⓐ Ⓑ Ⓒ Ⓓ
25. Ⓐ Ⓑ Ⓒ Ⓓ	59. Ⓐ Ⓑ Ⓒ Ⓓ	93. Ⓐ Ⓑ Ⓒ Ⓓ	127. Ⓐ Ⓑ Ⓒ Ⓓ
26. Ⓐ Ⓑ Ⓒ Ⓓ	60. Ⓐ Ⓑ Ⓒ Ⓓ	94. Ⓐ Ⓑ Ⓒ Ⓓ	128. Ⓐ Ⓑ Ⓒ Ⓓ
27. Ⓐ Ⓑ Ⓒ Ⓓ	61. Ⓐ Ⓑ Ⓒ Ⓓ	95. Ⓐ Ⓑ Ⓒ Ⓓ	129. Ⓐ Ⓑ Ⓒ Ⓓ
28. Ⓐ Ⓑ Ⓒ Ⓓ	62. Ⓐ Ⓑ Ⓒ Ⓓ	96. Ⓐ Ⓑ Ⓒ Ⓓ	130. Ⓐ Ⓑ Ⓒ Ⓓ
29. Ⓐ Ⓑ Ⓒ Ⓓ	63. Ⓐ Ⓑ Ⓒ Ⓓ	97. Ⓐ Ⓑ Ⓒ Ⓓ	131. Ⓐ Ⓑ Ⓒ Ⓓ
30. Ⓐ Ⓑ Ⓒ Ⓓ	64. Ⓐ Ⓑ Ⓒ Ⓓ	98. Ⓐ Ⓑ Ⓒ Ⓓ	132. Ⓐ Ⓑ Ⓒ Ⓓ
31. Ⓐ Ⓑ Ⓒ Ⓓ	65. Ⓐ Ⓑ Ⓒ Ⓓ	99. Ⓐ Ⓑ Ⓒ Ⓓ	133. Ⓐ Ⓑ Ⓒ Ⓓ
32. Ⓐ Ⓑ Ⓒ Ⓓ	66. Ⓐ Ⓑ Ⓒ Ⓓ	100. Ⓐ Ⓑ Ⓒ Ⓓ	134. Ⓐ Ⓑ Ⓒ Ⓓ
33. Ⓐ Ⓑ Ⓒ Ⓓ	67. Ⓐ Ⓑ Ⓒ Ⓓ	101. Ⓐ Ⓑ Ⓒ Ⓓ	
34. Ⓐ Ⓑ Ⓒ Ⓓ	68. Ⓐ Ⓑ Ⓒ Ⓓ	102. Ⓐ Ⓑ Ⓒ Ⓓ	

MSAT – Additional Answer Sheet

1. Ⓐ Ⓑ Ⓒ Ⓓ	35. Ⓐ Ⓑ Ⓒ Ⓓ	69. Ⓐ Ⓑ Ⓒ Ⓓ	103. Ⓐ Ⓑ Ⓒ Ⓓ
2. Ⓐ Ⓑ Ⓒ Ⓓ	36. Ⓐ Ⓑ Ⓒ Ⓓ	70. Ⓐ Ⓑ Ⓒ Ⓓ	104. Ⓐ Ⓑ Ⓒ Ⓓ
3. Ⓐ Ⓑ Ⓒ Ⓓ	37. Ⓐ Ⓑ Ⓒ Ⓓ	71. Ⓐ Ⓑ Ⓒ Ⓓ	105. Ⓐ Ⓑ Ⓒ Ⓓ
4. Ⓐ Ⓑ Ⓒ Ⓓ	38. Ⓐ Ⓑ Ⓒ Ⓓ	72. Ⓐ Ⓑ Ⓒ Ⓓ	106. Ⓐ Ⓑ Ⓒ Ⓓ
5. Ⓐ Ⓑ Ⓒ Ⓓ	39. Ⓐ Ⓑ Ⓒ Ⓓ	73. Ⓐ Ⓑ Ⓒ Ⓓ	107. Ⓐ Ⓑ Ⓒ Ⓓ
6. Ⓐ Ⓑ Ⓒ Ⓓ	40. Ⓐ Ⓑ Ⓒ Ⓓ	74. Ⓐ Ⓑ Ⓒ Ⓓ	108. Ⓐ Ⓑ Ⓒ Ⓓ
7. Ⓐ Ⓑ Ⓒ Ⓓ	41. Ⓐ Ⓑ Ⓒ Ⓓ	75. Ⓐ Ⓑ Ⓒ Ⓓ	109. Ⓐ Ⓑ Ⓒ Ⓓ
8. Ⓐ Ⓑ Ⓒ Ⓓ	42. Ⓐ Ⓑ Ⓒ Ⓓ	76. Ⓐ Ⓑ Ⓒ Ⓓ	110. Ⓐ Ⓑ Ⓒ Ⓓ
9. Ⓐ Ⓑ Ⓒ Ⓓ	43. Ⓐ Ⓑ Ⓒ Ⓓ	77. Ⓐ Ⓑ Ⓒ Ⓓ	111. Ⓐ Ⓑ Ⓒ Ⓓ
10. Ⓐ Ⓑ Ⓒ Ⓓ	44. Ⓐ Ⓑ Ⓒ Ⓓ	78. Ⓐ Ⓑ Ⓒ Ⓓ	112. Ⓐ Ⓑ Ⓒ Ⓓ
11. Ⓐ Ⓑ Ⓒ Ⓓ	45. Ⓐ Ⓑ Ⓒ Ⓓ	79. Ⓐ Ⓑ Ⓒ Ⓓ	113. Ⓐ Ⓑ Ⓒ Ⓓ
12. Ⓐ Ⓑ Ⓒ Ⓓ	46. Ⓐ Ⓑ Ⓒ Ⓓ	80. Ⓐ Ⓑ Ⓒ Ⓓ	114. Ⓐ Ⓑ Ⓒ Ⓓ
13. Ⓐ Ⓑ Ⓒ Ⓓ	47. Ⓐ Ⓑ Ⓒ Ⓓ	81. Ⓐ Ⓑ Ⓒ Ⓓ	115. Ⓐ Ⓑ Ⓒ Ⓓ
14. Ⓐ Ⓑ Ⓒ Ⓓ	48. Ⓐ Ⓑ Ⓒ Ⓓ	82. Ⓐ Ⓑ Ⓒ Ⓓ	116. Ⓐ Ⓑ Ⓒ Ⓓ
15. Ⓐ Ⓑ Ⓒ Ⓓ	49. Ⓐ Ⓑ Ⓒ Ⓓ	83. Ⓐ Ⓑ Ⓒ Ⓓ	117. Ⓐ Ⓑ Ⓒ Ⓓ
16. Ⓐ Ⓑ Ⓒ Ⓓ	50. Ⓐ Ⓑ Ⓒ Ⓓ	84. Ⓐ Ⓑ Ⓒ Ⓓ	118. Ⓐ Ⓑ Ⓒ Ⓓ
17. Ⓐ Ⓑ Ⓒ Ⓓ	51. Ⓐ Ⓑ Ⓒ Ⓓ	85. Ⓐ Ⓑ Ⓒ Ⓓ	119. Ⓐ Ⓑ Ⓒ Ⓓ
18. Ⓐ Ⓑ Ⓒ Ⓓ	52. Ⓐ Ⓑ Ⓒ Ⓓ	86. Ⓐ Ⓑ Ⓒ Ⓓ	120. Ⓐ Ⓑ Ⓒ Ⓓ
19. Ⓐ Ⓑ Ⓒ Ⓓ	53. Ⓐ Ⓑ Ⓒ Ⓓ	87. Ⓐ Ⓑ Ⓒ Ⓓ	121. Ⓐ Ⓑ Ⓒ Ⓓ
20. Ⓐ Ⓑ Ⓒ Ⓓ	54. Ⓐ Ⓑ Ⓒ Ⓓ	88. Ⓐ Ⓑ Ⓒ Ⓓ	122. Ⓐ Ⓑ Ⓒ Ⓓ
21. Ⓐ Ⓑ Ⓒ Ⓓ	55. Ⓐ Ⓑ Ⓒ Ⓓ	89. Ⓐ Ⓑ Ⓒ Ⓓ	123. Ⓐ Ⓑ Ⓒ Ⓓ
22. Ⓐ Ⓑ Ⓒ Ⓓ	56. Ⓐ Ⓑ Ⓒ Ⓓ	90. Ⓐ Ⓑ Ⓒ Ⓓ	124. Ⓐ Ⓑ Ⓒ Ⓓ
23. Ⓐ Ⓑ Ⓒ Ⓓ	57. Ⓐ Ⓑ Ⓒ Ⓓ	91. Ⓐ Ⓑ Ⓒ Ⓓ	125. Ⓐ Ⓑ Ⓒ Ⓓ
24. Ⓐ Ⓑ Ⓒ Ⓓ	58. Ⓐ Ⓑ Ⓒ Ⓓ	92. Ⓐ Ⓑ Ⓒ Ⓓ	126. Ⓐ Ⓑ Ⓒ Ⓓ
25. Ⓐ Ⓑ Ⓒ Ⓓ	59. Ⓐ Ⓑ Ⓒ Ⓓ	93. Ⓐ Ⓑ Ⓒ Ⓓ	127. Ⓐ Ⓑ Ⓒ Ⓓ
26. Ⓐ Ⓑ Ⓒ Ⓓ	60. Ⓐ Ⓑ Ⓒ Ⓓ	94. Ⓐ Ⓑ Ⓒ Ⓓ	128. Ⓐ Ⓑ Ⓒ Ⓓ
27. Ⓐ Ⓑ Ⓒ Ⓓ	61. Ⓐ Ⓑ Ⓒ Ⓓ	95. Ⓐ Ⓑ Ⓒ Ⓓ	129. Ⓐ Ⓑ Ⓒ Ⓓ
28. Ⓐ Ⓑ Ⓒ Ⓓ	62. Ⓐ Ⓑ Ⓒ Ⓓ	96. Ⓐ Ⓑ Ⓒ Ⓓ	130. Ⓐ Ⓑ Ⓒ Ⓓ
29. Ⓐ Ⓑ Ⓒ Ⓓ	63. Ⓐ Ⓑ Ⓒ Ⓓ	97. Ⓐ Ⓑ Ⓒ Ⓓ	131. Ⓐ Ⓑ Ⓒ Ⓓ
30. Ⓐ Ⓑ Ⓒ Ⓓ	64. Ⓐ Ⓑ Ⓒ Ⓓ	98. Ⓐ Ⓑ Ⓒ Ⓓ	132. Ⓐ Ⓑ Ⓒ Ⓓ
31. Ⓐ Ⓑ Ⓒ Ⓓ	65. Ⓐ Ⓑ Ⓒ Ⓓ	99. Ⓐ Ⓑ Ⓒ Ⓓ	133. Ⓐ Ⓑ Ⓒ Ⓓ
32. Ⓐ Ⓑ Ⓒ Ⓓ	66. Ⓐ Ⓑ Ⓒ Ⓓ	100. Ⓐ Ⓑ Ⓒ Ⓓ	134. Ⓐ Ⓑ Ⓒ Ⓓ
33. Ⓐ Ⓑ Ⓒ Ⓓ	67. Ⓐ Ⓑ Ⓒ Ⓓ	101. Ⓐ Ⓑ Ⓒ Ⓓ	
34. Ⓐ Ⓑ Ⓒ Ⓓ	68. Ⓐ Ⓑ Ⓒ Ⓓ	102. Ⓐ Ⓑ Ⓒ Ⓓ	

MSAT – Additional Answer Sheet

1. Ⓐ Ⓑ Ⓒ Ⓓ   35. Ⓐ Ⓑ Ⓒ Ⓓ   69. Ⓐ Ⓑ Ⓒ Ⓓ   103. Ⓐ Ⓑ Ⓒ Ⓓ
2. Ⓐ Ⓑ Ⓒ Ⓓ   36. Ⓐ Ⓑ Ⓒ Ⓓ   70. Ⓐ Ⓑ Ⓒ Ⓓ   104. Ⓐ Ⓑ Ⓒ Ⓓ
3. Ⓐ Ⓑ Ⓒ Ⓓ   37. Ⓐ Ⓑ Ⓒ Ⓓ   71. Ⓐ Ⓑ Ⓒ Ⓓ   105. Ⓐ Ⓑ Ⓒ Ⓓ
4. Ⓐ Ⓑ Ⓒ Ⓓ   38. Ⓐ Ⓑ Ⓒ Ⓓ   72. Ⓐ Ⓑ Ⓒ Ⓓ   106. Ⓐ Ⓑ Ⓒ Ⓓ
5. Ⓐ Ⓑ Ⓒ Ⓓ   39. Ⓐ Ⓑ Ⓒ Ⓓ   73. Ⓐ Ⓑ Ⓒ Ⓓ   107. Ⓐ Ⓑ Ⓒ Ⓓ
6. Ⓐ Ⓑ Ⓒ Ⓓ   40. Ⓐ Ⓑ Ⓒ Ⓓ   74. Ⓐ Ⓑ Ⓒ Ⓓ   108. Ⓐ Ⓑ Ⓒ Ⓓ
7. Ⓐ Ⓑ Ⓒ Ⓓ   41. Ⓐ Ⓑ Ⓒ Ⓓ   75. Ⓐ Ⓑ Ⓒ Ⓓ   109. Ⓐ Ⓑ Ⓒ Ⓓ
8. Ⓐ Ⓑ Ⓒ Ⓓ   42. Ⓐ Ⓑ Ⓒ Ⓓ   76. Ⓐ Ⓑ Ⓒ Ⓓ   110. Ⓐ Ⓑ Ⓒ Ⓓ
9. Ⓐ Ⓑ Ⓒ Ⓓ   43. Ⓐ Ⓑ Ⓒ Ⓓ   77. Ⓐ Ⓑ Ⓒ Ⓓ   111. Ⓐ Ⓑ Ⓒ Ⓓ
10. Ⓐ Ⓑ Ⓒ Ⓓ   44. Ⓐ Ⓑ Ⓒ Ⓓ   78. Ⓐ Ⓑ Ⓒ Ⓓ   112. Ⓐ Ⓑ Ⓒ Ⓓ
11. Ⓐ Ⓑ Ⓒ Ⓓ   45. Ⓐ Ⓑ Ⓒ Ⓓ   79. Ⓐ Ⓑ Ⓒ Ⓓ   113. Ⓐ Ⓑ Ⓒ Ⓓ
12. Ⓐ Ⓑ Ⓒ Ⓓ   46. Ⓐ Ⓑ Ⓒ Ⓓ   80. Ⓐ Ⓑ Ⓒ Ⓓ   114. Ⓐ Ⓑ Ⓒ Ⓓ
13. Ⓐ Ⓑ Ⓒ Ⓓ   47. Ⓐ Ⓑ Ⓒ Ⓓ   81. Ⓐ Ⓑ Ⓒ Ⓓ   115. Ⓐ Ⓑ Ⓒ Ⓓ
14. Ⓐ Ⓑ Ⓒ Ⓓ   48. Ⓐ Ⓑ Ⓒ Ⓓ   82. Ⓐ Ⓑ Ⓒ Ⓓ   116. Ⓐ Ⓑ Ⓒ Ⓓ
15. Ⓐ Ⓑ Ⓒ Ⓓ   49. Ⓐ Ⓑ Ⓒ Ⓓ   83. Ⓐ Ⓑ Ⓒ Ⓓ   117. Ⓐ Ⓑ Ⓒ Ⓓ
16. Ⓐ Ⓑ Ⓒ Ⓓ   50. Ⓐ Ⓑ Ⓒ Ⓓ   84. Ⓐ Ⓑ Ⓒ Ⓓ   118. Ⓐ Ⓑ Ⓒ Ⓓ
17. Ⓐ Ⓑ Ⓒ Ⓓ   51. Ⓐ Ⓑ Ⓒ Ⓓ   85. Ⓐ Ⓑ Ⓒ Ⓓ   119. Ⓐ Ⓑ Ⓒ Ⓓ
18. Ⓐ Ⓑ Ⓒ Ⓓ   52. Ⓐ Ⓑ Ⓒ Ⓓ   86. Ⓐ Ⓑ Ⓒ Ⓓ   120. Ⓐ Ⓑ Ⓒ Ⓓ
19. Ⓐ Ⓑ Ⓒ Ⓓ   53. Ⓐ Ⓑ Ⓒ Ⓓ   87. Ⓐ Ⓑ Ⓒ Ⓓ   121. Ⓐ Ⓑ Ⓒ Ⓓ
20. Ⓐ Ⓑ Ⓒ Ⓓ   54. Ⓐ Ⓑ Ⓒ Ⓓ   88. Ⓐ Ⓑ Ⓒ Ⓓ   122. Ⓐ Ⓑ Ⓒ Ⓓ
21. Ⓐ Ⓑ Ⓒ Ⓓ   55. Ⓐ Ⓑ Ⓒ Ⓓ   89. Ⓐ Ⓑ Ⓒ Ⓓ   123. Ⓐ Ⓑ Ⓒ Ⓓ
22. Ⓐ Ⓑ Ⓒ Ⓓ   56. Ⓐ Ⓑ Ⓒ Ⓓ   90. Ⓐ Ⓑ Ⓒ Ⓓ   124. Ⓐ Ⓑ Ⓒ Ⓓ
23. Ⓐ Ⓑ Ⓒ Ⓓ   57. Ⓐ Ⓑ Ⓒ Ⓓ   91. Ⓐ Ⓑ Ⓒ Ⓓ   125. Ⓐ Ⓑ Ⓒ Ⓓ
24. Ⓐ Ⓑ Ⓒ Ⓓ   58. Ⓐ Ⓑ Ⓒ Ⓓ   92. Ⓐ Ⓑ Ⓒ Ⓓ   126. Ⓐ Ⓑ Ⓒ Ⓓ
25. Ⓐ Ⓑ Ⓒ Ⓓ   59. Ⓐ Ⓑ Ⓒ Ⓓ   93. Ⓐ Ⓑ Ⓒ Ⓓ   127. Ⓐ Ⓑ Ⓒ Ⓓ
26. Ⓐ Ⓑ Ⓒ Ⓓ   60. Ⓐ Ⓑ Ⓒ Ⓓ   94. Ⓐ Ⓑ Ⓒ Ⓓ   128. Ⓐ Ⓑ Ⓒ Ⓓ
27. Ⓐ Ⓑ Ⓒ Ⓓ   61. Ⓐ Ⓑ Ⓒ Ⓓ   95. Ⓐ Ⓑ Ⓒ Ⓓ   129. Ⓐ Ⓑ Ⓒ Ⓓ
28. Ⓐ Ⓑ Ⓒ Ⓓ   62. Ⓐ Ⓑ Ⓒ Ⓓ   96. Ⓐ Ⓑ Ⓒ Ⓓ   130. Ⓐ Ⓑ Ⓒ Ⓓ
29. Ⓐ Ⓑ Ⓒ Ⓓ   63. Ⓐ Ⓑ Ⓒ Ⓓ   97. Ⓐ Ⓑ Ⓒ Ⓓ   131. Ⓐ Ⓑ Ⓒ Ⓓ
30. Ⓐ Ⓑ Ⓒ Ⓓ   64. Ⓐ Ⓑ Ⓒ Ⓓ   98. Ⓐ Ⓑ Ⓒ Ⓓ   132. Ⓐ Ⓑ Ⓒ Ⓓ
31. Ⓐ Ⓑ Ⓒ Ⓓ   65. Ⓐ Ⓑ Ⓒ Ⓓ   99. Ⓐ Ⓑ Ⓒ Ⓓ   133. Ⓐ Ⓑ Ⓒ Ⓓ
32. Ⓐ Ⓑ Ⓒ Ⓓ   66. Ⓐ Ⓑ Ⓒ Ⓓ   100. Ⓐ Ⓑ Ⓒ Ⓓ   134. Ⓐ Ⓑ Ⓒ Ⓓ
33. Ⓐ Ⓑ Ⓒ Ⓓ   67. Ⓐ Ⓑ Ⓒ Ⓓ   101. Ⓐ Ⓑ Ⓒ Ⓓ
34. Ⓐ Ⓑ Ⓒ Ⓓ   68. Ⓐ Ⓑ Ⓒ Ⓓ   102. Ⓐ Ⓑ Ⓒ Ⓓ